palgrave macmillan law masters

# family law

*Series editor*: **Marise Cremona**

palgrave macmillan law masters

# family law

## kate standley

Lecturer in Law at the
University of Essex

Sixth edition

**Series editor**: Marise Cremona
*Professor of European Law*
*European University Institute*
*Florence*
*Italy*

First edition 1993
Second edition 1997
Third edition 2001
Fourth edition 2004
Fifth edition 2006

Sixth edition 2008 published by
PALGRAVE MACMILLAN
Houndmills, Basingstoke, Hampshire RG21 6XS and
175 Fifth Avenue, New York, N.Y. 10010
Companies and representatives throughout the world

PALGRAVE MACMILLAN is the global academic imprint of the Palgrave Macmillan division of St. Martin's Press, LLC and of Palgrave Macmillan Ltd. Macmillan® is a registered trademark in the United States, United Kingdom and other countries. Palgrave is a registered trademark in the European Union and other countries.

ISBN-13: 978–0–230–53746–0
ISBN-10: 0–230–53746–4

This book is printed on paper suitable for recycling and made from fully managed and sustained forest sources. Logging, pulping and manufacturing processes are expected to conform to the environmental regulations of the country of origin.

A catalogue record for this book is available from the British Library.

| 10 | 9 | 8 | 7 | 6 | 5 | 4 | 3 | 2 | 1 |
|----|----|----|----|----|----|----|----|----|----|
| 17 | 16 | 15 | 14 | 13 | 12 | 11 | 10 | 09 | 08 |

Printed and bound in Great Britain by
Cromwell Press Ltd, Trowbridge, Wiltshire

# Contents

# Preface to the Sixth Edition

It is now 15 years since the first edition of *Family Law* was published in 1993. A great deal has happened in family law during that time. In 1993 the Children Act 1989 had been in force for only about two years and I wrote in the Preface to the first edition that it was 'still too early to estimate the success and impact of that Act'. It can now be said, however, that the Act has had a considerable impact and has been 'successful'. On the other hand, the Child Support Act 1991 – which had only just come into force when the first edition was written – has been 'unsuccessful' as it introduced a radically new child support maintenance system which has failed and which is to be replaced by a new regime.

Since the first edition there have been many major changes in family law. Civil partnerships have been introduced, transsexuals have gained new rights, and cohabitants (opposite-sex and same-sex) have acquired more rights, in particular in respect of protection against domestic violence and the right to adopt children jointly. With more couples choosing cohabitation as a life style, family law has had to move with the times, although in respect of their property and financial rights it has moved perhaps rather too slowly.

During the 15 years since the first edition, a radically new divorce law was proposed and almost came into force but was abandoned by the Government at the eleventh hour. Over the years there has been an increasing emphasis on settlement, with mediation, in particular, being recognised as a better way of solving family disputes. The voice of the child is being increasingly heard in family proceedings, although some think not enough. Changes have been made to the law to deal with the problem of intractable contact disputes, in order to improve the facilitation and enforcement of contact. The Human Rights Act 1998, which came into force in October 2000, has also added another dimension to family law.

Since 2006 when the fifth edition of *Family Law* was published, there have been further changes. Thus, for example, the provisions on special guardianship orders have come into force and so too have the new provisions governing family assistance orders. Changes to the law on domestic violence to give victims greater protection have also come into force. The provisions of the Children Act 2004 in respect of improving inter-agency work to protect children from harm have placed new responsibilities on public authorities. With regard to the case-law, the important case of *Miller* v. *Miller* on property and finance on divorce was handed down by the House of Lords in 2006, but too late to include in the previous edition. There have been other important cases, in particular a series of cases heard by the Court of Appeal on the new special guardianship order, and decisions of the House of Lords on the Hague Convention on Abduction.

Since the previous edition there has been considerable activity at Government level, as well as structural changes in Government organisation. At the request of the Government, the Law Commission has made proposals for reform of the law governing property and finance for cohabitants with the aim of removing the injustice and unfairness that can occur. There has been Government consultation on a wide range of family matters, including giving children more of a voice in private law proceedings, making it mandatory for unmarried fathers to be named on children's birth certificates, and it has conducted a review of the new provisions in section 58 of the Children Act 2004 restricting the use of corporal punishment by parents on children. Changes to the Statement of Arrangements form, which must be completed when parents divorce, have been discussed, as well as changes of divorce terminology in order to remove some of the rather archaic sounding words, such as 'petitioner' and 'respondent'. There has been discussion about creating a single family court. Discussions have also taken place about procedure in public law children's cases and a new protocol is to come into force in 2008. The Government has also conducted an important consultation on the child support system.

What does the future hold? Changes are due to come into force in respect of the child support system by 2010, and changes may eventually be taken forward by the Government to give cohabitants rights in respect of property and finance on family breakdown and on death. There are other changes that some family lawyers, practising and academic, would like to see in the future, in particular reform of the ground for divorce and of the law governing property and finance on divorce. However, at the time of writing there are no proposals to reform the law in these areas. Increasingly, however, the 'Europeanisation' of family law is being discussed.

Despite the numerous changes in family law, my aim in writing this book remains as it was when I wrote the first edition, which is to provide a readable, comprehensive and up-to-date account of the subject. I have taught many students family law (and child law) at the University of Essex since the first edition was published – and I think they have found it useful. Some of them have gone on to work in the family law field.

During the 15 years since the first edition was published my own family life has changed. My children who were 15 and 16 then are now adults forging their own lives. Throughout this time, however, I have been very lucky indeed to have had such a happy marriage, despite the odd 'contretemps' at the bridge table! My husband John has without fail provided me with support, humour and numerous cups of coffee during the hours I have spent researching and writing this book over the years. This book is dedicated to him.

Kate Standley
*2008*

# Table of Cases

**Practice Directions and Practice Notes**

# Table of Statutes

**Table of Rules**

**Other (Miscellaneous) Legislation**

# Part I

# Family Law –
# An Introduction

# Chapter 1

## Family Law Today

### 1.1    Family Law – Changes and Trends

Family law is an area of law which changes rapidly. Major legislative developments have taken place, and there have also been important case-law developments.

#### (a)    Legislative Developments

Since the early 1990s there have been many important legislative developments. Of particular importance was the Children Act 1989, which came into force in October 1991, and made far-reaching changes to the civil law relating to children (see Chapter 11). In 1993 the Child Support Act 1991 moved child maintenance from the courts into the Child Support Agency (see 13.2).

In the mid-1990s Part IV of the Family Law Act 1996 introduced a new range of remedies to protect a wider class of family members from domestic violence (see Chapter 6). During the 1990s, as a result of widespread dissatisfaction with divorce law, a radically new divorce law was due to come into force in the year 2000, but the proposals were abandoned because they were essentially unworkable in practice (see 7.2).

In the first few years of the new millennium there were further important legislative developments. Of particular importance was the Human Rights Act 1998 which came into force in October 2000 (see 1.5). Changes were also made to the way in which child support maintenance is calculated by the Child Support Agency (see 13.2), and pension sharing on divorce was introduced (see 8.8). Since December 2003 unmarried fathers have been able to acquire parental responsibility by registering their child's birth with the mother (see 10.6). Radical changes have also been made to the law of adoption by the Adoption and Children Act 2002, which came fully into force on 30 December 2005 (see Chapter 16). That Act has also made important changes to the Children Act 1989, including in particular the introduction of special guardianship orders (see 16.20). Changes have also been made to the civil and criminal law by the Domestic Violence, Crime and Victims Act 2004 to give greater protection to victims of domestic violence (see Chapter 6).

In the last few years the Government has shown its willingness to accept and provide for 'non-traditional' families by enacting the Civil Partnership Act 2004 and the Gender Recognition Act 2004. The Civil Partnership Act introduced a civil partnership registration scheme for same-sex partners (see 2.10), and the Gender Recognition Act allows transsexual persons to enter into a valid marriage in their newly acquired sex (see 2.7).

More recent changes include the Children Act 2004 which, among other things, makes changes to the structural framework governing the practice of child protection (see 15.2). Other developments include the introduction of new civil remedies to protect victims of forced marriages (see 2.6), and restrictions on the use of corporal punishment of children by their parents (see 9.5). Reforms have also been made to improve the facilitation and enforcement of contact on family breakdown because of the intractable problems that some contact disputes can create (see 12.5).

In respect of reforms on the Government's agenda, radical changes to the child support system are proposed which include the abolition of the Child Support Agency (see 13.2). Reforms are also proposed to improve the care system for children and young people (see 15.1). The Government is also discussing whether to make it mandatory for unmarried fathers to be named on children's birth certificates (see 10.6). Changes to the law to give children a greater voice in private law proceedings (such as for residence and contact) are also proposed (see 9.6). A particularly important issue for family law has been discussion about the introduction of a proposed new scheme for property and financial relief for cohabitants on relationship breakdown, in order to remove the unfairness that cohabitants may suffer (see 4.12).

Structural changes have taken place in Government organisation. Thus the Department for Constitutional Affairs is now the Ministry of Justice, and the Department for Education and Skills has become the Department for Children, Schools and Families.

Concerns which are not currently being addressed by the Government, but which many family lawyers think should be, are reforms of the ground for divorce (see 7.2), and of the law governing the distribution of property and finance on divorce (see 8.14).

### (b)    Case-Law Developments

There have been important case-law developments in recent years. There have been two important decisions of the House of Lords dealing with the approach that the courts should adopt in proceedings for property and financial orders on divorce (see 8.6). Other decisions of the House of Lords have dealt with the rights of transsexuals (see 2.7), the threshold conditions for making care and supervision orders, the status of care plans for children in care (see 15.7) and the power of the court to enforce the payment of child support (see 13.2). The House of Lords has also handed down some important decisions on the law governing international child abduction (see Chapter 14).

As a result of their obligations under the Human Rights Act 1998, courts now have to exercise their powers in the light of the European Convention for the Protection of Human Rights and Fundamental Freedoms, and human rights' arguments have been used in some cases (see 1.5). The law on the succession by a homosexual to the tenancy of his deceased partner has, for example, been extended by the House of Lords in order to bring the law into line with the Human Rights Act 1998 (see 5.4), and so has the law governing the rights of transsexuals (see 2.7).

### (c)    The Handling of Family Disputes – Developments

*Encouraging Agreement Rather Than Bringing Court Proceedings*    It is generally recognised by those in the family justice system that court proceedings are not the best way of dealing with family disputes, in particular disputes about finance and property on divorce and about arrangements for children on family breakdown. Going to court can be expensive, time-consuming, unpredictable and can increase hostility between the parties and have an adverse affect on children. As a result, mediation, an alternative form of dispute resolution to that of going to court, has been increasingly promoted (see below). There are also other ways in which agreement is promoted (see below).

*Openness and Transparency*    In the last few years there has been discussion about the need for openness and transparency in family proceedings, so that the public can see what is happening and understand how family judges reach their decisions. Open and informed public debate has been increasingly seen as performing an essential role in fostering public confidence in the family justice system. Justice must not only be done, but must be seen to be done.

In 2006 the Department for Constitutional Affairs (now the Ministry of Justice) published a consultation document on the matter (see *Confidence and Confidentiality: Improving Transparency and Privacy in Family Courts*, CP 11/06). The responses to the consultation paper (published in March 2007) showed widespread support for making more information available on how the family justice system works, including allowing children on reaching adulthood to have access to court decisions about disputes between their parents on relationship breakdown. Resolution (the organisation of family solicitors) has backed the proposals.

The Government has considered giving the media an automatic right to attend family courts, but it has decided against it in cases involving children because it would jeopardise children's rights to privacy and anonymity (see *Confidence and Confidentiality: Openness in Family Courts – A New Approach*, CP 10/07, 2007, Cm 7131, Ministry of Justice). Instead, the Government says that the emphasis will be on improving the information coming out of family courts rather than allowing greater access into them.

### (d)    The International Dimension

Family law has an increasingly international dimension. Not only do the courts in England and Wales have to deal with such matters as the recognition of foreign marriages and divorces and applications for ancillary relief after a foreign divorce, but many family matters are governed not by national law but by international conventions. Thus there are, for example, international conventions governing child abduction, inter-country adoption, the protection of minors, the reciprocal enforcement of maintenance and the jurisdiction of the courts in family matters in the European Union.

The European Convention for the Protection of Human Rights and Fundamental Freedoms has added a further international dimension, particularly as a result of the Human Rights Act 1998 (see below). The United Nations Convention on the Rights of the Child 1989 also performs an important role in protecting and promoting children's rights (see 9.2).

The international dimension has also had an impact on family law reform. For instance, when the Law Commission was discussing reform of divorce in England and Wales, it made a close study of divorce law in other countries. The increasing recognition of same-sex couples in many European countries by way of permitting gay marriages and allowing same-sex couples to register their partnership has been relevant when reforms have been discussed in England and Wales. Developments in Australia and New Zealand in respect of cohabitants and property ownership have been discussed in the contexts of reforms in England and Wales, and the child support scheme in England and Wales is based on models used in Australia and the USA.

### (e)    Demographic and Family Changes

There have been important demographic and social changes which impact on family law. Many people cohabit, fewer people marry and divorce is common. Increasing numbers of families are lone-parent families. Many children are brought up by a single parent. Many children are born outside marriage. There are also increasing numbers of elderly persons.

A particularly important change in family law has been the recognition given by legislators and courts to different forms of family living. The traditional family (married couple and children) is no longer the only family form, and families are also becoming increasingly complex. There are gay and lesbian families, step-families and multiple step-families. There are civil partnerships. Some parents adopt children. People can become special guardians. It is now possible for children to have multiple numbers of persons with parental responsibility. The recognition and acceptance by the Government of these increasingly complex family forms has resulted in an increasingly complex set of statutory provisions.

The driving forces behind the changes which have taken place in family life are articulated by Mr Justice Munby in the following extract:

> ▶ **Mr Justice Munby, 'Families old and new – the family and Article 8' [2005]** *Child and Family Law Quarterly* **487**
>
> 'There have been very profound changes in family life in recent decades. They have been driven by four major developments. First, there have been enormous changes in the social and religious life of our country. The fact is that we live in a secular and pluralistic society. But we also live in a multi-cultural community of many faiths. . . .
>
> Secondly, there has been an increasing lack of interest in – in some instances a conscious rejection of – marriage as an institution. There is no lack of interest in family life (or at least in intimate relationships) but the figures demonstrate a striking decline in marriage. At the same time, it has never been easier for the married to be divorced. The truth is that, for all practical purposes, we permit divorce on demand.
>
> Thirdly, there has been a sea-change in society's attitudes towards same-sex unions. . . .
>
> Fourthly, there have been enormous advances in medical and in particular reproductive science so that reproduction is no longer confined to "natural" methods. . . .'

## 1.2  The Discretionary Nature of Family Law

A distinguishing feature of family law is its discretionary nature. Each case depends on its own facts. Judges have to reach conclusions based on the circumstances of each case. Sometimes this can involve a difficult balancing exercise. Judges have a wide discretion, in particular in disputes about children on family breakdown and in proceedings about property and finance on divorce. It is important that judges have wide discretion in family matters, because family life is infinitely variable – no two cases are the same.

Discretion has advantages and disadvantages. Its main advantage is its flexibility. Its disadvantages are that it creates unpredictability and it can be a time-consuming exercise which can increase the cost of litigation. There is also a risk of arbitrariness, as judges may reach different conclusions in cases which are factually similar. The unpredictability and arbitrariness of judicial discretionary decision-making were some of the justifications given for moving child maintenance disputes out of the courts and into the Child Support Agency (see 13.2).

In some areas of the law checklists of factors are provided in family law statutes in order to help guide judges when exercising their discretion and in reaching their decisions.

There is a statutory checklist of factors which must be taken into account in children's cases under the Children Act 1989, and in property and finance on divorce cases under the Matrimonial Causes Act 1973. A statutory checklist of factors has also been introduced into the adoption legislation.

The discretionary nature of family law has an impact on appeals. Thus, because there may be several reasonable solutions to a family law dispute, the appeal courts are unwilling to overturn decisions made by the lower courts – unless the decision is wrong in law, or is outside a band of reasonable decisions and is therefore plainly wrong (*G v. G (Minors) (Custody Appeal)* [1985] 1 WLR 647; and see *Piglowska v. Piglowski* [1999] 1 WLR 1360, [1999] 2 FLR 763).

## 1.3  The Importance of Reaching Agreement

Most private law family matters (such as those involving divorce, residence and contact) are settled by the parties themselves, and, despite the impression given by the number of reported cases, most cases do not go to court. If family lawyers are consulted, they work within a conciliatory framework. Resolution, an organisation of solicitors and family justice professionals who believe in a constructive and non-confrontational approach to family law, encourages the amicable resolution of family disputes and has a Code of Practice which governs the way in which family law solicitors conduct their work. Members of Resolution must subscribe to the Code of Practice. The principles in the Code have been adopted by The Law Society in its *Family Law Protocol*, which family law practitioners must follow, with the aim of making private family law processes less confrontational and encouraging a conciliatory approach. Solicitors must encourage the parties to put the interests of their children first, and not use them as an emotional bargaining chip. They must aim to reduce delay, keep costs down and be sensitive to the risk of domestic violence. The *Protocol* requires solicitors to avoid inflaming the situation, to explore the possibility of mediation and to keep the other party to the dispute properly informed.

### (a)  Mediation and Conciliation

Mediation is a form of alternative dispute resolution whereby a mediator helps the parties identify the issues in dispute with the aim of reaching agreement. The mediator acts as an impartial third party to the dispute. It is the parties themselves who make the decision. It is not imposed by the mediator. The mediator merely acts as a facilitator. The process is confidential and non-coercive. Mediation has many advantages. It avoids the cost, trauma, uncertainty and delay of court proceedings. It helps improve communication between the parties and reduces conflict and bitterness. It may also empower the parties and make them better able to deal with disputes in the future.

Mediation can take place out-of-court or in-court, and is available from independent mediation agencies, and from some law firms. In ancillary relief proceedings on divorce, the district judge performs a mediatory role. Mediation can also play an important role at the appeal level. In *Al-Khatib v. Masry* [2004] EWCA Civ 1353, [2005] 1 FLR 381 Thorpe LJ in the Court of Appeal said that there was no family case that was not potentially open to successful mediation. He said, however, that it was important for there to be judicial supervision of the mediation process, and that the selection of an appropriate mediator was crucial in a difficult case.

The Law Society's *Family Law Protocol* requires solicitors at an early stage to explain to clients the benefits of mediation, to keep the suitability of mediation under review throughout the case and to encourage clients to go to mediation wherever appropriate. The *Protocol* states, however, that some cases are unsuitable for mediation (for instance, child protection, child abduction and domestic violence cases, and cases where emergency action is required).

The UK College of Family Mediators is the umbrella organisation responsible for setting professional and ethical standards in mediation practice outside the court system. Two of the major mediation bodies are National Family Mediation and the Family Mediators' Association.

The Government has invested a considerable amount of time and money in promoting mediation, and with this end in view has established the Family Mediation Council (FMC) in order to campaign for greater public awareness of, and access to, mediation. It has also set up a family mediation helpline and website. In order to promote mediation, before legal aid is granted, the Legal Services Commission requires a applicant to have considered mediation. The Government has also introduced a mediation hotline for persons wishing to find mediation services in their area. Some family law solicitors are also choosing to train as mediators.

However, despite the increasing promotion of mediation as the best way of solving most family law disputes, the Government has no plans to make it compulsory. It merely wishes to encourage its use. Compulsion would run counter to the essential nature of mediation, which is that it is a solution to family law disputes entered into voluntarily by the parties. However, mediation is compulsory in some countries (for example, in Australia, New Zealand, Norway and some states in the USA and Canada).

Despite the Government's attempts to promote mediation, however, it appears that it is not being used as extensively as it might be. The National Audit Office has found (see its report, *Legal Aid and Mediation for People Involved in Family Breakdown*, March 2007) that only 20 per cent of persons funded by legal aid for family breakdown cases (excluding those involving domestic violence) chose to use mediation. The report made recommendations to the Legal Services Commission in order to increase its use.

*Conciliation*   'Conciliation' is the term sometimes used for mediation in disputes about children, in particular residence and contact disputes. In certain circumstances the district judge must refer children's cases to conciliation, and both parents and any child aged over nine must attend (see *District Judges' Direction (Children: Conciliation)* [2004] 1 FLR 974).

### (b)  Collaborative Family Law

Like mediation and conciliation, this is a form of alternative dispute resolution which is used by some family lawyers and their clients. It was developed in North America during the 1990s. It is used only by clients who agree to use it, after they have received legal advice about all the other options available. With collaborative family law, the clients and their lawyers sign a participation agreement in which they agree to a commitment to make a transparent search for fair solutions, and not go to court. The clients and their lawyers then conduct round-table negotiations in order to find the best outcome. The process is transparent, and written correspondence is actively discouraged. The clients set both the pace and scope of the negotiations, but with assistance from their lawyers. Parties can also seek the assistance of mediation and counselling. If either client decides to go to court, both clients must consult new lawyers.

The Central London Collaborative Forum was launched in October 2007 by some London law firms with the aim of encouraging parties to 'big money cases' on divorce (see Chapter 8) to adopt a collaborative approach to resolving disputes.

## 1.4  The Courts Administering Family Law

### (a)  The Courts

There are three tiers of court with jurisdiction to hear family cases: magistrates' family proceedings courts (FPCs); county courts; and the Family Division of the High Court. Some proceedings can be heard in any of these courts, but others must be heard in a particular court. For instance, divorce proceedings must be heard in a divorce county court, and child abduction and other cases with an international dimension must be heard in the High Court. Proceedings under the Children Act 1989 and applications for orders for protection against domestic violence under Part IV of the Family Law Act 1996 can generally be heard in any tier of court, although some cases must be heard only in the High Court.

*(i) Family Proceedings Courts (FPCs)*    These courts are staffed by lay magistrates who are specially trained in family work and who are assisted by the clerk of the court. Sometimes district judges sit with lay magistrates. Broadly speaking all family matters, except divorce, and cases which are complex (as defined by specified criteria), can be heard in FPCs. They have concurrent powers with the other family courts in private and public law proceedings under the Children Act 1989 and in adoption proceedings under the Adoption and Children Act 2002, but they cannot deal with divorce matters. Public law cases under the Children Act 1989 must start in the FPC, but may be transferred to the county court to minimise delay, to consolidate with other family proceedings, or where the matter is exceptionally grave, complex or important. Private law proceedings can commence in any FPC or county court, but can be transferred laterally between courts, and vertically to the High Court in some circumstances.

*(ii) County Courts*    These courts deal with most family law matters. There are five types of county court:

| Type of County Court | Jurisdiction |
| --- | --- |
| Non-Divorce County Court | Cannot deal with children's matters but can deal with domestic violence. |
| Divorce County Court | All actions for divorce, nullity and judicial separation must start here. All private law proceedings can start here, but contested matters must be transferred to family hearing centres for trial. |
| Family Hearing Centres | Contested private law matters are dealt with here (for example, applications for residence and contact orders, domestic violence injunctions). |
| Adoption Centres | These are specialised centres with jurisdiction to issue, process and hear adoption applications. |
| Care Centres | These have full jurisdiction in all public and private law matters (such as in respect of care and supervision orders, divorce, adoptions). |

Some Care Centres also deal with inter-country adoptions. Some courts have jurisdiction in matters relating to civil partnerships. The Principal Registry of the Family Division is the Care Centre for London. Difficult, lengthy or serious cases can be transferred from a county court to the Family Division of the High Court. Some county courts also have jurisdiction to hear High Court cases, which are generally heard in Care Centres where High Court judges sit periodically.

*(iii) The Family Division of the High Court*    The High Court hears a wide range of different cases, including wardship cases, and cases with an international dimension. The High Court also has an inherent parental type of jurisdiction which is used, for example, when deciding whether or not a child should have medical treatment (see 10.9). It also hears cases transferred from county courts or magistrates' family proceedings courts. These are usually complex and particularly difficult cases requiring the expertise of the High Court. The President of the Family Division is the Rt Hon Sir Mark Potter P, who took over from the Rt Hon Dame Elizabeth Butler-Sloss P in April 2005.

*Reforming the Family Court System*    In February 2005 a consultation document, *A Single Civil Court?*, was published by the Department for Constitutional Affairs to look at the case for establishing a single Family Court by unifying the jurisdictions of the Family Division of the High Court, county courts and FPCs. In June 2005 a consultation paper was published by Her Majesty's Court Service (HMCS) discussing the introduction of 'Family Court Centres' whereby FPCs and county courts would work together as one unit to provide a more flexible service. Pilot studies have been conducted to test the proposed new scheme. Specialist domestic violence courts have been recently introduced to provide a better and more co-ordinated service for cases of domestic violence.

### (b)    The Problem of Delay

A major concern in the family justice system is the problem of delay. Public law proceedings for care and supervision orders, in particular, take a long time to be finally decided. Changes have been made, however, with the aim of reducing delay. In November 2003 a *Protocol* was published with the aim of speeding up public law proceedings and setting a guideline of 40 weeks for care cases. Problems still remain, but a new *Protocol*, the *Public Law Outline*, is to be introduced in 2008 with the aim of determining proceedings more speedily.

### (c)    CAFCASS

CAFCASS (the Children and Family Court Advisory and Support Service), which was established under s.11 Criminal Justice and Court Services Act 2000, looks after the best interests of children involved in family proceedings. The principal functions of CAFCASS officers (or Welsh family proceedings officers) are: to safeguard and promote the welfare of children in family proceedings; to make provision for children to be represented in family proceedings; and to provide information, advice and other support for children and their families (s.12(1)). CAFCASS advises courts, for example, on issues such as residence and contact for children on family breakdown, and placing children in local authority care. In April 2005 the functions of CAFCASS relating to Wales were devolved to the National Assembly for Wales.

CAFCASS also performs an increasing role in encouraging divorcing and separating parents to reach agreement. In fact its *Annual Report for 2006–2007* (published in July 2007) reported that there had been a 33.6 per cent increase in family court adviser time spent on dispute resolution work, and that in about 60 per cent of the cases where it had intervened full or partial agreement had been achieved.

CAFCASS has also been given a new role in respect of facilitating contact on family breakdown (see 12.5). It also carries out risk assessments of children in order to establish whether they are at risk of abuse or domestic violence (see 12.5). Checks have to be made of local authority child protection registers and with other relevant agencies. Where there is a risk of significant harm, the case will be referred to the child protection department of the relevant local authority.

CAFCASS officers are independent of the courts, social services, education and health authorities. They are qualified in social work and are experienced in working with children and families. The following officers are provided by CAFCASS:

- *Children and Family Reporters* When parents cannot agree about residence and contact arrangements for children on family breakdown, the court will usually appoint a Children and Family Reporter who will meet and talk with the family and help and encourage parents to agree about arrangements for their children. The Children and Family Reporter may be asked by the court under s.7 Children Act 1989 to write a report explaining what enquiries have been made and making recommendations about arrangements for the children. The Children and Family Reporter is responsible for conveying the child's wishes and feelings to the court.
- *Children's Guardians* are responsible for investigating the case and safeguarding and promoting the child's welfare before the court in public law proceedings for care and supervision orders and emergency protection and child assessment orders under the Children Act 1989.
- *Reporting Officers* are responsible for ensuring that the required consents to adoption and to placements for adoption have been given freely.
- *Guardians Ad Litem* are usually, but not exclusively, CAFCASS officers appointed by the court under rule 9.5 of the Family Proceedings Rules 1991 to represent the interests of children who have been made a party to private law proceedings (such as for residence and contact).

CAFCASS and CAFCASS CYMRU (based at the National Assembly for Wales) have teams of 'inhouse' lawyers who work in children's cases. In certain cases where a guardian *ad litem* is appointed for a child by the court in private law proceedings the case must be referred to the CAFCASS High Court Team (if the child lives in England) or to National Assembly lawyers (if the child lives in Wales).

CAFCASS has a national Children's Rights Director, and Children's Rights Champions in each of its regions.

### (d)    Other Personnel in the Family Justice System

In addition to lawyers and barristers, and CAFCASS officers (see above), social workers are also involved (for instance, in child protection cases), and so are the police (for instance, in domestic violence cases and child protection cases). The Official Solicitor to the Supreme Court may be involved in some cases. He or she is appointed by the Minister of Justice to look after the best interests of incapacitated adults or children who are unable to look after their own best interests in court.

## 1.5 Family Law and the Human Rights Act 1998

The Human Rights Act (HRA) 1998 is relevant to family law, as courts and public authorities must abide by its provisions. The Act came into force in October 2000 as a result of changes proposed by the Government in its White Paper *Rights Brought Home: The Human Rights Bill* (1998, Cm 3782). The effect of the Act is to weave the European Convention for the Protection of Human Rights and Fundamental Freedoms (ECHR) into the fabric of English law. The Act makes a considerable number of Convention rights directly enforceable in the UK. The Act gives UK citizens the right to rely upon the Convention in any proceedings which come before the UK courts, and courts and public authorities must act in accordance with it.

### (a) The Courts and the Human Rights Act 1998

When deciding any question which has arisen in connection with a Convention right the courts in the UK must 'take into account' the judgments, decisions and opinions of the European Court of Human Rights (s.2 HRA 1998). The courts, so far as it is possible, must read and give effect to primary and secondary legislation in a way which is compatible with Convention rights (s.3). If the High Court, Court of Appeal or House of Lords determines that a UK legislative provision is not compatible with the Convention, and cannot be read to make it compatible, then it may make a 'declaration of incompatibility' to that effect (s.4).

As courts are public authorities for the purposes of the HRA they must not act in a way which is incompatible with a Convention right (s.6). Thus in family cases, the court must ensure that it considers and upholds Convention rights, for otherwise it may itself be in breach of the Convention.

### (b) Public Authorities and the Human Rights Act 1998

It is unlawful for a public authority to act in a way which is incompatible with a Convention right, except where it could not have acted any differently as a result of there being incompatible primary legislation, or where the relevant primary or secondary legislation could not be read or given effect to so as to make it compatible with Convention rights, and the public authority was acting so as to give effect to or enforce those provisions (s.6). There is no definition of 'public authority' in the Act, but it includes, for instance, Government departments, local authorities, the National Health Service, the police and any other body or person exercising a public function. Because of the obligations imposed on public authorities by the HRA 1998, the Convention is especially important in the public law area of family law, in particular child protection and adoption where the courts and local authority social services departments must ensure compliance with the Convention.

### (c)    Asserting a Convention Right

Any person who is the victim of an unlawful act (or proposed act) of a public authority (because it is a breach of a Convention right) may bring free-standing court proceedings against the public authority under the Human Rights Act, or rely on a Convention right in any other legal proceedings (s.7). In practice, most claims in family law are brought as supporting arguments in family proceedings. If an applicant proves that a public authority has acted in breach of a Convention right, then the court may grant such relief or remedy, or make such order, within its powers as it considers just and appropriate, including awards of damages (s.8). Awards of damages under s.8 are usually low, however, because the court takes into account the levels of damages set by the European Court of Human Rights, which tend to be much less than those awarded under domestic law.

### (d)    Convention Rights

The following Convention rights are those most likely to impact on family law: the right to life (art. 2); the right not to be subjected to torture or to inhuman or degrading treatment (art. 3); the right to a fair trial (art. 6); the right to a private and family life (art. 8); the right to freedom of thought, conscience and religion (art. 9); the right to marry and found a family (art. 12); the right to an effective remedy (art. 13); and the right to enjoy Convention rights without discrimination (art. 14).

The Convention and decisions of the Court of Human Rights have been raised in a wide variety of different family situations, for instance:

- Transsexuals have argued that the UK's failure to allow them to change their birth certificates and to marry in their newly acquired sex is a breach of their right to family life under art. 8 and the right to marry under art. 12 (see 2.7).
- Children and parents have argued that corporal punishment of children by parents and teachers is inhuman and degrading treatment under art. 3 (see 9.5).
- Unmarried fathers have argued that their lack of automatic parental responsibility is a breach of the right to family life under art. 8 and is thereby discriminatory under art. 14 (see 10.6).
- Parents have argued in child protection cases that local authorities have breached their right to family life under art. 8 and that the procedures used have breached their right to a fair hearing under art. 6 (see 15.3).
- In contact cases and in relocations applications to take a child out of the UK, parents have argued that there has been a breach of their right to family life under art. 8 (see 14.4).
- In negligence cases involving children who have been harmed by local authority action or inaction, children have argued that striking out their claims in negligence is a breach of their right not to suffer inhuman and degrading treatment under art. 3 and a breach of their right to an effective remedy under art. 13 (see 15.12).
- In the child support context, it has been argued that the lack of an effective remedy in the courts for a person entitled to child support is a breach of their right to a fair trial under art. 6 (see 13.2).

(e)   The Right to Family Life (Article 8)

The right to life in art. 8 ECHR is particularly relevant to family law:

---

**Article 8 European Convention for the Protection of Human Rights**

'1. Everyone has the right to respect for his private and family life, his home and his correspondence.
2. There shall be no interference by a public authority with the exercise of this right except such as is in accordance with the law and is necessary in a democratic society in the interests of national security, public safety or the economic well-being of the country, for the prevention of disorder or crime, for the protection of heath or morals, or for the protection of the rights and freedoms of others.'

---

The essential object of art. 8 is to protect the individual against arbitrary interference by public authorities. In addition, national authorities have positive obligations to promote family life under art. 8. In respect of the right to family life, regard must be had to the fair balance that has to be struck between the competing interests of the individual and the wider community, and States Parties enjoy a margin of appreciation (see below).

In a dispute about the right to family life under art. 8 the court must ask itself whether there is a family life, and if so: was the right to respect for family life interfered with by a public authority; and, if so, was that interference in accordance with the law, in pursuit of a legitimate aim, and necessary in a democratic society?

### What is 'Family Life' for the Purposes of Article 8?

There is no definition of 'family life' in the European Convention. Whether or not there is a family life depends on the facts and circumstances of each case. Although the European Court of Human Rights (ECtHR) has made no attempt to define family life, because of the need for flexibility, it has nevertheless laid down the following propositions in respect of 'family life' for the purposes of art. 8:

▷   The existence or non-existence of family life is a question of fact depending on the real existence of close personal ties *(see Lebbink v. The Netherlands (Application No. 45582/99)* [2004] 2 FLR 463, where the ECtHR held that mere biological kinship, without any further legal or factual elements indicating the existence of a close personal relationship, could not be regarded as sufficient to attract the protection of art. 8; and *K and T v. Finland* (2000) 31 EHRR 484, [2000] 2 FLR 793).

▷   The bond between natural parents and children is a strong indicator of the existence of family life, and that bond amounting to family life cannot be broken by subsequent events, save in exceptional circumstances *(Ahmut v. The Netherlands* (1997) 24 EHRR 62).

▷   Family life is not limited to relationships based on marriage or blood, or relationships recognised in law. It can include cohabitants *(Abdulaziz, Cabales and Balkandali v. United Kingdom* (1995) 7 EHRR 471), even if they do not live together *(Kroon v. The Netherlands* (1995) 19 EHRR 263). It can include relationships between near relatives, such as between grandparents and grandchildren (*Marckx* v. *Belgium* (1979) 2 EHRR 330); and between nephew and uncle (*Boyle* v. *United Kingdom* (1995) 19 EHRR 179). It can also include a relationship between foster-parent and foster-child (*Gaskin* v. *UK* (1990) 12 EHRR 36).

▸ When deciding whether a cohabitation relationship amounts to family life, the following factors are relevant: whether the couple live together; the length of their relationship; and whether they have demonstrated their commitment to each other by having children together or by any other means. A family life was found to exist in *X, Y and Z* v. *United Kingdom* (1997) 24 EHRR 143, [1997] 2 FLR 892, where X, a female-to-male transsexual, and his female partner Y had a child (Z) by artificial insemination by donor, and X was involved throughout the process and acted as Z's father in every respect.

▸ As the ECtHR considers the Convention to be a 'living instrument' which must be interpreted in the light of societal changes (see *Selmouni* v. *France* (2000) 29 EHRR 403), the courts must adapt themselves to changing social conditions when interpreting family life (for example, the decline in marriage, the increase in cohabitation, the acceptance of same-sex relationships and developments in reproductive science).

▸ Family life can include the potential for family life, for instance the potential relationship which might have developed between an unmarried father and his child; or where the child is in the process of being adopted.

▸ When deciding whether family life exists, the ECtHR will give regard to the relevant principles of international law, and interpret art. 8 so far as possible to be in harmony with those principles (including the principles in the United Nations Convention on the Rights of the Child 1989 and the Hague Convention on the Protection of Children and Co-operation in Respect of Intercountry Adoption 1993).

▸ When deciding whether family life exists, it must be viewed in the context of the relevant social, religious and cultural setting.

### The European Court's Approach to Article 8

The European Court of Human Rights has laid down the following propositions in respect of art. 8:

▸ Although the main aim of art. 8 is to protect the individual against arbitrary action by public authorities (*Kroon* v. *The Netherlands* (1995) 19 EHRR 263), there are also positive obligations inherent in an effective 'respect' for family life under art. 8. In *Marckx* v. *Belgium* (1979) 2 EHRR 330, the ECtHR said: 'Article 8 does not merely compel the State to abstain from such interference; in addition to this primarily negative undertaking, there may be positive obligations inherent in an effective "respect for family life".'

▸ As well as a substantive right to respect for family life, there is also a procedural right inherent within art. 8.

▸ In respect of the substantial and procedural rights under art. 8, regard must be had to the fair balance that has to be struck between the competing interests of the individual and of the community as a whole; and the State enjoys a certain margin of appreciation (see *Keegan* v. *Ireland* (1994) 18 EHRR 342).

▸ The right to family life is not an absolute right, but a qualified right. Under art. 8(2) State interference into family life is justifiable if: it is in accordance with the law; it is in pursuit of a legitimate aim; and it is necessary in a democratic society. Thus, any intervention must be relevant and sufficient; must meet a pressing social need; and must be proportionate to that need (see, for example, *Olsson* v. *Sweden (No. 1)* (1988) 11 EHRR 259). Under the principle of proportionality (see below), the more serious the intervention into family life, the more compelling must be the justification (*Johansen* v. *Norway* (1997) 23 EHRR 33).

▶ In respect of a State's obligation to take positive measures, art. 8 includes an obligation on national authorities to take measures to reunite parents with their children (see, for example, *Ignaccola-Zenide* v. *Romania* (2001) 31 EHRR 7; and *Nuutinen* v. *Finland (Application No. 32842/96)* (2000) 34 EHRR 358, [2005] 2 FLR 596), unless it is contrary to the interests of those concerned, particularly the best interests of the child (see *Ignaccola-Zenide*) – as the right to family life is not an absolute right. (See also *Gil and Aui* v. *Spain (Application No. 56673/00)* [2005] 1 FLR 190.)

▶ When carrying out the balancing exercise under art. 8(2) between the interests of children and parents and/or the wider public, the court will take into account the paramountcy of the best interests of the child.

### (f)    The Margin of Appreciation

Claims against Member States under the Convention have sometimes failed because the Court of Human Rights has recognised a wide 'margin of appreciation' in the State's decision-making process – in other words, a reasonable discretion is permitted within States to exercise their powers while remaining in compliance with the Convention. The margin of appreciation possessed by the UK meant that for many years transsexuals failed in their claims before the European Court of Human Rights (see 2.7). Where a common approach or practice in respect of a particular matter exists between the different Member States the margin of appreciation will be narrow, but where there are disparities of approach or practice the margin will be wider.

### (g)    The Principle of Proportionality

The principle of proportionality is an important principle in the jurisprudence of the European Court of Human Rights, which must be applied by courts and public authorities in the UK. This principle requires that any interference with a Convention right must be proportionate to the legitimate aim pursued. The principle of proportionality would be breached, for example, if a care order were made to protect a child from significant harm when an alternative remedy would be adequate (see 15.7). In other words, 'a sledge-hammer must not be used to crack a nut'.

The following case provides a recent example of how human rights arguments, including in particular the principle of proportionality, are used by the courts in England and Wales:

▶ *Baiai* v. *Secretary of State for the Home Department* [2007] EWCA Civ 478, [2007] 2 FLR 627

The Court of Appeal had to consider whether a rule (which required persons subject to immigration control to obtain the Home Secretary's permission to marry in the UK, unless they intended to enter into an Anglican marriage) was human rights compliant. It held that this policy was a breach of the ECHR. It was a breach of the right to marry under art. 12, and was discriminatory under art. 14 (as it discriminated against persons who wished to enter into a non-Anglican marriage). The Court of Appeal held that, while art. 12 did not guarantee an absolute right to marry, the right was recognised as an important and fundamental right, not lightly to be interfered with. It held that, while immigration control was a legitimate ground for interfering with art. 12, it did not mean that the State was free to choose whatsoever means of controlling immigration that it considered prudent or necessary, irrespective of its impact on art. 12. The scheme was held to fail the test of proportionality.

(h)   Procedural Fairness (Article 6 ECHR)

Article 6 ECHR provides that in the determination of 'his civil rights and obligations' everyone is entitled to a fair hearing by an independent and impartial tribunal established by law. Article 6 is particularly relevant in the context of child protection cases (see 15.3). In *Re K (Procedure: Family Proceedings Rules)* [2004] EWCA Civ 1827, [2005] 1 FLR 764, for example, an appeal was allowed because of procedural unfairness which was not compliant with art. 6 and art. 8.

## Summary

1   There have been many important legislative developments in family law, in particular the Children Act 1989, the Child Support Act 1991, Part IV of the Family Law Act 1996, the Adoption and Children Act 2002, the Civil Partnership Act 2004 and the Gender Recognition Act 2004.

2   There have been important case-law developments, in particular in respect of ancillary relief on divorce, care plans in respect of children in care, the rights of transsexuals, and the rights of same-sex partners to succeed to their deceased's partner's tenancy on death.

3   Areas of concern and debate include in particular: the vulnerability of cohabitants in respect of property entitlement; delay in the family justice system; giving children a voice in court proceedings; the child support system; and the difficulty of facilitating and enforcing contact on family breakdown.

4   International law is increasingly important in family law.

5   Demographic and social changes, in particular the decline of marriage and the rise in cohabitation, have had an impact on family law.

6   Family law has changed dramatically in the last few years to give 'non-traditional' families and other family members rights, in particular same-sex partners and transsexuals.

7   In family law cases judges have considerable discretion. Cases turn on their own facts.

## Summary cont'd

8  The settlement of family cases by mediation and negotiation is encouraged in order to avoid the disadvantages of going to court, and to reduce hostility and bitterness between the adult parties – which can be harmful for children.

9  Family cases are heard in magistrates' family proceedings courts, county courts and the Family Division of the High Court.

10  The Children and Family Courts Advisory and Support Service (CAFCASS) provides officers to assist the court in family cases.

11  The Human Rights Act 1998 came into force in October 2000. The effect of the Act is to weave the European Convention for the Protection of Human Rights and Fundamental Freedoms into the fabric of English law. Of particular importance in family law cases is art. 8 (the right to family life).

## Further Reading and References

Bainham, 'Changing families and changing concepts – reforming the language of family law' [1998] CFLQ 1.

Booth and Kennedy, 'The "traditional family" and the law' [2005] Fam Law 482.

Cretney, 'The family and the law – status or contract?' [2003] CFLQ 403.

Cretney, *Family Law in the Twentieth Century: A History*, 2003, Oxford University Press.

Cretney and The Rt Hon Dame Elizabeth Butler-Sloss (eds.), *Family Law – Essays for the New Millennium*, 2000, Family Law.

Dewar, 'The normal chaos of family law' (1998) 61 MLR 467.

Eekelaar, 'Family law – keeping us on message' [1999] CFLQ 387.

Fisher, 'Privacy and open justice in the family courts – Parts 1 and 2' [2007] Fam Law 247 and 326.

Harris-Short, 'Family law and the Human Rights Act 1998: judicial restraint or revolution?' [2005] CFLQ 329.

Maclean (ed.), *Family Law and Family Values*, 2005, Hart Publishing.

Munby, The Honourable Mr Justice, 'The family justice system' [2004] Fam Law 574.

Munby, The Honourable Mr Justice, 'Families old and new – the family and Article 8' [2005] CFLQ 487.

Murphy, *International Dimensions in Family Law*, 2005, Manchester University Press.

Potter, Sir Mark, President of the Family Division, 'The Family in the 21st Century', 28/8/06 – Judiciary of England and Wales – Publications and Media (see website below).

Probert, ' "Family law" – a modern concept?' [2004] Fam Law 901.

Ryden, 'Miscarriages of justice, privacy and art. 8 – Parts 1 and 2' [2007] Fam Law 237 and 331.

Walsh, *Working in the Family Justice System: The Official Handbook of the Family Justice Council* (2nd edn), 2006, Family Law.

Wasoff and Dey, *Family Policy*, 2000, The Gildredge Press.

# Websites

## Government Services

**Department for Children, Schools and Families**: www.dcsf.gov.uk
**Department for Work and Pensions**: www.dwp.gov.uk
**Department of Health**: www.doh.gov.uk
**Home Office**: www.homeoffice.gov.uk
**House of Lords' Debates**: www.parliament.the-stationery-office.co.uk/pa/ld/ldhansrd.htm
**Judiciary of England and Wales**: www.judiciary.gov.uk
**Law Commission**: www.lawcom.gov.uk
**Ministry of Justice**: www.justice.gov.uk
**Office for National Statistics**: www.statistics.gov.uk
**United Kingdom Parliament**: www.parliament.uk

## Courts and Law Reports

**British and Irish Legal Information Institute**: www.bailii.org
**European Court of Human Rights**: www.echr.coe.int
**Her Majesty's Courts Service**: www.hmcourts-service.gov.uk
**House of Lords**: www.parliament.uk
**House of Lords' Judgments**: www.publications.parliament.uk/pa/ld/judgmt.htm
**Incorporated Council of Law Reporting**: www.lawreports.co.uk

## Other Legal Materials

**Joseph Rowntree Foundation (research reports, research materials)**: www.jrf.org.uk
**Official Documents**: www.official-documents.co.uk
**SOSIG (Social Sciences Information Gateway)**: www.sosig.ac.uk
**Statute Law Database**: www.statutelaw.gov.uk
**UK Official Publications**: www.ukop.co.uk

## Other Websites

**CAFCASS**: www.cafcass.gov.uk
**Central London Collaborative Forum**: www.centrallondoncollaborativeforum.com
**Families Need Fathers**: www.fnf.org.uk
**Family Justice Council**: www.family-justice-council.org.uk
**Family Mediation Helpline**: www.familymediationhelpline.co.uk
**Family Mediators' Association**: www.fmassoc.co.uk
**Fathers 4 Justice**: www.fathers-4-justice.org
**The Law Society**: www.lawsoc.org.uk
**Legal Services Commission**: www.legalservices.gov.uk
**National Association of Citizens Advice Bureaux**: www.nacab.org.uk
**National Audit Office**: www.nao.org.uk
**Resolution**: www.resolution.org.uk
**UK College of Family Mediators**: www.ukcfm.co.uk

**Websites cont'd**

Abbreviations of Law Journals

**CFLQ**: *Child and Family Law Quarterly.*
**Fam Law**: *Family Law Journal.*
**IFLJ**: *International Family Law Journal.*
**IJLP&F**: *International Journal of Law Policy and the Family.*
**LQR**: *Law Quarterly Review.*
**LS**: *Legal Studies.*
**MLR**: *Modern Law Review.*

# Part II

# Marriage, Civil Partnership and Cohabitation

# Chapter 2

# Marriage and Civil Partnership

This chapter looks at the status relationships of marriage and civil partnership and considers the legal consequences which attach to them. Cohabitation and its legal consequences are considered in Chapter 3.

## 2.1  Marriage

**Article 12 of the European Convention for the Protection of Human Rights**

'Men and women of marriageable age have the right to marry and to found a family according to the national laws governing the exercise of this right.'

▶ **Sir Mark Potter P in *Wilkinson* v. *Kitzinger and Others (No. 2)* [2006] EWHC 2022 (Fam), [2007] 1 FLR 295**

'The common law definition of marriage is that stated by Lord Penzance in *Hyde* v. *Hyde* (1866) . . . "The voluntary union for life of one man and one woman, to the exclusion of all others." This definition has been applied and acted upon by the courts ever since: see for instance *Corbett* v. *Corbett (otherwise Ashley)* [1971] . . . As stated by Lord Nicholls of Birkenhead in *Bellinger* v. *Bellinger (Lord Chancellor Intervening)* [2003] UKHL 21 . . : "Marriage is an institution, or a relationship, deeply embedded in the religious and social culture of this country. It is deeply embedded as a relationship between two persons of the opposite sex."'

Marriage today must be seen against a background of increasing cohabitation. Many couples choose to live together rather than marry. As a result, marriage is on the decline. There are also other trends. Many marriages are second marriages. The age at which people marry for the first time has risen. Many marriages break down and end in divorce.

Concern about the institution of marriage being undermined is sometimes raised when law reform is discussed, whether it be about the introduction of more liberal divorce laws, reform of cohabitants' property rights, or reforms giving greater pre-eminence to pre-marital agreements. In the discussions leading up to the introduction of civil partnerships there was concern about the institution of marriage being further undermined.

Same-sex partners cannot enter into a marriage, and overseas same-sex marriages are not recognised in the UK (see 2.8). However, same-sex partners can, if they wish, enter into a civil partnership under the Civil Partnership Act 2004 and thereby acquire rights and obligations which are virtually identical to those of married couples (see 2.10).

It is now possible for a transsexual person to enter into a valid marriage in his or her acquired gender as a result of reforms introduced by the Gender Recognition Act 2004 (see 2.7).

Marriage is not a contract which can be created and terminated at the will of the parties. It is an arrangement in which the State has an interest. For this reason, there are legal rules governing the creation of a marriage (see below), and rules governing its dissolution (see

Chapter 8). The legal effect of marriage is to give the parties various rights, obligations and privileges (see 2.9).

## 2.2 Contracting a Valid Marriage – Capacity to Marry

To contract a valid marriage the parties must have the capacity to marry and must comply with certain legal formalities relating to the creation of the marriage, otherwise the marriage may be void.

Section 11 Matrimonial Causes Act (MCA) 1973 provides that the parties have capacity to marry if:

(a) they are not within the prohibited degrees of relationship;
(b) they are both over the age of 16;
(c) neither of them is already married; and
(d) one of them is male and the other female.

### (a) Not Within the Prohibited Degrees of Relationship

A marriage is void if the parties are within what are called the 'prohibited degrees of relationship' (s.11(a)(i)). Marriages between certain relatives related by blood or by marriage (affinity) are prohibited by the Marriage Act 1949, as amended by the Marriage (Prohibited Degrees of Relationship) Act 1986. There are fewer restrictions on relationships created by marriage, and the Government has recently removed the restrictions in respect of 'in-law marriages' (see below).

A person is prohibited from marrying the following blood relatives: parent; grandparent; child; grandchild; brother or sister; uncle or aunt; nephew or niece. There are fewer restrictions on marrying a relative who is not a blood relative but where the relationship is created by marriage. Thus a person can marry his or her: step-child; step-parent; step-grandparent; or parent-in-law. However, certain restrictions exist. A person cannot marry a step-child unless both parties are aged 21 or over, and the step-child was not at any time before the age of 18 brought up by that person as a step-child. An adopted child is in the same degrees of prohibited relationships in respect of his or her birth-parents, but fewer restrictions apply to a relationship acquired by adoption (for example, a person can marry an adopted brother or sister).

*'In-Law' Marriages* Restrictions on certain 'in-law' marriage have recently been removed as a result of the following decision of the European Court of Human Rights:

▶ *B and L v. United Kingdom (Application No. 36536/02)* [2006] 1 FLR 35

A father-in-law and his daughter-in-law claimed that the bar on 'in-law' marriages was a breach of their fundamental right to marry under art. 12 ECHR. The daughter-in-law (L) wished to marry her 60-year-old father-in-law (B). She had previously been married to his son, but the marriage had broken down and she had developed a relationship with his father. The Superintendent Registrar refused to give them permission to marry, because B's son (L's former husband) was still alive. They took their case to the ECtHR, which allowed their claim, holding that the UK was in breach of art. 12. The prohibition was neither rational nor logical and served no useful purpose of public policy.

After the decision, the UK Government was forced to change the law to remove the bar on marriages between parties such as those in *B and L*, in order to remedy the incompatibility with the ECHR. It did so by passing the Marriage Act 1949 (Remedial Order) 2007, which has amended Sched. 1 to the Marriage Act 1949 so that the provisions forbidding the marriage of a person to the parent of his or her former spouse and the marriage of a person to the former spouse of his or her child are now repealed.

### (b)    Over the Age of 16

A marriage is void if either party is under the age of 16 (s.2 Marriage Act (MA) 1949; s.11(a)(ii) Matrimonial Causes Act 1973). If either party is under 18, the Marriage Act 1949 requires that consent to the marriage must be given by: parent(s) with parental responsibility; special guardians; any person with whom the child lives under a residence order (in substitution for parental or guardian consent); a local authority if the child is in care (in addition to parental and guardian consent); and, if a residence order is no longer in force, but was in force immediately before the child attained the age of 16, the consent of the person(s) with whom the child lived under that order (s.3). If the child is a ward of court, the court's consent is also required (s.3(6)). Consent can be dispensed with if a person whose consent is needed is absent or is inaccessible or suffers from a disability (s.3(1)(a)). If a person refuses to give consent, the court can give consent (s.3(1)(b)), but such applications are exceedingly rare – in fact almost non-existent. If a marriage is solemnised without consent, it will usually be valid (s.24).

At one time (in fact as late as the early 1960s) parents would sometimes invoke the wardship jurisdiction (see 9.7) to prevent their young daughters entering into marriage with an unsuitable person. Although this jurisdiction is still available, it is unlikely to be resorted to, and the High Court is unlikely to exercise it. However, wardship is sometimes used for the purpose of preventing a 16- or 17-year-old, who lacks capacity, from entering into an unsuitable marriage, or to protect a young person who is being forced to marry (see 2.6).

### (c)    Not Already Married

A party to a marriage must not be already married, otherwise the marriage is void (s.11(b) MCA 1973). Marriage is 'the voluntary union for life of one man and one woman to the exclusion of all others' (Lord Penzance in *Hyde* v. *Hyde* (1866) LR 1 P & D 130). A spouse who remarries without an earlier marriage being terminated may commit the crime of bigamy. Even if the parties reasonably believe that the other party is dead, the marriage is still void, and even if the spouse subsequently dies, the later marriage remains void. Where a spouse has disappeared and/or is thought to be dead, the other spouse can apply for a decree of presumption of death and dissolution of marriage, which, if granted, prevents the second marriage being bigamous even if the first spouse reappears (see 7.10).

### (d)    Respectively Male and Female

The parties to a marriage must be respectively male and female, otherwise the marriage is void (s.11(c) MCA 1973). Same-sex marriages are not permitted in the UK, but same-sex partners can, if they wish, enter into a civil partnership (see 2.10). There have been changes to the law governing the rights of transsexuals to marry (see 2.7).

## 2.3 Contracting a Valid Marriage – Preliminary Formalities

In addition to having the capacity to marry, the parties must satisfy certain preliminary formalities before the marriage can take place. The purpose of these preliminaries is to establish that the required consents have been given and that there are no lawful impediments to the marriage taking place. The marriage ceremony itself must also comply with certain formalities, and the marriage must be registered.

Two systems of preliminary formalities exist: (a) one for all marriages other than those celebrated in the Church of England; and (b) one for Church of England marriages.

### (a) Civil Preliminaries for All Marriages (Other Than Those Celebrated in the Church of England)

All marriages, other than Church of England marriages, must be preceded by preliminary formalities for which the superintendent registrar of the relevant district is responsible under the Registration Act 1953. A marriage can be solemnised in a register office or in any venue that has been approved for the purpose of civil marriage, but only after the grant of: (i) a superintendent registrar's certificate; or (ii) a Registrar-General's licence.

*(i) A Superintendent Registrar's Certificate*  Both parties must give notice of the marriage in prescribed form to the superintendent registrar in the district (or districts) in which each of them has resided for at least the previous seven days (s.27(1) MA 1949), and also the register office where the ceremony is to take place (if this is different). Both parties must attend the register office in person to give notice. A fee must be paid. The notice must be accompanied by a solemn declaration that there are no lawful impediments to the marriage, that the residence requirements have been satisfied and that the required consents have been given. Notice of the marriage is entered in a marriage notice book, and is publicly displayed in the register officer. At the end of a 15-day period from the giving of notice, and provided there has been no objection to the marriage, the superintendent registrar issues a certificate, after which the marriage must be solemnised within three months from the date of entry of the notice in the marriage notice book (s.31 MA 1949). The Registrar-General has the power in exceptional circumstances to reduce the 15-day period (s.31(5A) MA 1949).

Persons who are housebound due to illness or disability (which is likely to last for at least three months), and persons detained in prison or detained due to mental ill-health, can marry on the authority of a superintendent registrar's certificate in the place where they are residing or are detained (see the Marriage Act 1983).

*(ii) Registrar-General's Licence*  This procedure is available only in exceptional circumstances, such as when a person is seriously ill and not expected to recover and cannot be moved to a place where the marriage can be solemnised. It authorises the solemnisation of marriage in a place other than a register office, or an Anglican church or a place registered for worship (Marriage (Registrar-General's Licence) Act 1970).

### (b) Church of England Preliminaries

A Church of England marriage can be solemnised after the publication of banns (which the vicar deals with), or the grant of a superintendent registrar's certificate, or Registrar-

General's licence (see above). Most marriages usually take place, however, after the publication of banns.

## 2.4 Contracting a Valid Marriage – The Marriage Ceremony

### (a) Formalities in Respect of the Marriage Ceremony

The marriage ceremony must comply with certain formalities, which differ depending on whether the marriage is a civil or a religious one.

*(i) Civil Marriages*   Once the preliminary formalities have been satisfied (see above), the marriage can be solemnised in a register office or in 'approved premises' (a venue which has been approved for the purposes of conducting a civil marriage), or, in special cases, in the place where the person is housebound or detained. Under the Marriage Act 1994 'approved premises' are premises approved for marriage by local authorities in accordance with regulations laid down by the Secretary of State. Many hotels, stately homes, castles and other places are 'approved premises'. The ceremony, whether in a register office or approved premises, is public and secular, but may be followed by a religious ceremony in a church or chapel (s.46 MA 1949). It is the civil ceremony, however, which is legally binding. At the civil ceremony, the parties must declare that there are no lawful impediments to the marriage and they must exchange vows. The ceremony must be witnessed by at least two witnesses in the presence of the superintendent registrar and a registrar of the district in which the premises are situated. Some registrars remind the parties of the solemn nature of the vows they are making.

*(ii) Church of England Marriages*   After complying with the preliminary formalities (see above), the marriage is solemnised by a clergyman according to the rites of the Church of England in the presence of at least two witnesses.

*(iii) Quaker and Jewish Marriages*   A Quaker or Jewish marriage cannot be solemnised until the civil preliminary formalities above have been satisfied. Quakers must also make special declarations when giving notice (s.47 MA 1949). Both parties to a Jewish marriage must profess to belong to the Jewish faith (s.26(1)(d) MA 1949). Quaker and Jewish marriages are celebrated according to their own religious rites, but they need not take place in a registered building, or in public, or before an authorised person. There are special rules for the registration of Quaker and Jewish marriages.

*(iv) Other Religious Marriages*   Other religious marriages can be solemnised after the parties have complied with the civil preliminary formalities above. The certificate will state where the ceremony is to be held, which will usually be a 'registered building' in the district where one of the parties resides. A 'registered building' is a building registered by the Registrar-General as 'a place of meeting for religious worship' (s.41 MA 1949). Some Sikh and Hindu temples and Muslim mosques are registered. If a marriage takes place in a building which is not registered for the purpose of marriage, the marriage may be void, or there may be no marriage at all (see below).

A non-Anglican religious marriage must be attended either by a registrar or an 'authorised person' and must take place in the presence of at least two witnesses and be open to the public. The ceremony can take any form, provided that during the ceremony the required declarations are made.

### (b) Effect of Non-Compliance with Formalities

Breach of the formality requirements can attract criminal sanctions. Giving a false declaration is an act of perjury. A false declaration, however, may not necessarily prevent a person from obtaining ancillary relief under Part II of the Matrimonial Causes Act 1973 (see *J* v. *S-T (Formerly J) (Transsexual: Ancillary Relief)* [1997] 1 FLR 402, where a transsexual committed an act of perjury by entering into a marriage after having concealed his true gender from the registrar).

*Void Marriage or 'Non-Marriage'?* A failure to comply with marriage formalities results in the marriage being void, or there being no marriage at all (a 'non-marriage'). The distinction is important, because in the case of a 'non-marriage' a decree of nullity cannot be granted so that it will not be possible to apply for property and finance orders in ancillary relief proceedings (see Chapter 8). The following cases provide examples:

▶ *Ghandi* v. *Patel* [2002] 1 FLR 603

A Hindu marriage ceremony conducted by a Brahmin priest in a London restaurant was held not to be a void marriage but a 'non-marriage' – there was no marriage at all.

▶ *Gereis* v. *Yagoub* [1997] 1 FLR 854

The marriage ceremony took place in a Coptic Orthodox Church not licensed for marriages and was conducted by a priest not licensed to conduct marriages. In nullity proceedings one of the parties submitted that a decree of nullity should not be granted as there was no marriage at all. The court rejected this submission, and held that the church ceremony bore all the hallmarks of an ordinary Christian marriage and that the marriage had been treated as a subsisting marriage by all those who had attended. There was a marriage, but it was void and a decree of nullity was granted under s.11(a)(iii) MCA 1973.

▶ *Alfonso-Brown* v. *Milwood* [2006] 642 (Fam), [2006] 2 FLR 265

A 'marriage' which had taken place in Ghana was held to be no marriage at all, as both parties lacked the necessary intent at the time of the ceremony and neither party had believed that the ceremony was anything other than an engagement ceremony.

*The Common Law Presumption of Marriage from Long Cohabitation* A marriage which fails to comply with the required formalities may be upheld under the common law presumption of marriage from long cohabitation:

▶ *Chief Adjudication Officer* v. *Bath* [2000] 1 FLR 8

The marriage was invalid because it had taken place in a Sikh temple not registered for marriages. As a result Mrs Bath was not entitled to a widow's pension. However the marriage was upheld as valid under the presumption of marriage from long cohabitation. The Court of Appeal said that the presumption can be rebutted, but only by positive, not merely clear, evidence, and that guilty knowledge by both parties was needed for a marriage to be void because of improper formalities under s.49 MA 1949.

▶ *Pazpena de Vire* v. *Pazpena de Vire* **[2001] 1 FLR 460**

The parties had married by proxy in Uruguay. Neither party was present at the marriage ceremony. The couple came to live in England where they lived as husband and wife for 35 years. The wife petitioned for a decree of divorce, or alternatively for a decree of nullity on the ground that the marriage had been defective. The High Court held that there was a valid marriage by reason of the presumption of long cohabitation.

(See also *A-M* v. *A-M* (*Divorce: Jurisdiction: Validity of Marriage*) [2001] 2 FLR 6.)

## 2.5 Void and Voidable Marriages – The Law of Nullity

The law of nullity is laid down in Part I of the Matrimonial Causes Act (MCA) 1973. Like divorce, an annulment is granted in two stages: decree nisi followed by decree absolute (s.1(5)). Only on the grant of the decree absolute is the marriage annulled. A decree can be sought at any time – there is no bar on seeking a decree during the first year of marriage (s.3), as there is for divorce. On or after the grant of the decree, the court has jurisdiction to make finance and property orders under Part II of the MCA 1973 (see Chapter 8).

Nullity petitions are relatively uncommon when compared with divorces. Only 406 petitions for nullity of marriage were filed in the courts in 2006 (*Judicial and Court Statistics 2006*, Cm 7273, 2007, Ministry of Justice).

A decree of nullity can be sought on the ground that the marriage is (a) void or (b) voidable.

### (a) Grounds on Which a Marriage is Void

A void marriage is one that is void *ab initio* (right from the beginning). A decree of nullity is not technically necessary to dissolve a void marriage, but is useful because it gives the court jurisdiction to make finance and property orders equivalent to those which can be made on divorce (see Chapter 8). A third party may bring proceedings in respect of a void marriage. A void marriage is different from a 'non-marriage' (see above). A marriage is void on the following grounds:

**Section 11 Matrimonial Causes Act 1973**

'A marriage celebrated after 31st July 1971 shall be void on the following grounds only, that is to say –

(a) that it is not a valid marriage under the provisions of the Marriage Acts 1949 to 1986, that is to say where –
   (i) the parties are within the prohibited degrees of relationship;
   (ii) either party is under the age of sixteen; or
   (iii) the parties have intermarried in disregard of certain requirements as to the formation of marriage;
(b) that at the time of the marriage either party was already lawfully married;
(c) that the parties are not respectively male and female;
(d) in the case of a polygamous marriage entered into outside England and Wales, that either party was at the time of the marriage domiciled in England and Wales.'

These grounds have been dealt with above. For the purposes of s.11(a)(iii) not every breach of the formality requirements of the Marriage Acts necessarily invalidates a marriage.

There are no 'bars' (statutory defences) for void marriages as there are for voidable marriages. As far as children are concerned, a child born after a void marriage is treated in law as a legitimate child if at the time of conception (or at the time of the marriage ceremony, if later) one party (or both parties) reasonably believed that the marriage was valid (s.1 Legitimacy Act 1976, as amended).

### (b)    Grounds on Which a Marriage May be Voidable

A voidable marriage is a marriage which is a valid and subsisting marriage until annulled by a decree of nullity (s.16 MCA 1973). A marriage is void on the following grounds:

---

**Section 12 Matrimonial Causes Act 1973**

'A marriage celebrated after 31st July 1971 shall be voidable on the following grounds only, that is to say –

(a) that the marriage has not been consummated owing to the incapacity of either party to consummate it;

(b) that the marriage has not been consummated owing to the wilful refusal of the respondent to consummate it;

(c) that either party to the marriage did not validly consent to it, whether in consequence of duress, mistake, unsoundness of mind or otherwise;

(d) that at the time of the marriage either party, though capable of giving a valid consent, was suffering (whether continuously or intermittently) from mental disorder within the meaning of the Mental Health Act 1983, of such a kind or to such an extent as to be unfitted for marriage;

(e) that at the time of the marriage the respondent was suffering from venereal disease in a communicable form;

(f) that at the time of the marriage the respondent was pregnant by some person other than the petitioner;

(g) that an interim gender recognition certificate under the Gender Recognition Act 2004 has, after the time of marriage, been issued to either party to the marriage;

(h) that the respondent is a person whose gender at the time of the marriage had become the acquired gender under the Gender Recognition Act 2004.'

---

Subsections (g) and (h) were added by the Gender Recognition Act 2004 (see 2.7). Certain bars exist (see below).

### (i) Non-Consummation

Cases involving non-consummation sometimes arise in the context of forced marriages (see 2.6) or certain religious marriages. With some religious marriages the civil ceremony takes place first, followed later by a religious ceremony. Only after the religious ceremony are the parties deemed to be married in the eyes of their religion. In some of the reported cases a decree of nullity has been sought because the religious ceremony has not taken place, and the marriage has not been consummated (see *Kaur* v. *Singh* [1972] 1 All ER 292; and *A* v. *J (Nullity)* [1989] 1 FLR 110). As an alternative to non-consummation a party to a forced marriage may petition for a decree of nullity on the ground of lack of consent (see below).

*Consummation*    Consummation is the first act of intercourse after marriage. It must be 'ordinary and complete, not partial and imperfect' (Dr Lushington in *D-E* v. *A-G* (1845) 1 Rob Eccl 279 at 298). It takes place whether or not a condom is used (*Baxter* v. *Baxter* [1948] AC 274), and whether or not ejaculation takes place (*R* v. *R* [1952] 1 All ER 1194).

*Incapacity to Consummate (s.12(a))*    The petition can be based on the petitioner or the respondent's incapacity to consummate. The inability must be permanent and incurable. The court can order a medical examination. Incapacity to consummate includes not just physical incapacity, but 'an invincible repugnance to the respondent due to a psychiatric or sexual aversion' (*Singh* v. *Singh* [1971] 2 WLR 963).

*Wilful Refusal to Consummate (s.12(b))*    To establish wilful refusal there must be 'a settled and definite decision come to without just excuse' and the whole history of the marriage must be looked at (Lord Jowitt LC in *Horton* v. *Horton* [1947] 2 All ER 871 at 874). Refusal can be express or inferred (for example, by a refusal to go through the religious ceremony required). In *Kaur* v. *Singh* [1972] 1 WLR 105 a marriage was arranged between two Sikhs. The civil ceremony took place, but the husband refused to arrange the religious ceremony. The wife was granted a decree of nullity on the ground of her husband's wilful refusal to consummate the marriage. (See also *Jodla* v. *Jodla* [1960] 1 WLR 236.)

Unlike incapacity to consummate, the petition cannot be brought on the basis of the petitioner's own refusal to consummate (see s.11(b)). This means that a wife who has been forced into an arranged marriage, but who refuses to consummate the marriage, cannot petition on this ground; she must prove incapacity to consummate or that she entered into the marriage under duress.

Probert (2005) argues that non-consummation should cease to be a ground for voidable marriages, particularly as it may cause problems for transsexuals. She says that non-consummation as a ground for avoiding a marriage is a legacy of ecclesiastical law, and should be abolished in order to 'define marriage in a way that is relevant for the twenty-first century' (p.385). Consummation has no relevance, however, to civil partnerships.

### (ii) Lack of Consent (s.12(c))

*Duress*    To establish duress the petitioner used to have to prove that his or her will had been overborne by a fear of danger to life, limb or liberty. This principle was laid down by the Court of Appeal in *Szechter (Orse Karzov)* v. *Szechter* [1971] 2 WLR 170, and was applied in *Singh* v. *Kaur* (1981) Fam Law 152, where a decree of nullity was refused because the petitioner was unable to prove a threat of danger to life, limb or liberty. In the following case, however, the Court of Appeal adopted a more sympathetic approach, and relaxed the strict rule:

> ▶ *Hirani* v. *Hirani* (1983) 4 FLR 232
>
> The petitioner, a 19-year-old girl, had entered into an arranged marriage with a man she had never met – because her parents threatened to throw her out of the house if she did not go ahead with the ceremony. The Court of Appeal held, granting the decree of nullity, that there was no requirement that a threat to life, limb or liberty had to be proved. The test for duress was a subjective test. The question to be asked by the court was whether the particular petitioner taking account of his or her personal qualities submitted to the duress. The petitioner's will had been overborne with the result that her consent to the marriage had been vitiated, and she was entitled to a decree.

*Hirani* v. *Hirani* is relevant to the issue of forced marriages (see 2.6 below).

**Lack of Consent – Mistake**  The mistake must be in respect of the identity of the other party (not as to his or her qualities); or there must be a mistake as to the nature of the ceremony (such as where a party mistakenly thinks that the ceremony is an engagement ceremony).

**Lack of Consent – Lack of Capacity to Consent**  Lack of consent may be due to a lack of capacity to consent to the marriage.

Steps may have to be taken to prevent a person who lacks capacity from entering into an unsatisfactory marriage. The inherent jurisdiction of the High Court (see 9.7) can be invoked to protect a vulnerable adult who lacks the capacity to marry (see, for example, *Re PS (Incapacitated Vulnerable Adult)* [2007] EWHC 623 (Fam)). Lack of capacity usually arises owing to mental disorder or mental illness, but it may also arise because of coercion in the context of a forced marriage. The following cases deal with the issue of capacity to marry:

> ▶ *Re E (An Alleged Patient); Sheffied City Council* v. *E and S* [2004] EWHC 2808 (Fam), [2005] 1 FLR 965
>
> The local authority sought to prevent a 21-year-old woman, for whom they had responsibility, marrying a man with a history of sexually violent crimes. The local authority claimed that, as she functioned at the level of a 13-year-old child, she lacked capacity to enter into a marriage. A preliminary issue arose as to the questions to be put to experts in order to establish whether she had the necessary capacity. Munby J held that the law remained as set out by Singleton LJ in the *Estate of Park, Deceased, Re, Park* v. *Park* [1954] P 112, which is that a person must understand the nature of the marriage contract, which means that he or she must be mentally capable of understanding the duties and responsibilities that normally attach to marriage.

> ▶ *M* v. *B, A and S (By the Official Solicitor)* [2005] EWHC 1681 (Fam), [2006] 1 FLR 117
>
> The local authority was concerned that the parents of a young woman aged 23 (with a severe learning disability and who attended special school) were organising an arranged marriage for her in Pakistan. The local authority therefore applied for declarations that the daughter lacked capacity to marry and that it was not in her best interests to leave the jurisdiction. Sumner J made the declarations sought, and held that in appropriate circumstances the court has jurisdiction to grant an injunction restraining those persons responsible for an adult who lacks capacity from entering into a contract of marriage, if such an order is required to protect the adult's best interests.

> ▶ *Re SA (Vulnerable Adult With Capacity: Marriage)* **[2005] EWHC 2942 (Fam), [2006] 1 FLR 867**
>
> The local authority feared that a 17-year-old girl (who was profoundly deaf, unable to speak, and who had the intellect of a 13- or 14-year-old) might be taken by her family to Pakistan for the purposes of an arranged marriage. Munby J made an order under the inherent jurisdiction of the High Court requiring the girl to be properly informed, in a manner she would understand, about any specific marriage prior to entering into it. He held that the inherent jurisdiction could be exercised in relation to a vulnerable adult who was not incapacitated by mental disorder or mental illness, but who was (or was reasonably believed to be) incapacitated due to being subjected to constraint, coercion or undue influence; or for some other reason deprived of the capacity to give genuine consent.
>
> ▶ *X City Council* **v. *MB, NB and Mab (By His Litigation Friend The Official Solicitor)* [2006] EWHC 168 (Fam), [2006] 2 FLR 968**
>
> A 25-year-old man who, as a result of autism, lacked capacity to marry was given protection by Munby J under the inherent jurisdiction of the High Court on the application of the local authority, in order to prevent him being taken abroad by his parents to be married in Pakistan.

**(c)**  Voidable Marriages – Statutory Bars

Section 13 Matrimonial Causes Act 1973 lays down the following bars (statutory defences) to nullity petitions in cases of *voidable* marriage:

*Approbation by the Petitioner*   The court cannot grant a decree on any ground in s.12 if the respondent proves that: the petitioner knew that he or she could have avoided the marriage, but whose conduct in relation to the respondent led the respondent reasonably to believe that the petitioner would not do so; and the court considers that it would be unjust to the respondent to grant the decree (s.13(1)).

*The Three-Year Bar*   The court cannot grant a decree on ground (c), (d), (e), (f) or (h) of s. 12 MCA 1973 (see p.30, above) unless proceedings are instituted within three years of the marriage (s.13(2)). But the court can grant leave to apply after that three-year period if the petitioner has suffered from a mental disorder within the meaning of the Mental Health Act 1983 and it would in all the circumstances be just to grant leave (ss.13(4), (5)).

*Six-Month Bar*   A decree cannot be granted on ground (g) (issue of interim gender recognition certificate) unless proceedings were instituted within six months of the issue of the interim gender recognition certificate (s.13(2A)).

*Ignorance*   A decree cannot be granted on grounds (e), (f) and (h) unless the court is satisfied that the petitioner was ignorant of those facts at the time of the marriage (s.13(3)).

## 2.6    Forced Marriages

### (a)    The Problem of Forced Marriages

A forced marriage is one which is conducted without the valid consent of one or both of the parties and where duress is a factor. It is not the same as an arranged marriage – one where the families of both spouses take a leading role in choosing a marriage partner, but where the choice of whether to accept the arrangement remains with the potential spouses. In *NS* v. *MI* [2006] EWHC 1646 (Fam), [2007] 1 FLR 444, where a decree of nullity was granted to the petitioner in a forced marriage case as she had satisfied the test set out in *Hirani* v. *Hirani* (see above), Munby J said that, while forced marriages were utterly unacceptable, arranged marriages were to be respected and supported.

About 300 forced marriages are reported to the Foreign & Commonwealth Office each year. Most cases involve young women being pressured into marriage, but a small number involve the coercion of men. Many cases involve couples from southern Asia, in particular Bangladesh and Pakistan. In some cases they are used for immigration purposes, because by marriage a person acquires British citizenship and can gain entry into the UK. Forced marriages can involve a wide range of behaviour, including emotional threats, imprisonment, violence, abduction and blackmail. Police forces take forced marriages very seriously and have policy guidelines for dealing with them.

The courts do not tolerate forced marriages. In *Re K; A Local Authority* v. *N and Others* [2005] EWHC 2956 (Fam), [2007] 1 FLR 399 Munby J described forced marriage as 'a gross abuse of human rights' and as 'a form of domestic violence that dehumanises people by denying them their right to choose how to live their lives'. It was, he said, 'an appalling practice'.

The Government does not tolerate forced marriage and has introduced new civil remedies to protect victims (see below).

*What Can Victims Do?*    A person who enters into a forced marriage can have the marriage annulled on the ground that he or she did not consent to the marriage due to duress (see 2.5 above). The inherent jurisdiction of the High Court can be used to protect an adult who is being forced into marriage; or the wardship jurisdiction in the case of a person under the age of 18 (see 9.7). As Munby J said in *Re K* (above) the courts 'will not hesitate to use every weapon in its arsenal if faced with what is, or appears to be, a case of forced marriage'. Public funding is available so that cases can be brought before the court. Forcing someone to marry may be a criminal offence. It may also be a tort (that of trespass to the person or false imprisonment) and give a victim a right to obtain damages and/or injunctive protection. A new civil remedy has been introduced (see further below).

The following case involved the annulment of a forced marriage:

▶ *P v. R (Forced Marriage: Annulment)* [2003] 1 FLR 661

The petitioner, a 20-year-old girl, had been forced to enter into a marriage in Pakistan. Her brother threatened her with violence and she believed that if she did not go ahead with the marriage she would be unable to return to England. Her parents told her that it would bring shame and disgrace on the family if she did not go ahead with the marriage, and during the ceremony her mother forced her to nod by pushing her head forward three times. She signed the marriage certificate out of fear. On her return to England, she petitioned for a decree of nullity. Coleridge J held that she had not validly consented to the marriage, as her consent had been vitiated by force, both physical and emotional. Coleridge J said that in forced marriage cases the proper course of action was for a decree of nullity to be sought under s.12(c) and that in appropriate cases the court should grant a decree, and thereby, as far as possible, remove any stigma which would not be removed by petitioning for a divorce. Public funding should be available in forced marriage cases, so that they could be transferred to the High Court and investigated properly and fully in open court.

A petitioner alleging a forced marriage is required to establish duress by giving oral evidence in open court; but where a petitioner may be reluctant to give evidence (because her family is present) the court will do whatever it can to afford the petitioner protection (*per* Munby J in *NS* v. *MI* [2006] EWHC 1646 (Fam), [2007] 1 FLR 444). A Muslim petitioner will be required to remove her veil when giving evidence, but appropriate arrangements will be made (such as screens and a woman judge, if possible) to enable her to do so without breaching her religious principles (*per* Macur J in *Re S (Practice: Muslim Women Giving Evidence)* [2007] 2 FLR 461, where a young Muslim woman was granted a decree of nullity because she had entered into a forced marriage following a two-year campaign of family pressure).

### (b)  Forced Marriages – Reform of the Law

As a result of concerns about forced marriages, in January 2005 the Home Office and the Foreign & Commonwealth Office established a specialist unit, the Forced Marriage Unit, in order to focus on preventative action and to work closely with community organisations, particularly women's groups. The Unit is responsible for developing Government policy on forced marriages and provides support and information for those persons at risk. It deals with about 300 cases a year, the majority of which involve families of Pakistani and Bangladeshi origin. Some of the cases involve children, sometimes as young as 13.

The Government has discussed whether a new criminal offence of forcing someone to marry should be introduced, but this has been rejected in favour of introducing new civil remedies for victims (see below).

*(i) A New Criminal Offence?*   Under the criminal law, parents and other persons who force a person into marriage can be prosecuted for various offences (for example, kidnapping, false imprisonment, assault, or harassment), but there is no specific criminal offence of forcing someone to marry. In September 2005 the Home Office and the Foreign & Commonwealth Office published a consultation paper (*Forced Marriage: A Wrong Not a Right*) in order to discuss whether a new criminal offence of forcing someone to marry should be introduced. However, after the consultation process had taken place, the idea was shelved by the Government, as the police, the Crown Prosecution Service and the Probation Service offered little support for the proposal. Although creating a new criminal offence had various advantages (for instance, it might create a change of culture, have a deterrent effect, make the law clear, and empower young people), these were felt to be outweighed by the disadvantages. Persons and organisations who responded to the

consultation (see the report published in June 2006) considered that the creation of a new offence could drive forced marriages underground, isolate victims and cause racial segregation at a time of heightened racial tension. In May 2007 the Forced Marriage Unit announced, however, that it had not necessarily ruled out the possibility of introducing a new criminal offence.

*(ii) New Civil Remedies – The Forced Marriage (Civil Protection) Act 2007*    In November 2006 Lord Lester introduced a Private Member's Bill into the House of Lords, the Forced Marriage (Civil Protection) Bill, which received the Royal Assent in July 2007. The Act inserts a new Part 4A into the Family Law Act 1996 to give the High Court and county courts jurisdiction to make forced marriage protection orders (FMPOs) (s.63M).

A FMPO is an order which provides legal protection to actual or potential victims of forced marriages or attempted forced marriages (s.63A(1)). A forced marriage is one where a person has not given full and free consent (s.63A(4)). 'Force' includes not just physical coercion, but coercion by threats or other psychological means (s.63A(6)). The courts have wide powers to include in a FMPO such prohibitions, restrictions or requirements or other such terms as are considered appropriate; and the terms of the order can in particular relate to conduct outside England and Wales as well as (or instead of) conduct within England and Wales (ss.63B(1) and (2)). For example, an order could be made prohibiting a parent taking an unwilling daughter outside England and Wales for the purpose of marriage, or prohibiting a family contacting or molesting a daughter who has taken refuge from her family. In an appropriate case, the court can accept an undertaking from the respondent, instead of making a FMPO (s.63E); but it cannot do so if it would have attached a power of arrest (see below) to a FMPO, had it made one (s.63E(3)).

An application for a FMPO can be made by: a person who needs protection; a relevant third party (as specified by order of the Lord Chancellor, such as a relative, or local authority); or any other person who has leave of the court (s.63C(2)). The court also has jurisdiction to make a FMPO of its own motion (that is, where no application has been made for one) (s.63C(1)).

When deciding whether to exercise its powers under s.63 and, if so, in what manner, the court must consider all the circumstances of the case including the need to secure the health, safety and well-being of the person to be protected (s.63A(2)). In ascertaining that person's well-being the court must, in particular, have regard to that person's wishes and feelings (so far as they are readily ascertainable) as the court considers appropriate in the light of the person's age and understanding (s.63A(3)).

The court can make an *ex parte* FMPO (s.63D). In other words, it can make an order where it is just and convenient to do so, even though the respondent has not been given notice of proceedings.

The court can attach a power of arrest to a FMPO if it considers that the respondent has used or threatened violence against the person being protected (s.63H). The effect of a power of arrest is to give a police constable the power to arrest without warrant a person whom he has reasonable cause for suspecting to be in breach of an order. A respondent who breaches an order can be brought back to the original court for it to consider the alleged breach. Failure to comply with a FMPO, or an undertaking, is contempt of court, which can result in a fine or imprisonment.

A FMPO can be made for a specified period or until varied or discharged (s.63F). The court has the power to vary or discharge an order (s.63G).

## 2.7   Transsexuals and Marriage

Transsexualism is a medically recognised gender identity disorder (gender dysphoria). Persons with this disorder may opt to have a gender reassignment, which involves hormonal treatment, and, in some cases, surgery. These treatments are available on the National Health Service. Advances in medical science and recognition of transsexualism as a genuine medical problem have resulted in the law having to grapple with the issue of what should be the legal effects of acquiring a reassigned sex. One question which has arisen is whether a transsexual person can enter into a valid marriage in his or her reassigned sex. The starting point in the development of the law was the case of *Corbett* v. *Corbett*:

---

▶ *Corbett* v. *Corbett (Otherwise Ashley)* [1971] P 83, [1970] 2 WLR 1306

The petitioner, a man, petitioned for a decree of nullity on the ground that the marriage was void as the respondent was male. The respondent had been born male but had undergone gender reassignment surgery and hormone treatment and lived as a woman. Ormrod J held, granting the decree, that the marriage was void because both parties were male, as a person's biological sex was fixed at birth and could not be altered by a sex-change operation. Ormrod J held that the respondent was male by chromosomal, gonadal and genital criteria, and it was irrelevant that the respondent considered himself philosophically, psychologically and socially to be a woman.

---

The biological test laid down in *Corbett* was applied in subsequent cases (see, for example, *W* v. *W (Nullity: Gender)* [2001] 1 FLR 324), but transsexuals began to take their cases to the European Court of Human Rights. They claimed that they were discriminated against because the restricted biological approach to gender adopted in *Corbett* was applied to, and adversely affected, other areas of their lives:

---

▶ *Rees* v. *United Kingdom* (1986) 9 EHRR 56, [1987] 2 FLR 111

The applicant, a female-to-male transsexual, claimed that UK law violated art. 8 ECHR (right to a private and family life) by failing to provide measures that would legally constitute him as a male and allow him full integration into social life. He argued that the discrepancy between his apparent and legal sex as stated on his birth certificate caused him embarrassment and humiliation whenever the certificate was required to be produced. He also argued that the UK was in breach of art. 12 (right to marry and found a family) as he could not marry a woman. The ECtHR held by 12 votes to 3 that there had been no breach of art. 8, and unanimously that there had been no breach of art. 12. Although the ECtHR said that it was conscious of the distress suffered by transsexuals, this was an area of law where States enjoyed a wide margin of appreciation (a wide discretion). The ECtHR stressed the need, however, for appropriate legal measures to be kept under review, having regard to scientific and societal developments.

---

In *Cossey* v. *United Kingdom* [1991] 2 FLR 492 the ECtHR adopted the same reasoning as in *Rees* and dismissed the claim by the male-to-female transsexual – but by a smaller majority. In *B* v. *France* [1992] 2 FLR 249, where the facts were different from *Rees* and *Cossey*, a French transsexual was successful before the ECtHR as it found that French bureaucracy had made the applicant's daily life unbearable. Despite the requirement in *Rees* that the law should be kept under review, in the following case the ECtHR took the same approach it had taken in *Cossey* and *Rees*:

▶ *Sheffield and Horsham* v. *UK* [1998] 2 FLR 928

The claimants, male-to-female transsexuals, argued that the UK was in breach of arts. 8 and 12 ECHR because of the difficulties and embarrassment they encountered, in particular in respect of their birth certificates and other records recording their original gender. Miss Horsham also wished to marry a male partner in The Netherlands but had been informed that her marriage would not be recognised in English law. The ECtHR held by 11 votes to 9 that there had been no violation of art. 8. The applicants' cases were similar to *Rees* and *Cossey*, and there had been no scientific or legal developments which persuaded the court that it should depart from those decisions. The UK was still entitled to rely on a margin of appreciation to defend its refusal to recognise a post-operative transsexual's identity. The ECtHR held by 18 votes to 2 that there had been no violation of art. 12. It reiterated the principles in *Rees*, and held that the right to marry guaranteed by art. 12 referred to the traditional marriage between persons of the opposite biological sex. However, in the *Horsham* case, the Court forcefully stressed the need for contracting States to keep this area under review, because of increasing social acceptance of transsexualism and growing recognition of the problems which post-operative transsexuals encounter.

The following, a slightly different case, also involved a transsexual:

▶ *X, Y and Z* v. *United Kingdom* [1997] 2 FLR 892

The female-to-male transsexual (X), whose female partner (Y) had had a child (Z) by artificial insemination by donor, was unable to be registered as the child's father as this was not permitted under English law because he was not a man, applying the biological test laid down in *Corbett* (above). He claimed violations of arts. 8 and 14, but his application failed. The ECtHR, while recognising that 'family life' for the purposes of art. 8 was not confined solely to families based on marriage, held that there was a wide margin of appreciation and that, where the community had interests in maintaining a coherent system of family law which prioritised the best interests of the child, it could be justifiably cautious about changing the law. The applicant was not prevented from acting as the child's father in a social sense and could apply for a joint residence order with his partner, and thereby acquire parental responsibility for the child.

In the following case the ECtHR took a different approach to transsexuals, and it was this case that led to a change of the law in the UK:

▶ *Goodwin* v. *United Kingdom* (2002) 35 EHRR 18, [2002] 2 FLR 487

The applicant, a male-to-female transsexual, claimed that the UK had violated arts. 8 and 12 ECHR because it failed to recognise the legal status of transsexual persons in respect of employment, social security, State pensions, car insurance and marriage.

The European Court of Human Rights held, unanimously, that the UK was in breach of art. 8 (right to family life) and art. 12 (right to marry). In respect of art. 8, the unsatisfactory situation whereby post-operative transsexuals lived in an intermediate zone as not quite one gender or the other was no longer sustainable. The UK could no longer claim that the matter fell within their margin of appreciation. As there were no significant factors of public interest to weigh against the interest of the applicant in obtaining legal recognition of gender reassignment, the fair balance inherent in the Convention tilted in her favour. Accordingly there had been a breach of art. 8.

In respect of art. 12, the term 'man and woman' in relation to the fundamental right to marry in art. 12 could not still be assumed to refer to a determination of gender by purely biological criteria. A test of gender based purely on biological factors (as laid down by Ormrod J in *Corbett*) was not appropriate to the current understanding of transsexualism, and could no longer be decisive in denying legal recognition to the change of gender of a post-operative transsexual. There were other important factors, such as the acceptance of the condition of gender identity disorder by the medical profession, the provision of treatment including surgery, and the assumption by transsexual people of the social role of the assigned gender. As the applicant had no possibility of marrying a man but yet lived as a woman, was in a relationship with a man and would only wish to marry a man, the very essence of her right to marry had been infringed and there was no justification for barring her from enjoying that right under the circumstances. Accordingly there had been a breach of art. 12.

In *I v. United Kingdom* [2002] 2 FLR 518, heard with *Goodwin*, the applicant was a male-to-female transsexual who had not been admitted to a nursing course because she had failed to show her birth certificate (which stated she was male). The UK government, as in *Goodwin*, raised the margin of appreciation defence, but the ECtHR, applying the same reasoning as in *Goodwin*, held that there were violations of arts. 8 and 12.

In *Goodwin*, the ECtHR was referred to *Re Kevin: Validity of Marriage of Transsexual* [2001] Fam CA 1074, a decision of the Australian Family Court, where Chisholm J had strongly criticised the reasoning in *Corbett* and had upheld the validity of a marriage between a woman and a female-to-male transsexual. Chisholm J said that sex was to be determined at the date of marriage, having regard to all relevant factors, including life experiences and self-perception.

*Changing Attitudes to Transsexualism*   As a result of the decisions in *Goodwin* and *I v. UK* (above), the UK was obliged to comply with its Convention obligations and decide whether to reform the law in order to permit the amendment of birth certificates and the recognition of gender change. Before *Goodwin* had been decided, however, certain Government developments had already begun to open up the possibility of a different approach to transsexualism being adopted. In April 1999 the Home Office set up an Interdepartmental Working Group on Transsexual People, which reported to Parliament in July 2000 (*Report of the Interdepartmental Working Group on Transsexual People*, Home Office, 2000). After the decision in *Goodwin* the Interdepartmental Working Group on Transsexual People was reconvened in 2002, and the Government announced that it would introduce legislation to reflect the decisions in *Goodwin* and *I v. UK*, which would include not only changes in respect of birth certificates, inheritance provision and pension rights, but which would give transsexuals the right to marry a person of the opposite sex to their post-operative sex. Measures would also be introduced so that transsexuals would be better protected from constantly and unnecessarily having to reveal their history.

Subsequent to these developments the House of Lords in the following case had to consider the legal position of transsexuals in the light of the obligations imposed by the Human Rights Act 1998:

▶ *Bellinger* v. *Bellinger (Lord Chancellor Intervening)* [2003] UKHL 21, [2003] 1 FLR 1043

Mr Bellinger and Mrs Bellinger (a male-to-female transsexual) had married in 1981 and lived happily since then. Mrs Bellinger sought a declaration in the High Court under s.55 Family Law Act 1986 that the marriage was a valid and subsisting marriage. Johnson J in the High Court, and the Court of Appeal by a majority, refused to grant the declaration, applying the biological test of gender laid down in *Corbett* v. *Corbett* (above). Mrs Bellinger appealed to the House of Lords, arguing that the Court of Appeal's decision was incompatible with the ECHR and was therefore unlawful under s.7 HRA 1998. As the UK courts must take account of the judgments of the ECtHR when determining any question arising in connection with a Convention right (s.2(1) HRA 1998), the *Goodwin* case (above) became relevant to the appeal before the House of Lords. Under the HRA 1998 a court is a public authority (s.6(3)) and must act in accordance with the ECHR (s.6(1)), and, so far as it is possible to do so, primary legislation must be read and given effect to in a way which is compatible with Convention rights (s.3(1)). Under s.4 HRA 1998 the House of Lords also had the power to declare s.11(c) MCA 1973 incompatible with the ECHR.

The House of Lords held, dismissing the appeal, that to allow the appeal would represent a major change in the law which was better dealt with by Parliament rather than by the courts, particularly as the Government had already said that it would introduce legislation on the matter. But it made a declaration under s.4 HRA 1998 that s.11(c) MCA 1973 was incompatible with arts. 8 and 12 ECHR.

After the decisions in *Goodwin* and *Bellinger*, the Government was put under pressure to consider reforming the law in order to improve the legal position of transsexuals. As a result the Gender Recognition Act 2004 was enacted.

*The Gender Recognition Act 2004* The Gender Recognition Act (GRA) 2004 gives legal recognition in their acquired gender to transsexuals who can show that they have taken decisive steps towards living fully and permanently in their acquired gender. The Act came into force on 4 April 2005.

Under the GRA 2004 a transsexual person aged at least 18 can obtain a gender recognition certificate issued by the Gender Recognition Panel (s.1). If a full gender recognition certificate is issued, the person's gender becomes for all purposes the acquired gender (s.9). The practical effect of a gender recognition certificate is to provide a transsexual person with legal recognition in the acquired gender. Thus, he or she is entitled to a new birth certificate reflecting the acquired gender, and is able to enter into a valid marriage or valid civil partnership in his or her new gender.

Before issuing a certificate, the Gender Recognition Panel must be satisfied that the applicant (s.2): has, or has had, gender dysphoria; has lived in the acquired gender throughout the preceding two years; and intends to continue to live in the acquired gender until death. The Gender Recognition Panel can only issue an interim gender recognition certificate to a married applicant (s.4). If within six months of the issue of the interim certificate the marriage is ended, the applicant can seek a full certificate (s.5). The GRA 2004 also amends the law of nullity (see below).

*Parenthood*   Section 12 GRA 2004 provides that, although a person is regarded as being of the acquired gender, that person retains their original status as father or mother of a child. This provision ensures the continuity of parental rights and responsibilities.

*Annulling a Marriage or Civil Partnership to a Transsexual Partner*   The GRA 2004 lays down provisions in respect of nullity of a marriage. Thus, a party to a marriage can have the marriage annulled under the Matrimonial Causes Act 1973 on the ground that it is voidable on the basis that one of the parties is seeking a certificate from the Gender Recognition Panel (s.12(g) MCA 1973) or on the ground that he or she married a transsexual person in ignorance of that fact (s.12(h) MCA 1973). Proceedings must be instituted within three years of the marriage and the petitioner must have been ignorant of the facts at the time of marriage (ss.13(2) and (3) MCA 1973). The same rules apply to civil partnerships.

## 2.8 Recognition of an Overseas Marriage

*(i) Recognition of an Overseas Marriage*   A marriage contracted overseas (in other words, out of the jurisdiction of the UK) may be recognised as valid in England and Wales under the Family Law Act 1986, provided: each of the parties has the capacity to marry according to his or her place of domicile; and the formalities required by the law of the place where the marriage was celebrated were complied with. An overseas marriage celebrated by local custom may be recognised, as it was in *McCabe* v. *McCabe* [1994] 1 FLR 410, where a marriage which had taken place in Ghana (involving a bottle of whisky and a sum of money) was upheld as valid, with the result that the petitioner was entitled to a divorce in the English courts. Special rules apply in certain cases, for instance where a party is serving in HM Forces (see Foreign Marriages Acts 1892–1947).

*(ii) A Same-Sex Overseas Marriage is Not Recognised in the UK*   A same-sex marriage entered into legally overseas will not be recognised by the courts in England and Wales as being a valid marriage in the UK – although it may be recognised as a valid civil partnership. This is so, even though it is now possible for same-sex couples to enter into a civil partnership in the UK (see 2.10). In the following case, a lesbian couple unsuccessfully applied to have their Canadian marriage recognised in England and Wales:

▶ *Wilkinson* v. *Kitzinger and Others (No. 2)* [2006] EWHC 2022 (Fam), [2007] 1 FLR 295

Wilkinson (the petitioner) and Kitzinger (the respondent) were a lesbian couple living in England who had married in British Columbia, Canada. They wished their Canadian marriage to be regarded as a valid marriage in the UK. An application for a declaration as to marital status was made under s.55 Family Law Act 1986. They argued that ss.212–218 of the Civil Partnership Act 2004 (which treat an overseas marriage as a civil partnership) and s.11(c) Matrimonial Causes Act 1973 (parties to a marriage must be male and female) violated their human rights under the following articles of the European Convention for the Protection of Human Rights: art. 8 (right to family life); art. 12 (right to marry); and art. 14 (discrimination in respect of an ECHR right). In the alternative, they argued that the common law definition of marriage should be developed so as to recognise same-sex marriages; and they sought a declaration under s.4(2) Human Rights Act 1998 that the relevant statutory provisions above were incompatible with arts. 8, 12 and 14 ECHR.

Sir Mark Potter P dismissed the petition as there had been no violation of the parties' human rights. There was no consensus, he said, about same-sex marriages in Europe, and the ECtHR had declared itself slow to trespass into this area. There was no breach of art. 8 because, according to the jurisprudence of the ECtHR, the right to family life did not extend to childless same-sex couples. There was no breach of art. 12 because Strasbourg jurisprudence referred to marriage in the traditional sense – as a marriage between a man and a woman. The 'living instrument' doctrine, by which the ECHR is to be interpreted in the light of present-day conditions, could not be applied to art. 12 to bring it within the scope of Convention issues which were plainly outside its contemplation. The difference in treatment of same-sex couples was reasonable, legitimate and proportionate. Parliament had enacted the Civil Partnership Act 2004 as a policy choice creating a legal status for same-sex partners, but at the same time demonstrating support for marriage. Sir Mark Potter P said that this Act had accorded to same-sex partners all the advantages of civil marriage, save in name.

Bamforth (2007), commenting on *Wilkinson* v. *Kitzinger*, has discussed whether civil partnership and marriage should be seen as parallel institutions for legal purposes and whether the existence of two mutually exclusive institutions is permissible under the European Convention for the Protection of Human Rights. He concluded, however, that the prospect of bringing a successful human rights challenge to the civil partnership scheme was not great.

## 2.9  The Legal Consequences of Marriage

On marriage, the parties acquire a legal status from which various rights and duties flow.

### (a)  Separate Legal Personalities

Each spouse has a separate legal personality. This means that a husband and a wife can each own property solely (or jointly) and can bring proceedings in tort and contract separately against each other or against third parties (Law Reform (Married Women and Tortfeasors) Act 1935; s.1 Law Reform (Husband and Wife) Act 1962). They can also enter into contracts with each other. In *Balfour* v. *Balfour* [1919] 2 KB 571 the Court of Appeal held that an agreement between a husband and a wife in respect of maintenance was unenforceable because there was no intention to enter into legal relations; but this is an old case, and attitudes have changed. Today there is a considerable emphasis in family law on the importance of reaching agreement, and a contract may be upheld, provided there is no inequality of bargaining power or some other vitiating factor. In fact, pre-marital and post-marital contracts are increasingly being recognised – even though divorce courts retain a supervisory jurisdiction to scrutinise them (see Chapter 8).

As spouses have separate legal personalities, they can make unilateral decisions about their own medical treatment. This includes the right of a wife to abort a child born of the marriage. In *Paton* v. *British Pregnancy Advisory Service Trustees* [1979] QB 276 the husband applied for an injunction to prohibit the defendant carrying out an abortion on his wife, but his application failed.

## (b)   Financial Obligations

Parties to a marriage have a mutual duty to maintain each other during the marriage (and in some cases after marriage), and they can obtain financial provision orders from the court against the other party if he or she fails to provide such maintenance. In practice, however, applications are rare – because any dispute is likely to arise in the context of divorce, when the divorce court has powers to determine the allocation of any finance or property in dispute (see Chapter 8). Spouses have a duty to provide maintenance for any child of the family (see Chapter 13).

Married couples can apply for financial orders from (i) the magistrates' family proceedings court, or (ii) the county court or the High Court under the following statutory provisions:

*(i) An Application for Financial Provision in the Family Proceedings Court*   Under the Domestic Proceedings and Magistrates' Courts Act 1978 the family proceedings court has jurisdiction to make periodical payments and lump sum orders on the application of a spouse (or of its own motion) if the respondent spouse (s.1(1)): has failed to provide reasonable maintenance for the applicant; or has failed to provide, or to make proper contribution towards, reasonable maintenance for any child of the family; or has behaved in such a way that the applicant spouse cannot reasonably be expected to live with the respondent; or has deserted the applicant. Orders can be made in favour of the applicant or to or for the benefit of a child, but most child maintenance cases are dealt with by the Child Support Agency (see 13.2). When considering whether to make an order and, if so, in what manner, the magistrates must have regard to all the circumstances of the case (including certain specified matters), but with first consideration being given to the welfare of any child of the family (s.3). The court must not dismiss the application or make a final order, however, until it has considered whether it should exercise any of its powers under the Children Act 1989 (s.8). The magistrates have the power to make consent orders (s.6), and can also make periodical payments orders where the parties have been living apart by agreement and one of the parties has been making periodical payments (s.7). Orders can be varied or revoked (s.20).

*(ii) Financial Provision in the County Court or High Court*   Under s.27 Matrimonial Causes Act 1973 the county court or High Court can make orders for periodical payments and lump sums where the applicant spouse proves that the other spouse has failed to provide reasonable maintenance for the applicant (s.27(1)(a)), or has failed to provide, or to make a proper contribution towards, reasonable maintenance for any child of the family (s.27(1)(b)). An order may be made in favour of the applicant and/or to or for the benefit of any child of the family, but most child support claims are dealt with by the Child Support Agency (see 13.2). The statutory criteria laid down in s.25 Matrimonial Causes Act 1973 (see 8.4) govern the exercise of the court's discretion.

*(iii) Agreements about Maintenance*   Married couples can enter into agreements about maintenance, but an agreement cannot be conclusive, as the court has the power to vary or revoke the terms of an agreement and can insert new terms. Also, any provision in an agreement prohibiting the right of one of the parties to apply to the court for an order for financial provision is void. Private maintenance agreements are not precluded by the child

support legislation, but any provision in an agreement restricting the right of a person to apply to the Child Support Agency is void (see 13.2).

### (c)  The Criminal Law

For the purposes of giving evidence, the spouse of the accused is a competent witness for the prosecution, the accused and any co-accused, except where the spouses are jointly charged, when neither is competent to give evidence for the prosecution if either of them is liable to be convicted (s.80 Police and Criminal Evidence Act 1984). A person has the right to refuse to give evidence against a spouse except where the spouse is charged with personal violence against the other spouse or against a child under 16, or a sexual offence against a child under 16 (s.80). A husband can commit the crime of rape against his wife, as the common law rule that by marriage a wife impliedly consents to intercourse was overturned by the House of Lords in *R* v. *R* [1992] 1 AC 599, where Lord Keith said that marriage 'is in modern times regarded as a partnership of equals and no longer one in which the wife must be the subservient chattel of the husband'.

### (d)  Property Rights

As each party to a marriage has a separate legal personality, each party may own property solely or jointly. During a marriage, the rules governing property ownership are the same as those which apply to other persons, with the exception of some special statutory provisions which apply only to spouses (see 4.2). The position is different, however, on divorce (see Chapter 8). Married persons, unlike cohabitants, also enjoy statutory rights of occupation of the family home ('home rights') under s.30 of Part IV of the Family Law Act 1996 (see 4.2).

**Property Rights on Death**   Each spouse is free to make a will leaving his or her property to whomsoever he or she wishes. On intestacy (that is, where there is no will) the surviving spouse succeeds to the estate of the deceased spouse. A surviving spouse can apply under the Inheritance (Provision for Family and Dependants) Act 1975 for reasonable provision from the other party's estate without having to prove dependency or that he or she was being maintained by the deceased party (see 5.3). Marriage automatically revokes an existing will unless it has been made in contemplation of marriage (see 5.1).

### (e)  Children

Parents who are married have 'automatic' parental responsibility in law for their children (see 10.5). They can apply for residence and contact orders (and other orders under s. 8 Children Act 1989) (see 11.4). Spouses have a duty to provide maintenance for any child of the family. They can apply for financial provision for a child under Sched. 1 to the Children Act 1989 (see 13.5), and spouses can seek child support (see 13.2).

### (f)  Protection Against Domestic Violence and Harassment

Spouses (and former spouses) can seek remedies under Part IV of the Family Law Act 1996 and under the Protection from Harassment Act 1997 (see Chapter 6) to protect them from violence in the home.

### (g)    Rights on the Breakdown of a Marriage

On marriage breakdown, a married person can petition for divorce, nullity or judicial separation under Part I of the Matrimonial Causes Act 1973 (see Chapter 7); and can apply to the court under Part II of the 1973 Act for property and financial orders, including orders in respect of the matrimonial home and orders in respect of pension entitlement (see Chapter 8).

### (h)    Rights in Respect of Adoption

Married couples can jointly (and in some circumstances solely) apply to adopt a child. They also have rights in respect of giving consent to (or refusing to give consent to) the adoption of their child (see Chapter 16).

### (i)    Citizenship and Immigration

Under the British Nationality Act 1981 a person who marries a British citizen does not automatically acquire British citizenship, but can apply for naturalisation under conditions which are more favourable than those which apply to other persons, including cohabitants. As far as children are concerned, a child born in the UK is a British citizen if either of his or her married parents is a British citizen. Under the Immigration Act 1971 a British citizen has the right to live in and to enter and leave the UK. Whether or not a non-British spouse of a British citizen is able to live in and enter and leave the UK is governed by the immigration rules, but a person may be refused permission to enter the UK if the marriage is a 'sham', in other words one entered into merely for the purpose of circumventing the immigration rules.

### (j)    Taxation; Pensions

Transfers between parties to a marriage are exempt from inheritance tax, and a transfer between spouses does not give rise to a chargeable gain for the purpose of capital gains tax. There is an exemption from capital gains tax on the disposal of a dwelling house which has been the main or only residence of a married couple. A married person can benefit from a deceased spouse's pension rights.

## 2.10    Civil Partnerships

### (a)    Introduction

In some countries same-sex couples can enter into a valid marriage (for example, in The Netherlands, Canada, Belgium and Spain). In others they can enter into a registered civil partnership (for example, in Denmark, Sweden, Finland, Portugal, France and Germany). Some of these civil partnership schemes are also open to opposite-sex couples (such as in France). Under the Civil Partnership Act (CPA) 2004 (which came into force on 5 December 2005) same-sex partners in the UK can now register their partnership and by doing so acquire rights and obligations similar to those of married couples. Although the Government has been keen to stress that civil partnership is not 'gay marriage', there are in fact very few differences between civil partnership and marriage. As Sir Mark Potter P said in *Wilkinson* v. *Kitzinger* (see p.41, above), the 2004 Act had accorded to same-sex partners all the advantages of civil marriage, save in name.

Before the CPA 2004 came into force various informal registration schemes were available in England and Wales enabling same-sex (and opposite-sex) couples to declare their partnership (for example, the London Partnership Register introduced in 2001). The disadvantage of these informal schemes, however, was that they created no legally recognised status and consequently had no legal effects.

Because of the disadvantages for same-sex couples compared with married couples, there was increasing discussion about implementing new laws to permit civil partnership registration. Discussion was fuelled largely by pressure from the gay community, in particular the gay pressure group Stonewall, who felt that same-sex couples suffered many disadvantages as a result of being treated as separate individuals rather than as a couple. Visiting a partner in hospital or organising a partner's funeral arrangements, for example, created difficulties, because of confusion as to whether a partner was next-of-kin. Same-sex couples were also denied employment benefits and pension rights, and some found themselves unable to remain in their partner's home on death, or to succeed to their deceased partner's estate on intestacy. In fact, the House of Lords, even before civil partnerships were introduced, had recognised that same-sex cohabitants were being discriminated against (see *Fitzpatrick* v. *Sterling Housing Association* [2001] AC 27, [2000] 1 FLR 271; and *Ghaidan* v. *Godin-Mendoza* [2004] UKHL 30, [2004] 2 FLR 600).

As a result of increasing concern about the difficulties for same-sex couples, a civil partnership bill was introduced into the House of Commons in October 2001 by Jane Griffiths MP, and another into the House of Lords in January 2002 by Lord Lester. However, these went no further, as the Government had decided to conduct a full review of civil partnerships. Eventually, in December 2002 the Government announced that it proposed to introduce a same-sex partnership registration scheme, and in June 2003 the Women and Equality Unit of the Department of Trade and Industry published a consultation paper, *Civil Partnership: A Framework for the Legal Recognition of Same-Sex Couples*, setting out proposals for reform:

▶ *Civil Partnerships: A Framework for the Legal Recognition of Same-Sex Couples* (June 2003), para. 1.2

'Civil partnership registration would be an important equality measure for same-sex couples in England and Wales who are unable to marry each other. It would provide for the legal recognition of same-sex partners and give legitimacy to those in, or wishing to enter into, interdependent same-sex couple relationships which are intended to be permanent. Registration would provide a framework whereby same-sex couples could acknowledge their mutual responsibilities, manage their financial arrangements and achieve recognition as each other's partner. Committed same-sex relationships would be recognised and registered partners would gain rights and responsibilities which would reflect the significance of the roles they play in each other's lives. This in turn would encourage more stable family life.'

The Government was keen to emphasise, however, that civil partnership would not undermine the institution of marriage or offend religious beliefs. Furthermore, civil partnerships would not be available to opposite-sex partners:

## (b) The Civil Partnership Act 2004

The Civil Partnership Act (CPA) 2004 enables same-sex partners who register their partnership according to the required formalities in the Act to acquire the status of civil partner. The effect of registration is to give civil partners various rights, responsibilities and obligations broadly analogous to those possessed by married couples. If the partnership breaks down, it can be dissolved in a procedure similar to divorce. Decrees of separation, nullity and presumption of death are also available, and the court has jurisdiction to make finance and property orders on civil partnership breakdown equivalent to those it can make on divorce. Civil partners have rights and responsibilities in respect of children, and provision is made in respect of residence and contact. They also have rights on death. Thus, the surviving civil partner can register the other partner's death, and can claim a survivor's pension. Civil partners are entitled to bereavement benefits and compensation for fatal accidents or criminal injuries. They also have rights to succeed to a tenancy on the death of their partner, and have rights of inheritance on intestacy like those of married couples. In respect of taxation, civil partners have the same rights as married couples.

According to the Office for National Statistics, 15,672 civil partnerships were registered between December 2005 (when civil partnership registration became available) and September 2006. The overwhelming majority of registrations (14,084) took place in England. Most partnerships registered were male (in England, 62 per cent of civil partnerships). London and the South East were the two regions with the biggest number of civil partnership registrations. The number of persons entering into a civil partnership in the first nine months of the new scheme was much higher than the Government had originally estimated.

The Government's Women and Equality Unit produces information about civil partnerships.

*(i) Eligibility – Who can Enter into a Civil Partnership?*   Section 3(1) CPA 2004 provides that in order to be able to register a civil partnership: (a) both parties must be of the same-sex; (b) either party must not already be a civil partner or lawfully married; (c) each party must be aged at least 16; and (d) the parties must not be within the prohibited degrees of relationship (as determined by s.3(2) and Part I of Schedule 1 to the Act). Where a party is aged under 18, parental (or guardian) consent is required (s.4(1)).

*(ii) Formation of a Civil Partnership*   Local registration services are responsible for registration, a process which is similar to that for civil marriages. As with civil marriages,

preliminary formalities must be satisfied. Thus, under s.8(1) CPA 2004, each party must have lived in England and Wales for at least 7 days immediately before giving notice and each party must give the Register Office notice of their intention to register their partnership. Each party must make a declaration that there is no impediment to the formation of the partnership and that the residence requirement is satisfied (s.8(4)). Notice of the proposed registration must be published (s.10) and after a 15-day waiting period (ss.11 and 12), and in the absence of any objections (s.13), the registration authority in whose area registration of the partnership is to take place can issue a 'civil partnership schedule' (s.14). The 15-day waiting period can be reduced in special cases (such as where there is military posting or illness) (s.20). Special provision exists for housebound persons (s.18) and hospital patients or prisoners (s.19).

Once the preliminaries above are satisfied, registration can take place. Registration can only take place at the Register Office; it cannot take place in religious premises (s.6(1)). Registration is completed when each party has signed the civil registration document at the invitation of, and in the presence of, the civil partnership registrar; and in the presence of each other and two witnesses (s.2(1)). The civil partnership document must then be signed, in the presence of the civil partners and each other, by each of the two witnesses and the civil partnership registrar (s.2(4)). There must be no religious service at the registration (s.2(5)). There is no requirement that the parties make a verbal commitment to each other, as there is in the case of marriage.

*(iii) Legal Consequences of Civil Partnership Registration*    During the partnership, and on its breakdown, civil partners have the same rights and responsibilities as married couples (see 2.9, above). Thus, for example, they can apply for financial provision in the magistrates' family proceedings courts during their relationship (see s.72(3) and Sched. 6 CPA 2004). They have the same rights as married couples with respect to giving evidence in criminal proceedings. A civil partner who is not the biological parent of a child can apply for parental responsibility for the child in the same way as a step-parent (see 10.7). Civil partners can apply for residence and contact orders (and other orders under s. 8 Children Act 1989) (see 11.5). Civil partners have a duty to provide maintenance for any child of the family; and they can apply for financial provision for a child in the same way as married couples (see Chapter 13).

*(iv) Civil Partnership Agreements*    Civil partners can enter into a civil partnership agreement, which is the equivalent of an engagement to marry. The same rules which apply to engagements (see 4.3) also apply to civil partnership agreements. Thus, a civil partnership agreement does not have contractual effect (s.73 CPA 2004) and the same rules about rights in property apply on the termination of a civil partnership agreement as those which apply on the termination of an engagement (s.74). Thus, where a party to a civil partnership agreement makes a gift to the other party on the condition (express or implied) that it is to be returned if the agreement is terminated, he or she is not prevented from recovering the property merely because of his or her terminating the agreement (s.74(5)).

*(v) Dissolution of a Civil Partnership*    Under ss.37–64 CPA 2004 county courts and the High Court have jurisdiction to make dissolution orders and nullity orders (see below), and separation and presumption of death orders. Dissolution is a court-based process like

divorce, and, with the exception of adultery, the grounds for dissolution are the same as those for divorce. The applicant for a dissolution order must prove that the partnership has irretrievably broken down on the basis of one or more of the following facts (s.44(5)): (a) unreasonable behaviour; (b) two-years' separation with consent to the dissolution; (c) five-years' separation; and (d) desertion for at least two years. Like divorce, an application for dissolution cannot be made until one year has passed from the date of formation of the civil partnership (s.41). Attempts at reconciliation are permitted. For example, a period of up to six-months' cohabitation can be disregarded when calculating periods of separation or desertion (s.42). Provision is also made for the refusal of a dissolution order in five-year separation cases and for the protection of respondents in separation cases (ss.47 and 48).

The terminology for dissolution, however, is different from that of divorce. Thus, there is no decree nisi or decree absolute, as there is for divorce, but instead a conditional order followed by a final order.

*(vi) Nullity*　The court has the power under ss.49 and 50 CPA to make nullity orders in respect of a void or voidable civil partnership.

*Void Partnerships*　A partnership is void if (s.49): the parties were not eligible to register as civil partners (that is, they were within the prohibited degrees of relationship, either party was aged under 16, or aged 16 or 17 and the required consents had not been given); or there was non-compliance with formalities.

*Voidable Partnerships*　A partnership is voidable if (s.50): there was lack of valid consent (because of duress or mistake); mental disorder; or pregnancy by a third party. These mirror the grounds for nullity in Part I of the Matrimonial Causes Act 1973, except for the non-inclusion of non-consummation and venereal disease. Thus, there is no requirement that a civil partnership be consummated. Certain bars exist in respect of voidable partnerships (s.51).

*(vii) Ancillary Relief on Dissolution, Nullity and Separation*　Under s.72 and Sched. 5 CPA 2004 the court has discretionary powers on or after making a dissolution order (and a nullity or separation order) to make finance and property orders similar to those which the court can make on divorce (see Chapter 8). Thus the courts make periodical payments and lump sum orders, and orders for the sale or transfer of property, as well as orders in respect of pensions. The court also has the power to make finance and property orders after the overseas dissolution, annulment or legal separation of a civil partnership (s.72(4) and Sched. 7).

*(viii) Recognition of Overseas Civil Partnerships, Dissolutions etc*　Sections 233–238 CPA 2004 make provision for the recognition of overseas civil partnerships, and for the recognition of overseas civil partnership dissolutions, annulments and separations. These are equivalent to the provisions governing the recognition of overseas marriages (see 2.8) and overseas divorces (see 7.9). However, overseas same-sex marriages are not recognised in the UK (see *Wilkinson* v. *Kitzinger* at 2.8, above).

# Summary

1 To contract a valid marriage the parties must have the capacity to marry and must comply with preliminary formalities and formalities in respect of the marriage ceremony. Failure to comply with these requirements may render the marriage void (s.11 Matrimonial Causes Act 1973).

2 Parties have the capacity to marry if they are: not within the prohibited degrees of relationship; are aged 16 or over; are not already married; and are respectively male and female (s.11 MCA 1973).

3 Parties to a civil or religious marriage (other than a Church of England marriage) must obtain a superintendent registrar's certificate or Registrar-General's licence. Special provision exists for housebound and detained persons.

4 A Church of England marriage can take place after the publication of banns, or the grant of a superintendent registrar's certificate or a Registrar-General's licence.

5 The marriage ceremony must be celebrated according to certain formalities. A civil ceremony takes place in the Register Office or approved premises. A religious marriage must take place in a church or other place registered for religious worship.

6 A decree of nullity can be sought under Part I of the Matrimonial Causes Act 1973 on the ground that a marriage is void (s.11) or voidable (s.12). There is no prohibition on seeking a decree during the first year of marriage (s.3), as there is for divorce.

7 In some circumstances a marriage is not void, but is no marriage at all – as there was no semblance of a marriage.

8 In certain restricted circumstances a marriage may be upheld under the common law presumption of marriage from long cohabitation.

9 The grounds for a void marriage are laid down in s.11 MCA 1973.

10 The grounds for a voidable marriage are laid down in s.12 MCA 1973. Statutory bars (defences) in respect of voidable marriages are laid down in s.13 MCA 1973.

11 A decree of nullity gives the court jurisdiction to make orders for ancillary relief under Part II of the Matrimonial Causes Act 1973 (see Chapter 8).

12 There have been important developments in the European Court of Human Rights and House of Lords in respect of the rights of transsexuals. As a result, the Gender Recognition Act 2004 has introduced provisions to remove the discrimination that transsexual persons suffer, and a transsexual person who acquires a full gender recognition certificate under the GRA 2004 can enter into a valid marriage or valid civil partnership in his or her acquired gender.

13 An overseas marriage is recognised as valid in England and Wales if each party has the capacity to marry according to his or her domicile, and the formalities of the place where the marriage was celebrated have been complied with.

14 An overseas same-sex marriage cannot be recognised in England and Wales as a valid UK marriage, but can be recognised as a valid civil partnership.

15 Spouses have separate legal personalities. They can own property separately and can bring actions in tort and contract against each other, and separately or jointly against third parties. Husbands and wives have a mutual duty to provide each other with financial support, and either party may apply for financial provision from the courts. Married persons enjoy certain tax advantages. Married parents both have parental responsibility. Married couples have rights and remedies under the criminal and civil law to protect themselves and their children against domestic violence.

## Summary cont'd

**16** The Civil Partnership Act 2004 permits same-sex partners to enter into a registered civil partnership, and thereby acquire rights, obligations and privileges which are virtually the same as those possessed by married couples.

## Further Reading and References

Bamforth, '"The benefits of marriage in all but name"? Same-sex couples and the Civil Partnership Act 2004' [2007] CFLQ 133.

Barlow, Duncan, James and Park, *Cohabitation, Marriage and the Law: Social Change and Legal Reform in the 21st Century*, 2005, Hart Publishing.

Bessant, 'Transsexuals and marriage after *Goodwin* v. *United Kingdom*' [2003] Fam Law 111.

Borkowsi, 'The presumption of marriage' [2002] CFLQ 251.

Cretney, *Same Sex Relationships: From 'Odious Crime' to 'Gay Marriage'*, 2006, Oxford University Press.

Duncan, Barlow and James, 'Why don't they marry? Cohabitation, commitment and DIY marriage' [2005] CFLQ 383.

Gaffney-Rhys, '*M* v. *B, A and S (By the Official Solicitor)* – protecting vulnerable adults from being forced into marriage' [2006] CFLQ 445.

Gilmore, '*Bellinger* v. *Bellinger* – Not quite between the ears and the legs – transsexualism and marriage in the Lords' [2003] CFLQ 295.

Kirby, 'Equal treatment of same-sex couples in English family law?' [2007] Fam Law 413.

Lewis, 'Marriage and cohabitation and the nature of commitment' [1999] CFLQ 355.

McKnorrie, 'Marriage is for heterosexuals – may the rest of us be saved from it' [2000] CFLQ 363.

Probert, 'Lord Hardwicke's Marriage Act – vital change 250 years on?' [2004] Fam Law 585.

Probert, 'How would *Corbett* v. *Corbett* be decided today?' [2005] Fam Law 382.

Probert, '*Hyde* v. *Hyde*: defining or defending marriage?' [2007] CFLQ 322.

Probert and Barlow, 'Displacing marriage – diversification and harmonisation within Europe' [2000] CFLQ 153.

## Websites

**Foreign & Commonwealth Office**: www.fco.gov.uk

**Women and Equality Unit**: www.womenandequalityunit.gov.uk

# Chapter 3
## Cohabitation

3.1 Introduction

(a) Cohabitation Today

Many couples choose to cohabit rather than marry, and the numbers who choose to do so are increasing. According to the 2001 Census, there were more than two million cohabiting couples in England and Wales (compared to more than 10 million married couples), a 67 per cent increase from the previous Census 10 years earlier. In 2006 (according to the Office for National Statistics) 14 per cent of the 17.1 million families living in the UK were cohabiting couple families (compared with 9 per cent in 1996). Many children are born of cohabiting parents. According to the 2001 Census, the number of cohabiting couple households with dependent children doubled from the previous Census with more than 1.25 million children dependent on cohabitants. The Government Actuary's Department has predicted that by 2031 there will be 3.8 million cohabiting couples living in the UK.

Cohabitation can take many forms. With some couples it is a precursor to marriage. With others it is a lifestyle choice freely chosen as an alternative to marriage. Some people cohabit in the sense of sharing a home, but they are not cohabitants in the sense of being a couple. They may be better described as 'homesharers'.

Over the years there has been increasing social acceptance of cohabitation and the law has to some degree kept up with changing social attitudes. In the early development of the law it was opposite-sex, not same-sex, cohabitants who were given statutory recognition. Thus, in the 1970s opposite-sex cohabitants were given the same statutory rights as married couples to be able to apply for injunctive protection against domestic violence. Opposite-sex cohabitants, unlike same-sex cohabitants, were also given statutory rights to succeed to a tenancy on the death of their partner (but same-sex cohabitants now have this right; see *Ghaidan* v. *Godin-Mendoza* [2004] UKHL 30, [2004] 2 FLR 600 at 5.4).

(b) The Problem of Defining Cohabitation for Legal Purposes

One of the difficulties for the law, whether it be judge-made or statute, is defining the term 'cohabitation' or 'cohabitant' for the purposes of giving cohabitants legal rights and obligations. This is because, unlike marriage and civil partnership, there is no proof by registration of the status of cohabitant. In fact the parties to a cohabiting relationship may themselves take differing views as to whether or not they are cohabitants.

Statutory provisions giving cohabitants rights and obligations define cohabitation in terms of a quasi-marital or civil partnership relationship, and sometimes with a minimal duration and residence requirement. Thus, in order to apply for reasonable provision from a deceased cohabiting partner's estate under the Inheritance (Provision for Family and Dependants) Act 1975, a cohabitant must have lived in the same household as the deceased for at least two years as if he or she was the husband or wife or civil partner of the deceased (see 5.3). The definition of 'cohabitant' for the purposes of bringing a claim in tort under the Fatal Accidents Act 1976 is similarly defined. For the purposes of obtaining protection against domestic violence under Part IV of the Family Law Act 1996, however, the term 'cohabitant' is defined less restrictively – in order to provide injunctive protection for a wider class of cohabiting persons. Thus, there is no minimum duration requirement in respect of living together, and no requirement that the parties live in the same household. Instead, cohabitants are defined as two persons who are neither married to each other nor are civil partners of each other, but who are living together as husband and wife as if they are civil partners (see 6.6).

Sometimes judges may have to decide whether a couple are cohabiting (for example, for the purpose of obtaining welfare benefits). In *Kimber* v. *Kimber* [2000] 1 FLR 33 it was held that the following factors or 'signposts' could be used to determine whether persons were cohabitants: living together in the same household; sharing a daily life; permanence and stability of the relationship; handling of finances; existence of a sexual relationship; existence of children; intentions and motivation of the parties; and the perception of the relationship by the reasonable man.

Defining cohabitation is important for determining eligibility for legal remedies. However, there are policy issues which may be relevant here. One is that to give a wide category of cohabitants the same legal rights and remedies as married couples (and civil partners) might undermine the institution of marriage. Another is that to give a wide category of cohabitants legal rights and remedies might undermine the autonomy of cohabiting couples, as some couples may have made a conscious decision not to marry in order to avoid the rights and obligations which the State imposes on married couples and civil partners.

Eligibility for remedies under the Law Commission's proposed scheme for property and financial provision for cohabitants (see 4.12) will be an important issue that will have to be addressed by the Government if it decides to take the proposals forward. The Law Commission has suggested a duration requirement of two to five years' cohabitation in order to qualify for relief, but this will have to be discussed further.

### (c)   The Vulnerability of Cohabitants

Some cohabitants believe that there is something called a 'common law marriage', which gives opposite-sex cohabitants quasi-marital rights (see Probert, 2007). This is a myth. In fact, heterosexual cohabitants can be in a disadvantageous position compared with married couples, and so can same-sex cohabitants who are not civil partners. Cohabitants are in an especially vulnerable position in respect of property entitlement on relationship breakdown and on the death of their partner. They can suffer disadvantages on relationship breakdown in respect of ownership and occupation of the family home, and in respect of other assets, such as pensions and investments. On the termination of a marriage or civil partnership, the court has power under statute to adjust the parties' property and finance under a discretionary regime (see Chapter 8), but no such provision exists for cohabitants. Cohabitants must instead use the general rules of property law (see Chapter 4), and/or apply under Schedule 1 to the Children Act 1989 if they have children (see 13.5). Cohabitants are also vulnerable on the death of their partner, for a surviving cohabitant has no right to inherit from the other party's estate if he or she makes no will. Instead any property goes to the deceased's children or parents. It is therefore particularly important for cohabitants to make a will. During their relationship cohabitants are also vulnerable as there is no legal obligation to provide financial support for each other. Married couples and civil partners, on the other hand, have mutual maintenance obligations and the courts have the power to make maintenance orders in their favour. Cohabitants also suffer tax disadvantages compared with married couples and civil partners.

In order to give cohabiting couples more information about their rights and obligations (including helping them to understand that there is no such thing as a 'common law marriage'), a public information campaign, the 'Living Together' campaign, was launched by the Government in 2004.

In July 2007 the Law Commission (the Government's reform body) published proposals for reform of the law relating to the financial and property consequences of cohabitation breakdown (see 4.12).

Children of cohabiting couples can also be in a more vulnerable position than children whose parents are married, because cohabiting relationships are more likely to break down than are married ones. According to a Social Justice Policy Group Report, almost half of cohabiting parents separate before their child's fifth birthday, compared to one in twelve married parents. Furthermore, on cohabitation breakdown the court has no power to oversee arrangements for children of cohabiting parents, whereas it has in the case of parents who divorce (see 12.3).

## 3.2    Cohabitants – Rights and Obligations

Cohabitants have the following rights and obligations:

*(i) Financial Obligations*    Cohabitants, unlike married couples and civil partners, have no mutual duty during their relationship, or on relationship breakdown, to provide each other with financial support. Consequently, they have no right to apply to the court for orders in respect of financial provision. However, cohabiting parents (whether or not they have parental responsibility) have a duty to maintain their children, and maintenance for children can be sought against a cohabiting parent by applying to the Child Support Agency, and in some cases to the court (see Chapter 13). Cohabitants can also apply to the court for lump sum orders and property orders to or for the benefit of a child (see 13.5).

*(ii) Property Rights*    The law governing the property rights of cohabitants, particularly ownership, is determined by the general law of property (see Chapter 4). With the exception of provisions for cohabitants to obtain occupation orders in respect of the home in the context of domestic violence (see 6.5), and transfers of a tenancy on the death of a partner (see 5.4), no special family law statutory provisions exist for cohabitants equivalent to those for married couples and civil partners during their relationship, on relationship breakdown and on death. Cohabitants must rely instead on equitable doctrines, such as trusts and proprietary estoppel, to establish interests. Cohabitants, unlike married couples and civil partners, have no statutory rights of occupation of the family home.

*(iii) Property Rights on Death*    A cohabitant has no right to succeed to his or her deceased partner's estate on intestacy, but a surviving cohabitant can apply under the Inheritance (Provision for Family and Dependants) Act 1975 (see 5.3) for financial provision out of

the deceased cohabitant's estate, or claim a beneficial interest in the deceased cohabitant's property under a trust (see Chapter 4). The Law Commission in its proposals to reform the law governing property and finance for cohabitants (see 4.12) has not, however, recommended that the law be changed to give a surviving cohabitant rights on the intestacy of a deceased partner. However, on the death of a cohabiting partner, the surviving partner can succeed to the tenancy belonging to the deceased. In *Ghaidan* v. *Godin-Mendoza* [2004] UKHL 30, [2004] 2 FLR 600 a majority of the House of Lords held that same-sex cohabiting couples had the same rights as unmarried opposite-sex cohabiting couples to succeed to a tenancy on the death of a partner under the Rent Act 1977.

*(iv) Property and Finance on Relationship Breakdown*    On relationship breakdown cohabitants have a duty to maintain their children, but there is no maintenance duty between the partners themselves. The courts have no powers, as they have on divorce, to adjust their property entitlements according to their needs and resources. Cohabitants can therefore be in a vulnerable position on relationship breakdown in respect of property (whether it be the family home, investments or pension provision). Because of the disadvantages which exist for cohabitants in respect of their property rights, particularly on relationship breakdown and on death, the Law Commission has made proposals for reform (see 4.12).

*(v) Cohabitants and Children*    Cohabiting parents have the same maintenance obligations to their children as married couples and civil partners (see Chapter 13), whether or not the unmarried father has parental responsibility. Only a cohabiting mother has automatic parental responsibility in law for her children, but a cohabiting father may acquire it in various ways (see 10.6).

Only the unmarried mother, not the father, has a duty to register the child's birth. An unmarried father can be named on his child's birth certificate, but there is no obligation to do so. The Government is considering reforms, however, to make it compulsory for unmarried fathers to be named on birth certificates, in order to encourage them to recognise their responsibilities, in particular their child maintenance obligations (see 10.6).

A cohabiting parent (with or without parental responsibility) can apply for section 8 orders under the Children Act 1989 (for example, in respect of residence or contact). Eligibility to apply depends only on the applicant being the biological parent of the child (see 11.4).

Under the law of adoption (see Chapter 16) cohabiting couples can now make joint or sole applications for adoption. However, unmarried fathers without parental responsibility have no statutory right to consent to adoption.

*(vi) Protection against Violence*    Cohabitants and former cohabitants (opposite-sex and same-sex) can apply for non-molestation orders and occupation orders under Part IV of the Family Law Act 1996 to protect themselves and their children against domestic violence (see Chapter 6).

*(vii) British Citizenship and Immigration*    Under the British Nationality Act 1981 it is more difficult for a non-British cohabitant partner of a British citizen to gain British citizenship by virtue of that partnership. It may also be more difficult to obtain permission to enter and remain in the UK.

In respect of children, under s.9 Nationality, Immigration and Asylum Act 2002 (which came into force on 1 July 2006) children born to unmarried parents can now take their nationality from their father, subject to proof of the relationship. However, this new provision applies only to children born on or after 1 July 2006 – it is not retrospective. A child born before that date to an unmarried British father and a non-British mother does not automatically gain British citizenship. The parents will need to get married before the child's eighteenth birthday, thereby making the child 'legitimate' and giving the child an automatic right to citizenship; or apply for discretionary registration of the child as a British citizen.

## 3.3 Cohabitation Contracts

Cohabitants can enter into a cohabitation contract to regulate their affairs (for example, to make arrangements about the allocation of property and other matters should their relationship break down). In practice, however, few do so. Cohabitation contracts were once considered to be contrary to public policy, as they undermined the sanctity of marriage. This is no longer the case, but cohabitation contracts remain open to challenge in the courts and may not be upheld, for instance, if there is no intention to create legal relations, or there is duress, undue influence, misrepresentation or lack of independent legal advice (see, for example, *Sutton* v. *Mishcon de Reya and Gawor & Co* [2003] EWHC 3166 (Ch), [2004] 1 FLR 837, where Hart J held that the cohabitation agreement was not valid as it was an agreement about sexual relations rather than an agreement about property). Cohabitants wishing to enter into a cohabitation contract should seek legal advice.

The Law Commission in its recommendations for reforming the law on property and financial relief for cohabitants (see 4.12) has recommended that there should be a new statutory provision making it clear that cohabitation contracts are not contrary to public policy. In fact under its proposals cohabitation contracts in respect of property and finance would become more common, because cohabitants would be able to enter into agreements to opt out of the proposed statutory remedies.

## 3.4 Cohabiting Persons Who Are Not 'Couples'

Some people cohabit, but they are not couples. They are 'homesharers'. Such persons are not treated in the same way as married and cohabiting couples or civil partners, although they can obtain protection against domestic violence under Part IV of the Family Law Act 1996 as associated persons living in the same household (see Chapter 6). They can be particularly vulnerable in respect of property entitlement on the death of the other homesharer and can suffer tax disadvantages. A few years ago the Law Commission conducted a study of homesharers with a view to giving them property remedies, but, because it could not find a legal 'template' which would fit all homesharers, and because any reforms might prejudice cohabitants, the project went no further (see 4.12). Instead, the Law Commission has concentrated on reforming the law of property for cohabiting couples, not homesharers (see 4.12).

The disadvantages which homesharers can suffer was demonstrated by the case of Joyce and Sybil Burden, two elderly sisters who claimed that they were discriminated against in respect of inheritance tax under UK law because they did not have the same inheritance rights as same-sex couples. After their claim failed before the English courts they took their case to the European Court of Human Rights in Strasbourg, arguing that UK inheritance tax laws discriminated against them under art. 14 of the European Convention for the Protection of Human Rights taken in conjunction with art. 1 of Protocol 1 (right to the protection of property). However, their claim failed (see *Burden and Burden v. United Kingdom (Application 13378/05)* (December 2006)). The ECtHR held that the UK had not exceeded the wide margin of appreciation afforded to it, and that the difference of treatment for the purposes of the grant of inheritance tax exceptions was reasonably and objectively justified for the purpose of art. 14.

## Summary

1   Many couples choose to cohabit rather than to marry or enter into a civil partnership.

2   Opposite-sex and same-sex cohabitants are given some protection under the law (for example, in respect of remedies against domestic violence), but they are vulnerable under the law, in particular in respect of property rights on relationship breakdown and on the death of their partner.

3   Cohabitants have no mutual maintenance duty to each other, unlike spouses and civil partners, but they have a maintenance obligation to their children.

4   Only the unmarried mother has automatic parental responsibility for the child of a cohabiting relationship. Fathers without parental responsibility can acquire it (for example, by being registered on the child's birth certificate with the mother).

5   Cohabitants can enter into cohabitation contracts, but these are open to challenge in the courts.

6   Homesharers (persons who are cohabiting but who are not a 'couple') may also suffer disadvantages (for example, in respect of inheritance tax).

## Further Reading and References

Bailey-Harris, 'Law and the unmarried couple – oppression or liberation?' [1996] CFLQ 137.

Barlow, Duncan, James and Park, *Cohabitation, Marriage and the Law: Social Change and Legal Reform in the 21st Century*, 2005, Hart Publishing.

Duncan, Barlow and James, 'Why don't they marry? Cohabitation, commitment and DIY marriage' [2005] CFLQ 383.

Hale LJ, 'Unmarried couples in family law' [2004] Fam Law 419.

Kirby, 'Equal treatment of same-sex couples in English family law?' [2007] Fam Law 413.

Lewis, 'Marriage and cohabitation and the nature of commitment' [1999] CFLQ 355.

McKnorrie, 'Marriage is for heterosexuals – may the rest of us be saved from it' [2000] CFLQ 363.

Probert, 'Why couples still believe in common-law marriage' [2007] Fam Law 403.

Probert and Barlow, 'Displacing marriage – diversification and harmonisation within Europe' [2000] CFLQ 153.

## Websites

**Living Together Advice**: www.advicenow.org.uk/
**OnePlusOne – Married or Not**: www.oneplusone.org.uk/marriedornot

# Part III

# Family Property

# Chapter 4

# Family Property

Introduction

This chapter deals with the law governing family property, in particular ownership and occupation of the family home. Family property on death is dealt with in Chapter 5.

*Different Regimes for Married Couples (and Civil Partners) and Cohabitants*   During the subsistence of the relationship the rules governing the property rights of spouses, civil partners and cohabitants are very similar, but on relationship breakdown the position is radically different. This is because, whereas the courts have wide discretionary powers under family law statutes to redistribute and re-allocate the property and finances of married couples and civil partners according to their needs and resources, there is no such provision for cohabiting couples. Instead, cohabiting couples (and other family members) must rely on the general principles of property law to determine any property or financial dispute which arises on relationship breakdown. A cohabitant who does not own property may find himself or herself in a vulnerable position on relationship breakdown, in particular in respect of ownership and occupation of the family home. Cohabitants are also in a vulnerable position on the death of their cohabiting partner, for, if there is no will, they have no right to succeed to their deceased partner's estate (see 5.2). Because cohabitants, and their children, can be in a vulnerable position on relationship breakdown in respect of property and finance, and because the law can create unfairness, the Law Commission has made proposals for reform of the law (see 4.12).

*Two Sorts of Ownership in English Law*   There are two sorts of ownership in English law: ownership in law; and ownership in equity. Ownership in equity involves owning property as a beneficiary under a trust. A person can own property in law or in equity, or in both law and equity. Thus, for example, the male partner may be the legal owner of the house, but he may also hold it on trust for himself and his female partner, the beneficiary, in equity. Many spouses and cohabitants, however, own their home jointly as co-owners both in law and in equity.

*Co-ownership*   Co-owners can own property as joint tenants or as tenants in common. Joint tenants each own the whole property, not an individual share. This means that on the death of a joint tenant the surviving joint tenant is entitled to the whole property, unless there is any intention to the contrary, such as in a will. A joint tenancy can be severed and converted into a tenancy in common by: giving notice in writing; mutual agreement; alienation; or by conduct. A joint tenancy is also severed on bankruptcy. Tenants in common, unlike joint tenants, each own a separate share of the property. On the death of a tenant in common, the surviving tenant in common is not entitled to the whole property, but the deceased's share passes according to the will, or according to the laws of intestacy (see Chapter 5).

## 4.2 Property Rights of Married Couples and Civil Partners

The general principles of property law (contract and trusts) apply to ownership of property during marriage and civil partnership, but with some special statutory provisions (see below).

Property disputes between spouses and civil partners are more likely, however, to occur on breakdown of the marriage or partnership, whereupon the court can decide any dispute by using its wide discretionary powers under the Matrimonial Causes Act 1973 and the Civil Partnership Act (CPA) 2004 (see Chapter 8 and 2.10).

### (a) Ownership of Property During Marriage and Civil Partnership

There is no presumption of joint ownership of property in the case of married couples or civil partners. Each spouse or civil partner can own property separately. Thus, any property brought into the marriage or civil partnership belongs to the party who owns it, and so does any property acquired during the relationship by a particular party. In 1988 the Law Commission discussed the possibility of introducing a presumption of joint ownership of household goods for married couples (*Family Law: Matrimonial Property*, Law Com No. 175), but no changes were introduced, even though the Law Commission had found the rules for determining ownership to be 'arbitrary, uncertain and unfair' – as most married couples intended property to be jointly owned even though according to the law it was not.

### (b) Statutory Provisions for Spouses and Civil Partners

In addition to the general principles of property law, the following statutes lay down special provisions in respect of property ownership for married couples and civil partners during the subsistence of their relationship. When divorce was less common than it is today these provisions played a greater role. Today they are rarely invoked.

*Improvements to Property*   Under s.37 Matrimonial Proceedings and Property Act 1970 a spouse can acquire a share, or an enlarged share, of property (or the proceeds of sale of such property) if he or she makes a substantial improvement in money or money's worth to that property – subject to any intention to the contrary. Few applications are made under s.37. Civil partners have the same right under s.65 Civil Partnership Act 2004.

*Power of the Court to Declare Property Interests*   Under s.17 Married Women's Property Act 1882 the High Court and county courts have jurisdiction on the application of a spouse to make such order as they think fit as to the ownership or possession of any property. The court can only declare property interests under s.17 – it cannot create them (*Pettitt* v. *Pettitt* [1970] AC 777). Unlike the divorce court, however, the court cannot adjust property interests. Having declared any interest, the court can order the sale of property and order the proceeds of sale to be divided in accordance with the parties' interest (s.7(7) Matrimonial Causes (Property and Maintenance) Act 1958). A former spouse can apply under s.17, provided the application is made within three years of the termination of the marriage by divorce or annulment (s.39 Matrimonial Proceedings and Property Act 1970). An application under s.17 can be made in respect of money or property that is not in possession (s.7(1) Matrimonial Causes (Property and Maintenance) Act 1958). Applications under s.17 are rare in practice, because any property dispute on relationship breakdown can be dealt with in a more flexible way by the divorce court.

The court has the same powers as those above in respect of civil partners (s.66 CPA 2004). An application by a former civil partner must be made within three years of the dissolution or annulment of the partnership (s.68 CPA 2004). An application can be made under s.66 in respect of money or property that is not in possession (s.67 CPA 2004).

*Property Bought by a Wife from Savings*   Section 1 Married Women's Property Act 1964 provides that any property bought by a wife with savings from housekeeping money given to her by her husband belongs to them both in equal shares. This provision is archaic and discriminatory. However, although the Law Commission has recommended its repeal (see *Family Law: Matrimonial Property*, Law Com No. 175, 1988), and a bill (the Family Law (Property and Maintenance) Bill) was introduced in the House of Commons in November 2005 to repeal this provision, it remains on the statute book.

### (c)   Occupation of the Home – 'Home Rights' of Spouses and Civil Partners

A non-entitled spouse or civil partner has statutory rights of occupation of the home ('home rights') by virtue of s.30 of Part IV of the Family Law Act 1996 (see further in Chapter 6). Section 30 provides that a spouse or civil partner who has no rights of ownership in the home (by virtue of a contract or trust or under any enactment) has the right to occupy the home if the other spouse or civil partner is so entitled (under a contract, trust etc) (s.30(1)).

'Home rights' are: if in occupation, a right not to be evicted or excluded from the home by the other spouse or civil partner, except with leave of the court given by an order under s.33 of the Act; or, if not in occupation, a right with leave of the court so given to enter into and occupy the home (s.30(2)). 'Home rights' arise only in respect of a dwelling house which is (was, or was intended to be) the parties' matrimonial or civil partnership home (s.30(7)). The person with 'home rights' has other rights. Thus any payment or other thing done by that person in or towards satisfaction of any liability of the other party (the owner) in respect of rent, mortgage payments or other outgoings affecting the home is as good as if made or done by the owner (s.30(3)). Any mortgage payments by the party with 'home rights' may be treated as being made by the other party, but this does not affect any claim by the person with 'home rights' against the other party to an interest in the home by virtue of the payment (s.30(5)). Under Part IV of the Family Law Act 1996 spouses and civil partners have a right to take part in possession proceedings when the home is subject to a mortgage (ss.54–56), and the Act also makes provision for the transfer of tenancies on relationship breakdown (s.53 and Sched. 7).

A non-entitled spouse or civil partner's 'home rights' are a charge on the other party's estate or interest (s.31). A charge is binding on a third party (for example, a purchaser or a mortgagee), but only if it has been protected by a notice on the register made under the Land Registration Act 2002 or any enactment replaced by that Act (s.30(10)).

### 4.3   Engagements to Marry and Civil Partnership Agreements

Statutory provisions apply in respect of property where the parties are engaged to marry or have entered into a civil partnership agreement.

(a)   Engagements to Marry

The Law Reform (Miscellaneous Provisions) Act 1970 makes provision in respect of the property rights of engaged couples, including ownership of engagement gifts and ownership of the engagement ring.

An engagement is not a contract giving rise to legal rights and no action lies for breach of such an agreement, whatever the law applicable to the agreement (s.1 Law Reform (Miscellaneous Provisions) Act 1970).

On the termination of an engagement, any rule of law relating to the beneficial entitlement of spouses applies to any property in which either or both parties had a beneficial interest during their engagement (s.2(1)). Thus, s.37 Matrimonial Proceedings and Property Act 1970 and s.17 Married Women's Property Act (MWPA) 1882 apply (see p.62). An application under s.17 MWPA 1882 can be brought by a formerly engaged person within three years of the termination of the engagement (s.2(2)). An application can be brought under s.17 where an engagement is invalid because a party is already married (see *Shaw* v. *Fitzgerald* [1992] 1 FLR 357).

With respect to engagement gifts, the fact that one party was responsible for terminating the engagement does not affect any express or implied arrangement in respect of the return of engagement gifts (s.3(1)). Ownership is determined by the general law. It depends on the intention of the donor of the gift. In the absence of any express intention, the court may decide to infer that a gift from a particular relative belongs to the party to the engagement who is related to that relative (by analogy with *Samson* v. *Samson* [1982] 1 WLR 252 where this rule was applied to wedding gifts).

An engagement ring is presumed to be an absolute gift (s.3(2)) – which means that it can be kept on the termination of the engagement unless there is an express or implied condition to the contrary (for instance, that it should be returned because it is a family heirloom).

(b)   Civil Partnership Agreements

Under the Civil Partnership Act 2004 similar provisions to those which apply to engagements (above) apply to civil partnership agreements. Thus a civil partnership agreement is not a contract enforceable in law (s.73), and the following statutory provisions which apply to civil partners apply to the parties to a civil partnership agreement (s.74): s.65 (contribution by civil partner to property improvement); and ss.66 and 67 (disputes between civil partners about property, see p.63). Applications under ss.66 and 67 by a former party to a civil partnership agreement must be brought within three years of the termination of the agreement (s.73(4)). A party to a civil partnership agreement who makes a gift of property to the other party on the condition (express or implied) that it is to be returned if the agreement is terminated is not prevented from recovering the property merely because of his or her having terminated the agreement (s.73(5)).

4.4   The Property Rights of Cohabitants

(a)   Ownership of Property

During their relationship, and on relationship breakdown, the property rights of cohabitants (opposite-sex and same-sex) are governed by the general rules of property law. There are no special statutory provisions for cohabitants as there are for married couples and civil partners (see above). Cohabitants are in a particularly disadvantageous position on relationship breakdown, as there is no discretionary jurisdiction as there is on breakdown of marriage or civil partnership to adjust their property rights according to their needs and resources. A cohabitant is also in a vulnerable position on death if his or her deceased partner has made no will (see Chapter 5).

A cohabitant, or former cohabitant, who wishes to claim a share, or enlarged share, of property will have to rely on the law of equity. Applications for a claim to a share in property are usually made under the Trusts of Land and Appointment of Trustees Act 1996. Cases are heard in the civil or chancery courts and from a property law, not a family law, perspective. Bringing a case is expensive and time-consuming, and the law of trusts is not entirely satisfactory for determining such disputes.

The following case is often cited as the classic example of the disadvantage of being a cohabitant on relationship breakdown:

> ▶ *Burns* v. *Burns* [1984] Ch 317
>
> The female cohabitant (she had taken her partner's name) cohabited with her partner for nearly 20 years. She brought up the children and looked after the home. On relationship breakdown, she brought a claim against her former partner (the owner of the home) arguing that she had an interest in the home under a trust. Her claim was dismissed by the Court of Appeal because there was no evidence of any intention that she was to have an interest. Looking after the home and bringing up the children were held to be insufficient evidence to enable the court to infer an intention. While expressing considerable sympathy for her, the Court of Appeal felt that the matter was one for Parliament, not the courts.

In *Hammond* v. *Mitchell* [1991] 1 WLR 1127, *sub nom H* v. *M (Property: Beneficial Interest)* [1992] 1 FLR 229, by contrast, the female cohabitant was successful in obtaining an interest in the home under a trust on facts very similar to those in *Burns*. This was because the court accepted her evidence that she and her partner had exchanged a few words about ownership of the home, and these words were held to be sufficient evidence to infer an intention that she was to have a half-share in the home. The different outcomes in these two cases demonstrate the unfairness and arbitrary nature of the law.

### (b)    Occupation of the Home

A non-owning cohabitant, unlike a spouse or civil partner, has no statutory right of occupation of the home (see p.63). Rights of occupation are instead dependent on a cohabitant having a right of ownership, a right under a tenancy, or having a licence (permission) to remain in occupation. Cohabitants and former cohabitants who are victims of domestic violence can, however, apply for an occupation order under Part IV of the Family Law Act 1996 which, if granted, will give the applicant a right of occupation for the duration of the order (see 6.5).

## 4.5 Ownership of Property Other Than Land

Family members may own a wide range of property other than land (for example, a pension, investments, a car and household goods). Property other than land is called 'personal' property.

The rules governing personal property apply to spouses and civil partners (unless the court determines otherwise on divorce, annulment, or dissolution of the partnership), and to cohabitants and other family members during their relationship and after relationship breakdown – but with the exception of some special statutory provisions for spouses, civil partners, engaged couples and parties to a civil partnership agreement (see pp.62–3, above).

Ownership of personal property depends on whether there is an interest under a contract or an interest in equity under a trust. As a general rule, title to property passes to the person who purchases it, provided there is a valid contract and no contrary intention (for instance, that the property is to be jointly owned or to belong to someone else). In the case of gifts of property, ownership passes to the recipient, provided the donor intended to transfer the gift and it was handed over.

*Acquiring a Right of Ownership*   A person who has no right under a contract can claim an interest in personal property under an express, resulting or constructive trust. For example, a person who has paid money into a bank account held in the name of another person can claim an interest in that account in equity under a resulting trust proportionate to that payment, or can claim an interest under an express trust. The following cases provide examples of claims to personal property using the law of trusts:

▶ *Paul v. Constance* **[1977] 1 WLR 527**

The female claimant was held to have an interest by way of express trust in the bank account held in her cohabitant's sole name, as she had been authorised to draw on the account and he had told her on several occasions that the money in the account was as much hers as his.

▶ *Rowe v. Prance* **[1999] 2 FLR 787**

The female claimant was held to be entitled to a half-share in a valuable yacht owned by her former partner with whom she had had a close relationship for 14 years. She had not contributed financially to its purchase, but her partner had referred to the yacht as 'our boat', had spoken of 'a share of the boat together' and had said 'your security is your interest in it'. The claimant had given up rented accommodation and put furniture in storage in order to move into the boat which they intended to sail round the world together. The court accepted this evidence as sufficient to constitute the man as an express trustee of the boat, so that she was entitled to a share. No writing was required to establish a trust – as the property in dispute was not land.

Despite the successful outcomes for the cohabitants in the cases above, cohabitants should be wary of taking a case to court and should try to settle any dispute. Taking a case to court is costly, time-consuming and unpredictable. In *Hammond* v. *Mitchell* (see p.65, above) Waite J said that cohabitants on relationship breakdown should be encouraged to do their best to settle disputes about chattels (property other than land) on the understanding that in ordinary cases the court will divide them equally, in other words according to the maxim 'equality is equity'.

*Bank Accounts*    Disputes about bank accounts may arise in respect of ownership of the funds in the account and property purchased with the funds. If a bank account is in one person's name, then *prima facie* any money in the account belongs to that person, that is unless there is a contrary intention or another person has made a contribution to the fund. If a bank account is held in joint names, then *prima facie* any money in the account belongs to both parties as beneficial joint tenants of the whole fund, that is unless there is a contrary intention, such as that the account was put into joint names for the sake of convenience. However, even a joint account initially opened for convenience may be held to be regarded as a true joint account after a period of time (*Re Figgis, deceased* [1969] 1 Ch 123).

As a general rule, any property bought with funds from a bank account belongs to the purchaser. Thus, for example, if a husband draws money from a joint bank account to purchase shares in his name, then *prima facie* they belong to him. However, where the parties have pooled their resources, the court may adopt the approach in *Jones* v. *Maynard* [1951] Ch 572 where Vaisey J treated the joint account as a 'common pool' and held that investments purchased by the husband with money from an account held jointly with his wife belonged to them both in equal shares, even though the husband had made larger contributions to the joint account than his wife.

## 4.6   Settling Disputes About the Family Home

Disputes tend to arise in respect of the family home, rather than in respect of other property, because a home is a valuable financial asset and because it provides a roof over the family's head. Disputes about the family home may arise in the following situations:

- ▶ *On Relationship Breakdown*   If the parties are spouses or civil partners any dispute can be settled by the court using its statutory discretionary powers on divorce or dissolution, nullity or judicial separation (see Chapter 8). Cohabitants, on the other hand, have to use the law of equity to settle a dispute (see, for example, *Hammond* v. *Mitchell* [1991] 1 WLR 1127 and *Burns* v. *Burns* [1984] Ch 317, at p.65, above).
- ▶ *On Death*   If there is a will, then that determines the parties' property rights. Where there is no will (on intestacy), surviving spouses and civil partners have a statutory right to succeed to the deceased's estate (see 5.2). Cohabitants, on the other hand, have no rights of succession, but they can bring a claim under the Inheritance (Provision for Family and Dependants) Act 1975 (see 5.3), or claim an interest under a trust (see, for example, *Hyett* v. *Stanley* [2003] EWCA Civ 942, [2004] 1 FLR 394 where the surviving cohabitant was held to be entitled to an interest in her deceased partner's property under a constructive trust arising as a result of a statement he made during his lifetime; and see also *Churchill* v. *Roach* [2004] 2 FLR 989).
- ▶ *Where the Interests are Not Defined*   Where there has been no mention of the parties' respective interests on the conveyance, the court may have to determine the matter (see, for example, *Springette* v. *Defoe* [1992] 2 FLR 388; and *Stack* v. *Dowden* [2007] UKHL 17, [2007] 1 FLR 1858).
- ▶ *Where a Third Party Seeks Possession*   Where a third party (such as a purchaser, mortgagee or trustee in bankruptcy) seeks possession of the home, a spouse, civil

partner, cohabitant or other family member may claim an interest in the home under a trust in order to defeat the claim to possession (see, for example, *Lloyds Bank plc v. Rosset* [1991] 1 AC 107, [1990] 2 FLR 155 and *Midland Bank plc v. Cooke* [1995] 2 FLR 915, both of which involved claims by married women, see pp.71 and 74).

A dispute about property can be dealt with in the following ways:

*(i) On Divorce (Nullity and Judicial Separation) or on Dissolution (Annulment and Separation) of a Civil Partnership*    The courts have powers under the Matrimonial Causes Act 1973 and the Civil Partnership Act 2004 to adjust the parties' property rights according to statutory guidelines without the need to apply the rules of property law (except where a third party might be involved) (see Chapter 8 and 2.10).

*(ii) By Seeking an Order Under the Trusts of Land and Appointment of Trustees Act 1996*    Under s.14 Trusts of Land and Appointment of Trustees Act (TLATA) 1996 the court has the power to make orders for the sale and possession of land, including the family home, and declarations of interests in property; and also orders postponing sale. For example, in *Oxley v. Hiscock* [2004] EWCA Civ 546, [2004] 2 FLR 669 the female cohabitant sought a declaration under s.14 TLATA 1996 that the proceeds of sale were held by the man on trust for them both in equal shares.

*Orders for Sale*    Under s.14 TLATA 1996 any trustee or beneficiary under a trust of land, or any secured creditor of a beneficiary, can apply to the court for an order for sale of the property. When deciding whether or not to order sale, the court must take into account (s.15): the intentions of the person(s) who created the trust; the purposes for which the trust is held; the welfare of any child who occupies or who might reasonably be expected to occupy any land subject to the trust as his home; and the interests of any secured creditor or beneficiary.

Applications for orders for sale are sometimes made on bankruptcy. In cases decided under the law prior to the 1996 Act the wishes of the trustee in bankruptcy would usually prevail over the interests of the family (see *Re Citro (A Bankrupt)* [1991] Ch 142 and *Lloyds Bank plc v. Byrne* [1993] 1 FLR 309). However, as s.15 now requires the court to take account of the welfare of any child this may tip the balance in favour of the family rather than the trustee in bankruptcy (see Neuberger J in *The Mortgage Corporation v. Silkin and Another, The Mortgage Corporation v. Shaire* [2000] 1 FLR 973). In *F v. F (S Intervening) (Financial Provision: Bankruptcy: Reviewable Disposition)* [2002] EWHC 2814 (Fam) Coleridge J ordered postponement for 10 years of the intervenor's interest in the matrimonial home, or until such time as it was no longer required as a home for the children.

*(iii) By Seeking a Declaration*    The High Court and the county court have jurisdiction to make declarations in respect of property rights, but the more usual practice is to use one of the procedures above.

### 4.7    Acquiring a Right of Ownership in the Family Home Under a Trust

A person can claim a right of ownership in the family home under a trust, even if there is nothing in writing to that effect. Section s.53(1) Law of Property Act 1925 provides that writing is required for interests in land and declarations of trusts of land, but s.53(2) provides that writing is not required for the creation of an implied, resulting or constructive trust. Similar rules apply in respect of contracts for the sale of land. Thus, while s.2(1) Law of Property (Miscellaneous Provisions) Act 1989 provides that contracts for the sale of land must be in writing, s.2(5) provides that writing is not required for the creation of an implied, resulting or constructive trust. As s.2(5), like s.53(2) of the Law of Property Act 1925, was intended to allow a range of equitable remedies, an interest in land can also be claimed under the equitable doctrine of proprietary estoppel (Beldam LJ in *Yaxley* v. *Gotts and Gotts* [1999] 2 FLR 941, and see 4.8).

Resulting trusts and constructive trusts each have their own set of principles and their own body of case-law. They are quite different and separate doctrines.

### (a)   Acquiring an Interest Under a Resulting Trust

A resulting trust arises as a presumption of equity where a person makes a financial contribution to the purchase of property. In the absence of a contrary intention (for example, that the financial contribution was a gift or a loan, or that other shares were intended) a person who contributes money to the purchase of property acquires an interest under a resulting trust proportionate to his or her contribution. Thus, for example, a person who does not own the home but who has made a financial contribution to it can claim an interest in the home under a resulting trust proportionate to that contribution. Resulting trusts were claimed in the following cases:

▶ *Sekhon* v. *Alissa* [1989] 2 FLR 94

The house had been bought in the name of the defendant daughter. She had contributed to the purchase price, but her mother had paid the balance. The mother claimed a share in the house under a resulting trust, arguing that, although it was bought in her daughter's name, it was purchased as a joint commercial venture and they both intended to own it in proportion to their respective financial contributions. The daughter attempted to rebut the presumption of resulting trust by arguing that her mother's financial contribution was intended as a gift or a loan. The court had to decide what was the actual or presumed intention of the parties at the time of the conveyance. Was the mother's financial contribution a gift or an unsecured loan, or was she intended to have a beneficial interest in the property? The Court of Appeal held that the law presumed a resulting trust in the mother's favour, and on the facts the presumption was not rebutted by the daughter's allegation that the money was a gift or a loan.

▶ *Springette* v. *Defoe* [1992] 2 FLR 388

The parties, two elderly cohabitants, had bought their council house, but there was nothing in the registered transfer quantifying their respective beneficial interests. Each party had paid half the mortgage instalments, but the claimant, Miss Springette, had paid most of the balance of the purchase price. When the relationship broke down she issued an originating summons claiming that she was entitled to 75 per cent of the proceeds of sale, as this represented her contribution to the purchase. At first instance, the trial judge granted them an equal share of the beneficial interest, on the basis that it was their uncommunicated belief or intention that they were to share the property equally. The Court of Appeal allowed the claimant's appeal, holding that, as there was no discussion between the parties as to their respective beneficial interests, there was no evidence to rebut the presumption that the claimant was entitled to a 75 per cent share of the beneficial interest under a resulting trust.

However, despite the use of the resulting trust in the cases above, most cases in the law reports are based on a constructive trust. Resulting trusts are rarely invoked. The demise of the resulting trust as a mechanism for claiming a share in the home is due, in part, to the fact that the claimant obtains only a share proportionate to his or her contribution to the purchase price. Its demise may also be due to the fact that the courts have held that only initial contributions to the purchase of property can give rise to an interest under a resulting trust, not contributions made after its purchase (see, for example, *Curley* v. *Parkes* [2004] EWCA Civ 1515).

*The Presumption of Advancement*    Under this presumption of law, a transfer of property by a husband to his wife, or a father to his child, is presumed to belong to the wife, or child, absolutely. This presumption could be used to rebut a presumption of resulting trust (for instance, if a husband gives his wife money to purchase a house, she could argue that she has an absolute interest in the house because the money is an absolute gift to her and does not raise an inference of resulting trust in the husband's favour). However, as the presumption is archaic and discriminatory (because it applies only to gifts by husbands and fathers), it has little relevance today and is unlikely to be relied on. In *McGrath* v. *Wallis* [1995] 2 FLR 114 Nourse LJ said that in its application to a house acquired for joint occupation it was a judicial instrument of last resort which could be easily rebutted. Clause 2 of the Family Law (Property and Maintenance) Bill, introduced into the House of Commons in November 2005, made provision for the presumption of advancement to be abolished but this provision has not become law.

### (b)    Acquiring an Interest Under a Constructive Trust

An interest in the home (or any other property) can be claimed under a constructive trust. Unlike a resulting trust, there is no need for any financial contribution to have been made. Instead, the emphasis is on finding an express or implied agreement or intention that the non-owner is entitled to a beneficial interest under a trust. It is not possible, however, to impose a constructive trust merely to do justice. In *Springette* v. *Defoe* [1992] 2 FLR 388 at 393, Dillon LJ said: '[T]he court does not as yet sit, as under a palm tree, to exercise a general discretion as to what the man in the street, on the general view of the case, might regard as fair.' If there is no intention or arrangement to share, the court cannot ascribe to the parties intentions which they never had.

*A Two-Stage Exercise*    The court conducts a two-stage exercise. First, it looks at the evidence to establish whether there is a constructive trust. Next, if a trust is established, it must consider all the circumstances of the case in order to decide what share of the beneficial interest the claimant should have. As the size of the share is not proportionate to the size of any financial contribution, but depends on all the circumstances of the case, it may be advantageous to base a claim on a constructive trust, rather than a resulting trust.

The leading case on constructive trusts of the home is *Lloyds Bank plc* v. *Rosset*, where Lord Bridge laid down the approach to be adopted by the courts:

▶ *Lloyds Bank plc v. Rosset* **[1991] 1 AC 107, [1990] 2 FLR 155**

The home had been purchased in the husband's sole name. His wife had helped to renovate it, but she had made no financial contribution to its purchase or renovation. Mr Rosset charged the house to a bank as security for a loan, which Mrs Rosset knew nothing about. When Mr Rosset went into debt, Lloyds Bank claimed possession of the home and an order for sale. Mrs Rosset, by way of defence to the bank's claim, argued that she had a beneficial interest in the house under a constructive trust and that this interest coupled with her actual occupation gave her an overriding interest under s.70(1)(g) Land Registration Act 1925 which would defeat the bank's claims. (The 1925 Act has now been repealed and replaced by the Land Registration Act 2002.)

The House of Lords held, dismissing her appeal, that her activities in relation to the renovation of the house were insufficient to justify the inference of a common intention that she was entitled to a beneficial interest under a constructive trust. Lord Bridge summarised and encapsulated the law as laid down in the two earlier House of Lords' decisions of *Pettitt* v. *Pettitt* [1970] AC 777 and *Gissing* v. *Gissing* [1971] AC 886, and referred also to the Court of Appeal decision in *Grant* v. *Edwards* [1986] Ch 638 (the leading case on detriment).

**LORD BRIDGE:** 'The first and fundamental question which must always be resolved is whether, independently of any inference to be drawn from the conduct of the parties in the course of sharing the house as their home and managing their joint affairs, there has at any time prior to acquisition, or exceptionally at some later date, been any agreement, arrangement or understanding reached between them that the property is to be shared beneficially. The finding of an agreement or arrangement to share in this sense can only, I think, be based on evidence of express discussions between the partners, however imperfectly remembered and however imprecise their terms may have been. Once a finding to this effect is made it will only be necessary for the partner entitled to the legal estate to show that he or she has acted to his or her detriment or significantly altered his or her position in reliance on the agreement in order to give rise to a constructive trust or proprietary estoppel.

In sharp contrast to this situation is the very different one where there is no evidence to support a finding of an agreement or an arrangement to share, however reasonable it might have been for the parties to reach such an agreement if they had applied their minds to the question, and where the court must rely entirely on the conduct of the parties both as the basis from which to infer a common intention to share the property beneficially and as the conduct relied on to give rise to a constructive trust. In this situation direct contributions to the purchase price by the partner who is not the legal owner, whether initially or by payment of mortgage instalments, will readily justify the inference necessary to the creation of a constructive trust. But, as I read the authorities, it is at least extremely doubtful whether anything less will do.'

Lord Bridge's words (above) in *Rosset* have formed the basis of the courts' approach to constructive trusts in subsequent cases. There must be both a common intention and detrimental reliance. In respect of common intention, Lord Bridge said that there were two situations in which proof of a common intention can arise:

1. *Where there is an express agreement, arrangement or understanding that the property is to be shared beneficially* Lord Bridge gave the 'excuse cases' of *Eves* v. *Eves* and *Grant* v. *Edwards* (see below) as examples of cases in this situation.
2. *Where there is no such express agreement, arrangement or understanding, but where an agreement can be inferred* It is more difficult to establish a claim here, particularly as

the courts have been unwilling to accept anything other than direct financial contribution to the purchase of the property as evidence of an inferred intention.

**Examples From the Case-Law**

▶ *Eves* v. *Eves* [1975] 1 WLR 1338

The house was purchased in the man's name, but he told his partner that he would have put it in her name had she been 21. He admitted later in evidence that this was an excuse. She did extensive and substantial decorative work on the house. The Court of Appeal held that she had a beneficial interest, as, despite the lack of writing, the parties had orally made their intentions plain.

▶ *Grant* v. *Edwards* [1986] Ch 638

The male cohabitant told his partner that he had not put her name on the title as it might be detrimental to her pending divorce proceedings. This was an excuse. He paid the deposit and the mortgage and she made a substantial contribution to household expenses. The Court of Appeal, applying *Eves* v. *Eves*, held that she was entitled to a beneficial interest in the house under a constructive trust. There was a common intention that she should have such an interest and evidence of conduct (substantial contribution to housekeeping and bringing up the children), which amounted to an acting on that intention (that is, detrimental reliance), and on which it would not have been reasonable to have expected her to embark unless she was to have an interest.

▶ *Cox* v. *Jones* [2004] EWHC 1486 (Ch), [2004] 2 FLR 1010

The claimant, a female cohabitant, had made no direct financial contribution to the purchase price of the property in dispute which was owned by her cohabitant, and had made no contribution to the mortgage repayments. But she had spent time renovating it. Mann J found that there was an express arrangement between the parties that she was to have a share of the house, and that she had acted to her detriment by putting her practice as a barrister to one side to spend her time and energy on renovating the property that was to be their home. Mann J granted her a 25 per cent share of the beneficial interest in the property, applying *dicta* of Chadwick LJ in *Oxley* v. *Hiscock* [2004] EWCA Civ 546, [2004] 2 FLR 669 that her share of the interest in the house must be 'fair having regard to the whole course of dealing between them in relation to the property'.

▶ *Hyett* v. *Stanley* [2003] EWCA Civ 942, [2004] 1 FLR 394

The female cohabitant on the death of the male cohabitant was held to have a beneficial interest in the farm held in his name. The man's statement made in 1992 raised a clear inference that there was an understanding between him and the female applicant of a common intention that she was to have a beneficial interest in the farm. The detriment was assuming the risk of joint liability.

*Detrimental Reliance*  The claimant, having established a common intention or arrangement (express or inferred) that he or she is to have a beneficial interest in the property, must go on to establish that he or she suffered some detriment as a result of relying on that intention. Detriment is needed because it provides the consideration required to satisfy the maxim of equity that 'equity will not assist a volunteer' (someone who has not provided consideration). The detriment must follow the establishment of the common intention. Thus, in *Churchill* v. *Roach* [2004] 2 FLR 989 the female cohabitant's claim to property belonging to her deceased cohabitant's estate on the basis of a constructive trust failed, as the acts relied on as constituting detriment had occurred before the common intention was established.

Detrimental reliance in most cases, however, is usually fairly easily proved. Bringing up a family, and running a home, for example, can be used as evidence of detriment. The more difficult hurdle is proving the existence of a common intention that the claimant is to have a beneficial interest in the property in order to establish a constructive trust.

*Indirect Financial Contributions*    In *Rosset* (see p.71, above) Lord Bridge said that, on his reading of the authorities, he doubted whether anything less than a direct financial contribution to the purchase price would be sufficient to establish a share in the property in cases where there was no express intention that the claimant should have a beneficial interest. Because the decision in *Rosset* is binding on the lower courts, the courts have shown themselves to be unwilling to infer an intention to share in cases where there has merely been an indirect financial contribution to the purchase of the house (in other words, payment of household bills and other living expenses, or bringing up the children so that the other party can go out to work).

In 2002, the Law Commission in its Report, *Sharing Homes*, suggested that judges should be more generous in their approach and take indirect contribution into account. In *Le Foe* v. *Le Foe and Woolwich plc; Woolwich plc* v. *Le Foe and Le Foe* [2001] 2 FLR 970, decided before *Sharing Homes* was published, Nicholas Mostyn QC (sitting as deputy High Court judge) held that the wife who had made no direct financial contribution to the purchase of the house was nevertheless entitled to half the beneficial interest in the home under a constructive trust on the basis of an inferred common intention arising by virtue of her indirect contribution – she had contributed to domestic expenditure which had enabled her husband to pay the mortgage. Nicholas Mostyn QC said that Lord Bridge in *Rosset* had not intended to rule out the possibility that indirect contributions could give rise to a beneficial interest in the home, as his Lordship had not stated the proposition that he had advanced in absolute terms.

Bailey-Harris, commenting on *Le Foe* (at [2001] Fam Law 741), said that, in the absence of legislation, it was questionable whether the injustice created by precedents could legitimately be rectified by a judge at first instance, however laudable his motives. However, as unfairness and injustice may result if beneficial interests cannot be inferred from indirect contributions, perhaps the courts may become more willing to take them into account.

*Quantifying the Share of the Beneficial Interest*    Once the court is satisfied that the claimant is entitled to a beneficial interest under a constructive trust, it must then go on to determine the size (the quantum) of that interest. A broad-brush approach is taken when deciding on the share. The court takes account of all the circumstances of the case, including financial and non-financial circumstances and the intentions of the parties. There is some lack of clarity here, however. In *Oxley* v. *Hiscock* (see p.74), Chadwick LJ adopted a broad test based on fairness, but his test was disapproved of by the House of Lords in *Stack* v. *Dowden* (see p.74) as being too broad. However, as *Stack* v. *Dowden* was a different sort of case from *Oxley* v. *Hiscock* (as Mr Stack and Ms Dowden were joint owners in law), Chadwick LJ's 'fairness test' may still apply in sole ownership cases. In joint names' cases intentions are relevant to deciding whether the presumption of equal shares should be rebutted. In sole ownership cases, on the other hand, intentions relate to the first hurdle, that of establishing whether the non-owner has a beneficial interest at all (see Lord Bridge in *Rosset*, above). For this reason, a more flexible approach based on fairness may be justified in sole ownership cases.

---

▶ *Midland Bank plc v. Cooke* [1995] 2 FLR 915

The husband purchased the matrimonial home for £8,450, with £6,450 from a mortgage, £1,000 of his own savings and another £1,000 which was a wedding gift from his parents. His wife made no direct contribution to the purchase, except for the £500 which represented her half-share of the wedding gift, but she made considerable financial contributions to the upkeep of the house and to the household. She claimed a beneficial interest in the home. At first instance, the county court judge held that her beneficial interest in the house amounted to a sum equivalent to 6.47 per cent of the value of the property, representing her half-share of the wedding gift of £1,000. The Court of Appeal allowed her appeal, holding that, as she and her husband had agreed to share everything equally, including the house, she was entitled to half the beneficial interest. In respect of establishing the share of the beneficial interest, Waite LJ said that the court was permitted to undertake a survey of the whole course of dealing between the parties in respect of their ownership and occupation of the house and their sharing of its burdens and advantages.

▶ *Oxley v. Hiscock* [2004] EWCA Civ 546, [2004] 2 FLR 669

The female cohabitant applied under s.14 Trusts of Land and Appointment of Trustees Act 1996 for a declaration that the proceeds of sale were held by the man on trust for the parties in equal shares. Chadwick LJ conducted an extensive review of the authorities, and held, in respect of calculating the share of the beneficial interest, that each party 'is entitled to that share which the court considers fair having regard to the whole course of dealing between them in relation to the property'. Applying the broad-brush approach adopted in *Midland Bank v. Cooke* (above), the Court of Appeal held that a fair division of the sale of the property was 60 per cent to the man and 40 per cent to the woman – as equal division would have given insufficient weight to the disparity in the parties' financial contributions.

---

*Quantifying the Beneficial Interests Where the Parties are Joint Legal Owners*    Where the parties are joint owners in law of the home, but there is no declaration of their beneficial interest (their interest in equity under a trust), the principle of law here is that it is presumed that the parties own it equally in equity. In order to rebut this presumption, the defendant must prove that some share other than 50:50 was intended. However, only where the facts of the case are very unusual is the presumption of equal shares likely to be rebutted, as they were found to be in *Stack* v. *Dowden*, the leading case:

---

▶ *Stack v. Dowden* [2007] UKHL 17, [2007] 1 FLR 1858

The parties had cohabited for 20 years. The family home was registered in their joint names but the transfer deed contained nothing about their interests in equity. They had failed to draw up a declaration of trust. The purchase price other than the mortgage advance had been provided by Ms Dowden. When the relationship broke down, Mr Stack left the house and Ms Dowden remained there with the children. Mr Stack successfully sought an order for sale of the property and was granted a 50:50 division of the proceeds of sale. The Court of Appeal allowed Ms Dowden's appeal and held that she was entitled to 65 per cent of the proceeds of sale (as she had made a greater financial contribution to the purchase of the house), applying the fairness test laid down by Chadwick LJ in *Oxley* v. *Hiscock* (see p.74, above). Mr Stack appealed to the House of Lords.

The House of Lords unanimously dismissed his appeal (Lord Neuberger dissenting as to reasoning) and held that, where a house is conveyed into joint names in the domestic consumer context, then *prima facie* joint and equal beneficial interests arise unless and until the contrary is proved. The burden was on the defendant to rebut the presumption by showing that equal beneficial shares were not intended. In the domestic context, factors other than financial contributions could be taken into account. Looking at the facts of the case, there were many factors to which the defendant could point to indicate that the parties had a contrary intention that the shares in equity were owned jointly. For instance, when the property was bought, both parties knew that the defendant had paid more than the claimant, and they had kept their financial affairs separate. The defendant had therefore made good her case for a 65 per cent share.

In respect of the test for assessing the share of the beneficial interest, intentions were relevant in joint owner cases and Chadwick LJ's 'fairness test' in *Oxley* v. *Hiscock* was not appropriate.

**BARONESS HALE**: 'The search is to ascertain the parties' shared intentions, actual, inferred or imputed, with respect to the property in the light of their whole course of conduct in relation to it.'

*Stack* v. *Dowden* was the first case to go to the House of Lords involving a dispute between cohabitants about ownership of the family home. However, as the couple were joint legal owners of the home, the case does not improve the position for sole-owning cohabitants who may suffer unfairness in respect of the home (and other property interests) on family breakdown. The Law Commission has, at the request of the Government, made proposals for reform (see 4.12). In the meantime, however, the House of Lords in a suitable case (one involving a claim by a non-owning cohabitant for a share in the home owned by the other cohabitant) may decide to move with the times and develop the law to allow a more flexible approach in a constructive trust case in order to give a non-owner an interest. On the other hand, such a radical change of the law should perhaps be a matter for Parliament, not the courts.

Although there were changes to the Land Registry form in 1998, so that cases like *Stack* v. *Dowden* are much less likely to arise, it is important, particularly for cohabitants, to ensure that the shares in which the house is owned are clearly stated on the Land Registry transfer form, or on a separate deed.

For a case involving no declaration of the beneficial interests in the context of bankruptcy, see *Supperstone* v. *Hurst* [2005] EWHC 1309 (Ch), [2006] 1 FLR 1245.

## 4.8    Acquiring an Interest by Way of Proprietary Estoppel

An interest in the home (or other property) can be acquired under the equitable doctrine of proprietary estoppel, which can be invoked despite the absence of the written formalities required for creating interests in land (see pp.68–9, above). The doctrine is based on preventing unconscionable conduct. The doctrine in its broadest form was described by Balcombe LJ in *Wayling* v. *Jones* [1995] 2 FLR 1029, at 1031, as follows:

'Where one person (A) has acted to his detriment on the faith of a belief, which was known to and encouraged by another person (B), that he either has or is going to be given a right in or over B's property, B cannot insist on his strict legal rights if to do so would be inconsistent with A's belief.'

Thus there must be proof of an agreement or an expectation created or encouraged by one party upon which the other party has acted to his or her detriment. Thus there must be a promise, and a sufficient link between the promises relied upon and the conduct which constitutes the detriment. Once it has been established that promises were made, and there has been conduct by the claimant of such a nature that inducement may be inferred, the burden of proof shifts to the defendant (the party creating the expectation of an interest in property) to show that his actions did not induce the other party to act in reliance of this expectation (*Greasley* v. *Cooke* [1980] 1 WLR 1306).

In *Gillett* v. *Holt and Another* [2000] 2 FLR 266 the Court of Appeal stated that, as proprietary estoppel is a flexible doctrine which is based on preventing unconscionable conduct, the facts must be looked at in the round. It held that detriment is not a narrow or technical concept but one which must be approached as part of a broad inquiry, and that reliance and detriment should not be treated as being divided into separate watertight compartments.

Although the doctrines of constructive trust and proprietary estoppel are similar, in that they are both equitable doctrines providing relief against unconscionable conduct, the doctrines are separate – they have not been assimilated with each other (see *Hyett* v. *Stanley* [2003] EWCA Civ 942, [2004] 1 FLR 394). However, in *Oxley* v. *Hiscock* (see p.74, above) Chadwick LJ thought that it might be more satisfactory to accept that there is no difference between constructive trusts and proprietary estoppel, once it is accepted that the court in both situations is imputing a common intention as to the parties' respective shares to do what is fair in the light of all the material circumstances.

*What Remedy to Grant?*   Once an estoppel is proved, the court must consider all the circumstances of the case and exercise its discretion to decide what remedy to give. The courts, however, adopt a cautious approach. Equitable relief will only be 'the minimum equity to do justice' (Scarman LJ in *Crabb* v. *Arun District Council* [1976] Ch 179, at 198). For this reason, a claim based on estoppel may not be so advantageous as one based on a trust, because the claimant may not gain a right of ownership, but merely a licence to occupy the property or an order for financial compensation. In *Gillett* v. *Holt* (above), a right to a freehold interest in the property in dispute was granted but in the following case a different approach was taken:

▶ *Matharu* v. *Matharu* [1994] 2 FLR 597

A father bought a house which subsequently became the matrimonial home of his son and daughter-in-law. The son made extensive improvements to the house but later died. The father sought possession of the house against his daughter-in-law, but his action was dismissed at first instance on the ground that his daughter-in-law was entitled to an unquantifiable beneficial interest in the property by virtue of a proprietary estoppel in her favour. The Court of Appeal allowed the father's appeal in part, holding that, although an estoppel had been proved, the defendant daughter-in-law had not acquired a beneficial interest but merely a licence to remain in the property for life or for such shorter period as she might decide.

In *Van Laethem* v. *Brooker and Caradoc Estates Ltd* [2005] EWHC 1478 (Ch), [2006] 2 FLR 495 the woman claimant was held to be entitled to an interest by way of proprietary estoppel in the mansion which had been purchased in the man's name, and an interest by way of constructive trust in relation to the associated development land.

*Disadvantages of Estoppel*    Estoppel's main disadvantage compared with trusts, as we have seen above, is that the court may not necessarily grant the claimant a right of ownership. In *H* v. *M (Property Acquired by Wife's Parents)* [2003] EWHC 625 (Fam), [2004] 2 FLR 16 Baron J held that to acquire an interest by way of proprietary estoppel, proof of a promise of acquisition of a beneficial interest was essential. Baron J held that the claimants had been promised the right to live in the property as long as they wished, but not that they would acquire a beneficial interest in it.

Another disadvantage of estoppel compared with trusts is that an estoppel arises only when the remedy is granted, whereas a beneficial interest under a trust arises when the claimant acted to his or her detriment on the basis of the common intention. Thus, interests under a trust arise earlier than they do with estoppel, which may be important if third party interests are involved.

## 4.9   A Claim Based on Contract

An interest in property may be acquired under a contract, provided the legal requirements for creating a valid contract are satisfied. If a contract is for the sale or disposition of land it must be in writing (s.2 Law of Property (Miscellaneous Provisions) Act 1989), but this requirement does not prevent the creation of a resulting or constructive trust, or the creation of an interest by way of proprietary estoppel (see *Yaxley* v. *Gotts and Gotts* [1999] 2 FLR 941). The following cases are examples:

> ▶ *Tanner* v. *Tanner* [1975] 1 WLR 1341
>
> The claimant purchased a house for occupation by the defendant, his female partner, and their children. The defendant moved into the house, but when the relationship broke down the applicant sought possession on the basis that the defendant was only a bare licensee under a licence which he had revoked. The Court of Appeal held that there was an implied contractual licence under the terms of which the defendant was entitled to occupy the house while the children were of school age, or until some other circumstance arose which would make it unreasonable for her to remain in possession.
>
> ▶ *Layton* v. *Martin* [1986] 2 FLR 277
>
> The Court of Appeal held that there was no intention to create a legally enforceable contract, with the result that the claimant mistress failed in her claim against the deceased's estate even though she had accepted the man's offer that, if she were to live with him, he would give her emotional security, and also financial security on his death. Despite living with him for five years after he had made the offer, and for 13 years in total, her claim failed.

## 4.10    Tenancies

### (a)    Transferring a Tenancy

Under s.53 and Sched. 7 of Part IV of the Family Law Act 1996, the High Court and the county court have jurisdiction to transfer tenancies on divorce, dissolution of a civil partnership, and on the breakdown of cohabitation. With civil partners it can only do so where the court has jurisdiction to make a property adjustment order under the Civil Partnership Act 2004. With cohabitants, they must merely have ceased living together as husband and wife – there is no mention of them ceasing to live in the same 'household'.

A tenancy is transferred by the court making 'a Part II order' which it has power to make whether a spouse, civil partner or cohabitant is solely or jointly entitled under a tenancy, provided the house was a matrimonial home in the case of a married couple, or, in the case of cohabitants, was a home in which the cohabiting couple lived together as husband and wife (para. 2 of Sched. 7 and s.62(1)). Paragraph 1 of Sched. 7 makes it clear that 'cohabitant' includes a 'former cohabitant'. There is no requirement that cohabitants must have lived together for a minimum period, although the court is required to take into account the length of the relationship when deciding whether or not to order a transfer. These provisions also apply to civil partners, so that a tenancy of the civil partnership home can be transferred to one of the parties to the civil partnership, provided it was their home, and irrespective of whether they were solely or jointly entitled under the tenancy.

In determining whether to make a Part II order, and, if so, in what manner, the court must consider all the circumstances of the case including (see para. 5): the circumstances in which the tenancy was granted, or the circumstances in which either of them became tenant; the housing needs and housing resources of the parties and of any relevant child; their respective financial resources; the likely effect of any order (or no order) on the health, safety or well-being of the parties and of any relevant child; the conduct of the parties in relation to each other and otherwise; and the suitability of the parties as tenants.

Where the parties are cohabitants and only one of them is entitled to occupy the house under the tenancy, the court must also consider (see para. 5): the nature of their relationship; the length of time they have lived together as husband and wife; whether there are any children who are children of both parties or for whom both parties have or have had parental responsibility; and the length of time that has elapsed since the parties ceased to live together. Where the parties are council tenants, the housing policy of the local housing authority is a factor which the court can take into account (see *Jones* v. *Jones* [1997] 1 FLR 27).

Tenancies for the benefit of a child can be transferred under Schedule 1 to the Children Act 1989 (see 13.5).

### (b)    Succeeding to a Tenancy on the Death of a Tenant

See 5.4.

## 4.11    Property Claims for the Benefit of Children

Under s.15 and Schedule 1 to the Children Act 1989, property orders can be sought for the benefit of children. See 13.5.

## 4.12 Property Law Reform for Cohabitants

### (a) The Pressing Need for Reform

Over the past 20 years or so there has been increasing dissatisfaction with the law governing the property rights of cohabitants on relationship breakdown, and on the death of a cohabiting partner. There have been calls for reform from, for instance, The Law Society, Resolution, judges, lawyers and academics. In 2007 the Law Commission published a *Report* (see pp.85–8, below) in which it made proposals for reform (but which contained no draft Bill). As the Law Commission's project was undertaken at the request of the Government, reform is likely to take place, but when is not yet known. As Baroness Hale has said, implementation will depend not only on 'whether the proposals find favour with the Government, but also on whether the resources can be found to translate them into workable legislative form' (see para. 47 in *Stack v. Dowden*, above).

When so many couples today choose cohabitation rather than marriage, it does seem that something needs to be done to reform the law in order to remove the unfairness that some cohabitants, and their children, may suffer. As long ago as 1984 in the case of *Burns v. Burns* (see p.65, above) the Court of Appeal had drawn attention to the unfairness of the law but had said that any change of the law was a matter for Parliament, not the courts. Since 1984, changing social and economic conditions have made reform even more pressing.

Cohabitants, unlike married couples and civil partners, are in a particularly disadvantageous position on relationship breakdown as the courts have no discretionary powers to adjust their property interests. Instead, they must turn to the law of property, in particular the law of trusts. This is costly and time-consuming, and the law is sometimes insufficiently flexible to do justice between the parties and is complex and difficult to understand. As Carnwarth LJ said in the Court of Appeal in *Stack v. Dowden* [2005] EWCA Civ 857, [2006] 1 FLR 254:

> 'To the detached observer, the result may seem like a witch's brew, into which various esoteric ingredients have been stirred over the years, and in which different ideas bubble to the surface at different times. They include implied trust, constructive trust, resulting trust, presumption of advancement, proprietary estoppel, unjust enrichment, and so on. These ideas are likely to mean nothing to laymen, and often little more to the lawyers who use them.'

Developments to give cohabitants rights on relationship breakdown have taken place in other countries. For instance, in New South Wales, Australia, there are legislative provisions giving cohabitants (and other persons living in domestic relationships, such as personal carers) the right to apply to the court for various orders which the court can make by exercising adjustive powers similar to those of the divorce court, although these powers are narrower as the court exercises its discretion by looking at past contributions rather than future needs. Pawlowski (2003) argues that these reforms provide a useful model for legislative reform in the UK. New Zealand has introduced more radical legislative reforms, whereby the same adjustive criteria apply to cohabitants as apply to divorcing couples, so that, unless the parties have contracted out of the statutory scheme, or they do not satisfy the eligibility requirements, then the rights and obligations of unmarried couples, whether opposite-sex or same-sex, are the same as those of married couples.

**(b)** The Case for Reform

The arguments for and against reform of the law for cohabitants are set out below. In addition, the law itself has its own set of problems (see pp.81–2, below):

### Arguments in Favour of Reform of the Law for Cohabitants

▶ Many cohabitants suffer unfairness and injustice in respect of property, particularly on relationship breakdown. For instance, a case with the same facts as *Burns* v. *Burns* (see p.65, above) would be decided in the same way today even though that case was decided in 1984.
▶ The law should keep up to date with changing social conditions. Many couples choose to cohabit and many cohabitation relationships break down.
▶ Children of cohabitants may be left in a vulnerable position because the home belongs to the other parent.
▶ Some members of the public are under an assumption (a mistaken one) that there is something called a 'common law marriage' whereby cohabitants acquire the same rights as married couples after a period of cohabitation.
▶ There has been law reform for same-sex cohabitants (by the Civil Partnership Act 2004), and so there should be law reform for other cohabitants.
▶ Some cohabiting couples cannot marry for a variety of religious or practical reasons.
▶ The law of trusts, which many claimants rely on, is doctrinally unsatisfactory, difficult to understand and not designed to deal with relationship breakdown. Property entitlement should be determined by a family law, not a property law, regime.
▶ Bringing court proceedings is a costly and lengthy process.

### Arguments Against Reform of the Law for Cohabitants

▶ The social reality is that most cohabitants own their home jointly, and so very few cohabitants actually suffer any inequity and unfairness.
▶ The rules of trusts and proprietary estoppel may be imperfect, but they have the advantage of being sufficiently flexible to keep up with changing social conditions and being able to respond to the wide variety of factual situations which arise.
▶ Codification of the law would create its own set of problems. Reform raises difficult policy issues, in particular whether reform will undermine the institution of marriage and whether cohabitants should be able to contract out of any new regime. Other important questions that would have to be addressed are whether a cohabiting relationship should be of a minimum duration before legal rights and responsibilities arise, and whether it should make any difference if there are children involved.
▶ Opposite-sex cohabitants can choose to marry and thereby acquire the same rights and remedies in respect of the home and other property as divorcing couples can on relationship breakdown. Same-sex cohabitants can enter into a registered civil partnership.
▶ Many cohabitants do not wish to have an adjustive quasi-divorce regime forced upon them in respect of their property interests. That may be the very reason for choosing not to marry. Because of the conflicting policy objectives of autonomy and paternalism it would be necessary to allow cohabitants to contract out of a new statutory regime if they wished to do so. But clarification of the law on cohabitation contracts might prove difficult, and might open a 'can of worms' – for if cohabitants are allowed to contract out of any new regime, then spouses and civil partners should perhaps be allowed to do the same.
▶ To give cohabitants similar rights to married couples undermines the institution of marriage.

It is generally felt that the advantages in favour of reform strongly outweigh the disadvantages, because cohabitants (and their children) can suffer considerable injustice. In fact a research study conducted by Douglas, Pearce and Woodward into dealing with property issues when cohabitation relationships break down (*A Failure of Trust: Resolving Property Issues on Cohabitation Breakdown*) found major instances of injustice caused by the current operation of the law of trusts:

> ▶ **Douglas, Pearce and Woodward, *A Failure of Trust: Resolving Property Issues on Cohabitation Breakdown* (2007), Cardiff University Research Paper, Conclusion**
>
> 'Retrospective private ordering in cohabitation breakdown cases, set against a fog of uncertainty and complexity rather than the "shadow of the law", has led to a position where trusts law may now serve to perpetuate rather than redress injustice. Even if the parties reach some sort of rough and ready compromise, ignoring or sidestepping the "true" legal position, this comes at a cost, both actual and figurative. Whatever the fate of the Law Commission's or other similar proposals, the present study has thus indicated that maintenance of the status quo is unarguable. However controversial it may be, reform of the current law to meet the legitimate interests of separating cohabitants is both justified and overdue.'

*Drawbacks of the Law*    Cohabitants may have to resort to the law of trusts to establish an interest in property, for instance the family home (see 4.7, above), but trusts have the following disadvantages:

- The principles governing constructive trusts, in particular, are unsatisfactory as they are based on intentions and arrangements which are often vague and which arose many years earlier. For this reason, is may be difficult to establish evidence of intention.
- A claimant may be forced to trawl back through the relationship to find evidence of the intention needed for a constructive trust, instead of being encouraged to look at future needs and resources – which is the approach adopted on divorce and on dissolution of a civil partnership.
- The requirement of a direct financial contribution to establish an interest under a constructive trust where there is no express intention to share (see Lord Bridge in *Rosset*, at p.71, above) has resulted in some cohabitants (particularly women) failing to acquire an interest in the home even though they have spent many years contributing to its upkeep and looking after the family. On divorce, on the other hand, these sorts of contributions are taken into account by the court (see 8.4). Furthermore, there is some lack of uncertainty about the status of indirect contributions to the purchase of the home (such as looking after the children or paying for household goods).
- Because of the vagueness and unsatisfactory nature of the relevant legal principles, unsatisfactory and unjust distinctions may be made. In *Hammond* v. *Mitchell* (see p.65, above) the female cohabitant was granted a half-share in the family home on the basis of a short conversation she had had with her partner many years earlier, but the female cohabitant in *Burns* v. *Burns* (see p.65, above) failed to establish a beneficial interest in the home, despite her substantial contribution over many years to the household and family.

- A claimant may be tempted to fabricate the evidence. In *Rosset* (see p.71, above) Lord Bridge had said that express evidence of an intention to share the beneficial interest could be based on 'discussions between the partners, however imperfectly remembered and however imprecise their terms may have been'. This may encourage perjury. In *Hammond* v. *Mitchell* Waite J said that 'both parties were prone to exaggeration' and 'neither side had the monopoly of truth'. Bailey-Harris, commenting on *Rowe* v. *Prance* said that one is 'commonly left with the impression that the establishment of an interest . . . turns primarily on whose account of conversations is believed by the judge' ([1999] Fam Law 623, at 624). This is unsatisfactory.
- The terminology adopted by the courts is vague. In *Rosset*, Lord Bridge referred to 'any agreement, arrangement or understanding'. The term 'understanding' is particularly vague.
- The test for establishing the share of the beneficial interest is somewhat unclear. Does the 'fairness test' adopted by Chadwick LJ in *Oxley* v. *Hiscock* apply (see p.74, above)?
- There is some judicial uncertainty about whether Lord Bridge's interpretation in *Rosset* of earlier authorities was correct, or whether he had set the hurdle too high. Is his requirement of direct financial contribution the correct approach? Did he intend his words to act as a template for later cases, or were his words intended to be somewhat tentative? In *Stack* v. *Dowden* (see p.74, above) Baroness Hale (at para. 63) was of the opinion that there was undoubtedly an argument for saying that Lord Bridge's words in *Rosset* were *obiter dicta* and that his Lordship had set the first hurdle of establishing a beneficial interest rather too high.

The drawbacks of the law were recognised by the Law Commission in the following extract taken from its 2006 Consultation Paper (see further at p.84, below):

> ▶ *Cohabitation: The Financial Consequences of Relationship Breakdown* (Law Com No. 17, 2006)
>
> 'The rules contained in the general law have proved to be relatively rigid and extremely difficult to apply, and their application can lead to what many would regard as unfairness between the parties. The formulation of a claim based on these rules is time-consuming and expensive, and the nature of the inquiry before the court into the history of the relationship results in a protracted hearing for those disputes that are not compromised. The inherent uncertainty of the underlying principles makes effective bargaining difficult to achieve as parties will find it hard to predict the outcome of contested litigation.'

### (c)   Reform Proposals

The major proposals for reform have come from the Law Commission, but other proposals for reform have also come from (i) the Law Society and (ii) the Solicitors' Family Law Association (now called Resolution). Their proposals are similar to those recommended by the Law Commission.

*(i) The Law Society's Proposals*    In July 2002 The Law Society (see *Cohabitation: The Case for Clear Law; Proposals for Reform*) made proposals for reform because the law was unfair and

because long-term cohabitation was increasingly common. It recommended that cohabitants (same-sex and opposite-sex) should be permitted to obtain court orders similar to those available for divorcing couples.

Eligibility would be based on living together for at least two years in a relationship analogous to that of husband and wife, or on whether the couple had children. A statutory checklist list of factors (such as the existence of a sexual relationship, the provision of financial support, whether they had a child) would assist the court in determining whether the parties were cohabitants. ·

The court would have the power to make property adjustment orders and lump sum orders. Applications would be determined having regard to the principle that fair account should be taken of any economic advantage derived by either party from contributions by the other, and of any economic disadvantages suffered by either party in the interests of the other party or of the family. Cohabitants would also be allowed to apply for maintenance in limited circumstances (for example, to provide resources for training, retraining or to reflect capital payments which could not be made by way of a lump sum). Only in exceptional cases would maintenance orders last for more than four years.

The proposals included a range of other rights for cohabitants (for instance, in respect of transfers of tenancies, occupation of the home, succession, tax and immigration rights), but these would not be as great as those possessed by married couples. The Law Society recommended that the existing law relating to property disputes (for example, trusts) should continue to be available for cohabitants who, for whatever reason, were unable to invoke the remedies proposed.

**(ii) The Solicitors' Family Law Association Proposals** The Solicitors' Family Law Association (now called Resolution) has recommended changes to the law (see its policy document, *Fairness for Families*) similar to those proposed by The Law Society. Thus, cohabitants (opposite-sex and same-sex) should be able to apply for a financial relief order from the court if they had cohabited for at least two years and/or they had children. The court would exercise its discretion by taking into account all the circumstances of the case with the aim of doing what was fair and reasonable between the parties, which would include taking into account the level and extent of their commitment to each other. There would be a presumption, however, that cohabitants should be self-supporting, where possible. The court would have the power to make lump sum orders and transfer of property orders, and also limited-term maintenance orders for up to three years from the date of separation.

(d) Reform of the Law – The Work of the Law Commission

The Law Commission (the Government's law reform body) has spent many years addressing reform of property law to remove the injustices for cohabitants and other homesharers. As long ago as 1994 it announced that the law was unsatisfactory, arbitrary and unjust, and said that it would make proposals for reform. Its proposals were eagerly awaited for many years, but it was not until July 2002 that it published a discussion paper, *Sharing Homes*, with the aim of providing a framework for future debate. The Law Commission's findings in its 2002 paper, however, turned out to be a considerable disappointment, particularly for those who had been in favour of reforming the law for cohabitants, not homesharers generally.

*(i) The Law Commission's Homesharers Project*   In *Sharing Homes: A Discussion Paper* (Law Com No. 278, 2002) the Law Commission discussed its findings in respect of its home-sharers' project, a project which was both narrow (as it concentrated solely on the home) and broad (as it concentrated on homesharers generally). In fact the breadth of the project was responsible for its failure.

In *Sharing Homes* the Law Commission chose a 'contribution-based' model for reform, which it applied to two hypothetical scenarios (one involving a son living at home with his parents who makes a financial contribution to the household budget, the other a mother who cohabits for a long time with the father of their child but who makes no direct financial contribution to the purchase of the house). Applying the contribution-based model to these two scenarios, the Law Commission said that the son would acquire an interest in the home, but the female cohabitant would not. A contribution-based approach would therefore do nothing to improve the law for cohabitants, because it was insufficiently flexible to take account of the different types of relationship. The Law Commission concluded that the basis for distinguishing between the different scenarios could not be expressed in a suitably principled or rational manner.

The Rt Hon Lord Justice Thorpe ([2002] Fam Law 891), commenting on *Sharing Homes*, said that the Law Commission should have taken a relationship-based, rather than a property-based, approach to the project. He also said that the law commissioner in charge of the project should have been a family lawyer, not a property lawyer. He criticised the Commission's approach as being cautious, and said that the responsibility for any Parliamentary reform should lie within the family justice system.

*(ii) The Law Commission's Cohabitation Project*   In 2005 it was announced that the Law Commission, at the request of the Lord Chancellor, was to conduct a two-year study with a view to reforming the law to remove the disadvantages, in particular the financial hardships, which cohabitants and their children suffer on relationship breakdown and on death. The project was referred to the Law Commission because of concerns expressed in Parliament during the passage of the Civil Partnership Act 2004 (see 2.10).

*The 2006 Consultation Paper*   In 2006 the Law Commission published a Consultation Paper, *Cohabitation: The Financial Consequences of Relationship Breakdown* (Law Com No. 179, 2006) in which it asked for responses to its suggested proposals for reforming the law relating to the property and financial consequences of cohabitation breakdown. The Commission proposed a scheme based on a principle of 'economic advantage' (not a discretionary regime like that on divorce). Thus, a cohabitant would be able to make a claim where it could be shown that the respondent 'had been enabled to retain some economic benefit (in terms of a gain in capital, income, or earning capacity) at the point of separation; and that gain has been caused at least in part by contributions made by the applicant' (para. 6.134). The advantage of such an approach, the Commission said, was that the court would be able to take into account a wider range of contributions than it could under the current law.

Some of the major concerns and difficulties raised in the consultation paper related to the question of eligibility for the scheme and whether parties should be able to opt in or opt out of any new scheme. The consultation paper was followed in 2007 by the publication of the Law Commission's Report.

*The 2007 Report – The Proposed New Scheme*    In July 2007 the Law Commission concluded its two-year project on cohabitation reform by publishing its Report, *Cohabitation: The Financial Consequences of Relationship Breakdown* (Law Com No. 307), in which it made recommendations for the introduction of a new scheme of remedies for cohabitants in respect of property on family breakdown and on death. The proposals would apply only to England and Wales. In Scotland, statutory remedies for cohabitants on separation have been available since May 2006.

The new scheme would apply in place of the law of implied trusts and proprietary estoppel on which cohabitants currently have to rely (see 4.7 and 4.8, above). The Law Commission said that the new remedies would also benefit children, and remove the need to use Schedule 1 to the Children Act 1989 (see 13.5) as a means of seeking a transfer of property order for the benefit of a child.

The scheme would not be equivalent to that available on divorce (or on dissolution of a civil partnership) (see Chapter 8). Instead, it would focus on the economic impact of the contributions that the parties have made to their relationship.

*Key Features of the Scheme*    The key features of the scheme are that a remedy would be available only if:

- the couple had satisfied certain eligibility requirements;
- the couple had not agreed to disapply the scheme; and
- the applicant had made qualifying contributions to the relationship giving rise to certain enduring consequences at the point of separation.

*Eligibility*    The parties must have cohabited and had a child together; or have cohabited for a specified minimum number or years. The Commission recommended that the minimum duration period be set at between 2 and 5 years.

*Opting Out of the Scheme*    In order to preserve the autonomy of cohabitants to determine the consequences of relationship breakdown for themselves, the Law Commission recommended that couples should be able to make binding opt-out agreements, which would disapply the scheme and leave the parties free to make their own arrangements about what would happen to their assets in the event of separation.

A set of safeguards would be put in place. Thus, an opt-out agreement would have to satisfy certain formal requirements in order to be binding (for example, to be in writing and signed by the parties). The court would have the power to set aside an agreement where its enforcement would cause manifest unfairness, having regard to the circumstances at the time the agreement was made, or when it came into force, which were unforeseen when the agreement was made. The Law Commission recommended that *pro forma* agreements should be available, and that parties should be able to enter into opt-out agreements whether or not they were eligible cohabitants at the time the agreement was made. It recommended that there should be a period between the legislation being enacted and implementation of the scheme during which cohabitants should be able to make an opt-out agreement. It also recommended that minors should be capable of entering into opt-out agreements, but that they should be voidable (in accordance with the general principles of contract law) at the instance of a party who was a minor at the time the agreement was made.

The Commission rejected an 'opt-in' scheme, because it considered that such a scheme would not deal effectively with the hardships created by the current law (as individuals would be no more likely to protect themselves by 'opting-in' to the scheme than they are to marry under the current law). It also took the view that an 'opt-in' scheme would also effectively create a new status of 'registered cohabitant'.

The Law Commission also recommended that, in order to remove any doubt, any new legislation should include a provision stating that cohabitation contracts governing the financial arrangements of a cohabiting couple during their cohabitation, or following their separation, shall not be regarded as contrary to public policy.

*Financial Relief Available*    The Law Commission proposed that the courts should have the power to make the following range of orders:

- lump sums, including payment by instalment, secured lump sums, lump sums paid by way of pension attachment and interim payments;
- property transfers;
- property settlements;
- orders for sale; and
- pension sharing.

Unlike on divorce, periodical payments (maintenance) should not generally be available. Thus, according to the Law Commission, cohabitants would not be expected to meet each other's future needs by means of maintenance payments and there would be no principle that the parties should share their assets equally.

*Applicable Principles*    In order to obtain a remedy, the Law Commission recommended that an applicant must prove that he or she had made a 'qualifying contribution' to the parties' relationship which had given rise to certain enduring consequences at the point of separation. The applicant would have to prove that the respondent had retained a benefit, or that he or she had suffered a continuing economic disadvantage, as a result of qualifying contributions made to the relationship:

- A *'qualifying contribution'* would be any contribution arising from the cohabiting relationship which was made to the parties' shared lives or to the welfare of members of their families. Contributions would not be limited to financial contributions, and would include future contributions, in particular to the care of the parties' children following separation.
- A *'retained benefit'* would take the form of capital, income or earning capacity that had been acquired, retained or enhanced.
- An *'economic disadvantage'* would be a present or future loss. It would include a diminution in current savings as a result of expenditure, or of earnings lost during the relationship, lost future earnings, or the future cost of paid child-care.

The court would be able to make an order to adjust the retained benefit, if any, by reversing in so far as was reasonable and practicable having regard to a statutory list of discretionary factors (see below). If, after the reversal of any retained benefit, the applicant would still bear any economic advantage, the court could make an order sharing that loss equally between the parties, in so far as it was reasonable and practicable to do so, having regard to the discretionary factors. Thus the value of any award would depend on the extent of the retained benefit or continuing economic disadvantage.

*The 'Discretionary Factors'*   The court would have the power to grant such financial relief as might be appropriate, giving first consideration to the welfare while a minor of any child of both parties who had not attained the age of 18; and taking into account the following discretionary factors:

- the financial needs and obligations of both parties;
- the extent and nature of the financial resources which each party has or is likely to have in the foreseeable future;
- the welfare of any children who live with, or might reasonably be expected to live with, either party; and
- the conduct of each party, defined restrictively but so as to include cases where a qualifying contribution can be shown to have been made despite the express disagreement of the other party.

In making an order to share economic disadvantage, the court would be required not to exercise any of its powers so as to place the applicant, for the foreseeable future, in a stronger economic position than the respondent.

*Additional Recommendations*   The Law Commission recommended that:

- procedural rules and costs rules would need to be carefully framed to protect the parties from oppressive litigation and to preserve court time and resources;
- the rules should in particular prevent eligible cohabitants from bringing claims under the general law of implied trusts, estoppel and contract on the basis of facts which constituted qualifying contributions under the new scheme;
- mediation should wherever possible be promoted as an alternative to court proceedings;
- the scheme should include anti-avoidance provisions modelled on those in s.37 Matrimonial Causes Act 1973, and there should be similar provisions for the enforcement of orders;
- claims for financial relief should be brought within two years of the parties' separation, but with the court having the power to extend this period where the circumstances of the case were exceptional.

*Financial Provision on Death*   The Law Commission did not recommend any changes to the law of intestacy, but it recommended that amendments be made to the Inheritance (Provision for Family and Dependants) Act 1975 (see 5.3).

The Law Commission concluded (see the Executive Summary of the Report, at para. 1.20) as follows:

> 'We consider that a scheme based on these principles would provide a sound basis on which to address the hardship and other economic unfairness that can arise when a cohabiting relationship ends. It would respond, more comprehensively than the current law can, to the economic impact

of the contributions made by parties to the relationship, and so to needs which arise in consequence. Where there are dependent children, the scheme would enable a remedy to be provided for the benefit of the primary carer, and so better protect those children who share their primary carer's standard of living. By making adequate provision for the adult parties, the scheme would give more leeway to the court than it currently has to apply Schedule 1 to the Children Act 1989 for the benefit of the parties' children.'

Stuart Bridge, the Law Commissioner in charge of the project, stated (at [2007] Fam Law 785):

'As media coverage of this project over the last 2 years has indicated, this is contentious territory, attracting a high level of public interest. We consider that our recommended scheme strikes the right balance between protecting the vulnerable and respecting freedom of choice. While some may disagree with that assessment, and with technical aspects of our recommendations, we hope that the Report will provide a firm basis on which the reform agenda can now be taken forward.'

Reforming the law, however, raises difficult issues. As Stuart Bridge himself said (at [2007] Fam Law 998): 'Family relationships are complex and the financial effect of relationship breakdown is correspondingly difficult to quantify and to apportion fairly between the parties.'

However, in March 2008 the Government announced that the proposals would be shelved in order to see how the Scottish reforms would work before any changes were made in England and Wales. Resolution (the organisation of family solicitors) is in favour of reforming the law and supports the proposals.

## 4.13   Homelessness and the Family

Homelessness can arise in many different situations. A victim of domestic violence may be forced to leave the family home. A child leaving care may have no accommodation. A family relationship may break down and one of the parties may have to move out.

Persons who are homeless can apply to their local housing authority for public sector housing. Housing authorities are responsible for managing, regulating and controlling housing vested in them, and they have statutory duties and powers towards homeless persons under Part VII of the Housing Act 1996 (as amended by the Homelessness Act 2002). When exercising their duties and powers, local housing authorities are required to comply with the *Homelessness Code of Guidance for Local Authorities* (2006) (ss.169(1) and 182(1)). Housing authorities also have statutory duties to work jointly with other housing authorities, social services and other statutory, voluntary and private sector partners. Thus, for instance, if homelessness persists, any children in the family could be in need and the family could seek assistance from social services who have powers and duties under the Children Act 1989 (see further at Chapter 15).

The duties and powers of housing authorities vary depending on whether an applicant is homeless or intentionally homeless, and whether or not the applicant has a priority need. In some cases there is merely a duty to provide advice. In others there is a full housing duty, in other words a duty to provide accommodation. The duty to ensure that suitable accommodation is available for people who have a priority need, if they are eligible for assistance and are unintentionally homeless, is known as the 'main homelessness duty'.

*Human Rights*   As local housing authorities are public authorities for the purposes of the Human Rights Act 1998 they must ensure that they exercise their powers and duties in line with the European Convention for the Protection of Human Rights (ECHR). Thus, for example, a failure on the part of a housing authority to provide suitable accommodation, or the adoption of an unlawful Homelessness Allocation Policy might, depending on the circumstances, constitute a breach of art. 8 ECHR (the right to family life) (see, for example, *R (Aweys and Others)* v. *Birmingham City Council* [2007] EWHC 52 (Admin), [2007] 1 FLR 2066).

In *R (Morris)* v. *Westminster City Council* [2004] EWCH 2191 (Admin), which dealt with the question of priority need in the context of immigration, Keith J held that the housing authority had breached the applicant mother's rights under art. 14 ECHR to enjoy respect for family life under art. 8 ECHR without discrimination; and he made a declaration under s.4 Human Rights Act 1998 that the provisions of s.185(4) of Part IV of the Housing Act 1996 were incompatible with the ECHR. Keith J held that s.185(4) was incompatible with art. 14 (right not to suffer discrimination) to the extent that it had required a dependent child of a British citizen to be disregarded when determining whether a British citizen had a priority need for accommodation, when that child was subject to immigration control. In this case the housing authority had refused to treat the mother as having a priority need (even though she had acquired British citizenship after coming from Mauritius) on the basis that her dependent daughter was at the time subject to immigration control. This was held to be a breach of the ECHR.

### (a)  Local Housing Authority Duties

Under Part VII of the Housing Act 1996 local authority housing departments must provide assistance for certain eligible persons (s.185) who are homeless or threatened with homelessness. Housing authorities are required to maintain a register of qualifying persons (s.162), and an allocation scheme operates (ss.159 and 167). The Homelessness Act 2002 (ss.1–4) imposes a duty on local housing authorities to formulate a homelessness strategy.

Housing authorities have the following range of duties depending on the circumstances of the applicant:

- to make inquiries to establish whether an applicant who is homeless or threatened with homelessness is eligible for assistance and, if so, what duty is owed (s.184(1));
- to provide advice and information (s.179);
- to provide interim accommodation pending a decision as to a duty (if any) owed to an applicant if the local housing authority has reason to believe that the applicant may be homeless, eligible for assistance and has a priority need (s.188);
- to provide temporary housing, and advice and assistance to find long-term accommodation for an applicant who is homeless, eligible for assistance and who has a priority need, but who is intentionally homeless (s.190);
- to provide advice and assistance to an applicant who is homeless, eligible for assistance, but who has no priority need and who is intentionally homeless (s.190);
- to take reasonable steps to ensure that in the case of an applicant who is threatened with homelessness (but who is eligible for assistance, not threatened with homelessness intentionally, and has a priority need) that his accommodation does not cease to be available for his occupation (s.195) – but, if there is no priority need or intentionality, the duty is merely to provide advice and assistance to help secure that the applicant's accommodation does not cease to be available for his occupation;

▶ to give advice and assistance with the power (not the duty) to secure accommodation for an applicant who is homeless, eligible for assistance, not intentionally homeless, but who has no priority need (s.192);

▶ to provide accommodation where the applicant is homeless, eligible for assistance, not intentionally homeless and has a priority need (s.193) – unless the housing authority refers the case to another housing authority because of the local connection factor (see p.91, below).

### (b)  When is a Person Homeless?

An applicant is homeless if he (or she) has no accommodation available for his occupation in the UK or elsewhere which he (ss.175(1), (2)):

▶ is entitled to occupy by virtue of an interest in it or by virtue of an order of the court;

▶ has an express or implied licence to occupy;

▶ occupies as a residence by virtue of any enactment or rule of law giving him or her the right to remain in occupation or restricting the right of another person to recover possession;

▶ has occupation but cannot secure entry to it; or

▶ where the accommodation is a movable structure and there is no place where he is entitled to place it and reside in it.

A person who has accommodation is treated as being homeless if it would not be reasonable for him or her to continue to occupy that accommodation (s.175(3)). Violence may provide a reason for not continuing to occupy accommodation (see further below).

### (c)  The Full Housing Duty

The full or main homelessness duties in ss.193(2) and 195(2) (to secure suitable accommodation; or to take reasonable steps to prevent the loss of accommodation) are owed only to eligible persons who have (i) a priority need for accommodation, and who (ii) are not intentionally homeless.

*(i) Priority Need*    Those categories of applicants who qualify as having a priority need has been extended over the years. Section 189(1) and the Homelessness (Priority Need for Accommodation) (England) Order 2002 provide that the following categories of applicant have a priority need for accommodation:

▶ a pregnant woman or a person with whom she resides or might reasonably be expected to reside;

▶ a person with whom dependent children reside or might reasonably be expected to reside;

▶ a person who is vulnerable as a result of old age, mental illness or handicap or physical disability or other special reason, or with whom such a person resides or might reasonably be expected to reside;

▶ a person aged 16 or 17 who is not a 'relevant child' or a child in need to whom a local authority owes a duty under s.20 Children Act 1989;

- a person under 21 who was (but is no longer) looked after, accommodated or fostered between the ages of 16 and 18 (except a person who is a 'relevant student');
- a person aged 21 or more who is vulnerable as a result of being looked after, accommodated or fostered (except a person who is a 'relevant student');
- persons who are vulnerable as a result of having been in HM's armed forces, or have served a custodial sentence, or have been committed for contempt of court or any other kindred offences or having been remanded in custody;
- a person who is vulnerable as a result of ceasing to occupy accommodation because of violence from another person or threats of violence from another person which are likely to be carried out;
- a person who is vulnerable for any other special reason, or with whom such person resides or might reasonably be expected to reside;
- a person who is homeless or is threatened with homelessness as a result of an emergency such as flood, fire or other disaster.

*(ii) Intentionality*    A housing authority is under no duty to provide accommodation for a person who is intentionally homeless. A person is homeless intentionally if he (or she) deliberately does or fails to do anything in consequence of which he ceases to occupy accommodation that is available for his occupation and which it would have been reasonable for him to continue to occupy (s.191). The *Guidance* states that a person fleeing violence will not be treated as being intentionally homeless. However, if a person is evicted because of violence or threats of violence to an associated person (defined in s.178), that will be considered deliberate for the purposes of s.191. The *Guidance* states that a person who loses his home or who was obliged to sell it because of real financial difficulties (including because of family breakdown) should not be categorised as having made a deliberate act or omission for the purposes of s.191.

A housing authority can satisfy the full housing duty by providing accommodation from its own stock or by arranging for it to be provided by a housing association or a landlord in the private rented sector. However, the duty to provide accommodation requires a housing authority to provide 'suitable' accommodation (see *R v. Ealing London Borough Council ex parte Surdona* [1999] 1 FLR 650 where the duty to provide accommodation was not discharged by providing accommodation for a family in separate dwellings, as families should be able to live together as a unit).

### (d) Referral to Another Local Housing Authority – The Local Connection

Section 198 gives a housing authority the right to pass the housing duty on to another housing authority, if the applicant (or any person who might reasonably be expected to reside with the applicant) has no local connection with the authority to whom the application was made but has a local connection with the district of the other authority. Referral to another housing authority is not permitted, however, where the applicant (or any person expected to reside with the applicant) will run the risk of violence or domestic violence in the district of the other housing authority (s.198). A 'local connection' is established if the applicant is (or was) normally resident in that district of his own choice, or is employed there, or has family associations there, or special circumstances exist (s.199). Pending referral, or a decision about a referral, to another housing authority, the requesting authority has an interim duty to provide accommodation (s.200(1)).

### (e)    Domestic Violence and Other Violence

Applicants who suffer domestic violence, or other violence, are given special treatment under the homelessness legislation. They are treated as being homeless even if they have accommodation, as s.177(1) provides that it is not reasonable for a person to continue to occupy accommodation if it is probable that this will lead to domestic or other violence against: the applicant; a member of the applicant's family who normally resides with the applicant; or any other person who might reasonably be expected to live with the applicant.

Domestic violence or other violence includes actual or threatened violence; but violence is only 'domestic' if the victim and the perpetrator are 'associated persons' (s.177(1A)). The term 'associated persons' is defined in s.178 Housing Act 1996 and is similar to the definition of associated persons in s.62(3) of Part IV of the Family Law Act 1996 which provides remedies against domestic violence (see Chapter 6). The following persons are defined as being associated with each other (s.178): spouses and former spouses; civil partners and former civil partners; cohabitants and former cohabitants; persons who are living, or who have lived, in the same household; relatives; engaged and formerly engaged couples; parties, and former parties, to a civil partnership agreement; and parents who have, or who have had, parental responsibility in relation to a child. Parents who have adopted a child (or persons with whom a child has been placed for adoption) and the child's natural parent(s) or grandparent(s) are associated persons (s.178(2)). Unlike the definition in s.62(3) of Part IV of the Family Law Act 1996, however, the definition of 'associated persons' in s.178 does not include a person in an intimate relationship (see 6.6). However, such a person (for example, a girl being harassed by a former boyfriend) may still be owed a duty by a housing authority as a person suffering from 'other violence' rather than 'domestic' violence.

The *Homelessness Code of Guidance* provides the following guidance in respect of violence, including domestic violence:

- Domestic violence (actual or threatened) is not confined to instances in the home but extends to violence outside the home (para. 8.19).
- The term 'violence' should not be given a restrictive meaning and 'domestic violence' should be understood to include threatening behaviour, violence or abuse (psychological, physical, sexual, financial or emotional) between persons who are, or who have been, intimate partners, family members or members of the same household, regardless of gender or sexuality (para. 8.21).
- An assessment of the likelihood of violence being carried out should not be based on whether there has been actual violence in the past; and must be based on the facts of the case and devoid of any value judgment about what an applicant should or should not do, or should or should not have done, to mitigate the risk of any violence (for example, to seek police help, or to apply for an injunction against the perpetrator) (para. 8.22).
- Inquiries into cases where violence is alleged will need careful handling (para. 8.22).
- In cases involving violence, housing authorities may wish to inform applicants of the option of seeking an injunction, but should make it clear that there is no obligation on the applicant to do so (para. 8.23).
- Housing authorities should recognise that injunctions ordering a person not to molest, or enter the home of, an applicant may not be effective in deterring

perpetrators from carrying out further violence or incursions, and applicants may not have confidence in their effectiveness. Consequently, applicants should not be expected to return home on the strength of an injunction (para. 8.23).

▶ Where there would be a probability of violence if the applicant continued to occupy his or her present accommodation, the housing authority must treat the applicant as homeless and should not expect him or her to remain in, or return to, the accommodation. In all cases involving violence, the safety of the applicant and his or her household should be the primary consideration at all stages of the decision-making as to whether or not the applicant remains in their own home (para. 8.24).

Referral to another housing authority (see above) is not permitted if there is a risk of violence or domestic violence to the applicant in the area of that other housing authority (s.198).

### (f)  Homeless Families with Children

If there are dependent children an applicant has a priority need and the local housing authority has a duty to provide accommodation for the family, provided the applicant is eligible for assistance and is not intentionally homeless (see above).

The *Homelessness Code of Guidance* provides that, although there must be actual dependence on the applicant, the child need not be wholly and exclusively dependent on him; and, although there must be actual residence (or a reasonable expectation of residence) with some degree of permanence or regularity, the child need not be wholly and exclusively resident (or expected to reside wholly and exclusively) with the applicant. Dependent children need not necessarily be the applicant's own children, but there must be a parent–child relationship. The *Guidance* provides that the child does not need to have full-time residence with the applicant in order to qualify as a dependent child. It also provides that, if a shared residence order is in force, or an agreement about shared residence, it should not lead the local authority to conclude that it would be reasonable for the child to live with the other parent, rather than the applicant. Housing authorities are required to consider that, when parents separate, it is often in the best interests of the child to maintain a relationship with both parents.

*Intentional Homelessness*   There is no duty to provide accommodation for intentionally homeless families with children, but they are entitled to advice and assistance and temporary accommodation. If homelessness continues, the children may be in need for the purposes of Part III of the Children Act 1989, and help can be sought from a local authority social services department. Housing authorities must have arrangements in place to ensure that social services are alerted as quickly as possible where the applicant has children aged under 18 and the housing authority considers the applicant may be intentionally homeless (s.213A Housing Act 1996). If social services decide that the child's needs would best be met by helping the family to obtain accommodation, they can ask the housing authority for reasonable assistance in this matter and the housing authority must respond (s.27 Children Act 1989).

*Housing Applications by Children Are Not Permitted*   A child cannot apply for local authority housing if the child's parent has failed to obtain local authority accommodation:

> ▶ *R v. Oldham Metropolitan Borough Council ex parte G and Related Appeals* [1993] AC 509
>
> The father's application for housing had been rejected by the housing authority, because, although he had priority need, he was found to be intentionally homeless (he had deliberately failed to pay the mortgage). The father made a fresh application in the name of his 4-year-old son. The House of Lords held that the application had been properly rejected, as to allow such an application would render the intentional homelessness provisions redundant where there were dependent children.

*The Relationship Between the Housing Legislation and the Children Act 1989*   Local housing departments and local authority social services departments are required to work together when dealing with cases of homelessness involving children (see s.213A Housing Act 1996). However, there is no guarantee that a social services department will find housing for families where they do not qualify for housing under the housing legislation, as s.17(6) Children Act 1989 gives local authorities the power, not the duty, to provide accommodation (see the *Barnet* case below, and 15.6).

> ▶ *R v. Northavon District Council ex parte Smith* [1994] 2 AC 402
>
> The father applied for housing from Northavon housing authority but was found to be homeless intentionally. He then applied to the local social services department (Avon) with a view to their performing their duty under s.17(6) Children Act 1989 to safeguard the welfare of his children by making cash payments to cover rent and deposits. Avon social services refused to do this, but invoked their power under s.27 Children Act 1989 and asked Northavon housing authority to help with the provision of housing. Northavon refused, on the basis that they had performed their duties under the housing legislation and that it would be a contradiction to offer the family housing in the light of the intentional homelessness decision. The father applied for judicial review to quash Northavon's decision but his application failed. The House of Lords held that there was a duty for the authorities to co-operate with each other, but that an action for judicial review was not the way to obtain that co-operation.
>
> ▶ *R (G) v. Barnet London Borough Council; R (W) v. Lambeth London Borough Council; R (A) v. Lambeth London Borough Council* [2003] UKHL 57, [2004] 1 FLR 454
>
> The House of Lords held that local authority social services departments have no duty under Part III of the Children Act 1989 to provide accommodation for particular children in need, as this would subvert the provisions of the housing legislation (see 15.6).

Under s.13 Homelessness Act 2002 housing authorities are required to refer homeless persons with dependent children who are ineligible for homelessness assistance, or who are intentionally homeless, to social services, provided the person consents. If homelessness persists, any child in the family could be in need. In such cases, if social services decide the child's needs would be best met by helping the family to obtain accommodation, they can ask the housing authority for reasonable assistance in this, and the housing authority must respond.

*Housing and Residence Orders*   The existence of a residence order in favour of an applicant for housing is a highly material consideration for a local housing authority when exercising its powers and duties under the Housing Act 1996, but it is not the only factor to be taken into account and will not be the determinative factor as to the allocation of housing.

The following two cases involved shared residence orders and local authority housing. The first case involved the question of the allocation of housing, the second the question of whether or not a parent who was the subject of a shared residence order had a priority need:

▶ *R (Bibi)* v. *Camden London Borough Council* [2004] EWHC 2527 (Admin)

The parents had a 50/50 shared residence order in respect of their two children. The father had been given a three-bedroom house by Camden LBC, but the mother was offered only one-bedroom accommodation, on the basis that the children were not part of her household, and because of the acute shortage of three-bedroom accommodation in the borough, and the under-occupation which would result if both parents were granted three-bedroom accommodation. The mother successfully applied for judicial review. Davis J quashed the decision of the housing authority, on the ground that it was flawed – as it failed to address the question of the position of the children with regard to the mother's own housing needs. There was no obvious basis for the conclusion that the children's main housing was with their father, and it was illogical that he was the primary-carer because he was working. The shortage of housing stock and the issue of under-occupation were relevant factors which could be taken into account, but, like the existence of the residence order, they could not be decisive. Davis J was keen to emphasise that his decision was very much dependent on the shared residence order providing for 50/50 sharing, and the fact that the order had been put into practice by the parents.

▶ *Holmes-Moorhouse* v. *Richmond-upon-Thames London Borough Council* [2007] EWCA Civ 955

A consent order was made in family proceedings that the three minor children of the claimant father were to reside with him for one week in two and to spend the other with the mother. As the father had been made homeless by his separation from the mother, he applied for accommodation on the basis that he had a priority need (under s.189(1)(b) Housing Act 1996). The local housing authority turned him down on the basis that the children would merely be staying with him rather than residing with him; but he contended that the family court's decision established that his children might reasonably be expected to reside with him. His appeal to the county court under s.204 against the local authority's decision was dismissed, and so he appealed to the Court of Appeal.

The Court of Appeal held, allowing his appeal, that a shared residence order made by a family court in uncontested proceedings (that is, under a consent order) did not determine the question of whether a parent in whose favour the order was made had a priority need for housing as a homeless person with dependent children who might reasonably be expected to reside with him. The Court of Appeal held, however, that where a shared residence order was made in contested proceedings, the order would be determinative, because the court would have been obliged to have regard to the capacity of the parents to accommodate the children and would have given the local authority the opportunity to comment on that issue.

In this case, therefore, the basis on which the local authority had rejected the claimant's application for accommodation was not a valid ground for rejection, for otherwise it would be open to the council in such cases to say that the child was merely staying with one or other parent. The Court of Appeal ordered that the local housing authority should consider the matter afresh, bearing in mind that those concerned had already agreed that the children should live with more than one parent.

# Summary

**1** There are two sorts of ownership in English law: ownership in law; and ownership in equity under a trust.

**2** Property can be owned jointly by the parties as joint tenants or as tenants in common.

**3** During a marriage or civil partnership the parties have the same property rights as cohabitants and other persons, with the exception of certain special statutory provisions which exist for married couples and civil partners. Who owns what therefore depends on the general principles of property law (contract and trusts).

**4** Married couples and civil partners with no right of ownership in the home have 'home rights' under s.30 of Part IV of the Family Law Act 1996, which are rights to remain in occupation of the home, and to enter in and occupy the home. 'Home rights' are binding on third parties if the home right is registered as a notice on the register.

**5** Special statutory provisions apply in respect of the property rights of engaged couples and civil partners who have entered into a civil partnership agreement.

**6** There are no special statutory provisions for cohabitants in respect of property rights. They must rely on the general rules of property, in particular the equitable doctrines of resulting and constructive trusts, and proprietary estoppel.

**7** For spouses, civil partners, cohabitants and other family members, ownership of personal property (property other than land) depends on the law of contract and trusts. As a general rule, property passes to the purchaser. Rights in personal property can be acquired expressly or impliedly (under a trust, estoppel or contract) and in many cases without written formalities.

**8** Funds in a bank account presumptively belong to the party or parties in whose name the account is held, but the presumption can be displaced by proof of a contrary intention.

**9** As far as the family home is concerned, trusts in respect of land and contracts for the sale of land must be in writing (s.53 Law of Property Act 1925; and s.2 Law of Property (Miscellaneous Provisions) Act 1989). However, interests in land can be acquired under resulting or constructive trusts, or under the doctrine of proprietary estoppel without the requirement of writing (s.53(2) Law of Property Act 1925; and s.2(5) Law of Property (Miscellaneous Provisions) Act 1989).

**10** Orders for the sale and possession of land, and declarations of trusts in respect of land, can be sought under s.14 Trusts of Land and Appointment of Trustees Act 1996.

**11** A presumption of resulting trust gives a claimant a share of the beneficial interest in property proportionate to his or her financial contribution, subject to any contrary intention.

**12** A constructive trust arises where there is an express or implied agreement, arrangement or understanding that the claimant has an interest in property and the claimant has acted to his or her detriment on the basis of that agreement, arrangement or understanding.

**13** An interest in the family home (and any other property) can be acquired under the doctrine of proprietary estoppel where the claimant has acted to his detriment on the basis of a belief encouraged by the other party that he is to have an interest in the property in question and it would be inequitable to deny the claimant an interest.

**14** Tenancies can be transferred between married partners, civil partners and cohabitants (including former spouses, civil partners and cohabitants) under s.53 and Sched. 7 of Part IV of the Family Law Act 1996.

## Summary cont'd

**15** There has been increasing dissatisfaction with the law governing the property rights of cohabitants. There have been calls for reform to remove the perceived unfairness that exists, and in July 2007 the Law Commission published a report making proposals for reform of the law.

**16** Under Part VII of the Housing Act 1996 local housing authorities have powers and duties in respect of persons who are homeless. A full housing duty is owed to persons who are eligible for assistance, and who have priority need and who are not intentionally homeless. In other cases, there is only an obligation to provide advice or assistance. Domestic violence is taken seriously by local housing authorities, and victims of violence, or of threatened violence, are not treated as being intentionally homeless if they leave the home.

## Further Reading and References

Bailey-Harris (ed.), *Dividing the Assets on Family Breakdown*, 1998, Family Law.

Barlow, Callus and Cooke, 'Community of property – a study for England and Wales' [2004] Fam Law 47.

Barton, 'Cohabitants, contracts and commissioners' [2007] Fam Law 407.

Bridge, 'Money, marriage and cohabitation' [2006] Fam Law 641.

Bridge, 'Cohabitation: why legislative reform is necessary' [2007] Fam Law 911.

Bridge, 'Financial relief for cohabitants: how the Law Commission's scheme would work' [2007] Fam Law 998.

Bridge, 'Financial relief for cohabitants: eligibility, opt out and provision on death' [2007] Fam Law 1076.

Burles, '"Promises, promises" – *Burns* v. *Burns* 20 years on' [2003] Fam Law 834.

Douglas, Pearce and Woodward, 'Dealing with property issues on cohabitation breakdown' [2007] Fam Law 36.

Douglas, Pearce and Woodward, *A Failure of Trust: Resolving Property Issues on Cohabitation Breakdown*, Cardiff Research Papers, No. 1 (July 2007) (available at www.law.cf.ac.uk/researchpapers/index).

Fox, 'Reforming family property – comparisons, compromises and common dimensions' [2003] CFLQ 1.

Maclean *et al*, 'When cohabiting parents separate – law and expectations' [2002] Fam Law 373.

Miles, 'Property law v. family law: resolving the problems of family property' (2003) *Legal Studies* 624.

Pawlowski, 'Sharing homes – legislation down under' [2003] Fam Law 336.

Pawlowski, 'Family home: doing justice to the parties' [2006] Fam Law 462.

Probert, 'Trusts and the modern woman – establishing an interest in the family home' [2001] CFLQ 275.

Probert, 'Cohabitation: contributions and sacrifices' [2006] Fam Law 1060.

Probert, 'Cohabitation and joint ownership: the implications of *Stack* v. *Dowden*' [2007] Fam Law 924.

Probert and Barlow, 'Displacing marriage – diversification and harmonisation within Europe' [2000] CFLQ 153.

Rt Hon Lord Justice Thorpe, 'Property rights on family breakdown' [2002] Fam Law 891.

## Websites

**Law Commission**: www.lawcom.gov.uk
**The Law Society**: www.lawsoc.org.uk

# Chapter 5

# Family Property on Death

This chapter deals with what happens to property on the death of a family member. It looks first at the legal rules governing the devolution of property on death. Next, it considers the legal steps family members can take under the Inheritance (Provision for Family and Dependants) Act 1975 when a deceased person has failed to make financial provision, or adequate provision, for certain family members and dependants. Finally, it deals with succession to a tenancy on death. Reference should also be made to Chapter 4, as the equitable doctrines of trusts and estoppel can be used to claim a share of a deceased person's estate (see, for example, *Churchill* v. *Roach* [2004] 2 FLR 989). The appointment of a guardian for a child is dealt with at 10.4.

The rules relating to property on death are complex. Only an outline is provided here.

## 5.1 Devolution of Property by Will

There is complete freedom of testamentary disposition in England and Wales. Any adult person of sound mind may make a will disposing of his or her property to whomsoever he or she chooses. A will is valid if it is made in writing and is signed by the person making the will in the presence of at least two witnesses, each of whom must attest and sign the will, or acknowledge the signature of the person making it (ss.7 and 9 Wills Act 1837). A will is revoked by the testator's marriage or civil partnership, unless it was made in contemplation of a marriage or a civil partnership to a particular person and the testator did not intend the will to be revoked (ss.18 and 18B Wills Act 1837). In the case of divorce or nullity, or dissolution or annulment of a civil partnership, then subject to any contrary intention in the will, any legacies and gifts to a former spouse or former civil partner lapse. However, a former spouse or former civil partner may still have a claim for reasonable financial provision from the deceased's estate under the Inheritance (Provision for Family and Dependants) Act 1975 (see 5.3).

## 5.2 Devolution of Property on Intestacy

### (a) Spouses and Civil Partners

If a spouse or civil partner dies intestate (without making a will), but leaves a surviving spouse or civil partner, the estate (after the payment of debts and expenses) is distributed or held on trust according to the following rules of intestate succession which are laid down in the Administration of Estates Act 1925 (as amended):

▶ *If the deceased leaves children (or grandchildren)* The surviving spouse or civil partner receives: the deceased's personal chattels; a fixed sum of £125,000; and a life-interest (the income) in one-half of the balance of the estate. The other half is held on trust for the children (or grandchildren), who during their minority can be paid maintenance out of income and lump sums out of capital. When they reach majority they are entitled to the capital.

▷ *If the deceased leaves no children (or grandchildren), but parents* The surviving spouse or civil partner receives: the deceased's personal chattels; a fixed sum of £200,000; and an absolute interest in one-half of the balance of the estate. The deceased's surviving parents receive the other half of the estate.

▷ *If the deceased leaves no children (or grandchildren) and no surviving parents, but has siblings* The surviving spouse or civil partner receives: the deceased's personal chattels; a fixed sum of £200,000; and one-half of the balance of the estate. The deceased's siblings receive the other half of the estate.

▷ *If there are no children (or grandchildren) and no blood relatives* The surviving spouse or civil partner receives the whole estate.

▷ *If there is no surviving spouse or civil partner, and no children (or grandchildren) and no blood relatives* The estate passes to the Crown, although the Crown can make discretionary provision for dependants and other persons for whom the deceased might reasonably have been expected to provide.

A consultation paper, *Administration of Estates – Review of the Statutory Legacy*, published in 2005 by the Department for Constitutional Affairs, proposed that the current statutory legacies of £125,000 and £200,000 should be raised to £350,000 and £650,000 respectively, but these proposals have not been implemented.

### (b)   Rights in The Home

Where the home was owned by the spouses or civil partners as joint tenants, it devolves to the surviving spouse or civil partner. Where it was owned by them as tenants in common, the deceased's share forms part of his or her estate and passes according to the will or according to the laws of intestacy. On intestacy, however, the Intestates' Estates Act 1952 allows a surviving spouse or civil partner in certain circumstances to retain the home.

### (c)   Cohabitants on Intestacy

Where a cohabitant (opposite-sex or same-sex) dies without making a will, the surviving cohabitant has no automatic right to succeed to the deceased's estate. It passes to the children, or otherwise to the parent(s) of the deceased. This is with the exception of any property which was jointly owned by the parties as joint tenants (such as the home or a bank account), when ownership passes to the survivor. As cohabitants are in a vulnerable position on intestacy, it is important to make a will. However, cohabitants can make a claim under the Inheritance (Provision for Family and Dependants) Act 1975 (see 5.3, below). The Law Commission in its proposals to reform the law of property and finance for cohabitants has not recommended any changes to the rules of intestacy for cohabitants (see further below, and at 4.12).

### (d)   Succession and Human Rights

In *Haas* v. *The Netherlands (Application No. 36983/97)* [2004] 1 FLR 673 the applicant, who was born out of wedlock, claimed that his lack of a right to succeed to his father's estate (which had gone to a nephew as sole heir) breached his fundamental human rights under the European Convention for the Protection of Human Rights. His claim failed, as the Court of Human Rights held that art. 8 (right to family life), art. 13 (right to an effective remedy before a national authority) and art. 14 (discrimination in respect of a Convention right) did not apply to the facts of the case.

## 5.3    The Inheritance (Provision for Family and Dependants) Act 1975

Under the Inheritance (Provision for Family and Dependants) Act 1975 the court can make financial provision orders for certain family members and dependants out of a deceased person's estate where the deceased has failed under his or her will or under the laws of intestacy (or both) to make reasonable financial provision for them. The Act only applies if the deceased was domiciled in England and Wales at the time of death (s.1(1)). An application must be brought within six months of the date on which probate or letters of administration were taken out, or otherwise with the permission of the court (s.4).

The Act is concerned with dependency; it is not concerned with deciding how the assets should be fairly divided (see Goff LJ in *Re Coventry (deceased)* [1980] Ch 461, at 486). In *Jelley* v. *Iliffe and Others* [1981] Fam 128, Stephenson LJ said that the purpose of the Act is to remedy 'wherever reasonably possible, the injustice of one who has been put by a deceased person in a position of dependency upon him, being deprived of any financial support, either by accident or by design of the deceased, after his death'.

When considering an application, the court conducts a two-stage exercise. First it has to make an objective assessment of the facts to establish whether or not the deceased made reasonable financial provision for the applicant. If the answer is 'no', then it must go on to consider what financial provision should be made. When answering these questions, the court draws a distinction between spouses (and civil partners) and other applicants. For applicants other than spouses and civil partners, reasonable financial provision is such provision as would be reasonable for the applicant to receive by way of maintenance, but for spouses and civil partners other considerations can be taken into account by the court. Spouses and civil partners are treated more favourably under the Act than other applicants.

### (a)    Applicants

The following persons can make a claim under the 1975 Act:

*(i) The spouse or civil partner of the deceased (s.1(1)(a))*    This also includes a party who entered into a marriage or civil partnership in good faith but which was void (ss.25(4) and 25(4A)).

*(ii) The former spouse or civil partner of the deceased, provided he or she has not formed a subsequent marriage or civil partnership (s.1(1)(b))*    A subsequent marriage or civil partnership is deemed to have taken place whether or not the previous or subsequent marriage, or civil partnership, is void or voidable (s.25(5)).

*(iii) The cohabitant (opposite-sex or same-sex) of the deceased (s.1(1)(ba))*    A person only qualifies as a cohabitant for the purposes of s.1(1)(ba) if he or she was living in the same household as the deceased during the whole period of two years ending immediately before the date when the deceased died, and was living as the husband or wife or civil

partner of the deceased (ss.1(1A) and 1(1B)). A person who does not come within this definition (such as a former cohabitant or a cohabitant who lived with the deceased for a shorter period of time) can apply under s.1(1)(e) (see below).

The definition of cohabitant was purposively construed in *Gully* v. *Dix* [2004] EWCA Civ 139, [2004] 1 FLR 918, where the Court of Appeal held that occasional periods of separation need not alter the fact that the parties were 'living in the same household'. Here, although the applicant had separated from the deceased for the last three months of his life – due to his intolerable behaviour – she was nevertheless held to be a cohabitant within the definition in s.1(1A). In *Churchill* v. *Roach* [2004] 2 FLR 989, on the other hand, the applicant was held not to be a cohabitant, as she had not lived with the deceased for the full two-year period. In *Re Watson (Deceased)* [1999] 1 FLR 878 Neuberger J held that, when considering the definition of cohabitant, the court should 'ask itself whether, in the opinion of a reasonable person with normal perceptions, it could be said that the two people in question were living together as husband and wife', but that when considering that question, 'one should not ignore the multifarious nature of marital relationships'.

Although cohabitants are now treated more favourably under the Act than they once were – because they no longer have to prove dependency on the deceased – they are not treated as favourably as spouses and civil partners as the courts powers are limited only to providing such financial provision which is reasonable in all the circumstances of the case for the applicant's *maintenance*. Bailey-Harris and Wilson (2003) question whether the different treatment of cohabitants is a breach of arts. 8 and 14 of the European Convention on Human Rights.

*The Law Commission's Proposals to Reform the 1975 Act in Respect of Cohabitant Applicants*  The Law Commission in its *Report, Cohabitation: The Financial Consequences of Relationship Breakdown* (Law Com No. 307, July 2007) (see further at 4.12) recommended reforms so that cohabitants are treated in the same way as married couples and civil partners under the 1975 Act, in order to remove the perceived injustices that cohabitants suffer. Thus, the Law Commission recommended that reasonable financial provision should mean such financial provision as it would be reasonable in all the circumstances of the case for the applicant to receive, *whether or not* that provision is required for the applicant's maintenance. The Law Commission's recommendations would also bring cohabitants into line with spouses and civil partners, by providing that the court should have regard to the provision which the applicant cohabitant might reasonably be expected to receive in proceedings for financial relief on separation (that is, under the proposed new scheme for cohabitants) if the applicant and the deceased had separated on the day on which the deceased had died. The Commission also proposed the amendment of the definition of 'cohabitant' in the 1975 Act to bring it into line with the definition to be used in the new scheme for financial relief for cohabitants on relationship breakdown. However, the Law Commission made no proposals to reform the intestacy laws for cohabitants.

*(iv) A child of the deceased (s.1(1)(c))*  Marital and non-marital children, and adopted children, can apply under this section, whether born before or after the deceased's death (s.25(1)) and whether or not a minor or an adult.

*Adult Children*  Adult children of the deceased can apply under s.1(1)(c), but they may find it difficult to succeed, particularly if they are young and able-bodied, are in employment and are capable of maintaining themselves. For example, in *Re Jennings (Deceased)* [1994] Ch 286, *sub nom Re Jennings (Deceased), Harlow* v. *National Westminster Bank plc and Others* [1994] 1 FLR 536 an application by the adult child of the deceased failed. Each case, however, depends on its own facts. In *Re Abram (Deceased)* [1996] 2 FLR 379 the adult son successfully claimed against his deceased mother's estate, as he had worked for her in the family business for many years and for long hours, and had received only a minimal wage. In *Garland* v. *Morris* [2007] EWHC 2 (Ch), [2007] 2 FLR 528, on the other hand, an adult daughter's claim against her deceased father's estate was dismissed, as she had failed to establish that it was unreasonable in all the circumstances for her father to make provision for her (she had neither spoken to nor met her father at any time in the 15 years preceding his death, and had made no real effort to do so, and she had received all of her mother's estate).

At one time the court took the view that an adult child applicant would have to prove special circumstances, or that the deceased had a moral obligation to him or her, in order to succeed. However, the courts no longer adopt such a restricted approach. In *Re Hancock (Deceased)* [1998] 2 FLR 346 the Court of Appeal held that, although the presence of special circumstances or a moral obligation may be relevant factors, particularly where the applicant is in employment or possessed of earning capacity, their absence does not necessarily preclude a successful claim. In *Espinosa* v. *Bourke* [1999] 1 FLR 747 the Court of Appeal allowed the 55-year-old daughter's appeal as the judge had erred in elevating moral obligation to a threshold requirement.

The existence of a moral obligation may still be determinative, however, as it was in *Re Pearce (Deceased)* [1998] 2 FLR 705 where the 29-year-old son succeeded in his claim against his deceased father's estate, as his father was held to have a moral obligation to him. He had done substantial work on his father's farm, and his father had made representations that he would inherit it.

In *Garland* v. *Morris* (above) it was held that, while 'moral obligation' was not a necessary precondition to a claim under the 1975 Act, it was an important consideration in practice. It was held in the circumstances of the case that the father had been entitled to conclude that the claimant daughter no longer had any reasonable claim to his bounty. (The daughter had lived in close contact with her mother, had made no effort to contact her father for many years, and had succeeded to the whole of her mother's estate.)

*(v) Any person (not being a child of the deceased) who, in the case of any marriage or civil partnership to which the deceased was at any time a party, was treated by the deceased as a child of the family in relation to that marriage or civil partnership (s.1(1)d))*   A step-child or foster-child can apply under this section, whether or not a minor.

*(vi) Any person (not being a person included in the paragraphs above) who immediately before the deceased's death was being maintained either wholly or partly by the deceased (s.1(1)(e))* Persons such as relatives, friends and carers can apply under this section, and so can cohabitants who do not come within s.1(1)(ba) above – provided the applicant can prove that he or she was being maintained, wholly or partly, by the deceased. The word 'maintenance', according to Browne-Wilkinson LJ in *Re Dennis (Deceased)* [1981] 2 All ER 140, at 145, 'connotes only payments which, directly or indirectly, enable the applicant to discharge the cost of his daily living at whatever standard of living is appropriate to him'.

Section 1(3) provides that an applicant is only to be regarded as having been maintained by the deceased for the purposes of this section if the deceased, otherwise than for full valuable consideration, was making a substantial contribution in money or in money's worth towards the applicant's reasonable needs. An application can therefore be struck out on the ground that there was no dependency. In order to decide whether there was dependency, the court balances what the deceased was contributing against what the applicant was contributing, and, if the applicant made a greater or equal contribution, the claim is struck out (see Stephenson LJ in *Jelley* v. *Iliffe and Others* [1981] Fam 128). Although dependency is a question of fact, not of discretion, the court will look at the problem in the round and apply a common-sense sort of approach, avoiding fine balancing distinctions (see Butler-Sloss LJ in *Bishop* v. *Plumley* [1991] 1 All ER 236, where the Court of Appeal allowed the applicant's appeal despite the beneficiaries' argument that the claimant had given full valuable contribution by reason of her exceptional care of their father).

In *Bouette* v. *Rose* [2000] 1 FLR 363 a mother brought a successful claim against the estate of her deceased daughter.

### (b)  'Reasonable Financial Provision'

The applicant must prove that the deceased's will or the law of intestacy (or both, if there is partial intestacy) failed to make 'reasonable financial provision' for the applicant (s.1(1)). The test is not whether reasonable provision has been made, but the more rigorous test of whether the failure to make provision was unreasonable (Judge Roger Cooke in *Re Abram (Deceased)* [1996] 2 FLR 379). However, spouses and civil partners are treated more generously than other applicants, as 'reasonable financial provision' for them means 'such financial provision as it would be reasonable in all the circumstances of the case for a husband or wife or civil partner to receive, whether or not that provision is required for his or her maintenance' (ss.1(2)(a) and (aa)). With other applicants, 'reasonable financial provision' means such financial provision as it would be reasonable in all the circumstances of the case for the applicant to receive for his or her maintenance (s.1(2)(b)). There is no definition of 'maintenance' in the Act. What constitutes 'maintenance' depends on the facts of each case, but it may be construed broadly, as it was in *Rees* v. *Newbery and the Institute of Cancer Research* [1998] 1 FLR 1041, where the provision of accommodation by the deceased for 10 years at less than market rent was held to be maintenance for the purposes of the 1975 Act.

### (c)  Orders That May be Made

The court has the power to make a wide range of orders, which include (s.2): periodical payments; a lump sum (which can be paid in instalments); a transfer of property; a settlement of property; acquisition of property and its transfer to the applicant or for the settlement of the applicant; and a variation of an ante-nuptial or post-nuptial settlement. The court can make an interim order if immediate financial assistance is needed (s.5). Periodical payments orders can be varied, discharged, suspended or revived (s.6). A periodical payments order made in favour of a former spouse or former civil partner, or a spouse or civil partner subject to a decree or order of judicial separation (where separation was continuing at death), ceases to be effective on that person's remarriage or civil partnership, except in respect of any arrears due (s.19(1)).

### (d) The Exercise of Discretion – Matters to be Taken into Account

When deciding whether or not the deceased made reasonable financial provision for the applicant, and in what manner to exercise its powers, the court must have regard to the following matters laid down in s.3(1):

'(a) the financial resources and financial needs which the applicant has or is likely to have in the foreseeable future;
(b) the financial resources and financial needs which any other applicant . . . has or is likely to have in the foreseeable future;
(c) the financial resources and financial needs which any beneficiary of the estate of the deceased has or is likely to have in the foreseeable future;
(d) any obligations and responsibilities which the deceased had towards any applicant . . . or towards any beneficiary of the estate of the deceased;
(e) the size and nature of the net estate of the deceased;
(f) any physical or mental disability of any applicant . . . or any beneficiary of the estate of the deceased;
(g) any other matter, including the conduct of the applicant or any other person, which in the circumstances of the case the court may consider relevant.'

The weight given to each factor depends on the circumstances of each case. For example, where an application is brought by an adult child against a deceased parent, needs and resources under s.3(1)(a) and obligations and responsibilities under s.3(1)(d) are likely to be crucial (see, for example, *Espinosa* v. *Bourke* [1999] 1 FLR 747). Additional factors must be considered in certain cases (see below).

### (e) Additional Matters to be Considered in Special Cases

In addition to the matters in s.3(1) above, the court must take into account certain special matters in some cases.

*(i) Applications by Spouses and Civil Partners and Former Spouses and Civil Partners under ss.1(1)(a) and (b)* The court must consider the applicant's age, the duration of the marriage or civil partnership, and the applicant's contribution to the welfare of the family, including any contribution made by looking after the home or caring for the family (s.3(2)).

In the case of an applicant spouse (or civil partner) the court must also consider what provision the applicant might reasonably have expected to receive if, on the date of death the marriage (or civil partnership) had been terminated by divorce (or a dissolution order), instead of by death – unless at the date of death a decree of judicial separation (or separation order) was in force and separation was continuing (s.3(2)). In *Moody* v. *Stevenson* [1992] Ch 486, for example, the court made a similar order to that which the husband would have received in ancillary relief proceedings on divorce. In *Davis* v. *Davis* [1993] 1 FLR 54, on the other hand, although it was clear that, if the marriage had ended in divorce, the divorce court would have ordered a clean break capital settlement, the Court of Appeal held that the wife's life interest in her deceased husband's estate was reasonable financial provision in the circumstances and her claim failed. The Court of Appeal has stressed, however, that the 'hypothetical divorce' approach in s.3(2) is only one of the factors for the court to consider, and is subject to the overriding consideration of what is reasonable in all the circumstances (see *Re Krubert (Deceased)* [1997] 1 FLR 42).

**White v. White *Applies but with Caution***   In *Fielden and Another* v. *Cunliffe* [2005] EWCA Civ 1508 the Court of Appeal held that there was no reason why the principles laid down by the House of Lords in *White* v. *White* [2001] 1 AC 596, [2000] 2 FLR 981 (in respect of applications for ancillary relief on divorce) (see 8.6) should not be applied to a claim by a spouse under the 1975 Act. The Court of Appeal held, however, that caution was necessary when considering the *White* cross-check of equality in cases under the 1975 Act, as a deceased spouse who left a widow was entitled to bequeath his estate to whomsoever he pleased, and was only obliged to make reasonable financial provision for his widow. It held that, depending on the value of the estate, the concept of equality might bear little relation to such provision. The Court of Appeal allowed the executors' appeal and reduced the amount of financial provision awarded to the surviving spouse from £800,000 to £600,000, as the judge had wrongly applied the principle in *White* (having presumed a starting point of a 50:50 split of the estate).

*(ii) Applications by Cohabitants Under s.1(1)(ba)*   The court must have regard to the applicant's age, the duration of the cohabitation and the contribution which the applicant made to the welfare of the deceased's family, including any contribution made by looking after the home or caring for the family (s.3(2A)).

*(iii) Applications by Children Under s.1(1)(c) or (d)*   The court must consider the manner in which the applicant was, or might be expected to be, educated or trained (s.3(3)). The court must also consider whether the deceased had assumed any responsibility for the applicant's maintenance (and, if so, its extent, basis and duration, and whether the deceased did so knowing that the applicant was not his own child), as well as the liability of any other person to maintain the applicant (s.3(3)).

*(iv) Applications by Dependants under s.1(1)(e)*   The court must consider the extent, basis and duration of the deceased's responsibility for maintenance (s.3(4)).

**(f)   Special Provisions Relating to Divorce, Nullity, Separation and Dissolution of a Civil Partnership**

Where within 12 months of decree absolute of divorce a party to the marriage dies and an application has been made for a financial provision order or property adjustment order under s.23 or s.24 Matrimonial Causes Act 1973 (whether or not the proceedings have been determined by the date of death), the court can, if just to do so, treat the application for an order under s.2 Inheritance (Provision for Family and Dependants) Act 1975 as if the decree of divorce (or nullity) had not been made absolute (s.14). Similar provisions also apply in the case of a decree of judicial separation (see ss.14(1), (2)) and in respect of dissolution, nullity and separation in respect of a civil partnership (s.14A).

As part of the 'clean-break' policy on divorce (see 8.5), the divorce court on or after the grant of a decree nisi of divorce (or nullity or judicial separation) can on the application of either spouse make an order, if just to do so, prohibiting the other spouse from making an application under the 1975 Act on the applicant's death (see s.15 Inheritance (Provision for Family and Dependants) Act 1975). A s.15 restriction is usually included in a clean-break order. The court has the same powers when making a dissolution order, nullity order, separation order or presumption of death order under the Civil Partnership Act 2004 (see s.15ZA Inheritance (Provision for Family and Dependants) Act 1975). The same rule applies when the court is making financial provision and property adjustment orders after an overseas divorce or an overseas dissolution of a civil partnership, including overseas annulments and separations (ss.15A and 15B).

### (g)  Other Powers Under the 1975 Act

Where an application has been made under the 1975 Act and the applicant is entitled to secured periodical payments under the Matrimonial Causes Act 1973 or under Sched. 5 to the Civil Partnership Act 2004, the court may, on application, vary or discharge the periodical payments order or revive the operation of any provision thereof which has been suspended under s.31 of the 1973 Act or Part 2 of Sched. 5 of the 2004 Act (s.16).

A maintenance agreement between the applicant and the deceased providing for maintenance on and after death can be varied or revoked (s.17). The court can in certain circumstances set aside a disposition made by the deceased within six years of death with the intention of defeating an application under the 1975 Act (s.10). Where a contract was made by the deceased without full valuable consideration with the intention of defeating an application for financial provision under the 1975 Act, the court can direct the personal representatives not to pass or transfer the whole or part of any money or property involved (s.11).

To facilitate making payment to an applicant, the court can treat a deceased's interest in property under a joint tenancy, or a joint interest existing immediately before death, as a severable share of the net estate where just in all the circumstances to do so, provided the application is made within six months of the date on which a grant of representation to the deceased's estate was first taken out (s.9) (see, for example, *Jessop* v. *Jessop* [1992] 1 FLR 59).

### 5.4  Succession to a Tenancy on Death

Succession to a tenancy on death is governed by Sched. 1 to the Rent Act 1977 (statutory tenancies), and by s.17 Housing Act 1988 (assured tenancies). Under these Acts a spouse, civil partner and a surviving cohabitant (opposite-sex or same-sex who had lived in a settled relationship with the deceased) can apply for a transfer of the deceased's tenancy on his or her death.

Under para. 2 of Sched. 1 to the Rent Act 1977 a spouse (or civil partner) or a cohabitant (living as a husband or wife, or as a civil partner of the deceased) can succeed to the deceased spouse's or cohabitant's tenancy. Under para. 3(1) a family member of the deceased tenant can succeed to the tenancy. A person who succeeds to a tenancy under para. 2 is in a better position than a family member who succeeds under para. 3 because he or she succeeds to a statutory tenancy, whereas a family member succeeds only to an assured tenancy. Statutory tenants are in a better position because they enjoy security of tenure and may register a fair rent for the property, whereas assured tenants are subject to a different form of security of tenure and may be charged a market, rather than a fair, rent.

Until recent amendments to the Rent Act 1977 and the Housing Act 1988, only spouses and heterosexual cohabitants could succeed to a deceased partner's tenancy under the Rent Act 1977 and s.17 Housing Act 1988. However, the following two cases heard by the House of Lords led to a change in the law, the second decision being influenced by the European Convention for the Protection of Human Rights as a result of the coming into force of the Human Rights Act 1998 (see 1.5):

▶ *Fitzpatrick* v. *Sterling Housing Association* [2001] AC 27, [2000] 1 FLR 271

The House of Lords held by a majority of 3 to 2 that a surviving same-sex cohabitant could succeed to the tenancy of the deceased tenant, on the basis that he or she could be construed as a member of the deceased tenant's 'family' under para. 3(1) of Sched. 1 to the Rent Act 1977. It unanimously held that the surviving homosexual partner could not be construed as a 'spouse' of the deceased under para. 2(2), because he could not be regarded as 'living with the original tenant as his or her husband or wife'.

▶ *Ghaidan* v. *Godin-Mendoza* [2004] UKHL 30, [2004] 2 FLR 600

Mr Godin-Mendoza had lived in a long, close and loving and monogamous homosexual relationship with his deceased partner, who was the protected tenant of a flat owned by Mr Ghaidan, the landlord. Mr Ghaidan brought possession proceedings, and Mr Godin-Mendoza claimed by way of defence that he was entitled to succeed to the tenancy under Sched. 1 to the Rent Act 1977. At first instance, the judge held that he could only succeed to a tenancy under para. 3(1), applying *Fitzpatrick* (above), but the Court of Appeal allowed his appeal, holding that there had been a breach of art. 14 of the European Convention for the Protection of Human Rights (discrimination) in conjunction with art. 8 (right to family life), and that the court had a duty under s.3 Human Rights Act 1998 to give effect to the Rent Act in a way which was compliant with the ECHR. The landlord, Mr Ghaidan, appealed.

The House of Lords dismissed the appeal (Lord Millett dissenting), holding that same-sex cohabitants are in the same position as married couples when it comes to security of tenure. It held that para. 2(2) of Sched. 1 to the Rent Act 1977, when construed with reference to s.3 Human Rights Act 1998, violated the surviving partner's right under art. 14 ECHR taken together with art. 8. It held that it was possible under s.3 Human Rights Act 1998 (which provides that primary and subordinate legislation must be read and given effect in a way which is compatible with the ECHR) to read para. 2(2) in a way which was compatible with the ECHR, in other words as though the survivor of a homosexual relationship was the surviving spouse of the defendant.

The principles in *Ghaidan* also apply to s.17 Housing Act 1988 (which provides for the transfer of tenancies on death). However, in *Nutting* v. *Southern Housing Group Ltd* [2004] EWHC 2982 (Ch), [2005] 1 FLR 1066 a homosexual partner failed to defeat a claim to possession of his deceased partner's tenancy as he was not a 'spouse' for the purposes of s.17 Housing Act 1988. His relationship with the deceased had not been sufficiently permanent.

## Summary

1 Any adult person of sound mind can make a will leaving his or her property on death to whomsoever he or she chooses. A will is valid if it is made in writing and signed by the testator in the presence of two witnesses who must attest the will (ss.7 and 9 Wills Act 1837). A will is revoked by marriage or civil partnership, unless made in contemplation of a particular marriage or civil partnership.

2 Where a spouse or civil partner has not made a will, his or her property passes under the rules of intestacy which are laid down in the Administration of Estates Act 1925, as amended.

3 A cohabitant has no right to succeed to a deceased's partner's estate on his or her intestacy, and the Law Commission (see further at 4.12) has made no proposals to change this rule. It is therefore particularly important for cohabitants to make a will.

4 Under the Inheritance (Provision for Family and Dependants) Act 1975 certain family members and other dependants (including spouses, civil partners, former spouses, former civil partners and cohabitants) can apply for financial relief out of the deceased's estate where the deceased has failed to make reasonable financial provision either under the will or under the law of intestacy (or both). The Law Commission has made proposals recommending reforms to give cohabitants new rights under the 1975 Act (see also 4.12).

5 Under the Rent Act 1977 and s.17 Housing Act 1988 the deceased's tenancy can on death be transferred to a surviving spouse, or civil partner, or a surviving opposite-sex or same-sex cohabiting partner.

## Further Reading and References

Bailey-Harris and Wilson, '*Mendoza* v. *Ghaidan* and the rights of the *de facto* spouse' [2003] Fam Law 575.

Borkowski, '*Re Hancock (Deceased)* and *Espinosa* v. *Bourke* – moral obligations and family provision' [1999] CFLQ 305.

Cownie and Bradney, 'Divided justice, different voices: inheritance and family provision' (2003) *Legal Studies* 566.

Wilson and Bailey-Harris, 'Family provision: the adult child and moral obligation' [2005] Fam Law 555.

# Chapter 6

## Domestic Violence and Occupation of the Family Home

---

**The Legislation**

**Part IV of the Family Law Act 1996** Provides civil remedies for protection against domestic violence and makes provision in respect of occupation of the family home.

**Protection from Harassment Act 1997** Creates two criminal offences of harassment and gives the court power to grant injunctions restraining a defendant from pursuing any course of conduct which amounts to harassment.

**Domestic Violence, Crime and Victims Act 2004** Amends the two Acts above to give greater protection to victims of domestic violence, and makes changes to the criminal law.

---

Both the civil law and the criminal law provide protection for victims of violence in the home, but this chapter deals mainly with the civil law.

## 6.1 Introduction

The Government is committed to fighting domestic violence and to giving support to its victims. As a result, domestic violence has been high on the political agenda because of the prevalence of violence in the home, the suffering that victims experience, and the financial costs involved. In furtherance of these aims, the Domestic Violence, Crime and Victims Act 2004 has recently made amendments to the legislation in order to improve protection for victims of domestic violence. The following extract provides some data about the incidence and cost of domestic violence:

---

*Specialist Domestic Violence Court Programme: Guidance*, **published by HM Court Service, Crown Prosecution Service, and Home Office, 2005**

- Domestic Violence accounts for 17 per cent of reported crime.
- On average, two women a week are killed by a male partner or former partner: in 2003/2004 nearly 40 per cent of all female homicide victims were killed by their current or ex-partner compared with about 5 per cent of male homicide victims.
- About one in four women and one in six men have been a victim of domestic violence since the age of 16, although women are likely to suffer greater injury and be classed as chronic victims.
- 89 per cent of those suffering four or more attacks are women.
- One incident is reported to the police every minute.
- In 2001 in England and Wales, domestic violence was estimated to cost a total of £23 billion. £3 billion was spent on public services, £2.7 billion was absorbed by employers and workers and £17 billion represented the cost of human and emotional suffering. £1 billion was spent by the Criminal Justice System, accounting for a quarter of its budget for dealing with violent crime. £300 million is spent by civil legal services.

---

*What is Domestic Violence?*    Domestic violence – violence in the home – can take many forms. It includes not just physical assault, but psychological and emotional molestation or harassment, and may also involve pestering, nagging, making nuisance telephone calls and intimidation. The Home Office has defined domestic violence as: 'Any violence between current or former partners in an intimate relationship, wherever and whenever the violence occurs. The violence may include physical, sexual, emotional or financial abuse' (Home Office Circular 19/2000).

*A Widespread Problem*    Despite the difficulty of establishing what goes on behind closed doors, violence in the home is thought to be a widespread social problem existing at all levels of society, involving not just spouses and cohabitants, but other family members. According to the Home Office, although domestic violence is chronically under-reported, domestic violence accounts for 17 per cent of all violent crime and has more repeat victims than any other crime. For women aged between 19 and 44, domestic violence is the leading cause of death, greater than that for cancer and for car accidents. Victims of violence suffer on many levels – in respect of health, housing and education – and lose the freedom to live their lives in the way they wish, and without fear.

*The Causes of Domestic Violence*    Various factors may cause violence. Personality factors, such as psychopathic tendencies, aggression or jealousy, may play a part, as may social factors, such as poverty, housing and unemployment. Alcohol and drugs also often play a part.

*Housing Problems*    Violence can create housing problems. Some victims will seek temporary accommodation in a refuge (there are 400 in the UK for women, and a few for men). Some will apply to their local housing authority for public sector housing (see 4.13). Some will end up divorcing (or dissolving their civil partnership), whereupon the court has jurisdiction to adjudicate on any dispute about ownership and occupation of the home (see Chapter 8). In some cases, the court will remove the perpetrator from the home and allow the victim back in (see 6.5, below).

*Children and Domestic Violence*    The civil law and the criminal law provide protection for children who witness or suffer domestic violence. Sometimes local authority intervention will be needed (see Chapter 15). As violence in the home can be damaging to children who witness it, the word 'harm' in the Children Act 1989 has been amended so that it now includes 'impairment suffered from seeing or hearing the ill-treatment of another'. The Children Act 1989 also makes provision for exclusion orders which can be used to exclude a suspected child-abuser from the home (see 15.10). Violence in the home can also cause harm for children on contact visits, and in the last few years there has been a greater recognition of the problem of contact and domestic violence (see 12.5). CAFCASS officers and Welsh family proceedings officers have a legal duty to carry out risk assessments to assess whether children are suffering, or at risk of suffering, harm, which includes domestic violence (see 12.5).

*Specialist Domestic Violence Courts*    Specialist domestic violence courts have been established in some parts of the UK in the last two or three years, with the aim of bringing more perpetrators of domestic violence to justice and to ensure that victims and their families are given vital support. These courts promote a combined approach to tackling domestic violence by the police, crown prosecutors, magistrates, courts and probation officers. Specialist support is provided for victims by Independent Domestic Violence Advisors (IDVAs) who are responsible for ensuring that the safety of the victim is co-ordinated across the criminal justice system and for giving expert advice on accessing essential services, such as victim and witness agencies, housing, health, counselling and child care. Evidence shows that specialist domestic violence courts: enhance the effectiveness of court and support services for victims; make support for victims and information-sharing easier; and bring more perpetrators to justice (see *Specialist Domestic Violence Court Programme Guidance*, HM's Court Service, Crown Prosecution Service and Home Office, 2005).

*Domestic Violence Forums*   These have been set up in most areas with the aim of: raising awareness of domestic violence; promoting co-ordination between agencies in preventing and responding to domestic violence; and encouraging the development of services for victims. They work together with Local Safeguarding Children Boards (see 15.1).

*The Domestic Violence, Crime and Victims Act 2004*   The Domestic Violence, Crime and Victims Act (DVCVA) 2004 has amended the civil and the criminal law relating to domestic violence in order to give greater protection to victims. In its consultation paper, *Safety and Justice: Proposals on Domestic Violence* (Cm 5847, Home Office, June 2003), the Government set out a new strategy for domestic violence based on three elements: prevention; protection and justice for victims and their families; and support for victims to rebuild their lives.

The DVCVA 2004 has made amendments to Part IV of the Family Law Act 1996 (see below). These include: extending the class of persons who can apply for remedies; making breach of a non-molestation order a criminal offence; and restricting the use of undertakings. The 2004 Act has also amended the Protection from Harassment Act 1997 (see 6.8), in particular to give the court power to make restraining orders even if the defendant has been acquitted of harassment; and to establish a register of persons subject to a restraining order so that the police can take immediate action to protect victims.

The DVCVA 2004 also makes changes to the criminal law (see below).

## 6.2  Domestic Violence – The Criminal Law

Domestic violence is a serious and frequently reported crime which the police treat as seriously as any other crime. Police forces are required to draw up clear policy statements about intervention in domestic violence cases and to have special domestic violence units. Police forces are also required to support victims of domestic violence by, for instance, finding temporary accommodation for them, and keeping them informed about the case. Police forces are involved in local domestic violence initiatives, including Domestic Violence Forums (see above); and police domestic violence units work closely with solicitors, Women's Aid and other organisations. They also have powers and duties where children are at risk of, or are suffering, domestic violence.

The police have a wide range of powers in respect of domestic violence. Under the common law the police can enter premises to prevent or deal with breaches of the peace, and they have a power of arrest in such circumstances. Under s.17 Police and Criminal

Evidence Act 1984 a constable can enter premises to arrest or to save life or limb or to prevent serious damage to property. A perpetrator of violence can be prosecuted for: common assault (s.39 Criminal Justice Act 1998); assault occasioning actual bodily harm (s.47 Offences Against the Person Act 1861); rape (s.1(1) Sexual Offences Act 1956); indecent assault (ss.14 and 15 Sexual Offences Act 1956); affray (s.3(1) Public Order Act 1986); criminal damage (s.1(1) Criminal Damage Act 1971); and harassment (s.2 Protection from Harassment Act 1997). Under s.51 Criminal Justice and Public Order Act 1994 it is an offence to intimidate a witness, or to harm, or threaten to harm, a witness. Offences can also be committed under the Telecommunications Act 1984, which prohibits the sending of grossly offensive, indecent, obscene or menacing communications, and under the Malicious Communications Act 1988, which prohibits the sending of indecent or grossly offensive letters which are intended to create distress or anxiety. Victims of domestic violence may be entitled to compensation under the Criminal Injuries Compensation Scheme.

*Changes to the Criminal Law Introduced by the Domestic Violence, Crime and Victims Act 2004*  The DVCVA 2004 makes the following changes to the criminal law.

- *Creates a New Criminal Offence of Causing or Allowing the Death of a Child or a Vulnerable Adult (s.5 DVCVA 2004)* This new offence is limited to cases where the victim has died of an unlawful act; it does not apply to accidental deaths (such as a cot death). It applies only where a member of a household has frequent contact with the victim, and could therefore be reasonably expected both to have been aware of any risk to the victim, and to have had a duty to protect the victim from harm. The member of the household must have failed to take reasonable steps to protect the victim; and the victim must have been at significant risk of serious physical harm. A person who visits the household frequently can be a member of the household (s.5(4)(a)). Only persons over the age of 16 may be guilty of the offence, unless he or she is the mother or father of the victim (s.5(3)).
- *Makes Common Assault an Arrestable Offence (s.10(1) DVCVA 2004)* under Schedule 1 to the Police and Criminal Evidence Act 1984, so that the police have the power to arrest a person on suspicion of assault and/or battery without an arrest warrant.
- *Makes Changes in Respect of Restraining Orders Under the Protection from Harassment Act 1997* See 6.8.

*Drawbacks of the Criminal Law for Family Members*  Although police intervention may be required, recourse to the criminal law can be a rather heavy-handed instrument in family disputes. In fact, some victims, having contacted the police, do not wish criminal proceedings to be brought because they fear that they may lose their partner, their home, their financial stability and even their children. Punishing a violent partner may also have a disastrous emotional and financial impact on a family. There may also be evidential difficulties proving violence. Victims may be unwilling to co-operate with the police and may withdraw their evidence, because of feelings of disloyalty, or because prosecution and possible conviction will ruin any chance of reconciliation, or because they fear further violence. However, the police are now much more proactive in domestic violence cases, and prosecutions may be brought even where the victim does not wish the prosecution to proceed. In many cases, however, civil remedies may be a better solution than criminal proceedings.

## 6.3 Civil Remedies Under Part IV of the Family Law Act 1996

Under Part IV of the Family Law Act 1996 magistrates' family proceedings courts, county courts and the High Court have jurisdiction to grant the following orders to protect victims of domestic violence:

> *A Non-Molestation Order* This is an order containing a provision prohibiting the respondent from molesting another person who is associated with the respondent; and/or a provision prohibiting the respondent from molesting a relevant child (s.42(1)).
>
> *An Occupation Order* This is an order made under ss.33, 35, 36, 37 or 38 of Part IV of the Family Law Act 1996. It is an order regulating, prohibiting, and governing the occupation of the family home by the respondent.

Part IV of the Family Law Act 1996 was introduced because the family remedies available before the Act came into force were considered to be unnecessarily complex, confusing and lacking integration. The new law was based on the recommendations of the Law Commission in its Report, *Family Law: Domestic Violence and Occupation of the Family Home*, Law Com No. 207, 1992.

In order to give greater protection to victims of violence, and to extend the remedies to a wider range of victims, Part IV of the Family Law Act 1996 has been amended by the Domestic Violence, Crime and Victims Act 2004.

## 6.4 Part IV of the Family Law Act 1996 – Non-Molestation Orders

Under s.42 of Part IV of the Family Law Act 1996 magistrates' family proceedings courts, county courts and the High Court can make a non-molestation order (NMO) prohibiting the respondent from molesting another person who is associated with the respondent and/or from molesting a relevant child (s.42(1)).

*(i) Applicants* The applicant must be 'associated' with the respondent, and the child must be a 'relevant child' (see definitions at 6.6, below). The court can make the order on an application, or of its own motion (in any family proceedings) (s.42(2)), or when it is considering whether to make an occupation order (s.42(4A)). An order made under the court's own motion powers ceases to be effective, however, if proceedings are withdrawn or dismissed (s.42(8)). A child can apply for a NMO, but a child under 16 needs leave of the court to do so, which it can only grant if the child has sufficient understanding to make the application (s.43).

*(ii) What is 'Molestation'?* 'Molestation' is not defined in the Act, but has been interpreted on a case-by-case basis by the courts. It has been widely interpreted to include not just violence, but pestering, harassment and threatening behaviour. In *C* v. *C (Non-Molestation Order: Jurisdiction)* [1998] Fam 70, [1998] 1 FLR 554 Stephen Brown P held that there 'has

to be some conduct which clearly harasses and affects the applicant to such a degree that the intervention of the court is called for'. Here, the husband was granted a NMO to prevent his wife publishing offensive articles about him in the national press at the time when their divorce proceedings were being heard. The wife appealed against the order, and her appeal was allowed, as the material complained of came nowhere near molestation as envisaged by s.42. Stephen Brown P held that, if the husband thought the information was untrue, he should have instituted defamation proceedings.

*(iii) Criteria for Making a Non-Molestation Order*   When deciding whether to make a NMO, and, if so, in what manner, the court must have regard to all the circumstances of the case, including the need to secure the health, safety and well-being of the applicant and of any relevant child (s.42(5)).

*(iv) Orders without Notice (ex parte Orders)*   As urgent action is often needed in domestic violence cases, the court, where just and convenient to do so, may make an order without the respondent being given notice of the proceedings (s.45(1)). When deciding whether to make such an order, the court must consider all the circumstances of the case, including (s.45(2)): the risk of significant harm to the applicant or any relevant child by the respondent if an order is not immediately made; and the likelihood of the applicant being deterred or prevented from pursuing the application if an order is not immediately made. It must also consider: whether there is reason to believe that the respondent is aware of the proceedings but deliberately avoiding service; and whether the applicant or relevant child will be seriously prejudiced by the delay in effecting service of proceedings or in effecting substituted service.

If a NMO is made without notice (*ex parte*), the court must give the respondent an opportunity to make representations relating to the order at a full hearing, as soon as is just and convenient (s.45(3)).

*(v) Terms and Duration of the Order*   A NMO can refer to molestation in general and/or to particular acts of molestation (s.48(6)). It may be made for a specified period or until further order (s.48(7)). Although the aim of the order is to give the parties a temporary breathing space, in *Re B-J (Power of Arrest)* [2000] 2 FLR 443 the Court of Appeal held that an order can be made for an indefinite period in appropriate circumstances. A NMO made in other family proceedings ceases to have effect if those proceedings are withdrawn or dismissed (s.42(8)).

*(vi) Undertakings*   Instead of making a NMO the court may accept an undertaking (a promise to the court) from any party to the proceedings (s.46(1)). An undertaking is enforceable as if it were a court order (s.46(4)). However, as a result of an amendment by the DVCVA 2004, the court must not accept an undertaking instead of making a NMO in any case where: it appears that the respondent has used or threatened violence against the applicant or a relevant child, and a NMO is necessary so that any breach may be punishable as a criminal offence under s.42A (s.46(3A)). The court's powers under s.42 in respect of undertakings do not prejudice the powers of the High Court and county court (s.42(5)). The advantage of an undertaking is that it carries less stigma than a court order, as the court does not make findings of fact about the respondent's behaviour.

*(vii) Attaching a Power of Arrest*   The jurisdiction of the court to attach a power of arrest to a NMO was abolished as from 1 July 2007 (see Sched. 10, para. 38 DVCVA 2004), but a power of arrest can still be attached to an occupation order (see 6.5, below).

*(viii) Variation and Discharge*   A NMO may be varied or discharged on the application of the respondent or by the person on whose application the order was made (s.49).

*(ix) Breach of an Order*   Breach of a NMO may be dealt with in civil proceedings for contempt of court or as a criminal offence under s.42A Family Law Act 1996.

*Civil Proceeding for Contempt of Court*   In civil proceedings for contempt the contemnor can be ordered to pay a fine or serve a prison sentence. In *Rafiq* v. *Muse* [2000] 1 FLR 820, for example, a 21-year-old man who had repeatedly harassed and threatened his mother was sentenced to imprisonment for breaches of non-molestation injunctions.

The courts have been increasingly willing to impose prison sentences (and longer sentences) for breaches of non-molestation orders (and occupation orders), to send out the clear message that domestic violence will not be tolerated. In *H* v. *O (Contempt of Court: Sentencing)* [2004] EWCA Civ 1691, [2005] 2 FLR 329 the Court of Appeal said that Parliament and society generally now regarded domestic violence and other violence associated with harassment and molestation as demanding rather more deterrent punishment than formerly. In *Robinson* v. *Murray* [2005] EWCA Civ 935, [2006] 1 FLR 365, where there had been three breaches of NMOs and occupation orders, the Court of Appeal endorsed the approach in *H* v. *O* (above), but held that, if a case warrants a sentence near the top of the range, then the appropriate course is probably to bring proceedings under the Protection from Harassment Act 1997. In *Lomas* v. *Parle* [2003] EWCA Civ 1084, [2004] 1 FLR 812 the Court of Appeal held that the sentence for breach of a NMO in that case had been too lenient, and also drew attention to the unsatisfactory nature of the current interface between the criminal courts and the family courts in respect of breaches of orders under Part IV of the Family Law Act 1996 (and under the Protection from Harassment Act 1997).

*The Criminal Offence of Breaching a Non-Molestation Order*   Since 1 July 2007, breach of a NMO is now a criminal offence (s.42A(1) Family Law Act 1996, introduced by s.1 DVCVA 2004). Under s.42A a person is guilty of an offence if, without reasonable excuse, he does anything that he is prohibited from doing by a NMO. If the NMO was made without notice (see above), there is no criminal offence unless the person was aware of the existence of the NMO (s.42A(2)). A person convicted of the offence cannot be punished for contempt of court, and vice versa (ss.42A(3), (4)). A person found guilty of an offence can be fined or imprisoned for up to 5 years (s.42A(5)). The effect of making the new offence subject to a maximum 5-year prison term is that it automatically becomes an arrestable offence (under s.24(1) Police and Criminal Evidence Act 1984). For this reason, it has been no longer possible for the court (since 1 July 2007) to attach a power of arrest to a NMO. This new criminal offence of breaching a NMO does not apply where a power of arrest was attached to an order before 1 July 2007.

Bessant (2005) has voiced concern about this new criminal offence, on the ground that victims may be deterred from seeking a non-molestation order for fear of being involved in criminal proceedings.

## 6.5 | Part IV of the Family Law Act 1996 – Occupation Orders

There may come a point where a victim of domestic violence is no longer able to tolerate living under the same roof as the perpetrator and will have to leave home and seek alternative accommodation with a relative or friend or in a refuge for victims of violence. A victim of domestic violence may decide to apply for an occupation order under Part IV of the Family Law Act 1996; for example to remove the perpetrator from the house and to allow her back in, and possibly to exclude the perpetrator from an area around the house. Occupation orders, however, are not routinely made, and they are a temporary, not a permanent, remedy – as they are limited in duration.

Under ss.33 and 35–38 of Part IV of the Family Law Act 1996 magistrates' family proceedings courts, county courts and the High Court can make occupation orders (s.39). They can be made by the court on an application, or of the court's own motion in any 'family proceedings' (ss.39(1), (2)) (see definition at 6.6, below). An occupation order does not affect a person's claim to any legal or equitable interest in the home in any subsequent proceedings (including subsequent proceedings under Part IV) (s.39(4)).

*Categories of Applicant*   Part IV of the Family Law Act 1996 creates two categories of applicant:

> **An 'Entitled' Applicant**  This is a person who has a right to occupy the home: by virtue of a beneficial estate or interest or contract; or by virtue of any enactment giving him the right to remain in occupation; or who has 'home rights' under s.30 of the Act (see 4.2).
>
> **A 'Non-Entitled' Applicant**  This is a person who has no right to occupy the home by virtue of a beneficial estate, interest, contract, or enactment, or by having 'home rights'.

The courts' powers to make occupation orders are much greater for entitled applicants. The basic scheme in respect of occupation orders of the home is as follows:

> An *entitled* applicant *where the respondent is a person associated with the applicant (whether or not the respondent is entitled)* must apply under **s.33**.
>
> An *unentitled* applicant *where the respondent is entitled, and they are former spouses or former civil partners*, must apply under **s.35**.
>
> An *unentitled* applicant *where the respondent is entitled, and they are cohabitants or former cohabitants (opposite-sex or same-sex)*, must apply under **s.36**.
>
> If *neither* the applicant *nor* the respondent is entitled, and they are *spouses or former spouses, or civil partners or former civil partners*, the applicant must apply under **s.37**.
>
> If *neither* the applicant *nor* the respondent is entitled, and they are *cohabitants or former cohabitants (opposite-sex or same-sex)*, the applicant must apply under **s.38**.

(a)    'Entitled' Applicants (s.33)

*(i) 'Entitled' Applicants*    An entitled person (see above) can apply for an occupation order under s.33(1)(a), provided the dwelling-house is (or was or was intended to be) the home of the applicant and an 'associated person' (s.33(1)(b)). 'Dwelling-house' includes a building, caravan, house-boat, structure, and any yard, garden, garage or outhouse belonging to it (s.63(1)).

The term 'associated person' includes a wide range of persons (see definition at 6.6, below), not just spouses, civil partners, cohabitants and family members, but a person living in the same household. A party to an engagement or a civil partnership agreement can apply, and also within three years of the termination of the engagement or agreement (s.33(2)).

*(ii) Powers of the Court*    The order may (s.33(3)):

- enforce the applicant's entitlement to remain in occupation as against the respondent;
- require the respondent to permit the applicant to enter and remain in the home, or part of it;
- regulate the occupation of the home by either or both parties;
- prohibit, suspend or restrict the respondent's exercise of any right to occupy the home;
- restrict or terminate the 'home rights' of the respondent on the application of the spouse or civil partner of the respondent;
- require the respondent to leave the home, or part of it;
- exclude the respondent from a defined area in which the home is included.

*Other Powers*    The order may declare that the applicant is an entitled person (s.33(4)). If the applicant has 'home rights' (see 4.2) and the respondent is the other spouse or civil partner, the court where just and reasonable to do so can, when making an order during the subsistence of a marriage or civil partnership, include a provision in the order that those rights are not to be brought to an end by the death of the other spouse or civil partner or by the termination of the marriage or civil partnership (ss.33(5), (8)).

*(iii) How the Court Exercises its Powers*    In exercising its powers, the court must first apply the 'balance of harm test' below. If the balance lies in favour of making an order, the court must make it. If the balance does not so lie, then the court must exercise its discretion and consider whether to make an order by considering the factors listed in s.33(6) (see below).

*The Balance of Harm Test (s.33(7))*    The court *must* make an order if it appears that the applicant or any relevant child is likely to suffer *significant* harm attributable to conduct of the respondent if an occupation order under s.33 is not made, *unless* it appears that (s.33(7)):

the respondent or any relevant child is likely to suffer significant harm if the order is made (s.33(7)(a)); *and*
the harm likely to be suffered by the respondent or child in that event is *as great as, or greater than*, the harm attributable to conduct of the respondent which is likely to be suffered by the applicant or child if the order is not made (s.33(7)(b)).

'Harm' is defined in s.63(1). In relation to an adult it means ill-treatment or the impairment of health. In relation to a child it means ill-treatment or the impairment of health or development. 'Ill-treatment' includes forms of treatment which are not physical, and, in relation to a child, includes sexual abuse.

'Health' includes physical and mental health. 'Development' means physical, intellectual, emotional, social or behavioural development. Where the question of whether harm suffered by the child is significant turns on the child's health or development, the court must compare his health or development with that which could reasonably be expected of a similar child (s.63(3)).

The balance of harm test was applied in the following cases:

▶ *Chalmers v. Johns* [1999] 1 FLR 392

The parties were cohabitants who had an adult son and a 7-year-old daughter. Their relationship had always been tempestuous. There had been acts of violence by each party against the other, resulting in minor injuries. Alcohol use, particularly by the mother, had been responsible for much of this. The mother left the family home with the daughter and moved into temporary council accommodation. She applied for an occupation order under s.33 as an entitled applicant (she was a joint tenant of the home with the respondent). The judge made an interim occupation order requiring the father to vacate the family home seven days later. The judge recognised that this was not an ordinary domestic violence case, but, applying the balance of harm test, made the order on the basis that the mother and child were likely to suffer significant harm attributable to the father if the order was not made. The father appealed.

The Court of Appeal allowed the appeal, as the judge had incorrectly applied the statutory provisions. The mother and child were not likely to suffer significant harm attributable to the conduct of the father if the order was not made. There was no real risk of violence or any other harm befalling the child. The case was one in which the court should exercise its discretion by considering all the circumstances of the case and the prescribed matters in s.33(6). Occupation orders which overrode proprietary rights (the father was a joint tenant) were justified only in exceptional circumstances. The fact that the final hearing was to take place very shortly weighed against making such a Draconian order at an interlocutory hearing, particularly as there was no evidence that any further domestic disharmony could not be managed by the imposition of injunctive orders. The trial judge had not clearly focused upon the alternative nature of the adjoining subsections of s.33(6) and s.33(7), but had treated them as if they were both simultaneously applicable to the facts of the case. Had she directed herself more closely to the statutory language, she would have seen that this was a case which came nowhere near s.33(7).

▶ *B v. B (Occupation Order)* [1999] 1 FLR 715

The wife left the matrimonial home, where she and her husband lived as council tenants, taking with her their baby daughter, and leaving her husband in the matrimonial home with his 6-year-old son from a previous marriage. She was granted an occupation order. The husband appealed. The Court of Appeal allowed his appeal, as the balance of harm test had not been satisfied – as the husband's child would suffer more harm if an order was made than the wife and their baby daughter would suffer if an order was not made. While the husband's behaviour fully justified the order being made, his position as a full-time carer of his son had to be considered. If an order was made, his 6-year-old son would be placed in unsuitable temporary council accommodation and he would have to change schools. The Court of Appeal stressed, however, that each case turns on its facts and that it did not intend to give out the message that other fathers in the same position as the husband could expect to remain in occupation.

▶ *G v. G (Occupation Order: Conduct)* **[2000] 2 FLR 36**

The wife's application for an occupation order was refused by the trial judge who held that, as the husband's conduct had been unintentional, the likelihood of harm could not be attributed to him. The wife appealed. The Court of Appeal held that the important factor, when applying the balance of harm test, was the effect of the conduct upon the applicant or child, not the intention of the respondent. Lack of intent might be a relevant consideration, but it did not mean that harm could not be attributed to the respondent's conduct without lack of intention. The judge had therefore erred in law in considering that the harm likely to be suffered by the children could not be attributed to the husband because it was not intentional. However, having concluded that the making of an order was not mandatory under s.33(7) on the facts, the judge had correctly proceeded to consider whether to make an order under s.33(6) in the exercise of his discretion. Even though criticisms could be made of the judge, his conclusion was in broad terms tenable. It was not a case where the applicant had suffered violence at the hands of her husband; and occupation orders excluding a person from their house were Draconian orders to be used only in exceptional circumstances.

▶ *Banks v. Banks* **[1999] 1 FLR 726**

The wife, aged 79, suffered from manic-depression and dementia, and her verbal and physical abuse were a potential threat to her husband. The husband sought an occupation order to exclude her from the matrimonial home. Judge Geddes in the county court refused to make an occupation order because the harm to the wife if the order was made would be significantly greater than the harm to the husband if it was not. A final decision on the parties' occupation rights could be made in the divorce proceedings. He also refused to make a non-molestation order because her behaviour was a symptom of her mental condition and not something over which she was capable of control.

*The Discretionary Exercise Under s.33(6)*    If, applying the balance of harm test, the balance does not lean in favour of making the order, then the court must go on to conduct the discretionary exercise under s.33(6) which requires the court when deciding whether or not to exercise its powers under s.33(3) (see above), and, if so, in what manner, to have regard to all the circumstances including:

(a) the housing needs and housing resources of each of the parties and of any relevant child;
(b) the financial resources of each of the parties;
(c) the likely effect of any order, or of any decision by the court not to exercise any of the powers under s.33(3), on the health, safety or well-being of the parties and of any relevant child; and
(d) the conduct of the parties in relation to each other and otherwise.

*(iv) Duration of the Order*    The order may be made for a specified period, or until the occurrence of a specified event, or until further order (s.33(10)). There is no time-limit on the duration of the order, as there is for non-entitled applicants (see below).

(b)    Non-Entitled Applicants

A non-entitled applicant is a person who has no property right (see above). Non-entitled applicants must apply under ss.35–38 of the Act.

*(i) Section 35 – Non-Entitled Former Spouse or Former Civil Partner v. Entitled Former Spouse or Former Civil Partner*   A former spouse or civil partner who is not entitled can apply against an entitled former spouse or civil partner (the respondent) (ss.35(1), (2)). The dwelling-house must be (have been or be intended to be) the matrimonial home or civil partnership home (ss.35(1), (2)).

*Mandatory Provisions (ss.35(3), (4))*   If the applicant is in occupation of the home, the order must: give the applicant the right not to be evicted or excluded from the home or any part of it by the respondent for a specified period; and must prohibit the respondent from evicting or excluding the applicant during that period (s.35(3)). If the applicant is *not* in occupation, it *must*: give the applicant the right to enter into and occupy the home for a specified period; and require the respondent to permit the exercise of that right (s.35(4)).

When exercising its powers to decide whether to make an order containing any of the mandatory provisions in s.35(3) or (4) above, and, if so, in what manner, the court must have regard to all the circumstances, including the following matters (s.35(6)):

(a)–(d)   are the same as the first four criteria which apply to entitled applicants under s.33(6) (see above);

(e)   the length of time that has elapsed since the parties ceased to live together;

(f)   the length of time that has elapsed since the marriage or civil partnership was dissolved or annulled; and

(g)   the existence of any pending proceedings between the parties for: an order under s.23A or s.24 Matrimonial Causes Act 1973 (property adjustment orders in connection with divorce proceedings); a property adjustment order under Part 2 of Sched. 5 to the Civil Partnership Act 2004; an order under para. 1(2)(d) or (e) of Sched. 1 to the Children Act 1989 (orders for financial relief against parents); or relating to the legal or beneficial ownership of the home.

*Discretionary Provisions (s.35(5))*   An order made under s.35 *may* also (s.35(5)): regulate the occupation of the home or part of it; prohibit, suspend or restrict the respondent's right to occupy it; require the respondent to leave the home or part of it; or exclude the respondent from a defined area in which the home is included. In deciding whether to exercise its power to include one or more of these provisions and, if so, in what manner, the court must have regard to all the circumstances including the matters mentioned in s.33(6)(a)–(d) above.

The balance of harm test laid down in s.35(8) must also be applied. Thus, if the court decides to make an order under s.35 and it appears that if the order does not include a discretionary provision under s.33(5) the applicant or any relevant child is likely to suffer significant harm attributable to the conduct of the respondent, then the court *must* include a s.33(5) discretionary provision, unless the respondent or any relevant child is likely to suffer significant harm if the provision is included and that harm is as great or greater than the harm attributable to the respondent's conduct which is likely to be suffered by the applicant or child if the provision is not included.

*Duration*   The order must be limited to a specified period not exceeding six months, but can be extended on one or more occasions for a further specified period not exceeding six months (s.35(10)). While an order is in force an applicant is treated as possessing home rights and ss.30(3)–(6) apply (s.35(13)) (see 4.2). An order cannot be made after the death of either party, and an order ceases to be effective on either party's death (s.35(9)).

*(ii) Section 36 – Non-Entitled Cohabitant or Former Cohabitant v. Entitled Cohabitant or Former Cohabitant*   A cohabitant or former cohabitant with no right to occupy the dwelling-house (or who has an equitable interest in the dwelling-house or its proceeds of sale but in whom the legal estate is not vested) may apply for an occupation order against an entitled cohabitant or former cohabitant, provided the dwelling-house is the home in which they cohabit (or have cohabited or intend to cohabit) (ss.36(1), (2)).

Both opposite-sex and same-sex cohabitants and former cohabitants (opposite-sex and same-sex) can apply under s.36 (see definition at 6.6, below).

*Mandatory Provisions*   An order must contain the provisions laid down in ss.36(3), (4). These are the same as the mandatory provisions for a s.35 order (see above). In deciding whether to make an order containing a mandatory provision, and, if so, in what manner, the court must have regard to all the circumstances of the case, including (s.36(6)):

(a)–(d)  are the same as those for entitled applicants (see s.33(6)(a)–(d), above);
(e)      the nature of the parties' relationship and in particular the level of commitment involved in it;
(f)      the length of time during which they have cohabited;
(g)      whether there are or have been any children who are children of both parties or for whom both parties have or have had parental responsibility;
(h)      the length of time that has elapsed since the parties ceased to live together; and
(i)      the existence of any pending proceedings for an order under para. 1(2)(d) or (e) of Sched. 1 to the Children Act 1989 (orders for financial relief against parents); or relating to the legal or beneficial interest of the dwelling-house.

*Discretionary Provisions (s.36(5))*   These are the same as the discretionary provisions for a s.35 order (see above). When considering whether or not to make a s.36(5) discretionary provision, and (if so) in what manner, s.36(7) requires the court to have regard to all the circumstances including those mentioned in s.36(6)(a)–(d) (above) and the balance of harm test, laid down in s.36(8). Under the balance of harm test the court must ask whether the applicant or any child is likely to suffer significant harm attributable to the respondent's conduct if a s.36(5) discretionary provision is not made, and whether the harm likely to be suffered by the respondent or child, if the provision is included, is as great or greater than the harm attributed to the respondent's conduct which is likely to be suffered by the applicant or child if the provision is not included. There is no obligation, however, to make the provision even if the balance leans in favour of doing so – the balance of harm test is merely part of the discretionary exercise.

*Duration*   The order must be limited so as to have effect for a specified period not exceeding six months, but may be extended on one occasion for a further specified period not exceeding six months (s.36(10)). An order cannot be made after the death of one of the parties and ceases to have effect on the death of either party (s.36(9)).

*(iii) Section 37 – Neither Spouse or Civil Partner or Former Spouse or Civil Partner is Entitled to Occupy*
Where one spouse or civil partner (or former spouse or former civil partner) occupies the matrimonial home or civil partnership home but neither of them is entitled to remain in occupation, either party may apply against the other for an occupation order under s.37 (ss.37(1), (2); s.37(1A)). The order may contain a provision (s.37(3)): requiring the respondent to permit the applicant to enter and remain in the dwelling-house or part of it; regulating the occupation of the house by either or both parties; requiring the respondent to leave the house, or part of it; or excluding the respondent from a defined area in which the house is included (s.37(4)). When exercising its powers, the factors in s.33(6) and the balance of harm test in s.33(7) apply as they apply to the exercise by the court of its powers under s.33(3) above (s.37(4)).

*Duration*   The order is limited to six months, but may be extended on one or more occasions by a further specified period not exceeding six months (s.37(5)).

*(iv) Section 38 – Neither Cohabitant or Former Cohabitant is Entitled to Occupy*   Where both cohabitants or both former cohabitants (opposite-sex or same-sex) occupy a dwelling-house which is the home in which they live, or have lived, together as husband and wife, but neither party is entitled, either party may apply against the other for an occupation order (ss.38(1), (2)). The provisions which the order *may* contain are the same as those for a s.37 order above (s.38(3)). In deciding whether to exercise its powers to include a s.38(3) provision, and if so in what manner, the court must have regard to all the circumstances including four factors (a)–(d) which are the same as those in s.33(6)(a)–(d) (see above), and it must apply the balance of harm test laid down in s.38(5) (s.33(4)). The balance of harm test requires the court to ask whether the applicant or relevant child is likely to suffer significant harm attributable to the respondent's conduct if the s.38(3) provision is not included in the order, and whether the harm likely to be suffered by the respondent or child is as great or greater than the harm attributable to the respondent's conduct which is likely to be suffered by the applicant or child if the provision is not included (s.38(5)). There is no obligation, however, to make the provision even if the balance leans in favour of doing so – the balance of harm test is merely part of the discretionary exercise.

*Duration*   The order is limited to a specified period not exceeding six months, but can be extended on one occasion by a further specified period of up to six months (s.38(6)).

### (c)   Occupation Orders – Ancillary Powers

On or after making an occupation order under s.33, s.35 or s.36 (but not s.37 or s.38) the court has various ancillary powers (s.40(1)). It can impose repair and maintenance obligations, require a party to pay the rent, mortgage or other outgoings, and impose obligations in respect of the furniture or other contents of the house (for example, grant the use or possession of furniture or other contents, and order a party to take reasonable care of them). It can also require a party to keep the house, furniture and any other contents secure. When deciding whether and, if so, how to exercise these ancillary powers, the court must consider all the circumstances of the case, including the parties' financial needs and resources, and their present and future financial obligations, including their financial obligations to each other and any relevant child (s.40(2)). Ancillary orders are only effective for the duration of the occupation order (s.40(3)).

In the following case, the Court of Appeal drew attention to the lack of any power in the Act to enforce these ancillary powers:

▶ *Nwogbe* v. *Nwogbe* **[2000] 2 FLR 744**

An occupation order had been made on terms that the husband was to pay the monthly rent, water rates, council tax and other expenses relating to the property (under s.40). He defaulted on the payments. The Court of Appeal held that there was no power to commit a defaulter to prison, and there was no power to enforce the order. It was not possible to make an attachment of earnings order, or for the wife to take action as a judgment debtor (as the payments were to a third party). Such orders were therefore of no value to a person remaining in occupation. The Court of Appeal held that the lack of any enforcement powers was a serious omission requiring urgent Parliamentary attention.

### (d) Restrictions on the Powers of Magistrates

The magistrates' family proceedings court cannot hear an application or make an occupation order where the proceedings involve a disputed question about a party's right to occupy the home, unless it is not necessary to determine that question in order to deal with the application or to make the order (s.59(1)). The magistrates' court can also decline jurisdiction if it considers the case can be dealt with more conveniently by another court (s.59(2)).

### (e) Undertakings, Orders Without Notice, and Enforcement

The rules for undertakings, orders without notice, and enforcement are the same as those for non-molestation orders (see above), except that the restriction on accepting an undertaking (see s.46(3A)) does not apply to occupation orders.

### (f) Attaching a Power of Arrest to an Occupation Order

Under s.47, the court can attach a power of arrest to an occupation order. The power differs depending on whether the occupation order was made with or without notice.

*Orders On Notice*   If it appears to the court that the respondent has used or threatened violence against the applicant or a relevant child, it *must* attach a power of arrest to one or more provisions of the order, unless it is satisfied that the applicant or any child will otherwise be adequately protected (ss.47(1), (2)). The Court of Appeal has held that a power of arrest can be imposed which is to have an effect for a shorter period than the other provisions in the order, but that it is usually preferable for the power of arrest to have effect for the same period as the order (*Re B-J (Power of Arrest)* [2000] 2 FLR 443).

*Orders Without Notice (ex parte Orders)*   The court *may* attach a power of arrest to one or more provisions of the order, but only if the respondent has used or threatened violence against the applicant or a relevant child, and there is a risk that the applicant or child will suffer significant harm as a result of the respondent's conduct if the power of arrest is not attached to those provisions immediately (s.47(3)). A power of arrest can be imposed which is to have effect for a shorter period than the other provisions of the order (s.47(4)). The court can vary or discharge a power of arrest attached to an order without notice, whether or not an application for variation or discharge has been made (s.49(4)).

### Effect of a Power of Arrest

A power of arrest permits a constable to arrest, without a warrant, a person whom he has reasonable cause to suspect is in breach of any provision in an order to which the power of arrest is attached (s.47(6)). The respondent must be brought before a judge or justice of the peace within 24 hours, and, if the matter is not disposed of, the respondent may be remanded in custody or on bail (s.45(7)).

In the following case it was held that a power of arrest can be attached even though the respondent is a minor:

▶ **Re H (Respondent Under 18: Power of Arrest) [2001] 1 FLR 641**

An occupation order was made, with a power of arrest attached, ordering a 17-year-old son who had been violent and abusive to his parents to leave the house where he was living with his parents and not to return, to enter, or attempt to enter, it. He appealed to the Court of Appeal, arguing that the court had no power to attach the power of arrest, as there was no power to imprison a minor for contempt of court, including the breach of an occupation order. The Court of Appeal, dismissing the appeal, held that s.47(2) could not be read in such a way as to disapply or modify the mandatory duty to attach a power of arrest, even though the respondent was under 18. In the circumstances there was no adequate protection without a power of arrest – although the relationship and the comparative age of the parties are relevant in deciding whether there should be such protection. There was a duty to attach a power of arrest in the circumstances. There was, however, a serious gap in the law in respect of the courts' extremely limited powers to deal with persons under 18 for contempt of court, and policy-makers should give this urgent attention.

### (g)  Variation and Discharge

An occupation order may be varied or discharged on an application by the respondent or by the person on whose application the order was made (see s.49).

### (h)  Applications by Children

A child under 16 can apply for an occupation order (or non-molestation order) with leave of the court, which the court can only grant if the child has sufficient understanding to make the proposed application (s.43). Applications by children are rare in practice. With occupation orders there is the added difficulty that a child cannot hold a legal estate in land. But a child may have a beneficial interest in land under a trust and thereby possess an entitlement to property.

### 6.6  Part IV of the Family Law Act 1996 – Definitions

Section 62 of Part IV of the Family Law Act 1996 is important because it defines the persons who come under the umbrella of the Act.

*'Cohabitants' and 'Former Cohabitants'*   Cohabitants (and former cohabitants) include opposite-sex and same-sex cohabitants. Cohabitants are defined as two persons who are neither married to each other nor are civil partners of each other but who are living together as husband and wife or as if they were civil partners; but it does not include cohabitants who have subsequently married each other or become civil partners of each other (s.62(1)).

*'Relevant Child'*   A relevant child is: any child who is living with, or who might reasonably be expected to live with, either party to the proceedings; any child in relation to whom an order under the Adoption and Children Act 2002 or the Children Act 1989 is in question in the proceedings; and any other child whose interests the court considers relevant (s.62(2)). This broad definition highlights the importance of protecting any child from domestic violence. Thus, the child need not be related to the applicant, nor be a child of the family.

*'Associated' Persons*   An applicant for a non-molestation order must be associated with the respondent, and so must an entitled applicant for an occupation order who is not a spouse, civil partner or cohabitant or a former spouse, civil partner or cohabitant. Associated persons are (s.62(3)):

- spouses, or former spouses;
- civil partners, or former civil partners;
- cohabitants, or former cohabitants (opposite-sex or same-sex);
- persons who live, or have lived, in the same household, otherwise than merely by reason of one of them being the other's employee, tenant, lodger or boarder;
- relatives (see further below);
- engaged, or formerly engaged, couples;
- parties to a civil partnership agreement (whether or not that agreement has been terminated);
- persons who have, or have had, an intimate personal relationship with each other which is or was of significant duration;
- in relation to any child, they are both persons falling within s.62(4) – that is, he or she is a parent of the child or he or she has or has had parental responsibility for the same child;
- parties to the same family proceedings (see definition below), other than proceedings under Part IV of the Family Law Act 1996.

*Engagements and Civil Partnership Agreements*   Written evidence of the engagement is required, unless the court is satisfied that the engagement is evidenced by an engagement ring or engagement ceremony (s.44). Written evidence is also required of a civil partnership agreement, unless the agreement is evidenced by a gift by one party to the agreement as a token of the agreement or by a civil partnership agreement ceremony (s.44). If an engagement or civil partnership agreement has been terminated, the application for a non-molestation or occupation order must be brought within three years of its termination (ss.33(2), 42(4)).

*Associated Persons Having an Intimate Personal Relationship*   The extension of the definition of 'associated persons' to persons who have, or who have had, an intimate personal relationship of significant duration may cause difficulties. However, the court is likely to adopt a purposive interpretation, in order to bring a person within the protective jurisdiction of the Act. A person whose relationship is not of significant duration can consider seeking protection under the Protection from Harassment Act 1997, or ancillary to other court proceedings (for example, in tort proceedings for assault and battery).

*A Purposive Approach to Associated Persons*   A purposive approach was given to the interpretation of associated persons in the following case in order to bring the applicant under the protective umbrella of the legislation:

▶ *G v. F (Non-Molestation Order: Jurisdiction)* [2000] 2 FLR 233

A woman applied for a non-molestation order against a man with whom she spent four or five nights a week but with whom she did not strictly live. The justices refused to make the order, holding that they were not associated persons as they maintained separate households, did not have children and the relationship was not stable. Wall J held, allowing the appeal and ordering a rehearing that, although the parties lived in separate households, they could be described as being cohabitants within the meaning of s.62(3)(b). There was a sexual relationship, some form of financial support and the respondent's evidence demonstrated that from his perspective they were cohabiting. Wall J said that it would be most unfortunate if the term 'associated persons' was construed too narrowly to exclude borderline cases where swift and effective protection for victims of domestic violence was required. Where domestic violence is concerned, Wall J said that Part IV of the Family Law Act 1996 should be given a purposive construction. Jurisdiction should not be refused unless the facts were plainly incapable of being brought within the statute.

*A 'Relative'*   A 'relative' in relation to a person is (s.63(1)):

▷ the father, mother, step-father, step-mother, son, daughter, step-son, step-daughter, grandmother, grandfather, grandson or granddaughter of that person or of that person's spouse or former spouse, civil partner or former civil partner; or
▷ the brother, sister, uncle, aunt, niece or nephew (whether of the full blood or of the half blood or by marriage or civil partnership) of that person or of that person's spouse or former spouse, civil partner or former civil partner, and includes, in relation to a person who is cohabiting or has cohabited with another person, any person who would be any of the above relatives if the parties were married to each other or were civil partners of each other.

*Adopted Children*   If a child has been adopted or an adoption agency has power to place him for adoption or he has become the subject of a placement order (under the Adoption and Children Act 2002), two persons are associated with each other if: one of them is the natural parent of the child (or a parent of such a natural parent); and the other is the child or any person who has become a parent of a child under an adoption order or has applied for an adoption order, or a person with whom the child has at any time been placed for adoption (ss.62(5), (7)).

*'Family Proceedings'* 'Family proceedings' mean any proceedings under (ss.63(1), (2)):

- the inherent jurisdiction of the High Court in relation to children;
- Part IV of the Family Law Act 1996;
- the Matrimonial Causes Act 1973;
- the Adoption and Children Act 2002;
- the Domestic Proceedings and Magistrates' Courts Act 1978;
- Part III of the Matrimonial and Family Proceedings Act 1984;
- Parts I, II and IV of the Children Act 1989;
- s.30 Human Fertilisation and Embryology Act 1990;
- Schedules 5 to 7 of the Civil Partnership Act 2004.

## 6.7 Injunctions Ancillary to Legal Proceedings

County courts and the High Court have jurisdiction (under s.38 County Courts Act 1984 and s.37 Supreme Court Act 1981) to grant injunctions ancillary to civil proceedings where it appears to the court to be just and convenient to do so. These powers may be useful if a victim of domestic violence does not come within the definition of associated person (see above). However, the court can only grant an injunction ancillary to civil proceedings if the applicant has a legal or equitable right which is capable of being protected, such as a cause of action in tort, or a proprietary interest. The House of Lords has held that it is not sufficient if another member of the family has such a right (see *Hunter v. Canary Wharf Ltd* [1997] AC 655, [1997] 2 FLR 342). An injunction was granted in the following case:

> ▶ *Tameside Metropolitan Borough Council v. M (Injunctive Relief: County Courts: Jurisdiction)* [2001] Fam Law 856
>
> Local authority social workers, who were working on a case involving four young children who had been taken into care, were threatened with violence by the children's parents, who followed them and damaged their cars. On the application of the local authority, the county court granted injunctive protection, as the local authority had a statutory right by virtue of the care order granted by the court, and it was just and convenient to grant injunctive protection so that the local authority would be able to implement its care plan in accordance with its parental responsibility for the children. The local authority's alternative application for injunctive relief under the Protection from Harassment Act 1997 was dismissed, as the local authority was held not to be a 'person' for the purposes of that Act.

## 6.8 The Protection from Harassment Act 1997

The Protection from Harassment Act 1997 was enacted primarily to provide protection from harassment and other similar conduct arising in the context of 'stalking' (the obsessive harassment of one person by another), but it is sometimes used by victims of domestic violence. The Act creates criminal offences, and also provides civil remedies (injunctions and damages). It has been amended by the Domestic Violence, Crime and Victims Act 2004 (see below).

---

### The Protection from Harassment Act 1997 and Part IV of the Family Law Act 1996 – A Comparison

▶ Only 'associated persons' can apply for injunctive protection under Part IV of the Family Law Act (FLA) 1996, whereas any person can apply under the Protection from Harassment Act (PHA) 1997.

▶ Remedies under the FLA 1996 specifically relate to occupation of the home, but those under the PHA 1997 do not.

▶ Damages can be awarded under the PHA 1997, but not under the FLA 1996.

▶ A power of arrest cannot be attached to an order under the PHA 1997, but can to an occupation order under the FLA 1996.

▶ A warrant of arrest can be issued under both statutes.

▶ Breach of an injunction under s.3 PHA 1997 and breach of a non-molestation order under the FLA 1996 are both criminal offences.

▶ Applications under the FLA 1996 are family proceedings and are governed by the Family Proceedings Rules 1991, whereas applications under the PHA 1997 are civil proceedings.

▶ Special provision for orders without notice is made in the FLA 1996, but not in the PHA 1997.

---

Section 1(1) Protection from Harassment Act 1997 prohibits harassment by providing that a person must not pursue a course of conduct which amounts to harassment of another, and which he knows or ought to know amounts to harassment of another. There is no definition of 'harassment' in the Act, but s.7(2) provides that references to harassing a person include alarming the person or causing the person distress. The Act may therefore be used to prosecute persons for acts other than stalking. In order for there to be harassment the Act requires there to be 'a course of conduct' – a single incident is not sufficient to bring a person within the Act. The Court of Appeal has held that, because the Protection from Harassment Act 1997 was passed to protect persons from stalking (an act performed by persons with an obsessive nature), a person may be convicted of an offence under the Act even if he or she suffers from an identifiable mental illness (see *R* v. *Colohan* [2001] EWCA Civ 1251, where the defendant was convicted despite his defence that his schizophrenia took him out of the Act, as he did not have the necessary mental state).

*Course of Conduct* In order for there to be harassment there must be a 'course of conduct,' which s.7(3) defines as 'conduct on at least two occasions'. As 'conduct' can include speech (s.7(4)), verbal violence can constitute harassment. Course of conduct was considered in the following case:

---

▶ *R* v. *Hills* [2001] 1 FLR 580

After the woman left the defendant he was charged with harassment under the 1997 Act. The course of conduct consisted of various assaults during a seven-month period, but centred on two separate and individual assaults which took place approximately six months apart. The defendant was convicted but appealed against his conviction. The Court of Appeal allowed his appeal, holding that a course of conduct requires proof of a cogent link between the two (or more) incidents constituting harassment. As the case centred on two separate and individual incidents, the necessary cogent link between the two assaults had not been established. The case was held to be far from the stalking type of offence for which the 1997 Act was intended. The Court of Appeal held that, where a couple were frequently coming back together and having sexual intercourse, it was unrealistic to think that the behaviour fell within the stalking category. The Court of Appeal applied *Lau* v. *Director of Public Prosecutions* [2000] 1 FLR 799, which concerned two incidents between a girlfriend and a boyfriend, and where it was held that, although two incidents could be enough to establish harassment, the fewer the occasions and the wider they were spread the less likely it would be that a finding of harassment could reasonably be made for the purposes of the Act.

### (a)  Criminal Offences

The Act creates two levels of criminal offence, each of which must involve a 'course of conduct' (ss.1, 2(1) and 7(3)). The first offence is the s.2 offence whereby a person pursues a course of conduct which amounts to harassment of another, and which he knows or ought to know amounts to harassment of the other (s.2(1)). A person who is found guilty of this offence is liable to a fine or imprisonment for a term of up to six months (s.2(2)). The second offence is the more serious s.4 aggravated indictable offence of harassment – that of causing another person to fear on at least two occasions that violence will be used against him (s.4(1)). The s.4 offence carries more serious penalties.

*Defences*   The s.2 and s.4 criminal offences are subject to statutory defences (ss.1(3) and 7(3)): that the course of conduct was pursued for the purpose of preventing or detecting crime; or that the pursuit of the course of conduct was reasonable (see ss.1(3) and 4(3)).

*Restraining Orders (s.5)*   The criminal court can impose a restraining order, an injunctive-style order, on an offender convicted of a s.2 or a s.4 criminal offence (s.5(1)), prohibiting him from further conduct which amounts to harassment, or which will cause the victim fear of violence. However, s.12 Domestic Violence, Crime and Victims Act 2004 removes the words 'of a s.2 or s.4 criminal offence' so that the criminal courts can make a restraining order on conviction of any offence (such as an assault), not just on conviction of an offence under the 1997 Act. A restraining order may have effect for a specified period or until further order (s.5(3)). Breach of a restraining order without reasonable excuse is a criminal offence (s.5(5)), which can result in a fine, or imprisonment for up to five years (s.5(6)). Under s.5A (inserted by s.12(5) Domestic Violence, Crime and Victims Act 2004) the courts have new powers to make a restraining order where a person has been acquitted of an offence, where the court believes such an order is necessary to protect a person from harassment by the defendant.

### (b)  Civil Remedies

In addition to the two criminal offences described above, the Act creates civil remedies. Section 3 creates a statutory tort of harassment by providing that a person who is, or may be, the victim of harassment, as prohibited by s.1 of the Act, can bring a claim in civil proceedings against the person responsible for the harassment (s.3(1)). Damages can be awarded, including damages for anxiety caused by the harassment and any financial loss resulting from the harassment (s.3(2)). Furthermore, where in such civil proceedings the High Court or a county court grants an injunction for the purpose of restraining the defendant from pursuing any conduct which amounts to harassment, and the complainant considers that the defendant has done anything which is prohibited by the injunction, the complainant may apply for the issue of a warrant for the arrest of the defendant (s.3(3)). Breach of an injunction restraining the defendant from pursuing any conduct which amounts to harassment is a criminal offence (s.3(6)). It is not, however, punishable as a contempt of court (s.3(7)).

In an application for a civil remedy under s.3 the standard of proof is the civil standard of proof (on the balance of probabilities), not the criminal standard (Tugendhat J in *Hipgrave and Hipgrave* v. *Jones* [2004] EWHC 2901 (QB), [2005] 2 FLR 174). As the 1997 Act provides remedies for the protection of privacy, it is relevant for the court when interpreting the Act to have regard to art. 8 of the European Convention for the Protection of Human Rights (right to a private and family life), and an order under the Act could also interfere with freedom of expression (art. 10) and rights of assembly and association (art. 11) (Tugendhat J in *Hipgrave*, above).

Damages can be awarded under the 1997 Act without the need to seek an injunction. Thus, for example, in *Singh* v. *Bhakar and Bhakar* [2007] 1 FLR 889 a young Sikh girl, who had suffered harassment by her mother-in-law after she joined her husband in his extended family home, was successful in obtaining damages of £35,000 in the county court under s.3 of the 1997 Act for the depression caused by the maltreatment.

## Summary

1 Domestic violence is a widespread phenomenon existing at all levels of society.

2 The criminal law provides protection for victims of domestic violence, and the police treat domestic violence as a serious crime.

3 The civil law provides remedies for victims of domestic violence. Under Part IV of the Family Law Act 1996 magistrates' courts, county courts and the High Court have jurisdiction to make occupation orders and non-molestation orders for a wide class of applicants, including spouses, former spouses, civil partners, former civil partners, cohabitants (opposite-sex and same-sex), former cohabitants, family members and other persons who come within the definition of 'associated persons'.

4 In respect of occupation orders made under Part IV of the Family Law Act 1996, the court makes a distinction between 'entitled persons' (those with a right of occupation) and 'non-entitled persons' (those with no such right).

5 The court can accept undertakings from respondents in some circumstances under Part IV of the Family Law Act 1996.

6 Orders can be made without notice under Part IV of the Family Law Act 1996.

7 County courts (under s.38 County Courts Act 1984) and the High Court (under s.37 Supreme Court Act 1981) have jurisdiction to grant injunctions ancillary to other proceedings where it is just and convenient to do so, but the applicant must have a right in law or in equity which is capable of being protected.

8 The Protection from Harassment Act 1997 makes harassment a criminal offence and provides civil remedies for protection against harassment.

9 The Domestic Violence, Crime and Victims Act 2004 has made changes to the civil and criminal law in order to give greater protection to victims of domestic violence and their families.

## Further Reading and References

Bessant, 'Enforcing non-molestation orders in the civil and criminal courts' [2005] Fam Law 640.

Burton, '*Lomas* v. *Parle* – coherent and effective remedies for victims of domestic violence: time for an integrated domestic violence court?' [2004] CFLQ 317.

Hayes, 'Criminal trials where a child is the victim: extra protection for children or a missed opportunity?' [2005] CFLQ 307.

## Websites

**Crime Reduction Website**: www.crimereduction.gov.uk

**Home Office**: www.homeoffice.gov.uk

**Women and Equality Unit**: www.womenandequalityunit.gov.uk

**Women's Aid**: www.womensaid.org.uk

Part IV

# Divorce and its Consequences

# Chapter 7
## Divorce

**The Legislation**

**Matrimonial Causes Act 1973** Part I makes provision in respect of the grounds for divorce. Part II makes provision in respect of finance and property on divorce (see Chapter 8).

**Domicile and Matrimonial Proceedings Act 1973** Governs the jurisdiction to hear divorces.

**Family Law Act 1986, Part II** Makes provision in respect of the recognition of foreign divorces.

**Family Proceedings Rules 1991** Lays down the procedural rules governing divorce proceedings, and proceedings for property and finance on divorce.

This chapter deals first with the development of divorce law, and then with the current law governing the obtaining of a divorce. Financial and property matters on divorce are dealt with in Chapter 8. Residence and contact arrangements for children are dealt with in Chapter 12. Financial provision for children is dealt with in Chapter 13.

Although divorces are common, the number of divorces is dropping. According to figures from the Office for National Statistics (August 2007) the number of divorces granted in 2006 in England and Wales fell by 6.5 per cent to 132,562. This was the second consecutive year in which the divorce rate had dropped and was the lowest since 1984. The average age for divorce was 43.4 years for men and 40.9 years for women, and one in five men and women divorcing had had a previous marriage ending in divorce; 69 per cent of divorces were granted to women, and for all divorces behaviour was the most common fact proved.

## 7.1 The Development of Divorce Law

### (a) The Grounds for Divorce

Until the mid-nineteenth century the courts had no jurisdiction to grant decrees of divorce, although the ecclesiastical courts had the power to annul marriages and to grant a limited sort of divorce called a divorce *a mensa et thoro*, which relieved the spouses of the legal obligation to live together, but did not terminate the marriage. The Christian idea of marriage as an indissoluble life-long union prevailed. Anyone who wished to divorce could only do so by private Act of Parliament, which was a complex, lengthy and expensive procedure available only to a small minority of people.

In order to remedy the inadequacies of the Act of Parliament procedure, the Matrimonial Causes Act 1857 was passed permitting judicial divorce. It did so by establishing the Court for Divorce and Matrimonial Causes which had jurisdiction to grant decrees of divorce, nullity and judicial separation. However, divorce continued to be difficult to obtain as there was only one ground, which was adultery by the respondent – a ground which was acceptable to the Church because of biblical precedent for it. In addition to adultery, the petitioner also had to prove the absence of any collusion, condonation or connivance between the parties to the marriage. Divorce was therefore only available to an innocent petitioner if the respondent had committed the matrimonial offence of adultery. However, divorce under the 1857 Act remained particularly difficult for wives, as, unlike husbands, they had to prove 'aggravated adultery' (adultery plus an additional factor, such as incest, cruelty, bigamy, sodomy or desertion). Eventually, however, after considerable pressure for reform by the female emancipation movement, aggravated adultery was abolished by the Matrimonial Causes Act 1923.

After considerable criticism of the fact that adultery was the only ground for divorce, the following grounds were added by the Matrimonial Causes Act 1937: cruelty; desertion for a continuous period of at least three years; and incurable insanity. Divorce therefore continued to require proof of a matrimonial offence (except in cases of incurable insanity). In response to concerns that the more liberal divorce law would undermine the institution of marriage, the 1937 Act introduced an absolute bar on divorce in the first three years of marriage, unless the petitioner had suffered exceptional hardship, or the respondent had shown exceptional depravity. The aim of the three-year bar was to deter trial marriages and hasty divorces. Condonation, connivance and collusion remained as bars.

Later on, particularly at the end of the Second World War, there was a sharp increase in the number of people wishing to divorce, and a growing dissatisfaction with the law. It seemed wrong to have to prove a matrimonial offence, thereby apportioning blame, when both spouses might be responsible for marriage breakdown. It seemed wrong for a restrictive divorce law to perpetuate a dead marriage which had completely broken down. It was also easy to abuse the system, for example by fabricating adultery. In response to dissatisfaction with the law, a Royal Commission, the Morton Commission, was established to look at divorce, and in its *Report* in 1956 (Cmd. 9678) it recommended the retention of the matrimonial offence doctrine as the basis for a good divorce law. This was a considerable set-back for the proponents of reform, and it was not until the 1960s with the publication of two reports, one by the Church of England and the other by the Law Commission, that proposals for change began to be made. In 1963 the Archbishop of Canterbury appointed a Committee to study divorce, which in its report (*Putting Asunder*, 1966) recommended that the doctrine of the matrimonial offence be abolished and be replaced by a principle of irretrievable breakdown of marriage, which would be proved by holding an inquest into the causes of breakdown. Shortly after the publication of *Putting Asunder*, the Law Commission published a Report (*Reform of the Grounds of Divorce: The Field of Choice*, Cmnd. 3123, 1966) in which it stated that the objectives of a good divorce law should be:

'To buttress, rather than to undermine the stability of marriage; and when, regrettably a marriage has irretrievably broken down, to enable the empty legal shell to be destroyed with the maximum fairness, and the minimum bitterness, distress and humiliation.'

The Law Commission concluded that a divorce law based on a matrimonial offence failed to satisfy these objectives, and, while it agreed with the Archbishop's Committee that irretrievable breakdown should be the sole ground for divorce, it rejected the Committee's proposal that breakdown should be established by holding an inquest into its causes, as this would be distressing for the parties, expensive, time-consuming and essentially untriable. The Law Commission proposed instead that breakdown should be established on proof of one or more of five facts, three of which would be based on the old matrimonial offences, and the other two on periods of separation. The five facts proposed were: adultery plus intolerability; unreasonable behaviour; desertion for a period of at least two years; two-years' separation with consent to the divorce; and five-years' separation. The Law Commission also recommended that a new divorce law should incorporate certain policy objectives. It should encourage reconciliation, prevent injustice to economically vulnerable spouses and protect children. It also recommended that the bar on divorce within the first three years of marriage should be replaced with a one-year bar, as the three-year bar prolonged poor marriages or encouraged allegations of exceptional hardship or depravity which were difficult to adjudicate, and caused hostility and bitterness between the parties. It also caused duplication of proceedings, as an unhappily married spouse would petition for a decree of judicial separation followed not long afterwards by a petition for divorce. The Law Commission recommended a one-year bar, as it felt that to have no bar at all would undermine the sanctity of marriage.

The Law Commission's recommendations were eventually enacted in the Divorce Reform Act 1969, which came into force on 1 January 1971, but which was later re-enacted as Part I of the Matrimonial Causes Act 1973. Except for certain amendments (notably the 'clean-break' provisions introduced by the Matrimonial and Family Proceedings Act 1984) the reforms introduced by the Divorce Reform Act 1969 remain the law today. We therefore have a hybrid law of divorce made up of fault and no-fault grounds. The retention of fault means that the matrimonial offence doctrine remains, and in fact is particularly prevalent, as many divorces are sought on the basis of the fault grounds of adultery or unreasonable behaviour as these enable a petitioner to obtain a 'quick' divorce. The Law Commission's belief that most couples would use the separation grounds has not been realised in practice.

Since the introduction of the current grounds for divorce nearly forty years ago, there has been increasing dissatisfaction with the law, and in 2000 a radically new form of divorce was to have been introduced, but this was abandoned because it was found to be unworkable in practice. It remains the case, however, that divorce law is still considered to be unsatisfactory, and in need of reform (see 7.11, below).

### (b) Divorce Procedure

Changes have also taken place over the years in respect of divorce procedure. Initially, because divorce was considered a serious matter, proceedings were heard only in London and only by senior judges. Later on, however, the position changed, with the result that all undefended divorces today are now heard by specially designated divorce county courts (or the Divorce Registry in London). Defended divorces, however, continue to be heard in the High Court. At one time, divorces were heard in open court with the petitioner giving oral evidence to prove the ground alleged. However, it became increasingly recognised that hearing divorces in open court was not only distressing for the parties, as they would have their intimate marital details exposed in public, but it was also unnecessarily expensive and time-consuming. Divorce was failing to achieve one of its major policy aims, namely the burial of a dead marriage with the minimum of distress and humiliation.

With the huge increase in the divorce rate, particularly after the introduction of the more liberal grounds for divorce by the Divorce Reform Act 1969, the courts became overloaded, even though most undefended divorces were taking as little as ten minutes to be heard. Eventually, a new divorce procedure, the 'special procedure', was introduced with the aim of achieving simplicity, speed and economy. It was introduced in 1973 only for childless couples divorcing with consent, but was extended in 1975 to all childless couples, except those petitioning on the basis of unreasonable behaviour. In 1977 it was extended to all undefended divorces.

All undefended divorces today are therefore dealt with in what is essentially an administrative procedure with minimal judicial involvement. The district judge examines the papers in order to establish whether the fact alleged in the petition is proved, whether the marriage has irretrievably broken down and whether there is any reason for not granting a divorce. A list of petitioners who have satisfied the district judge is drawn up and is later read out in open court by the judge's clerk, after which the judge pronounces decree nisi of divorce on block. This judicial pronouncement is the last vestige of the public hearing of divorce. If a divorce is undefended neither party need attend court. Defended divorces, on the other hand, which are virtually non-existent, are still required to be heard in open court with the parties giving oral evidence.

## 7.2    An Attempt at Reform

In the late 1980s, as a result of increasing dissatisfaction with the law, proposals began to be made to reform divorce law, both the grounds and procedure. These proposals were eventually enacted in Parts I, II and III of the Family Law Act 1996, but they were never implemented, and were finally abandoned, because they proved to be unworkable in practice. As a result, the law remains in an unsatisfactory state, as the same criticisms of divorce law remain.

### (a)    The Background to the Proposed Reforms

In the 1980s, the Government established a committee, the Booth Committee on Procedure in Matrimonial Causes (chaired by Hon Mrs Justice Booth), whose remit was to look at divorce procedure with the aim of making recommendations to mitigate the intensity of divorce disputes, to encourage settlement and to provide further for the welfare of the children of the family. The Committee, which reported its findings in 1985, found, among other things, that under the special procedure the registrar (now the district judge) could do no more that merely 'rubber stamp' divorce applications, as the registrar was not in a position in most cases to make findings of fact, such as to establish the effect of the respondent's behaviour on the petitioner. The Committee felt that the law was little respected and little understood and that the special procedure increased bitterness. With these criticisms in mind the Booth Committee recommended various reforms, including allowing joint applications for divorce and a system of initial hearings in which the parties would be able to reach a settlement or identify areas of dispute. The Committee also recommended changes of terminology to make the law more understandable.

It was concern, however, not about divorce procedure, but about the ground for divorce which ultimately led to proposals for reform. In 1988 the Law Commission published a discussion paper, *Facing the Future: A Discussion Paper on the Ground for Divorce* (Law Com No. 170), in which it looked at the grounds for divorce and discussed whether divorce law had succeeded in satisfying the objectives for a good divorce law which it had laid down in its 1966 Report, *Reform of the Grounds of Divorce: The Field of Choice* (Cmnd. 3123), namely to: buttress, rather than to undermine the stability of marriage; and when a marriage had irretrievably broken down, to enable the empty legal shell to be destroyed with the maximum fairness, and the minimum bitterness, distress and humiliation. The Law Commission also considered whether divorce law avoided injustice to economically weak spouses, protected children's interests, and was understandable and respected.

The Law Commission came to the conclusion that, although the 1969 reforms were a considerable improvement on the previous law, a major aim of those reforms – to move away from fault – had not been achieved in practice, as most divorces were sought on the basis of adultery and unreasonable behaviour. As a result, many parties continued to apportion blame with one party being unfairly stigmatised when both parties were often to blame. Allegations of fault also encouraged the parties to adopt entrenched and hostile positions, which made agreement about ancillary matters more difficult. The Law Commission concluded that the law had not achieved its objectives. It was neither easily understandable nor respected. Proving a fact had become a meaningless formality, with petitioners exaggerating a fact in order to obtain a divorce. The law was also illogical because in some cases, although a marriage had clearly irretrievably broken down, it was not possible to grant a decree, as a fact could not be proved. The Commission also felt that divorce law created a juggernaut effect, because once the parties had started out on the divorce process there was little scope for reconciliation, conciliation and negotiation. Most of all, the Law Commission felt that the law failed to recognise that divorce is not a final product but part of a massive transition for the parties and their children. Having identified the weaknesses in the law, the Law Commission proposed reforms of divorce law which, it claimed, would introduce a truly, and not artificially, no-fault divorce which would encourage the parties to reach agreement and consider and face up to the consequences of marital breakdown.

The Law Commission discussed various options for reform, but concluded that a no-fault model was best. After discussing the advantages and disadvantages of different no-fault models (divorce on proof of marriage breakdown, separation, or divorce by mutual consent, or by unilateral demand), it recommended the retention of irretrievable breakdown as the ground for divorce, but with divorce available at the end of a period of time. The Commission felt that divorce over a period of time had many advantages. It would encourage the parties to co-operate and to consider the practical consequences of divorce, and would reinforce the idea that divorce is a process and not an event. It also considered that conciliation and mediation would fit in well with the proposed model, as would the procedural reforms recommended by the Booth Committee (see p.138, above).

The Law Commission's Discussion Paper was followed in 1990 by its Report, *Family Law: The Ground for Divorce* (Law Com No. 192), in which it outlined in more detail its recommendation for a divorce over a period of time. The Report also included a draft Bill.

In 1993 the Government published a Consultation Paper, *Looking to the Future: Mediation and the Ground for Divorce* (Cm 2424), in which it adopted most of the Law Commission's and Booth Committee's proposals, and also proposals for an increased role for mediation. In the Consultation Paper it stated that divorce law was not working well for various reasons. It allowed a divorce to be obtained too quickly and easily without the parties being required to consider the consequences. It did nothing to save marriages. It could make things worse for children. It was unjust and exacerbated bitterness and hostility. It was confusing, misleading, open to abuse, discriminatory and it also distorted the parties' bargaining positions.

In 1995, the Government published a White Paper, *Looking to the Future: Mediation and the Ground for Divorce. The Government's Proposals* (Cm 2799), in which it laid down the objectives for a better divorce law, which were to support the institution of marriage, to include practicable steps to prevent the irretrievable breakdown of marriage, to ensure that the parties understood the practical consequences of divorce before taking any irreversible decision, and to keep the costs to the parties and the taxpayer to a minimum. Where divorce was unavoidable, divorce law should minimise the bitterness and hostility between the parties and reduce the trauma for the children.

### (b) The Proposed Reform – 'Divorce Over a Period of Time'

'Divorce over a period of time,' which was enacted as Part II of the Family Law Act 1996, emphasised that divorce is a process, not an event, and introduced no-fault divorce. It required couples, in most cases, to have sorted out ancillary matters (finance, property and children) before being able to obtain a divorce. Parties were to be given more information about divorce, and greater emphasis was to be placed on mediation.

Irretrievable breakdown was to remain the sole ground for divorce, which would be proved if: the applicant(s) had made a statement of marriage breakdown; a required period for reflection and consideration had passed; and one or both parties had declared that, having reflected on the breakdown, and having considered arrangements for their future, their marriage could not be saved. A series of steps would have to be taken in order to obtain a divorce. An applicant would first have to attend an 'information meeting' at which information about divorce (but not legal advice) would be given, and marriage counselling provided, if needed. At least three months later, one or both of the parties would have to send a 'statement of marital breakdown' to the court. The court would then have the power to make directions requiring the parties to attend a meeting at which mediation would be explained, and to make interim ancillary relief orders and interim orders under the Children Act 1989. Once the statement of marital breakdown had been lodged with the court, a period for reflection and consideration would then have to pass (nine months in some cases, fifteen in others), during which the applicant(s) were required to spend time reflecting on whether their marriage could be saved and, if not, then on making arrangements in respect of ancillary relief and the welfare of any children. At the end of that period, an application for a 'divorce order' could be made, which the court could grant if it was satisfied that: the marriage had irretrievably broken down; the information meeting requirements had been complied with; arrangements for the future had been made; there was no order preventing divorce; and the requirements in respect of the welfare of the children had been satisfied.

The court would have had the power to make an 'order preventing divorce' if it considered that dissolution of the marriage would result in substantial financial or other hardship to the other party, or to a child of the family, and it would be wrong in all the circumstances for the marriage to be dissolved. The court would also have had the power to make separation orders.

### (c) The Decision Not to Introduce the Reforms

'Divorce over a period of time' was due to come into force on 1 January 1999, but implementation was suspended until 2000 until after the Government had received the results of a pilot scheme to see how the information meetings would work in practice. However, the results of the pilot scheme turned out to be disappointing. Only 7 per cent of those attending information meetings were diverted into mediation and very few couples attended the meetings together. The information meetings had failed to achieve the Government's stated objectives of saving savable marriages and encouraging mediation. Because the proposals had failed to fulfil the policy objectives in Part I of the Act of saving savable marriages and, where they had broken down, bringing them to an end with the minimum of distress to the parties and any children, the reforms were never introduced and Part II of the Family Law Act was eventually repealed.

The Government's decision not to implement the reforms was greeted with considerable relief by those who thought the proposals were inherently flawed – as they were unnecessarily complicated and unworkable in practice. One of the main criticisms was that the reforms placed impractical and impossible demands on divorcing couples. Couples in the throes of marriage breakdown would have found it difficult, and in some cases impossible, to make arrangements for the future. Cretney (1995) thought that the Government seemed 'curiously naive' about what was likely to happen during the period of reflection (at p.304). He said that some couples would not spend time considering whether their marriage could be saved or making arrangements for the future, but would instead spend time conceiving children, or exploiting their emotional or financial advantage or brooding on their grievances. Freeman (1997) was critical of the length of the divorce process because he thought it would create 'more conflict, more tension, more domestic violence, unnecessary abortions and more children who [would] experience their parents' divorce while still of pre-school years' (at p.414). Eekelaar (1999) criticised the need for information meetings, and considered them a form of 'social engineering'. The Solicitors' Family Law Association (now called 'Resolution') considered the new law to be cumbersome and confusing, and said it would create delay and uncertainty, which were contrary to the best interests of divorcing couples and their children.

Thus, despite more than a decade-long attempt at reform, the new divorce law that was to be introduced never came to fruition. As a result, we still have an unsatisfactory law of divorce in England and Wales which is considered to be in need of reform. Currently, however, there are no proposals to reform it. In Scotland, however, where divorce law is similar to that in England and Wales, the law has been changed so that the five-year separation ground for divorce had been reduced to two years, and the two-year separation with consent ground reduced to one year. The aim is to encourage the use of the separation grounds, and thereby lessen the acrimony and conflict which are associated with fault-based divorces, and allow parents and children to move on.

---

### Major Milestones in the Development of Divorce Law

| | |
|---|---|
| **1857** | The Matrimonial Causes Act 1857 introduces judicial divorce by establishing the Court for Divorce and Matrimonial Causes with jurisdiction to grant decrees of divorce, nullity and judicial separation. Adultery is the sole ground for divorce, but women must prove 'aggravated adultery' (adultery plus cruelty, bigamy, sodomy or desertion). |
| **1923** | The Matrimonial Causes Act 1923 abolishes aggravated adultery in order to equalise the position of women with men. |
| **1937** | The Matrimonial Causes Act 1937 introduces additional grounds, so that a divorce can be obtained on the ground of: adultery; cruelty; desertion for a continuous period of at least three years; or incurable insanity. A bar on divorce in the first three years of marriage is introduced. |

| Major Milestones in the Development of Divorce Law | |
|---|---|
| 1 January 1971 | The Divorce Reform Act 1969 comes into force introducing irretrievable breakdown as the sole ground for divorce, but which can be established only on proof of: adultery; unreasonable behaviour; two-years' separation with consent to the divorce; desertion; or five-years' separation. The three-year bar on divorce is reduced to one. The Divorce Reform Act is later re-enacted as Part I of the Matrimonial Causes Act 1973 (which is the law which applies today). |
| 1973 | The 'special procedure' (administrative divorce) is introduced for undefended divorces by childless couples who are divorcing with consent. It is extended in 1977 to all undefended divorces. |
| 1 January 1999 | A new law of divorce ('divorce over a period of time') is due to come into force under Part II of the Family Law Act 1996, but its implementation is suspended so that the Government can conduct a pilot study to see how the information meetings work in practice. |
| 2000 | The proposed new divorce law is abandoned. |

## 7.3  The Current Law of Divorce

### (a)  Introduction

The law of divorce is laid down in the Matrimonial Causes Act (MCA) 1973, Part I of which deals with obtaining a divorce (or an annulment or judicial separation), and Part II with finance and property orders on divorce (annulment or judicial separation) (see Chapter 8). Procedural rules governing divorce are found in the Family Proceedings Rules 1991.

An undefended divorce is obtained by means of what is essentially an administrative paper exercise. It can be granted in a matter of weeks without the need, in most cases, for either party to attend court. Sorting out ancillary matters (property, finance and children), if the parties cannot reach agreement, takes much longer. Obtaining a divorce is a two-stage process. A decree nisi of divorce must be obtained first, followed by a decree absolute. Only on the grant of decree absolute is the marriage terminated. The procedure for defended divorces is different, but divorces are rarely defended. The parties to a divorce are called the 'petitioner' and the 'respondent'.

### (b)  Jurisdiction

The jurisdictional rules for hearing a petition for divorce (or for nullity or judicial separation) in the courts in England and Wales are laid down in s.5 Domicile and Matrimonial Proceedings Act 1973 and Council Regulation (EC) (No. 2201/2003) Concerning Jurisdiction and the Recognition and Enforcement of Judgments in Matrimonial Matters and in Matters of Parental Responsibility (Brussels II Revised). The rules are complex, but in very general terms the courts in England and Wales have jurisdiction to grant a divorce if either spouse is domiciled in England or Wales when the proceedings are begun, or is habitually resident in England or Wales throughout the period of one year ending with the date on which proceedings are begun.

In *Mark* v. *Mark* [2005] UKHL 42, [2005] 2 FLR 1193 the House of Lords held that, for the purpose of jurisdiction to entertain a divorce petition under s.5(2) Domicile and Matrimonial Proceedings Act 1973, residence in England and Wales need not be lawful residence. Thus a person can be habitually resident or domiciled in England and Wales even if his or her presence in the UK is a criminal offence under the Immigration Act 1971.

*Staying Divorce Proceedings*   The Domicile and Matrimonial Proceedings Act 1973 gives the divorce courts in England and Wales the power to stay (stop) divorce proceedings where divorce proceedings are pending in another country (see, for example, *S v. S (Divorce: Staying Proceedings)* [1997] 2 FLR 100 where the High Court granted the husband's application for a stay of proceedings, as the court in New York was the more appropriate forum for the divorce).

### (c)  The 'One-Year Bar' on Divorce

Divorce proceedings cannot be commenced within the first year of marriage (s.3(1) MCA 1973). This is an absolute bar – there is no discretion to waive it. Despite the one-year bar, a petitioner can base the divorce petition on matters which happened during the first year of marriage (s.3(2)). A decree of nullity or of judicial separation can, on the other hand, be sought during the first year of marriage.

### (d)  Encouraging Reconciliation

As part of the policy objective of divorce law to encourage the saving of savable marriages, certain provisions in Part I of the MCA 1973 aim to encourage reconciliation. Thus, the court can adjourn divorce proceedings at any stage if there is a reasonable possibility of a reconciliation between the parties (s.6(2)), and certain periods of resumed cohabitation are ignored when establishing whether or not the marriage has irretrievably broken down (see below).

### 7.4  The Ground for Divorce and the Five Facts

Under Part I of the Matrimonial Causes Act 1973 there is only one ground for divorce, which is that the marriage must have irretrievably broken down (s.1(1)). To establish irretrievable breakdown, the petitioner must prove the existence of one or more of the following five 'facts'. In common parlance, these are mistakenly referred to as the 'grounds' for divorce:

---

**The Five Facts for Divorce**

Section 1(2) of the Matrimonial Causes Act 1973 requires the petitioner to prove to the court that:

'(a)  the respondent has committed adultery and the petitioner finds it intolerable to live with the respondent;

(b)  the respondent has behaved in such a way that the petitioner cannot reasonably be expected to live with the respondent;

(c)  the respondent has deserted the petitioner for a continuous period of at least two years immediately preceding the presentation of the petition;

(d)  the parties to the marriage have lived apart for a continuous period of at least two years immediately preceding the presentation of the petition . . . and the respondent consents to a decree being granted; or

(e)  the parties to the marriage have lived apart for a continuous period of at least five years immediately preceding the presentation of the petition.'

If a 'fact' is proved, the court must grant a decree nisi of divorce unless it is satisfied that the marriage has not irretrievably broken down (s.1(4)). The court must be satisfied that the marriage has irretrievably broken down, *and* that at least one of the above five facts is proved. This requirement has led to some rather unsatisfactory decisions, and the Law Commission when discussing reform of divorce (see above) considered it to be illogical. In *Richards* v. *Richards* [1972] 1 WLR 1073, for example, the petitioner satisfied the court that her marriage had irretrievably broken down, but she failed to satisfy the court that her mentally ill husband had behaved in such a way that she could not reasonably be expected to live with him. Similarly, in *Buffery* v. *Buffery* [1988] 2 FLR 365 the Court of Appeal was satisfied that the marriage had irretrievably broken down, but was not satisfied that unreasonable behaviour had been proved.

Each of the five facts will be considered in turn. Divorce procedure is dealt with below (at 7.7).

### (a)    Adultery (s.1(2)(a))

Adultery involves an act of voluntary heterosexual intercourse between two people who are not married to each other, but at least one of whom is married. For the purposes of a divorce, adultery is usually proved by the respondent acknowledging adultery on the Acknowledgment of Service form. Where there is no admission of adultery, proof of adultery is needed, for which the degree of proof has been held to be slightly higher than on the balance of probabilities (*Serio* v. *Serio* (1983) 4 FLR 756). The person with whom it is alleged the respondent committed adultery is called the 'corespondent', and he or she must be made a party to the divorce unless not named in the petition or the court otherwise directs (r.2.7(1) Family Proceedings Rules 1991).

In addition to proving adultery, the petitioner must also prove that he or she finds it intolerable to live with the respondent (s.1(2)(a)). This requirement was added to buttress the stability of marriage (a policy aim of the law), so that an act of adultery would be insufficient on its own to end a marriage. The Court of Appeal has held that, as adultery and intolerability are two separate and unrelated facts, the tolerability need not relate to the adultery (see *Cleary* v. *Cleary* [1974] 1 WLR 73, where a decree was granted even though it was the respondent's behaviour after the adultery, not the adultery itself, which had made it intolerable for the petitioner to live with the respondent). The test of intolerability is a subjective one, namely whether the particular petitioner finds it intolerable to live with the respondent, not whether a reasonable petitioner would so find it. In practice, the petitioner must simply answer the question 'Do you find it intolerable to live with the respondent?'

As part of the policy objective of divorce law to encourage reconciliation, a petition based on adultery cannot be heard if the parties have lived together for more than six months (in one period, or several periods aggregated) after the petitioner discovered the adultery (s.2(1)), but the period of living together is disregarded by the court when it is determining whether the petitioner finds it intolerable to live with the respondent (s.2(2)).

### (b)    Behaviour (s.1(2)(b))

The petitioner must prove that the respondent has behaved in such a way that the petitioner cannot reasonably be expected to live with the respondent. Although this fact is commonly referred to as 'unreasonable behaviour', this is a misnomer, because under s.1(2)(b) it is the effect of the respondent's behaviour on the petitioner which is relevant, not whether the respondent's behaviour is unreasonable. The test for establishing unreasonable behaviour is objective, as the court must establish whether the petitioner can reasonably be expected to live with the respondent, but it is also subjective in that the court must consider the effect of the respondent's behaviour on the particular petitioner. In *Ash* v. *Ash* [1972] Fam 135 Bagnall J said that the question to be asked was:

> '[C]an this petitioner, with his or her character and personality, with his or her faults and other attributes, good and bad, having regard to his or her behaviour during the marriage, reasonably be expected to live with this respondent?'

Bagnall J said, by way of example, that a violent or alcoholic petitioner could reasonably be expected to live with a respondent with similar attributes. In *Livingstone-Stallard* v. *Livingstone-Stallard* [1974] Fam 47 Dunn J adopted the following test:

> 'Would any right-thinking person come to the conclusion that this husband has behaved in such a way that this wife cannot reasonably be expected to live with him, taking into account the whole of the circumstances and the characters and personalities of the parties?'

This test was approved by the Court of Appeal in *O'Neill* v. *O'Neill* [1975] 1 WLR 1118, and endorsed by the Court of Appeal in *Buffery* v. *Buffery* [1988] 2 FLR 365.

In *Birch* v. *Birch* [1992] 1 FLR 564 the wife petitioned for divorce on the basis of her husband's unreasonable behaviour, claiming that his attitude to her was dogmatic, nationalistic and dictatorial. She said that she was sensitive and had taken a passive role during their 20-year marriage, and had put aside her own interests until the children had grown up. Her petition was dismissed, but the Court of Appeal allowed her appeal and granted a decree because the judge had used an objective test when the correct test was a subjective one.

Divorces are granted for a wide range of behaviour, including both acts and omissions. In *O'Neill* v. *O'Neill* (above), for example, the petitioner stated that her husband had a withdrawn personality, had doubted the paternity of their children, and had spent two years 'improving' the matrimonial home, which included mixing cement on the living-room floor and leaving the lavatory door off for about eight months. Financial irresponsibility can constitute unreasonable behaviour (see, for example, *Carter-Fea* v. *Carter-Fea* [1987] Fam Law 131), and so can violent or drunken behaviour (see, for example, *Ash* v. *Ash*, above).

Some behaviour, however, may be too trivial and a decree may be refused, as it was in *Buffery* v. *Buffery* (see above) where the wife alleged that her husband was insensitive, never took her out, and that they had nothing to talk about and nothing in common after their children had grown up and left home. Her petition was dismissed, as her husband's behaviour was found to be insufficient to satisfy the behaviour ground. An accumulation of trivial incidents may, however, constitute unreasonable behaviour as they did in *Livingstone-Stallard* v. *Livingstone-Stallard* (see above), where Dunn J held that the wife 'was subjected to a constant atmosphere of criticism, disapproval and boorish behaviour on the part of her husband'. However, as each case depends on its own facts, an accumulation of various minor matters will not necessarily result in a decree being granted. In *Butterworth* v. *Butterworth* [1997] 2 FLR 336, for example, the decree of divorce was set aside by the Court of Appeal as the petition was severely defective. The husband had denied the wife's allegations that he was a violent, possessive, sexually demanding and jealous alcoholic who had stopped her going to church. The Court of Appeal stressed that English divorce law still gave the respondent the right to oppose a divorce, and to have the allegations in the petition properly proved. The Court of Appeal held that the court had not applied the correct test for unreasonable behaviour, or anything like it.

*What if the Behaviour is not the Respondent's Fault?*    Sometimes the court will have to decide whether to grant a divorce where the behaviour is not the respondent's fault, for example, where the respondent is mentally or physically ill. Whether a divorce will be granted depends on the circumstances of the case, and, although the court will be cognisant of the fact that marriage entails a commitment which includes caring for a sick spouse, it is likely to be sympathetic to the plight of a petitioner and the fact that illness can place severe strains on a marriage. A divorce may therefore be granted even though a respondent is not responsible for his or her own 'behaviour'. Thus, in *Katz* v. *Katz* [1972] 1 WLR 955 the wife succeeded in obtaining a decree where her husband suffered from manic-depression. In *Thurlow* v. *Thurlow* [1976] Fam 32 the wife, an epileptic, suffered from a severe neurological disorder. She was bed-ridden and bad-tempered, threw objects at her husband and wandered the streets causing him distress. He worked full-time and found it difficult to care for her, and the stress affected his health. Rees J granted a decree, stating that:

> 'If the behaviour stems from misfortune such as the onset of mental illness or from disease of the body or from accidental physical injury the court would take full account of all the obligations of the married state. These would include the normal duty to accept and to share the burdens imposed upon the family as a result of the mental and physical ill-health of one member. It would also consider the capacity of the petitioner to withstand the stresses imposed by the behaviour, the steps taken to cope with it, the length of time during which the petitioner had been called upon to bear it, and the actual or potential effect upon his or her health.'

*Reconciliation Provisions*    As with the other four facts, certain periods of time are ignored in order to encourage reconciliation and promote the policy aim of supporting the institution of marriage. Thus, spouses are permitted to live together for up to six months (in one period or several aggregated) after the last instance of behaviour alleged, without losing the right to petition for divorce; and the court must ignore this period when determining whether the petitioner can reasonably be expected to live with the respondent (s.2(3)). If the spouses live together for more than six months after the last proven instance of behaviour, the court can, however, take that into account when determining what is reasonable.

## (c)    Desertion (s.1(2)(c))

The respondent must have deserted the petitioner for a continuous period of at least two years immediately preceding the presentation of the petition. Divorces based on desertion are rare. To divorce on the basis of desertion, there must be: factual separation; an intention by the respondent to desert; no consent by the petitioner to the desertion; and no just cause to desert.

Constructive desertion is possible, in other words where a spouse's behaviour is so bad that the other spouse is forced to leave the home. Desertion is also possible even if the parties are living under the same roof. To encourage reconciliation, a period of up to six-months' resumed cohabitation does not prevent the desertion being continuous (s.2(5)).

### (d)   Two-Years' Separation with Consent to the Divorce (s.1(2)(d))

The parties must have lived apart for a continuous period of at least two years immediately preceding the presentation of the petition, and the respondent must consent to the decree being granted. The respondent must have the capacity to consent and must be given such information as will enable him or her to understand the effect of a decree being granted (s.2(7)). The respondent can notify the court of his or her consent by filing a notice to that effect signed by the respondent personally, but a respondent normally signifies his or her consent on the Acknowledgement of Service form signed by the respondent personally (and his or her solicitor, if any), and this is treated as notice of consent. Consent may be withdrawn at any time before decree nisi, whereupon the proceedings must be stayed. At any time before decree absolute the respondent can apply to have the decree nisi rescinded if the petitioner has misled the respondent about any matter which the respondent took into account in deciding whether to give consent (s.10(1)).

The respondent may be able to postpone decree absolute (see 7.5, below).

*Parties Must Live in Separate Households*   The parties will not be treated as separated if they are living in the same household (s.2(6)). Whether they live in separate households is a question of fact. However, separation is possible even if the parties are living under the same roof – as 'household' is not the same as 'house'. In *Fuller* v. *Fuller* [1973] 1 WLR 730, for example, a decree was granted where the husband lived as a lodger with his wife and her new male friend. In *Mouncer* v. *Mouncer* [1972] 1 WLR 321, on the other hand, a decree was refused because they were not living in separate households – although they slept in separate bedrooms, they ate their meals with the children and shared household chores. Each case depends on its facts.

*Reconciliation Provisions*   When calculating the period of separation, no account is taken of a period of up to six months (in one period or several aggregated) during which the parties resumed living together, but there must still be an aggregated period of actual separation for at least two years (s.2(5)). If the period of resumed cohabitation is more than six months, the two-year period of separation starts to run again.

### (e)   Five-Years' Separation (s.1(2)(e))

The parties must have lived apart for a continuous period of at least five years immediately preceding the presentation of the petition. The petitioner must establish factual separation, but there can be separation even though the spouses live under the same roof. To protect the respondent, the court can delay decree absolute or refuse decree nisi (see below). A reconciliation period of up to six months can be ignored, provided the parties have separated for an aggregated period of at least five years, but, if the reconciliation is for more than six months, then the five-year period begins to run again (s.2(5)). In practice, few spouses petition for divorce on this fact because most petitioners do not wish to wait for five years to obtain a divorce.

## 7.5 Protection for Respondents

Sections 10 and 5 of the Matrimonial Causes Act 1973 provide protection for 'innocent' respondents – those being divorced on the basis of two- or five-years' separation, and who have therefore committed no matrimonial offence.

### (a) Section 10 Matrimonial Causes Act 1973

Under s.10(2) a respondent to a divorce based on two- or five-years' separation can ask the court to consider whether his or her financial situation after divorce will be satisfactory. If such an application is made, the court may refuse to grant a decree absolute unless it is satisfied: that the petitioner should not be required to make financial provision for the respondent; or that the provision made by the petitioner is reasonable and fair, or the best that can be made in the circumstances (s.10(3)). The court may, however, grant a decree absolute in any event if it is desirable to do so without delay, and it has obtained a satisfactory undertaking from the petitioner that he or she will make such financial provision as the court may approve (s.10(4)).

Few applications are made under s.10, but an application may be useful as a tactical manoeuvre to put pressure on a petitioner to sort out the parties' financial position, particularly where there may be a problem enforcing an ancillary relief order. In *Garcia* v. *Garcia* [1992] 1 FLR 256, for example, an application under s.10 was used to enforce maintenance payments for a child where the petitioner had failed to keep up with those payments under a Spanish separation agreement. The Court of Appeal held that the protection afforded to respondents under s.10 was not confined to future financial provision, but could be used to remedy past financial injustice and unfulfilled past obligations, as the duty of the court in a s.10 application was to consider all the circumstances of the case (s.10(3)).

Section 10 applications were sometimes used to provide protection for respondents (particularly wives) who would be losing pension entitlements as a result of divorce (see, for example, *Griffiths* v. *Dawson & Co* [1993] 2 FLR 315 and *Jackson* v. *Jackson* [1993] 2 FLR 848), but, as the pension position on divorce has been improved, there is no longer any need to use s.10 for this purpose (see 8.8).

### (b) Section 5 Matrimonial Causes Act 1973

Under s.5 a respondent to a divorce based on five-years' separation has a complete defence to divorce. The aim of s.5 is to safeguard the position of 'innocent' spouses who do not wish to be divorced. In practice it is rarely invoked, and even if it is, rarely succeeds. Under s.5, the court has the power to rescind a decree nisi if the respondent proves that he or she will suffer grave financial or other hardship if the divorce is granted; and that it would be wrong in all the circumstances to grant the divorce. The alleged hardship must arise as a result of the dissolution of the marriage, not from the fact of marriage breakdown or separation. Hardship can include the loss of the chance of acquiring a benefit which the respondent might acquire if the marriage were not dissolved (s.5(3)). Such a loss might include, for example, loss of a right to succeed under the other spouse's will or intestacy. Most of the cases brought under s.5 have been in relation to pension rights (see, for example, *Le Marchant* v. *Le Marchant* [1977] 1 WLR 559; *Mathias* v. *Mathias*

[1972] Fam 287; and *Archer* v. *Archer* [1999] 1 FLR 327), but because of changes to the law in respect of pensions on divorce (see 8.8) this is no longer necessary. Section 5 refers not just to financial hardship, but to 'other hardship', but defences based on 'other hardship' are extremely rare. 'Other hardship' could include religious or social hardship, for example that the respondent will suffer ostracism in the community because of social or religious attitudes to divorce (see, for example, *Banik* v. *Banik* [1973] 1 WLR 860 and *Rukat* v. *Rukat* [1975] Fam 63).

Defences under s.5 are extremely rare, and even rarer now that pension provision on divorce has been improved. Even where the defence has been pleaded, they have rarely been successful as financial loss to the respondent can usually be compensated for in other ways (for example, by State benefits or a proposal put forward by the petitioner). In *K* v. *K (Financial Relief: Widow's Pension)* [1997] 1 FLR 35, for example, the High Court adjourned proceedings on an application under s.5 by the wife, who would lose her widow's pension on divorce, in order to allow her husband to make a reasonable financial proposal. In most cases the court will consider it best to end the marriage, despite the possibility of the respondent suffering hardship.

## 7.6 Protection for Children

Where there are children of the family aged under 16, or over 16 which the court directs should be included (for instance, because of disability), the court must consider the proposed future arrangements for the children (s.41 Matrimonial Causes Act 1973) (see 12.3).

## 7.7 Divorce Procedure

Divorce procedure differs according to whether a divorce is undefended or defended. In practice, virtually all divorces are undefended – because of the expense and futility of defending a divorce. The rules of procedure are laid down in the Family Proceedings Rules (FPR) 1991.

### (a) Undefended Divorce

An undefended divorce is obtained by way of what is essentially a paper exercise. There is usually no need for the parties, or their legal representatives (if any), to attend court.

*The Divorce Petition* The petition is the central document in divorce proceedings, as it informs the respondent and the court of the basis on which the petitioner is seeking a decree of divorce and of the orders that he or she will be seeking as part of the divorce.

To commence divorce proceedings, the petitioner (the spouse seeking the divorce) must present a divorce petition to a divorce county court (in London, the Divorce Registry) alleging that the marriage has irretrievably broken down and alleging at least one of the five facts (see p.143, above). The petition cannot be presented to the court before one year has expired from the date of the marriage (s.3(1)). This is a strict rule (see *Butler* v. *Butler* [1990] FLR 114). However, anything that happened during that one-year period (such as evidence of unreasonable behaviour or adultery) can be used as evidence in the divorce proceedings (s.3(2)).

The petition must contain specified information (see r.2.3 FPR 1991), for example, the names and addresses of the parties and any children under 16 or in full-time education, the occupations of the parties and details of the marriage. The petition must also contain a statement that the marriage has irretrievably broken down, the fact or facts relied on and brief particulars of such individual fact or facts. It must conclude with a prayer for dissolution of the marriage, any claim for costs, and a prayer setting out any ancillary relief claimed (such as property and/or financial orders) and any child support maintenance claimed from the Child Support Agency. The petition must give the names and addresses of the persons who are to be served with the petition as well as the petitioner's address for service (or the solicitor's address, if the petitioner has a solicitor). Where the petition alleges that the respondent has committed adultery, the person with whom the adultery is alleged to have been committed must be made a corespondent, unless that person is not named in the petition or the court otherwise directs (r.2.7(1) FPR 1991).

The petition is sent to the court with the following documents: the marriage certificate; the Statement of Arrangements for the Children (Form M4); certified copies of any court orders; and any certificate in respect of public funding. If a solicitor is acting in the divorce proceedings, the solicitor must also file with the court a reconciliation certificate (Form M3) stating whether or not he has discussed with the petitioner the possibility of a reconciliation and has given details of persons qualified to help to effect a reconciliation (r.2.6(3) FPR 1991). A solicitor is not obliged to discuss reconciliation with the client (see s.6(1) Matrimonial Causes Act 1973). A court fee must be paid when the petition is filed.

*After the Petition is Filed at Court*   When the petition and other documents are received by the court, the petition is filed at court and given a number. Once filed at court, a copy of the petition is served by the court on the respondent (and any corespondent). This is accompanied by forms known as: Notice of Proceedings (Form M5) (explaining the effect of the petition and informing the respondent of the procedure involved); and an Acknowledgement of Service (Form M6).

The Acknowledgment of Service is a straightforward question-and- answer form which the respondent (or his or her solicitor) must complete, sign and return to the court within seven days of receiving the divorce papers, failing which a further copy of the petition may be served upon him personally and a sworn written statement filed to prove such service. In the Acknowledgement of Service the respondent must state whether the petition has been received, whether he or she intends to defend the divorce, whether consent to the divorce is given if sought on the basis of two-years' separation with consent, and also whether he or she intends to apply for ancillary relief and/or for orders in respect of the children. The Acknowledgement of Service may be signed by either the respondent or his solicitor, save that, where the fact relied upon is two-years' separation with consent of the respondent and the respondent does in fact consent, then the respondent must sign in person.

Once the Acknowledgement of Service has been returned to the court and the respondent does not wish to defend, the petitioner (or petitioner's solicitor) must file a written request for 'directions for trial' together with a written statement and questionnaire in specified form, sworn by the petitioner providing evidence of the fact(s) relied on. The district judge gives 'directions for trial' by entering the cause in the special procedure list and thereafter considers the evidence filed by the petitioner for procedural regularity and to establish that there is sufficient evidence to prove the fact alleged. The district judge may request further information or evidence, if needed. If he is satisfied that the fact is proved and that the marriage has irretrievably broken down, he files a certificate to that effect and a date, time and place are fixed for the judge to pronounce decree nisi. Both parties receive a certificate and notice of the date and place for the pronouncement of decree nisi by the judge or district judge in open court, which neither the parties nor their legal representatives need attend. The process of pronouncement is a mere formality. The decrees are listed together in batches and collectively read out by the clerk of the court before the judge or district judge (or by the judge or district judge) who will give his or her consent orally or by nodding.

If the district judge is not satisfied that the case for divorce is made out, he can ask the petitioner to file further evidence or he can remove the case from the special procedure list and require that it be heard before the judge.

*Decree Nisi Followed by Decree Absolute*    The decree nisi of divorce does not terminate the marriage. It is terminated only on the grant of the decree absolute, which is automatically granted on the application of the petitioner, who can apply for it six weeks or more after decree nisi by lodging a notice on Form M8. A fee must be paid. If the petitioner fails to apply for the decree absolute, the respondent may apply at any time after three months have elapsed from the earliest date on which the petitioner could apply for it (s.9(2)). However, the court cannot grant the respondent a decree absolute without a hearing and adjudication by a judge or district judge, after giving at least four-days' notice of the hearing to the petitioner (r.2.50 FPR 1991). These rules are strict. If a decree absolute is obtained in breach of the rules, the divorce is void (see *Dennis* v. *Dennis* [2000] 2 FLR 231).

A decree nisi may be rescinded by the court, but only if both parties to the marriage who are of sound mind consent to this (and with sound advice, where appropriate) (Singer J in *S* v. *S (Rescission of Decree Nisi: Pension Sharing Provision)* [2002] 1 FLR 457, where both parties wished to rescind the decree nisi in order to be subject to the new pension law on divorce).

*Purpose of Gap Between Decree Nisi and Decree Absolute*    The purpose of this gap is to enable a respondent to appeal, and the Queen's Proctor and other persons to intervene to show just cause why a decree should not be made absolute (s.8 Matrimonial Causes Act 1973). Intervention by the Queen's Proctor was much more of a possibility under the old divorce law, where, if the parties were found to have colluded, the decree absolute would be refused. Such intervention is now rare. However, the Queen's Proctor intervened in *Bhaijii* v. *Chauhan (Queen's Proctor Intervening)* [2003] 2 FLR 485 where bogus allegations of behaviour had been used to secure divorces in cases where marriages had been entered into in order to circumvent immigration rules. The petitioners in five divorces had presented a false case and the respondents had connived at it. The Queen's Proctor opposed the grant of a decree of divorce in each case. (See also *Moynihan* v. *Moynihan (Nos. 1 and 2)* [1997] 1 FLR 59.)

*Children*    If there are children, the divorce cannot be made absolute until the district judge has considered whether the court should exercise any of its powers under s.41 Matrimonial Causes Act 1973 (see 12.3). Where a divorce is sought on the basis of two- or five-years' separation, a decree absolute may be refused where a respondent has not been satisfactorily financially provided for by the petitioner (see 7.5, above).

### (b) Defended Divorce

Defended divorce proceedings begin in the same way as an undefended divorce, but the respondent in the Acknowledgement of Service indicates an intention to defend. Notice of an intention to defend must be given within seven days from service of the petition, inclusive of the day of service (r.10 FPR 1991). Such an indication does not of itself cause the proceedings to become defended, but must be followed by the filing of an answer within 21 days after the expiry of the time-limit for giving notice of the intention to defend (that is, within 28 days of service of the petition). There is then exchange of pleadings by counsel and the hearing takes place in open court with oral evidence being given and cross-examination of both parties. (For a rare case involving a defended divorce, see *Hadjimilitis (Tsavliris)* v. *Tsavliris (Divorce: Irretrievable Breakdown)* [2003] 1 FLR 81.)

## 7.8 Effects of Divorce

Once a decree absolute has been granted, the marriage is dissolved and each party is free to remarry. A decree absolute has other legal consequences. Financial provision and property adjustment orders made under Part II of the Matrimonial Causes Act 1973 in favour of the parties to the marriage can take effect, and orders for settlement or variation of a settlement can take effect in respect of any child of the family. All other orders for children take effect as soon as they are made. Divorce also has an effect on a will made by either party to the marriage. Social security and pension rights and taxation are affected, and both parties lose rights under certain matrimonial legislation, in particular rights of occupation of the home ('home rights'). However, as far as children are concerned, each parent retains parental responsibility on divorce and there is an obligation to provide children with financial support.

## 7.9 Recognition of an Overseas Divorce

Part II of the Family Law Act 1986 lays down rules for the recognition in the UK of divorces (and annulments and separations) obtained overseas. The Act makes a distinction between divorces obtained in judicial or other proceedings and those otherwise obtained. Recognition is much broader for divorces obtained in proceedings. An overseas divorce granted in proceedings is recognised in the UK if it is effective under the law of the country where it was obtained, and at the commencement of those proceedings either party was habitually resident or domiciled in that country or was a national of that country (s.46(1)). An overseas divorce obtained otherwise than in proceedings is recognised in the UK if it is effective in the country where it was obtained and at the date it was obtained one or both parties were domiciled there, or one party was domiciled there and the other party was domiciled in a country which recognised the divorce, and in any case neither party was habitually resident in the UK for one year immediately preceding the divorce (s.46(2)) (see, for example, *Wicken* v. *Wicken* [1999] Fam 224, [1999] 1 FLR 293 where Holman J held that a 'divorce letter' was effective under Gambian law to dissolve the marriage and could be recognised as a divorce).

The English courts have a discretion to refuse recognition of an overseas divorce whether or not it was obtained in proceedings. Thus, for example, it may under s.51(3) refuse to recognise an overseas divorce if reasonable steps have not been taken for giving notice of the proceeding to a party to the marriage (see *Duhur-Johnson* v. *Duhur-Johnson (Attorney-General Intervening)* [2005] 2 FLR 1042 where a Nigerian divorce was refused recognition as a valid overseas divorce because the husband had not taken reasonable steps to give notice of the divorce proceedings to his wife).

An overseas divorce may not be recognised in England and Wales where recognition would be manifestly contrary to public policy (s.52). In *Eroglu* v. *Eroglu* [1994] 2 FLR 287 the wife, who wished to divorce in England, argued that her Turkish divorce should not be recognised in England and Wales on the basis of public policy, since it had been obtained by fraud (they had divorced in Turkey so that her husband could avoid Turkish national service). However, the English court held that the Turkish divorce was valid and dismissed the English petition. Thorpe LJ said that it is difficult to argue that a divorce should not be recognised on public policy grounds. (See also *D* v. *D (Recognition of Foreign Divorce)* [1994] 1 FLR 38.) In *H* v. *H (The Queen's Proctor Intervening)(Validity of Japanese Divorce)* [2006] EWHC 2989 (Fam), [2007] 1 FLR 1318 a Japanese divorce by agreement (a Kyogi rikon) was recognised as a valid divorce 'obtained by means of proceedings' for the purposes of s.46(1) of the 1986 Act. There was no reason to refuse recognition on the grounds of public policy.

A foreign divorce obtained other than in proceedings may be refused recognition, for example, where no document of divorce exists, or where it would be manifestly contrary to public policy. Recognition may also be refused where a foreign divorce is irreconcilable with a previous decision about the subsistence or validity of the marriage or there was no subsisting marriage under UK law.

*Recognition of Divorces Within the EU*   Special rules apply to the recognition of divorces with the European Union. Council Regulation (EC) (No. 2201/2003) Concerning Jurisdiction and the Recognition and Enforcement of Judgments in Matrimonial Matters and in Matters of Parental Responsibility (Brussels II Revised) applies (see, for example, *D* v. *D (Nature of Recognition of Overseas Divorce)* [2005] EWHC 3342 (Fam), [2006] 2 FLR 825 where Bodey J made a declaration that the Greek divorce was recognised in England and Wales under Brussels II, which had the effect of dissolving the parties' marital status).

*Is a Talaq a Valid Overseas Divorce?*   A talaq is a unilateral Islamic divorce whereby the husband can divorce his wife by merely uttering the words 'I divorce you' three times without being in the presence of another person and without the wife's consent. The validity of a talaq was considered in the following case:

▶ *Sulaiman* v. *Juffali* [2002] 1 FLR 479

A Muslim couple had married according to Sharia law in Saudi Arabia where they were domiciled, but they lived together as husband and wife in London. The wife petitioned for divorce, but the next day the husband pronounced a talaq in England which was then registered in the Sharia court in Saudi Arabia. The wife applied for a summary determination as to whether the talaq (which was valid in Saudi Arabia, their place of domicile) was valid in the UK. The High Court in England held that the talaq did not dissolve the marriage, as divorces obtained in the UK other than by proceedings in a civil court were not recognised. The talaq was held not to be an overseas divorce within the meaning of s.45(1) Family Law Act 1986, as it had not been obtained in Saudi Arabia even though it was accepted that it complied with all the formalities required by Sharia law in Saudi Arabia. The talaq had clearly been obtained in England other than in a court, and thus fell foul of the Family Law Act 1986.

*Transnational Divorces*   Some divorces are 'transnational', in that they take place in two different countries. The Jewish 'get' and the Muslim talaq (above) are examples. The English courts have refused to recognise transnational divorces even though this creates a 'limping marriage' (one which is recognised as valid in one country but not in another). Thus, in *R* v. *Secretary of State for the Home Department ex parte Ghulum Fatima* [1986] AC 527 the House of Lords refused to recognise a Muslim talaq. However, the courts' power to recognise or fail to recognise a foreign divorce, even a talaq, is discretionary, and in *El Fadl* v. *El Fadl* [2000] 1 FLR 175 a talaq divorce registered with the Sharia court in Lebanon was recognised by the English High Court, and the wife's petition for an English divorce dismissed. Recognition of the talaq was not held to be contrary to public policy, even though such a divorce might offend English sensibilities. In *Berkovits* v. *Grinberg (Attorney-General Intervening)* [1995] Fam 142 the court, applying *Fatima* (above), refused to recognise a Jewish 'get' written by the husband in London but delivered to his wife in Israel.

## 7.10   Other Decrees

Under Part I of the Matrimonial Causes Act 1973 the court has jurisdiction to grant decrees of nullity (see Chapter 2), decrees of judicial separation and decrees of presumption of death.

### (a)   Decree of Judicial Separation

Under s.17 Matrimonial Causes Act 1973 divorce county courts and the High Court can grant a decree of judicial separation provided a petitioner can prove one of the five facts in s.1(2) (adultery, unreasonable behaviour, etc, see 7.4, above). There is no need to prove irretrievable breakdown of marriage. The effect of a decree is to relieve the petitioner of the obligation to continue living with the respondent (s.18(1)), but the spouses are not obliged to separate. Where a decree of judicial separation is in force and separation is continuing, the surviving spouse is not entitled to succeed to the deceased spouse's property on his or her intestacy, but judicial separation does not affect a will (s.18(2)). On the grant of a decree, the court has jurisdiction to make orders for ancillary relief under Part II of the Matrimonial Causes Act 1973 (see Chapter 8). Divorce is not precluded by a previous judicial separation and the divorce court can treat the decree of judicial separation as proof of one or more of the five facts alleged for divorce (s.4). Decrees are rarely sought, but a decree may be useful for a spouse who does not wish to divorce (such as for religious reasons) or who cannot divorce because one year of marriage has not elapsed. The procedure is virtually the same as that for seeking a decree of divorce (see 7.7, above).

(b)    Decree of Presumption of Death

Where a spouse is missing and thought to be dead, the other spouse can petition for a decree of presumption of death and dissolution of marriage under s.19 Matrimonial Causes Act 1973. If a decree is granted, the petitioner can contract a valid new marriage, which remains valid, even if the spouse who is presumed dead subsequently reappears. The court will grant a decree if it is satisfied that reasonable grounds exist for supposing the petitioner's spouse is dead. A spouse is presumed dead if he or she has not been seen for a continuous period of at least seven years. The petitioner must, however, have made reasonable enquiries to establish whether the other spouse is alive.

## 7.11    The Future of Divorce

▶ **Stephen Cretney,** *Family Law in the Twentieth Century,* **2003, p.391:**

'English divorce law is in a state of confusion. The theory of the law remains that divorce is a matter in which the State has a vital interest, and that it is only allowed if the marriage can be demonstrated to have irretrievably broken down. But the practical reality is very different: divorce is readily and quickly available if both parties agree, and even if one of them is reluctant he or she will, faced with a divorce petition, almost always accept the inevitable: there is no point in denying that the marriage has broken down if one party firmly asserts it has.'

It is clear from the more than decade-long attempt to reform the law that finding a coherent and workable new divorce law is a difficult task. Despite the Government's decision not to implement the reforms in Part II of the Family Law Act 1996, it is still recognised by judges and academics that the current law is unsatisfactory, confusing and in need of reform – although there seems to be no pressure for reform from the public in general, and in particular from those who have experienced the divorce process.

The Rt Hon Dame Elizabeth Butler-Sloss, at her inaugural press conference on becoming President of the Family Division (she has now retired), described the current practice of obtaining a divorce on the ground of unreasonable behaviour as a 'hypocritical charade' and stressed the need for the introduction of a truly no-fault divorce. In July 2001, the Lord Chancellor's Advisory Board on Family Law in its final report regretted the missed opportunity to reform divorce, and urged that serious consideration be given to replacing the current adversarial, partly fault-based divorce regime. It said that the serious defects in the current law identified by the Law Commission still remained. In particular, allegations of adultery and unreasonable behaviour caused unnecessary conflict between the parties, and their distress and anger impacted on children.

The grounds for divorce are also inconsistent with the settlement culture which exists in respect of ancillary relief proceedings and arrangements for children on divorce. The current grounds for divorce are not conducive to agreement. It is difficult to disagree with Kay (2004) who states:

'Over two-thirds of divorces granted in England and Wales in 2002 were based on facts that clearly have connotations of blame and guilt, and where proceedings can be commenced in haste, without thought for the consequences of the breakdown and the legal ending of marriage. Taken as a whole, these statistics make a compelling case for reform.'

Kay also points out that, although divorce law is acknowledged to be unsatisfactory, it has nevertheless been replicated in virtually the same form for civil partners under the Civil Partnership Act 2004.

The possibility of introducing a purely administrative divorce has been considered by Cretney, who has questioned whether the proposed reforms under the Family Law Act 1996 went far enough, and whether the law should move away from judicial divorce completely. He asked ([2002] Fam Law 900, at 903):

'Should we not accept that the routine processing of marriage breakdown is no longer a judicial function and that it should accordingly be removed altogether from the courts and the judicial system, leaving them with more time to deal with the problems that do require their expertise and procedures? If we believe that respect for the law and the legal system is important, and that the 1996 reforms would have made the law even more complex and difficult to understand, should we not begin to ask whether there is not a simpler and better alternative?'

Booth ([2004] Fam Law 617), referring to the fact that Scotland proposed to change its divorce law to reduce the time periods required to prove separation (from one year to two with consent, and from five years to two without consent) and that France had announced changes to its divorce law, said that it was perhaps time to look again at reforming divorce law in England and Wales, and be a bit more radical and think about introducing divorce on demand.

With the increasing emphasis on mediation, conciliation and settlement, it might also be time to think again about the possibility of introducing divorce by mutual consent, whereby a divorce can be granted on the application of both parties to a marriage where they are in agreement that their marriage has irretrievably broken down. This option was dismissed rather cursorily by the Law Commission in 1988 in its Discussion Paper, *Facing the Future: A Discussion Paper on the Ground for Divorce* (Law Com No. 170), on the basis that it would undermine the institution of marriage.

At the present time there are no proposals to reform divorce law. However, Resolution (an organisation of family law solicitors who favour conciliatory approaches to solving family disputes) has been campaigning for many years for no-fault divorce to be introduced – because the current law of divorce does not sit well with the non-confrontational approach adopted and promoted in the rest of the family justice system. It has called for reform to be put back on the agenda (see [2007] Fam Law 1053). Whether it will be, remains to be seen.

## Summary

1 Divorce is common. There are about 150,000 divorces a year in England and Wales.

2 Legislative divorce was introduced into England and Wales by the Matrimonial Causes Act 1857. The sole ground for divorce was adultery.

3 The Matrimonial Causes Act 1937 extended the grounds for divorce to include not just adultery but cruelty, three-years' desertion and incurable insanity. It also introduced a bar on marriage in the first three years of marriage.

4 The Divorce Reform Act 1969 introduced new grounds for divorce: irretrievable breakdown of marriage, plus proof of one or more of the following: adultery (plus intolerability); unreasonable

## Summary cont'd

behaviour; two-years' desertion; two-years' separation with consent to the divorce; and five-years' separation. These provisions were re-enacted in Part I of the Matrimonial Causes Act 1973 and remain the law today.

5   All divorces were once heard in open court, but in the 1970s the special procedure (an administrative form of divorce) was introduced for all undefended divorces.

6   As a result of dissatisfaction with the current law, Part II of the Family Law Act 1996 was enacted introducing a new form of divorce – 'divorce over a period of time'. However, the reforms were not implemented because of Government concerns that the changes might not work in practice and might not achieve their stated objectives.

7   The current law of divorce is laid down in Part I of the Matrimonial Causes Act 1973.

8   There is one ground for divorce: irretrievable breakdown of marriage (s.1(1)), which is established on proof of one or more of the following five facts (s.1(2)): (a) adultery; (b) unreasonable behaviour; (c) desertion for a period of at least two years; (d) two-years' separation with consent to the divorce; and (e) five-years' separation. There must be both proof of irretrievable breakdown and proof of at least one fact.

9   Divorce is not possible within the first year of marriage (s.3(1)).

10  Under s.10 a respondent to a two-year or five-year separation divorce can ask the court to delay decree absolute until it is satisfied about financial arrangements made by the petitioner for the respondent.

11  Section 5 provides a complete defence to divorce for a respondent to a petition brought on the basis of five-years' separation, if the respondent can prove that the dissolution of the marriage will cause him or her grave financial or other hardship, and it would be wrong to grant the divorce.

12  Undefended divorces are dealt with under what is an essentially administrative procedure. It is commenced by the petitioner presenting a divorce petition to a divorce county court (or the Principal Registry in London). There is usually no need to attend court. The other party is called the 'respondent'. Divorce involves a two-stage process: decree nisi followed by decree absolute. Only after decree absolute is the marriage terminated. Defended divorces, which are extremely rare, are heard in open court.

13  Part II of the Family Law Act 1986 lays down rules for the recognition in the UK of divorces obtained overseas. Overseas divorces are more likely to be recognised if they were obtained in court proceedings.

14  Under s.17 Matrimonial Causes Act 1973 the court has jurisdiction to grant a decree of judicial separation if one of the five facts in s.1(2) is proved. Under s.19 it has jurisdiction to grant a decree of presumption of death.

15  Although it is generally agreed that divorce law is unsatisfactory, there is uncertainty as to what form any changes should take. At the time of writing (2008) there are no proposals to reform the law.

## Further Reading and References

Booth, 'Divorce' [2004] Fam Law 617.

Cretney, 'The Divorce White Paper – some reflections' [1995] Fam Law 302.

Cretney, 'Marriage, divorce and the courts' [2002] Fam Law 900.

**Further reading cont'd**

Day Sclater and Piper (eds.), *Undercurrents of Divorce*, 1999, Dartmouth.

Eekelaar, 'Family law – keeping us "on message" ' [1999] CFLQ 387.

Freeman (ed.), *Divorce – Where Next?*, 1996, Dartmouth.

Freeman, 'Divorce gospel style' [1997] Fam Law 413.

Hasson, 'Setting a standard or reflecting reality? The "role" of divorce law, and the case of the Family Law Act 1996' [2003] IJLP&F 338.

Kay, 'Whose divorce is it anyway? – the human rights aspect' [2004] Fam Law 892.

Reece, *Divorcing Responsibility*, 2003, Jordans.

Thorpe, Rt Hon Lord Justice and Clark (eds.), *No Fault or Flaw: The Future of the Family Law Act 1996*, 2000, Jordans.

# Chapter 8
## Finance and Property on Divorce

## 8.1 Introduction

On marriage breakdown it will usually be necessary for the divorcing couple to distribute and reallocate their property and financial assets, whether it be the family home, a pension, the car, investments or other assets. Most couples will sort out matters themselves, but some will end up taking their case to court.

The distribution of finance and property on divorce by the court is referred to as 'ancillary relief' – because the relief is ancillary to the petition for divorce (or nullity or judicial separation). Obtaining a divorce and sorting out ancillary matters involve separate court proceedings. A decree of divorce can be obtained in a short time, a matter of weeks, but disputes about property and finance take much longer to sort out.

### A Settlement Culture

Despite the impression given by the number of reported cases, most couples do not litigate about property and finance but reach agreement with or without the assistance of a solicitor and/or mediator. If legal advice is sought, solicitors adopt a conciliatory approach. Resolution (an organisation of family law solicitors) encourages solicitors to adopt a conciliatory approach in order to reduce the cost, unpredictability and trauma of having to go to court. It has a *Code of Practice* which is based on encouraging settlement. Solicitors who deal with divorce matters are required to follow The Law Society's *Family Law Protocol*, a set of guidelines which aim to make the process less confrontational. Solicitors are required to adopt conciliatory approaches and to encourage the parties to put the interests of their children first. They must explore the possibility of using mediation to settle disputes. In addition to mediation and conciliatory approaches, settlement is facilitated in other ways. Thus the parties can enter into a pre-marital or post-marital agreement, and the court can make consent orders.

Despite the emphasis on settlement, however, spouses are not completely free to make their own arrangements, as the court has the power to scrutinise any agreement, and, if necessary, overturn it. Furthermore, ordinary contractual principles do not apply to agreements to compromise an ancillary relief application; the divorce court has a discretion to determine whether agreement has been reached (see *Xydhias* v. *Xydhias* [1999] 1 FLR 683). In ancillary relief proceedings the court exercises its own discretionary review of all the circumstances; and spouses are not permitted to agree to oust the jurisdiction of the divorce court.

Over the years there has been a gradual move towards a greater recognition of private agreement, and less State intervention in the divorce process. Not only is it easier to obtain a divorce than it once was, but there has been an increasing emphasis on mediation, and a greater willingness on the part of the courts to accept pre- and post-marital agreements. However, despite a shift towards private agreement, Cretney says ([2003] Fam Law 399, at 403–405) that the 'family justice system still seems reluctant to accept that it should shed its "paternal" role in purporting to supervise or assess the arrangements a married couple makes when they have concluded that their relationship has broken down'. He says that it is 'far from clear what purpose (save, perhaps, a symbolic one)' is served by this supervision and assessment, and he argues that '[t]he more the courts distance themselves from unnecessary intervention into family life the better'.

Despite the emphasis on settlement, however, some couples still manage to spend vast sums of money on legal costs, particularly where there are substantial assets to fight over (see, for example, *F* v. *F (Ancillary Relief: Substantial Assets)* [1995] 2 FLR 45 where the wife's costs were £733,521 and the husband's £777,182; and *White* v. *White* [2000] 2 FLR 981 where the parties' costs in the House of Lords alone exceeded £500,000). In *Moore* v. *Moore* [2007] EWCA Civ 361, [2007] 2 FLR 339 the parties spent £1.5 million on legal fees primarily to decide whether the English or Spanish courts would hear their ancillary relief application – even though the parties had agreed that the relevant law was English law. Judges now have greater powers, however, to control the proceedings with the aim of reducing costs and encouraging the parties to reach agreement.

*A Wide Range of Different Family Situations*   The courts exercise their discretion over a wide spectrum of family life. In *Dart* v. *Dart* [1996] 2 FLR 286, Butler-Sloss LJ said that the Matrimonial Causes Act 1973 'provides the jurisdiction for all applications for ancillary relief from the poverty-stricken to the multi-millionaire'. If the parties are wealthy, orders in respect of vast sums of money may be made. At the opposite end of the spectrum, on the other hand, the court may have to consider finance and property issues in the context of State benefits and local authority housing. In low-income cases 'the assessment of the needs of the parties will lean heavily in favour of the children and the parent with whom they live' (Butler-Sloss LJ in *Dart* v. *Dart*). In *B* v. *B (Financial Provision: Welfare of Child and Conduct)* [2001] EWCA Civ 2308, [2002] 1 FLR 555, for example, the parties' sole asset of £124,000, which represented the proceeds of sale of the matrimonial home, was ordered to be transferred to the wife because of the need to rehouse her and the child.

*Judicial Discretion*   The system governing disputes about matrimonial assets on divorce in England and Wales is based on judicial discretion. There is no community of property regime as there is in some European countries, whereby each spouse on marital breakdown is entitled to a fixed share of the property assets, subject to any agreement to the contrary. Under Part II of the Matrimonial Causes Act (MCA) 1973 the court has wide discretionary powers to redistribute matrimonial assets, which Waite LJ in *Thomas v. Thomas* [1995] 2 FLR 668 described as 'almost limitless'. However, these powers are not completely 'limitless' because the guidelines in s.25 MCA 1973 and the clean-break provisions govern and restrict the exercise of judicial discretion. As far as case-law is concerned, previously decided cases do not create precedents in the strict sense – because the court must reach a decision based on the unique facts of each case. In *Piglowska* v. *Piglowski* [1999] 2 FLR 763 Lord Hoffmann warned against a rigid application of guidelines in earlier cases.

A discretion-based system has the great advantage of flexibility, in that the judge can tailor an order to fit the facts of the case, but it can create uncertainty and unpredictability, and involve the court in a time-consuming and expensive exercise. Because of these disadvantages, there has been discussion from time to time about moving away from a discretion-based system (see 8.14, below), but there are currently no proposals to change the law.

## 8.2 Procedure in Ancillary Relief Proceedings

The rules of procedure are laid down in the Family Proceedings Rules 1991. These rules aim to reduce delay and costs by facilitating settlement and allowing the court to have control over the conduct of proceedings. The Law Society's *Family Law Protocol* provides guidance on the conduct of ancillary relief with the emphasis being on the settlement of disputes. The *Practice Direction (Ancillary Relief Procedure) (25 May 2000)* [2000] 1 FLR 997, and the *Pre-Application Protocol* annexed to it, outline the steps that parties must take with the aim of resolving disputes justly and speedily, safeguarding the interests of children and ensuring that costs are not out of proportion to the assets available.

The spouse who applies for ancillary relief is called the 'applicant', and the other spouse the 'respondent'. Cases are heard by a district judge in the divorce county court (in London, the Principal Registry) seized of the divorce petition, but complex or serious cases can be referred to the judge, or transferred to the High Court. Except for maintenance pending suit and any order to or for the benefit of a child of the family, orders do not take effect until decree absolute. In an international case, the court can stay (stop) the proceedings if it considers it more appropriate for the matter to be determined outside England and Wales (see, for example, *W* v. *W (Financial Relief: Appropriate Forum)* [1997] 1 FLR 257).

The parties must attend a first appointment, followed by a financial dispute resolution hearing at which the district judge will help the parties to reach agreement. If agreement cannot be reached, the case will proceed to a full hearing. To encourage agreement, written estimates of costs are provided at each hearing (on Form H), so that the parties are fully aware of the costs being incurred. In order to encourage agreement, the court also has the power to make costs orders in ancillary relief proceedings when this is justified by the litigation conduct of one of the parties (see r.2.71 Family Proceedings Rules 1991, and *President's Direction (Ancillary Relief: Costs) (20 February 2006)* [2006] 1 FLR 865).

*Proceedings Usually Take Place in Private*  Despite a move to greater openness in the family justice system, ancillary relief proceedings are usually heard in private. Rule 2.66 of the Family Proceedings Rules 1991 provides that hearings for ancillary relief 'shall, unless the court otherwise directs, take place in chambers'.

*A Duty of Full and Frank Disclosure* Both parties have a duty to make full and frank disclosure of all their assets, documents and other relevant up-to-date information, for without this the court will be unable to exercise its discretion justly. The Law Society's *Family Law Protocol* emphasises this, and so do the courts. Failure to make full and frank disclosure is a serious matter and can result in an order being set aside (*Jenkins* v. *Livesey (Formerly Jenkins)* [1985] AC 424, see 8.12). The court is permitted to draw appropriate adverse inferences from any failure to make full and frank disclosure (see *Baker* v. *Baker* [1995] 2 FLR 829). A costs penalty can be imposed on a dishonest party, but the court is unlikely to reduce a party's share of the assets as a penalty (*P* v. *P (Financial Relief: Non-Disclosure)* [1994] 2 FLR 381). (For a case where there was serious non-disclosure, and other grave misconduct, see *Al-Khatib* v. *Masry* [2002] EWCH 108 (Fam), [2002] 1 FLR 1053.)

*The Overriding Objective* The district judge is required to engage in active case management to ensure that couples co-operate in the conduct of proceedings, so as to further the overriding objective which is that cases must be dealt with justly (r.2.51 Family Proceedings Rules 1991). To further the overriding objective, the district judge must, so far as is practicable, deal with cases in such a way as to ensure that the parties are on an equal footing and to save expense. The district judge must also deal with the case in a way which is proportionate to the amount of money involved, the importance and complexity of the issues, and the financial position of each party. The district judge must also ensure that the case is dealt with expeditiously and fairly.

To further the overriding objective that cases be dealt with justly, the district judge must engage in active case management, which includes: encouraging the parties to co-operate and to mediate; identifying issues; regulating disclosure; helping the parties to settle; and fixing timetables. The parties themselves are required to help the court to further the overriding objective.

*To Commence Proceedings* A prayer for orders for ancillary relief must be made by the petitioner in the divorce petition, but an application for ancillary relief will be activated by filing Form A at the court (Notice of Intention to Proceed with an Application for Ancillary Relief). A fee must be paid. The respondent can file an answer, or (more usually) make an application for ancillary relief on Form A. Once Form A is lodged at the court, the court must fix a first appointment (not less than 12 weeks and not more than 16 weeks after the date of filing Form A) and give notice of that date (on Form C) to the applicant and to the respondent. The date of the first appointment cannot be cancelled except with the court's permission, and, if cancelled, the court must immediately fix a new appointment.

*Before the First Appointment* Both parties must exchange with each other, and each file with the court, a statement in Form E signed by the party who made the statement, and sworn to be true. Form E is an important form. It provides a comprehensive statement of financial means, including income, assets and outgoings, and includes supporting documents. Form E must be exchanged and filed not less than 35 days before the date of the first appointment. At least 14 days before the first appointment, each party must file with the court and serve on the other party: a concise statement of the issues between the parties; a chronology; a questionnaire setting out by reference to the concise statement of issues any further information and documents requested from the other party or a statement that no information and documents are required; and a notice on Form G (Notice of Response to First Appointment) stating whether that party will be in a position to proceed on that occasion to a financial dispute resolution (FDR) appointment.

*The First Appointment (r.2.61D Family Proceedings Rules 1991)* The aim of the first appointment is to define the issues and make directions (if needed), so that the parties can reach agreement, if possible. Both parties must attend, unless the court orders otherwise. The district judge has various powers, such as to direct that further documents be produced, to give directions about the valuation of assets, to order that the case be adjourned for out-of-court mediation or private negotiation, or to make an interim order. The district judge must direct that the case be referred to a FDR appointment unless it is not appropriate in the circumstances. The district judge may treat the first appointment as the FDR appointment.

*The Financial Dispute Resolution (FDR) Appointment (r.2.61E Family Proceedings Rules 1991)* Both parties must attend the FDR appointment, unless the court orders otherwise. Not later than seven days before the appointment, the applicant must file with the court details of all offers and proposals, and responses to them. The aim of the FDR appointment is for discussion, negotiation and conciliation to take place. The emphasis is on encouraging the parties to settle, and they must use their best endeavours to reach agreement. If agreement is not possible, the case proceeds to a final hearing.

In *Rose v. Rose* [2002] EWCA Civ 208, [2002] 1 FLR 978 the Court of Appeal held that, although the FDR appointment can take many forms, depending on the style and practice of the judge, the judicial evaluation of the appointment should never be superficial or ill-considered. It held that the FDR appointment is an invaluable tool for dispelling unreasonable expectations, but that in a finely balanced case it is no substitute for a trial and should not be used to discourage either party to go to trial where the case can only be resolved in such a way.

*The Final Hearing* The hearing usually takes place before the district judge in chambers in private, but the district judge can refer the case to a judge.

## 8.3 Orders That Can be Granted

Under Part II of the Matrimonial Causes Act 1973 the court can make the following orders:

(a) **maintenance pending suit (s.22)**;
(b) **financial provision orders (s.23):** periodical payments orders; lump sum orders (including pension attachment orders under ss.25B and C);
(c) **property adjustment orders (s.24):** transfer of property; settlement of property; and variation of a settlement;
(d) **pension sharing orders (s.24B)**.

### (a) Maintenance Pending Suit (s.22)

This is interim maintenance which terminates when the divorce suit is determined (or earlier if the court so orders). The court must exercise its discretion to make such order as is 'reasonable' (s.22). Although the exercise of discretion is not governed by the factors in s.25 (see below), the court performs a similar exercise. The court has a wide discretion and in an appropriate case may make a substantial order (see, for example, *M* v. *M (Maintenance Pending Suit)* [2002] EWHC 317 (Fam), [2002] 2 FLR 123 where the wife was awarded £330,000 per annum maintenance pending suit plus school fees). In *A* v. *A (Maintenance Pending Suit: Provision of Legal Fees)* [2001] 1 FLR 377 Holman J, referring to the non-discrimination principle in *White* v. *White* (see p.178, below), held that maintenance pending suit need not be restricted to daily living expenses, but can, depending on the circumstances, include a sum to fund the costs of the proceedings. In *A* v. *A* there had been a long marriage, and complex issues involving bigamy and polygamy. Holman J warned, however, that the courts should be cautious about including a costs element in maintenance pending suit. (See also *G* v. *G (Maintenance Pending Suit: Costs)* [2003] 2 FLR 71, where maintenance pending suit also included a sum for legal costs.)

### (b) Financial Provision Orders (s.23)

The following orders can be made in favour of a spouse and to or for the benefit of any child of the family aged under 18, or any other 'child' over 18 who is undergoing education or training or who has special circumstances (such as a disability) (ss.23(1), 29(1), (3)).

*(i) Periodical Payments Order (Maintenance)* A periodical payments order can be ordered in favour of a spouse and/or to or for the benefit of any child of the family. But most child maintenance disputes are dealt with by the Child Support Agency (see 13.2), not the court. Periodical payments can be secured or unsecured. If unsecured, payment is made from unsecured income. If secured, capital assets or other property are charged as security for payment. Periodical payments made in favour of a spouse terminate on his or her remarriage (s.28(1)), but not cohabitation, even if settled and long-term. In *Atkinson* v. *Atkinson* [1988] Ch 93 the Court of Appeal refused to equate long-term or settled cohabitation with remarriage after divorce, because of the difficulty the courts would have in making qualitative judgments about what constituted settled cohabitation. In *Fleming* v. *Fleming* [2003] EWCA Civ 1841, [2004] 1 FLR 667 the Court of Appeal reaffirmed the rule in *Atkinson*, holding that it did not need to be revisited and that it remained as sound as it did 15 years before, notwithstanding social changes in respect of cohabitation.

*(ii) Lump Sum Order (A Capital Order)* A lump sum order can be made in favour of a spouse and to or for the benefit of any child of the family (s.23(1)). It can be made to enable liabilities and expenses reasonably incurred by a spouse or a child prior to the application to be met (ss.23(3)(a), (b)). It can be ordered to be paid in instalments (s.23(3)(c)), and can incur interest (s.23(6)).

The advantage of a lump sum is that it can be used to affect a clean break between the parties. Sometimes a lump sum will be ordered to represent 'capitalised maintenance' (that is, a sum which is invested to provide an income). The *Duxbury* calculation, a computer program, has been used as a guide to calculate capitalised maintenance needs by taking account of certain variables (such as inflation, life expectancy, income tax, capital growth and income from investments) in order to calculate the lump sum which will be needed to produce sufficient income for the payee. However, while the court has recognised the usefulness of the *Duxbury* program, it has not allowed it to restrict its discretionary powers. Thus, in *A* v. *A (Elderly Applicant: Lump Sum)* [1999] 2 FLR 969, for example, the lump sum calculated by the *Duxbury* technique was reduced, because it would be unjust to the husband, who had made a significant contribution to the parties' lengthy marriage and which needed recognition in monetary terms. The *Duxbury* formula was also held to be inappropriate in *Fournier* v. *Fournier* [1999] 2 FLR 990 where the wife had a life expectancy exceeding 40 years.

A lump sum made in favour of a spouse is a final order which cannot be varied under s.31 (see 8.12). However, in *Westbury* v. *Sampson* [2001] EWCA Civ 4807, [2002] 1 FLR 166 the Court of Appeal held that the court has the power under s.31(1) to vary the quantum (as opposed to the scheduling) of a lump sum order payable by instalments, but that this power should only be exercised sparingly in exceptional circumstances. Only one lump sum order can be made; the plural reference to 'lump sums' in s.23(1)(c) is merely to allow payment by instalment.

A lump sum order made in favour of a child, unlike one made in favour of a spouse, is not a final order, as the court's power to make orders for children is 'exercisable from time to time' (s.23(4)). In practice, however, lump sums in favour of children are rarely made.

*Adjourning an Application Where a Capital Sum will Become Available in the Future* To avoid the potential injustice caused by the finality of lump sum orders and the policy requirement that matters should be dealt with once and for all, the court can adjourn proceedings in order to do justice where there is a real possibility of capital from a specific source becoming available in the near future (see *Michael* v. *Michael* [1986] 2 FLR 389; and *Milne* v. *Milne* (1981) FLR 286). The courts have sometimes left lump sum claims open where a party is expected to inherit a significant sum on the death of a relative in the reasonably near future (see *MT* v. *MT (Financial Provision: Lump Sum)* [1992] 1 FLR 363). In *D* v. *D (Lump Sum Order: Adjournment of Application)* [2001] 1 FLR 633, however, Connell J stressed that the discretion to adjourn should be exercised rarely. In practice, it is therefore uncommon for the courts to leave lump sum applications open. Another situation where the court might be prepared to adjourn proceedings is where a pension is about to be paid.

Where a lump sum application has been adjourned, because one of the parties is likely to receive an inheritance, the court can in the exercise of its discretion order a lump sum to be paid, even though the recipient spouse has subsequently remarried. Singer J so held in *Re G (Financial Provision: Liberty to Restore Application for Lump Sum)* [2004] EWHC 88 (Fam), [2004] 1 FLR 997, where he awarded the wife a lump sum of £460,000, after her husband had inherited £2.1 million, on the basis that, although her remarriage was relevant, it did not affect or diminish her ongoing contribution to the welfare of the children. She had a reasonable need for a lump sum to repay her debts, to allow her to purchase a car and to cover the purchase of suitable accommodation.

## (c) Property Adjustment Orders (s.24)

*(i) A Transfer of Property Order (s.24(1)(a))* This order directs a spouse to transfer specified property to the other spouse and/or to or for the benefit of a child of the family. Any

property can be transferred, but the order is often used to transfer the matrimonial home. The transferee may be given a charge over the house for a fixed amount or a percentage of the value which is to be realised at a later date, or may be ordered to pay the transferor a lump sum representing the latter's share in the matrimonial home. A transfer of property is a useful way of effecting a 'clean break' (see 8.5, below) – for example, one spouse could be ordered to transfer investments to the other spouse so that spouse can live on the income; or one spouse could be ordered to transfer the matrimonial home to the other spouse with that spouse agreeing to forego any claim for spousal maintenance.

*(ii) A Settlement of Property Order (s.24(1)(b))*    This order directs a spouse to settle property for the benefit of the other spouse and/or any child of the family. Under a settlement, property is held on trust for certain persons who have an interest in the property. Settlement of property orders are rarely made (but see *E v. E (Financial Provision)* [1990] 2 FLR 233, where £1.25 million was ordered to be transferred to the wife and children from a settlement held on discretionary trusts). A settlement of property order is sometimes made to give the children a roof over their heads during their dependency but to enable the house to be transferred back to the owner once the children become independent (this order is known as a *Mesher* order; see 8.7, below).

*(iii) A Variation of Settlement (Ante-Nuptial or Post-Nuptial) Order (ss.24(1)(c), (d))*    This order can be made for the benefit of the parties and/or any child of the family. Such orders are rare.

*(iv) Order for the Sale of Property (s.24A)*    The court can make an order for the sale of property (or proceeds of the sale of property) in which one spouse has, or both spouses have, a beneficial interest – but only if it has made a secured periodical payments, or lump sum or property adjustment order. The power to order sale is a useful enforcement mechanism where there is, or is likely to be, non-compliance with an order (for example, the court could order that property belonging to a spouse who has failed to pay a lump sum be sold and direct that the proceeds of sale be paid to the spouse who should have received it; s.24A(2)(a)). The court can defer sale until a specified event has occurred or until a specified period of time has expired (s.24A(4)). It can also order that property be offered for sale to a specified person or persons (s.24A(2)(b)). A third party with an interest in the property in dispute (such as a mortgagee) must be allowed to make representations to the court, and the third party's interest must be included as one of the circumstances of the case when the court performs its discretionary exercise (s.24A(6)).

*Property Adjustment Orders and Bankruptcy*    In the following case, an important case arising in the context of bankruptcy, the Court of Appeal held that a property adjustment order, whether made following contested proceedings or by consent, was made for consideration in money or in money's worth, and for that reason could not be set aside as a transaction at an undervalue under s.339 Insolvency Act 1986:

▶ *Hill* v. *Haines* [2007] EWCA Civ 1284

On divorce, the husband was ordered to transfer the home to the wife. One month after the order for transfer became effective, a bankruptcy order was made against the former husband on his own petition. The trustees in bankruptcy applied to the county court for a declaration that the transfer of the home on divorce was a transaction at an undervalue under s.339 Insolvency Act 1986 and was therefore void. At first instance the district judge held that it was not a transaction at an undervalue as there was consideration for the transfer consisting of the satisfaction or partial satisfaction of the wife's claims for ancillary relief. The decision of the district judge was overturned in the Chancery Division by Judge Pelling QC (sitting as a deputy High Court judge), but the Court of Appeal unanimously allowed the wife's appeal, holding that there had been no transaction at an undervalue under s.339 of the 1986 Act. Sir Andrew Morritt, the Chancellor, held that Parliament could not have intended that a court order of this type (one of the most commonly made in matrimonial proceedings) could be capable of automatic nullification on the suit of a trustee in bankruptcy of the husband against whom a bankruptcy order was subsequently made on his own petition. The Court of Appeal upheld the reasoning of the district judge and restored the original order.

(d) Pension Orders

See 8.8 below.

8.4 The Exercise of Discretion in Ancillary Relief Proceedings

▶ Baroness Hale in *Miller* v. *Miller; McFarlane* v. *McFarlane* [2006] UKHL 24, [2006] 1 FLR 1186 at para. 122:

'There is much to be said for the flexibility and sensitivity of the English law of ancillary relief. It avoids the straitjacket of rigid rules which can apply harshly or unfairly in an individual case. But it should not be too flexible. It must try to achieve some consistency and predictability. This is not only to secure that so far as possible like cases are treated alike but also to enable and encourage the parties to negotiate their own solutions as quickly and cheaply as possible.'

The court in ancillary relief proceedings has wide discretionary powers. Property law principles, such as the laws of trusts, are not relevant and will not be investigated by the court, except where there is a genuine third-party interest in any property (*Tee* v. *Tee and Hillman* [1999] 1 FLR 613).

In addition to applying the s.25 criteria, and considering whether to effect a clean break (see 8.5, below), the House of Lords has held that the court must seek to achieve a fair outcome between the parties and must not discriminate between husband and wife or favour the breadwinner over the spouse who looks after the home and the children (*White* v. *White* [2001] 1 AC 596, [2000] 2 FLR 981; see 8.6, below).

### The Section 25 Factors

When exercising its powers to make orders under Part II of the Matrimonial Causes Act 1973 (except maintenance pending suit) the court must apply the following factors (or matters) laid down in s.25 Matrimonial Causes Act 1973:

**Section 25(1)** 'It shall be the duty of the court in deciding whether to exercise its powers . . ., and, if so, in what manner, to have regard to all the circumstances of the case, first consideration being given to the welfare while a minor of any child of the family who has not attained the age of eighteen.'

In many cases the first consideration will be to give the child a home with the parent with whom the child is to live. It should be noted that the child's welfare is the 'first', not the 'paramount' consideration of the court as it is under the Children Act 1989 and under the adoption legislation.

The court must also take into account the following factors:

**Section 25(2)** 'As regards the exercise of the powers of the court in relation to a party to the marriage, the court shall in particular have regard to the following matters –

(a) The income, earning capacity, property and other financial resources which each of the parties to the marriage has or is likely to have in the foreseeable future, including in the case of earning capacity any increase in that capacity which it would in the opinion of the court be reasonable to expect a party to the marriage to take steps to acquire.
(b) The financial needs, obligations and responsibilities which each of the parties to the marriage has or is likely to have in the foreseeable future.
(c) The standard of living enjoyed by the family before the breakdown of marriage.
(d) The age of each party to the marriage and the duration of the marriage.
(e) Any physical or mental disability of either of the parties to the marriage.
(f) The contribution which each of the parties has made or is likely in the foreseeable future to make to the welfare of the family, including any contribution by looking after the home or caring for the family.
(g) The conduct of each of the parties, if that conduct is such that it would in the opinion of the court be inequitable to disregard it.
(h) In the case of proceedings for divorce or nullity of marriage, the value to each of the parties to the marriage of any benefit which by reason of the dissolution or annulment of the marriage, that party will lose the chance of acquiring.'

The list of factors in s.25(2) is not arranged in any hierarchy – no one factor is more important than another – and the weight or importance attached to these factors depends upon the facts of the particular case (Lord Nicholls in *White* v. *White*, citing *Piglowska* v. *Piglowski*). In practice, however, financial needs and financial resources are often particularly important.

The list of factors in s.25(2) is not exclusive – other factors can be taken into account, as s.25(1) refers to 'all the circumstances of the case'. Cultural factors can be taken into account. Thus, in *A* v. *T (Ancillary Relief: Cultural Factors)* [2004] EWHC 471 (Fam), [2004] 1 FLR 977, where the spouses were Iranian Muslims bound by Sharia law, the High Court considered how the matter would be dealt with in Iran (an approach which accorded with that taken by the Court of Appeal in *Otobo* v. *Otobo* [2002] EWCA Civ 949, [2003] 1 FLR 192).

The court is also required under s.25(2) to take into account pension arrangements and loss of pension arrangements on divorce (and nullity) (see 8.8, below).

*(a) 'The income, earning capacity, property and other financial resources which each of the parties to the marriage has or is likely to have in the foreseeable future, including in the case of earning capacity any increase in that capacity which it would in the opinion of the court be reasonable to expect a party to the marriage to take steps to acquire.'*

A wide interpretation is given to financial resources. The court is 'not obliged to limit its orders exclusively to resources of capital or income which are shown actually to exist' (Waite LJ in *Thomas* v. *Thomas* [1995] 2 FLR 668, at 670). In an appropriate case, the court may impute a notional earning capacity, or infer that unidentified resources are available from a spouse's expenditure or style of living. Future earning potential is a particularly important consideration when the court is deciding whether to affect a clean break (see 8.5, below).

In *Schuller* v. *Schuller* [1990] 2 FLR 193 the Court of Appeal said that the word 'resources' is entirely unqualified – there are no words of limitation on it. The court can therefore take into account a wide range of resources, such as business profits, interest on investments, insurance policies, pension rights and welfare benefits. Damages for personal injury have been taken into account as resources under s.25(2)(a) (*Wagstaff* v. *Wagstaff* [1992] 1 WLR 320; *C* v. *C (Financial Provision: Personal Damages)* [1995] 2 FLR 171); and so has a beneficial interest under a discretionary trust (*Browne* v. *Browne* [1989] 1 FLR 291). The income of a new spouse or cohabitant may be taken into account (*Macey* v. *Macey* (1982) FLR 7). The fact that each spouse may have a different income will not affect the outcome of the case, unless other s.25 factors prevail (see *Foster* v. *Foster* [2003] EWCA Civ 565, [2003] 2 FLR 299, where the wife earned more than twice as much as the husband, but where the shortness of the marriage affected the outcome).

As future financial resources must be considered, the court may postpone making an order if financial resources are likely to be available in the relatively near future, for instance: gratuities receivable upon retirement or upon termination of employment; inheritances (*Michael* v. *Michael* [1986] 2 FLR 389; *H* v. *H (Financial Provision: Capital Allowance)* [1993] 2 FLR 335); interests under a trust; and assets tied up in a business which are realisable at a later date.

The court is required to take into account any pension scheme which a party to a marriage has or is likely to have, and in relation to the benefits in a pension scheme, s.25(2)(a) must be read as if the words 'in the foreseeable future' were omitted (s.25B(1)).

*Obligations to a New Partner*  The court can in the exercise of its discretion take account of the fact that a party is living with a new partner, as this may affect the parties' financial resources and financial needs under s.25(2)(a). Thus, in *Atkinson* v. *Atkinson (No. 2)* [1996] 1 FLR 51 the wife's periodical payments were reduced when she began to cohabit with a new partner after the original order had been made. However, each case depends on its facts, and in *S* v. *S* [1987] 1 FLR 71 a lump sum of £400,000 was ordered to be paid to the wife even though she was living with a wealthy boyfriend; and in *Duxbury* v. *Duxbury* [1987] 1 FLR 7 the wife's cohabitation was ignored in calculating capitalised maintenance where her husband was a millionaire.

*Inherited Assets*  As Lord Nicholls confirmed in *White* v. *White* (see 8.6, below), inherited assets stand on a different footing from other assets acquired during marriage, and fairness generally requires that a spouse should be allowed to keep inherited property, unless the other party's financial needs cannot otherwise be satisfied – in which case, applying the s.25 guidelines, it may be necessary to have recourse to the inherited property. Whether inherited assets can be invaded therefore depends on the circumstances of the case. In some cases inherited property may count for little, but in others it may be of the greatest significance. For example, in *H* v. *H (Financial Provision: Special Contribution)* [2002] 2 FLR 1021 and *M* v. *M (Financial Provision: Valuation of Assets)* [2002] Fam Law 509 inherited assets were quarantined from the pool of assets to be divided. But in *Norris* v. *Norris* [2002] EWHC 2996 (Fam), [2003] 1FLR 1142 and *GW* v. *RW (Financial Provision: Departure from Equality)* [2003] 2 FLR 108 inherited assets were treated as a factor in the s.25 exercise and taken into account as contributions and resources along with the other circumstances of the case. In *Norris* v. *Norris*, where the marriage had lasted 23 years, and there were assets of £7.7 million, of which £3.6 million derived from the wife's family trusts and other gifts, Bennet J said that in his judgment 'merely because inherited property has not been touched or does not become part of the matrimonial pot is not necessarily, without more, a reason for excluding it from the court's discretionary exercise'. Similarly, in *GW* v. *RW* Nicholas Mostyn QC (sitting as a deputy High Court judge) followed Bennett J's analysis in *Norris* and held that it must be 'an artifice and contrary to the express words of s.25(2)(a) . . . to exclude the non-marital assets from the pool of assets to be divided'.

Fairness may, however, require that different types of inheritance be treated differently:

> ▶ *P* v. *P (Inherited Property)* [2004] EWHC 1364 (Fam), [2005] 1 FLR 576
>
> The bulk of the matrimonial assets was a farm which had been in the husband's family for generations. Munby J said that fairness might require quite a different approach if the inheritance was a pecuniary legacy that accrued during the marriage than if it was a landed estate that had been with one spouse's family for generations and had been brought into the marriage with the expectation that it would be retained *in specie* for future generations. But Munby J said that a reluctance to realise landed property must, however, be kept within limits. On the facts, Munby J held that the proper approach was to make an award based on the wife's reasonable needs for accommodation and income, as any other approach would compel a sale of the farm, which would have devastating implications for the husband.

Inherited assets may, depending on the circumstances of the case, be treated as part of the pool of assets to be divided between the parties on divorce, as they were in the following case:

> ▶ *S* v. *S* [2007] EWHC 1975 (Fam)
>
> The parties had been married for 20 years. The district judge divided the family assets (worth about £2 million) equally, but ring-fenced two assets inherited by the wife from her family, which resulted in an award with a 17 per cent differential in favour of the wife. The husband's appeal was allowed by Baron J, who ordered equal division of the assets, on the basis that it was quintessentially a needs case, not a big money case, as given the parties' ages and lifestyles, all the money would be required to fund the parties' long-term future. Baron J held that the district judge had been plainly wrong to have ring-fenced the wife's inherited assets, as all the assets which had come into the marriage had to be available to cover the parties' requirements. He held that, as time went by in a marriage, all assets became amalgamated.

*(b) 'The financial needs, obligations and responsibilities which each of the parties to the marriage has or is likely to have in the foreseeable future.'*

Financial needs can include, for example, the provision of accommodation and general living expenses. If there are children, the financial needs of the parent with whom the children are to live may be greater than those of the other parent, particularly if the primary-carer is not working. Obligations and responsibilities to a new partner or new family may be taken into account.

In *White* v. *White* (2000) (see 8.6, below), where the parties were wealthy, the House of Lords held that needs in s.25(2)(b) in the sense of 'reasonable requirements' should not be allowed to prevail over the general principle that the division of matrimonial assets should be fair in all the circumstances, for otherwise wives in particular would be discriminated against. However, although there has been a spate of reported 'big money' cases where it is possible, because of the size of the assets, to distribute them equally (or nearly equally), most cases are still needs-based and involve courts making decisions where there are often insufficient assets to be distributed between the parties on divorce.

*Obligations to a Second Family*    Obligations to a second family can be taken into account, depending on the facts of the case and applying all the s.25 criteria. As far as the principle of equality is concerned (see *White* v. *White*, below) different approaches have been taken. In *S* v. *S (Financial Provision: Departing from Equality)* [2001] 2 FLR 246 Peter Collier QC (sitting as a High Court judge) considered that obligations to a second family could justify a departure from equality, whereas in *H-J* v. *H-J (Financial Provision: Equality)* [2002] 1 FLR 415 Coleridge J held that such an approach would normally be wrong in principle.

*(c) 'The standard of living enjoyed by the family before the breakdown of marriage.'*

Although the court must take this factor into account, in practice it is often not possible for the parties to enjoy the same standard of living after divorce as they did before it – unless there are substantial assets available for distribution.

*(d) 'The age of each party to the marriage and the duration of the marriage.'*

The needs and resources of a couple whose marriage has been of short duration (and possibly childless) are likely to differ from those who are divorcing after a long marriage. In *Foster* v. *Foster* [2003] EWCA Civ 565, [2003] 2 FLR 299 the Court of Appeal held that the duration of a marriage will obviously be relevant in cases where one party's earning capacity has been seriously affected by a long period of time devoted to home-making and rearing children.

The duration of the marriage will be an important consideration when the court is considering the question of whether non-marital assets (such as inheritances or investments accrued before marriage) are part of the pool of assets available for distribution on divorce. With a short marriage, such property may not be considered part of the pool of assets to be divided, but in a long marriage they may become part of that pool. Thus, the longer the marriage the less likely the court is to categorise different types of property as 'matrimonial' or 'non-matrimonial' (see *Miller* v. *Miller* at 8.6, below). However, each case depends on its facts and other factors, in addition to the length of the marriage, will be relevant to the question of whether assets are 'matrimonial' or not. The length of the marriage was considered in the following two case-law examples:

> ▶ *Foster* v. *Foster* [2003] EWCA Civ 565, [2003] 2 FLR 299
>
> After a three-year marriage, the husband and wife were awarded 39 per cent and 61 per cent of the assets respectively, taking into account the fact that the wife had contributed more income.
>
> ▶ *GW* v. *RW (Financial Provision: Departure from Equality)* [2003] EWHC 611 (Fam), [2003] 2 FLR 108
>
> The principle of assumed equality of contribution laid down in *White* v. *White* (see 8.6, below) was held by Nicholas Mostyn QC (acting as a High Court judge) not to apply to a 12-year marriage, and the wife was awarded an unequal share (40 per cent) of the assets. The fact that the husband had brought capital assets into the marriage, and had a developed career, high earnings and a high earning capacity justified a departure from equality.

*Pre-Marital Cohabitation*   At one time the court would refuse to take into account a period of pre-marital cohabitation when calculating the duration of a marriage – as it took the view that marital obligations and needs began on marriage, not before (see *Foley* v. *Foley* [1981] 2 All ER 857). Only in very exceptional circumstances would pre-marital cohabitation be taken into account, as it was in *Kokosinski* v. *Kokosinski* [1980] Fam 72 where the parties had cohabited because they had been unable to marry for political reasons.

Today, however, as social attitudes to cohabitation have changed, the courts' attitude has changed and they may decide to take a settled and committed period of pre-marital cohabitation into account when calculating the duration of a marriage, particularly where that cohabitation has seamlessly and immediately preceded the marriage. Pre-marital cohabitation was taken into account when calculating the duration of the marriage in: *GW* v. *RW (Financial Provision: Departure from Equality)* [2003] EWHC 611 (Fam), [2003] 2 FLR 108; *Co* v. *Co (Ancillary Relief: Pre-Marriage Cohabitation)* [2004] EWHC 287 (Fam), [2004] 1 FLR 1095; and *M* v. *M (Financial Relief: Substantial Earning Capacity)* [2004] EWHC 688 (Fam), [2004] 2 FLR 236.

A period of cohabitation after divorce may be taken into account at the discretion of the court (see, for example, *Chatterjee* v. *Chatterjee* [1976] Fam 199). Cohabitation by one of the parties after divorce may be taken into account in variation proceedings (see *K* v. *K (Periodical Payment: Cohabitation)* [2005] EWHC 2886 (Fam), [2006] 2 FLR 468).

*(e) 'Any physical or mental disability of either of the parties to the marriage.'*

*(f) 'The contribution which each of the parties has made or is likely in the foreseeable future to make to the welfare of the family, including any contribution by looking after the home or caring for the family.'*

In *Vicary* v. *Vicary* [1992] 2 FLR 271 Purchas LJ held that no distinction should be made between a wife who had contributed directly to a business and one who had supplied the infrastructure and support for the family while her husband was able to prosper and accumulate wealth. The wife's contributions to the family were also considered to be important in *Piglowska* v. *Piglowski* [1999] 1 WLR 1360, [1999] 2 FLR 763. In *White* v. *White* (see 8.6, below) the House of Lords endorsed the importance of taking into account the contribution made to caring for the home, and held that to ignore it would be discriminatory and unfair to wives in particular. In *Lambert* v. *Lambert* [2002] EWCA Civ 1685, [2003] 1 FLR 139 (see 8.6, below) the Court of Appeal held that there should be an end to the sterile suggestion that the breadwinner's contribution was more important than the homemaker's. A failure to make a contribution may be taken into account (see *West* v. *West* [1978] Fam 1, where the wife refused to set up home with her husband but looked after the children at her parents' house).

### (g) 'The conduct of each of the parties, if that conduct is such that it would in the opinion of the court be inequitable to disregard it.'

Only conduct of an extreme kind is taken into account, as to do otherwise would contradict one of the policy aims of divorce law which is not to apportion blame. In *Wachtel* v. *Wachtel* [1973] Fam 72 Lord Denning MR said that conduct must be 'obvious and gross'. In *Duxbury* v. *Duxbury* [1987] 1 FLR 7 the Court of Appeal refused to take adultery into account, as Ackner LJ held that the s.25 exercise was essentially a financial, not a moral, exercise.

In *Miller* v. *Miller* (see 8.6, below) the House of Lords held that, where conduct is not inequitable, the court should not seek to weigh the parties' respective conduct or attitudes in an attempt to assess responsibility for the breakdown of the marriage, or to attribute 'legitimacy' or 'reasonableness' to the wish of one party to continue the marriage against the wishes of the other. The House of Lords held that the lower courts had therefore been wrong to take into account the husband's alleged responsibility for the breakdown of the marriage (he had left his wife for another woman) under the guise of having regard to all the circumstances of the case, given that it was conduct which fell far short of 'conduct which it would be inequitable to disregard' under s.25(2)(g).

---

#### Examples of Cases Where Conduct Was Taken Into Account

▶ Malicious persecution by a schizophrenic spouse (*J (HD)* v. *J (AM) (Financial Provision: Variation)* [1980] 1 WLR 124).
▶ Alcoholism causing disagreeable behaviour and neglect of the home (*K* v. *K (Conduct)* [1990] 2 FLR 225).
▶ Inciting a spouse's murder (*Evans* v. *Evans* [1989] 1 FLR 351).
▶ Assisting a spouse's suicide (*K* v. *K (Financial Provision: Conduct)* [1988] 1 FLR 469).
▶ Stabbing a spouse (*H* v. *H (Financial Provision: Conduct)* [1994] 2 FLR 801).
▶ An accumulation of serious misconduct, namely failing to make full and frank disclosure, dissipating matrimonial assets and abducting a child (*Al-Khatib* v. *Masry* [2002] EWHC 108 (Fam), [2002] 1 FLR 1053).
▶ Violently attacking the wife in the matrimonial home in front of the children resulting in the husband receiving a 12-year sentence of imprisonment was held to be, not merely conduct that it would be inequitable to disregard, but conduct at the very top end of the scale (*H* v. *H (Financial Relief: Attempted Murder as Conduct)* [2005] EWHC 2911 (Fam), [2006] 1 FLR 990).

---

Even where conduct is serious, however, the court can discount it and take other factors into account, as it did in *A* v. *A (Financial Provision: Conduct)* [1995] 1 FLR 345 where, even though the depressed and suicidal husband had assaulted his wife with a knife, which constituted conduct which it would be inequitable to disregard, other s.25 factors were taken into account.

If the court does consider that the conduct is sufficiently serious to be taken into account, it does not necessarily mean that the 'guilty' party will receive nothing. In *Clark* v. *Clark* [1999] 2 FLR 498 the wife had married a husband 36 years her senior. She had refused to consummate the marriage, and had induced her husband to buy property, most of which was transferred into her name. She relegated him to a caravan in their garden, and later made him a virtual prisoner in his own home. The court considered that this was conduct which it was inequitable to regard, but nevertheless made an order in her favour. In *H* v. *H (Financial Provision: Conduct)* [1998] 1 FLR 971, where the husband's conduct was held to be too inequitable to ignore (he had transferred money for three years into a Swiss bank account), Singer J said that the approach to be taken was not to fix a sum as a 'penalty', but to carry out an evaluation based on all the relevant factors taken in the round.

*Domestic Violence*    This is not necessarily taken into account as conduct under s.25(2)(g) unless the violence is particularly severe. Inglis ([2003] Fam Law 181) has argued, however, that the courts should consider changing their approach and treat domestic violence as conduct which it is inequitable to disregard. He says that the 'message received by litigants is that most domestic violence is unimportant', and that this approach is unsustainable today when there is a greater recognition of the harm caused to adults and children by domestic violence.

*Non-Disclosure*    A failure to make full and frank disclosure (or any other misconduct in respect of the process of the case) generally only affects costs (see *Tavoulareas* v. *Tavoulareas* [1998] 2 FLR 418; and *Young* v. *Young* [1998] 2 FLR 1131), but in a serious case (as in *Clark*; and *Al-Khatib*, above) it can be taken into account when assessing the substantive order. Depending on the circumstances, the court may decide to dismiss the application, as it did in *S-T (Formerly J)* v. *J* [1998] Fam 103, *sub nom J* v. *S-T (formerly J) (Transsexual: Ancillary Relief)* [1997] 1 FLR 402, where a transsexual's deception as to his sexual identity led to his application for ancillary relief (in nullity proceedings) being dismissed on grounds of public policy.

*Bigamy*    Although bigamy is a criminal offence and a ground for nullity under s.11 Matrimonial Causes Act 1973 (see 2.5), a party to a bigamous marriage is not necessarily barred from applying for ancillary relief, even though it is the general policy of the law not to allow a person to profit from his own crime. In *Whiston* v. *Whiston* [1995] 2 FLR 268 a bigamist was barred from seeking ancillary relief on grounds of public policy, but a different approach was taken in the following case:

▶ *Rampal v. Rampal (No. 2)* [2001] EWCA Civ 989, [2001] 2 FLR 1179

The Court of Appeal allowed a bigamist to pursue a claim for ancillary relief, distinguishing *Whiston* (above) on the basis that the bigamist in that case had been much more culpable. The Court of Appeal said that bigamy was a relevant factor in the s.25(2) exercise, but not a complete bar to a claim. It said, however, that striking out a claim would not be a violation of art. 6 of the European Convention for the Protection of Human Rights (a right to a fair trial).

Sharp ([2003] Fam Law 414) has argued that *Rampal* was wrongly decided, as *Whiston* had laid down a universal rule precluding bigamists from applying for ancillary relief.

*(h) 'In the case of proceedings for divorce or nullity of marriage, the value to each of the parties to the marriage of any benefit which by reason of the dissolution or annulment of the marriage, that party will lose the chance of acquiring.'*

On divorce a spouse may lose certain property rights and interests, such as the benefit of a pension, the surrender value of an insurance policy, future business profits, or the right to succeed to the other spouse's estate. The court can take these and other lost benefits into account. It might, for example, decide to increase an order for financial provision to compensate for the loss of future benefits, or make a deferred lump sum order, or adjourn proceedings. The position in respect of pensions on divorce is governed by special rules (see 8.8, below).

## 8.5  The 'Clean Break'

A major policy aim of the law governing ancillary relief is that a spouse cannot expect a 'meal ticket' for life. For this reason the court is required to determine cases in such a way as to effect, where possible, a 'clean break' between the parties. Various provisions in Part II of the Matrimonial Causes Act 1973 require the court to effect a clean break. These were inserted into the Act by Part II of the Matrimonial and Family Proceedings Act 1984 after the Law Commission in its *Report on the Financial Consequences of Divorce* (Law Com No. 112) had recommended that greater weight should be given to a divorced wife's earning capacity and to the desirability, where possible, of spouses becoming financially self-sufficient on divorce. The clean break was introduced to encourage the parties to put the past behind them and to begin a new life which would not be overshadowed by the relationship which had broken down (Lord Scarman in *Minton* v. *Minton* [1979] AC 593).

Baroness Hale had this to say about the clean break in *Miller* v. *Miller* (see below at 8.6), where an immediate clean break could be fairly achieved because of the amount of wealth available for distribution:

> ▶ **Baroness Hale in *Miller* v. *Miller; McFarlane* v. *McFarlane* [2006] UKHL 24, [2006] 1 FLR 1186 (at para. 133):**
>
> 'Section 25A is a powerful encouragement towards securing the court's objective by way of lump sum and capital adjustment (which now includes pension sharing) rather than by continuing periodical payments. This is good practical sense. Periodical payments are a continuing source of stress for both parties. They are also insecure. With the best will in the world, the paying party may fall on hard times and be unable to keep up with them. Nor is the best will in the world always evident between formerly married people. It is also the logical consequence of the retreat from the principle of the life-long obligation. Independent finances and self-sufficiency are the aims. Nevertheless, section 25A does not tell us what the outcome of the exercise required by section 25 should be. It is mainly directed at how that outcome should be put into effect.'

The court encourages the parties to go their separate ways after divorce, provided it is fair and appropriate for them to do so. Thus, under s.25A(1) the court when exercising its powers to make finance and property orders in favour of a spouse must consider 'whether it would be appropriate so to exercise those powers that the financial obligations of each party towards the other will be terminated as soon after' the divorce as the court 'considers just and reasonable'. However, despite this obligation, there is no presumption that a clean break must be ordered (Butler-Sloss LJ in *Barrett* v. *Barrett* [1988] 2 FLR 516; and Hale J in *SRJ* v. *DWJ (Financial Provision)* [1999] 2 FLR 176). The Court of Appeal has also warned against treating the clean break as a legal principle (*Clutton* v. *Clutton* [1991] 1 FLR 242).

In *Miller* v. *Miller* (see further at 8.6, below) the House of Lords held that the policy of the clean break did not prevail over the need to ensure that a fair result was obtained in ancillary relief proceedings. In *D* v. *D and B Ltd* [2007] EWHC 278 (Fam), [2007] 2 FLR 653 Charles J said that the cases of *White* and *McFarlane* showed that the unfairness that could result from a clean break needed careful consideration. He also said that, although an agreement between the parties that there should be a clean break carried great weight (referring to *Edgar* v. *Edgar* [1980] 1 WLR 1410, (1981) 2 FLR 19, and *X* v. *X (Y and Z Intervening)* [2002] 1 FLR 508), the court still had a duty to consider whether or not there should be a clean break.

The court can effect a clean break between the parties in an application for periodical payments by:

- dismissing the application;
- dismissing the application with a direction that the applicant shall not make any further application (s.25A(3));
- making a limited term periodical payments order (s.25A(2));
- making a limited term periodical payments order with a direction that no application can be made in variation proceedings for an extension of that term (s.28(1A));
- ordering a lump sum representing capitalised periodical payments as a means of discharging a party's liability to make further periodical payments (ss.31(7A) and (7B)).

The court also has a duty to consider a clean break in s.31 variation proceedings, when the court can make a limited term order 'to enable the party in whose favour the order was made to adjust without undue hardship to the termination of those payments' (s.31(7)).

The court's duty to consider whether to effect a clean break, however, is subject to the overarching objective of fairness laid down by the House of Lords in *White* v. *White* (see 8.6, below) (and see also *F* v. *F (Clean Break: Balance of Fairness)* [2003] 1 FLR 847).

Despite the court's duty to consider a clean break, it may be unwilling to effect one where it would make unrealistic expectations of a spouse's capacity for economic independence. The following are examples of clean-break cases:

> ▶ *M* v. *M (Financial Provision)* [1987] 2 FLR 1
>
> Heilbron J held that it would be inappropriate, unjust and unrealistic to terminate periodical payments to the wife under s.25A(2), because of her age (she was 47) and her inability to find employment, despite her genuine attempt to do so. She had also lost the chance of a secure future which her husband's pension would have provided, and, in any event, her husband could apply for variation of the order should his financial position deteriorate.

▶ *Flavell v. Flavell* **[1997] 1 FLR 353**

Ward LJ said that considerable caution should be exercised before making a limited term order, and he endorsed the circuit judge's approach that it is not usually appropriate to provide for the termination of periodical payments in the case of a woman in her mid-50s and that a fixed term order to effect a clean break will only usually be justified where she has substantial capital of her own and/or consistent and significant earning capacity.

▶ *C v. C (Financial Provision)* **[1989] 1 FLR 1**

A clean break was considered appropriate as the wife had considerable earning capacity, but the court made a deferred order, whereby the lump sum and maintenance would terminate after three years.

In cases where there is ill-health, the court may be unwilling to order a clean break (see *M v. M (Property Adjustment: Impaired Life Expectancy)* [1993] 2 FLR 723; and *Purba v. Purba* [2000] 1 FLR 444). Although the first consideration of the court in ancillary relief proceedings is the welfare of any child of the family (s.25(1)), a clean break can be imposed where there are children (*Suter v. Suter and Jones* [1987] Fam 111).

*A Nominal Order*   In some cases, the court may decide to make a nominal order (such as for £10 per annum) which acts as a 'backstop' which can be varied in the future should circumstances change. In *Whiting v. Whiting* [1988] 1 WLR 565 a nominal order was upheld on appeal by a majority of the Court of Appeal, even though the wife had qualified as a teacher and had a steady job. Balcombe LJ, however, dissented, saying that to make a nominal order just in case something should happen in the future was to negate entirely the aim of the clean break. A nominal order was made in *SRJ v. DWJ (Financial Provision)* [1999] 2 FLR 176, as the Court of Appeal considered that a clean-break order was inappropriate on the facts. However, in *K v. K (Periodical Payment: Cohabitation)* [2005] EWHC 2886 (Fam), [2006] 2 FLR 489 a nominal order was not appropriate, despite the impact of the wife's cohabitation post-divorce.

**8.6**   The Discretionary Exercise – The Impact of *White* v. *White* and *Miller* v. *Miller*

There have been two important cases heard by the House of Lords on the question of how the courts should exercise their discretion in ancillary relief cases on divorce. The first was *White v. White* [2001] 1 AC 596, [2000] 2 FLR 981. The second was *Miller v. Miller; McFarlane v. McFarlane* [2006] UKHL 24, [2006] 1 FLR 1186. Both cases were 'big money' cases, but the principles laid down in them apply to all divorce cases.

The problem with the s.25 guidelines is that they give only limited guidance on how the court should exercise its powers in ancillary relief cases. The first consideration is the welfare of any children of the family and the court must consider the feasibility of a clean break, but beyond that 'courts are largely left to get on with it for themselves' (Lord Nicholls in *Miller*). The courts must exercise their discretion having regard to all the circumstances of the case.

### (a) White v. White (2000)

Before the important decision of the House of Lords in *White* v. *White* [2001] 1 AC 596, [2000] 2 FLR 981 (see further below) the Court of Appeal had adopted a 'reasonable requirements' approach in 'big money' cases, whereby the main breadwinner (usually the husband) would be ordered to pay an amount which was sufficient to satisfy the other spouse's reasonable requirements even though he could afford to pay more. This approach resulted in many wives receiving a substantially smaller proportion of the matrimonial assets than their husband.

In the late 1990s, however, the Court of Appeal began to question whether the 'reasonable requirements' approach in 'big money' cases was the proper approach as it might be causing injustice. Thus, in *Dart* v. *Dart* [1996] 2 FLR 286, for example, where the wife was awarded a mere £4 million of her husband's £400 million fortune, Butler-Sloss LJ wondered whether the courts might have given too much weight to reasonable requirements over the other s.25 criteria. However, the Court of Appeal held that any challenge to the reasonable requirements approach should be made by Parliament, not the courts. (See also *Gojkovic* v. *Gojkovic* [1990] 1 FLR 140, where the wife, who had contributed to the family business, received only £1.3 million of the £4 million available for distribution.)

The reasonable requirements approach was also reinforced by the courts' endorsement of the *Duxbury* formula (see 8.3, above), which was based on calculating income needs. It was also reinforced by the courts' acceptance of the 'millionaire's defence', whereby a wealthy spouse (usually the husband) was not obliged to disclose details of property and financial assets if there was sufficient money available to satisfy the other spouse's reasonable needs (see *Thyssen-Bornemisza* v. *Thyssen-Bornemisza (No. 2)* [1985] FLR 1069). (It should be noted that in *J* v. *V (Disclosure: Offshore Corporation)* [2003] EWHC 3110 (Fam), [2004] 1 FLR 1042 Coleridge J said that there may still be a place for the millionaire's defence after the decision in *White* v. *White* (see below) in cases where the marriage is of short to medium duration, and the wealth has largely come from sources other than the efforts of the respondent during the course of the marriage.)

Although the reasonable requirements approach was considered to be unsatisfactory – because it discriminated against wives, and prioritised needs when there was no hierarchy prescribed in the s.25 factors (see 8.4) by the Matrimonial Causes Act 1973 – it was not until the decision of the House of Lords in *White* v. *White* in the year 2000 that the reasonable needs or reasonable requirements approach was finally rejected.

---

▶ **White v. White [2001] 1 AC 596 , [2000] 2 FLR 981**

After 33 years of marriage the wife obtained a divorce and sought enough capital to set herself up independently in farming, arguing that her equal contribution to their farming business throughout their long marriage justified her claim to an equal share of the assets. Her husband argued that she should only be given enough to satisfy her reasonable needs or requirements, applying the approach adopted in the Court of Appeal. Their overall assets were assessed at approximately £4.6 million. They had three children who were adult and independent.

At first instance, the judge adopted a reasonable needs approach and, on the basis that it was impractical for the wife to continue farming, awarded her one-fifth of their joint assets, and ordered that the farming business remain with her husband. The Court of Appeal allowed the wife's appeal and increased her award to £1.5 million. Butler-Sloss LJ said that cases where a wife was an equal business partner were in a wholly different category from other 'big money' cases such as *Dart* v. *Dart* (see above) and *Conran* v. *Conran* [1997] 2 FLR 615 where the origin of the wealth was clearly on one side and the emphasis was rightly on contribution, not entitlement. The Court of Appeal also held that it was not the function of the judge to criticise the wife's plans to carry on farming. Both parties appealed to the House of Lords.

The House of Lords held, dismissing the appeals, that, although the judge had been mistaken in regarding reasonable requirements as the determinant factor, the award made by the Court of Appeal was within the ambit of reasonable discretion. The House of Lords, with Lord Nicholls giving the leading opinion, laid down the following statements of principle:

▶ The objective implicit in s.25 is to achieve a fair outcome in financial arrangements on divorce, giving first consideration to the welfare of any children.

▶ Fairness requires the court to take into account all the circumstances of the case. In seeking to achieve a fair outcome, there is no place for discrimination between husband and wife in their respective roles. Fairness requires that their division of labour should not prejudice or advantage either party when considering their contributions to the welfare of the family under s.25(2)(f). If each in their different spheres contributed equally to the family, then in principle it matters not who earned the money and built up the assets. There should be no bias in favour of the money-earner and against the homemaker and the child-carer.

▶ Before making an order for division of assets, a judge should check his tentative views against the yardstick of equality of division. As a general rule, equality should be departed from only if, and to the extent that, there is good reason for doing so. The need to consider and articulate reasons for doing so will help the parties and the court to focus on the need to ensure the absence of discrimination.

▶ Section 25(2) does not rank the matters listed therein in any hierarchy and other matters may also be important. Financial needs is only one of the several factors to be taken into account in determining a fair outcome. When considering s.25(2)(b), confusion will be avoided by courts ceasing to employ the expression 'reasonable requirements' and returning to the statutory language of 'needs', which preserves the necessary degree of flexibility.

▶ Lord Nicholls, who laid down the propositions above, dismissed, however, the idea that there should be a presumption of equality – as this would be an impermissible judicial gloss on s.25, and the introduction of such a presumption was a matter for Parliament.

The result of *White* was that the criterion of 'reasonable requirements' was rejected and replaced by 'the yardstick of equality of division' in order to ensure fairness and abolish discrimination. The yardstick of equality created a presumption that there should be equality of division of assets on divorce – unless there was good reason to the contrary. The yardstick acted as a check on any tentative views of what the parties should receive. *White* recognised that marriage is a partnership of equals and that the homemaker should not be discriminated against in favour of the breadwinner. Discrimination was the antithesis of fairness. This was a principle of universal application which was to be applied to all cases, whether 'big money' ones or not. In *Miller* v. *Miller* (see p.180, below), however, Lord Nicholls, who had given the leading opinion in *White*, said that the yardstick of equality was 'to be applied as an aid, not a rule' (at para. 16).

*Reaction to* White   The decision provoked considerable comment from lawyers and academics. Duckworth and Hodson (2001) thought that the decision would increase the impetus for recognising formal agreements between spouses, especially pre-marital contracts. Eekelaar ([2001] Fam Law 30) said that the equality of sharing approach in *White* might deter people from marrying. In his view the equality idea in *White* was no great advance because the decision provided no suggestions as to what sorts of reasons might justify departing from equality. Cretney ([2001] Fam Law 3) thought that the House of Lords had gone too far. He questioned whether the House of Lords might not have been a 'trifle rash' in overturning the settled practice of the courts, particularly in a case which was highly untypical of other 'big money' cases. He also questioned whether the change of approach should have been decided by the House of Lords, but should instead have been a matter for Parliament.

Another criticism that might be made is that, although the House of Lords in *White* (and in *Piglowska*) had emphasised the importance of the statute and had rejected the primacy given to reasonable needs in the s.25 exercise, in *White* it somewhat contradictorily introduced a yardstick, or check, of equal division which has no basis in the statute. Furthermore, since the non-discrimination principle laid down in *White* is derived from s.25(2)(f) of the statutory guidelines, the House of Lords appears to have elevated that factor, when it had stressed in *Piglowska* v. *Piglowski* that there was no hierarchy in the s.25 factors. Although the House of Lords in *White* said that there must be no gloss put on s.25 in respect of reasonable needs, it appears to have imposed a gloss in respect of fairness and equality. The relationship between s.25 of the Matrimonial Causes Act 1973 and the principles enunciated in *White* is therefore left rather unclear. Perhaps any glosses on s.25 would have been better left to Parliament. It is also unfortunate, and somewhat unsatisfactory, that the principles identified by Lord Nicholls (equality, fairness and discrimination) arose in an atypical ancillary relief case, one in which *both* parties to the marriage were engaged in a family business.

In *Charman* v. *Charman (No. 4)* [2007] EWCA Civ 503, [2007] 1 FLR 1246 (see p.185) Sir Mark Potter P said (at para. 117) that the decision in *White* had undoubtedly not resolved 'the problems faced by practitioners in advising clients or by clients in deciding upon what terms to compromise'.

**The Case-Law After White v. White**   After *White* v. *White* the courts were no longer able to order division of matrimonial assets on the basis of reasonable needs. As a result, the courts began to order more equal divisions of matrimonial assets, at least in 'big money' cases. However, after *White* husbands began to argue that the presumption of equality should be departed from where they had made a 'special contribution' to the matrimonial assets by way of their hard work and exceptional business skills (see further below).

### (b)   *Miller* v. *Miller; McFarlane* v. *McFarlane* (2006)

In 2006 in the case of *Miller* v. *Miller* (heard with *McFarlane* v. *McFarlane*) the House of Lords had the opportunity once again to consider 'the most intractable of problems: how to achieve fairness in the division of property following a divorce' (Lord Nicholls at para. 1 in *Miller*), but this time in the light of the principles laid down by the House in *White* v. *White* (above). It also had the opportunity (in *McFarlane*) to consider for the first time whether the principles in *White* should also apply to the power of the court to order periodical payments on divorce. In *Miller* the House of Lords made important statements about conduct and special contribution. *Miller* involved a short marriage, *McFarlane* a long one. *White* had involved a long marriage, one of over 30 years.

▶ *Miller v. Miller; McFarlane v. McFarlane* [2006] UKHL 24, [2006] 1 FLR 1186

In *Miller* the husband (aged 41) and wife (aged 36) had been married for less than three years, and had no children. At the time of the marriage the husband was an exceptionally successful businessman earning about £1 million a year, and the wife earned £85,000 a year. The matrimonial home was purchased by the husband for £1.8 million and he subsequently bought a second property in joint names in the South of France. During the marriage the husband acquired shares in a new firm which subsequently proved to be extremely valuable. The wife gave up work to concentrate on furnishing their two homes. The husband left his wife for another woman, whom he subsequently married. Singer J in the High Court held that the award should not be limited to putting the wife 'back on her feet', but should recognise that the husband had, by marriage, despite its short duration, given her a reasonable and legitimate expectation that she would be able to leave the marriage significantly better off in terms of accommodation and spendable income than when she had entered it. Singer J therefore ordered the husband to transfer the matrimonial home (worth £2.3 million) to his wife and to pay her a lump sum of £2.7 million. The husband appealed to the Court of Appeal, which held, dismissing the appeal, that the judge had been entitled to take into account the husband's responsibility for the breakdown of the marriage and the wife's legitimate expectation of a higher standard of living. The husband appealed to the House of Lords. (For the facts of the *McFarlane* appeal, see below.)

The House of Lords held, *inter alia*, dismissing the husband's appeal, and applying the principles in *White* (see p.178, above) that:

In ancillary relief cases the redistribution of resources from one party to the other following divorce was justified on the basis of the following three principles:

▶ the needs (generously interpreted) generated by the relationship between the parties;
▶ compensation for relationship-generated disadvantage; and
▶ the sharing of the fruits of the matrimonial partnership.

These principles, each of which looked at factors linked to the parties' relationship, rather than to extrinsic, unrelated factors, could guide a court in making an award. Any, or all of them, might justify redistribution of resources, but the court must be careful to avoid double counting. Which of the three would be considered first depended on the circumstances of the case. In general it could be assumed that the marital partnership did not stay alive for the purpose of sharing future resources unless this was justified by needs and compensation. The ultimate object was to give each party an equal start on the road to independent living.

The House of Lords held that, in the circumstances of the case, the needs generated by the relationship were comparatively small, as was the need for compensation, but the wife was entitled to some share of the assets, including the considerable increase in the husband's wealth during the marriage. Had the yardstick of equality been applied to all the assets which had accrued during the marriage, the wife would have obtained more. But here there were reasons to depart from the yardstick of equality, either on the basis that the substantial growth was attributable to contacts and capacities that the husband brought to the marriage, or on the basis that the assets were business assets generated solely by the husband during a short marriage.

The House of Lords also considered: the role of conduct in ancillary relief cases; the role of special contribution; the distinction between matrimonial and non-matrimonial property; and whether periodical payment can be made to afford compensation as well as to meet financial needs (see further below).

*Miller* v. *Miller* 'makes plain that the three elements of needs, compensation and sharing are to be separately considered and that the order of their determination will vary from case to case' (Thorpe LJ in *Moore* v. *Moore* [2007] EWCA Civ 361, [2007] 2 FLR 339).

In *Miller* the term 'yardstick of equality' was referred to as 'the equal sharing principle' and to 'sharing entitlement' which, as Sir Mark Potter P in *Charman* v. *Charman (No 4)* [2007] EWCA Civ 503, [2007] 1 FLR 1246 (at para. 65) recognised, created more than a yardstick for use as a check. In *White* the House of Lords held that the court must conduct the s.25 exercise and test the result against a yardstick of equality, but in *Miller* it applied the equal sharing principle and then went on to decide whether it should be departed from if needs or compensation supplied a reason to do so. Thus, after *Miller* it appears that the starting point is equality of sharing rather than a check once a tentative calculation has been made.

### (c) Matrimonial and Non-Matrimonial Property and Short and Long Marriages

In exercising their discretion in ancillary relief cases the courts may sometimes be required (particularly in 'big money' cases) to consider whether or not to ring-fence certain assets from the pool of assets and treat them as non-matrimonial assets. Depending on the facts of the case, property acquired before marriage and inheritances and gifts received during marriage may be deemed not to be part of the pool of assets to be divided by the court on divorce. The length of the marriage will be an important factor here, as property (such as an inheritance owned by one of the spouses) may become part of the pool of assets to be distributed at the end of a long marriage, but not at the end of a short one (unless the parties' needs require those assets to be treated as such).

However, in *Miller* v. *Miller* there were conflicting opinions about matrimonial and non-matrimonial property. Baroness Hale, with whom Lord Hoffmann agreed, said that, as English law was based on a system of separate property ownership, there remained some scope for one party to acquire and retain separate property which was not automatically to be shared equally between them. If assets were not 'family assets' (assets not generated by the joint efforts of the parties), then the duration of the marriage might justify a departure from the yardstick of equality of division. The nature and source of the property and the way in which the parties had run their lives might be taken into account in deciding how that property should be shared. However, Baroness Hale held that these arguments would be irrelevant in the great majority of cases, and should not be taken too far.

Lord Nicholls, on the other hand, said that in respect to matrimonial property (that is, the matrimonial home and property acquired during the marriage other than by way of inheritance or gift) the equal sharing principle applied as much to short marriages as to long marriages, being no less a partnership of equals. However, in respect to non-matrimonial property (that is, property which the parties brought with them into the marriage or acquired by inheritance or gift during the marriage), following a short marriage fairness might well require that the claimant should not be entitled to an equal share. In a longer marriage non-matrimonial property represented a contribution made to the marriage by one of the parties whose weight would, in some circumstances, diminish, in others not. In all cases the nature and source of the parties' property were, as circumstances of the case, matters to be taken into account when determining the requirements of fairness, but Lord Nicholls said that the courts should be exceedingly slow to reintroduce a distinction between 'family' assets and 'business or investment' assets. Exceptional earnings were a contribution to marriage which could justify a departure from equality of division only where it would be inequitable to proceed otherwise. Where it became necessary to distinguish matrimonial property from non-matrimonial property, the court might do so with the degree of particularity or generality appropriate in the particular case.

Lord Mance said that the duration of the marriage could not be discounted as a relevant factor, nor could the financial arrangements of the parties during the marriage. Once needs and compensation had been addressed, divorce itself would not justify the court disturbing principles by which the parties had chosen to live their lives while married.

For a case post-*Miller* involving the distribution of matrimonial and non-matrimonial assets, and where an allowance was made for the husband's substantial financial contribution over and above the norm, see *S v. S (Non-Matrimonial Property: Conduct)* [2006] EWHC 2973 (Fam), [2007] 1 FLR 1496.

**(d)   Special Contributions**

After *White* v. *White* (see above) husbands began to argue that their special or exceptional or 'stellar' business contribution justified a departure from the yardstick of equality laid down by the House of Lords in *White*. In other words they would argue that, as they had been responsible for the accumulation of matrimonial assets, they were entitled to more than half of them on divorce. The husband successfully used this argument in *Cowan* v. *Cowan* [2001] EWCA Civ 679, [2001] 2 FLR 192 where after a long marriage the wife was awarded only a 38 per cent share of the assets (worth over £11 million) on the basis that equal division would not be fair in the circumstances, in particular because of the husband's special business talent and the great wealth he had thereby produced. The Court of Appeal so held, even though its approach seemed to contradict the non-discrimination principle laid down in *White*.

After *Cowan* v. *Cowan* courts began to take into account special contributions by husbands as a justification for departing from equality. However, the emphasis on contribution endorsed by the Court of Appeal in *Cowan* began to create difficulties. Not only did it lead to detailed evidence of contribution being put forward – which increased the length and cost of litigation and was contrary to the policy objective of encouraging agreement – but the courts began to adopt different approaches to contribution. Some judges accepted special contribution as a justification for departing from equality of division of matrimonial assets, but others began to express concerns about this approach. Coleridge J, in particular, began to express concern. In *H-J* v. *H-J (Financial Provision: Equality)* [2002] 1 FLR 415 Coleridge J awarded the wife 50 per cent of the assets on the basis that there was nothing special about the husband's contributions and that to hold otherwise would drive a wedge into the heart of the principles underlying *White*. In *G* v. *G (Financial Provision: Equal Division)* [2002] EWHC 1339 (Fam), [2002] 2 FLR 1143 Coleridge J expressed disquiet about the growing forensic practice of routinely arguing special contribution in 'big money' cases, which, he said, invited recrimination and was not conducive to settlement. Coleridge J found that the husband had failed to establish special contribution, and held that fairness dictated that, as far as possible, the parties should leave the marriage on terms of broad financial equality. As a result of a long marriage of more than 30 years, the wife was awarded almost half the matrimonial assets, despite her husband's substantial business contribution.

The difficulties created by *Cowan* (of allowing arguments based on special contribution to justify a departure from equality) were eventually addressed by the Court of Appeal in *Lambert* v. *Lambert*:

> ▶ *Lambert* v. *Lambert* [2002] EWCA Civ 1685, [2003] 1 FLR 139
>
> The parties had been married for 23 years. Their matrimonial assets were worth £20.2 million, and two years after their separation the sale of shares in the husband's business had produced more than £26 million. The husband argued that he had made an exceptional business contribution in generating the family fortune. His wife claimed 50 per cent of the assets arguing that she had been the principal homemaker and parent during the marriage, and that she had played a significant role in the husband's business. Connell J, applying *Cowan*, awarded her 37.5 per cent of the assets, on the basis that her contribution had been modest, in fact merely 'ornamental'. The husband's contribution, on the other hand, to the welfare of the family by creating such a substantial fortune was held by Connell J to be 'really special' or 'exceptional'. The wife appealed, arguing *inter alia* that the judge had fallen into the trap of gender discrimination by concluding that the husband's contribution as a money maker was special and therefore greater than her contribution, and that this justified a departure from equality. She argued that there had been insufficient consideration of her needs. The husband argued that the Court of Appeal should be slow to interfere with the exercise of judicial discretion.
>
> The Court of Appeal allowed the wife's appeal and awarded her 50 per cent of the assets. Thorpe LJ said that there 'must be an end to the sterile assertion that the breadwinner's contribution weighs heavier than the homemaker's'. However, Thorpe LJ said that he did not consider that the decision of Coleridge J in *H-J* v. *H-J* (above) had created a presumption of equality. He said that it was possible for the court to order unequal division, even where the parties' contributions had been equal, because other s.25(2) factors might prevail and because of the overarching need to achieve fairness.
>
> **THORPE** LJ: '[I]f the decision of this court in *Cowan* has indeed opened what Coleridge J descried as a forensic Pandora's box, then it is important that we should endeavour to close and lock the lid. . . . However, for the present, given the infinite variety of fact and circumstance, I propose to mark time on a cautious acknowledgement that special contributions remain a legitimate possibility but only in exceptional circumstances.'

The Court of Appeal in *Lambert* therefore endeavoured to confine the doctrine of exceptional or special contribution, endorsed by the Court of Appeal in *Cowan*, within narrow bounds. The Court of Appeal recognised that domestic contribution is just as special as business contribution.

After *Lambert* the courts took a variety of approaches to the division of matrimonial assets. Thus, for example, in *Norris* v. *Norris* [2002] EWHC 2996 (Fam), [2003] 1 FLR 1142 the wife claimed more than half the assets on the basis that she had made an exceptional contribution (primary-carer of the child, domestic contribution and financial contribution from her inherited wealth), but Bennett J found to the contrary, applying *Lambert*. In *L* v. *L (Financial Provision: Contributions)* [2002] FLR 642 the wife claimed she had played a pivotal role in the success of the business, but Connell J found to the contrary and awarded her only 37 per cent of the matrimonial assets because of her husband's special contribution. (See also *GW* v. *RW (Financial Provision: Departure from Equality)* [2003] EWHC 611 (Fam), [2003] 2 FLR 108 where a departure from equality was held to be justified.)

In the following case the wife was awarded more than 50 per cent of the assets on the basis of the special circumstances of the case:

▶ *Parra v. Parra* [2002] EWCA Civ 1886, [2003] 1 FLR 942

The wife was awarded 54 per cent of the assets. The parties were joint owners of a business and the matrimonial home had been bought by their joint efforts. The Court of Appeal held that the parties had effectively opted for a regime of community of property. Thorpe LJ stated that the outcome of ancillary relief cases depended on the exercise of judgment using a broad- brush approach which obviated the need to investigate minute detail and findings on minor issues in dispute. He suggested that the introduction into the statutory guidelines (in s.25(2) Matrimonial Causes Act 1973) of a 'no-order' principle (like that in s.1(5) Children Act 1989) might contribute to the elimination of unnecessary litigation.

Special contribution remains a legitimate argument in ancillary relief cases after the decision in *Miller* v. *Miller*, but, because of the risk of discriminating against the contribution of the 'homemaker' in favour of the contribution of the 'breadwinner', the House of Lords in *Miller* heavily circumscribed the situations in which it would be appropriate to find that one party had made a special contribution which would justify a departure from the principle of equality. The House of Lords approved the words of Thorpe LJ in *Lambert* (above), who had acknowledged that 'special contribution remains a legitimate possibility but only in exceptional circumstances'. After *Miller* it is therefore clear that departing from equality must be kept within narrow bounds.

In *Miller* the House of Lords held that the question of contribution should be approached in much the same way as conduct. In other words, it should be regarded as a factor leading to a departure from equality of division only in wholly exceptional cases when it would be inequitable to disregard it. Lord Nicholls said that he echoed the powerful observations of Coleridge J in *G* v. *G (Financial Provision: Equal Division)* [2002] EWHC 1339 (Fam), [2002] 2 FLR 1143 (see p.183, above) that parties should not seek to promote a case of special contribution unless the contribution was so marked that to disregard it would be inequitable. Baroness Hale, however, was of the opinion that the contributions which should be taken into account were only those which had been made, and were to be made, to the 'welfare of the family', and not contributions to accumulated wealth. Only if there was such a disparity in the parties' respective contributions to the welfare of the family that it would be inequitable to disregard it, should contribution be taken into account in determining their shares.

Special contribution was considered in the following case:

▶ *Charman v. Charman (No. 4)* [2007] EWCA Civ 503, [2007] 1 FLR 1246

The parties had been married for almost 28 years and were 54 years old. Their substantial assets had been generated solely during the marriage as a result of the husband working in the insurance industry. The assets amounted to £131 million, and there was a separate trust for the children worth at least £30 million. The wife conceded that the husband had made a special contribution in the generation of the fortune and sought 45 per cent of the matrimonial assets. The husband offered her £20 million. At first instance, Coleridge J awarded her £48 million, representing 36.5 per cent of the assets, basing his departure from equality both on special contribution by the husband, and on the greater risks inherent in the assets remaining with the husband. The husband appealed to the Court of Appeal on the basis that the judge had made insufficient allowance for his special contribution. He argued, in particular, that the methodology employed by the judge was flawed because the judge had begun with the hypothesis of equal division, and then factored his special contribution into the equation by way of a discount, whereas he should have proceeded through the s.25 Matrimonial Causes Act 1973 exercise, allowing for his special contribution within that exercise. He also argued that the offshore trusts should not have been treated as his financial resources as they were intended for the benefit of future generations.

The Court of Appeal dismissed the appeal, and the husband's application for leave to appeal to the House of Lords was refused.

### The Principles in White v. White and Miller v. Miller Apply to Cases Other Than 'Big Money' Cases

The approaches laid down in *White* and in *Miller* are not just relevant to 'big money' cases. In *White* Lord Nicholls said that the non-discriminatory treatment of husbands and wives in their respective roles is to be treated as a principle of universal application. The first duty of the court is to apply the s.25 criteria in search of the overarching objective of fairness, and this rule applies to all cases. However, in cases which are not 'big money' cases the housing needs of the child and primary-carer will often dominate, and only if there are sufficient assets left over will the other spouse be able to purchase accommodation. In practice, equality of division will usually be impossible in 'small money' cases particularly where there are children (see, for example, *Cordle* v. *Cordle* [2001] EWCA Civ 1791; and *B* v. *B (Financial Provision: Welfare of Child and Conduct)* [2001] EWCA Civ 2308, [2002] 1 FLR 555).

(e) Big Money Cases and Periodical Payments

Although *White* v. *White* involved capital provision (a lump sum), the House of Lords held in *Miller and McFarlane* that the overriding objective of fairness laid down in *White* v. *White* could also apply to periodical payments (income) in an exceptional case. In *McFarlane* the facts were exceptional as there was a huge surplus of available income after the needs of the parties had been met:

▶ *Miller v. Miller; McFarlane v. McFarlane* [2006] UKHL 24, [2006] 1 FLR 1186

In the *McFarlane* case the parties had been married for 16 years and had three children. Both parties were qualified professionals and, until shortly before the birth of their second child, earned similar sums of money. The wife gave up her highly-paid career to care for the family, while the husband continued his professional career, with a salary increasing considerably from year to year. The family had insufficient capital available to achieve a clean break, but the husband earned substantially more than would be needed to meet his own and the wife's budgeted household expenditure. The district judge made a periodical payments order of £250,000 a year to the wife (representing one-third of the husband's current income), on the basis of an estimated income requirement of £128,000, on the ground that fairness required her to have a share of her husband's future earnings, which had been made possible by her past contributions to his career. The periodical payment was reduced by the High Court, but the Court of Appeal allowed the wife's appeal in part, restoring the award to £250,000, but limiting the term to 5 years. The Court of Appeal held that in exceptional cases, and on the basis of term rather than joint lives orders, periodical payments could be used to accumulate capital. (The *McFarlane* appeal to the Court of Appeal was conjointly heard with the *Parlour* appeal (see *Parlour* v. *Parlour* [2004] EWCA Civ 872, [2004] 2 FLR 893), but in the *Parlour* case there was no appeal to the House of Lords.) Mrs McFarlane appealed to the House of Lords.

The House of Lords held, allowing her appeal, that a periodical payments order could be made to afford compensation as well as to meet financial needs. If capital had been equally shared and was enough to provide for need and compensate for disadvantage, there should be no continuing financial provision. However, a clean break was not to be achieved at the expense of a fair result. Thus, if a claimant was owed compensation and capital assets were not available, the social desirability of a clean break would not be sufficient reason for depriving a claimant of that compensation. There was no reason to limit periodical payments to a fixed term in the interests solely of achieving a clean break.

The House held that the case was a paradigm case for an award of compensation in respect of the significant future economic disparity sustained by the wife, arising from the way the parties had conducted their marriage. Equal division of the capital was not enough to provide for needs or compensate for disadvantage, but unusually the husband's very substantial earning power was far in excess of the family's financial needs after separation. The wife, having given up her own highly paid career to look after the family, was not only entitled to generous income provision, including sums which would enable her to provide for her own old age and insure the husband's life, but was also entitled to a share in the very large surplus, on the principles both of sharing and compensation. The Court of Appeal had been wrong to set a five-year time-limit on the order, on the basis that the wife would save the whole surplus above her requirements and that she would have the burden of justifying continuing payments at the end of the order, especially given the high threshold. The burden should be on the husband to justify a reduction, at which stage the court could consider whether a clean break was practicable, which would depend on the amount of capital generated by the husband.

Cooke ([2004] Fam Law 906) was critical of the decision of the Court of Appeal in *McFarlane* for extending the principles in *White* to income, as she said it perpetuated 'dependency and perhaps animosity'.

**(f)** How the Court Conducts the Discretionary Exercise After *White* and *Miller*

Charles J in the following case usefully summarises how the courts must now exercise their discretion in ancillary relief cases in the wake of *White* v. *White* and *Miller* v. *Miller*:

▶ **Charles J in *H* v. *H* [2007] EWHC 459 (Fam), [2007] 2 FLR 548:**

'To my mind it is clear [from *White* v. *White* and *Miller* v. *Miller*] that:

(i)   the court must apply the statutory provisions;
(ii)  the overall aim is to reach a fair result;
(iii) the claimant is not a supplicant, each party to a marriage is entitled to a fair share, and the search is always as to the requirements of fairness in the particular case;
(iv)  there is no gender discrimination;
(v)   the yardstick of equality is to be applied as an aid and not a rule;
(vi)  fairness has a broad horizon and inherent flexibility; and
(vii) in identifying the rationale for awards in *Miller and McFarlane* the House of Lords through both Lord Nicholls of Birkenhead and Baroness Hale of Richmond are not

setting rigid rules or formulae but are identifying principles guiding the court's approach and thus its reasoning in applying the MCA 1973 . . .

In my view when reading and applying the guidance given by the House of Lords it is important not to forget the facts and circumstances of the cases they were dealing with and to see how they were applied in them. Also it should be remembered that Baroness Hale of Richmond expresses common ground with Lord Nicholls of Birkenhead as to the three principles of need, compensation and sharing and that the only divergence between them that is identified by Lord Mance relates to the identification of the matrimonial property to which the yardstick of equality may readily be applied.'

### (g) What Have *White* and *Miller* Added? Have They Improved the Law?

In *RP* v. *RP* [2006] EWHC 3409 (Fam), [2007] 1 FLR 2105 Coleridge J said that the rationales highlighted in *Miller* v. *Miller*, particularly by Baroness Hale, were very helpful in ensuring that the court achieved a fair result and did not 'become stuck or formulaic in its approach as it had done from time to time in the past (for example, when the *Duxbury* formula tended to overwhelm consideration of all the s.25 factors)'. However, he said that care needed to be taken to ensure that the passages in *Miller* were not treated 'as some kind of quasi statutory amendment'. They were, Coleridge J said, 'commentary of the House of Lords on a well trodden statute, now in its fourth decade'. He said that the word 'compensation' did not appear in the statute, and that 'talk of "compensation" ' in respect of the circumstances of the case in *RP* had 'added nothing except confusion and the real risk of double counting'.

Coleridge J's judgment in *RP* contains some express, and implicit, concerns about the decision of the House of Lords in *Miller*. He described it as a 'high profile case' which had sent 'seismic reverberations throughout the whole [family justice] system'. However, he said that the case had created 'very real uncertainty as to outcome' and, as a result, the 'consensual disposal of individual cases in this huge and, sadly, ever growing area of litigation' had become 'that much harder to achieve and that much more costly'. Coleridge J said that 'considerable confusion' still existed. He said there had been two decisions of the House of Lords in six years after three decades of silence (1970–2000), and he made a plea for 'a period of reflective tranquillity'.

One is certainly left wondering whether the three principles (of needs, compensation and sharing) laid down in *Miller* have added an unhelpful gloss to the law which has arguably created unnecessary obfuscation rather than clarification of the law. Coleridge J's emphasis on the importance of referring to the statute must be borne in mind.

In *Charman* v. *Charman (No. 4)* [2007] EWCA Civ 503, [2007] 1 FLR 1246 Sir Mark Potter P (at para. 120) said that it remained to be seen whether the impact of the decision in *Miller and McFarlane* would be as great as had been the decision in *White* in very big money cases. He stated (at para. 12) that specialist practitioners had not received the decision in *Miller* as one that had introduced 'the benefit of predictability and improvement of the prospect of compromise' (and he referred to the response to *Miller* of the National Chair of Resolution, at [2007] Fam Law 203). If this was the case, then Sir Mark Potter P considered it to be 'highly unfortunate'.

Cooke ([2007] CFLQ 98) states that what was most needed from the decision of the House of Lords in *Miller and McFarlane* was a 'decisive theoretical lead' on the issues which had been left unresolved in respect of the yardstick of equality in *White*. However, she says that, because of conflicting opinions in the House of Lords, the theoretical difficulties were not fully addressed or resolved, thereby leaving the operation of s.25 Matrimonial Causes Act 1973 'the subject of considerable uncertainty'. She says that 'the pressing need to find a coherent rationale for the yardstick of equality' was not met by *Miller*.

Predicting what is special contribution, and when it should be taken into account, and determining what are matrimonial and non-matrimonial assets are likely to continue to create difficulties for lawyers and the courts. As Cooke (above) says, although 'the concept of non-matrimonial property is firmly embedded in law and practice . . . we do not know how it is defined'. Furthermore, it is difficult to predict the extent to which the duration of a marriage will impact on special contribution and what is, or is not, matrimonial property.

## 8.7  The Family Home on Divorce

The future of the family home on divorce is an important matter, not just because of its financial value but because it provides accommodation for the family. The provision of accommodation will be a primary consideration for the court when deciding how to distribute the matrimonial assets, and the provision of a home for any children will be particularly important. However, although the housing needs of both parties must be taken into account, the outcome in the case will depend on all the circumstances, as the following two cases show:

▶ *M v. B* [1998] 1 FLR 53

The Court of Appeal allowed the husband's appeal, as the judge had failed to take into account the importance of the parent who was not the primary-carer having a home of his own where the children could enjoy contact. The wife should have a cheaper house so that her husband would also have enough to buy a property of his own where the children could visit him. Thorpe LJ said that 'it is one of the paramount considerations, in applying the section 25 criteria, to endeavour to stretch what is available to cover the need of each for a home, particularly where there are young children involved'.

▶ *Piglowska v. Piglowski* [1999] 1 WLR 1360, [1999] 2 FLR 763

The question for the House of Lords, like that in *M v. B* (above), was whether the wife should have a cheaper house so that her husband could buy himself a house in England, even though he had accommodation in Poland. Lord Hoffman said that to treat *M v. B* as a case laying down the rule that both spouses invariably have a right to purchase accommodation was a misuse of authority and he distinguished *M v. B* on the basis that the children in *Piglowska* were adults, so that there was no question of the husband needing a home to receive them. Lord Hoffmann said that there was no reason why the courts should not take into account the rationality of a party's intentions which gave rise to their needs (here whether it was reasonable for the husband to wish to return to live in England when he already had accommodation in Poland). His Lordship said that judges are free to make value judgments about the facts of cases. The House of Lords warned against treating earlier cases as binding precedents and restored the order of the trial judge which had given particular weight to the wife's need to stay in the matrimonial home (s.22(2)(b)) and the fact that she not only looked after the home and cared for the family but had made a substantially greater financial contribution to the matrimonial assets (s.25(2)(f)).

When deciding what should happen to the home on divorce the court has various options available, depending on the facts. It might, for example, order one spouse to transfer the house, or his or her share of the house, to the other spouse with or without the other spouse making any compensating payment. It might order a transfer but make it subject to a charge in favour of the transferor, representing the value of the transferor's interest in the home which will be realised on sale at a later date (see, for example, *Knibb* v. *Knibb* [1987] 2 FLR 396; and *Popat* v. *Popat* [1991] 2 FLR 163). The house might be transferred to effect a clean break. It might, for instance, be transferred to the wife with her forbearing to claim periodical payments.

**A Mesher Order**   This is an order made under s.24(1)(b) whereby the house is settled on trust for one or both of the spouses in certain shares, but with sale postponed until a future event, such as until the children have reached a particular age or have finished full-time education, or until the death, remarriage or cohabitation of the other spouse. *Mesher* orders were once popular with the courts, but they have become less popular because of their drawbacks. One drawback is that some spouses (usually wives) may find that they have insufficient funds from the eventual proceeds of sale to rehouse themselves. Another drawback is that children often continue to need accommodation after the event triggering sale has occurred. It is possible, however, for the court to take this into account, as it did in the following case:

▶ *Sawden* v. *Sawden* [2004] EWCA Civ 339

The two adult children continued to live in the former matrimonial home. The Court of Appeal added another condition to the *Mesher* order, which provided that the home could only be sold in the event of both children leaving the property and settling independently in homes of their own. Thus, the children could remain indefinitely in the home, if they wished, without their father enforcing sale and claiming his 45 per cent of the proceeds of sale.

Another disadvantage of *Mesher* orders is that they are contrary to the clean break as, until sale, the parties are tied together as joint owners, thereby restricting their chances of financial self-sufficiency.

Despite their drawbacks, the Court of Appeal in *Clutton* v. *Clutton* [1991] 1 WLR 359 said that a *Mesher* order might be appropriate where the family assets were sufficient to provide both parties with a roof over their heads if the matrimonial home were sold at a later date, but where the interest of the parties required the children to stay in the matrimonial home. However, Lloyd LJ stressed that, where there were any doubts about a wife's eventual ability to rehouse herself, then a *Mesher* order should not be made. The Court of Appeal held that a *Martin* order (see below) did not suffer from the same disadvantage.

After *White* v. *White* (see 8.6, above), it was thought that the courts might be prompted into making more use of *Mesher* orders, because of the emphasis on fairness (see, for example, Hodson *et al* [2003] Fam Law 37; and Fisher [2002] Fam Law 108), but the courts are still aware of the disadvantages of *Mesher* orders, particularly for wives. Thus, for example, in *B* v. *B (Mesher Order)* [2002] EWHC 3106 (Fam), [2003] 2 FLR 285, heard after *White*, a *Mesher* order was held not to be appropriate in the circumstances – because of the wife's inability to generate capital at the date of the suggested *Mesher* triggering event and because it would impose a significant financial burden on her.

**A Martin Order**    This is an order giving one spouse a right to occupy the house until that party's death, remarriage or cohabitation, after which the proceeds of sale are divided in certain shares (see, for example, *Harvey* v. *Harvey* [1982] Fam 83). A *Martin* order effectively gives the party in occupation a life interest in the house, unless a specified event occurs.

**An Order for Sale**    Under s.24A MCA 1973 the court can order that the matrimonial home be sold, but this power is only ancillary to the court's power to make a financial provision or property adjustment order. Thus, for example, the court could order sale of the home so that one of the parties receives a lump sum from the proceeds of sale.

   If the house is in joint names the signatures of both parties will be required for sale. However, if it is in the name of one spouse, and there is a danger that the sole owner may sell it before the divorce court has exercised its powers, the non-owner spouse should register his or her 'home rights' (see 4.2). Where the house has been sold, an application can be made under s.37 Matrimonial Causes Act 1973 to have the transaction set aside (see 8.12, below).

**Tenancies of the Home**    Section 53 and Sched. 7 to the Family Law Act 1996 make provision for the transfer of tenancies on divorce. A tenancy can also be transferred under s.24 Matrimonial Causes Act 1973. Where the tenancy is a joint council tenancy, the court in ancillary proceedings can take into account the effect on either party of the local authority's housing policy (*Jones* v. *Jones* [1997] Fam 59, [1997] 1 FLR 27).

## 8.8    Pensions on Divorce

Pensions, like the family home, can be a valuable financial asset. Loss of a pension as a result of divorce can therefore be a substantial loss, particularly for wives, as many of them may have made no arrangement, or inadequate arrangement, in respect of pension provision. Although pension entitlement is something which the divorce courts have always been able to take into account as part of the s.25 discretionary exercise (see above), amendments to the Matrimonial Causes Act 1973 have improved the pension position on divorce. Loss of pension rights can be dealt with by the court on divorce (and on nullity) by: 'offsetting'; making a pension attachment order; or making a pension sharing order.

*(i) 'Offsetting'*    To allow for loss of a pension, the court in the exercise of its s.25 discretionary powers can make compensatory adjustments in respect of matrimonial assets other than the pension itself, for example by ordering that the matrimonial home be transferred and/or a larger lump sum be paid. In this way, rights under a pension scheme are left untouched but their value is taken into account by giving a party an appropriately enlarged share of the other party's assets.

*(ii) Pension Attachment Orders*    Since 1 August 1996 the divorce court has had the power to make a pension attachment order under ss.25B–25D Matrimonial Causes Act 1973 when exercising its powers under s.23. If an order is made, then once the pension becomes payable the person responsible for the pension arrangement must pay part of

the pension income and/or lump sum available under the pension arrangement to the other party to the marriage (s.25B(4)).

When considering whether to make an order, the court adopts a two-stage approach. First, it asks whether a financial provision order should be made to take account of any benefits or lost benefits under a pension scheme (s.25B(2)). If the answer is 'yes', then it must next decide whether to make an order requiring the trustees or managers of the pension fund to make payments out of the pension to the other spouse (s.25B(4)). Any payment ordered must not exceed the amount of payment due to the pension holder (s.25B(5)). Where the benefits under a pension include a lump sum payable in respect of the pension holder's death, the court can require the pension trustees or managers to pay the sum in whole or in part, or require the pension holder to nominate that the other spouse be entitled to payment in whole or in part (ss.25C(1), (2)). An attachment order must be expressed in percentage terms (s.25B(5)). The court cannot make an attachment order in relation to a pension arrangement which is the subject of a pension sharing order (ss.25B(7B), 25C(4)).

There is no automatic entitlement to a pension attachment order – the power to make orders is merely part of the court's discretionary powers to adjust the parties' matrimonial assets on divorce:

> ▶ *T v. T (Financial Relief: Pensions)* [1998] 1 FLR 1072
>
> The wife asked the judge to make a pension attachment order, earmarking part of her husband's pension to compensate for her lost pension rights, and she argued that the Matrimonial Causes Act 1973 obliged the court to compensate her. Singer J rejected her argument, holding that the Act required the court to consider: first, whether a periodical payments order or a lump sum was appropriate; and secondly, how pension considerations should affect the terms of any such order. He said that the answer to the second question might be 'not at all'. Singer J also said that an attachment order is subject to the same restrictions as a conventional order. It is a financial provision order under s.23, not a new or distinct species of order. Thus, it can be varied during the payer's lifetime and terminates on the payee's death or remarriage.

Pension attachment orders have several disadvantages. First, they undermine the policy of the clean break, as the parties remain financially tied to each other (as payments continue to be paid from the pension once it becomes payable). Secondly, it may be difficult for the court to force the pension holder to continue to make payments to the pension or to retire by a specified age. Thirdly, it is difficult for the court to predict the needs of the parties when the pension becomes payable, and the value of the pension. Fourthly, they can create uncertainty and insecurity as to when payments are to take effect and how long they will last. Pension sharing orders provide a better solution.

*(iii) Pension Sharing Orders*   Because of continuing concerns about pensions on divorce, pension splitting was introduced on 1 December 2000, as a result of amendments made to Part II of the Matrimonial Causes Act 1973 by the Welfare Reform and Pensions Act 1999 (for the background to the reforms, see the Consultation Paper, *Pension Sharing on Divorce: Reforming Pensions for a Fairer Future*, 1998). Pension

splitting enables a pension to be split at the time of the ancillary relief proceedings so that part of the pension fund can be allocated to the other spouse to invest as he or she thinks appropriate.

Under s.24B the court, on granting a decree of divorce (or nullity) or at any time thereafter (whether or not the decree is made absolute), may make a pension sharing order, which is an order that one party to the marriage's shareable rights under a specified pension arrangement be subject to pension sharing for the benefit of the other party, and which specifies the percentage value to be transferred (s.21A(1)). Thus the effect of the order is to credit the transferee with a percentage of the transferor's pension arrangement, which is reduced accordingly. The order cannot take effect until decree absolute (s.24B(2)). More than one order can be made, provided each is made in respect of a different pension arrangement (ss.24B(1), (3) and (4)). An order cannot be made where an attachment order in relation to a particular pension arrangement is in force (s.24B(5)). A pension sharing order can be made in respect of a pension which is already being paid. The provisions do not apply to the basic State retirement pension. Divorcing couples are not obliged to seek a pension sharing order. Offsetting and attachment orders (above) are available as alternative options. The s.25 guidelines apply.

*(iv) The Exercise of Discretion in Respect of a Pension*   The court's powers in respect of pension arrangements are governed by the factors in s.25 Matrimonial Causes Act 1973 (see 8.4, above), and the objective of the court is to achieve a fair result which does not discriminate against either spouse (applying *White* v. *White* and *Miller* v. *Miller*, above). In exercising its powers, the court has considerable discretion as to whether or not to make an order, and, if so, in what manner.

Section s.25B(1) expressly requires the court when conducting its s.25(2) exercise to have regard to: any benefits under a pension arrangement which a party to the marriage has or is likely to have; and any benefits under a pension arrangement which by reason of the divorce (or annulment), a party to the marriage will lose the chance of acquiring. When considering any benefits under a pension arrangement, there is no requirement that the courts take into consideration only those benefits which will be available in the foreseeable future (s.25B(1)). A pension can also be taken into account under s.25(2)(a) as a 'financial resource' which a party has or is likely to have in the future. If retirement is reasonably imminent, the court may decide to adjourn the proceedings.

## 8.9   Reaching Agreement

Most couples on divorce do not go to court to litigate about financial and property matters, but reach agreement. Some couples may make a pre-marital or post-marital agreement about what is to happen to their property and financial assets on marital breakdown.

Although spouses are free to enter into their own written agreements about finance and property on divorce, they are not completely free to do so, as the divorce court retains a supervisory role in respect of such agreements. Thus, the court has the power to alter them where circumstances change, and where there is no provision in the agreement for a child of the family (ss.34 and 35). Furthermore, any provision in an agreement restricting the right of either party to apply to the court for ancillary relief is void (s.34(1)). The court may insert new terms, or may vary or revoke the order.

The advantages of private agreements are that they promote amicable settlement and avoid the uncertainty and cost of litigation. However, they can have disadvantages as the following case shows:

> ▶ *Edgar v. Edgar* [1980] 1 WLR 1410, (1981) 2 FLR 19
>
> The parties entered into a separation agreement in which the husband, a multi-millionaire, agreed to pay his wife a lump sum of £100,000 and in which she agreed to seek no further provision. She entered into the agreement despite her solicitor's advice that she would obtain a better settlement in divorce proceedings. Later in ancillary relief proceedings on divorce she was granted a lump sum of £760,000. The husband appealed to the Court of Appeal.
>
> The Court of Appeal held, allowing his appeal, and setting the order aside, that the wife was bound by the terms of the original agreement. There was no evidence that she had been exploited. She had received legal advice and there had been no adverse conduct by her husband during negotiations leading up to the agreement. A large disparity between the sum agreed and the sum that she might have been awarded in divorce proceedings was insufficient on its own for the court to ignore the agreement. The court acknowledged that it had a duty to exercise its discretionary powers under s.25, but Ormrod LJ held that it was an important general principle that 'formal agreements, properly and faithfully arrived at with competent legal advice' should not be displaced unless there were 'good and substantial grounds' for concluding that an injustice would be done by holding the parties to the terms of their agreement. Ormrod LJ said that 'good and substantial grounds' included whether there was pressure from one side, exploitation of a dominant position, inadequate knowledge, bad legal advice or an unforeseen change of circumstances. His Lordship said that 'the existence of a freely negotiated bargain entered into at the instance of one of the parties and affording him or her everything for which he or she has stipulated must be a most important element of conduct which cannot lightly be ignored'.

*Edgar* v. *Edgar* emphasised the important policy objective of achieving finality and the undesirability of opening up arrangements which have already been settled by the parties. As a result of the decision, a spouse will not be permitted to resile from an agreement without good reason, for example where a spouse entered into the agreement under extreme pressure or with poor legal advice (see *Camm* v. *Camm* (1983) 4 FLR 577). In *J* v. *V (Disclosure: Offshore Corporation)* [2003] EWHC 3110 (Fam), [2004] 1 FLR 1042, for example, a pre-nuptial settlement was held to be of no significance, because its terms were unfair, and it had been signed on the eve of the marriage, without full legal advice, without proper disclosure and had made no provision for the arrival of children.

Each case, however, depends on its facts. In *G* v. *G (Financial Provision: Separation Agreement)* [2004] 1 FLR 1011 an agreement was upheld even though it had been drawn up without legal advice and at a time when emotional pressures were high and judgment was likely to be clouded. The Court of Appeal held that these facts had to be balanced by the consideration that both parties had previous experience of marital breakdown and had from the outset of their marriage elected to regulate their affairs contractually.

The *Edgar* v. *Edgar* principles also apply to a financial provision agreement made in the context of a financial provision application under s.15 and Schedule 1 to the Children Act 1989 (see 13.5, and *Morgan* v. *Hill* [2006] EWCA Civ 1602, [2007] 1 FLR 1480).

## (a)  Pre-Marital and Post-Marital Agreements

A pre-marital agreement is an agreement entered into by a man and woman on contemplation of marriage which deals with the financial arrangements that they are to make should their marriage end in divorce. People are increasingly making them, particularly where substantial assets are involved. Post-marital agreements are similar to pre-marital agreements except that they are made during marriage.

Although couples are free to make pre-marital (or post-marital) agreements governing the distribution of property and finance should their marriage break down, they are not completely free to do as they like (see above). Thus, the terms of the agreement cannot limit or oust the divorce court's powers to make property and finance orders (*Hyman* v. *Hyman* [1929] AC 601), and either party to the agreement can still opt to apply for property and finance orders on divorce.

At one time there was considerable judicial reluctance to uphold these agreements. They were considered to be contrary to public policy as they undermined the institution of marriage. In fact, only in 1995, Thorpe LJ had stated in *F* v. *F (Ancillary Relief: Substantial Assets)* [1995] 2 FLR 45 that such agreements were of 'very limited significance' in England and Wales. In recent years, however, there has been a change of attitude, and the benefits of such agreements are recognised as an important part of the settlement culture. However, they are not necessarily binding, as the court has the ultimate say and will take the agreement into account when conducting its discretionary exercise, either as one of the circumstances of the case under s.25 or as conduct which it would be inequitable to disregard under s.25(2)(g). Depending on the circumstances, however, the general approach of the courts is that agreements freely negotiated between the parties to a marriage should be upheld, unless they were unfairly entered into or they create injustice.

*Edgar* v. *Edgar* (above) is still the leading case on private agreement, but in *X* v. *X (Y and Z Intervening)* [2002] 1 FLR 508, where the wife was held to the agreement – because she had willingly entered into it with the benefit of expert advice – Munby J usefully listed the propositions which apply to such agreements:

- The court must apply the s.25 criteria and reach a just result, what Lord Nicholls in *White* v. *White* called the 'fair' result; but the fact that the parties have entered into an agreement is a very important factor in considering what is fair.
- The court will not lightly allow parties to depart from an agreement, and agreements should as a matter of general policy be upheld by the courts, unless contrary to public policy or subject to some vitiating feature such as lack of legal advice, duress or change of circumstances.
- The mere fact that one party might have done better by going to court is not of itself generally a ground for permitting that party to resile from an agreement. The court must nonetheless have regard to all the circumstances, including, in particular, the circumstances surrounding the making of the agreement, the extent to which the parties attached importance to it, and the extent to which the parties have acted upon it. The relevant circumstances are not limited to the purely financial aspects of the agreement, but social, personal, religious and cultural considerations can also be taken into account.

The following cases provide examples of the courts' approach:

▶ *M v. M (Pre-nuptial Agreement)* [2002] 1 FLR 654

The parties had entered into a pre-nuptial agreement in Canada, which the wife had signed contrary to legal advice that it was not in her best interests. She applied for ancillary relief in the English courts. Connell J awarded her a lump sum which was £600,000 greater than that agreed upon in the agreement, plus child maintenance and school fees. Although the husband was worth £7.5 million and the wife had sought £1.3 million by way of ancillary relief, Connell J allowed the existence of the agreement to affect the amount of the award, holding that it did not matter whether the court treated the agreement as a circumstance of the case, or as conduct which it would be inequitable to disregard under s.25(2)(g) Matrimonial Causes Act 1973. He said that under either approach, the court's duty was to look at the agreement and decide in the particular circumstances what weight to give it. Connell J held that it would have been unjust to the husband to ignore the existence of the agreement and its terms, as it would have been to the wife to hold her strictly to its terms.

▶ *K v. K (Ancillary Relief: Pre-nuptial Agreement)* [2003] 1 FLR 120

The existence of a pre-nuptial agreement signed the day before marriage but with independent legal advice was taken into account as one of the circumstances of the case under s.25 and as conduct which it would be inequitable to disregard under s.25(2)(g). The parties understood the agreement. They had been properly advised. There was no pressure to sign. They knew there was soon to be a child. There was no unforeseen change of circumstances which would make it unfair to hold one party to the agreement, and there was no injustice to the other party. However, the court gave the wife an award which was higher than that agreed upon in the agreement, because of the wife's enormous contribution to the upbringing of the child, and because under s.25(1) the child's welfare required him to have a home to live in with his mother and for there to be sufficient income to provide for his and his mother's maintenance. The child was entitled to be brought up in circumstances that bore some sort of relationship to the father's current resources and standard of living.

▶ *NA v. MA* [2006] EWHC 2900 (Fam), [2007] 1 FLR 1760

The husband was worth about £40 million. He and his wife had entered into a post-nuptial settlement, which included a term that the wife should have £3.3 million on divorce. The agreement had been signed a few months after the husband had discovered that his wife had committed adultery with one of his friends. The husband argued that the wife should be kept to the terms of the agreed settlement, but Baron J overturned the post-nuptial settlement, awarding the wife £9.176 million, on the ground that, although the wife had had independent legal advice, she had been forced to enter into the agreement under duress. Her will had been overborne by her husband exercising undue pressure or influence over her. Furthermore, the agreement had not been premised on fairness, having been calculated on the basis of what the husband was prepared to provide rather than upon what was a fair assessment of what might be appropriate or needed, and it had been non-negotiable.

Factors which are likely to be taken into account by the court when considering whether the parties should be bound by the terms of agreement will include: whether the parties understood the agreement; whether they had independent legal advice; whether there was any pressure to sign the agreement; whether there was full disclosure; whether the agreement was made very close to the marriage; and whether there was any abuse of a dominant position. The court is more likely to uphold an agreement if one or both of the parties has come from a jurisdiction where pre-nuptial agreements are commonplace and enforceable (for example, from Europe or some states in the USA).

There has been discussion about whether there should be reform to make pre-marital (and post-marital) agreements legally binding and to encourage their greater use (see 8.14, below).

### (b)  Consent Orders

Agreements about finance and property on divorce can be incorporated into a consent order, which the court has jurisdiction to make under s.33A Matrimonial Causes Act 1973. Consent orders encourage settlement and reduce the cost of litigation. However, they can only contain those orders which the court has power to make under Part II of the 1973 Act. In order to enable the court to exercise its discretionary powers, the parties must provide the court with prescribed information, such as the duration of the marriage, the ages of the parties and children, an estimate of the approximate value of their capital resources, accommodation arrangements for them and the children, and whether either party has remarried or intends to marry or cohabit (s.33A). Failure to provide this information can result in an order being set aside (see below). Although consent orders are based on an agreement, they are not treated as ordinary contracts (see *Potter* v. *Potter* [1990] 2 FLR 27). General contract principles do not determine the outcome of a case. It is the consent order itself which determines the rights and duties of the parties, not the agreement which the parties make before the order is made (*De Lasala* v. *De Lasala* [1980] AC 546 and *Xydhias* v. *Xydhias* [1999] 1 FLR 683).

When considering whether to make a consent order, the court does not just 'rubber-stamp' the proposed agreement. It considers all the circumstances and applies the s.25 guidelines and the clean-break provisions. However, the court will usually approve the agreement, as the fact that it has been drawn up and agreed to by the parties, usually with legal advice, is *prima facie* proof of its reasonableness. The terms of a consent order can be varied in variation proceedings, but only in respect of periodical payments (see below).

Consent orders may be set aside in some circumstances, for example if there has been non-disclosure (see 8.12, below).

### 8.10  Enforcing Ancillary Relief Orders

Ancillary relief orders can be enforced in various ways. Remedies for enforcement available in the High Court and county courts (the 'superior' courts) differ from those in the magistrates' family proceedings courts. The Lord Chancellor's Advisory Group on Ancillary Relief has drawn attention to the fragmented nature of the system for enforcing orders and has recommended that there should be a single process for enforcement (see *Report on Enforcement of Orders*, Lord Chancellor's Department, 1998).

### (a)  Enforcing Orders for Payment of Money

The enforcement procedures for enforcing orders for payment of money include:

- ▶ *Judgment Summons* The spouse wishing to enforce the order can apply for a judgment summons which requires the other party to attend before a judge to be examined as to his or her means. At the hearing, the judge will make such order as he thinks fit in relation to the arrears or outstanding payment. Committal to prison can be exercised but only for dishonesty or contempt of court, and only if the court, applying the criminal burden of proof, is satisfied that the defaulter has, or has had, the means to pay. In *Mubarak v. Mubarak* [2001] 1 FLR 698 the Court of Appeal held that the provisions and rules governing the judgment summons procedure were incompatible with art. 6 of the European Convention for the Protection of Human Rights (right to a fair trial), but held that the incompatibility could be corrected by a practice direction (see *President's Direction (Committal Proceedings) 16 March 2001* [2001] Fam Law 333). Other changes to the rules of court have been made since *Mubarak*. Thorpe LJ in *Mubarak* predicted that the judgment summons would become a largely obsolete method of enforcement in ancillary relief proceedings, as the criminal, not the civil, standard of proof applies. In *Corbett v. Corbett* [2003] EWCA Civ 559, [2003] 2 FLR 385, where a judgment summons was made against the husband for arrears in maintenance payments, the Court of Appeal allowed the husband's appeal and set aside a suspended order for imprisonment, as the process had been manifestly not compliant with the husband's rights under the European Convention for the Protection of Human Rights and the Human Rights Act 1998, and the process did not meet the standards laid down in *Mubarak*.

- *Order for Sale Under s.24A Matrimonial Causes Act 1973* This can be made to enforce a lump sum payment. The order can direct that the proceeds of sale, or part of them, be used to pay the lump sum.

- *Execution Against Goods* A writ of *fieri facias* (in the High Court) or a warrant of execution (in the county court) can be made authorising the sheriff (in the High Court) or the bailiff (in the county court) to seize sufficient of the other spouse's goods to pay the debt (excluding basic goods for domestic needs).

- *A Garnishee Order* directing a sum of money to be paid (for example a spouse's bank or building society may be ordered to pay a sum owed directly to the other spouse).

- *A Charging Order* imposing a charge on interests in property so that priority is gained over the property charged, and an order is sought that the property be sold. These are commonly made.

- *Appointment of Receiver* to receive rents, profits and other proceeds of property belonging to the defaulting spouse, or of a business carried on by that spouse. This is an exceptional remedy.

- *A Writ of Sequestration* preventing the defaulting spouse from dealing with property until the default has been made good.

- *An Attachment of Earnings Order* ordering that payments from the defaulter's earnings be paid to the collecting officer of the court (see the Attachment of Earnings Act 1971, as amended). There is a 'protected earnings rate' below which, having regard to the defaulter's resources and needs, the court thinks it reasonable that the earnings paid to him should not be reduced.

- *Registration in the Magistrates' Family Proceedings Court* A periodical payments order made by the High Court or county court can be registered in the magistrates' family proceedings court, whereupon it can be enforced as a magistrates' court order under the Magistrates' Courts Act 1980 (for example by warrant of distress, attachment of earnings, a fine or imprisonment). The advantage of doing this is that the magistrates' family proceedings court has an efficient administrative procedure for collecting payments owed.

- *The Maintenance Enforcement Act 1991* This Act improved the collecting and enforcement of maintenance payments. It gives the courts power to specify that payments of maintenance be made by standing order, or by attachment of earnings, or some other method.

### (b)    Enforcing Property Adjustment Orders

Where a spouse fails to co-operate in completing the required formalities for the transfer of the matrimonial home to the other spouse, an application can be made to the court for an order that, unless the transfer is completed within a specified time, then the document(s) will be executed by a district judge or judge.

In the case of a s.24A order for sale, if a party refuses to vacate the matrimonial home, an application can be made to the court for an order ordering that spouse to give up possession, so that the sale can proceed.

## 8.11    Protecting Matrimonial Property Pending Ancillary Relief Proceedings

### (a)    A Freezing Order

Sometimes a spouse may dispose, or attempt to dispose, of matrimonial assets in order to defeat a claim to ancillary relief, for example by selling them, giving them away, or sending them out of the UK. In order to protect property pending a hearing for ancillary relief, the court can make a 'freezing order' under s.37 Matrimonial Causes Act 1973 (see, for example, *Sherry* v. *Sherry* [1991] 1 FLR 307) or under the High Court's inherent jurisdiction. An applicant for a freezing order must have a good arguable case and show that there is a real risk that the respondent would seek to defeat or thwart the case by disposing of his or her assets unless restrained from doing so by the court. Overseas assets can be frozen, unless there may be problems enforcing an order in a foreign court. A freezing order does not usually freeze all the defendant's assets, but is restricted to the maximum amount of property likely to be awarded in divorce proceedings (*Ghoth* v. *Ghoth* [1992] 2 All ER 920). Although the jurisdiction to make freezing orders is wide, flexible and innovative, only in the most exceptional circumstances should the terms of a freezing order include a provision imposing an obligation on a spouse to make maintenance payments (see *Re M (Freezing Injunction)* [2006] 1 FLR 1031).

### (b)    A Search and Seize Order

Another order which is available to protect matrimonial assets pending ancillary relief proceedings is a search and seize order which allows a named person to enter premises to search for and seize documents which might be useful as evidence in court proceedings. It can only be granted by the High Court. The aim of the order is to ensure that the respondent does not dispose of evidence which may be useful at the ancillary relief hearing. It is sometimes used in cases of suspected non-disclosure (see, for example, *Emmanuel* v. *Emmanuel* [1982] 1 WLR 669). Strict rules apply to the grant of an order and to the way in which the entry and search powers can be exercised.

The above orders are considered to be draconian orders, which are granted only in the last resort in exceptional cases (see, for example, *Araghchinchi* v. *Araghchinchi* [1997] 2 FLR 142, where an application for these orders was refused even though the husband had been devious and dishonest). Where there is a danger that a party may leave the jurisdiction before a claim for ancillary relief has been settled, a writ *ne exeat regno* can be sought which directs the tipstaff, an officer of the court, to arrest the respondent and bring him or her before a judge. The respondent's passport may also be seized. These orders are rarely sought, and rarely made.

## 8.12 Challenging an Order for Ancillary Relief

An order for ancillary relief can be challenged by: (a) asking for a rehearing; (b) applying for variation under s.31 Matrimonial Causes Act 1973; (c) appealing, which may require an application for leave to appeal out of time; (d) applying to have the order set aside. It is also possible to have an application struck out under the rules of court and under the court's inherent jurisdiction (see *Rose* v. *Rose* [2003] EWHC 505 (Fam)).

### (a) A Rehearing

Where a party considers that there was something fundamentally wrong with the way in which the case was heard (for example, there was non-disclosure or perjury), an application can be made for a rehearing. Sometimes an appeal court will order a rehearing because the order is fundamentally flawed.

### (b) Variation

Under s.31 Matrimonial Causes Act 1973 the court has wide powers to vary or discharge certain orders (whether or not made by consent) or temporarily to suspend and revive any provision contained therein (s.31(1)). The most common applications for variation are in respect of periodical payments orders by recipients who wish to have payments increased, and by payers who wish to have them reduced. Not all ancillary relief orders made on divorce (or nullity) can be varied – only the following orders (s.32(2)):

- maintenance pending suit or interim maintenance;
- periodical payments (secured or unsecured);
- an order providing for the payment of a lump sum by instalments;
- any deferred order made by virtue of s.23(1)(c) (lump sum) which includes provision made by virtue of s.25B(4) or s.25C (provision in respect of pension rights);
- an order for the sale of property under s.24A;
- a s.24B pension sharing order made before decree absolute.

*Orders that Cannot be Varied*   Lump sum orders and property adjustment orders cannot be varied. They are 'once and for all' orders. The reason for the final nature of these orders is to create certainty, so that the parties can make plans for the future without worrying about whether an order will be overturned. Lump sum orders and property adjustment orders can, however, be appealed against or set aside (see below).

*How the Court Exercises its Variation Powers*   When exercising its powers the court must consider all the circumstances of the case, but must give first consideration to the welfare of any child of the family aged under 18, and any changes of circumstance, including any change in any of the matters to which the court was required to have regard when making the original order (s.31(7)). The court must also consider whether to effect a clean break. In other words, it must consider whether it is appropriate to vary a periodical payments order so that payments will be made for a limited term sufficient to enable the payee to adjust without undue hardship to the termination of those payments (s.31(7)(a)). For the purpose of effecting a clean break, the court can make a compensating lump sum or property adjustment order under s.31(7B) (see below). The court has various powers. It can remit payment of all or part of any arrears due under any periodical payments order, including maintenance pending suit and interim maintenance (s.31(2A)). Where a periodical payments order is for a limited term, it can extend the term, unless the original order prohibited it (s.28(1A)).

The court has a wide discretion in variation proceedings. It can take into account increases in the payer's capital and income resources. In *Flavell* v. *Flavell* [1997] 1 FLR 353 the Court of Appeal held that, when seeking variation of periodical payments, there is no need to show a change of circumstances, or an exceptional or material change of circumstances. It held that, as the court has an absolute discretion, it can look at the case afresh, and need not regard the original order as the starting point. However, it said that the court will be vigilant to ensure that the variation application is not a disguised form of appeal.

The Court of Appeal has held that an application for variation of periodical payments should be made well in advance of the cut-off date for a variation or extension of a periodical payments order (see *G* v. *G (Periodical Payments: Jurisdiction)* [1998] Fam 1, [1997] 1 FLR 368, where the Court of Appeal held that a wife was not able to apply after the child's eighteenth birthday for variation of a periodical payments order which had terminated on the child reaching 18).

*Cohabitation and Variation* The fact that a former spouse is cohabiting with a new partner may be an important factor in variation proceedings, and may result in a reduction, or termination, of periodical payments. In the following case Coleridge J held that the law should keep up with changing social conditions and treat cohabitation after divorce as a relevant factor:

▶ *K* v. *K (Periodical Payment: Cohabitation)* [2005] EWHC 2886 (Fam), [2006] 2 FLR 468

The former husband applied for a downward variation of a periodical payments order made some seven years earlier, asking for a nominal order with immediate effect. He did so on the basis that his wife had been cohabiting with a man for three years and because of his own imminent drop in income.

Coleridge J held that the court could place considerable weight on cohabitation as a factor in the case. The wife's settled cohabitation for three years had resulted in a reduction in her dependency on her former husband and constituted a relevant circumstance under s.31(7)(b). He said that there was no reason nowadays why the court should not order termination of periodical payments after a certain period of cohabitation. Section 28(3) of the 1973 Act did not prohibit this step, which would provide certainty for the parties and better reflect modern mores and social behaviour. Coleridge J concluded by saying that this was 'a troubling and messy area of the law' and that the current legislation 'enacted against an utterly different social fabric [was] not adequate to deal with it'. He said that '[i]f cohabitation is to be a social norm surely financial independence from a previous partner, whether married or not, must go with it?' As there was no sign that Parliament was going to change the law, he suggested that 'the court must nowadays grapple with this point and factor into its analysis and calculation not only numerically but in principle the existence of a lengthy and settled period of cohabitation and the likelihood of its continuing indefinitely'. Coleridge J reduced the periodical payments from £16,000 to £12,000 per annum and capitalised the payments at the sum of £100,000.

*Achieving a Clean Break*   In order to effect a clean break in variation proceedings, the court has power under s.31(7B) (on discharging a periodical payments order in favour of a party to a marriage, or on varying such an order so that payments are to be made for a fixed period) to substitute the periodical payments for one or more of the following orders as a means of effecting a variation: a lump sum order; a property adjustment order; a pension sharing order; and a direction that the person in whose favour the original order discharged or varied was made is not entitled to make any further application for a periodical payments order or an extension of the period to which the original order is limited by any variation made by the court. Thus, s.31(7B) allows a clean break to be achieved in variation proceedings which was not possible when the original order was made.

In *Pearce* v. *Pearce* [2003] EWCA Civ 1054, [2003] 2 FLR 1144, where the wife sought an increase in periodical payments and the husband sought to capitalise her maintenance (under ss.31(7A) and (7B)), the Court of Appeal held that, on dismissing an entitlement to future periodical payments, the court's function is not to reopen capital claims but to substitute for the periodical payments order such other order(s) as will both fairly compensate the payee and, at the same time, complete the clean break. It also held that, in surveying what substitute order(s) should be made, the court should give first consideration to the option of carving out of the payer's pension fund a pension for the payee that is equivalent to the discharged periodical payments order.

In exercising its powers to capitalise periodical payments, Baron J in *Lauder* v. *Lauder* [2007] EWHC 1227 (Fam), [2007] 2 FLR 802 said that 'the proper approach in this type of application is to apply the precise terms of the statute in the light of the factual matrix and give proper consideration to the recent guidance given by the House of Lords in the case of *Miller*'. In *Lauder* Baron J held, allowing the wife's appeal, that the district judge's award to the wife of periodical payments of £40,000 per annum (to be capitalised at £500,000) was plainly too low, given that the wife's needs had to be 'generously interpreted' and that, post-*Miller*, the court also had to take into account the wife's right to an element of compensation.

### (c)   Appeals and Permission to Appeal Out of Time

In order to encourage finality in litigation, appeals are only allowed in restricted circumstances. In *Piglowska* v. *Piglowski* [1999] 1 WLR 1360 the House of Lords emphasised the width of discretion conferred on trial judges in ancillary relief proceedings, and said that the appellate court should be slow to interfere. It held that appeals are only possible if there has been procedural irregularity, or irrelevant matters have been considered, or relevant matters ignored, or the decision is plainly wrong (applying *G* v. *G* [1985] 1 WLR 647). This is a high hurdle (see, for example, *Foster* v. *Foster* [2003] EWCA Civ 565, [2003] 2 FLR 299 where the Court of Appeal, referring to *dicta* in *Piglowska* on appeals, restored the decision of the district judge at first instance).

The Court of Appeal has held that, when considering appeals and applications for leave to appeal, the courts can encourage the parties to use mediation rather than continuing expensive and protracted litigation (see *dicta* in *Al-Khatib* v. *Masry* [2004] EWCA Civ 1353, [2005] 1 FLR 381; and *Moore* v. *Moore* [2004] EWCA Civ 1243, [2005] 1 FLR 666).

If the date for lodging the appeal has passed, leave of the court is needed to bring an appeal. With an application for leave to appeal out of time, the applicant is asking for the late appeal to be heard because unforeseen events have occurred since the original order was made, but after the time for lodging an appeal has expired. Sometimes an appeal out of time is combined with an application to set aside the original order (see below).

The courts are, however, unwilling to reopen litigation unless it is really necessary, because it increases costs and extends the duration of the conflict (see *Shaw* v. *Shaw* [2002] EWCA Civ 1298, [2002] 2 FLR 1204). For this reason, the number of cases in which permission is given to reopen litigation, whether by an application to appeal out of time or to have the order set aside, is exceptionally small because of the public interest in the finality of litigation.

Because of the need for certainty and finality in litigation and to prevent a flood of appeals, the courts are unwilling to grant leave to appeal out of time unless the principles in the following case are satisfied:

---

▶ *Barder* v. *Barder* [1988] AC 20, *sub nom Barder* v. *Barder (Caluori Intervening)* [1987] 2 FLR 480

A consent order was made in full and final settlement, in which the husband agreed to transfer his half-share in the matrimonial home to his wife. Four weeks after the order was made, but outside the time-limit for lodging an appeal, the wife killed the children and committed suicide. The husband sought leave to appeal out of time against the order (it could not be varied under s.31 as it was a property order), arguing that the basis on which the order had been made had been fundamentally altered by the unforeseen change of circumstances – the death of his wife and children.

The House of Lords held that he should be granted leave to appeal out of time and that the order should be set aside. Lord Brandon said, however, that leave to appeal should be granted only where the following four conditions were satisfied:

▶ the new events relied on had invalidated the fundamental basis or assumption on which the original order had been made, so that, if leave to appeal were granted, the appeal would be certain or very likely to succeed;
▶ the new events had occurred within a relatively short time of the original order being made – probably less than a year;
▶ the application for leave to appeal had been made promptly; and
▶ the grant of leave would not prejudice third parties who had acquired in good faith and for valuable consideration an interest in the property subject to the order.

---

Thus, there must be a material change of circumstances which has undermined or invalidated the basis of the order. Not every application will result in permission to appeal being granted and an order being set aside. The *Barder* principles are severe in order to ensure that the courts are not swamped by meritless applications.

The *Barder* principles apply to orders whether made in contested proceedings or by consent. The operative date for determining whether permission to appeal has been sought promptly is when the order was implemented, not when it was made (Ward J in *B v. B (Financial Provision: Leave to Appeal)* [1994] 1 FLR 219).

*The Supervening Event Must be an Unforeseeable Event*   In *Barder* it was held that the supervening event must be unforeseen. In *Maskell v. Maskell* [2001] EWCA Civ 858, [2003] 1FLR 1138 the Court of Appeal held, for instance, that becoming unemployed two months after an order for ancillary relief was made was not a *Barder* event – as it was foreseeable. Foreseeability of the event was also fatal to the claim in the following case:

---

▶ ***S v. S (Ancillary Relief: Consent Order)*** **[2002] EWHC 223 (Fam), [2002] 1 FLR 922**

The wife applied to have a consent order set aside six months after it had been made, because the House of Lords had given its decision in *White v. White* and she thought she would have obtained a better settlement if the propositions laid down in that case had been applied (see 8.6, above).

Bracewell J dismissed her application, holding that, while a change in the law, such as in *White*, could constitute a supervening event under the *Barder* principles, the supervening event must be an unforeseeable one. As *White* was a landmark case which was anticipated at the time the wife's case was being decided, she and her legal advisers should have known that it was foreseeable and that its impact was unavoidable. Bracewell J said that there were public policy arguments against setting aside a consent order on the basis of a change in the law, as this would lead to the floodgates opening.

---

### Examples of Situations Where Appeals Out of Time Have Been Allowed

▶ Fluctuations in property valuations where a party has delayed in effecting sale (*Heard v. Heard* [1995] 1 FLR 970; *Penrose v. Penrose* [1994] 2 FLR 621).

▶ Unforeseen death or serious illness (*Amey v. Amey* [1992] 2 FLR 89; *Reid v. Reid* [2003] EWHC 2878 (Fam), [2004] 1 FLR 736).

▶ Unexpected marriage or cohabitation (*Wells v. Wells* [1992] 2 FLR 66; *Chaudhuri v. Chaudhuri* [1992] 2 FLR 73; *Williams v. Lindley (Formerly Williams)* [2005] EWCA Civ 103, [2005] 2 FLR 710, where the wife became engaged within one month of a lump sum being ordered in her favour).

▶ Misrepresentation (*Ritchie v. Ritchie* [1996] 1 FLR 898).

---

*How the Court Exercises its Powers Once Permission to Appeal Has Been Granted*   This matter was considered in *Smith v. Smith (Smith and Others Intervening)* [1991] 2 FLR 432, [1992] Fam 62. Here a lump sum order had been made in favour of a wife, which represented half the family assets, but six months later she committed suicide leaving her whole estate, including the lump sum, to her daughter. In the Court of Appeal Butler-Sloss LJ stated that the correct approach was to start the s.25 exercise from the beginning and consider what order should be made on the basis of the new facts (here that the wife was known only to have a few months to live). Applying the s.25 guidelines to the facts, Butler-Sloss LJ reduced the lump sum.

In *Williams v. Lindley (Formally Williams)* [2005] EWCA Civ 103, [2005] 2 FLR 710 the

Court of Appeal held that great flexibility was needed in supervening event cases to accommodate the widely different facts and circumstances of each case and that the determinations required by *Barder* v. *Barder (Caluori Intervening)* (above) and *Smith* v. *Smith (Smith and Others Intervening)* (above) should not be too rigidly prescribed. It said that much would depend upon the impact of the supervening event, and the lapse of time between the order being invalidated and the consequential reassessment on the principles established in *Smith* v. *Smith (Smith and Others Intervening)*.

### (d) Setting the Original Order Aside

An application can be made to set aside an order which has been made on an improper basis, for example because of non-disclosure, fraud, duress or misrepresentation, or where changes of circumstances have occurred which were unforeseen when the original order was made. An application to set an order aside will often be made in conjunction with an appeal out of time (see above). However, because of the need for finality in litigation, the courts will not usually set aside an order unless the circumstances are exceptional.

Applications are sometimes made where there has been a failure to disclose information which is required by the rules of court. This occurred in the following case, which lays down the approach to be adopted by the court in applications to set aside:

> ▶ *Jenkins* v. *Livesey (Formerly Jenkins)* [1985] AC 424, *sub nom Livesey (Formerly Jenkins)* v. *Jenkins* [1985] 1 FLR 813
>
> A clean break consent order was made, in which the parties agreed that the husband would transfer to his wife his half-share in the matrimonial home, on her foregoing all claims to ancillary relief. Three weeks after the house had been transferred, the wife remarried and two months later put the house up for sale. The husband appealed out of time, asking for the consent order to be set aside on the grounds of misrepresentation and non-disclosure.
>
> The House of Lord allowed his appeal and held that parties who wished the court to exercise its discretionary powers under Part II of the 1973 Act were under a duty in contested or consent proceedings to make full and frank disclosure of all material matters, so that the court could exercise its discretion properly. However, because of the importance of encouraging a clean break, orders should not be lightly set aside. They should only be set aside if the failure to make full and frank disclosure led the court to make an order which was substantially different from the one it would have made had there been full and frank disclosure. As the wife's engagement was a material circumstance directly relevant to the parties' agreement about ancillary relief, she was under a duty to disclose it before the agreement was put into effect by means of the consent order. Her failure to disclose the engagement invalidated the order. The order was set aside, and the case remitted for a rehearing.
>
> The House of Lords stressed that non-disclosure of itself is not a sufficient ground for an order to be set aside. Like applications for appeals out of time, where the policy objective of finality is also upheld, the circumstances must be such that a fundamentally different order would have been made had the circumstances been known.

Although the House of Lords in *Jenkins* v. *Livesey* emphasised the important policy objective of finality in litigation, sometimes justice will prevail and an order will be set aside (see, for example, *T* v. *T (Consent Order: Procedure to Set Aside)* [1996] 2 FLR 640 where the order was set aside because of fraudulent non-disclosure by the husband, who, unbeknown to his wife, had sold his company for £1.6 million two months after the consent order had been made).

In *Harris* v. *Manahan* [1997] 1 FLR 205 the Court of Appeal had to consider whether a consent order could be set aside because a party had received bad legal advice. The Court of Appeal held that the requirements of public policy that there be finality in litigation also required, save in the most exceptional cases of the cruellest injustice, that bad legal advice should not be a ground for interfering with a consent order. The rationale for such an approach was that, once an agreement has been embodied in a consent order, the source of the obligation becomes the court's order rather than the agreement made by the parties (*De Lasala* v. *De Lasala* [1979] 2 All ER 1146). However, where any agreement about property and finance has not been embodied in a consent order, then the court may take into account the quality of any legal advice.

## 8.13  Applications for Ancillary Relief After a Foreign Divorce

Under Part III of the Matrimonial and Family Proceedings Act 1984 a person who has divorced outside England and Wales can apply for ancillary relief in the courts in England and Wales, but only if the court grants leave to apply, which it can do if there is a substantial ground for making the application (s.13). Under s.16 the court, when deciding whether to grant leave, must consider whether England and Wales is the appropriate venue for the application (s.16(1)) and must have regard to a number of specified matters (s.16(2)), such as: the connection that the parties have with England and Wales, the country where they were divorced and any other country; and any financial benefit the applicant or child of the family has received or is likely to receive by agreement or by operation of law in another country. Consideration of these matters in s.16 acts as a threshold to prevent unmeritorious applications and to avoid the abuse of the purpose of the provision (Coleridge J in *M* v. *L (Financial Relief After Overseas Divorce)* [2003] EWHC 328 (Fam), [2003] 2 FLR 425). Once leave has been granted, ss.17 and 18 provide that the court can exercise its ancillary relief powers under Part II of the Matrimonial Causes Act 1973 having regard to the s.25 factors (see 8.4). The overriding principle of fairness laid down in *White* v. *White* and endorsed in *Miller* v. *Miller* (see 8.6, above) will also apply.

Because of the need for finality in litigation and the principle of comity between nations, leave to apply for ancillary relief in the courts in the UK is only likely to be granted in exceptional cases. As the purpose of the 1984 Act is 'to remit hardships which have been experienced in the past in the presence of a failure in a foreign jurisdiction to afford appropriate financial relief' (Purchas LJ in *Holmes* v. *Holmes* [1989] Fam 47), the courts have used their leave powers sparingly. Thus, in *Hewitson* v. *Hewitson* [1995] 1 FLR 241, for example, the Court of Appeal refused to grant leave to the wife, because a court of competent jurisdiction in California had made the consent order, which had been negotiated by lawyers, and was designed to be comprehensive and final. She was not therefore entitled to 'two bites of the cherry.' In *M* v. *M (Financial Provision after Foreign Divorce)* [1994] 1 FLR 399 an application by a wife for ancillary relief in England after a French divorce was refused. However, in *A* v. *S (Financial Relief After Overseas UK Divorce and Financial Proceedings)* [2002] EWHC 1157 (Fam), [2003] 1 FLR 531, where the court in Texas, USA, had awarded the wife practically nothing on the basis of the doctrine of community of property, Bodey J took a generous approach, and, while recognising the need for caution when an overseas court had already ruled on the matter, nonetheless granted leave in order to do justice between the parties.

An application for leave to apply for ancillary relief in England and Wales is unlikely to succeed where the application is made solely for the purpose of enforcing a foreign order (see *Jordan* v. *Jordan* [1999] 2 FLR 1069, where the application was in essence an application to enforce a Californian court order). However, if the foreign enforcement procedures and reciprocal enforcement procedures have been exhausted, or are manifestly inadequate, leave may be granted (see *Lamagni* v. *Lamagni* [1995] 2 FLR 452 where the wife was granted leave because of her fruitless attempts to enforce Belgian court orders for financial relief in Belgium).

## 8.14 Reforming the Law on Ancillary Relief

### (a) Discussion of Reform

The discretionary system for allocating property and finance on divorce has been criticised from time to time, and proposals for reform have been discussed. While a discretionary regime has the advantage of flexibility, it has the disadvantages of being uncertain and unpredictable and is time-consuming and expensive. One of the drawbacks is that s.25 Matrimonial Causes Act 1973 – which governs the exercise of judicial discretion – provides no indication of how the discretionary powers should be exercised. It merely lists a number of factors which must be taken into account. There are no guiding principles.

Although the House of Lords in *White* v. *White* (see 8.6, above) held that the overarching objective in ancillary relief proceedings is that of fairness, and that there should be no discrimination between divorcing couples in respect of their different contributions, financial or domestic, the decision has not made the exercise of judicial discretion more predictable and the case has created its own set of uncertainties. In fact, Sir Mark Potter P in *Charman* v. *Charman (No. 4)* (see 8.6, above) was of the opinion that the decision in *White* had undoubtedly not resolved 'the problems faced by practitioners in advising clients or by clients in deciding upon what terms to compromise' (para. 117). Furthermore, the decision of the House of Lords in *Miller and McFarlane* has not resolved the uncertainties. *White* v. *White* and *Miller* v. *Miller* have not made it any easier to predict the outcome of cases, particularly those involving significant assets. As Cooke has said ([2007] CFLQ 98), crucial issues of principle were left unresolved in *White* v. *White* – and *Miller* v. *Miller* did not resolve them. Thus, problems still remain about how the *Miller* guiding principles (of needs, compensation and sharing) are to be applied, and how they relate to the s.25 guidelines. Difficulties also arise in respect of when and how special contribution should be taken into account as a justification for departing from equality. Also, can special contribution by the homemaker to the upbringing and welfare of the family count as special contribution, or does special contribution only apply to financial contributions by the breadwinner? If it applies only to financial contribution, then discrimination may still exist. There is also uncertainty about what constitutes matrimonial and non-matrimonial assets and whether the equal sharing principle applies only to matrimonial property or all property.

Discussions of reform of ancillary relief have focused on three main options: the greater use of pre-marital and post-marital agreements; the introduction of a presumptive 50:50

split of matrimonial assets; and the introduction of a set of policy objectives to help govern the exercise of judicial discretion. Pre-marital and post-marital agreements would work in tandem with a 50:50 split. Thus, a married couple would be able to contract out of a 50:50 split by making a pre- or post-marital agreement to the contrary. These three options for reform were looked at in 1991 by the Family Law Committee of the Law Society (see *Memorandum: Capital Provision on Divorce*, Law Society, 1991), but no reforms took place, as it was felt that more research was needed.

At the end of the 1990s there was renewed discussion about the same three options for reform by the Government (see *Supporting Families*, Home Office, 1998). These discussions were taken further by the Lord Chancellor's Ancillary Relief Advisory Group (chaired by the Rt Hon Lord Justice Thorpe), but the group concluded that there was a need for research and wide consultation, which would encompass both social and public policy issues (see *Report of the Lord Chancellor's Advisory Group on Ancillary Relief*, July 1998). Some of the Advisory Group, however, urged the retention of the status quo.

In July 2003 the Family Law Committee of The Law Society published a report (*Financial Provision on Divorce: Clarity and Fairness – Proposals for Reform*) in which it recommended, among other things, that s.25 Matrimonial Causes Act 1973 should have a series of guidelines for the sharing of assets added to it. It also recommended that changes should be made to make the law easier to understand (for example, 'applicant' and 'respondent' should no longer be used, but 'husband' and 'wife' or 'former husband' and 'former wife'; and forms should be amended to make them easier to understand). Judges should also be given extra powers to make interim lump sum and property orders which would help alleviate financial problems for the parties and make it easier for them to rehouse themselves, and pay for the cost of litigation. The committee was of the view that pre-marital contracts (see 8.9, above) should continue to be considered by the courts as one of the factors to be taken into account, but that they should not be given binding status because of the risks involved.

There have also been some developments in the European Union. The European Commission has been looking at matrimonial property rights with a view to harmonising the law throughout the EU. Harmonisation may have certain advantages, but European systems for distributing property and finance on divorce are quite different from those in England and Wales. Most European countries have regimes based on community of property, whereby a divorced spouse is entitled to a fixed share of the assets unless there is a pre-nuptial agreement to the contrary. There are no discretionary regimes based on needs and fairness.

### (b)  Options for Reform

*(i) Pre- and Post-Marital Agreements*   As the law currently stands, couples are free to make pre-marital and post-marital agreements about their matrimonial assets, but the court retains a supervisory jurisdiction and has a discretion to decide whether or not the terms of the agreement should be binding in the circumstances.

The question has arisen, however, as to whether there should be legislative reforms to make them legally binding. There has been a reluctance to do this because it would be contrary to public policy in that it would undermine the idea of marriage as a life-long indissoluble union. It would also remove the courts' supervisory jurisdiction to make financial solutions on marital breakdown. However, as the courts have become more willing to uphold them, and family lawyers are increasingly having to advise clients about them, particularly in 'big money' cases, then perhaps it is time to introduce legislative reform.

As long ago as 1997 Wilson J in *S v. S (Divorce: Staying Proceedings)* [1997] 2 FLR 100 said that, like other jurisdictions, such as in the USA and the European Union, 'we should be cautious about too categorically asserting to the contrary'. In 1998, the Government mooted the possibility of legislative reform to make such agreements legally binding, except, for example, where there were children, or there had been no independent legal advice, or non-disclosure, or duress (see the Consultation Document, *Supporting Families*, 1998, Home Office). In November 2004, Resolution (formerly the Solicitors' Family Law Association) recommended that s.25 Matrimonial Causes Act 1973 be amended to give the court a duty to treat pre-marital and post-marital agreements as legally binding, subject to the overriding safeguard of significant injustice to either party or to any minor child of the family (see *A More Certain Future – Recognition of Pre-Marital Agreements in England and Wales*). The advantages and disadvantages of making such agreements legally binding are as follows:

---

### Advantages of Making Marital Agreements Legally Binding

- ▶ Creates greater certainty, as the parties, not the courts, are responsible for regulating financial and property matters.
- ▶ Reduces the need for costly, time-consuming and, sometimes, traumatic litigation.
- ▶ Brings the law into line with the law in most of the rest of Europe.
- ▶ Brings the law into line with the law governing cohabitants, as they can enter into private agreements.
- ▶ Gives the parties autonomy to choose how to regulate their own affairs.
- ▶ Brings the law into line with the increasing emphasis on settlement and agreement on divorce.

### Disadvantages

- ▶ There may be problems drafting agreements, and lawyers risk having negligence claims brought against them for failing to draft them appropriately.
- ▶ A party may be unwilling to seek legal advice.
- ▶ There may be problems of non-disclosure, duress, mistake and inequality of bargaining power.
- ▶ It is difficult for agreements to make provision for future contingencies, for example the birth of children, ill-health of either party, loss of a job, or receipt of a windfall, such as an inheritance or a lottery win.
- ▶ The birth of children may cause particular problems, because, although it may be appropriate for a spouse to contract out of any financial obligation to the other spouse, the parental obligation to support and maintain children cannot be terminated by agreement.
- ▶ Although greater use of agreements will reduce lawyers' and court time spent in respect of ancillary relief, cases are likely to be brought attacking such agreements on various grounds (such as duress, non-disclosure, incapacity and hardship).
- ▶ It may be difficult to draft legislation to protect against injustice and unfairness, and any legislation may lead to complexity.
- ▶ Negligence claims against lawyers may increase because of problems drafting such agreements.

Although reform making these agreements binding would not be a universal panacea for solving all the problems inherent in the current discretionary system of ancillary relief, there is sound argument for reforming the law in order to encourage greater use of agreements. However, any reforms will have to make provision for agreements to terminate on the birth of a child and other triggering events (such as illness and unemployment), in order to avoid unfairness and injustice.

Although there are currently no proposals to reform the law, the decision of the House of Lords in *Miller* v. *Miller* (see 8.6) has arguably made the case for making pre-nuptial agreements binding even stronger. People may wish to safeguard their assets on entering into marriage, particularly where those assets are significant. Furthermore, the Law Commission's proposals for reforms of the law governing property and finance for cohabitants (see 4.12) make provision for cohabitation contracts, which makes the case for allowing married couples to make binding agreements even more persuasive. It would seem somewhat discriminatory to allow cohabitants to enter into binding contracts, but not married couples. Permitting pre-nuptial agreements to be binding (subject to certain safeguards) would also fit well with the settlement culture that pervades the family justice system. As Morley ([2006] Fam Law 772) says, the issue is fundamentally 'one of paternalism versus individual responsibility'. Referring to the case of *Hyman* v. *Hyman* [1929] AC 601 (which held that pre-nuptial agreements contravened public policy), Morley states that 'society has changed dramatically since 1929', and that '[j]ust because the courts are supposed to have an almost unfettered discretion does not prevent them from enforcing prenuptial agreements that comply with whatever rules the courts deem fit'.

In July 2007 the Pre-Nuptial Agreement Bill was introduced into the House of Commons by Quentin Davies MP as a private member's bill to provide for the enforceability of pre-nuptial agreements, but this was not taken forward by the Government.

*(ii) A 50:50 Split of Matrimonial Assets* Equal division of matrimonial assets, unless there is an agreement to the contrary, is common throughout Europe, where they are called 'community of property' regimes. Some states in the USA also have such an arrangement on divorce, and in New Zealand, too, if a marriage has lasted more than three years, then the matrimonial assets are shared equally between the spouses unless extraordinary circumstances render equality repugnant to justice. If a 50:50 division of assets on divorce were introduced in England and Wales, it would be a presumption which would be rebuttable if there was a pre-marital or post-marital agreement to the contrary.

While a 50:50 split has certain advantages, in particular that it creates certainty, it does have drawbacks. One drawback is that while such a split might create a fairer and more equitable result for middle and upper income families, it would be likely to create hardship for poorer families, because such a split would give many parties insufficient funds to rehouse themselves. This would cause hardship for children and injustice for the parties.

The possibility of introducing a 50:50 split has been discussed from time to time over the years (see above), but there are currently no proposals to change the law. Despite this, there has nevertheless been a move towards equality of division of assets in 'big money' cases (see *White* v. *White* at 8.6, above). According to Cretney: 'English law now has, by virtue of judicial decision rather than legislation, a matrimonial regime of community of property' ([2003] CFLQ 403). He expressed concern about this, however, stating that the decisions in *White* and *Lambert* raised 'in acute form, issues about the proper limits of judicial power'.

*(iii) A Set of General Principles*   The factors in s.25 (see 8.4) which govern the exercise of judicial discretion in ancillary relief proceedings contain no express articulation of the principles and policies which govern the distribution of assets on divorce, other than that the child's welfare is the court's first consideration. There is no mention of any policy of fairness or whether marriage is a partnership of equals or whether there should be no discrimination between husbands and wives.

Scotland has a discretionary system for allocating finance and property on divorce similar to that in England and Wales, but Scottish legislation lays down a set of general principles which courts must take into account when exercising their discretion. The introduction of a similar set of principles in England and Wales has been mooted from time to time. In 1998 the Government in its discussion paper, *Supporting Families* (Home Office, at para. 4.49), suggested the following set of general principles which the court could apply:

1. Seek first to promote the welfare of children by meeting their housing needs and those of their primary-carer.
2. Take into account any written agreement about financial arrangements.
3. Divide any surplus so as to achieve a fair result, recognising that fairness will generally require the value of the assets to be divided equally between the parties.
4. Try to determine financial relationships at the earliest date practicable.

The Lord Chancellor's Advisory Group on Ancillary Relief, which reported in 1998, said that it would not be appropriate to adopt the set of principles used in Scotland, but it was in unanimous agreement that there was a strong case for codifying in legislation the principles that are applied by the courts in England and Wales (see *Report of the Lord Chancellor's Advisory Group on Ancillary Relief*, July 1998).

Eekelaar (1998) has suggested a set of principles. The first would give priority to providing accommodation for the parties and children. After that, all property would be subject to a presumption of equal sharing, provided the parties have lived together for a minimum specified duration, and (unless the circumstances are exceptional) have brought up at least one child during that period. If the parties have lived together for less than the set period (he suggests 15 years), then the assets should not be divided 50:50, but in other proportions (perhaps 10:90 after 3 years, 20:80 after 6, 30:70 after 9, and 40:60 after 12). He says that such an approach could be used not just for divorcing couples, but also for cohabiting couples on relationship breakdown, at least for cohabitants who have children.

The House of Lords in *Miller* v. *Miller* laid down a set of general principles (of needs, compensation and sharing) (see 8.6), but uncertainties still remain.

(c)    The Future

Despite discussion about reform, there is no consensus as to what the nature of any reform should be and whether reform is needed at all. While some commentators believe that clear rules may reduce litigation and encourage agreement, others believe that there is no firm evidence that clearer rules make agreement easier. Some believe that the unpredictability of the present system may actually encourage agreement and settlement (see Davis, Cretney and Collins, 1994). Eekelaar (1998) has acknowledged that s.25 can be criticised, but he says that it is hard to find evidence of any strong dissatisfaction with the way it is working. He suggests that reform should only proceed after careful consideration of existing practice, and only on the basis of clear principle and policy.

What is clear from discussions of reform, however, is that it will be extremely difficult to reform the law in order to produce a fair, just and effective system for adjusting finance and property matters on relationship breakdown which is both predictable and also flexible enough to deal with the infinite variety of family circumstances. Reforms of child support have been riddled with the same problems (see 13.2).

Hodson ([2007] Fam Law 57), in the wake of *Miller* v. *Miller*, has suggested that one possible way forward is to adopt a formulaic approach in ancillary relief cases, not to replace the law, and not to produce binding outcomes – but 'to help cases along the road to a settlement'.

However, despite the difficulty of deciding the nature of any reforms, practitioners and judges clearly believe that reform is needed. Resolution (the organisation of family law solicitors) has called for a fundamental reform of the rules of ancillary relief ([2007] Fam Law 203), and Nicholas Mostyn QC has strongly criticised the law for its continuing uncertainty ([2007] Fam Law 573).

## Summary

1 The emphasis in respect of finance and property on divorce is on settlement, with an emphasis also on mediation and negotiation, and with court proceedings being sought only as the last resort.

2 If the parties cannot reach agreement, financial provision and property adjustment orders can be sought on divorce (and on nullity or judicial separation) in ancillary relief proceedings under Part II of the Matrimonial Causes Act 1973. Orders can be made for a spouse and/or to or for the benefit of a child of the family, although child maintenance must be sought in most cases from the Child Support Agency.

3 The procedure for ancillary relief applications is laid down in the Family Proceedings Rules 1991. The emphasis is on reaching agreement, saving cost and reducing delay. The district judge must 'actively manage' the case to achieve these aims. Both parties must personally attend a first appointment (unless the court orders otherwise). At this hearing the district judge will define the issues, recommend the parties to mediation, and set an appointment for the next hearing. The parties will then be encouraged to settle their dispute at a financial dispute resolution appointment. If the parties are unable to settle their differences, the case will proceed to a contested hearing.

4 There is a duty of full and frank disclosure.

5 The court in ancillary relief proceedings can make the following orders: maintenance pending suit (s.22); periodical payments order (s.23); lump sum order (s.23); property adjustment order (s.24); an order for the sale of property (s.24A); and orders in respect of pensions (ss.25B–D).

6 The court must apply the s.25 guidelines when considering whether to make an order, and, if so, in what manner. The court has considerable discretion.

## Summary cont'd

**7** The House of Lords in *White* v. *White*, a 'big money' case, said that the overarching objective in ancillary relief cases is that of fairness, and that there must be no discrimination between husbands and wives.

**8** The House of Lords in *Miller* v. *Miller* endorsed the principles laid down in *White* v. *White*, and identified three guiding general principles which apply in ancillary relief cases: needs; compensation; and sharing.

**9** The court must apply the clean break provisions when making orders in favour of spouses in original proceedings (s.25A) and in variation proceedings (s.31(7)).

**10** Various orders may be made in respect of the matrimonial home. Tenancies can be transferred under s.24 Matrimonial Causes Act 1973 or under s.53 and Sched. 7 of the Family Law Act 1996.

**11** Pensions can be taken into account by: 'offsetting'; making a pension attachment order; or making a pension sharing order.

**12** Private agreements may be made on divorce. The court has jurisdiction to make consent orders (a court order incorporating an agreement in respect of periodical payments, lump sum and property adjustment).

**13** Orders can be enforced in various ways.

**14** A 'freezing order' can be granted under s.37 Matrimonial Causes Act 1973 or under the High Court's inherent jurisdiction to protect matrimonial assets pending the outcome of ancillary relief proceedings. A 'seek and search order' can be granted by the High Court to gain entry to premises to take out and copy evidence relevant to ancillary relief proceedings. These orders are granted only in exceptional circumstances because of their Draconian nature.

**15** An order for ancillary relief can be challenged in the following ways: by asking for a rehearing; by applying to have the order varied under s.31; by appealing against the order, which may require an application for permission to appeal out of time; or by applying to have the order set aside.

**16** Applications for appeals out of time and applications to set orders aside are granted only in exceptional circumstances, because of the policy objective of finality in litigation. The court will not grant permission to appeal out of time unless the *Barder* principles are satisfied. An application to set aside an order will only be granted if the order is fundamentally unsound (such as for non-disclosure, fraud, mistake and so on).

**17** An application for permission to seek ancillary relief in the courts in England and Wales after a foreign divorce can be sought under Part III of the Matrimonial and Family Proceedings Act 1984.

**18** The law on ancillary relief has been criticised because the discretionary jurisdiction creates uncertainty and unpredictability. Reforms have been discussed, in particular a presumption in favour of a 50:50 split of matrimonial property, making pre-nuptial agreements enforceable, and introducing a set of policy guidelines to govern the exercise of judicial discretion. There are currently no proposals to change the law.

## Further Reading and References

Bailey-Harris, '*Lambert* v. *Lambert* – towards the recognition of marriage as a partnership of equals' [2003] CFLQ 417.

Barlow, Callus and Cooke, 'Community of property – a study for England and Wales' [2004] Fam Law 47.

**Further reading cont'd**

Barton and Hibbs, 'Ancillary relief and fat cat(tle) divorce' (2002) MLR 79.

Bird, '*Miller* v. *Miller*: Guidance or confusion?' [2005] Fam Law 874.

Booth, 'Ancillary relief – evolution or revolution?' [2005] Fam Law 712.

Brasse, 'It's payback time! *Miller*, *McFarlane* and the compensation culture' [2006] Fam Law 647.

Cooke, '*White* v. *White* – a new yardstick for the marriage partnership' [2001] CFLQ 81.

Cooke, '*Miller/McFarlane*: law in search of discrimination' [2007] CFLQ 98.

Cretney, 'Community of property imposed by judicial decision' (2003) LQR 349.

Cretney, 'Private ordering and divorce – how far can we go?' [2003] Fam Law 399.

Davis, Cretney and Collins, *Simple Quarrels*, 1994, Clarendon Press.

Davis, Pearce, Bird, Woodward and Wallace, 'Ancillary relief outcomes' [2000] CFLQ 43.

Douglas and Perry, 'How parents cope financially on separation and divorce – implications for the future of ancillary relief' [2001] CFLQ 67.

Duckworth and Hodson, '*White* v. *White* – bringing s.25 back to the people' [2001] Fam Law 24.

Edwards, 'Division of assets and fairness – "Brick Lane" – gender, culture and ancillary relief on divorce' [2004] Fam Law 809.

Eekelaar, 'Should s.25 be reformed?' [1998] Fam Law 469.

Eekelaar, 'Asset distribution on divorce – the durational element' (2001) LQR 552.

Eekelaar, ' Back to basics and forward into the unknown' [2001] Fam Law 30.

Eekelaar, 'Asset distribution on divorce – time and property' [2003] Fam Law 828.

Eekelaar, '*Miller* v. *Miller*: The descent into chaos' [2005] Fam Law 870.

Eekelaar, 'Property and financial settlement on divorce – sharing and compensation' [2006] Fam Law 754.

Francis and Fisher, 'Departure from equality: inherited property' [2005] Fam Law 218.

Greensmith, 'Let's play ancillary relief' [2007] Fam Law 203.

Hodson, 'Financial provision: a formula will do nicely, sir' [2007] Fam Law 57.

Miller, 'The effect of bankruptcy on property adjustment orders' [2007] Fam Law 930.

Morley, 'Enforceable prenuptial agreements: their time has come' [2006] Fam Law 772.

O'Donovan, 'Flirting with academic categorisations – *McFarlane* v. *McFarlane* and *Parlour* v. *Parlour*' [2005] CFLQ 415.

Scully, '*Parra* v. *Parra* – big money cases, judicial discretion and equality of division' [2003] CFLQ 205.

## Websites

**Family Mediation Helpline**: www.familymediationhelpline.co.uk
**Family Mediators' Association**: www.fmassoc.co.uk
**The Law Society**: www.lawsociety.org.uk
**Resolution**: www.resolution.org.uk
**UK College of Family Mediators**: www.ukcfm.co.uk

# Part V
# Children and Parents

# Chapter 9

## Children

This chapter looks at children's rights and also at the protection of children under the wardship and inherent jurisdictions of the High Court. It looks, in particular, at children's autonomy rights, at the corporal punishment of children, and at children's right to participate in court proceedings.

### 9.1 Introduction

#### (a) Children's Rights

At one time children did not have rights. However, during the twentieth century there was increasing recognition and acceptance that children do have rights. In fact they have a wide range of rights, including the right to make their own autonomous decisions if they are mature and intelligent enough to do so.

The first international document devoted to protecting children's rights was the 1924 Declaration of the Rights of the Child. It was after the end of the Second Word War, however, that the children's rights movement began to grow. In 1959 the United Nations passed the Declaration of the Rights of the Child. In 1979, during the International Year of the Child, the Children's Legal Centre was established, and in 1989 the United Nations Convention on the Rights of the Child was adopted (see 9.2, below).

A major impetus for children having rights was the children's liberationist movement in the 1960s and 1970s, which generated debate about the extent to which children should have rights. The children's liberationists took the view that children had the right to enjoy certain freedoms, in particular the right to be free to make decisions about themselves. Radical liberationists took the view that children had the right to enjoy the same freedoms as adults, but others took a more moderate view and argued that children have a right not to be forced into adulthood, and have rights to be protected and cared for. To give children too much autonomy might undermine and inhibit parental authority and have repercussions for children.

*Children – Rights or Interests?*  Some theorists have preferred not to talk about rights, because of theoretical difficulties in doing so. It has been argued, for instance, that it is inappropriate to talk about children having rights because they are often too powerless and dependent to enforce any rights they may have. Thus, under the 'will theory' children cannot have rights, because they do not have the necessary competence, or will, to make decisions. They need adults to champion their rights. Some theorists have preferred not to talk about children's rights, but about children's 'interests' (see Eekelaar, 1986), or to view children's rights in terms of the obligations adults owe them (see O'Neill in Alston *et al*, 1992).

*What Sorts of Rights?*  If children do have rights, then the next question to ask is: what sorts of rights do they have? One way to think about this is to adopt some sort of classification of rights. Various attempts have been made to do this. Freeman (1983) proposed four categories of rights: welfare rights; protective rights; rights grounded in social justice; and rights based on autonomy. Eekelaar (1986) preferred to talk about 'interests', and suggested that children have three types of interest: basic; developmental; and autonomy interests. Basic and developmental interests prevail over autonomy interests where this is necessary to protect the child. Bevan (1989) divided children's rights into two broad categories: 'protective' rights and 'self-assertive' rights. Fortin (2003, at p.17) says that she prefers Bevan's categorisation of rights, because it 'reflects the fundamental conflict currently underlying the whole of child law as it is developing in practice – that is the conflict between the need to fulfil children's rights to protection and to promote their capacity for self-determination'.

### (b) The Autonomy of Children

One of the central dilemmas for those involved with children, whether they be law reformers, lawyers, social workers or doctors, or parents, is the extent to which paternalistic approaches should be adopted or whether, and, if so, to what extent, children should have rights of self-determination or autonomy. We shall see in the chapters that follow that in the development of children's rights there has been a move away from authoritarian and paternalistic approaches towards more permissive and liberal ones. However, while some advocates of children's rights have argued in favour of greater autonomy for children, the law must strike a balance between recognising that children have greater rights of self-determination as they near adulthood, while at the same time recognising that they need the protection of the law.

### (c) Children's Commissioners

England and Wales each have a Children's Commissioner to act as a champion for children. The Children's Commissioner for Wales, who has been in office for longer than his English counterpart, has powers and duties under provisions in the Care Standards Act 2000, which were inserted into that Act by the Children's Commissioner for Wales Act 2001. Section 72A of the Care Standards Act 2000 provides that: 'The principal aim of the Commissioner in exercising his functions is to safeguard and promote the rights and welfare of children to whom [the Act] applies.'

The powers and duties of the Children's Commissioner for England are laid down in Part I of the Children Act 2004. In contrast to the Welsh Commissioner, the general function of the English Commissioner is to promote '*awareness* of the views and interests of children in England' (s.2(1)) – there is no mention of rights. Clucas (2005) is critical of the English provisions for failing to mention children's rights. She says that, even in s.2(11), which refers to the United Nations Convention on the Rights of the Child 1989, the word 'rights' is avoided (except in the title to the provision), and that reference is made instead to the 'interests of children'. She says that the 'excision of children's rights from the Act suggests a view that children are less-than-full persons' and that 'to move away from rights discourse and back to concern for welfare and compassion is a retrograde step'. Fortin (2006) is also critical of the fact that the Children's Commissioner for England is under no duty to promote children's rights. She is also critical of the fact that, while there is now 'a widespread perception [in the UK] that children have rights that ought to be respected', rights are nowhere mentioned in any statute which applies to children.

### (d)    The Minister for Children and Young People

In June 2003 the post of Minister for Children and Young People was created. Based in the Department for Education and Skills (DfES) (now called the Department for Children, Schools and Families), the Minister is responsible for children's services, child care and provision for children under five, and for family policy, including parenting support and family law.

### (e)    Lawyers and Officers of the Court for Children

Lawyers and barristers can represent children in children's cases, but children rarely instruct a lawyer on their own behalf. Instead, their views are put before the court by an officer of CAFCASS (see 1.4). Solicitors who work with or on behalf of children are required to obtain accreditation from The Law Society and be members of The Law Society's Children Panel (for example, if they represent children in care proceedings). There is no system of accreditation for family law barristers, although barristers who do family work are encouraged to become members of the Family Law Bar Association. The Association for Lawyers is a national association of lawyers working primarily in the area of public child care law.

*The Official Solicitor*    The Official Solicitor to the Supreme Court is a barrister appointed by the Minister of Justice to look after the best interests of incapable children who are unable to represent themselves in court (and also mentally incapable adults). The Official Solicitor acts as a next friend of the guardian *ad litem* in family proceedings and as a litigation friend in civil proceedings. Thus, for example, the Official Solicitor may represent a child or young person in proceedings under the inherent jurisdiction where he or she is incapable of giving consent to medical treatment (see 9.7).

## 9.2    The United Nations Convention on the Rights of the Child 1989

The United Nations Convention on the Rights of the Child 1989 (UNCRC) was created with the aim of encouraging governments worldwide to recognise the importance of children in society and to recognise that children have rights. It is the world's most ratified convention (the USA and Somalia are the only UN members who have not ratified it). It covers the social, economic and civil rights of children and young people, as well as their protection from abuse, discrimination, exploitation, abduction and armed conflict. The Convention has a website (see end of this chapter).

Although the Convention has been ratified by the UK, it does not have the same force in domestic law as the European Convention for the Protection of Human Rights which has been woven into the fabric of English law by the Human Rights Act 1998. This is because the UNCRC has not been incorporated into UK law and no court exists under the UNCRC to enforce its provisions. (An Act of Parliament is needed to make a Convention have direct effect in the UK.) There is therefore a problem enforcing its provisions. Some of the articles in the UNCRC also seem more like aspirations and moral values than enforceable legal rights. However, despite these drawbacks, the Convention is referred to by judges in England and Wales, and is of persuasive value in legal argument. Furthermore, the UN Committee on the Rights of the Child monitors the implementation of the UNCRC in Member States and by means of its reports puts pressure to bear on Member States to change the law where they fail to promote the rights and best interests of children (see further below).

The contents of the UNCRC have been classified in various ways. LeBlanc (1995) classified the rights into four groups: survival rights; membership rights; protection rights; and empowerment rights. Hammarberg (1990) suggested a classification based on four general aims (the 'four Ps'): participation of children in decisions involving their own destiny; protection of children from harm; prevention of harm; and provision and assistance for their basic needs.

The following articles of the UN Convention are particularly important as they lay down key principles:

### Article 2(1)

'States Parties shall respect and ensure the rights set forth in the present Convention to each child within their jurisdiction without discrimination of any kind, irrespective of the child's or his or her parent's or legal guardian's race, colour, sex, language, religion, political or other opinion, national, ethnic or social origin, property, disability, birth or other status.'

### Article 3(1)

'In actions concerning children, whether undertaken by public or private social welfare institutions, courts of law, administrative authorities or legislative bodies, the best interests of the child shall be a primary consideration.'

### Article 6

'1. States Parties recognise that every child has the inherent right to life.
2. States Parties shall ensure to the maximum extent possible the survival and development of the child.'

### Article 12

'1. States Parties shall assure to the child who is capable of forming his or her own views the right to express those views freely in all matters affecting the child, the views of the child to be given due weight in accordance with the age and maturity of the child.
2. For this purpose, the child shall in particular be provided the opportunity to be heard in any judicial and administrative proceedings affecting the child, either directly, or through a representative or an appropriate body, in a manner consistent with the procedural rules of national law.'

Under the UNCRC children also have rights, for example: to freedom of expression (art. 13); to freedom of association and freedom of peaceful assembly (art. 15); to a private and family life (art. 16); to freedom of thought, conscience and religion (art. 14); to education (art. 28); to enjoy minority rights (art. 30); to rest and leisure (art. 31); to an adequate standard of living (art. 27); to protection against economic exploitation (art. 32); and to social security benefits (art. 26).

Children also have a right to contact with both parents on a regular basis, except when a court decides that it is contrary to the child's best interests (art. 9). States Parties must also protect children from all forms of abuse, neglect, maltreatment, exploitation and sexual abuse while in the care of their parents or other persons (art. 19). Children must be protected against: drugs (art. 33); sexual exploitation (art. 34); other forms of exploitation (art. 36); abduction (art. 35); and cruel, inhuman or degrading treatment or punishment (art. 37). The UNCRC also lays down rights for refugee children (art. 22) and disabled children (art. 23), and rights to health care and medical provision for children (art. 24).

The UNCRC recognises the importance of the family unit, and the importance of parents in the upbringing of their children. It provides that respect must be afforded to the responsibilities, rights and duties of parents, members of the extended family or community and others who are legally responsible for children (art. 5). It also recognises the importance of both parents having common responsibilities for the upbringing and development of their children, and having the primary responsibility for bringing them up (art. 18). Parents and others responsible for children must ensure that the child's living conditions are the best that can be secured in the circumstances (art. 27(2)), and States Parties must take all appropriate measures to recover maintenance for children from parents having financial responsibility (art. 27(4)).

*The UN Committee on the Rights of the Child*    The UN Committee on the Rights of the Child is responsible under the UNCRC (see arts. 43 and 44) for monitoring the implementation of the UNCRC in Member States. It does so by responding, by way of report, to periodical reports submitted by Member States about the state of children's rights in their country. This reporting mechanism puts pressure on Member States to change their law when the UN Committee's Report (which is put into the public domain) criticises them for failing to promote the rights and best interests of children.

In July 2007 the UK Government submitted its consolidated third and fourth Report to the UN Committee, which was co-ordinated by the Department for Children, Schools and Families. The report included responses to the UN Committee's 2002 Report (available on the UNCRC website), and provided observations on developments made in respect of children's rights since that report. The UK's 2007 Report is available on the Every Child Matters website.

In the 2002 Report on the UK, the UN Committee expressed concerns about various aspects of children's rights in the UK. In particular, the Committee was concerned about the treatment of child offenders, the number of children living in poverty, the lack of participation by children in private law proceedings and the fact that the UK still permitted corporal punishment of children by their parents.

## 9.3  Children and the European Convention for the Protection of Human Rights

Children have rights under the European Convention for the Protection of Human Rights (ECHR), even though the Convention makes no express provision for, or reference to, children. Despite misplaced concerns (for example, by Herring (1999) and Fortin (1999)) about the impact of the ECHR on the welfare of children, and the possibility of tensions between the rights of parents and those of children, particularly in respect of the right to family life under art. 8, the European Court of Human Rights (ECtHR) has recognised that children do have rights under the Convention and that their best interests are paramount and can prevail over parental interests. In *Hoppe* v. *Germany (Application No. 28422/95)* [2003] 1 FLR 384 the ECtHR made clear its acceptance of the primacy of the child's interests where a balance is required to be struck between competing Convention rights.

In *Johansen* v. *Norway* (1997) 23 EHRR 33 the ECtHR held that 'particular weight should be attached to the best interests of the child . . . which may override those of the parent', and in *L* v. *Finland* [2000] 2 FLR 118 it stressed that the consideration of what is in the best interests of the child is of crucial importance. Again, in *Scott* v. *UK* [2000] 1 FLR 958, which concerned whether a mother's art. 8 rights had been breached by a local authority who had applied to free her child for adoption, the ECtHR stated that 'consideration of what is in the best interests of the child is always of crucial importance'. In *Yousef* v. *The Netherlands* [2003] 1 FLR 210 the ECtHR referred to the 'paramountcy of welfare' of the child. In *Keegan* v. *Ireland* (1994) 18 EHRR 342 the ECtHR held that a right to family life exists between a child and his parents 'even if at the time of his or her birth the parents are no longer cohabiting or if their relationship had then ended'.

Fortin (2003, at p.61) has said that 'a flexible interpretation of the Convention by the European Commission and the Court has extended the protection available to children in a surprisingly forceful way', and that '[t]he Convention's ability to promote children's rights has also been strengthened through the notion of positive obligations attaching to many of its provisions'.

The ECHR has played a greater role for children in domestic law as a result of the coming into force of the Human Rights Act 1998 in October 2000 (see 1.5 and, for example, *Re Roddy*, below). Human rights are used in legal argument and by judges when making their decisions. However, Fortin considers that human rights arguments are not being used enough in children's cases, largely as a result of the primacy of the welfare principle in domestic law (see [2006] 69 *Modern Law Review* 299).

## 9.4 The Autonomy of Children – The *Gillick* Case

*Gillick* v. *West Norfolk and Wisbech Health Authority* [1986] AC 112 was an important case for two main reasons. First, it gave greater recognition to the right of children to make decisions for themselves without parental interference. Secondly, it emphasised that it is better to talk about parental responsibilities, rather than parental rights (see 10.5). Children's autonomy rights have been considered by the courts mainly in the context of consent to medical treatment, but in *Re Roddy (A Child) (Identification: Restriction on Publication)* [2003] EWHC 2927 (Fam), [2004] 2 FLR 949 (below) they were considered in the context of the right to freedom of expression and in that case the child's autonomy rights were recognised as a human right under art. 8 (the right to a private and family life) of the European Convention for the Protection of Human Rights.

▶ *Gillick* v. *West Norfolk and Wisbech Health Authority* **[1986] AC 112**

A Department of Health and Social Security (DHSS) circular was sent to doctors advising them that they would not be acting unlawfully if in exceptional circumstances they prescribed contraceptives to girls under the age of 16 without first obtaining parental consent, provided they did so in good faith. Mrs Gillick, an ardent Roman Catholic with teenage daughters, brought an action against the DHSS and her local hospital authority seeking a declaration that the circular was illegal on two grounds. First, it enabled doctors to break the criminal law by causing or encouraging unlawful sexual intercourse under the Sexual Offences Act 1956. Secondly, the circular was inconsistent with her parental rights. Mrs Gillick was successful in the Court of Appeal. The defendants appealed to the House of Lords.

The House of Lords held, allowing the appeal, that:

(i) There was no rule of absolute parental authority over a child until a fixed age, but that parental authority dwindled as the child grew older and became more independent. The law recognised parental rights only in so far as they were needed for the child's protection, so that it was more appropriate to talk of duties and responsibilities than rights. Parental rights, if any, yielded to the right of the child to make his or her own decisions if of sufficient understanding and intelligence. Consequently a girl under 16 did not merely by reason of her age lack legal capacity to consent to contraceptive treatment.

(ii) Neither had any offence under the Sexual Offences Act 1956 been committed, as the *bona fide* exercise of a doctor's clinical judgment negated the necessary *mens rea* (mental element).

**LORD SCARMAN**: 'The underlying principle of the law was exposed by Blackstone [in his *Commentaries on the Laws of England*] and can be seen to have been acknowledged in the case-law. It is that parental right yields to the child's right to make his own decisions when he reaches a sufficient understanding and intelligence to be capable of making up his own mind on the matter requiring decision.'

*Gillick* was applied and upheld in the following case, despite the applicant's argument that, with the coming into force of the Human Rights Act 1998, *Gillick* could no longer be considered good law. The case focused on the question of medical confidentiality between doctors and children:

▶ *R (Axon) v. Secretary of State for Health* [2006] EWHC 37 (Admin), [2006] 2 FLR 206

The applicant, the mother of teenage daughters, applied in judicial review proceedings for the following declarations: (i) that a doctor is under no obligation to keep confidential the advice or treatment he proposes to give a young person aged under 16 in respect of contraception, sexually transmitted infections and abortion, and should therefore not provide such advice and treatment without a parent's knowledge unless to do so might prejudice the child's physical or mental health so that it was in the child's best interests not to do so; and (ii) that the Department of Health's *Best Practice Guidance for Doctors and Other Health Professionals on the Provision of Advice and Treatment to Young People Under 16 on Contraception, Sexual and Reproductive Health* (2004) was unlawful because it violated parents' rights under art. 8 of the European Convention for the Protection of Human Rights (ECHR).

Silber J dismissed the application, holding that the *Gillick* case (see above) was determinative of these issues. There was no different rule on waiving confidentiality when abortion advice or treatment was being discussed from when contraceptive advice or other treatment was under consideration. Silber J held that the very basis and nature of the information which a medical professional received relating to the sexual and reproductive health of any patient of whatever age deserved the highest degree of confidentiality. The proposed limitation on the young person's right to confidentiality might well be inconsistent with the current trend towards a 'keener appreciation of the autonomy of the child and the child's consequential right to participate in the decision making-process'. The guidelines laid down in *Gillick* did not infringe parental rights under the ECHR. Not only did a young person have his or her own right to respect for family life, and a significant and compelling right to confidentiality of health information under the ECHR which would compete with, and potentially override, any right to parental authority, but also the right to parental authority dwindled as a child matured. The *2004 Guidance* was not unlawful. *Gillick* did not establish as a matter of law that a medical professional should regard it as an exceptional practice, or unusual, to offer contraceptive advice or abortion advice or treatment to young people without first involving a parent.

Silber J stated, however, that nothing in his judgment was intended to encourage young people to seek or to obtain advice or treatment on sexual matters without first informing their parents and discussing matters with them.

In the '*Axon* case' the challenge to *Gillick* on the basis of human rights therefore failed and *Gillick* remains a landmark decision in the development of children's rights. It was a landmark case because it brought about a recognition that children, particularly those of sufficient age and understanding, should have a greater say in decisions concerning them. This recognition was also reflected in the drafting of the Children Act 1989. Thus, in s.8 order proceedings (see 11.4) and in care and supervision proceedings (see 15.7) the court must have regard to the ascertainable wishes and feelings of the child concerned (considered in the light of his age and understanding) (s.1(3)(a)). A child can also apply for s.8 orders, with leave of the court (s.10(8)). Under the Children Act 1989, a child with sufficient understanding to make an informed decision also has a right to refuse to consent to a medical or psychiatric examination, or other assessment (s.38(6)).

However, although *Gillick* had an impact on the content of the Children Act 1989, and the views and wishes of children of sufficient intelligence and understanding are given greater recognition, a child does not necessarily have the final say. It is always open to the court to overrule or discount a child's wishes. Furthermore, although there are many references to the child's welfare in the Children Act 1989, nowhere is there any reference to children's 'rights'. A child is not necessarily a party to proceedings, and the child's consent is not needed in respect of removal from the jurisdiction and for a change of surname.

**Gillick – *its Progeny*** Although *Gillick* was hailed as a landmark case for children's rights, it did not give children absolute rights. In fact, the House of Lords itself stressed that, as far as contraception was concerned, only in exceptional cases would there be no parental involvement. As subsequent case-law has shown, the scope of children's autonomy rights depends on all the circumstances of the case. The wishes of a '*Gillick* competent' child (a child who is mature and intelligent enough to make an informed decision) can be overridden. The child's welfare is the court's paramount consideration, and '*Gillick* competence' is only one of the circumstances of the case. Thus, the outcome of a case depends not just on whether a child is *Gillick* competent, but on the nature and seriousness of the decision to be taken.

### (a) Autonomy Rights and Medical Treatment

The issues of autonomy rights of children and *Gillick* competency have been considered in several reported cases where children have refused to consent to medical treatment (*Gillick* was about consent, not refusal). In these cases the courts have overridden the wishes of the child and authorised the treatment, even though the child concerned was mature enough to make an informed decision.

▶ *Re R (A Minor) (Wardship: Medical Treatment)* [1992] Fam 11

R, a girl aged 15 who had a serious mental illness, had been placed in an adolescent psychiatric unit. The local authority applied in wardship (see 9.7, below) for her to be given psychiatric treatment without her consent.

The Court of Appeal allowed the application, holding that she was not *Gillick* competent as her mental state fluctuated from day to day, but, even if she had been, the court would still have had the power to override her refusal. Lord Donaldson MR was also of the opinion that a *Gillick* competent child's refusal to have treatment could be overridden if a person with parental responsibility gave consent. The Court of Appeal held that a *Gillick* competent child could consent to medical treatment, but where such a child refused to give consent, then consent could be given by someone else with parental responsibility, including the court.

▶ *Re W (A Minor) (Medical Treatment: Court's Jurisdiction)* [1993] Fam 64, [1993] 1 FLR 1

W, a 16-year-old girl, suffered from anorexia nervosa. Her condition was rapidly deteriorating, but she refused treatment. The local authority applied to the court under its inherent jurisdiction (see 9.7, below) for it to authorise medical treatment for the girl, despite her refusal.

The Court of Appeal held, authorising the treatment, that the court has jurisdiction to override a *Gillick* competent child's refusal to consent to medical treatment, despite the provision of s.8 Family Law Reform Act 1969 (which allows 16- and 17-year-olds to give valid consent to surgical, medical and dental treatment), as the court under its inherent *parens patriae* jurisdiction had theoretically limitless powers extending beyond the powers of natural parents. Nolan LJ said: 'In general terms the present state of the law is that an individual who has reached the age of 18 is free to do with his life what he wishes, but it is the duty of the court to ensure so far as it can that children survive to attain that age.'

▶ *South Glamorgan County Council v. W and B* [1993] 1 FLR 574

The court had made an interim care order in respect of a severely disturbed 15-year-old girl with a direction under s.38(6) Children Act 1989 that she receive a psychiatric examination and assessment. When she refused to consent to the examination and assessment, the court under its inherent jurisdiction overrode her wishes and gave the local authority permission to take the necessary steps for her to be treated and assessed. The court so decided, despite the fact that s.38(6) expressly states that a child of sufficient understanding to make an informed decision may refuse to submit to the examination or other assessment, and notwithstanding that she was *Gillick* competent. The court had the power to override the wishes of a mature minor in respect of medical treatment, despite statutory provisions in the Children Act 1989 to the contrary.

In *Re K, W and H (Minors) (Medical Treatment)* [1993] 1 FLR 854, applying *Re R* (above), three teenage children in secure accommodation were held not to be *Gillick* competent, and, even if they had been, their refusal to consent to medical treatment would not have exposed the doctors to civil or criminal proceedings, as parental consent had been given. In *Re M (Medical Treatment: Consent)* [1999] 2 FLR 1097 Johnson J, following *Re W*, the leading authority, authorised that a 15-year-old girl undergo an urgent heart transplant operation, despite her refusal to give consent.

In several cases the High Court has authorised the treatment of children who are Jehovah's Witnesses, and who have refused to undergo life-saving medical treatment because of their religious beliefs (see *Re E (A Minor) (Wardship: Medical Treatment)* [1993]

1 FLR 386; *Re S (A Minor) (Consent to Medical Treatment)* [1994] 2 FLR 1065; *Re L (Medical Treatment: Gillick Competency)* [1998] 2 FLR 810; and see *Re P*, below).

These cases show that the *Gillick* competency principle is limited. A child has no absolute power of veto over medical treatment. The court can always intervene to override the child's wishes. Thus, while children may have greater rights of self-determination than they used to have, they do not have absolute autonomy. The cases show that refusal of treatment is treated quite differently from consent to treatment. *Gillick* was about consent.

*What if the Child is Nearly an Adult?*    In the following case it was held that where the child is nearly an adult, the court will give very careful consideration to the child's wishes about medical treatment:

> ▶ *Re P (Medical Treatment: Best Interests)* [2003] EWHC 2327 (Fam), [2004] 2 FLR 1117
>
> A Jehovah's Witness (aged nearly 17), with a medical condition (a tendency to bleed), objected, as did his parents, to the doctors using medical treatment involving blood or blood products. The hospital sought leave of the High Court to administer blood or blood treatments should his situation became immediately life-threatening.
>
> Johnson J held, authorising the treatment, that treatment imposed against the patient's will was to be avoided wherever possible, and that, in seeking to achieve what was best for the patient, his wishes had to be put at the forefront of the court's consideration. As a young man, who was nearly 17 with established convictions, his religious faith must demand the respect of all about him. However, Johnson J, referring to *dicta* in *Re W (A Minor) (Medical Treatment)* (above), held that, although there were weighty and compelling reasons why the order should not be made, and the court was reluctant to overrule the wishes of the patient, nonetheless, looking at the patient's interest in the widest possible sense, his best interests would be met by an order permitting the hospital to administer blood or blood treatments subject to there being no other form of treatment available.
>
> Johnson J held, *obiter dicta*, that there could be cases where the refusal of medical treatment by a child approaching 18 would be determinative. He said that in some cases the court would have to consider whether to override the wishes of a child approaching the age of majority, when the likelihood was that all that would have been achieved was the deferment of an inevitable death and for a matter only of months.

### (b)    Autonomy Rights and Human Rights

In the following cases the court had to consider the autonomy of children in the context of their human rights, as it had also done in the *Axon* case (see p.223, above):

> ▶ *Re Roddy (A Child) (Identification: Restriction on Publication)* [2003] EWHC 2927 (Fam), [2004] 2 FLR 949
>
> A young girl wished to publish in a national newspaper a story about the pregnancy she had experienced at the age of 12, and the subsequent birth and upbringing of her child. The local authority applied to prevent publication. Johnson J refused to prevent publication, but permitted the story to be published with conditions imposed to preserve the anonymity of the father and baby.
>
> Johnson J held that the same principles which applied in other areas of adolescent decision-making (see above) also applied to the question of whether a minor could exercise

her right to freedom of expression under art. 10 ECHR, and choose to waive her right to privacy under art. 8. It was the duty of the court to defend the right of the child, who had sufficient understanding to make an informed decision, to make his or her own choice. The court must recognise the child's integrity as a human being and acknowledge that, in order to respect the child's rights under the ECHR, the child must be allowed to make his or her own decision. The personal autonomy protected by art. 8 embraced the right to decide whether that which is private should remain private or should be shared with others. Article 8 thus embraced both the right to maintain one's privacy and the right not merely to waive that privacy, but to share what would otherwise be private with others, or with the world at large.

The court was first required to decide whether the child's rights were engaged, and then to conduct the necessary balancing exercise between the competing rights under arts. 8 and 10, considering the proportionality of the potential interference with each right considered independently. The rights of the newspaper publisher under art. 10 and the mother's rights under art. 10 and art. 9 had to be balanced against the art. 8 rights of the father and child. Since the mother's story raised important issues of public interest, the public interest had also to be taken into account in the balancing exercise.

▶ *R (On the Application of Begum) v. Headteacher and Governors of Denbigh High School* **[2006] UKHL 15**

The claimant, a Muslim girl, claimed that her school breached her right to freedom of religion under art. 9 of the European Convention for the Protection of Human Rights because she was excluded from school for wearing a jilbab (a form of Muslim dress which covers the arms and legs) rather than the shalwar kameez (tunic and trousers) which was permitted by her school. She sought declarations that she had been unlawfully excluded from school, and that she had been unlawfully denied the right to manifest her religion, and unlawfully denied access to a suitable and appropriate education. Her claim failed at first instance, but she was successful in the Court of Appeal. However, the House of Lords unanimously allowed the school's appeal, holding that its school uniform policy did not breach her right to manifest her religion.

## 9.5  The Corporal Punishment of Children

**Article 37  United Nations Convention on the Rights of the Child 1989**

'No child shall be subject to cruel, inhuman and degrading treatment or punishment.'

**Article 3  European Convention for the Protection of Human Rights and Fundamental Freedoms**

'No one shall be subject to inhuman or degrading treatment.'

Corporal punishment of children by their parents is permitted in limited circumstances, but it has been outlawed in schools. Childminders are also prohibited from using any form of corporal punishment in respect of children in their care.

### (a)  Corporal Punishment of Children by Parents

The development of society's attitude to the corporal punishment of children shows how differently children are treated today. At one time it was acceptable for parents to beat their children. Today, however, parents may commit a criminal offence if they use corporal punishment. Furthermore, physical chastisement of a child can constitute significant harm for the purposes of the Children Act 1989 and result in the child being placed in the care of a local authority (see Chapter 15). However, this will depend on the circumstances of the case. Thus, for example, in *Re F (Interim Care Order)* [2007] EWCA Civ 516 unreasonable physical chastisement of the children by their parent was held in the circumstances not to be classified as of a severity and seriousness persistent enough to justify the proportionate remedy of removing the children from their family and placing them for adoption.

In the UK corporal punishment of children by parents is not completely outlawed. This is because, in certain circumstances, the defence of reasonable chastisement can be used by parents as a defence to a criminal charge – although the circumstances in which this defence can be used have now been restricted. The defence of reasonable chastisement was laid down in the Victorian case of *R* v. *Hopley* (1860) 2 F&F 202 where Cockburn CJ held that the beating of a boy aged 13 by a teacher (which was supported by the parent) was 'reasonable' even though the boy later died. The Chief Justice stated: 'By the law of England, a parent . . . may for the purpose of correcting what is evil in the child, inflict moderate and reasonable corporal punishment.' Section 1(7) Children and Young Persons' Act 1933 subsequently gave statutory recognition to this defence.

In many countries, however, there is a total ban on parents using corporal punishment. Sweden, for instance, imposed a ban as long ago as 1979, and other countries have also outlawed it (for example, Austria, Croatia, Cyprus, Denmark, Finland, Germany, Iceland, Latvia, Norway, Romania and Ukraine). Over the years there has been increasing pressure to outlaw it in the UK, in particular by organisations such as End All Corporal Punishment of Children, and the National Society for the Prevention of Cruelty to Children (NSPCC). The UN Committee on the Rights of the Child in its last Report on the UK in October 2002 said that it was 'deeply concerned' about the fact that parents in the UK were permitted to inflict corporal punishment on their children.

*Pressure to Change the Law*   At the end of the 1990s the UK Government came under increasing pressure to change the law because of the following decision by the European Court of Human Rights:

▶ *A* v. *United Kingdom (Human Rights: Punishment of Child)* [1998] 2 FLR 959

The applicant, a boy aged 9, was beaten with a garden cane on a number of occasions by his step-father. The step-father was charged with assault occasioning actual bodily harm (under s.47 Offences Against the Persons Act 1861), but was acquitted because, although it was not disputed by the defence that the step-father had caned the boy on a number of occasions, the jury accepted his defence of 'reasonable chastisement' (see above). The applicant claimed before the European Court for the Protection of Human Rights (ECtHR) that the UK was in breach of art. 3 ECHR (right not to be subjected to torture or to suffer inhuman or degrading treatment or punishment) and art. 8 (right to a private and family life).

The ECtHR unanimously held that the UK was in breach of art. 3, because the reasonable chastisement defence did not give a child sufficient protection. It said that the ill-treatment must attain a minimum level of severity in order to fall within art. 3. On the facts, the step-father's ill-treatment of the child had reached that level taking into account the age of the child and the severity of the treatment. It held that the following factors were particularly important when establishing whether punishment was sufficiently severe to constitute ill-treatment for the purposes of art. 3: the nature and context of the defendant's treatment; its duration; its physical and mental effects in relation to the age and personal characteristics of the victim; and the reasons given by the defendant for administering the punishment.

Having concluded that there was a breach of art. 3, it held that there was no need to consider art. 8. The applicant was awarded £10,000 by way of damages.

As a result of the decision in *A* v. *UK*, the UK Government was obliged to consider the law with a view to reform, but it was not obliged to impose a complete ban on corporal punishment by parents – as the breach of art. 3 in *A* v. *UK* related to the degree of severity of the step-father's ill-treatment and to the unsatisfactory nature of the reasonable chastisement defence. The step-father's use of corporal punishment was not of itself a breach of art. 3.

After the decision in *A* v. *UK* the Government looked at corporal punishment, and in January 2000 published *Protecting Children, Supporting Parents: A Consultation Document on the Physical Punishment of Children* (Department of Health). In the consultation document the Government said that it was not in favour of outlawing corporal punishment completely. It said that, while harmful and degrading treatment of children could never be justified, it did not consider that the right way forward was to make all smacking and other forms of physical rebuke unlawful. It said that there was 'a common sense distinction to be made between the sort of mild physical rebuke which occurs in families, and which most loving parents consider acceptable, and the beating of a child' (para. 1(5)).

The Government said that a possible option would be to introduce new legislation defining the defence of 'reasonable chastisement' using the criteria laid down by the ECtHR in *A* v. *UK* (that is, the nature of the treatment, its context, duration and so on). However, this proposal was not taken up, and nothing was done, because, with the coming into force of the Human Rights Act 1998 in October 2000, it became no longer necessary for the Government to introduce legislation to define what constituted reasonable chastisement – in order to conform with the decision in *A* v. *UK*. This was because s.2(2) Human Rights Act 1998 requires courts in the UK to take account of the decisions of the ECtHR, and so the criteria laid down in *A* v. *UK* as to what constitutes inhuman and degrading treatment would be taken into account by the criminal courts in the UK when deciding on what constituted reasonable chastisement. In fact, before the Human Rights Act 1998 came into force, the Court of Appeal had already recognised and applied the decision in *A* v. *UK* in *R* v. *H* (*Reasonable Chastisement*) [2001] EWCA Civ 1024, [2001] 2 FLR 431, where it held that, when juries are considering the reasonableness or otherwise of chastisement, they must be instructed by the judge to consider the criteria laid down in *A* v. *UK*.

In November 2001 the Government published *An Analysis of Responses to Protecting Children, Supporting Parents: A Consultation Document on the Physical Punishment of Children*, in which it published its conclusions on the responses to the January 2000 consultation document (above). The Government concluded (at para. 76) that it did not believe that 'any further change to the law at this time would command widespread public support or that it would be capable of consistent enforcement', but that it intended to 'keep the reasonable chastisement defence under review in the future'. It said that the guidance issued by the Court of Appeal in *R* v. *H* (above) was sufficient to provide the protection guaranteed by art. 3 of the European Convention for the Protection of Human Rights.

The Scottish executive, on the other hand, was more proactive than England and Wales about reforming the law. It did not propose a complete ban, but made recommendations for it to be illegal to hit a child on the head, to shake a child, to hit a child with an implement, and to hit any child aged under three. It also proposed that the criteria for assessing what constitutes reasonable chastisement identified in *A* v. *UK* (above) should be implemented by legislation. These proposals were due to come into force by the end of 2002, but in May 2002 they were rejected by Scottish ministers who felt that it would be contrary to public opinion to introduce them and that not enough thought had been given to educating parents about the harmful effects of corporal punishment.

In England and Wales there were further developments. In October 2003 a private member's bill was introduced into the House of Commons by David Hinchcliffe MP to remove the defence of reasonable chastisement, but this went nowhere. At the end of 2004 renewed attempts were made to prohibit parents using corporal punishment but proposals for an absolute ban were defeated in the House of Commons. However, a last-minute amendment to the Children Bill 2004 by Lord Lester of Herne Hill in the House of Lords was accepted by the Government, whereby corporal punishment by parents would not be totally outlawed, but where the use of the defence of reasonable chastisement would be severely restricted. These reforms were enacted in s.58 Children Act 2004, which came into force on 15 January 2005.

---

**Section 58  Children Act 2004**

'(1) In relation to any offence specified in subsection (2), battery of a child cannot be justified on the ground that it constituted reasonable punishment.
(2) The offences referred to in subsection (1) are –
   (a)  an offence under section 18 or 20 of the Offences Against the Person Act 1861 . . . (wounding and causing grievous bodily harm);
   (b)  an offence under section 47 of that Act (assault occasioning actual bodily harm);
   (c)  an offence under section 1 of the Children and Young Persons' Act 1933 . . . (cruelty to persons under 16).
(3) Battery of a child causing actual bodily harm to the child cannot be justified in any civil proceedings on the ground that it constituted reasonable punishment.'

---

Section 58 does not outlaw all forms of corporal punishment, as parents can continue to raise the defence of reasonable punishment when charged with the offences of common assault or battery against a child (under s.39 Criminal Justice Act 1998). However, a defendant like the step-father in *A* v. *UK* would no longer be able to raise the defence – as the defence is not available for assault occasioning actual bodily harm. Thus, since 2004, when s.58 came into force, any injury which is more serious than common assault cannot be considered to be the result of reasonable punishment. Thus, any injury to a child caused by a parent or a person acting *in loco parentis* which amounts to more than a temporary reddening of the skin, and where the injury is more than transient and trifling, does not constitute reasonable punishment.

*The Review of Section 58*    During the passage of the Children Act 2004 the then Minister for Children (the Rt Hon Margaret Hodge MP) promised that the Government would conduct a review of s.58 after it had been in force for two years. The Government conducted the promised review by consulting parents, children, the police, the Crown Prosecution Service and seeking out evidence. The results were published in October 2007 (see the *Review of Section 58 of the Children Act 2006*, Cm 7232, Department for Children, Schools and Families). On the basis of the findings, the Government concluded that it was clear that s.58 had improved the legal protection of children, but it said that it did not intend to change the law to outlaw corporal punishment completely. It considered that, through its enactment of s.58, it had met its international obligations under both the UN Convention on the Rights of the Child and the European Convention for the Protection of Human Rights.

The Government found that, although smacking was less commonly used by parents, they still wished to retain the right to smack their children – although the numbers of parent who favoured retention of this right had dropped from 88 per cent (in 1998) to 52 per cent in 2007. The Government accepted, however, that the evidence showed that there appeared to be a lack of understanding about what the law did and did not allow. The Government concluded (at para. 57) that it would retain the law in its current form in the absence of evidence that it was not working. However, it said that it would: do more to help with positive parenting; ask the Crown Prosecution Service to monitor the situation with regard to the use of reasonable punishment; and recommend that the police take similar action to the CPS and remind staff of s.58, particularly those working in Child Abuse Investigation Units.

*Should Corporal Punishment be Outlawed Completely?*    Despite the restrictions imposed by s.58 on parental punishment of children, many organisations continue to believe it should be outlawed completely (for example the NSPCC, Save the Children, 11 Million, and the Children's Rights Alliance). The UN Committee on the Rights of the Child (see 9.2, above) has also recommended its complete abolition. In its 2002 Report on the UK the Committee expressed strong criticisms of the UK Government's proposals to limit, but not to ban, corporal punishment:

> 'The Committee is of the opinion that the Government's proposals to limit rather than to remove the "reasonable chastisement" defence do not comply with the principles and provisions of the Convention . . ., particularly since they constitute a serious violation of the dignity of the child. Moreover, they suggest that some forms of corporal punishment are acceptable, thereby undermining educational measures to promote positive and non-violent discipline.'

Various arguments can be put forward in favour of imposing a complete ban. One is that condoning corporal punishment creates a culture of abuse which can lead to children being harmed – in some cases very seriously. It can also be argued that the current law creates confusion for parents, advisers and prosecutors, because of the difficulty of distinguishing common assault and battery from the other offences for which there is no defence of reasonable punishment. Another argument in favour of a complete ban is that the current law is contrary to the human rights of children. It could be argued that the UK is in breach of the European Convention for the Protection of Human Rights as it may not be legitimate and proportionate to permit parents to use reasonable punishment as a defence to a charge of assault against a child when such a defence is not available between adults. Children may be being discriminated against under art. 14 in respect of their art. 3 right not to suffer inhuman and degrading treatment, and their art. 8 right to a private and family life.

### (b) Corporal Punishment in Schools

Corporal punishment of children is banned in all schools (by s.548 Education Act 1996). It was banned first of all in State schools (s.47 Education (No. 2) Act 1986), and later in independent schools. Thus the use of physical force or punishment by a teacher on a schoolchild can give rise to criminal or civil liability, and s.548 Education Act 1996 removes the defence of reasonable chastisement. However, a teacher can in certain limited circumstances use reasonable restraint on a schoolchild (s.550A Education Act 1996).

The following case was highly influential in leading to the abolition of corporal punishment in State schools:

▶ *Campbell and Cosans* v. *UK* (1982) 4 EHRR 293

Two mothers from Scotland claimed that the use of corporal punishment in State schools breached their son's rights not to suffer inhuman and degrading treatment under art. 3 ECHR.

The ECtHR found no breach of art. 3 – as the boys had not been punished or threatened with punishment – but held that there had been a breach of art. 2 of Protocol 1 to the ECHR, which provides that '[n]o person shall be denied the right to education', and that 'the State shall respect the right of parents to ensure such education and teaching in conformity with their own religious and philosophical convictions'. The ECtHR held that Jeffrey Cosan's right to education had been breached as he had been suspended from school for nearly a year, because his parents objected to corporal punishment. And both applicants' rights had been breached – because corporal punishment was not in conformity with their philosophical convictions.

In *Costello-Roberts* v. *UK* (1993) 19 EHRR 112 the applicant boy claimed that the corporal punishment he had suffered at his independent school breached arts. 3, 8 and 13 of the European Convention for the Protection of Human Rights. His claim failed, but in September 1999 corporal punishment in independent schools was eventually abolished.

In the following case parents objected on religious grounds to the abolition of corporal punishment in schools:

▶ *R (Williamson)* v. *Secretary of State for Education and Employment and Others* [2005] UKHL 15, [2005] 2 FLR 374

Headteachers, teachers and parents at certain Christian independent schools claimed in judicial review proceedings that the ban on corporal punishment in schools breached their rights to freedom of religion under the European Convention for the Protection of Human Rights. They claimed that it was a tenet of their fundamental Christian belief that parents (and teachers) should be able to administer physical punishment to children. They wished teachers to be able to administer reasonable chastisement because they believed it was conducive to the moral well-being of children. They claimed that s.548 Education Act 1996 did not completely abolish the use of corporal punishment in independent schools, and that, if it did so, it was a breach of art. 9(1) (right to freedom of religion) and art. 2 of Protocol No. 1 ECHR – which provides that '[n]o person shall be denied the right to education' and that 'the State shall respect the right of parents to ensure such education and teaching in conformity with their own religious and philosophical convictions'. Their application was rejected at first instance, and by the Court of Appeal. They appealed to the House of Lords.

The House of Lord held, dismissing their appeal, that there was no breach of the ECHR. Section 548 Education Act 1996 did not breach their rights to freedom of religion under art. 9(1) because the ban complied with art. 9(2) – which permits freedom of religion to be limited by law where 'necessary in a democratic society . . . for the protection of the rights and freedoms of others'. The statutory ban pursued a legitimate aim (to protect children from physical violence) and the means used to achieve that aim were appropriate and not disproportionate.

## 9.6 Children as Parties in Legal Proceedings

### Article 12  United Nations Convention on the Rights of the Child 1989

'1. States Parties should assure to the child who is capable of forming his or her own views the right to express those views freely in all matters affecting the child, the views of the child being given due weight in accordance with the age and maturity of the child.
2. For this purpose, the child shall in particular be provided the opportunity to be heard in any judicial and administrative proceedings affecting the child, either directly, or through a representative or an appropriate body, in a manner consistent with the procedural rules of national law.'

The rules for legal representation of children in court proceedings differ depending on whether the case arises in public law or private law. In public law cases (such as for care and supervision orders) a child has an automatic right to representation and a Children's Guardian (an officer of CAFCASS, see 1.4) and a solicitor are appointed for the child. In private law proceedings (such as for residence and contact orders), on the other hand, the child has no 'automatic' right to representation, although recent developments aim to give children, particularly older ones, greater rights of participation (see further below).

### (a) Private Law

*Bringing Proceedings*    As a general rule a child cannot bring proceedings (for example, in tort or contract) otherwise than through a 'next friend' (an adult who conducts the litigation for the child, such as a parent, relative or friend) or a Children's Guardian (an officer of CAFCASS). The next friend is responsible for instructing a solicitor, and for serving and accepting service of documents and so on, and must act in the child's best interests. However, in some circumstances children can conduct litigation themselves, provided they are mature and competent enough to do so.

*Applying for Court Orders Under the Children Act 1989*   A child can apply for a s.8 order under the Children Act 1989 (such as for residence or contact, see 11.4), but only with the permission of the court, which it can grant if it considers that the child has sufficient understanding to make the application (s.10(8) Children Act 1989). Although the test of sufficient understanding is that of *Gillick* competence (see 9.4, above), only older teenagers are likely to be held to have the required sufficiency of understanding (see *Re T (A Minor) (Child Representation)* [1994] Fam 49; and *Re C (Residence: Child's Application for Leave)* [1995] 1 FLR 927). Leave applications for s.8 orders are heard in the High Court (*Practice Direction* [1993] 1 FLR 668). At the leave application the court can hear the views of other parties who may be involved in the application.

Children can also bring proceedings under the inherent jurisdiction of the court (see 9.7, below) without a next friend or Children's Guardian, or can apply during such proceedings to discharge the next friend or Guardian.

*Rights of Representation for Children in Private Law Proceedings Under the Children Act 1989 and Under the Inherent Jurisdiction*   The usual way in which the voice of the child is conveyed to the court in private law proceedings (such as for residence and contact) is by means of a welfare report prepared by the Child and Family Reporter (a CAFCASS officer, see 1.4). Children do not have party status, or the legal representation that accompanies it, unless the court makes an order under rule 9 of the Family Proceedings Rules 1991. Under r.9.5 the court can appoint a Children's Guardian (an officer of CAFCASS), who will work in tandem with the lawyer acting on the child's behalf. In *Mabon* v. *Mabon* (see below) Thorpe LJ described this 'tandem model' as being essentially paternalistic. However, the child can ask the court for leave to remove the Children's Guardian so that he or she can instruct the lawyer himself or herself (r.9.2A(4)). The court must give permission to remove the Children's Guardian if it considers that the child concerned has sufficient understanding to participate in the proceedings without having a Guardian (r.9.2A(6)).

In the following case, the Court of Appeal held that the judge at first instance had been wrong not to permit three intelligent teenage boys to instruct their own solicitor:

▶ *Mabon* v. *Mabon and Others* [2005] EWCA Civ 634, [2005] 2 FLR 1011

Three teenage boys (aged 13, 15 and 17), who were living with their father on the breakdown of their parents' relationship, wished to be separately represented in court proceedings involving a residence dispute between their parents. The boys has three younger siblings, who were living with the mother, but the mother sought residence orders against the father in respect of all six children. A CAFCASS officer filed a report and was appointed Guardian of all six children. During the trial, however, the three oldest boys attended solicitors and sought to instruct them at the hearing. The boys' solicitor applied under r.9.2A Family Proceedings Rules 1991 for them to be separately represented, but the application was opposed by counsel for the Children's Guardian and refused by the judge. The boys appealed to the Court of Appeal.

The Court of Appeal unanimously allowed their appeal, on the ground that the judge had been plainly wrong. Thorpe LJ said that it was unthinkable to exclude young men from knowledge of and participation in legal proceedings that affected them so fundamentally. Thorpe LJ described the 'tandem model' for representation of children who were parties to family proceedings (see above) as essentially paternalistic. The Guardian's first priority was to advocate the welfare of the child he represented and his second priority was to put before the court the child's wishes and feelings. These priorities, his Lordship said, could in some cases conflict. Although the tandem model had many strengths and virtues, he said that at its heart lay a conflict between advancing the child's welfare and upholding the child's freedom of expression and participation in family life. His Lordship said that in the case of articulate teenagers courts must accept that the right to freedom of expression and participation in family life outweighed the paternalistic judgment of welfare, and that the case provided a timely opportunity to recognise the growing acknowledgment of the autonomy and consequential rights of children. Thorpe LJ said that in individual cases trial judges must equally acknowledge this shift of approach when they made a proportionate judgment of the sufficiency of the child's understanding.

In most cases, however, unlike the approach taken by the Court of Appeal in *Mabon*, the court will usually consider that the child's best interests will be sufficiently safeguarded by commissioning a welfare report (under s.7 Children Act 1989). Participating in proceedings can be a harrowing and traumatic experience for children. Not only are they exposed to the risk of having to make choices about their parents, but they are also open to being manipulated by one parent, or both. The courts are keen to ensure that children are protected from the potentially harmful effect of being involved in adversarial litigation.

▶ *Re N (Contact: Minor Seeking Leave to Defend and Removal of Guardian)* [2003] 1 FLR 652

Coleridge J held that an 11-year-old boy who wished to defend the contact proceedings did not have sufficient understanding to participate and give instructions on his own behalf without a Guardian. Complex issues were involved against a background of a long and stormy contact dispute. The child would not be able to understand the issues involved. Consequently, as he could not be fully informed about deciding on participation, he did not have sufficient understanding to participate. Coleridge J held that the test of competence was 'not whether the child was capable of articulating instructions but whether the child was of sufficient understanding to participate as party in the proceedings, in the sense of being able to cope with all the ramifications of the proceedings and giving considered instructions of sufficient objectivity'.

Whybrow (2004), commenting on *Re N*, said that the test of competence was set high and 'would render many adults incapable of conducting their family litigation, let alone children'. A different approach, however, was taken in the following case:

▶ *Re W (Contact: Joining Child as Party)* [2001] EWCA Civ 1830, [2003] 1 FLR 681

The district judge ordered that the child, a 7-year-old boy (who had expressed concern about staying in contact with his father), be joined as party to the contact proceedings, and that a solicitor be appointed to represent him and an independent social worker be instructed to report. The social worker charted the boy's increasing reluctance to see his father and, on the social worker's advice, the district judge made an order for no contact. The father appealed, and the Court of Appeal allowed his appeal, to the extent of allowing CAFCASS Legal (now

CAFCASS High Court Team) to be invited to act on the child's behalf, and held that the child had a right to a relationship with his father, even if he did not want it, and that his welfare demanded that efforts be made to make contact possible.

In *Re A (Contact: Separate Representation)* [2001] 1 FLR 715 the Court of Appeal held that there was no objection to a service such as the National Youth Advocacy Service (NYAS) representing a child in private proceedings (here a contact dispute).

***Court Guidance on Separate Representation of Children***  The *President's Direction (Representation of Children in Family Proceedings Pursuant to Family Proceedings Rules 1991, Rule 9.5) 5 April 2004* [2004] 1 FLR 1188 provides that making a child party to proceedings is a step to be taken only in cases involving an issue of significant difficulty. For this reason, it says that separate representation will occur in only a minority of cases. Before making a child a party, it says that consideration should be given as to whether an alternative route might be better. The *Direction* states that judges may be justified in making an order for a child to be a party, and have separation representation, for example, where: there is an intractable dispute about residence or contact; the child has interests incapable of being represented by any of the adult parties; the child's views cannot be adequately met by a report to the court; an older child is opposing a proposed course of action; or there are complex medical, mental health or other issues which necessitate separate representation of the child. The *Direction* also draws attention to the fact that granting separate representation to a child may cause delay.

The *Direction* (above) should be read together with *CAFCASS and the National Assembly for Wales Practice Note (Appointment by Guardians in Private Law Proceedings) June 2006* [2006] 2 FLR 143, which lists the types of case (where a Guardian has been appointed under r.9.5 Family Proceedings Rules 1991 or where the child is a party) which should be referred to CAFCASS High Court Team or Welsh Assembly lawyers. These include: complex adoption, and inter-country adoption, cases; medical cases where the child is old enough to have his or her views taken into account or difficult ethical issues are involved; human rights applications under s.7(1)(a) Human Rights Act 1998; complex international cases particularly where there is a dispute about jurisdiction; and applications in wardship and under the inherent jurisdiction.

### Is the Voice of the Child Being Heard Sufficiently in Court Proceedings?

There has been increasing discussion in recent years about whether the voice of the child is being heard enough in private law proceedings (in particular for residence and contact), and whether there should be a greater willingness to allow them to be joined as parties, and to be separately represented so that their voices can be heard. Timms ([2004] Fam Law 855) says that '[s]eparate representation of children can be a valuable and often underestimated facilitator in resolving parental disputes, and can divert children and families away from bitter and expensive court proceedings'.

The lack of a right to be involved in court proceedings, and to have separate representation, may breach the child's rights under the European Convention for the Protection of Human Rights in regard to art. 6 (right to a fair trial), art. 8 (right to family life), art. 10 (right to freedom of expression) and art. 12 (right to an effective remedy). In

*Re A (Contact: Separate Representation)* [2001] 1 FLR 715 Butler-Sloss P recognised that there were cases where children needed to be separately represented, and cases where her Ladyship suspected that the voices of children had not always been sufficiently heard. She said that the courts' attitude to separate representation needed to change as a result of arts. 6 and 8 of the European Convention on Human Rights.

The European Court of Human Rights has not ruled on the need for separate representation in children's cases, but in two cases brought against Germany involving contact disputes the ECtHR was critical of the German courts' failure to hear the children's views (see *Elsholz* v. *Germany* [2000] 2 FLR 486; *Sahin* v. *Germany* [2002] 1 FLR 119).

The lack of separate representation for children may also breach art. 12 of the United Nations Convention on the Rights of the Child 1989 (see 9.2), in particular art. 12(2), which requires the child to be given the opportunity to be heard in any judicial or administrative proceedings. In fact, the UN Committee on the Rights of the Child in its 2002 Report on the UK expressed concern about the lack of implementation of art. 12 in respect of the failure of the domestic courts to allow the child to be represented in private law proceedings. A research report (*Constructing Children's Welfare: A Comparative Study of Professional Practice*, ESRC, 2003) found that children's voices are not being heard in both private and public law family proceedings in the way that was intended by the Children Act 1989 or in line with the UNCRC.

There is concern not just about whether separate representation should be more widely available for children, but whether children's voices are being sufficiently heard at all. The wishes and feelings of the child may be overlooked by parents who are involved in a difficult conflict, and in some cases the court may decide not to commission a welfare report (under s.7 Children Act 1989). There have also been concerns that CAFCASS officers are not listening to children enough.

*Separate Representation of Children – Reform* Section 122 Adoption and Children Act 2002 amended the Children Act 1989 to allow court rules to be made so that children would be entitled to separate representation in proceedings for making, varying or discharging a s.8 order (see s.41(6A)), not just in public law proceedings. As a precursor to drawing up new rules of court, with the aim of improving outcomes for children involved in family proceedings, the Department for Constitutional Affairs (now the Ministry of Justice) conducted a consultation exercise in 2006 (Consultation Paper, *Separate Representation of Children*, CP/20/06, 2006). (For an interesting response to the Consultation Paper, see Wall LJ in [2007] Fam Law 124.) As part of its review, the Department for Constitutional Affairs commissioned research into the current rule permitting separate representation (see Douglas, Murch, Miles and Scanlan, *Research into the Operation of Rule 9.5 of the Family Proceedings Rules 1991*, Department of Constitutional Affairs, 2006). The Government said that its aim in reforming the law was to create a cultural change in respect of the availability of separate representation for children and to create greater consistency in its use between different courts. However, the Government made it clear in its Consultation Paper that it considered that only a small proportion of s.8 Children Act 1989 proceedings (such as for residence or contact) would be suitable for separate representation.

The responses to the consultation were published in July 2007 (*Separate Representation of Children: Summary of Responses to a Consultation Paper*, CP(R)20/06). In its conclusions to the Report the Government proposed to extend jurisdiction for deciding whether a child should be made a party to family proceedings to all levels of court. It also proposed that children would be provided with information during the course of proceedings to help them cope with associated anxieties and uncertainties. Furthermore, it also proposed that, subject to agreement with the judiciary, children who wished to speak to a judge or magistrate should be able to do so.

*Transparency for Children in Family Proceedings*   In 2007 the Government proposed that in all public and private law family cases a transcript of the court's judgment should be routinely prepared, kept and made available to children who were the subject of those proceedings at their request when they reached adulthood (*Confidence and Confidentiality: Openness in Family Courts: A New Approach*, Cm 7131, Ministry of Justice 2007). However, in respect of transparency and the media the Government has decided that the media should not be automatically allowed to enter family courts.

### (b)   Public Law Cases

In public law proceedings (such as for care and supervision orders) the system of representation for children operates with a Children's Guardian (an officer of CAFCASS) and a solicitor acting side by side (see Chapter 15). Thus, children involved in public law proceedings are made a party to the proceedings.

### 9.7   Protection for Children in Wardship and Under the Inherent Jurisdiction

The inherent jurisdiction, of which wardship is a part, is an ancient jurisdiction deriving from the right and duty of the Crown as *parens patriae* (parent or protector of the realm) to take care of persons who are unable to care for themselves – which includes not just children, but also incapacitated adults (see, for instance, in the context of capacity to marry, at 2.2). Only the High Court has jurisdiction in wardship and under the inherent jurisdiction.

*A Residual Role*   The High Court's inherent jurisdiction, including wardship, is now only used in cases which cannot be dealt with, or satisfactorily dealt with, under the Children Act 1989. Wardship and the inherent jurisdiction only have a residual role in children's cases.

   Before the Children Act came into force local authorities preferred to use the High Court's inherent jurisdiction, in particular wardship, to take a child into care despite the existence of statutory provisions for this purpose. The Children Act 1989, however, now provides that a local authority cannot use the inherent jurisdiction to: place a child in care or under its supervision (s.100(2)(a)); accommodate a child in care (s.100(2)(b)); make a child a ward of court (s.100(2)(c)); or give it power to determine a question about any aspect of parental responsibility for a child (s.100(2)(d)). However, local authorities can invoke the inherent jurisdiction in some circumstances.

*Applications by Local Authorities*   It remains possible for a local authority to use the inherent jurisdiction in circumstances other than those prohibited by s.100(2) Children Act 1989 (above), but only with leave of the High Court (s.100(3)), which it can grant if it is satisfied that: the result which is wanted cannot be achieved by any other order; and there is reasonable cause to believe that the child will suffer significant harm if the inherent jurisdiction is not exercised (s.100(4)). Local authorities have sometimes successfully invoked the inherent jurisdiction in order to obtain the court's permission for children to have medical treatment despite their refusal to consent to it (see 9.4, above). Hospitals and health authorities sometimes invoke the jurisdiction in difficult medical cases in order for the court to authorise medical treatment, or the termination of medical treatment, in the case of a child (or an incapacitated adult).

*Applications by Private Individuals*    Although there is no express prohibition in the Children Act against a private individual invoking the inherent jurisdiction, including wardship, it is now rarely invoked, as the Children Act 1989 introduced two new orders (the s.8 prohibited steps and specific issue orders, see 11.7 and 11.8) which are similar to the High Court's inherent powers. As a result, in private law cases, as in local authority cases, the inherent jurisdiction, including wardship, now only exists as a residual jurisdiction providing a safety net for complex and difficult cases (for example, international child abduction cases, see Chapter 14).

*Section 8 Orders*    As proceedings under the inherent jurisdiction (and in wardship) are 'family proceedings' for the purpose of the Children Act 1989, the High Court can make any s.8 order in the proceedings (see 11.4), except where the child is in care, when only a residence order can be made (s.9(1)). As a s.8 order cannot be made in favour of a local authority on an application by a local authority when a child is in care (ss.9(1) and (2)), a local authority who wishes to resolve a question about a child in care (such as in respect of medical treatment) must apply for leave to invoke the inherent jurisdiction (see above).

### (a)  Wardship

Wardship is part of the inherent jurisdiction of the High Court (see below). The essence of wardship is that, once a child is made a ward of court, the situation is frozen and the court stands *in loco parentis* for the child. As the court has parental responsibility for the child any major step in the child's life requires the court's prior consent. Thus, for example, a ward cannot marry, be adopted, leave the jurisdiction, or receive serious medical treatment without the court's consent. It is this supervisory role of the court which distinguishes wardship from the inherent jurisdiction. Wardship is also useful in urgent situations, for the High Court acquires powers in respect of the child automatically on the issue of the initial application. For this reason wardship is useful in abduction cases (see Chapter 14).

The governing principle in wardship proceedings is that the welfare of the child is the court's paramount consideration (see s.1(1) Children Act 1989).

Provided the High Court has jurisdiction to make the child a ward of court, it can exercise a wide range of powers. Under the Children Act 1989 it can: make any s.8 orders; make a s.37 direction that a local authority make enquiries about a child; appoint a guardian for the child; and make orders for financial provision under Sched. 1. It also has the power to grant injunctions.

### (b)  The Inherent Jurisdiction

The High Court has a general inherent power to protect children (and incapacitated adults, see 2.2) independent of the wardship jurisdiction. The inherent jurisdiction is sometimes used to obtain the court's permission to allow or refuse medical treatment, as the following examples show:

- By a local authority to obtain the court's permission to arrange medical treatment for a 16-year-old anorexic girl in its care (*Re W (A Minor) (Medical Treatment: Court's Jurisdiction)* [1993] Fam 64).
- For permission to give blood transfusions to a child whose parents are Jehovah's Witnesses and object to treatment on religious grounds (*Re O (A Minor) (Medical Treatment)* [1993] 2 FLR 149; *Re S (A Minor) (Medical Treatment)* [1993] 1 FLR 376).
- For guidance on the treatment of a severely handicapped child (*Re J (A Minor) (Medical Treatment)* [1992] 2 FLR 165).

The inherent jurisdiction can be invoked in cases other than medical cases. For example, in *Re M (Care: Leave to Interview Child)* [1995] 1 FLR 825 the High Court was asked to decide whether a solicitor should be permitted to interview two boys in care concerning a rape. The High Court has sometimes exercised its inherent jurisdiction to fill in gaps in Acts of Parliament, in order to protect the best interests of children. It is also sometimes used in the context of forced marriages (see 2.2).

### (c) Limits to Wardship and the Inherent Jurisdiction

The High Court may refuse to exercise its jurisdiction, or refuse to make a child a ward of court, where other interests prevail over the child's welfare, as the following cases show:

> ▶ *Re F (In Utero)* **[1998] Fam 122**
>
> The High Court refused to make an unborn child a ward of court, as this would place an unjustifiable fetter on the rights of the child's mother.
>
> ▶ *R (Anton)* v. *Secretary of State for the Home Department; Re Anton* **[2004] EWHC 273/2731 (Admin/Fam) [2005] 2 FLR 818**
>
> The High Court refused to make an injunction in wardship to prevent a child leaving the UK where the child and his family were subject to immigration control. Munby J held that the fact that the child was a ward of court could not limit or confine the exercise by the Secretary of State of his powers.
>
> ▶ *Re X (A Minor) (Wardship: Jurisdiction)* **[1975] Fam 47**
>
> An application was made to ward a child for the purpose of prohibiting the publication of a book which contained references to the salacious behaviour of her deceased father which might harm her if the book came to her knowledge. Jurisdiction was refused on the ground that freedom of speech and freedom of publication prevailed over the child's welfare.
>
> ▶ *R (Mrs)* v. *Central Independent Television plc* **[1994] Fam 192**
>
> A child was made a ward of court, on the application of her mother, in order to prevent a television programme being broadcast which discussed her father's conviction and imprisonment for indecency. The decision was overturned by the Court of Appeal. Waite LJ stated that no child, simply by virtue of being a child, is entitled to a right of privacy or confidentiality. As the programme had nothing to do with the care or upbringing of the child, there was nothing to put in the balance against the freedom to publish.

**(d)** Protecting Children from Media Intrusion and Harmful Publication

Applications to the High Court in wardship or under its inherent jurisdiction have sometimes been made in order to obtain an injunction to protect a child from intrusion by the media or from the publication of harmful material (see, for example, *Re Z (A Minor) (Freedom of Publication)* [1996] 1 FLR 191, [1997] Fam 1; and *Nottingham City Council* v. *October Films Ltd* [1999] 2 FLR 347). Jurisdiction is sometimes refused, however, on the ground that freedom of speech prevails (see above).

The Human Rights Act 1998 gives particular priority to the right to freedom of speech, as s.12(4) requires the courts, when considering whether to grant relief which, if granted, might affect the exercise of art. 10 European Convention for the Protection of Human Rights (the right to freedom of speech), to have particular regard to the importance of that right. The High Court in children's cases must now weigh this in the balance when considering the child's art. 8 right to a private and family life, and the child's welfare.

The following decision of the House of Lords is now the leading case on preventing publication in order to protect children, and cases decided before the Human Rights Act 1998 no longer need to be considered:

> ▶ *Re S (Identification: Restriction on Publication)* [2004] UKHL 47, [2005] 1 FLR 591
>
> The guardian of an eight-year-old child obtained an injunction under the inherent jurisdiction to restrain publication of the identity of the child's mother who had been charged with the murder of the child's older brother. The judge in the High Court (on the application of the newspaper) modified the injunction so that the newspaper could, in reports of the criminal trial, publish the identity of the mother and the deceased brother and reproduce their photographs. This decision was upheld by the Court of Appeal. The child appealed to the House of Lords, arguing that his right to respect for his private and family life under art. 8 ECHR meant that he was entitled to protection against harmful publicity concerning his family.
>
> The House of Lords unanimously dismissed his appeal, holding that cases decided before the Human Rights Act 1998 on the existence and scope of the High Court's inherent jurisdiction to restrain publicity no longer need to be considered. The foundation to restrain publicity now derives from rights under the European Convention for the Protection of Human Rights (ECHR). However, the case-law on the inherent jurisdiction is not wholly irrelevant, as it might remain of some interest in regard to the ultimate balancing exercise to be carried out under the provisions of the ECHR. Article 8 was engaged in the case, but the child would not be involved in the trial as a witness or otherwise. The impact of the trial on the child would be indirect. Competing rights of freedom of the press under art. 10 were also engaged but were not outweighed by the rights of the child under art. 8. Given the weight traditionally given to the importance of open reporting of criminal proceedings, it had been important for the judge, in carrying out the exercise required by the ECHR, to begin by acknowledging the force of the argument under art. 10 before considering whether the right of the child under art. 8 was sufficient to outweigh it.
>
> The House of Lords referred to the UN Convention on the Rights of the Child which protects the privacy of children directly involved in criminal proceedings, but not children indirectly affected by criminal trials.

For a case involving freedom of publication and the autonomy of the child see *Re Roddy (A Child) (Identification: Restriction on Publication)* [2003] EWHC 2927 (Fam), [2004] 2 FLR 949, discussed at 9.4 (above).

# Summary

1 It is recognised that children have rights and that parents have responsibilities.

2 Children have greater rights of self-determination than they once had, partly as a result of the decision of the House of Lords in *Gillick* (1986).

3 Various theories of children's rights have been put forward, but some theorists have argued that 'rights talk' is not appropriate in the context of children.

4 The UN Convention on the Rights of the Child 1989 (UNCRC) has been ratified by the UK but it is not part of English law and does not have its own court. Enforcing its provisions is therefore difficult. However, arguments based on the UNCRC can be used persuasively in court, and judges refer to it in their decisions.

5 In the *Gillick* case the House of Lords said that, where necessary, doctors could prescribe contraceptives to children under the age of 16 without parental consent.

6 Section 8 Family Law Reform Act 1969 allows children aged 16 and 17 to give valid consent to medical and dental treatment.

7 Cases since *Gillick* have shown that children's rights are not absolute, and that they cannot have the final say about medical treatment (and other matters), particularly if a course of action, or inaction, is contrary to their welfare.

8 *Gillick* was also important for emphasising that parents have responsibilities, not rights.

9 Parents are not prohibited from using corporal punishment on their children, but s.58 Children Act 2004 has outlawed the defence of reasonable punishment (chastisement) for all criminal charges except common assault or battery. Some proponents of children's rights still argue for an outright ban.

10 Corporal punishment is outlawed in all schools.

11 A child cannot bring private law proceedings other than through a next friend (for example, a parent, guardian, relative or friend) or a Children's Guardian. A child can apply for a s.8 order (residence, contact and so on) under the Children Act 1989 with leave of the court (s.10(8) Children Act 1989). In private law proceedings a Children's Guardian may be appointed, who will instruct a solicitor on behalf of the child, but under the Family Proceedings Rules 1991 the court can, on the application of the child, dismiss the Guardian so that the child can instruct the solicitor on his own. In public law proceedings the child has automatic rights of representation under s.41 Children Act 1989. There continues to be concern that the voice of the child is not being sufficiently heard in private law proceedings, in particular residence and contact proceedings, but the Government is proposing to increase the use of separate representation to a limited degree.

12 The High Court has an inherent jurisdiction (which includes wardship) to protect children. This is a parental type of jurisdiction. The welfare of the child is the court's paramount consideration in such cases (s.1(1) Children Act 1989). The High Court's powers are not invoked as much as they once were (following changes introduced by the Children Act 1989). There are restrictions on local authorities using the inherent jurisdiction and wardship, but they sometimes invoke this in difficult medical cases involving children. Wardship is useful in difficult and complex cases where urgent action is needed (such as in international child abduction cases). The High Court may refuse to exercise its jurisdiction where other interests prevail over the child's welfare. Freedom of speech under art. 10 ECHR may prevail, depending on the circumstances.

## Further Reading and References

Alston, Parker and Seymour (eds.), *Children, Rights and the Law*, 1992, Clarendon Press.

Bainham, 'Can we protect children and protect their rights?' [2002] Fam Law 279.

Bainham, *Children: The Modern Law* (3rd edn), 2005, Family Law.

Barton, '*A* v. *UK* – The thirty thousand pound caning – An "English vice" in Europe' [1999] CFLQ 63.

Bevan, *Child Law*, 1989, Butterworths.

Brazier and Bridge, 'Coercion or caring – Analysing adolescent autonomy' (1996) *Legal Studies* 84.

Bridge, 'Religion, culture and conviction – The medical treatment of young children' [1999] CFLQ 1.

Clucas, 'The Children's Commissioner for England: the way forward?' [2005] Fam Law 290.

Edwards, 'Imaging Islam . . . of meaning and metaphor symbolising the jilbab – *R (Begum)* v. *Headteacher and Governors of Denbigh High School*' [2007] CFLQ 247.

Eekelaar, 'The emergence of children's rights' (1986) 6 OJLS 161.

Eekelaar, 'The importance of thinking that children have rights' (1992) 6 IJLF.

Eekelaar, 'The interests of the child and the child's wishes: the role of dynamic self-determinism' (1994) 8 IJLF 42.

Fenwick, 'Clashing rights, the welfare of the child and the Human Rights Act' (2004) 67(6) *Modern Law Review* 889.

Fortin, 'The HRA's impact on litigation involving children and their families' [1999] CFLQ 237.

Fortin, 'Rights brought home for children' (1999) 62 *Modern Law Review* 350.

Fortin, *Children's Rights and the Developing Law* (2nd edn), 2003, Cambridge University Press.

Fortin, 'Accommodating children's rights in a post HRA era' [2006] 69 *Modern Law Review* 299.

Fortin, 'Children's rights – substance or spin?' [2006] Fam Law 757.

Fortin, 'Children's representation through the looking glass' [2007] Fam Law 500.

Freeman, *The Rights and Wrongs of Children*, 1993, Frances Pinter.

Freeman, 'Disputing children', chapter 20 in Katz, Eekelaar and Maclean (eds.), *Cross Currents*, 2000, Oxford University Press.

Hammarberg, 'The UN Convention on the Rights of the Child – and how to make it work' (1990) *Human Rights Quarterly* 97.

Herring, 'The Human Rights Act and the welfare principle in family law – conflicting or complementary?' [1999] CFLQ 223.

Hunter, 'Close encounters of a judicial kind: "hearing" children's "voices" in family law proceedings' [2007] CFLQ 283.

Huxtable, '*Re M (Medical Treatment: Consent)* – time to remove the "flak jacket"' [2000] CFLQ 83.

LeBlanc, *The Convention on the Rights of the Child: United Nations Lawmaking on Human Rights*, 1995, University of Nebraska Press.

Levy, 'Do children have human rights?' [2002] Fam Law 204.

Masson, 'Paternalism, participation, and placation: young people's experience of representation in child participation proceedings in England and Wales', in Dewar and Parker (eds.), *Family Law: Processes; Practices, Pressures*, 2003, Hart Publishing.

Mitchell, 'Whatever happened to wardship?' Part I [2001] Fam Law 130, Part II [2001] Fam Law 212.

Murch with Keehan, *The Voice of the Child in Private Law Proceedings*, 2003, Family Law.

Taylor, 'Reversing the retreat from *Gillick*? *R (Axon)* v. *Secretary of State for Health*' [2007] CFLQ 81.

Wall, Rt Hon Lord Justice, 'Separate representation of children' [2007] Fam Law 124.

Whybrow, 'Children, guardians and rule 9.5' [2004] Fam Law 504.

Williams, 'Effective government structures for children?: The UK's four Children's Commissioners' [2005] CFLQ 37.

Wilson, Sir Nicholas, 'The ears of the child in family proceedings' [2007] Fam Law 808.

## Websites

**Association of Lawyers for Children**: www.alc.org.uk

**Children are Unbeatable! Alliance**: www.childrenareunbeatable.org.uk

**Children's Commissioner (for England)**: www.11million.org.uk

**Children's Commissioner (for Wales)**: www.childcom.org.uk

**Children's Legal Centre**: www.childrenslegalcentre.com

**Children's Rights Alliance for England**: www.crae.org.uk

**Department for Children, Schools and Families**: www.dcsf.gov.uk

**End All Corporal Punishment of Children**: www.endcorporalpunishment.org

**Every Child Matters**: www.everychildmatters.gov.uk

**National Children's Bureau**: www.ncb.org.uk

**National Youth Advocacy Service**: www.nyas.net

**NSPCC**: www.nspcc.org.uk

**Save the Children**: www.savethechildren.org.uk

**UN Convention on the Rights of the Child**: www.unhchr.ch

**United Nations Convention on the Rights of the Child**: www.unicef.org/crc

# Chapter 10

## Parents

## 10.1  Introduction

In this chapter we look at the rights, responsibilities and obligations of parents. The word 'parent' includes many different types of persons. Married parents, unmarried parents, adoptive parents, step-parents and foster-parents are all 'parents'. The court in respect of wards of court and local authorities in respect of children in care are also 'parents' in the sense that they can stand *in loco parentis* to a child.

### (a)  Who is a Parent?

The word 'parent' is not defined in the Children Act 1989 (see Chapter 11). However, in *Re G (Children)* [2006] UKHL 43, [2006] 2 FLR 629 Baroness Hale considered the meaning of 'parent'. Her Ladyship said that parents could be classified as 'legal' and/or 'natural' parents, and that a person could be, or could become, a natural parent in one of three ways: by genetic parenthood (where the parent provides the gametes which produce the child); by gestational parenthood (where the parent conceives and bears the child); or by 'social and psychological parenthood'. Baroness Hale said that in the great majority of cases the child's mother would combine all three types of natural parenthood, and the father would combine two.

*The Importance of the Biological Bond Between Parent and Child*   In the following case the House of Lords considered the importance of the biological bond (the 'blood tie') between parent and child, while also acknowledging the importance of social and psychological parenting:

▶ *Re G (Children)* **[2006] UKHL 43, [2006] 2 FLR 629**

CG and CW were a lesbian couple who had two daughters (full sisters) by artificial insemination (by an unknown donor). CG was the children's genetic and gestational mother. When their relationship broke down CW applied for contact and shared residence. A shared residence order was made at first instance with CG being granted a 70 per cent share. CG moved to Cornwall in breach of a court order requiring the children to live in Leicester.

Bracewell J therefore made an order changing the children's primary place of residence to that of CW, as she had no confidence that CG would promote the 'essential close relationship' with CW and her family. CG's appeal to the Court of Appeal was dismissed and so she appealed to the House of Lords on the basis, *inter alia*, that it was wrong for the courts below to have attached no significance to the fact that she was the child's genetic and gestational mother.

The House of Lords unanimously overturned the decision of the Court of Appeal and reversed the children's living arrangements so that their primary home was once more with CG, the biological mother. It held that it was contrary to the welfare of the children to remove them from their biological mother.

**BARONESS HALE**: 'I am driven to the conclusion that the courts below have allowed the unusual context of this case to distract them from principles which are of universal application. First, the fact that CG is the natural mother of these children in every sense of that term, while raising no presumption in her favour, is undoubtedly an important and significant factor in determining what will be best for them now and in the future. Yet nowhere is that factor explored in the judgment below. Secondly, while it may well be in the best interests of children to change their living arrangements if one of their parents is frustrating their relationship with the other parent who is able to offer them a good and loving home, this is unlikely to be in their best interests while that relationship is in fact being maintained in accordance with the court's order.'

**LORD NICHOLLS**: 'I decry any tendency to diminish the significance of this factor. A child should not be removed from the primary care of his or her biological parents without compelling reason.'

### (b) The Importance of Parents

The Government recognises the importance of parents and is keen to support them. In its Consultation Document (*Supporting Families*, 1998, Home Office) the Government said that good parenting benefits us all and that all parents need support, advice and guidance on how to bring up their children (paras. 1.1 and 1.2). The Government has introduced new support initiatives, for instance the National Family and Parenting Institute which was established to provide parental guidance and to develop more and better parenting support. A national parenting telephone helpline was also established, and the Government is now promoting parenting classes for parents.

*The Parental Presumption*   The courts also recognise the importance of parents by upholding the principle that it is usually in a child's best interests to be brought up by his natural parents. In *Re KD (A Minor) (Ward: Termination of Access)* [1988] AC 806 at 812 Lord Templeman said:

'[T]he best person to bring up a child is the natural parent. It matters not whether the parent is wise or foolish, rich or poor, educated or illiterate, provided the child's moral and physical health are not endangered.'

The presumption in favour of parents was applied, for example, in *Re D (Residence: Natural Parent)* [1999] 2 FLR 1023 where a residence order made in favour of the child's aunt was overturned by Johnson J, because, although the child's welfare was the court's paramount consideration, there was a strong supposition that a child should remain with his natural parents.

The presumption in favour of parents is also enshrined in the Children Act 1989, which is based on a policy of minimum State intervention into family life. The importance of parents is also recognised in the decisions of the European Court of Human Rights, which by virtue of the Human Rights Act 1998 must be taken into account by the courts in England and Wales (see 1.5). In *Kosmopolou* v. *Greece (Application No. 60457/00)* [2004] 1 FLR 800 the ECtHR held that the bond between a child and his marital parents amounts to a right to family life under art. 8, and that this right arises from the moment of the child's birth and cannot be broken by subsequent events, except in exceptional circumstances. The ECtHR held that the mutual enjoyment of parent and child of each other's company constitutes a fundamental element of family life, even if the relationship between the parents has broken down; and that any interference must be justified under art. 8(2) applying the principle of proportionality and the principle of the best interests of the child.

Courts and public authorities must abide by the provisions of the European Convention for the Protection of Human Rights and must therefore do their best to foster co-operation between parents in order to maintain the bond between parent and child (see also *Johansen* v. *Norway* (1997) 23 EHRR 33; and *K and T* v. *Finland* (2001) 36 EHRR 255, [2001] 2 FLR 707). The failure of a court in England and Wales to enforce a contact order, or the failure of social services to allow a parent to have contact with a child in care, might amount to a breach of both a parent's and a child's right to family life under art. 8 ECHR, with the possibility of liability to pay damages by way of compensation.

The importance of parents is also recognised in arts. 5 and 8 of the UN Convention on the Rights of the Child 1989 (see 9.2).

## 10.2 Becoming a Parent – Assisted Reproduction and Surrogacy

### (a) Assisted Reproduction

Modern technological advances in the field of assisted reproduction have raised difficult legal and ethical issues. Because of these developments, the Warnock Committee into Human Assisted Reproduction and Embryology looked at assisted reproduction and in 1984 published its Report, the *'Warnock Report'* (Cmnd. 9314). Its findings resulted in the Human Fertilisation and Embryology Act (HFEA) 1990 being passed. Under this Act the Human Fertilisation and Embryology Authority is responsible for regulating treatment and research in the field of fertility treatment. It maintains a Code of Practice and issues licences to clinics to enable them to carry out treatment. The 1990 Act also makes provision as to who are the parents of a child born as a result of assisted reproduction, and gives the court jurisdiction to make parental orders (see below).

*The Human Tissues and Embryos Bill*   Because of developments in medical science, the 1990 Act has been reviewed by the Government, and is to be amended (see the Human Tissues and Embryos Bill). The Human Fertilisation and Embryology Authority will be replaced by a new body – the Regulatory Authority for Tissues and Embryos. The Bill will improve the regulation of the creation and use of all embryos outside the body. It will also recognise same-sex couples as legal parents of children conceived through the use of donated sperm, eggs or embryos.

*(i) Assisted Reproduction – Who is the Child's Mother?* Where a woman gives birth following an embryo or sperm and egg donation, she alone is treated as the child's mother (s.27(1) HFEA 1990). Different provisions apply in respect of surrogacy (see below).

*(ii) Assisted Reproduction – Who is the Child's Father?* Where a child is conceived by an embryo or by sperm and eggs being placed in his wife, or she is inseminated with sperm that was not her husband's, the husband is treated as the child's father, unless he did not consent to the embryo or sperm and eggs being placed in her or he did not consent to her insemination (s.28(2)). If the man is not the father of the child under s.28(2), and an embryo or the sperm and eggs are placed in the woman, or she was artificially inseminated in the course of treatment under a licensed arrangement, and the creation of the embryo carried by her was not brought about with the sperm of that man, the man shall be treated as the father of the child (s.28(3)). In *Re CH (Contact: Parentage)* [1996] 1 FLR 569 the child was conceived by artificial insemination by donor, as the husband had had a vasectomy. He was present at the birth and regarded himself as the child's father. The marriage broke down and the wife remarried. She sought to deny him contact with the child, *inter alia*, on the ground that he was not the biological father, but Callman J held that he was the child's biological parent under s.28 of the 1990 Act.

Where a man and a woman separate before a successful implantation takes place, even though it started out as a 'joint enterprise', the man may not be the legal father of the child under s.28(3):

---

▶ *Re R (IVF: Paternity of Child)* [2005] UKHL 33, [2005] 2 FLR 843

The mother and her unmarried partner sought fertility treatment involving donor sperm. The man signed the prescribed documents acknowledging that he intended to become the legal father of any child born as a result of the treatment. An implantation was successful, but the mother failed to inform the clinic after the pregnancy was confirmed that she had separated from her partner. Her former partner obtained a declaration of paternity but the Court of Appeal allowed the mother's appeal. The man appealed to the House of Lords.

The House of Lords dismissed his appeal, and held that, in conferring the relationship of parent and child on people who were related neither by blood nor marriage, the rules must be applied very strictly. If the 'joint enterprise' of fertility treatment had ended by the time the successful treatment had begun (because by that stage the couple had separated), the man was not the legal father of the resulting child.

---

*(iii) Assisted Reproduction – Deceased Fathers* The Human Fertilisation and Embryology (Deceased Fathers) Act 2003 inserts new provisions into the HFEA 1990 (see ss.28(5A)–(5I)), so that a man can be registered on the child's birth certificate as the father of a child conceived after his death using his sperm or using an embryo created with his sperm before his death. It also enables a man to be registered as the father of a child conceived after his death using an embryo created using donor sperm before his death. The provisions apply to unmarried and cohabiting fathers. Registration of the child does not confer upon the child any legal status or rights as a consequence of the registration. The father must give written consent to registration of his name on the birth register (a sample consent form is available on the Human Fertilisation and Embryology Authority's website, see end of chapter).

*(iv) Assisted Reproduction – Consent to Using Embryos*   With *in vitro* fertilisation (IVF) the genetic parent must consent to the use of an embryo (s.12 HFEA 1990). The issue of consent was considered in the following case:

---

▶ *Evans v. Amicus Healthcare Ltd; Hadley v. Midland Fertility Services Ltd* **[2003] EWHC 2161 (Fam), [2004] 1 FLR 67**

In each appeal the claimant had undergone IVF treatment with her respective partner, but after the relationships broke down the male partner in each case withdrew his consent to IVF treatment and to storage of the embryos, and wished them to perish. The claimants argued that the court had the power to override the withdrawal of consent and to permit the embryos to be used. Each claimant sought an injunction to restore the man's consent, and a declaration of incompatibility under the Human Rights Act 1998 arguing that the relevant provisions in the HFEA 1990 were in breach of the European Convention for the Protection of Human Rights (ECHR).

Wall J held that the court had no power to override the unconditional statutory right of either party to withdraw or vary consent to the use of embryos in connection with IVF treatment at any time before implantation in the woman. Where consent had originally been given for treatment together with a named partner it was neither effective nor valid once the parties had ceased to be together. The HFEA 1990 did not breach the claimants' right to family life under art. 8 ECHR. As the HFEA 1990 was enacted with sound policy reasons for requiring treatment to be consensual throughout, any interference by the State was both lawful and proportionate. There was no breach of art. 12 (right to marry and found a family) and art. 14 (discrimination in respect of a Convention right). Nor was there a breach of art. 2 (right to life), as an embryo is not a person in English law.

*Note*: Ms Evans (who had received IVF treatment prior to surgical removal of her ovaries due to a pre-cancerous condition but whose partner subsequently refused to consent to their use when their relationship broke down) sought leave to appeal to the Court of Appeal, but it upheld the decision of Wall J and refused leave to appeal (see [2004] EWCA (Civ) 727). She subsequently applied to the European Court of Human Rights (*Evans v. United Kingdom (Application No. 6339/05)* [2007] 1 FLR 1990) claiming that the requirement of the father's consent to the continued storage and implantation of the fertilised eggs was in breach of her rights under arts. 8 and 14 ECHR, and the rights of the embryos under art. 2. However, the ECtHR held by a majority of 13:4 that there had been no breach of her human rights or those of the embryo.

---

**(b)    Surrogacy**

Some couples may resort to surrogacy to have a child. Under a surrogacy arrangement a surrogate mother acts as a birth mother for the commissioning parents and agrees to hand the child over to them soon after birth (see, for example, *Re C (A Minor) (Wardship: Surrogacy)* [1985] FLR 846; and *Re P (Minors) (Wardship: Surrogacy)* [1987] 2 FLR 421). The practice of surrogacy is governed by the Surrogacy Arrangements Act 1985. Under the Act a surrogate mother is defined as a woman who carries a child in pursuance of an arrangement made before she began to carry the child, and with a view to any such child being handed over to, and parental responsibility being met (so far as practicable) by, another person or persons (s.1(2)). If surrogacy takes place in a licensed clinic it has the advantage of ensuring that any man who goes for treatment with the woman is treated as the father under s.28(3), whether or not he provides sperm.

Under the Surrogacy Arrangements Act 1985 surrogacy arrangements between private individuals are permitted (s.2(2)), but it is a criminal offence to set up a surrogacy agency commercially and to advertise and to negotiate a surrogacy arrangement for money (s.2(1)).

*Surrogacy – Parental Orders*　Under s.30(1) Human Fertilisation and Embryology Act 1990 married commissioning parents of a surrogacy arrangement can apply to the court for a 'parental order', which is an order for a child to be treated in law as a child of the parents' marriage. There is no need to apply to adopt the child. Where an application is made to the court for a parental order, a parental order reporter, an officer of CAFCASS (see 1.4) is appointed by the court to investigate the case.

The court can make a parental order in respect of a child of a married couple where one parent is the genetic parent (s.30(1)). The application must be made within six months of the child's birth (s.30(2)). At the time of the application and the making of the order the child's home must be with the married couple, and one or both parties must be domiciled in the UK or the Channel Islands or the Isle of Man (s.30(3)). Each spouse must have attained the age of 18 (s.30(4)). The court must be satisfied that the child's genetic father (whether or not the husband) and the woman who carried the child have freely, and with full understanding of what is involved, agreed unconditionally to the making of the order (s.30(5)), unless they cannot be found or are incapable of giving agreement (s.30(6)). The agreement of the mother who carried the child is ineffective if given less than six weeks after the child's birth (s.30(6)). The court must be satisfied that no money or other benefit (other than expenses reasonably incurred) has been given or received by the husband or wife in respect of the making of the order or the surrogacy arrangement (s.30(7)). In *Re C (Application by Mr and Mrs X Under s.30 of the Human Fertilisation and Embryology Act 1990)* [2002] EWHC 157 (Fam), [2002] 1 FLR 909 £12,000 paid to the surrogate mother by the commissioning parents (because they did not wish her to work during pregnancy) was held by Wall J to be expenses reasonably incurred under s.30(7).

As s.30 proceedings for a parental order are family proceedings for the purposes of the Children Act 1989 (s.30(8)(a)) the court may make any s.8 order under the Children Act in those proceedings, either on an application or of its own motion.

## 10.3　Parentage

### (a)　Establishing Parentage

Sometimes it may be necessary to establish a child's parentage. Usually it is paternity that needs to be established. Thus, for example, a man may need to prove that he is the father so that he can seek an order in respect of the child under the Children Act 1989 (for example, a parental responsibility order, or a contact or residence order). A mother, or the Child Support Agency, may need to prove paternity so that the father can be required to pay child maintenance. A person may need to prove that he or she is the child of a specified person for the purpose of amending his or her birth certificate, or to establish inheritance rights, or to acquire nationality or citizenship.

*(i) Presumptions of Parentage*　Certain presumptions exist in respect of parentage. Under the presumption of legitimacy a child born to a married woman is presumed to be the child of the married couple. The presumption applies to any child conceived or born during marriage, or born within the normal gestation period if the marriage is

terminated by death or divorce. Under the presumption of birth registration the entry of a particular man's name as the child's father on the birth register is *prima facie* evidence that he is the child's father (s.10 Births and Deaths Registration Act 1953).

Legal presumptions, however, have little relevance today, as parentage can be established with almost 100 per cent certainty by using DNA profiling. In fact the Court of Appeal has held (see below) that presumptions should not be relied on when scientific tests can be carried out.

*(ii) Directing a Scientific Test* Provisions governing the use of scientific tests for determining parentage in civil proceedings are laid down in ss.20–25 Family Law Reform Act 1969, as amended. Special provisions exist for determining parentage for child support purposes (see 13.2).

---

**Section 20(1)  Family Law Reform Act 1969**

'In any civil proceedings in which the parentage of any person falls to be determined, the court may, either of its own motion or on an application by any party to the proceedings, give a direction –

(a)  for the use of scientific tests to ascertain whether such tests show that a party to the proceedings is or is not the father or mother of that person; and

(b)  for the taking, within a period specified in the direction, of bodily samples from all or any of the following, namely, that person, any party who is alleged to be the father or mother of that person and any other party to the proceedings;

and the court may at any time revoke or vary a direction previously give by it under this subsection.'

---

'Bodily sample' means a sample of bodily fluid or bodily tissue taken for the purpose of scientific tests (s.25). The scientific test must be carried out by an accredited body (s.20(1A)), and the result reported to the court (s.20(2)). The court can draw such inferences as appear proper in the circumstances if a person fails to comply with any step required for the purpose of giving effect to a s.20 direction for scientific testing (s.23(1)).

*Consents Are Required (s.21)*  Adults and children aged 16 or over must give consent to the taking of a bodily sample from them (s.21(1)). The consent of a child aged 16 or over is as effective as if he were of full age; no other person's consent is needed (s.21(2)). In the case of a child under 16 the person with care and control of the child must give consent to a bodily sample being taken from the child, but if consent is not forthcoming the court can give its consent, provided it is in the child's best interests (s.21(3)). The court's power to give consent was introduced in April 2001 in response to the decision in *Re O and J (Paternity: Blood Tests)* [2000] 1 FLR 418 where Wall J had held that the court had no power to give consent under its inherent jurisdiction (see 9.7), and had stated that this gap in the law needed to be filled in order to protect the best interests of children and to comply with the Human Rights Act 1998.

*The Approach of the Courts*  In the following case the Court of Appeal outlined the principles applicable in cases on establishing parentage:

▶ *Re H and A (Paternity: Blood Tests)* [2002] EWCA Civ 383, [2002] 1 FLR 1145

The applicant applied for contact with, and parental responsibility for, twins who were living with their mother and her husband. The applicant believed that he was their father, as he had had a sexual relationship with the mother. When the mother challenged his claim to paternity he applied for a blood sample to be taken from the twins with the court's consent (under s.23(1)(b) Family Law Reform Act 1969). The judge refused the application, because of the possible disastrous disintegrative effects upon the mother's family unit if the applicant was proved to be the father. The father appealed.

The Court of Appeal allowed his appeal and remitted the case for a retrial, as there had been fundamental flaws in the judge's assessment of the individual factors which had to be brought into the essential balancing exercise. Thorpe LJ held that it was necessary to introduce into the balancing exercise the advantages of establishing scientific fact against the risks of perpetuating a state of uncertainty that bred rumour and gossip. The judge had also fallen into error in calculating the real chance of the applicant being the father as 1 per cent instead of 50 per cent, and that factor had tainted the judge's conclusion that the test offered no advantage to the applicant. The judge had also erred in finding that to order the test would drive the mother's husband from the family. The Court of Appeal doubted whether the judge had given sufficient weight to the importance of certainty.

The Court of Appeal held that the following two principles applied to cases on establishing parentage: that the interests of justice are best served by the ascertainment of the truth; and that the court should be provided with the best available science and not be confined to such unsatisfactory alternatives as presumptions and inferences.

*The Child's Rights and Best Interests*   A child has a right to know his true identity, and this is recognised in the UN Convention on the Rights of the Child. Article 7(1) provides that a child has 'as far as possible, the right to know and be cared for by his parents', and art. 8(1) provides that States Parties must 'respect the right of the child to preserve his or her identity, including . . . family relations'. If a child is illegally deprived of some or all of the elements of his identity States Parties must 'provide assistance and protection with a view to speedily re-establishing his or her identity' (art. 8(2)). In *Re H (Paternity: Blood Tests)* [2001] 2 FLR 65 Ward LJ said, referring to art. 7(1), that 'every child has a right to know the truth unless his welfare clearly justifies the cover-up'.

The right to family life in art. 8 of the European Convention for the Protection of Human Rights may also provide a justification for the truth to be known:

▶ *Re T (Paternity: Ordering Blood Tests)* [2001] 2 FLR 1190

The applicant, who believed he had fathered a child during a sexual relationship with a friend's wife, wanted blood tests to be taken for DNA sampling to prove his paternity as a preliminary to applying for parental responsibility and contact. He relied on the right to family life in art. 8 ECHR. Bodey J ordered the tests to be taken, as it was in the child's best interests to be sure about his father's identity, and suspicions about the child's identity were already in the public domain. Bodey J balanced the rights of the adults and the child under art. 8, but held that the child's right to know his true identity carried most weight. Any interference with the mother and her husband's rights to family life under art. 8 was proportionate to the legitimate aim of providing such knowledge to the child.

Although the court will usually direct a scientific test, because it is usually in the best interests of the child to know the truth, the court can refuse to do so where it is contrary to a child's best interests, as it did, for example, in *Re F (A Minor) (Blood Tests: Parental Rights)* [1993] 1 FLR 598 where a blood test would destabilise the child; and *Re K (Specific Issue Order)* [1999] 2 FLR 280 where the mother had an obsessional hatred of the applicant and the truth would cause the child emotional disruption.

In *Re D (Paternity)* [2006] EWHC 3545 (Fam), [2007] 2 FLR 26 (heard after the decision of the Court of Appeal in *Re H and A*, above) Hedley J held that it was in the best interests of the child (a boy aged 11 but not *Gillick* competent, see 9.4) that the truth be withheld, at least temporarily, owing to the turbulence in the child's life and his strong resistance to scientific testing.

*Delaying Tactics Not Permitted*    The court will not allow delaying tactics to undermine a claim to determine parentage and to establish parental rights (see *Blunkett* v. *Quinn* [2005] 1 FCR 103 where a former Home Secretary sought a parental responsibility order and contact order and the mother attempted to adjourn proceedings on the basis that he was not the father).

*Paternity Fraud*    Where a parent fraudulently assures another person that he or she is the child's parent, but knows this is not so, then he or she may be liable under the tort of deceit to pay damages to the wronged person. Thus, for example, in *A* v. *B (Damages: Paternity)* [2007] EWHC 1246 (QBD) the claimant was successful in obtaining damages against the defendant mother who had repeatedly and fraudulently assured him that he was the child's biological father with the result that he had provided maintenance for the mother and child for several years. (See also *P* v. *B (Paternity: Damages For Deceit)* [2001] 1 FLR 1041.) Such claims, however, are rare.

### (b)  Declarations of Parentage

A declaration of parentage may be required, for instance to impose (or deny) a child support obligation; or for the purpose of establishing citizenship, nationality, or inheritance rights, or to amend a birth certificate.

Under s.55A Family Law Act 1986 a person domiciled in England and Wales, or habitually resident in England and Wales for at least one year, can apply to a magistrates' family proceedings court, county court or the High Court for a declaration of parentage (or non-parentage). An applicant seeking a declaration that he is the parent of a named person, or that a named person is his parent, has an unqualified right to apply (s.55A(4)). Other applicants must prove a sufficient personal interest in the determination of the application before the court can hear their case (s.55A(3)). (There are exceptions for child support purposes, see 13.2.)

The court can refuse to hear an application which is not in the child's best interests (s.55A(3)). If it refuses to hear an application it can order that a further application may not be made without leave of the court (s.55A(6)).

*The Child's Involvement in Proceedings*    A failure to involve a child in proceedings for a declaration of status may be a breach of the child's rights under the European Convention for the Protection of Human Rights (ECHR):

> ▶ *Re L (Family Proceedings Court) (Appeal: Jurisdiction)* [2003] EWHC 1682 (Fam), [2005] 1 FLR 210
>
> A girl, aged 15, who had learned that her parentage was in doubt, applied for permission to appeal a declaration of parentage which had been made under s.55A Family Law Act 1986 for the purposes of child support (see s.20 Child Support Act 1991). She alleged breaches of her rights under art. 6 ECHR (right to a fair trial) and art. 8 ECHR (right to family life), as the declaration affecting her status had been made without reference to her or her mother. She had not been a party to proceedings, had not been given notice of proceedings, and had not been given the opportunity to be heard or to make representations.
>
> Munby J held that it was not disputed that she was fully entitled to invoke what she correctly described as a basic and fundamental human right. Information about one's biological father went to the very heart of a person's identity (see Scott Baker J in *Rose* v. *Secretary of State for Health and Human Fertilisation and Embryology Authority* [2002] EWHC 1593 (Admin), [2002] 2 FLR 962). As her human rights had been infringed the decision could not stand. She had not been given a fair hearing or a fair trial (art. 6), and the declaration breached her rights under art. 8. She was entitled to have the order made by the family proceedings court set aside.

*Adoption – Declaration of Parentage*    A declaration of parentage may be useful in the context of adoption, as it was in *M* v. *W (Declaration of Parentage)* [2006] EWHC 2341 (Fam), [2007] 2 FLR 270 where the petitioner, an adopted adult, applied for a declaration of parentage in respect of his natural father who had died in Australia and with whom he had never had any contact. Hogg J, granting the declaration, drew attention to the importance of adopted persons knowing about their background and said that the declaration would be of assistance to the petitioner, and his children, in relation to medical conditions or genetic make-up. Furthermore, the declaration would not affect the validity of the adoption order.

### (c)    Declarations of Legitimacy or Legitimation

Under s.56 Family Law Act 1986 a person may apply to the High Court or a county court for a declaration in respect of legitimacy or legitimation. However, an application under this provision can only be made by a 'child'. The court can make a declaration that: the applicant is the legitimate child of his or her parents; or that the applicant has (or has not) become a legitimated person.

## 10.4    'Alternative' Parents

Most children are brought up by parents with whom they have a biological link, but some are brought up by step-parents, foster-parents or guardians. Some children have adoptive parents.

### (a)    Step-Parents

With the high rate of divorce, but with many divorced persons remarrying, many children are brought up by step-parents. A step-parent is not a biological parent but a parent created by marriage. Step-parents have legal obligations towards their step-children, in particular to provide financial support. Step-parents can apply for parental responsibility (see 10.7). They can also apply for s.8 orders under the Children Act 1989 with leave of the court (see 11.4), and can apply for special guardianship (see 16.20). They can now apply for an adoption in their own right without making a joint application with the child's parent (see 16.7).

### (b) Foster-Parents

A foster-parent is a person who acts *in loco parentis* for a child on a fairly settled basis. There are two types of foster-parent: those who care for children under a private fostering arrangement; and those who look after children in local authority care. Although both types of foster-parent have no automatic parental responsibility for the child under the Children Act 1989, they may acquire it (see 10.7, below). Even where they have no such responsibility they have an obligation to care for the child, as they have a delegated form of parental responsibility under s.3(5) Children Act 1989. Because they have no parental responsibility foster-parents have no right to change a child's first name (*Re D, L and LA (Care: Change of Forename)* [2003] 1 FLR 339). Foster-parents can apply for s.8 orders under the Children Act 1989 (see 11.4), and for special guardianship orders (see 16.20).

### (c) Appointing a Guardian for a Child

A guardian of a child may be appointed but only in accordance with the provisions of s.5 Children Act 1989 (s.5(13)). Under s.5 a guardian can be appointed by (i) a parent, guardian or special guardian of the child, or (ii) by the court.

*(i) Appointment by Parent, Guardian or Special Guardian*  A parent with parental responsibility, a guardian, or a special guardian can appoint a guardian for the child (ss.5(3), (4)). Two or more persons may do so jointly (s.5(10)). To be effective the appointment must be (s.5(5)): made in writing, and be dated and signed by the person making the appointment; or if made in a will which is not signed by the testator, be signed at the direction of the testator in accordance with s.9 Wills Act 1837; or in any other case be signed at the direction of the person making it in his presence or in the presence of two witnesses who must each attest the signature.

*Revocation, Disclaimer and Termination of Appointment (s.6)*  An appointment of a guardian (including one made in an unrevoked will or codicil) is revoked if: the appointer makes a later appointment (including one made in an unrevoked will or codicil), unless it is clear (by express provision or necessary implication) that the purpose of the later appointment is to appoint an additional guardian (s.6(1)); or the appointer revokes the appointment by a written and dated instrument signed by him, or signed at his direction in his presence and in the presence of two witnesses each of whom must attest the signature (s.6(2)). An appointment (excluding one made in a will or codicil) is revoked if, with the intention of revoking it, the appointer destroys the instrument by which the appointment was made, or has some other person to destroy it in his presence (s.6(3)). An appointment made in a will or codicil is revoked if the will or codicil is revoked (s.6(4)).

A person who is appointed a guardian (other than by the court) can disclaim the appointment by an instrument in writing signed by him and made within a reasonable time of his first knowing that the appointment has taken effect (s.6(5)). An appointment made by an individual (including an appointment made in an unrevoked will or codicil) is revoked if the person appointed is the spouse of the appointer and the marriage has been dissolved or annulled by a court in England and Wales, or the divorce or annulment is entitled to recognition in England and Wales – unless a contrary intention appears in the appointment (s.6(3A)). The same rule applies on the dissolution or annulment of a civil partnership (s.6(3B)).

Any appointment of a guardian (by an individual or by the court) can be terminated by court order (s.6(7)) on: the application of any person with parental responsibility for the child (including a local authority); or on the application of the child concerned, with leave of the court; or by the court of its own motion in any family proceedings if it considers that the appointment should be brought to an end.

*(ii) Appointment by the Court*   The court can order that an applicant be appointed as a guardian of a child if (s.5(1)): the child has no person with parental responsibility; or a residence order has been made with respect to the child in favour of a parent, guardian, or special guardian, who has died while the order was in force; or where there is no residence order and the child's only last surviving special guardian has died. The court cannot appoint a guardian if a residence order was also made in favour of a surviving parent of the child (s.5(9)).

The court can also appoint a guardian under s.5(1) of its own motion in any family proceedings (see 11.9), that is without any application having been made (s.5(2)).

When exercising its powers to decide whether to appoint a guardian the child's welfare is the court's paramount consideration and the 'no-delay' (s.1(2)) and the 'no-order' provisions (s.1(5)) apply (see 11.3). As proceedings for the appointment of a guardian are family proceedings (see s.8(4)) the court can instead of, or in addition to, appointing a guardian, make a s.8 order under the Children Act 1989 (see 11.4).

*Termination of Court Order*   A court order appointing a guardian can be terminated by the court (s.6(7)): on the application of any person with parental responsibility for the child (including a local authority); or on the application of the child concerned, with leave of the court; or by the court of its own motion in any family proceedings.

### Effects of Guardianship

*When Does Guardianship Take Effect?*   The appointment of a guardian under s.5 takes effect on the appointer's death provided: the child concerned has no parent with parental responsibility for him (s.5(7)(a)); or where immediately before the appointer's death he had a residence order in force in his favour with respect to the child or he was the child's only (or last surviving) special guardian (except where the residence order was also made in favour of a surviving parent of the child (ss.5(7)(b) and (9)). If on the appointer's death the child concerned has a parent with parental responsibility for him, and there was no residence order in favour of the appointer, the appointment takes effect when the child no longer has a parent with parental responsibility for him (s.5(8)).

*Parental Responsibility*   A guardian has parental responsibility for the child (s.5(6)) (see 10.5). He must therefore make sure that the child is cared for and provided for, and see that the child is educated. A guardian also has the right to apply for orders under the Children Act 1989 and to consent to adoption. However, as a guardian, unlike a parent or step-parent, has no legal duty to provide financial support for the child (as this might deter people from becoming guardians), an application cannot be made against a guardian for child support and orders for financial relief. A guardian has no right to succeed to the child's estate on the child's intestacy, and a child cannot acquire British nationality under the British Nationality Act 1981 by virtue of the guardian being resident or settled in the UK.

### (d)  Special Guardians

See 16.20.

## 10.5  Parental Responsibility

'Parental responsibility', not 'parental rights', is the term used in the Children Act 1989 to describe parental interests in children. The term 'parental responsibility' was adopted to reflect the idea that children are persons to whom duties are owed rather than persons over whom power is wielded. The emphasis on parental responsibility, not rights, arose partly as a result of the influence of the *Gillick* case (see 9.4) where Lord Scarman had said that parental rights are derived from parental duty. 'Responsibility' reflects the trustee model of parenthood adopted by the House of Lords in *Gillick*.

   Eekelaar (1991) has identified two ideas enshrined in the concept of parental responsibility. One idea is that it encapsulates all the duties and powers relating to a child's upbringing, and embodies the idea that parents must behave dutifully towards the child. The other is that responsibility for a child's care rests with parents, not with the State.

*Parents Without Parental Responsibility Have Rights and Responsibilities*   Parents have parental rights and responsibilities for a child even though they may have no parental responsibility in law. Of particular importance is the parental duty to provide financial support, which arises whether or not a parent has parental responsibility. Parents without parental responsibility have succession rights; and they can apply for orders under Part II of the Children Act 1989 (such as for residence, contact and parental responsibility) (see Chapter 11). Parents, with or without parental responsibility, have a right to reasonable contact with a child who is in local authority care (see 15.8), and have a right to be consulted by a local authority when it reviews the child's case.

### (a)  Who Has Parental Responsibility?

Parental responsibility can be possessed by more than one person in respect of a particular child (s.2(5) Children Act 1989). It does not terminate just because another person acquires it (s.2(6)) – except on adoption. It is not lost when a child goes into local authority care. It continues after divorce, dissolution of a civil partnership, or if parents separate. It terminates on the child reaching the age of majority, and on adoption, and in some circumstances by court order.

*Parents*   Married parents each have parental responsibility for their child (s.2(1) Children Act 1989). In the case of unmarried parents, only the mother has parental responsibility (s.2(2)), but the father can acquire it (see below).

Parents whose marriage is void have parental responsibility, provided that at the time of the child's conception, or at the time of the marriage (if later), either or both of them reasonably believed that the marriage was valid (s.1 Legitimacy Act 1976). Parents who marry after their child's birth are treated as if they were married to each other at the time of the birth (s.2 Legitimacy Act 1976), and therefore have parental responsibility.

*Step-Parents*   A step-parent has no parental responsibility in law for a child but can acquire it in various ways (see below).

*Other Persons*   Under the Children Act 1989 the following persons also have parental responsibility: a guardian (see 10.4); a person in whose favour a residence order is made, but only for the duration of the order (see 11.5); a special guardian (see 16.20); a local authority when a child is in care (see 15.7) or when an emergency protection order is made (see 15.9). A person who adopts a child has parental responsibility (see Chapter 16).

### (b)  The Exercise of Parental Responsibility

*(i) Parental Responsibility Can be Exercised Jointly and Severally*   Persons with parental responsibility can act independently of each other in meeting their responsibility, unless the law requires otherwise. The following important decisions require the consent of both parents (and other persons with parental responsibility):

- *removing the child from the UK* (oral consent is sufficient, except where a residence order, care order, or a placement order is in force, when written consent is needed);
- *consenting to the child's adoption* (although consent can be dispensed with);
- *deciding about the child's education* (see, for example, *Re G (Parental Responsibility: Education)* [1994] 2 FLR 964 where the Court of Appeal held that the father's decision to send the child to boarding school was an important step in the child's life and the mother should have been consulted);
- *changing the child's surname* (there is a duty to consult and agree about a change, whether or not a parent has parental responsibility);
- *consent to serious or irreversible medical treatment* (such as sterilisation, circumcision and immunisation, see below).

If consent is not forthcoming the court's consent will have to be obtained by applying for a specific issue order under s.8 Children Act 1989 (see 11.8) or by invoking the wardship or the inherent jurisdiction (see 9.7).

Parents are prohibited from exercising parental responsibility in a way which is incompatible with a court order made under the Children Act 1989 (s.2(8)). Where persons who share parental responsibility cannot agree on a particular course of action an application can be made for a s.8 order (see 11.4), or in some cases in wardship or under the inherent jurisdiction (see 9.7).

*(ii) Parental Responsibility is Not Transferable*    A person with parental responsibility cannot surrender or transfer any of that responsibility, but may arrange for some or all of it to be met by one or more persons acting on his or her behalf (s.2(9)), including another person with parental responsibility (s.2(10)). Thus it is lawfully permissible to place the child with a person acting *in loco parentis* (for example a childminder, babysitter, friend or relative) or someone else with parental responsibility. However, as a person with parental responsibility cannot escape liability under the criminal or civil law by delegating responsibility to another person (s.2(11)), the onus is on parents to make proper arrangements for their children.

## 10.6  Unmarried Fathers and Parental Responsibility

### (a)  Unmarried Fathers Do Not Have 'Automatic' Parental Responsibility

An unmarried father has no parental responsibility automatically arising as a result of his being the child's natural parent (s.2(2)). Subject to a court order to the contrary, he therefore has no legal right to consent: to his child's adoption; to his child leaving the UK; to a change of his child's surname; or to a decision about his child's education or medical treatment.

Unmarried fathers were not given 'automatic' parental responsibility by the Children Act 1989 because the Government thought that it might be detrimental to some unmarried mothers and children. The reasoning behind the rule was explained by Balcombe LJ in *Re H (Illegitimate Child: Father: Parental Rights) (No. 2)* [1991] 1 FLR 214, at 218:

> 'The position of the natural father can be infinitely variable; at one end of the spectrum his connection with the child may be only the single act of intercourse (possibly even rape) which led to conception; at the other end of the spectrum he may have played a full part in the child's life from birth onwards, only the formality of marriage to the mother being absent. Considerable social evils might have resulted if the father at the bottom of the spectrum had been automatically granted full parental rights and duties.'

However, over the years there has been increasing criticism of the discrimination that unmarried fathers (and children) suffer as a result of not having parental responsibility. Many unmarried fathers are not even aware of the fact that they lack it, and may only learn so on relationship breakdown. Lack of parental responsibility has also caused problems for unmarried fathers in some areas of the law, for instance in child abduction cases (see Chapter 14).

The European Court of Human Rights has held, however, that the lack of automatic parental responsibility for unmarried fathers is not necessarily a breach of the European Convention for the Protection of Human Rights (ECHR):

---

▶ *B v. UK* [2000] 1 FLR 1

An unmarried father without parental responsibility complained that his inability to obtain a declaration that his child had been unlawfully removed from the UK (because he had no custody rights) was a breach of his right to family life under art. 8 ECHR and was therefore discriminatory under art. 14 ECHR.

The ECtHR dismissed his claim, and held that unmarried fathers in the UK are not discriminated against because they have no automatic parental responsibility. It held that, as the relationship between unmarried fathers and their children varies from ignorance and indifference to a close stable relationship indistinguishable from the conventional family-based unit, the UK Government had an objective and reasonable justification for the difference in treatment between married and unmarried fathers with regard to the automatic acquisition of parental rights.

The same view was taken by the ECtHR in *McMichael* v. *United Kingdom (Application No. 16424/90) (1995) 20 EHRR 205* where it held that, compared with married fathers, unmarried fathers inevitably varied in their commitment and interest in, or even knowledge of, their children. But it held that, as a general rule, unmarried fathers who had established family life with their children could claim equal rights of contact and custody as married fathers.

However, in *M* v. *United Kingdom (Application No. 6638/03) (The Times*, 15 September 2005) the ECtHR unanimously held that tax deductions granted to married fathers, but not to unmarried fathers, violated the discrimination provisions of art. 14 ECHR in conjunction with art. 1 of the First Protocol to the ECHR, which protects property.

### (b)   A Change of Attitude to Unmarried Fathers

As a result of concern about the lack of automatic parental responsibility for unmarried fathers and the injustices it could create, in March 1998 the Government published a consultation paper which discussed changing the law (*The Law on Parental Responsibility for Unmarried Fathers*, Lord Chancellor's Department). It concluded in the consultation document, however, that it would be wrong to give all unmarried fathers automatic parental responsibility, and recommended instead a compromise, whereby unmarried fathers would have parental responsibility if they registered the child's birth with the mother (see below).

The Government is currently consulting on the issue of whether unmarried fathers should be named automatically on birth certificates. This discussion has arisen in the context of reforms of the child support system, where it is felt that to name fathers on birth certificates automatically (except in cases where it would be contrary to the child or mother's best interests) might encourage more fathers to accept their child support responsibilities (see Chapter 13).

### (c)   The Unmarried Father – Acquiring Parental Responsibility

An unmarried father can acquire parental responsibility by:

- becoming registered as the father jointly with the mother on the child's birth certificate (see below);
- making a parental responsibility agreement with the mother (see below);
- obtaining a parental responsibility order from the court (see below);
- obtaining a residence order (see 11.5);
- becoming the child's guardian on the mother's death (see 10.4);
- adopting the child (see Chapter 16);
- obtaining a special guardianship order (see 16.20); or
- marrying the mother (s.1 Legitimacy Act 1976).

Once a father has acquired parental responsibility he has the same rights as a married father, except that his parental responsibility can be terminated by the court (see below). In this respect, unmarried fathers are still discriminated against.

*Acquiring Parental Responsibility by Becoming Registered at Birth as the Child's Father*   Under ss.4(1)(a) and 4(1A) Children Act 1989 an unmarried father has parental responsibility for his child if he is registered with the child's mother on the child's birth certificate under ss.10(1)(a)–(c) and 10A(1) Births and Deaths Registration Act 1953. These provisions came into force in December 2003. An unmarried father who is not so registered can acquire parental responsibility by other means (see below). Acquiring parental responsibility by birth registration is not permanent, however, as it can be terminated by court order (see below). The Government is currently considering changing the law to make it compulsory for unmarried fathers to be named on the child's birth certificate.

*Acquiring Parental Responsibility by Agreement with the Child's Mother*   Under s.4(1)(b) Children Act 1989 an unmarried father can enter into a parental responsibility agreement with the mother and thereby acquire parental responsibility for his child. The agreement is made on a prescribed form (Form C (PRA1)) which must be signed by both parties, witnessed and then registered in the Principal Registry of the Family Division. There is no judicial scrutiny of the agreement, but parental responsibility acquired in this way can be revoked by an order of the court (see below).

A local authority has no power to stop a mother of a child in care entering into a parental responsibility agreement with the child's father (see *Re X (Parental Responsibility Agreement: Children in Care)* [2000] 1 FLR 517).

*Acquiring Parental Responsibility by Parental Responsibility Order*   An unmarried father can apply to the court under s.4(1)(c) Children Act 1989 for an order giving him parental responsibility. When considering whether to grant the order the child's welfare is the court's paramount consideration (see s.1(1)). The no-delay principle (s.1(2)) applies. The 'order/no-order' test in s.1(5) must also be applied, but has little relevance in practice, because, if the circumstances justify making the order, then the court will make it – because of the important status it confers. In 2006, 8,702 parental responsibility orders were made (*Judicial and Court Statistics 2006*, Cm 7273, 2007, Ministry of Justice).

In *Re H (Minors) (Local Authority: Parental Rights) (No. 3)* [1991] Fam 151 Balcombe LJ held that the following factors are important when the court is considering whether or not to make a parental responsibility order: the degree of commitment which the father has shown towards the child; the degree of attachment which exists between the father and the child; and the father's reasons for applying for the order. However, although these factors have been applied in subsequent cases (see, for example, *Re CB (A Minor) (Parental Responsibility Order)* [1993] 1 FLR 920; and *Re G (A Minor) (Parental Responsibility Order)* [1994] 1 FLR 504), the Court of Appeal has stressed that they are only a starting point and that other factors can be taken into account (see *Re H (Parental Responsibility)* [1998] 1 FLR 855).

As the court recognises the important status conferred by an order, it will usually make the order unless it is clearly contrary to the child's welfare. Parental responsibility orders have been made even where: there may be problems enforcing the rights arising as a result of acquiring parental responsibility (*Re C (Minors) (Parental Rights)* [1992] 2 All ER 86); or where there is acrimony between the parents (*Re P (A Minor) (Parental Responsibility Order)* [1994] 1 FLR 578); or where parental responsibility cannot be exercised (*Re H (A Minor) (Parental Responsibility)* [1993] 1 FLR 484). Failure to provide maintenance does not of itself provide a reason for refusing an order (*Re H (Parental Responsibility: Maintenance)* [1996] 1 FLR 867). In *Re S (Parental Responsibility)* [1995] 2 FLR 648 the Court of Appeal stressed that, as a parental responsibility order granted an important status, it was wrong to place undue and false emphasis on the rights, duties and powers comprised in parental responsibility, because any abuse of its exercise could be controlled by making a s.8 order under the Children Act 1989 (see 11.4).

Despite the willingness of the courts to make parental responsibility orders, in exceptional cases they may be refused, as they were in the following cases:

▶ *Re M (Contact: Parental Responsibility)* [2001] 2 FLR 342

The child had multiple handicaps and special needs. To give the father parental responsibility would place stress on the mother and undermine her ability to care for the child, even though the father was committed to the child and his motivation for applying was for the recognition of his status as the child's father.

▶ *Re H (Parental Responsibility)* [1998] 1 FLR 855

The father had injured the child, and the child of a former partner, and had displayed cruel behaviour with an element of sadism.

▶ *Re P (Parental Responsibility)* [1998] 2 FLR 96

The father was found to be in possession of obscene photographs of young children.

▶ *Re P (Parental Responsibility)* [1997] 2 FLR 722

The father was serving a long prison sentence for several offences of robbery.

▶ *M v. M (Parental Responsibility)* [1999] 2 FLR 737

The father was held to be incapable of exercising parental responsibility because he had suffered serious head injuries in a motorcycle accident, and Wilson J took the view that the motivation factor (see above) required a father to be capable of reason.

### (d) Termination and Revocation of Parental Responsibility

Parental responsibility agreements and parental responsibility orders terminate when the child reaches 18, unless terminated earlier by court order (ss.91(7), (8) Children Act 1989).

A person who has acquired parental responsibility under s.4(1) Children Act 1989 (by birth registration, parental responsibility agreement or court order) can lose it only by court order (s.4(2A)). The court can revoke a parental responsibility order under s.4(2A) on the application of any person with parental responsibility for the child; or on the application of the child (with leave of the court) (s.4(3)). The court can grant leave to a child only if the child has sufficient understanding to make the proposed application (s.4(4)).

In revocation applications the child's welfare is the court's paramount consideration (s.1(1)). Parental responsibility will only be revoked in exceptional circumstances. The following case was a rare case where it was revoked:

> ▶ *Re P (Terminating Parental Responsibility)* [1995] 1 FLR 1048
>
> The child had suffered severe non-accidental injuries as a very young baby which were subsequently attributed to the father. Singer J terminated the father's parental authority, but said that parental responsibility should not be terminated except on strong grounds, as there was a strong presumption in favour of its continuance. Here the father had shown no attachment or commitment to the child. Singer J was keen to stress, however, that an application for termination of parental responsibility should not be used as a weapon by a dissatisfied unmarried mother.

Section 75(2) Civil Partnership Act 2004 amends s.4A(1) Children Act 1989 to permit civil partners to acquire parental responsibility for a child in the same way as a step-parent, in other words by parental responsibility agreement or by court order (see 10.7).

Although revocation of the father's parental responsibility in *Re P* seemed an appropriate response in the circumstances, the law continues, perhaps, to discriminate against unmarried fathers, because it would not have been possible for a married father in the same position as the father in *Re P* to have had his parental responsibility revoked. In *Re M (A Minor) (Care Order: Threshold Conditions)* [1994] 2 AC 424, for example, the married father had murdered the mother in the presence of the children, but there was no question of him losing his parental responsibility.

## 10.7  Step-Parents and Other Persons – Acquiring Parental Responsibility

### (a)  Step-Parents

Under s.4A Children Act 1989 (which came into force on 30 December 2005) a step-parent (by marriage or civil partnership) can acquire parental responsibility for a step-child by making a parental responsibility agreement or by obtaining a parental responsibility order. A step-parent can also acquire parental responsibility by obtaining a special guardianship order (see 16.20), or a residence order (see 11.5), or by adopting the child (see Chapter 16).

*Parental Responsibility Agreement*  Under s.4A(1)(a) the child's parent with parental responsibility, or both parents if the other parent has parental responsibility, may enter into a parental responsibility agreement with the step-parent to provide for the step-parent to have parental responsibility for the child. This involves filling in a prescribed form (Form C (PRA2)) (s.4A(2)). The agreement will take effect once it has been received and recorded at the Principal Registry of the Family Division.

*Parental Responsibility Order*  Under s.4A(1)(b) the court may, on the application of the step-parent, order that the step-parent shall have parental responsibility for the child. The welfare of the child will be the court's paramount consideration (under s.1(1) Children Act 1989) and the other principles in s.1 will apply, other than the welfare checklist (see 11.3).

*Termination of Parental Responsibility*  A step-parent's parental responsibility, acquired by agreement or court order, can be terminated by the court on the application of any person with parental responsibility, or, with leave of the court, the child (s.4A(3)). The court can grant leave to the child only if it is satisfied that the child has sufficient understanding to make the proposed application (s.4A(4)).

### (b) Other Persons

A person other than an unmarried father or step-parent can acquire parental responsibility by obtaining a residence order (see 11.5), or a special guardianship order (see 16.20), or by adopting the child (see Chapter 16).

## 10.8 Parental Responsibility and Parental Rights

Parental responsibility is defined in s.3(1) Children Act 1989 as:

> 'all the rights, duties, powers, responsibilities and authority which by law a parent of a child has in relation to the child and his property.'

This definition is not very helpful, however, as it does not define the precise nature and scope of parental responsibility. This must be deduced from statute and case-law.

### (a) What Rights Do Parents Have?

Despite the emphasis on parental responsibility in the Children Act, parents do possess parental rights. They have a right, for instance, to bring proceedings under the Children Act 1989, and a right to challenge a local authority's decision to institute care and supervision proceedings. In fact s.3(1) above mentions the word 'rights', and in the *Gillick* case (see 9.4) Lord Scarman, while recognising that 'responsibility' was a more appropriate term than 'rights', nevertheless stated that parental rights clearly exist but that the law had never treated such rights as 'sovereign or beyond review and control'. Parental rights include:

- a right to physical possession of the child;
- a right to contact with the child;
- a right to decide on the child's education;
- a right to choose the child's religion;
- a right to consent to medical treatment of the child;
- a right to consent to the child's marriage or civil partnership;
- a right to choose the child's surname and register the child's birth;
- a right to consent to the child's adoption;
- a right to discipline the child;
- a right to administer the child's property and enter into contracts on the child's behalf;
- a right to appoint a guardian for the child;
- a right to bring legal proceeding in respect of the child.

Parents also have duties to their children, in particular a duty to provide maintenance (see Chapter 13). Some of the rights above are also duties. For example, a parent has both a right and a duty to register the child's birth.

*Parental Rights are Not Absolute*   Parents rights are never absolute. They are subject to the principle that the child's welfare is the court's paramount consideration. Parental wishes can therefore be overridden by the court. In *Re Z (A Minor) (Freedom of Publication)* [1996] 1 FLR 191, [1997] Fam 1 Sir Thomas Bingham MR said that if the court's judgment 'is in accord with that of the devoted and responsible parent, well and good. If not, then it is the duty of the court . . . to give effect to its own judgment.' Thus the court can restrain a parent from doing any act which might adversely affect the child's welfare. For example, in *A v. M (Family Proceedings: Publicity)* [2000] 1 FLR 562 Charles J granted an injunction to stop the mother publishing information about what had happened in court proceedings involving herself, the father and the child. In adoption law parental consent to adoption can be dispensed with if this is in the child's best interests (see 16.11). In proceedings for residence, contact and other orders under the Children Act 1989 parental wishes are not paramount – the child's welfare prevails. In the context of medical treatment for the child parental wishes can be overridden (see below). Children who suffer significant harm can be taken into the care of the local authority whereupon parental responsibility is not removed but the local authority is 'in the driving seat' (see Chapter 15).

## (b) Important Parental Rights

The following parental rights are particularly important:

*(i) A Right to the Physical Possession of the Child*   The criminal and civil law relating to child abduction (see Chapter 14), and the restriction under s.13 Children Act 1989 on removing a child out of the UK (when the child is subject to a residence order) show that parents have a right to physical possession of their child. This is also emphasised by the fact that under the Children Act 1989 a parent can ask a local authority to hand the child back if the child is not subject to a care or emergency protection order. The right to physical possession also includes the right to decide where the child lives. Thus, for example, when a child is accommodated in local authority care under a voluntary arrangement a local authority may not place the child in accommodation against parental wishes (see *R v. Tameside Metropolitan Borough Council ex parte J* [2000] 1 FLR 942). The right to physical possession also includes the right to decide on travel and emigration.

*(ii) A Right to Have Contact with the Child*   The s.8 contact order and the presumption of reasonable contact when a child is in local authority care show that parents have a right to contact with their child. But this right is not an absolute or fundamental right (see *Re KD (A Minor) (Ward: Termination of Access)* [1988] AC 806). It is always subject, like all parental rights, to the welfare of the child and can be terminated by the court. However, the law encourages parent–child contact, as contact is generally considered to be beneficial for the child. Although the law encourages contact, the case-law has emphasised that contact is a right of the child (*M v. M* [1973] 2 All ER 81). For this reason contact is also a parental duty.

*(iii) A Right to Decide on Education*   Parents have a legal duty to ensure that a child aged between five and 16 receives efficient, full-time education (suitable to the child's age, ability and aptitude, and to any special needs) either by regular attendance at school or otherwise (s.7 Education Act 1996). The words 'or otherwise' mean that parents can lawfully educate their children at home, provided it is an efficient and suitable education. A parent who fails to comply with this duty can be prosecuted. Parents have a right to

express a preference as to which school the child shall attend and the admissions authority must comply with that preference, subject to certain exceptions (s.86(1) School Standards and Framework Act 1998). Parents have a right of appeal against a refusal of a place at a chosen school, and have a right to be provided with information about the school, such as the curriculum, discipline, school policy and so on. A parent also has a right to withdraw a child from religious education and from some sex education classes.

*(iv) A Right to Choose the Child's Religion*    Parents have a right to choose the child's religion (if any), at least until the child becomes '*Gillick* competent' (see 9.4). Parents have the right to choose to remove their child from religious instruction and school assemblies. The importance of religion is also reflected in statutory provisions relating to fostering and adoption placements, as the local authority and adoption agency must take into consideration the child's religious beliefs and background. However, parental wishes are not absolute, and in some circumstances the best interests of the child, not the religious wishes of parents, will prevail, for instance in the context of medical treatment (see below).

*(v) A Right to Consent to Medical Treatment*    See 10.9 (below).

*(vi) A Right to Consent to the Child's Marriage or Civil Partnership*    Where a child is aged over 16 but under 18 the child's parents and other persons with parental responsibility must give their consent to the marriage or civil partnership, although failure to do so is unlikely to invalidate it.

*(vii) A Right to Choose the Child's Surname and to Register the Child's Birth*    A child by convention takes the father's surname, although this is not compulsory. A parent can choose any surname for the child. Where a residence order is in force the child's surname cannot be changed without the written consent of all those with parental responsibility, or otherwise with permission of the court (see s.13(1) Children Act 1989, and 11.5).

Parents have a statutory duty to register the child's birth. Under the Births and Deaths Registration Act 1953, if the mother and father are married either parent can register the child's birth. If they are not married, only the unmarried mother has a duty to register the birth, and the registrar is not permitted to enter the name of any person as the child's father in the register, unless: both parents attend together and make a joint request to register the birth; or one of them makes a request to register the child's birth and provides a statutory declaration acknowledging paternity. If both unmarried parents are registered on the birth certificate the father has parental responsibility for the child with the mother (see 10.5). If a child is legitimated by the parents' subsequent marriage, the parents must re-register the child's birth (s.9 Legitimacy Act 1976).

*Proposals for Mandatory Birth Registration by Both Unmarried Parents*    Under the current law only the unmarried mother is under a duty to register the child's birth, although she and the father can do so jointly. However, the Government is considering whether to make it compulsory for unmarried fathers to be jointly named on the child's birth certificate with the mother, with the aim of making unmarried fathers acknowledge their obligations to their children, in particular their child support obligations (see the Green Paper, *Joint Birth Registration: Promoting Parental Responsibility*, Cm 7160, Department for Work and Pensions, June 2007). Unmarried fathers would face penalties for refusing to be named on their child's birth certificate. The Green Paper states that any change to the law would be subject to robust and effective safeguards being in place. Thus, the proposals contain a series of measures to protect vulnerable mothers and children, in cases of rape or child abuse. With increasing numbers of children being born outside marriage, and with one in five children not having a father named on their birth certificate (according to the Office for National Statistics, 2004) it seems a sensible measure – provided satisfactory controls can be put in place.

*(viii) A Right to Consent to the Child's Adoption*   Under the adoption legislation parents have a right to consent to their child's adoption, although consent may be dispensed with on certain grounds (see 16.11).

*(ix) A Right to Discipline the Child and to Administer Reasonable Punishment*   A parent has a right and a duty to discipline a child, but must inflict only reasonable punishment otherwise he or she may be guilty of a criminal offence (see 9.5).

*(x) Other Rights*   Parents have other rights. They can administer the child's property and enter into contracts on the child's behalf. They have a right to appoint a guardian for the child (see 10.4, above). They also have rights to apply for court orders in respect of their children, and have a right to apply to the Child Support Agency (see Chapters 11 and 13).

## 10.9   Parents and Children – Medical Treatment

The *Gillick* case (see 9.4) did not remove the right (and duty) of parents to consent to the child's medical treatment. In fact the Department of Health and Social Security circular, which was the object of Mrs Gillick's wrath, stated that doctors should act on the presumption that parents should be consulted before contraceptives were prescribed. If a child is a mature minor (that is 'Gillick competent'), parental consent to medical treatment may not be needed. Young persons aged 16 or 17 have a statutory right to give valid consent to medical, dental or other treatment under s.8 Family Law Reform Act 1969. However, the court has the power to override the wishes of a child (of whatever age and maturity), and also the wishes of a parent, if it considers the medical treatment, or the withdrawal of medical treatment, is in the best interests of the child.

### (a)   Disputes Between Parents and Doctors About Medical Treatment of a Child

Although a failure to obtain parental consent could result in a medical practitioner being liable for assault under the civil and criminal law, parental rights in medical matters are not absolute as they can be overridden by the court. Where there is a dispute between the medical profession and parents the court will be asked to intervene. The usual procedure is for the hospital or National Health Service Trust to seek a declaration from the High Court under its inherent jurisdiction (see 9.7). Another option, which is less often used, is to apply for a s.8 specific issue order under the Children Act 1989, which requires leave to apply (see 11.8).

If doctors treat (or fail to treat) a child in defiance of parental wishes, this may be a breach of the parents' and child's rights to family life under art. 8 of the European Convention for the Protection of Human Rights. In *Glass* v. *United Kingdom (Application No.*

*61827/00)* [2004] 1 FLR 1019, where doctors stopped giving medical treatment to a child who was severely mentally and physically disabled in contravention of his mother's wishes, the European Court of Human Rights held that the UK was in breach of art. 8, and awarded the mother and child damages. The ECtHR held that the NHS should have sought the intervention of the court before stopping medical treatment in contravention of the mother's wishes.

### (b)  The Governing Principles in Disputes Between Doctors and Parents

The following principles are applied by the court in cases where parents are in dispute with the medical profession:

- The best interests of the child test applies which includes emotional and other factors.
- There is a very strong presumption in favour of prolonging life, but there is no obligation on the medical profession to give treatment which would be futile. In *Re J (A Minor) (Wardship: Medical Treatment)* [1991] Fam 33, [1991] 1 FLR 366 Lord Donaldson MR said that account had to be taken of the pain and suffering and quality of life which the child will experience if life is prolonged, and the pain and suffering involved in the proposed treatment.

Thus, the court has to conduct a balancing exercise and weigh up the advantages and disadvantages of giving, or withholding, medical treatment in order to decide what is in the child's best interests. While the courts accord great respect to parental wishes, and they are usually put into the balancing exercise, parental wishes never prevail over the best interests of the child (but for a rare case where they seemed to do so, see *Re T (Wardship: Medical Treatment)* [1997] 1 FLR 502, below).

There are many reported cases involving disputes between parents and the medical profession about the medical treatment of children. The following are some examples:

▶ *Re C (HIV Test)* [1999] 2 FLR 1004

A specific issue order was granted under s.8 Children Act 1989 on the application of the local authority, so that an HIV test could be carried out on a baby, despite the mother and father's refusal to consent to the test.

▶ *Re B (A Minor) (Wardship: Medical Treatment)* [1990] 3 All ER 927

A baby born with Down's syndrome was ordered to have a life-saving operation to remove an intestinal blockage where the parents refused to consent to the operation.

▶ *Royal Wolverhampton Hospitals NHS Trust* v. *B* [2000] 1 FLR 953

A declaration was granted that the child be treated in accordance with the wishes of the paediatrician who thought that ventilation of the child was not in her best interests, despite parental wishes to the contrary.

▶ *A National Health Service Trust* v. *D* [2000] 2 FLR 677

A declaration was granted that the child need not be ventilated, and this was held not to breach art. 2 (right to life) and art. 3 (the right not to suffer inhuman and degrading treatment) under the ECHR.

▶ *Re R (A Minor) (Blood Transfusion)* [1993] 2 FLR 757

A specific issue order was granted on the application of a local authority ordering that a child with leukaemia be given medical treatment (including blood transfusions) despite the parents' religious objections as they were Jehovah's Witnesses.

▶ *Re A (Conjoined Twins: Medical Treatment)* [2001] 1 FLR 1

Conjoined twins were ordered to be separated despite their parents' wishes to the contrary, and the fact that separation would inevitably lead to the death of the weaker twin.

▶ *Re L (Medical Treatment: Benefit)* [2004] EWHC 2713 (Fam), [2005] 1 FLR 491

A declaration was granted that the hospital could give artificial ventilation, with an option to perform cardiac massage, to a 9-month-old baby with an incurable genetic disorder, who was unlikely to survive beyond one year, despite the mother's contention that the medical profession was giving up too soon and that her baby's health had not deteriorated.

▶ *Portsmouth NHS Trust v. Wyatt and Wyatt, Southampton NHS Trust Intervening* [2004] EWHC 2247 (Fam), [2005] 1 FLR 21

Hedley J made declarations that further aggressive treatment to prolong the life of a seriously ill one-year-old child was not in her best interests, despite her parents wishes to the contrary (but see *Portsmouth NHS Trust v. Wyatt and Wyatt, Southampton NHS Trust Intervening* [2005] EWHC 693 (Fam), [2005] 2 FLR 480 where the restriction was lifted as the child showed signs of improvement). (See also *Wyatt v. Portsmouth NHS Trust* [2005] EWCA Civ 1181, [2006] 1 FLR 554.)

▶ *Re T (Wardship: Medical Treatment)* [1997] 1 FLR 502

The parents (medical professionals) refused to give consent to their child having a life-saving liver transplant, as they did not wish to care for the child. The court under its inherent jurisdiction, applying the welfare principle, refused to overrule the parents' refusal to consent.

(c) Seriously Invasive Medical Treatment

Where the medical treatment of a child is seriously invasive the court's consent may be needed. For instance, sterilisation of a child usually requires the prior sanction of the High Court under its inherent or wardship jurisdiction (see *Practice Direction (Official Solicitor: Sterilisation)* [1993] 2 FLR 222), although an application by way of specific issue order was permitted in *Re HG (Specific Issue Order: Sterilisation)* [1993] 1 FLR 587.

In *Re B (A Minor) (Wardship: Sterilisation)* [1988] AC 199 the House of Lords authorised the sterilisation of a mentally retarded 17-year-old girl child under the wardship jurisdiction. By contrast, however, in *Re D (A Minor) (Wardship: Sterilisation)* [1976] Fam 185 sterilisation was refused, because the court felt that the girl might be able to give informed consent to the operation at a later date. Consent of the court is not required, however, where sterilisation is needed for therapeutic reasons, such as cancer of the womb (see, for example, *Re E (A Minor) (Wardship: Medical Treatment)* [1993] 1 FLR 386).

### (d)  Where Parents Cannot Agree About Medical Treatment

The consent of the court may be needed in respect of certain types of medical treatment of a child where the child's parents cannot agree about the treatment. This is so even though s.2(7) Children Act 1989 provides that each parent with parental responsibility can act independently of the other. Medical treatment, such as circumcision and immunisation, may, for example, need the court's consent if the child's parents cannot agree it. The following cases are examples:

▶ *Re J (Specific Issue Orders: Child's Religious Upbringing and Circumcision)* [2000] 1 FLR 571

The father, a Muslim, wished his son aged five to be circumcised, but the mother, a Christian, objected. The father applied for a specific issue order under s.8 Children Act 1989 so that the circumcision could be carried out. The Court of Appeal held that a parental dispute about circumcision is one of the exceptional cases where a disagreement between those who possess parental responsibility must be determined by the courts. The father's application was refused, as the best interests of the child prevailed over the parents' religious beliefs and wishes.

See also *Re S (Specific Issue Order: Religion: Circumcision)* [2004] EWHC 1282 (Fam), [2005] 1 FLR 236 where a Muslim mother's application for a specific issue order authorising her son's circumcision (which the Hindu father had objected to) was refused, as the child might be able to make his own informed choice about circumcision when he was older.

▶ *Re C (Welfare of Child: Immunisation)* [2003] EWCA Civ 1148, [2003] 2 FLR 1095

Sumner J granted fathers, who had parental responsibility and contact rights, specific issue orders ordering that their daughters be immunised, despite the mothers' opposition. Immunisation was held to be in the girls' best interests, applying the welfare paramountcy principle in s.1(1) Children Act 1989. Sumner J said that the court had to undertake a balancing exercise, but that a court asked to override parental wishes had to move extremely cautiously and balance the issue with great care. Sumner J held that the decision to order immunisation was not a breach of the right to family life under art. 8 ECHR, because art. 8(2) allowed a court to interfere with the rights of parents and children in order to protect the health of a child. The Court of Appeal dismissed the appeals, and upheld Sumner J's decision.

### (e)  Disputes Between Parents and Children About Medical Treatment

See Chapter 9.

## Summary

1  It is a judge-made presumption of law that the best person to bring up a child is the child's natural parent. This approach is also enshrined in the Children Act 1989 (see Chapter 11).

2  Some couples may have to resort to assisted reproduction techniques or to surrogacy to have a child. The Human Fertilisation and Embryology Act 1990 governs assisted reproduction. Under the Surrogacy Arrangements Act 1985 it is a criminal offence to make surrogacy arrangements on a commercial basis.

## Summary cont'd

3   Married commissioning parents of a surrogacy arrangement and married parents of a child conceived by assisted reproduction can apply for a parental order under s.30 Human Fertilisation and Embryology Act 1990, which is an order for a child to be treated in law as a child of the parents' marriage.

4   A child born of married parents is presumed to be the child of the husband. The same presumption does not apply to unmarried parents. These presumptions are not very relevant today because parentage can be proved virtually conclusively by DNA profiling. The court has held that scientific tests, not legal presumptions, should be used to prove parentage.

5   The court can direct that a scientific test take place to establish parentage (s.20 Family Law Reform Act 1969). The consent of the child is needed (if aged 16 and over), or the consent of the person with the care and control of the child if the child is aged under 16. If consent is not forthcoming the court can consent. The court will usually direct a scientific test because the child has a right to know his identity, and it is important that the truth be ascertained.

6   The court can grant a declaration of parentage under s.55 Family Law Act 1986.

7   A guardian can be appointed for a child (ss.5 and 6 Children Act 1989).

8   Married parents and unmarried mothers have 'automatic' parental responsibility for their child (ss.2 and 3 Children Act 1989).

9   The unmarried father has no parental responsibility (s.2(2) Children Act 1989), but can acquire it under s.4 Children Act 1989 by making an agreement with the mother on a prescribed form, or by obtaining a parental responsibility order, or by being registered on the child's birth certificate with the mother. Another option is for the unmarried father to apply for a s.8 residence order.

10   Parents have certain rights and duties at common law and under statute, but parental rights are not absolute.

11   Disputes between parents and doctors about medical treatment of a child can be decided by the High Court under its inherent jurisdiction or in wardship; or by making an application for a s.8 specific issue order under the Children Act 1989. The best interests of the child are paramount in these cases, and parental wishes, while respected by the courts, do not prevail. Serious and irreversible operations on the child (such as sterilisation and circumcision) may need the consent of the court. Parental disputes about medical treatment can be decided by making an application for a specific issue order under s.8 Children Act 1989, or by making an application under the High Court's inherent or wardship jurisdiction. Where a parent wishes to prevent the other parent doing something an application can be made for a s.8 prohibited steps order.

## Further Reading and References

Bainham, Day Sclater and Richards (eds.), *What is a Parent? A Socio-Legal Analysis*, 1999, Hart Publishing.

Bridge, 'Religion, culture and conviction: the medical treatment of children' [1999] CFLQ 217.

Cook, Day Sclater with Kaganas, *Surrogate Motherhood*, 2003, Hart Publishing.

Downie, '*Re C (HIV Test)* – the limits of parental autonomy' [2000] CFLQ 197.

Eekelaar, 'Are parents morally obliged to care for their children?' (1991) OJLS 340.

Eekelaar, 'Parental responsibility: State of nature or nature of the state?' (1991) JSWFL 37.

## Further reading cont'd

Eekelaar, 'Rethinking parental responsibility' [2001] Fam Law 428.

Jackson, 'Conception and the irrelevance of the welfare principle' (2002) MLR 176.

Lind, '*Evans* v. *United Kingdom* – judgment of Solomon: power, gender and procreation' [2006] CFLQ 576.

Maidment, 'Parental responsibility – Is there a duty to consult?' [2001] Fam Law 518.

Pedain, 'Doctors, parents and the courts: legitimising restrictions on the continued provision of lifespan maximising treatments for severely handicapped, non-dying babies' [2005] CFLQ 535.

Sheldon, '*Evans* v. *Amicus Healthcare*; *Hadley* v. *Midland Fertility Services*: Revealing cracks in the twin pillars' [2004] CFLQ 437.

## Websites

**Advice Now**: www.advicenow.org.uk

**Families Need Fathers**: www.fnf.org.uk

**Family and Parenting Institute**: www.familyandparenting.org

**Human Fertilisation and Embryology Authority**: www.hfea.gov.uk

**Parentline Plus**: www.parentlineplus.org.uk

# Chapter 11

## The Children Act 1989

The Children Act 1989

The Children Act 1989 contains both private and public law provisions relating to children. Private law governs the relationships between private individuals, usually parents, and includes rules on parental responsibility, guardianship and residence and contact. Public law, on the other hand, is the law governing State intervention into family life by local authority social services departments who have duties and powers to provide for children in need and to protect children who are suffering, or who are at risk of suffering, significant harm.

*Influences on the Act and its Principles and Policies*   The Children Act 1989 was an important Act not only because it consolidated much of the civil law relating to children, but because it introduced new principles and policies. Government reports and public inquiries relating to the management of child abuse by social workers and other agencies had a considerable influence on the Act. Of particular importance was *The Report of the Inquiry into Child Abuse in Cleveland 1987* (Cm 412, 1988), which severely criticised the over-zealous intervention of local authority social services in children's cases in Cleveland in the North East of England. The Report had an important influence on the public law provisions of the Act, in particular in respect of the emergency protection of children and the importance of promoting inter-agency co-operation.

The *Gillick* case (see 9.4) also had an impact on the Act, by giving children of sufficient age and understanding the right to bring proceedings and to have their views taken into account by the court. The concept of parental responsibility was also introduced by the Children Act (partly as a result of *Gillick*), in order to stress the positive ongoing nature of parental involvement in bringing up children and to remove the adversarial undertones of the word 'rights'.

An important policy in the Act is that of minimum State intervention. Thus, under the no-order provision in s.1(5) courts must decide whether or not an order is really necessary in the circumstances. The aim of the Act is to restrict intervention into family life by courts and local authorities unless really necessary for the child's welfare.

Another aim of the Act is to provide a flexible court structure and a flexible range of orders available in all family proceedings involving children (and which can be made on an application to the court or of the court of its own motion). Applications under the Act can be brought in magistrates' family proceedings courts, county courts and the High Court, but cases can be transferred between these courts if the matter is urgent or serious, or where proceedings should be consolidated.

*Strengths and Weaknesses*   The Children Act 1989 has generally been considered to be a 'successful' Act (and this was recognised by the inquiry which followed the tragic death of Victoria Climbié, see 15.2), but it has been criticised by some commentators for not putting children's interests sufficiently to the fore (see Freeman, 1998) and for failing to include any reference to children's rights (see Fortin, 2006). A major problem with proceedings under the Act, however, is that of delay. Delays can be particularly long in child protection cases, but steps have been taken to resolve the problem (see 15.1).

*Human Rights*    The Children Act 1989 must be construed and applied by courts and public authorities in a way which complies with the European Convention for the Protection of Human Rights as a result of the obligations on courts and other public authorities under the Human Rights Act 1998 (see 1.5).

*New Provisions*    New provisions have been inserted into the Children Act 1989 by the Adoption and Children Act 2002, in particular: to allow unmarried fathers to acquire parental responsibility if they register the child's birth with the mother (s.4(1)); to allow step-parents to acquire parental responsibility for a step-child (s.4A); and to give the court power to make special guardianship orders (ss.14A–G). These provisions are all in force. New provisions in respect of contact have also been inserted into the Act by Part 1 of the Children and Adoption Act 2006 (see 12.5). In respect of the public law governing children, amendments to the Act have been made by the Children (Leaving Care) Act 2000 (see further in Chapter 15).

The Children Act 1989 must not be confused with the Children Act 2004 (see 15.1), which does not replace, but supplements, the 1989 Act.

## 11.2    An Overview of the Act

Parts I to V of the Children Act 1989 are the parts most relevant to family lawyers, and so is Part XII ('Miscellaneous and General') which contains the interpretation section (s.105) defining the terms used in the Act. The Act also contains important schedules. Schedules 1 to 3 are particularly important for family law. The main provisions of the Act are as follows:

### Part I (Introductory)

Welfare principle and other principles applicable in proceedings under the Act (s.1). Parental responsibility (ss.2–4A). Parental responsibility agreements and parental responsibility orders for unmarried fathers (s.4); and step-parents (s.4A). Appointment of guardians for children (ss.5 and 6). Welfare reports (s.7).

### Part II (Orders with Respect to Children in Family Proceedings)

Section 8 orders (residence, contact, specific issue and prohibited steps), and the powers of the court in respect of these orders (ss.9–14), including new provisions in relation to contact (for example contact activity directions and conditions) (ss.11A–11P). Special guardianship orders (ss.14A–G). Orders for financial relief for children (s.15 and Schedule 1). Family assistance orders (s.16). Risk assessments (s.16A).

### Part III (Local Authority Support for Children and Families)

Local authority services for children in need, their families and others (ss.17–19). Payments and vouchers in respect of children in need (ss.17A and B). Provision of accommodation for children in need (ss.20 and 21). The duties of local authorities in relation to children looked after by them (ss.22 and 23). Advice and assistance for children (s.24). Advice and assistance for children and young persons who have left care (ss.23A–E, ss.24A–D). Secure accommodation (s.25). Case reviews (s.26). Co-operation between local authorities (s.27).

Advocacy services for children (s.27A). Consultation with local education authorities (s.28). Recoupment of cost of providing services (s.29).

### Part IV (Care and Supervision)

Care orders, supervision orders and education supervision orders (ss.31–40). Care plans (s.31A). Provision in respect of guardians *ad litem* for children in court proceedings (ss.41 and 42).

### Part V (Protection of Children)

Child assessment orders (s.43). Emergency protection orders (ss.44 and 45). Police removal of children (s.46). Local authority duty to investigate (s.47). Power to assist in discovery of children (s.48). Abduction of children in care (ss.49 and 50). Refuges for children at risk (s.51).

### Schedule 1 (Financial Provision for Children)

Orders for financial relief for children (para. 1); orders for financial relief for persons aged over 18 (para. 2); provisions relating to the courts' powers to make these orders (paras. 3–14); local authority contribution to a child's maintenance (para. 15).

### Schedule 2 (Local Authority Support for Children and Families)

Provision of services for families (Part I, paras. 1–11); children looked after by local authorities (Part II, paras. 12–20); contribution towards maintenance of children looked after by local authorities (Part III, paras. 21–25).

### Schedule 3 (Supervision Orders)

Powers of supervisor, psychiatric and medical examination and treatment (Part I, paras. 1–5); duration of supervision orders, information to be given to supervisor (Part II, paras. 6–11); education supervision orders (Part III, paras. 12–21).

---

## 11.3    The Part I Principles

Important principles are laid down in Part I of the Children Act 1989 which apply to most court applications involving children, whether brought by private individuals or public authorities. These principles are as follows:

### (a)    The Welfare Principle (s.1(1))

The paramountcy of the child's welfare is the governing principle in children's cases.

---

### Section 1(1)  Children Act 1989

'When a court determines any question with respect to—
(a) the upbringing of a child; or
(b) the administration of a child's property or the application of any income arising from it,
the child's welfare shall be the court's paramount consideration.'

The child's welfare is the paramount consideration in private law proceedings (such as for residence and contact orders) and in public law proceedings (such as for care and supervision orders). The Children Act 1989 does not expressly require the welfare principle to be applied in applications for leave to apply for a s.8 order (see 11.4) or in applications for financial relief for children under s.15 and Sched. 1 (see 13.5), but in practice the court will consider the child's welfare as part of all the circumstances of the case.

The paramountcy of the child's welfare is enshrined in art. 3(1) of the UN Convention on the Rights of the Child 1989, and it is recognised by the European Court of Human Rights even though there is no express reference to children in the European Convention for the Protection of Human Rights (see 1.5).

### (b) The 'Welfare Checklist' (s.1(3))

Section 1(3) contains a list of factors (a 'welfare checklist') which imposes some structure on the broad exercise of judicial discretion in the application of the welfare principle above. The court must have regard to the checklist when deciding whether to make, vary or discharge a s.8 order in contested proceedings (s.1(4)(a)), or to make, vary or discharge a special guardianship order, or a care or supervision order (s.1(4)(b)). Thus, the checklist must be applied in private law proceedings and in public law proceedings involving local authorities (except in emergency protection proceedings – as to apply the checklist would inhibit emergency action).

---

**Section 1(3)  Children Act 1989**

'. . . a court shall have regard in particular to—
(a)  the ascertainable wishes and feelings of the child concerned (considered in the light of his age and understanding);
(b)  his physical, emotional and educational needs;
(c)  the likely effect on him of any change in his circumstances;
(d)  his age, sex, background and any characteristics of his which the court considers relevant;
(e)  any harm which he has suffered or is at risk of suffering;
(f)  how capable each of his parents, and any other person in relation to whom the court considers the question to be relevant, is of meeting his needs;
(g)  the range of powers available to the court under this Act in the proceedings in question.'

---

The list is not exclusive – other factors may be taken into account – and the factors are not listed in any hierarchy of importance. Furthermore, as the Act does not refer to s.1(3) as a 'checklist', a judge is not required 'to read out the seven items in s.1(3) and pronounce his conclusion on each' (Staughton LJ in *H* v. *H (Residence Order: Leave to Remove from Jurisdiction)* [1995] 1 FLR 529). In *B* v. *B (Residence Order: Reasons for Decision)* [1997] 2 FLR 602, Holman J held that, although it is not always necessary or appropriate for a judge to go through the checklist item by item, it does represent an extremely useful and important discipline for judges to ensure that all the relevant factors and circumstances are considered and balanced. A failure to consider one or more of the factors may, however, provide a ground for an appeal.

'Harm' in s.1(3)(e) has the same meaning as it has in s.31 of the Act (see 15.7) and now includes harm caused by 'witnessing the ill treatment of another person'. Witnessing domestic violence can therefore constitute harm.

### (c)   The 'Minimum Intervention Principle' (s.1(5))

This principle was introduced as part of the general policy of the Act to place the primary responsibility for children on their parents.

---

**Section 1(5)  Children Act 1989**

'Where a court is considering whether or not to make one or more orders under this Act with respect to a child, it shall not make the order or any of the orders unless it considers that doing so would be better for the child than making no order at all.'

---

The aim of s.1(5) is to discourage courts making unnecessary orders and to ensure that they are only made if they will positively improve the child's welfare. Sometimes an order may exacerbate problems and increase hostility between parents, with harmful repercussions for the child. In public law cases, where the emphasis is on local authorities working in voluntary partnerships with parents in order to promote the welfare of children, it may sometimes be better not to make an order, or to make a different order.

Section 1(5) has been interpreted by some commentators and judges as creating a presumption in favour of making no order, and for this reason has been referred to as the 'no-order' principle. However, in *Re G (Children) (Residence Order: No Order Principle)* [2005] All ER 399 the Court of Appeal held that this is an incorrect interpretation, as it is perfectly clear that s.1(5) does not create a presumption either way. It merely requires the court to ask itself the question whether to make an order would be better for a child than making no order at all. The Court of Appeal held that the district judge had been wrong in refusing to make a residence order in the circumstances because he considered that s.1(5) raised a presumption against making an order. (See also *B v. B (A Minor) (Residence Order)* [1992] 2 FLR 327 where the trial judge's refusal to grant the applicant grandmother a residence order on the basis of s.1(5) was overturned by the Court of Appeal.)

### (d)   The 'No-Delay' Principle (s.1(2))

The Children Act recognises that delay is harmful for a child:

---

**Section 1(2)  Children Act 1989**

'In any proceedings in which any question with respect to the upbringing of a child arises, the court shall have regard to the general principle that any delay in determining the question is likely to prejudice the welfare of the child.'

---

To avoid delay, the progress of cases is determined by the court, which must draw up a timetable for s.8 order proceedings (s.11) and for care and supervision proceedings (s.32). The court can give directions and the rules of court make provision to avoid delay. Children's issues must be determined as soon as possible so that minimum disruption is caused to the child's life and the child is not left in limbo. Despite attempts to reduce delay, it continues to be a problem, particularly in child protection cases (see 15.1).

## 11.4 Section 8 Orders

Section 8 of the Children Act 1989 makes provision for the following orders which can be used in a wide range of different situations involving children:

- **Residence Order** (determining with whom the child should live);
- **Contact Order** (determining with whom the child should visit or stay);
- **Prohibited Steps Order** (preventing an action in respect of parental responsibility being taken);
- **Specific Issue Order** (determining an issue arising in respect of parental responsibility).

In 2006, 111,607 section 8 orders were made in private and public law proceedings in England and Wales, of which 31,712 were residence orders, 66,075 were contact orders, 9,617 were prohibited steps orders and 4,203 were specific issue orders (*Judicial and Court Statistics 2006*, Cm 7273, Ministry of Justice, 2007).

*Applicable Principles*   When considering whether to make, vary or discharge any s.8 order, the court must apply the welfare principle and the welfare checklist (see above). The no-delay principle and the no-order presumption (above) must also be applied.

*Applicants*   Parents (with or without parental responsibility) and guardians have an automatic right to apply for s.8 orders, but other persons, including children, need the court's leave to apply (see below). Restrictions exist in respect of applications by local authorities (see below).

*General Provisions*   The court can: make interim s.8 orders (s.11(3)); attach directions and conditions to a s.8 order (s.11(7)); and grant a s.8 order without the other party being given notice of the proceedings (if urgent action is needed).

*Restrictions*   Section 9 lays down restrictions which apply to s.8 orders:

- The court cannot make any s.8 order (other than a residence order) with respect to a child who is in the care of a local authority (s.9(1)).
- A local authority cannot apply for a residence or contact order and no court shall make such an order in favour of a local authority (s.9(2)). This prohibition is to prevent local authorities using s.8 orders instead of the care or supervision order provisions in Part IV of the Act.
- A person who is, or who was at any time during the last six months, a local authority foster-parent may not apply for leave to apply for a s.8 order with respect to the child

unless: he has the consent of the local authority; or he is a relative of the child; or the child has lived with him for at least one year preceding the application (s.9(3)).

- A court cannot make a specific issue order or prohibited steps order with a view to achieving a result which could be achieved by making a residence or contact order; or in any way which is denied by the High Court (by s.100(2)) in the exercise of its inherent jurisdiction with respect to children (s.9(5)).
- With the exception of an 'extended residence order' (see below), a court cannot make any s.8 order which is to have effect for a period which will end after the child has reached the age of 16, unless it is satisfied that the circumstances of the case are exceptional (s.9(6)).
- A court cannot make any s.8 order, other than one varying or discharging such an order, with respect to a child who has reached the age of 16 unless it is satisfied that the circumstances of the case are exceptional (s.9(7)).

## 11.5  Residence Orders

> A **residence order** is an order 'settling the arrangements to be made as to the person with whom the child is to live' (s.8(1)).

Residence orders are often sought on family breakdown (see 12.4) – although it is better if parents try to reach agreement about a child's residence arrangements.

Residence orders were introduced by the Children Act 1989 to replace custody orders, with the aim of removing the claim right implicit in, and the adversarial undertones of, the term 'custody'. The emphasis on residence rather than custody is to reinforce the fact that both parents have a continuing role to play in relation to a child. With residence orders it is a question of where the child should live, rather than to whom the child belongs.

In addition to the general provisions and restrictions applicable to s.8 orders (see above), the following provisions specifically apply to residence orders:

- The court can make a 'shared' residence order in favour of two or more persons who live in different households (s.11(4)) (see 12.4).
- If a residence order is made there are restrictions on changing the child's surname and taking the child out of the UK (ss.13(1) and (2)).
- If under a residence order the child is to live with one of two parents who each has parental responsibility for him the order ceases to be effective if the parents live together for a continuous period of more than six months (s.11(5)).
- The court can impose conditions on residence orders (s.11(7)).

*Local Authorities and Residence Orders*   A residence order is the only s.8 order that can be made in respect of a child in local authority care (s.9(1)) – as it would otherwise undermine a local authority's statutory powers. However, a residence order cannot be applied for by, or made in favour of, a local authority (s.9(2)), as this would allow a local authority to gain parental responsibility for a child by means other than a care order.

*Residence Orders and Parental Responsibility*   A residence order does not affect the parental responsibility of any other person who possesses such responsibility (s.2(1)). Thus, parental responsibility is retained whether or not a residence order is made.

A residence order confers parental responsibility on a person in whose favour it is made (if they do not already have such responsibility), but only for the duration of the order (s.12(2)). Parental responsibility acquired in this manner, however, is limited, as the person in whose favour the residence order is made does not have the right to give consent, or refusal of consent, to the child's adoption, or have the right to appoint a guardian (s.12(3)). Adoption and special guardianship orders also provide alternatives for persons who wish to acquire parental responsibility for a child (see Chapter 16).

If a residence order is made in favour of an unmarried father without parental responsibility, the court must also make a parental responsibility order under s.4 giving him such responsibility (s.12(2)).

*'Extended Residence Orders'*   A residence order in normal circumstances lasts until the child is 16 (s.9(6)), but under s.12(5) the court has the power to make an 'extended residence order' in favour of any person who is not the child's parent or guardian, which includes a power to direct, at the request of that person, that the order continues in force until the child reaches the age of 18 (unless the order is brought to an end earlier); and any power to vary a residence order is exercisable accordingly (s.12(5)). This provision came into force on 30 December 2005. It is useful for step-parents, relatives and foster-parents who wish to acquire parental responsibility which lasts until the end of the child's minority.

## 11.6   Contact Orders

A **contact order** is an order 'requiring the person with whom the child lives, or is to live, to allow the child to visit or stay with the person named in the order, or for that person and the child otherwise to have contact with each other' (s.8(1)).

The Children Act 1989 introduced the term 'contact' to replace that of 'access' in order to stress the importance of children maintaining links with their parents and other family members on family breakdown. The change of terminology was intended to shift the emphasis from the adult to the child. Contact orders are often applied for on family breakdown (see 12.5).

The general provisions and restrictions which apply to s.8 orders apply to contact orders (see above). In respect of local authorities, a contact order cannot be made in respect of a child in care and cannot be applied for by, or be made in favour of, a local authority (s.9). Contact in care is governed by s.34 of the Children Act (see 15.8). A s.8 contact order ceases to be effective if the parents live together for a continuous period of more than six months (s.11(6)).

**11.7**  Prohibited Steps Orders

A **prohibited steps order** is an order 'that no step which could be taken by a parent in meeting his parental responsibility for a child, and which is of a kind specified in the order, shall be taken by any person without the consent of the court' (s.8(1)).

The prohibited steps order, and the specific issue order (see below), give the court powers similar to those which before the Children Act were available only to the High Court under its inherent jurisdiction and in wardship (see 9.7).

A prohibited steps order is a flexible injunctive type of order which can be used in a wide range of circumstances, for example to prohibit a parent taking a child out of the UK or from taking a unilateral decision about the child's medical treatment or education, or from changing the child's surname. In *Re G (Parental Responsibility: Education)* [1994] 2 FLR 964, for example, a mother applied for a prohibited steps order to prevent her husband sending their son away to boarding school, but her application was refused.

In addition to the general provisions and restrictions which apply to s.8 orders (see above), a prohibited steps order cannot be made to achieve the same result which could be achieved by making a residence or contact order, and cannot be made in any way denied to the High Court (by s.100(2)) under its inherent jurisdiction (s.9(5)).

As a prohibited steps order is an order prohibiting 'a step which could be taken by a parent in meeting his parental responsibility' for a child, it cannot be used to restrict anything other than some aspect of parental responsibility. For example, it could not be used to restrict publicity about a child, since this is not within the scope of parental responsibility (this must be dealt with by the High Court under its inherent jurisdiction); or to prohibit a parent occupying the family home (see *Nottinghamshire County Council v. P* [1993] 2 FLR 134, [1994] Fam 18; and *Re D (Prohibited Steps Order)* [1996] 2 FLR 273).

**11.8**  Specific Issue Orders

A **specific issue order** is an order 'giving directions for the purpose of determining a specific question which has arisen, or which may arise, in connection with any aspect of parental responsibility for a child' (s.8(1)).

This order can be made to settle any dispute which has arisen, or may arise, in respect of the exercise of parental responsibility. It can be used, for example, to settle a dispute arising in respect of a child's education or medical treatment, or a decision to move a child abroad, or to change a child's surname. A specific issue order (like a prohibited steps order) gives the court similar powers to those possessed by the High Court under its inherent jurisdiction and in wardship (see 9.7). In addition to the general provisions and restrictions which apply to s.8 orders (see above), a specific issue order, like a prohibited steps order, cannot be made to achieve the same result which could be achieved by making a residence or contact order, and cannot be made in any way denied to the High Court (by s.100(2)) under its inherent jurisdiction (s.9(5)).

Specific issue orders have been sought by parents in a wide range of situations, for example:

> ▶ **To obtain permission for a child to be sterilised** (*Re HG (Specific Issue Order: Sterilisation)* [1993] 1 FLR 587).
> ▶ **To require a child to be brought up in the Muslim religion and be circumcised** (*Re J (Specific Issue Orders: Child's Religious Upbringing and Circumcision)* [2000] 1 FLR 571; *Re S (Specific Issue Order: Religion: Circumcision)* [2004] EWHC 1282 (Fam), [2005] 1 FLR 236).
> ▶ **To require a child to be informed about his paternity and the existence of his father** (*Re K (Specific Issue Order)* [1999] 2 FLR 280).
> ▶ **To resolve a parental dispute about a child's education** (*Re A (Specific Issue Order: Parental Dispute)* [2001] 1 FLR 121).

In respect of local authorities, a specific issue order cannot be made in respect of a child in local authority care (s.9(1)). A local authority will instead have to seek leave to invoke the court's inherent jurisdiction to decide a particular matter (ss.100(2)–(5)) (see 9.7). It has been held that a specific issue order cannot be made to deem a child to be in need for the purposes of Part III of the Children Act 1989 (see 15.6), as this is not an 'aspect of parental responsibility' for the purposes of the order – the appropriate remedy is judicial review (see *Re J (Specific Issue Order: Leave to Apply)* [1995] 1 FLR 669).

## 11.9 Power of the Court to Make Section 8 Orders in Family Proceedings of its Own Motion

In any family proceedings in which a question arises with respect to the welfare of any child the court may make a s.8 order with respect to the child if (s.10(1)): a person is entitled to apply; or a person has been given leave of the court to make the application; or the court considers that the order should be made even though no such application has been made.

'Family proceedings' are defined in ss.8(3), (4) as any proceedings under the following (but not including an application for leave under s.100(3) Children Act 1989):

▶ the inherent jurisdiction of the High Court in relation to children;
▶ Parts I, II and IV of the Children Act 1989;
▶ the Matrimonial Causes Act 1973;
▶ Schedule 5 to the Civil Partnership Act 2004;
▶ the Adoption and Children Act 2002;
▶ the Domestic Proceedings and Magistrates' Courts Act 1978;
▶ Schedule 6 to the Civil Partnership Act 2004;
▶ Part III of the Matrimonial and Family Proceedings Act 1984;
▶ the Family Law Act 1996;
▶ Sections 11 and 12 Crime and Disorder Act 1998.

Thus s.8 orders can be made in a wide range of proceedings involving children, for example in divorce proceedings, adoption proceedings, and proceedings for non-molestation orders and occupation orders in domestic violence cases.

**11.10**   Power of the Court to Make Section 8 Orders in Family
Proceedings on the Application of Certain Persons

In addition to the court having the power to make a s.8 order of its own motion in any
family proceedings (see above), the court may make an order with respect to a child on
the application of certain persons who are entitled to apply without leave of the court (see
below) or by certain persons with leave (s.10(2)).

**(a)**   Persons Entitled to Apply Without Leave of the Court

*(i) Any s.8 Order*   The following persons are entitled to apply for any s.8 order without leave
(s.10(4)): a parent, guardian, or special guardian of the child (s.10(4)(a)); a step-parent who
has parental responsibility for the child under s.4A Children Act 1989 (s.10(4)(aa)); and a
person in whose favour a residence order is in force with respect to the child (s.10(4)(b)).

*(ii) Residence and Contact Orders*   The following persons are entitled to apply for a
residence or contact order without leave (s.10(5)): a party to a marriage or civil partnership
(whether or not subsisting) in relation to whom the child is a child of the family (that is,
a step-parent or former step-parent) (ss.10(5)(a), (aa)); a person with whom the child has
lived for at least three years, which need not be continuous but must not have begun more
than five years before, or have ended more than three months before, applying for the
order (ss.10(5)(b), (10)); a person who has the consent of each person in whose favour a
residence order was made; a person who has the consent of the local authority when a
child is in care; and any other person who has the consent of each person (if any) with
parental responsibility for the child (s.10(5)(c)).
    Special provisions apply to local authority foster-parents (see below). An application
for a residence order can be made in respect of a child who is the subject of a special
guardianship order, but only with leave of the court to apply (s.10(7A)).

**(b)**   Applications for Leave to Apply for s.8 Orders

Different requirements apply to leave applications by children and to those by other
persons. Special provisions apply to foster-parents (see below).

*(i) Children – Leave to Apply*   A child needs leave of the court to apply for a s.8 order,
which the court may only grant if it is satisfied that the child has sufficient
understanding to make the proposed application (s.10(8)). The court can take into
account the likelihood of the proposed application succeeding, and on that basis refuse
leave even if the child has sufficiency of understanding (see Booth J in *Re SC (A Minor)
(Leave to Seek a Residence Order)* [1994] 1 FLR 96; and Johnson J in *Re H (Residence Order:
Child's Application for Leave)* [2000] 1 FLR 780). Leave applications by children are heard
in the High Court (*Practice Direction (Children Act 1989: Applications by Children)* [1993] 1
FLR 668).
    There has been conflicting judicial opinion as to whether the child's welfare is
paramount in a leave application. In *Re C (A Minor) (Leave to Seek Section 8 Orders)* [1994]
1 FLR 26 Johnson J applied the welfare principle, but in *Re SC (A Minor) (Leave to Seek
Residence Order)* [1994] 1 FLR 96 Booth J said that the child's welfare was not the

paramount consideration. In *Re C (Residence) (Child's Application for Leave)* [1995] 1 FLR 927 Stuart-White J considered these divergent views, and concluded that the child's welfare is an important, but not a paramount, consideration, and this approach was subsequently adopted by Johnson J in *Re H (Residence Order: Child's Application for Leave)* [2000] 1 FLR 780.

*(ii) Other Persons – Leave to Apply*  In leave applications by persons other than children the court must have particular regard to (s.10(9)): the nature of the proposed application; the applicant's connection with the child; any risk of the proposed application disrupting the child's life to such an extent that he would be harmed by it; and where the child is being looked after by a local authority, the local authority's plans for the child's future and the wishes and feelings of the child's parents.

The welfare principle does not apply to a leave application (*Re A and W (Minors) (Residence Order: Leave to Apply)* [1992] Fam 182, [1992] 2 FLR 154). The application will be refused if it is frivolous or vexatious, or otherwise an abuse of the court. The case must disclose a real prospect of success, and there must be a serious issue to be tried and a good arguable case (see Wall J in *Re M (Minors) (Contact: Leave to Apply)* [1995] 2 FLR 98). In *G v. F (Contact and Shared Residence: Applications for Leave)* [1998] 2 FLR 799, for example, a lesbian couple were granted leave to apply for contact and shared residence orders; and in *Re J (Leave to Issue Application for Residence Order)* [2003] 1 FLR 114 a grandmother was granted leave to apply for a residence order.

### (c) Foster-Parents – Applications for s.8 Orders

A person who has been a foster-parent at any time within the previous six months can, with leave of the court, apply for any s.8 order (including a residence order, see s.10(5A)) provided the applicant: has the local authority's consent, or is a relative of the child; or the child has lived with the applicant for at least one year preceding the application (s.9(3)). (See, for example, *C v. Salford City Council and Others* [1994] 2 FLR 926, where foster-parents applied for a residence order.)

In *Gloucestershire County Council v. P* [1999] 2 FLR 61 the Court of Appeal held that in exceptional circumstances the court acting of its own motion under s.10 may make a residence order in favour of foster-parents even though they are disqualified because they have failed to obtain local authority consent as required by s.9(3) (above). However, it stressed that foster-parent applications made without local authority support would be subject to careful scrutiny.

### 11.11 Jurisdiction to Make Section 8 Orders

Jurisdiction to make s.8 orders is governed by the Family Law Act 1986. The court has jurisdiction if on the date of application the child is habitually resident in England and Wales, or is present in England and Wales and is not habitually resident in any other part of the UK (s.2(2)). Habitual residence is not defined in the 1986 Act – case-law principles apply. The court may refuse jurisdiction where public policy considerations prevail over the child's welfare (for example in immigration cases, see *Re M (A Minor) (Immigration: Residence Order)* [1993] 2 FLR 858). The court can refuse to hear an application if the matter has already been determined in proceedings outside England and Wales (s.5(1)

Family Law Act 1986) and may, on application, stay the proceedings if proceedings relating to the same matters are continuing outside England and Wales, or if it would be more appropriate for those matters to be dealt with outside England and Wales (s.5(2)) (see, for example, *Re F (Residence Order: Jurisdiction)* [1995] 2 FLR 518; and *Re S (Jurisdiction to Stay Application)* [1995] 1 FLR 1093).

## 11.12   Other Orders Under the Children Act 1989

A wide range of orders other than s.8 orders can be made by the courts under the Children Act 1989.

### (a)   Part I Orders

*(i) Parental Responsibility Order – Fathers (s.4)*   The court can make a parental responsibility order giving an unmarried father parental responsibility (see 10.6).

*(ii) Parental Responsibility Order – Step-Parents (s.4A)*   The court can make an order giving a step-parent parental responsibility (see 10.7).

*(iii) Order Appointing a Guardian of a Child (s.5)*   The court can appoint a person to be a guardian of a child (see 10.4).

*(iv) Order for a Welfare Report (s.7)*   When considering any question with respect to a child under the Children Act, the court may request a report from a CAFCASS officer (see 1.4) or from a local authority officer (or such other person as the authority considers appropriate) on such matters relating to the child as are required to be dealt with in the report (s.7(1)).

### (b)   Part II Orders (Orders with Respect to Children in Family Proceedings)

*(i) Section 8 Orders*   See above.

*(ii) Contact Activity Directions and Conditions etc (ss.11A–P)*   See 12.5.

*(iii) Special Guardianship Orders (ss.14A–G)*   See 16.18.

*(iv) Orders for Financial Relief (s.15 and Schedule 1)*   See 13.5.

*(v) Family Assistance Orders (s.16)*   The aim of a family assistance order (FAO) is to provide short-term help to a family on family breakdown. Section 16 has been amended (by s.6 Children and Adoption Act 2006) to make FAOs more flexible and of longer duration so that they can be more usefully used in difficult contact cases. CAFCASS can now be involved, and there is no requirement that the circumstances are exceptional before an order can be made. The changes came into force on 1 October 2007. The following provisions now apply.

The court has the power to make a FAO on an application or of its own motion in any family proceedings (see definition at 11.9, above). The effect of an order is to require a

CAFCASS officer or Welsh family proceedings officer to be made available, or a local authority to make an officer of the local authority available to advise, assist and (where appropriate) befriend any person named in the order (s.16(1)). A FAO cannot be made unless the local authority agrees to making an officer available, or the child concerned lives or will live in the local authority's area (s.16(7)). *Practice Direction: Family Assistance Orders: Consultation (3/9/07)* [2007] 2 FLR 626 issued by the President of the Family Division provides that, before making a FAO, the court must obtain the opinion (oral or written) of a CAFCASS officer as to whether it is in the best interests of the child for a FAO to be made and, if so, how the order could operate and for what period. The *Practice Direction* also provides that, before making an order, the court must give any person whom it proposes be named in the order an opportunity to comment on any opinion given by the officer.

Only the following persons can be named in a FAO: a parent, guardian, or special guardian of the child; any person with whom the child is living or in whose favour a contact order is in force with respect to the child; the child himself (s.16(2)). An order can be made whether or not any other order is made in the family proceedings (s.16(1)), but the court can only make the order if it has obtained the consent of every person named in the order, other than the child (s.16(3)). A FAO may direct a person (or persons) named in the order to take such steps as may be specified with a view to the officer concerned to be kept informed of the address of any person named in the order and to be allowed to visit any such person (s.16(4)). If a FAO is made and is to be in force at the same time as a s.8 contact order with respect to the child, the order may direct the officer concerned to give advice and assistance as regards establishing, improving and maintaining contact to such of the persons named in the order as may be specified in the order (s.16(4A)). If a FAO is made at the same time as a s.8 order is in force with respect to the child, the FAO may direct the officer concerned to report to the court on such matters relating to the s.8 order as the court may require (including the question of whether the s.8 order ought to be varied or discharged) (s.16(6)). A FAO can be made to last for up to a period of 12 months (s.16(5)).

### (c) Risk Assessments

See 13.5.

### (d) Part IV Orders (Care and Supervision)

*(i) Care and Supervision Orders (s.31)*   Where a child is suffering, or is likely to suffer, significant harm the court can, if certain threshold criteria are satisfied and the child's welfare requires it, make a care order placing the child in the care of a local authority, or a supervision order placing the child under the supervision of a local authority officer or probation officer (s.35) (see 15.7).

*(ii) Order for Contact with a Child in Care (s.34)*   Where a child is in local authority care the authority must allow parents and certain other persons reasonable contact with the child, and the court can make orders in respect of such contact, including the termination of contact (see 15.8).

*(iii) Education Supervision Order (s.36)*   Where a child of compulsory school age is not being properly educated the court can, on the application of a local education authority, make

an education supervision order in favour of that authority (see, for example, *Essex County Council v. B* [1993] 1 FLR 866). These orders are rarely made.

*(iv) Order that a Local Authority Investigate the Child's Circumstances (s.37)*   Where in any family proceedings a question arises in respect of the child's welfare and it may be appropriate for a care or supervision order to be made, the court may direct that a local authority undertake an investigation into the child's circumstances (s.37(1)). (See, for example, *Re L (Section 37 Direction)* [1999] 1 FLR 984; and *Re CE (Section 37 Direction)* [1995] 1 FLR 26.)

### (e)   Part V Orders (Protection of Children)

*(i) Child Assessment Order (s.43)*   Where there is reasonable cause to suspect that a child is suffering, or is likely to suffer, significant harm and an assessment of the child's health and development or the way in which the child is being treated is needed the court can make a child assessment order (see 15.9).

*(ii) Emergency Protection Order (s.44)*   Where there is reasonable cause to believe that a child is likely to suffer significant harm the court can in certain circumstances make an emergency protection order, which authorises the removal from, or retention of the child in, certain accommodation (see 15.9).

### (f)   An Order Restricting an Application to the Court (s.91(14))

Under s.91(14), when disposing of any application under the Children Act 1989, the court (whether or not it decides to make an order) can order that no application for an order under the Children Act of any specified kind may be made with respect to the child by any person named in the order without the court's permission. The aim of a s.91(14) order is to prevent unnecessary and disruptive court applications which may be detrimental to a child's best interests. They are sometimes used in the context of a protracted contact dispute. The order is made to control persons who have made repeated and unreasonable applications to the court, or who are likely to act unreasonably in the future. In an exceptional case it may be made in respect of a first application (see *Re Y (Child Orders: Restricting Applications)* [1994] 2 FLR 699 where the father, who had killed the mother in front of the children, had applied for a contact order or discharge of a care order).

In exercising its discretion under s.91(14) the court balances the welfare of the child against the right of the litigant to have unrestricted access to the courts. The court will ensure that the degree of restriction in a s.91(14) order is proportionate to the degree of harm which it is intended to avoid (see *Re M (Section 91(14) Order)* [1999] 2 FLR 553). The court can lift an order where an applicant can show a need for renewed judicial investigation into the matter (see *Re A (Application for Leave)* [1998] 1 FLR 1).

The courts are greatly aware of the severity of making a s.91(14) order, and will only make them in the last resort where there is a clear evidential basis for doing so. In *B v. B (Residence Order: Restricting Applications)* [1997] 1 FLR 139 the Court of Appeal held that the power must be exercised with great care as it represents a substantial interference with the principle of public policy that all citizens enjoy a right of unrestricted access to the courts. In *Re B (Section 91(14) Order: Duration)* [2003] EWCA Civ 1966, [2004] 1 FLR 871 a s.91(14) order imposed for the duration of the child's minority (to prevent any further contact applications by the father) was reduced to two years, on the basis that the court should never abandon any endeavours to right the wrongs within the family dynamics. Sometimes an order may be imposed where there is violence in the home (see *Re F (Restrictions on Applications)* [2005] EWCA Civ 499, [2005] 2 FLR 950 where an order lasting two-and-half years was imposed on a father who wished to apply for contact, but against whom the mother had obtained injunctive protection under Part IV of the Family Law Act 1996).

As a result of their obligations under the Human Rights Act 1998 the courts must ensure that making a s.91(14) order does not infringe a person's rights under the European Convention for the Protection of Human Rights, in particular art. 6 (right of access to the court) and art. 8 (right to family life). In *Re P (A Minor) (Residence Order: Child's Welfare)* [2000] Fam 15, *sub nom Re P (Section 91(14) Guidelines) (Residence and Religious Heritage)* [1999] 2 FLR 573 the Court of Appeal held that making a s.91(14) order was not a breach of art. 6 ECHR – as it was only a partial restriction on disallowing claims before the court – but it ruled that, because of the severity of a s.91(14) order, the court should specify what type of court applications are restricted and for how long. Butler-Sloss LJ said:

> '[A s.91(14) order] is a partial restriction in that it does not allow [a parent] the right to an immediate *inter partes* hearing. It thereby protects the other parties and the child from being drawn into the proposed proceedings unless or until a court has ruled that the application should be allowed to proceed. On an application for leave, the applicant must persuade the judge that he has an arguable case with some chance of success. That is not a formidable hurdle to surmount. If the application is hopeless and refused the other parties and the child will have been protected from unnecessary involvement in the proposed proceedings and unwarranted investigations into the present circumstances of the child.'

Thus, s.91(14) does not impose an absolute bar on an application to the court (see also Wall LJ in *Stringer v. Stringer* [2006] EWCA Civ 1617, [2007] 1 FLR 1532).

In *Re S (Permission to Seek Relief)* [2006] EWCA Civ 1190, [2007] 1 FLR 482 the Court of Appeal held that:

- there was no power to attach a condition to a s.91(14) order beyond stating how long it is to last and identifying the type of relief to which it applied;
- a person subject to a s.91(14) order, because of his or her conduct, must have addressed that conduct if an application for permission to apply is to warrant a renewed judicial investigation or an arguable case;
- although it was clear from *Re P (A Minor)* (above) that an order can be made without a time-limit and expressed to last until a child reaches the age of 16, these powers should be the exception rather than the rule;
- before a s.91(14) order can be made, the person affected should have a proper opportunity to consider it and be heard on it.

# Summary

1   The Children Act 1989 contains much of the civil law, private and public, relating to children.

2   Part I lays down the general principles of the Act. Part II makes provision for private law orders. Parts III–V make provision in respect of the powers and duties of local authorities in respect of the care and protection of children.

3   The following welfare principles are laid down in s.1: the welfare principle (s.1(1)); the no-delay principle (s.1(2)); the 'welfare checklist' (s.1(3)); and the no-order principle (s.1(5)). The welfare checklist must be applied in contested s.8 order proceedings and in care and supervision proceedings under Part IV of the Act (s.1(4)).

4   The court can make the following s.8 orders: residence order; contact order; prohibited steps order; and specific issue order.

5   Section 8 orders can be made on application or by the court of its own motion in any family proceedings. Some persons have an automatic right to apply but other persons, including the child, need leave of the court (s.10). The court has jurisdiction to make s.8 orders if the child is habitually resident or present in England and Wales and is not habitually resident in any other part of the UK (s.2 Family Law Act 1986).

6   Under Part I of the Children Act 1989 the court can make the following private law orders: parental responsibility orders for unmarried fathers and step-parents (s.4 and s.4A); orders appointing a guardian (s.5). It can also order a welfare report (s.7).

7   Under Part II of the Children Act 1989, in addition to s.8 orders (see above), the court can make: special guardianship orders (ss.14A–G); orders for financial relief (s.15 and Sched. 1); and family assistance orders (s.16). The provisions governing family assistance orders (see s.16) have been amended so that a FAO can be more usefully used in difficult contact cases. New provisions have been introduced in respect of facilitating and enforcing contact (see ss.11A–11P). CAFCASS officers have a duty under Part II of the Act to conduct risk assessments of children (s.16A).

8   The court can make a range of public law orders, in particular care and supervision orders (see Part IV Children Act 1989), and orders for the emergency protection of children (see Part V).

9   The court can also make the following: an order that a local authority investigate the child's circumstances (s.37); and a s.91(14) order restricting an application to the court.

# Further Reading and References

Bailey-Harris, Barron and Pearce, 'The settlement culture and the use of the "no order" principle under the Children Act 1989' [1999] CFLQ 53.

Eekelaar, 'Beyond the welfare principle' [2002] CFLQ 237.

Fortin, 'Children's rights – substance or spin?' [2006] Fam Law 757.

Freeman, 'The next Children's Act' [1998] Fam Law 341.

# Website

**Statute Law Database**: www.statutelaw.gov.uk

# Chapter 12

## Children on Family Breakdown

Introduction

> ▶ *Parental Separation: Children's Needs and Parents' Responsibilities* (Cm. 6273, 2005)
>
> 'Parental separation affects many children and their families. Some three million of the twelve million children in the UK have experienced the separation of their parents. Each year between 150,000 and 200,000 parental couples separate. Where the process of separation is handled well, the adverse impact on children is minimised. Where separation goes badly and, in particular, where children are drawn into parental conflict, then the effects can be profoundly damaging for children.'

This chapter deals with the law governing residence and contact disputes when parental relationships break down. The law is laid down in the Children Act 1989 (see also Chapter 11). Disputes about maintenance and financial provision for children on family breakdown are dealt with in Chapter 13.

*Keeping Cases Out of the Court*   Children may suffer emotional trauma when their parents break up. They may suffer fear, anger, withdrawal, grief, depression and guilt. It is therefore better for children if parents do not make things worse by becoming involved in litigation, but instead make amicable arrangements for their children. Most parents do make their own arrangements, but some fail to reach agreement and end up applying to the court for residence and contact orders. Going to court, however, has many disadvantages. It can be costly, time-consuming, unpredictable and traumatic. Furthermore, the judge has considerable discretion and may refuse to make the order sought, or make a different order. Also, having a court order does not necessarily guarantee compliance. In fact, enforcing contact orders has proved particularly problematic, and the Government has recommended reforms (see 12.5, below).

If parents seek legal advice about residence and contact they will find that family law solicitors adopt a conciliatory, not a litigious, approach – because of the benefits of reducing hostility and bitterness where children are involved. Mediation, a form of alternative dispute resolution, is also increasingly promoted by the Government, the judiciary and family lawyers as a much better way of dealing with parental disputes about residence and contact. The House of Common's Constitutional Affairs Select Committee in its report on family justice (*Family Justice: The Operation of the Family Courts*, HC 116-1, March 2005) said that there must be a clear and unequivocal commitment to remove as many child contact and residence cases from the courts as possible, and for mediation (see 1.3) to have a greater role.

*Dissatisfaction of Some Fathers*   Some fathers are unhappy about how they are treated by the family justice system on family breakdown. They feel that the law is unjustly weighted in favour of mothers. Pressure groups, such as Fathers 4 Justice, have also been active in bringing to public attention fathers' grievances about the family justice system.

The House of Commons Constitutional Affairs Select Committee looked at this issue in 2005 as part of its review of the family justice system, but rejected claims that the family courts are consciously biased against non-resident parents, fathers in particular (*Family Justice: The Operation of the Family Courts*, HC 116-1, March 2005). The Committee did feel, however, that non-resident parents are often disadvantaged because of delay, lack of judicial continuity and lack of enforcement powers, particularly in the context of contact. It felt that perceptions of bias and unfairness were fuelled by a lack of transparency in family court proceedings, and it recommended that the press and public should be allowed into family courts so that the public can see what actually happens (subject to appropriate reporting restrictions and the judge's discretion to exclude the public in certain cases), but this proposal has now been rejected (see below).

*Family Proceedings Take Place in Private*   Residence and contact disputes are usually heard in private, even though the courts have been under pressure to hear them in public in order to dispel the belief that fathers are being discriminated against. In the following case, the Court of Appeal held that there is no obligation on the courts to hold family proceedings involving children in public, and that a decision to hold them in private does not breach the European Convention for the Protection of Human Rights (ECHR) (see also *Glaser* v. *UK* (2001) 33 EHRR 1, [2001] 1 FLR 153, below):

▶ *Pelling* v. *Bruce-Williams (Secretary of State for Constitutional Affairs Intervening)* [2004] EWCA Civ 845

The father, a campaigner on family justice issues, wanted residence proceedings to be heard in open court, but the judge delivered his judgment in private. The Court of Appeal held that, as regards art. 6 ECHR (right to a fair trial), it remained justifiable, in order to protect the privacy of the children and the parties and to avoid prejudicing the interests of justice, to hold residence proceedings in chambers and to limit the extent to which judgments were made available to the general public. As regards art. 10 ECHR (right to freedom of expression), the Court of Appeal held that the conduct of proceedings in chambers might properly be regarded as necessary in a democratic society for the protection of the rights of others, namely the rights of the respondent and the child under art. 8 (right to a private and family life).

The Government has discussed the possibility of opening up the family courts to the media in order to improve public confidence in the family justice system, but it has decided against it on the ground that it would jeopardise children's rights to privacy and anonymity (*Confidence and Confidentiality: Openness in Family Courts – A New Approach*, CP 10/07, 20/6/07, Cm 7131, Ministry of Justice). Instead, the Government says that the emphasis will be on improving the information coming out of family courts rather than on who can go into them.

*Continuing Parental Responsibility and the Duty to Maintain*   On relationship breakdown, parents continue to have parental responsibility (see 10.5). An important duty which parents have, whether or not they have parental responsibility, is the duty to provide financial provision for their children. Where a parent refuses to provide financial support, or insufficient support, an application can be made to the Child Support Agency and in some circumstances to the court (see Chapter 13).

*Parenting Plans*   These were launched by the Government in March 2002 to encourage parents to think about parenting arrangements after separation and divorce. Parenting plans contain information, guidance and ideas on issues that parents need to consider about their children on family breakdown, and include sections that parents can complete if they wish to record their decisions about arrangements for the children. They also contain lists of organisations that can assist parents and children on family breakdown. The completed plan, however, merely represents a statement of the parents' intentions. It is not a legal document and cannot be enforced by the court.

*Personnel in Private Law Cases*   In private law cases (such as those involving residence and contact disputes), in addition to lawyers there are other personnel who may be involved in proceedings. Of particular importance is the Children and Family Reporter, an officer of CAFCASS who has a duty to provide a welfare report under s.7 Children Act 1989 if required by the court to do so. The role of the Reporter is to provide the court with advice and recommendations on matters relating to the welfare of the child. Children and Family Reporters also perform an important conciliatory role in trying to help parents reach agreement about arrangements for children. They also have to conduct risk assessments, and the Government plans to give them new powers in respect of enforcing and facilitating contact (see 12.5). Another officer of CAFCASS is the Children's Guardian, who may be appointed by the court (under rule 9.5 Family Proceedings Rules 1991) to represent the interests of children who have been made party in private law proceedings (see 9.6).

*Welfare Reports*   Each case turns on its own facts and many cases will be finely balanced. The court has the power to order a welfare report under s.7 Children Act 1989 by a Children and Family Reporter, an officer of CAFCASS who has a duty to protect the child's best interests in the proceedings (see 1.4). A welfare report is important as it provides an independent assessment of the case. The recommendations in the report will be particularly important where a case is finely balanced. Judges must not depart from the recommendations without giving reasons (see *Re W (Residence)* [1999] 2 FLR 390). A failure to do so may provide grounds for an appeal (see *Re M (Residence)* [2004] EWCA Civ 1574, [2005] 1 FLR 656 where the Court of Appeal ordered a retrial, because the trial judge had not referred to the opinion of the CAFCASS officer, and had not, therefore, explained why he was departing from her recommendations).

*The Voice of the Child in Court Proceedings*   Children do not have automatic party status in residence and contact proceedings, but the Government has discussed giving them greater rights of self-representation (see 9.6).

## 12.2 Human Rights and Family Breakdown

The Human Rights Act 1998 requires courts (including family courts) to comply with the European Convention for the Protection of Human Rights (ECHR) and to take into account the decisions of the European Court of Human Rights (ECtHR) (see 1.5). In *Hoppe*

v. *Germany (Application No. 28422/95)* [2003] 1 FLR 384 the ECtHR identified the following general principles which courts must take into account when exercising their powers in the context of children on family breakdown:

- The mutual enjoyment by parent and child of each other's company constitutes a fundamental element of family life, even if the parents' relationship has broken down, and any measures which hinder such enjoyment amount to an interference with art. 8 (the right to family life).
- The task of the ECtHR is not to substitute itself for the domestic authorities in the exercise of their responsibilities regarding custody and access, but to review, in the light of the ECHR, their decisions in the exercise of their margin of appreciation.
- In determining whether the interference into family life was necessary in a democratic society for the purposes of art. 8(2), consideration of what lies in the best interests of the child is of crucial importance. A fair balance must be struck between the child's interests and those of the parent, and in striking such a balance particular importance must be attached to the best interests of the child, which, depending on their nature and seriousness, may override those of the parent.
- In cases concerning a person's relationship with his or her child there is a duty to exercise exceptional diligence in view of the risk that the passage of time may result in a *de facto* determination of the matter.
- The manner in which art. 6 (right to a fair trial) applies to proceedings before courts of appeal depends on the special features of the proceedings viewed as a whole. It does not always require a public hearing.
- The court must avoid delay in reaching a final decision.

In *Sahin* v. *Germany; Sommerfeld* v. *Germany (Application Nos. 30943/96 and 31871/96)* [2003] 2 FLR 671 the ECtHR held that, although national authorities enjoy a wide margin of appreciation when deciding on custody matters, a stricter scrutiny is called for regarding any further limitations, such as restrictions placed on parental rights of access. As regards hearing a child in court on the issue of access, the ECtHR held that domestic courts are not always required to hear the child. It depends on the facts of each case, having regard to the age and maturity of the child concerned.

*Human Rights and Contact*    As the ECtHR takes the view that the mutual enjoyment by parent and child of each other's company constitutes a right to family life under art. 8, save in exceptional circumstances (see above), the courts in the UK must do their best to enforce and facilitate contact, otherwise they risk being in breach of the ECHR, and a wronged parent may be entitled to damages. In *Hansen* v. *Turkey (Application No. 36141/97)* [2004] 1 FLR 142, for example, the ECtHR held that the failure of the Turkish authorities to take realistic coercive measures against the father (who had custody) to allow the mother to have access to her child was a breach of her art. 8 right to respect for her family life. The fines which had been imposed on the father were neither effective nor adequate.

However, the ECtHR has held that the duty on national authorities to enforce and facilitate contact is not absolute. The question to be asked is whether the national authorities concerned have taken all the necessary steps to enforce and facilitate contact as could reasonably be demanded in the circumstances (see *Sylvester* v. *Austria (Application Nos. 36812/97 and 40414/98)* [2003] 2 FLR 210; and *Zadwadka* v. *Poland (Application No.*

*48542/99)* [2005] 2 FLR 897). Each case depends on its own facts, and in *Glaser* v. *UK* (2001) 33 EHRR 1, [2001] 1 FLR 153 the ECtHR rejected a complaint that the UK authorities were in breach of the ECHR in the circumstances, by failing to take adequate steps to enforce contact against a mother. (For another case on contact, see *Kosmopoulou* v. *Greece* *(Application No. 60457/00)* [2004] 1 FLR 800.)

**Human Rights and Hearing Cases in Private**   The ECtHR has held that it is not a breach of art. 6 (right to a fair and public hearing) if family proceedings involving children are heard in private. In *Glaser* v. *UK* (2001) 33 EHRR 1, [2001] 1 FLR 153 the ECtHR held that this is not a breach of art. 6 as the requirement of 'public' hearings for the purpose of art. 6 is subject to exceptions, including the need to protect the privacy of children and other parties, and to avoid prejudicing the interests of justice. In *Glaser* the ECtHR also held that it was essential that custody and contact cases be dealt with speedily.

## 12.3  The Duty to Children in Divorce Proceedings

An important policy objective of the law of divorce is to protect the best interests of children. In furtherance of this objective, the petitioner must file with the divorce court a Statement of Arrangements for Children (Form M4) setting out required information about any child of the family under the age of 16 or over that age if he or she is still receiving education or training (r.2.2 Family Proceedings Rules 1991). The Statement of Arrangements covers the following issues: details of the child (names and dates of birth); home details; education and training; childcare details; maintenance; details for contact; details of health; details of care and other court proceedings. The petitioner must sign the form and, where possible, the information must be agreed by the respondent. The petitioner must also state on the form whether he or she intends to apply for any s.8 order under the Children Act 1989 (see 11.4 and below). (The form is available on HM Courts' Service website.)

A Statement of Arrangements for the Children is also required where there is a petition for nullity or judicial separation, or where a civil partner applies for dissolution of the partnership.

The purpose of the Statement of Arrangements form is to enable the court to fulfil its duty under s.41 Matrimonial Causes Act 1973 (the divorce legislation). Under s.41(1) Matrimonial Causes Act 1973 the district judge in the divorce court has a duty to consider whether, in the light of the arrangements made for the children, or proposed to be made, the court should exercise any of its powers under the Children Act 1989 with respect to any of the children (for these powers, see Chapter 11).

The court's duty under s.41 must be exercised in respect of any child of the family aged under 16, unless it directs otherwise (s.41(3)). A 'child of the family' includes not just the parents' own child but a non-marital child of one or both parties and any other child treated by the parties as a child of the family (but excluding a local authority foster-child) (s.52). Thus, the district judge must consider arrangements for natural and adopted children, privately fostered children and step-children. In *Re A (Child of the Family)* [1998] 1 FLR 347 the Court of Appeal said that the question of whether a child has been treated as a child of the family must be judged by an objective test, and it held that a 17-year-old girl who had been brought up by her divorcing grandparents was a 'child of the family', as her grandparents were her primary-carers, and their long-term commitment went beyond the ties that grandparents normally had for their grandchildren.

Having looked at the Statement of Arrangements the district judge will usually be satisfied that there is no need for the court to exercise any of its powers under the Children Act, and will certify to that effect. If not satisfied, he can direct that further evidence be filed, or order a welfare report, or order that one or both parents attend court. If the child's interests require it, and the court is not able to exercise any of its powers under the Children Act without further consideration of the case, the district judge can direct that the decree of divorce should not be made absolute (s.41(2)). In practice, however, the district judge usually accepts the statements on the form and makes no further enquiries before granting the final divorce decree. Even if there is a disputed issue the court will usually take the view that any disputed matter can be dealt with at a subsequent hearing, and it will not delay the divorce.

In practice, it is questionable whether the s.41 exercise does much to protect children's interests, as district judges rarely take action after scrutinising the proposed arrangements – often because they do not consider there is much they can reasonably do to remedy any problem they have identified (see research by Murch *et al*, 1999).

The Government has recommended that the s.41 procedure be reviewed, with the particular aim of requiring information to be made available to divorcing parents, and for the judiciary to be given the power to refer parties to mediation (see *The Final Report of the Child Contact Facilitation and Enforcement Group*, Department for Constitutional Affairs, December 2003; and *Making Contact Work*, Lord Chancellor's Department, February 2002). In August 2006 the Government published a consultation document in which it discussed producing a shorter version of the Statement of Arrangements for Children form (see para. 25, *A New Procedural Code for Family Proceedings*, CP19/06, 2006, HM Courts Service and Department for Constitutional Affairs).

## 12.4  Residence Disputes

An unresolvable dispute about residence arrangements for a child on family breakdown can be decided by applying for a residence order, which the High Court, county courts and magistrates' family proceedings courts have jurisdiction to make under s.8 Children Act 1989 (see also 11.5).

Residence disputes often go hand in hand with contact disputes, as the non-resident parent will usually wish to have contact with the child (see 12.5, below). Other parental disputes (for example about education, medical treatment, taking a child out of the UK and changing the child's name) can be decided by making an application for a prohibited steps or specific issue order which the courts can also make under s.8 Children Act 1989 (see 11.7 and 11.8). Some parents enter into disputes about financial provision for their children on family breakdown, in particular child support (see Chapter 13).

### (a)  Residence Orders

A **residence order** is an order 'settling the arrangements to be made as to the person with whom a child is to live' (s.8(1) Children Act 1989).

Before the Children Act 1989 came into force in October 1991 parental disputes about children on family breakdown were resolved in custody proceedings, where a sole or joint custody order would usually be granted with care and control to one parent (usually the mother) and access to the other (usually the father). However, in discussions leading up to the Children Act the Law Commission had criticised the term 'custody' (and 'care and control' and 'access'), because 'custody' created a parental claim right and had the potential to increase hostility and bitterness between parents which was detrimental for their children (see *Report on Guardianship and Custody*, Law Com No. 172, 1988). Residence orders were therefore introduced by the Children Act 1989 to replace custody with the aim of placing the emphasis on the child's living arrangements, and not on which of the parents had a greater claim to the child. The idea was to encourage the view that parents have responsibilities for their children, not claims to them.

Residence orders are often made, but they are not as commonly made as contact orders: 31,712 residence orders were made in England and Wales in 2006 compared with 66,075 contact orders (*Judicial and Court Statistics 2006*, Cm 7273, Ministry of Justice, 2007).

*Applicants*   The child's parents (married or unmarried, and with or without parental responsibility) can apply. Other persons (including the child) can apply, but only with leave of the court (s.10, and see further in Chapter 11).

*Applicable Principles*   See below.

*Other Powers*   The court can: attach conditions to a residence order (s.11(7)); make a 'shared residence order' (s.11(4)); order a welfare report on the child (s.7); and direct that a local authority investigate the child's circumstances (s.37).

*Duration*   The order cannot be made to last beyond the child's sixteenth birthday, except where there are exceptional circumstances (as there were, for example, in *A v. A (Shared Residence)* [2004] EWHC 142 (Fam), [2004] 1 FLR 1195). But the court now has the power to make an 'extended' residence order (see p.280 and 16.18).

*Appeals*   As a judge has wide discretion when exercising his powers, an appeal against a residence order is unlikely to be successful unless there has been an error of law or the exercise of judicial discretion was so unreasonable that no judge would have exercised it in that way. Even where there is judicial error the court may still refuse to overturn an order (see, for example, *Re R (Residence Order: Finance)* [1995] 2 FLR 612, where the mother's appeal against a shared residence order was dismissed, even though the trial judge had taken into account financial considerations which are not expressly provided for in the s.1(3) welfare checklist).

### (b)   Attaching a Condition to an Order (s.11(7)) – Restricting Residence

The court can attach a condition to a residence order (s.11(7)), but this power is used only in exceptional circumstances. While it is open to the court to restrict residence to a certain place by way of a condition in a residence order, this power will be used only in a very exceptional case as the courts regard such a restriction as 'an unwarranted imposition upon the right of a parent to choose where he/she will live within the UK' (Baroness

Hale in *Re G (Children)* [2006] UKHL 43, [2006] 2 FLR 629). In *B v. B (Residence: Condition Limiting Geographic Area)* [2004] 2 FLR 979, for example, a condition was imposed that the mother and child live within a specified geographic area, as the mother had made two applications to remove the child to Australia and her prime motive in moving the child's residence from the south to the north of England was to get away from the father.

### (c)  Shared Residence Orders (s.11(4))

Under s.11(4) Children Act 1989 the court can make a 'shared' residence order, which is a residence order 'made in favour of two or more persons who do not all live together', and which 'specifies the periods during which the child is to live in the different households concerned' (s.11(4)). When considering whether or not to make the order, the court must apply the welfare test and the other welfare provisions in s.1 Children Act 1989 (see 11.3).

In its *Report on Custody and Guardianship* (No. 172, 1988) the Law Commission had stated that the new residence order should be flexible enough to accommodate a wide range of situations, and that, although shared arrangements would rarely be practicable, evidence from the USA showed that they could work well in some circumstances. The Law Commission saw no reason why shared residence orders should be actively discouraged.

In cases decided shortly after the Children Act 1989 came into force judges were reluctant to make shared residence orders because they felt they might create uncertainty and insecurity for children. In *Re H (A Minor) (Shared Residence)* [1994] 1 FLR 717 the Court of Appeal held they should be made only in exceptional circumstances, and in *A v. A (Minors) (Shared Residence Order)* [1994] 1 FLR 669 Butler-Sloss LJ said that they should only be made if it could be shown that the shared order would provide a positive benefit for the child and there were no concrete issues between the parties which still needed to be resolved.

Over the years, however, judges have become more willing to make shared residence orders, and in the following case the Court of Appeal relaxed its earlier restrictions on making them, and held that it was no longer necessary to show exceptional circumstances in order to obtain an order:

▶ *D v. D (Shared Residence Order)* [2001] 1 FLR 495

A pattern had been established on marriage breakdown whereby the three children spent substantial periods of time with each parent, but where the arrangements were subject to a high degree of animosity between the parents and frequent legal proceedings had been brought to sort out the details. The father applied for a shared residence order, which was granted at first instance. The mother appealed. The Court of Appeal dismissed her appeal, and held that, contrary to earlier case-law, it was not necessary to show that exceptional circumstances existed before a shared order could be granted, and neither was it probably necessary to show a positive benefit to the child. What must be shown is that the order is in the child's best interests in accordance with the welfare principle in s.1 Children Act 1989. Here, on the facts, it was necessary to make the shared order to lessen the animosity between the parties.

Although it is no longer necessary to show exceptional circumstances, and the court will make a shared order even though the parents or carers are unwilling or unable to co-operate, they are not commonly made, despite their advantages – in particular that they can make existing shared arrangements more concrete, and they can confer parental responsibility on someone who does not already possess it. A shared order also has the advantage of emphasising the fact 'that both parents are equal in the eyes of the law, and that they have equal duties and responsibilities as parents' (Wall LJ in *Re P (Children)(Shared Residence Order)* [2005] EWCA Civ 1639, [2006] 2 FLR 347).

Whether a shared order will be made depends on the facts of each case, with the welfare of the child as the court's paramount consideration (s.1(1) Children Act 1989) and with the other s.1 welfare principles being applied. In the following case-law examples shared residence orders were considered:

▶ *Re F (Shared Residence Order)* [2003] EWCA Civ 592, [2003] 2 FLR 397

A shared order was made even though the parents' homes were a considerable distance apart. The Court of Appeal held that a shared residence order must reflect the underlying reality of where children live their lives.

▶ *Re H (Shared Residence: Parental Responsibility)* [1995] 2 FLR 883

A shared order was held to be of practical therapeutic importance because it conferred parental responsibility on the step-father.

▶ *A v. A (Shared Residence)* [2004] EWHC 142 (Fam), [2004] 1 FLR 1195

A shared order was made, even though the parents were not able to co-operate, as the children had already been spending 50 per cent of their time with each parent. Wall J made a shared order partly to 'reflect that fact that the parents are equal in the eyes of the law, and have equal duties and responsibilities towards their children'.

▶ *Re WB (Residence Order)* [1995] 2 FLR 1023

A shared order was refused, as it would give the unmarried father parental responsibility which would be likely to foment disputes between the parents which would be contrary to the children's welfare.

▶ *Re C (A Child)* [2006] EWCA Civ 235

The Court of Appeal, allowing the appeal, described the case as 'a paradigm' case of the circumstances in which a shared residence order should have been granted. The child had a strong attachment to both parents and was happy and confident in both homes, which were proximate to each other and close to the child's school. The child had a real familiarity with both homes and a sense of belonging in each, and he had a clear perception that he had two homes. There was a post-separation history of the child's care being shared.

▶ *Re P (Shared Residence Order)* [2005] EWCA Civ 1639, [2006] 2 FLR 347

The Court of Appeal held that, on the facts, it was a plain case for a shared residence order – as it would reflect the reality that the parents had established for the child (the father had contact with the child for 45 per cent of the child's time).

In *Re P* (above) the Court of Appeal held that, although it did not automatically follow that a shared residence order should be made merely because children divided their time between parents in proportions approaching equality, good reasons were required if a shared residence order was not to be made in the same proportions.

Although a shared residence order may provide an answer in cases where there are, or are likely to be, problems enforcing and facilitating contact, the Government has rejected the idea of introducing any presumption of shared residence. Where there is little contact, however, between the resident and non-resident parent, then the court is unlikely to make a shared order. In *A* v. *A (Shared Residence)* [2004] EWHC 142 (Fam), [2004] 1 FLR 1195 Wall J said that '[w]here children are living with one parent and are either not seeing the other parent or the amount of time to be spent with the other parent is limited or undecided, there cannot be a shared residence order'.

### (d) How the Court Exercises its Powers to Make a Residence Order

When determining whether or not to make a residence order the court must apply the principles in s.1 Children Act 1989 (see 11.3). Thus, it must apply the welfare principle (s.1(1)), the no-delay principle (s.1(2)) and the minimum intervention principle (s.1(5)). In contested proceedings it must also apply the s.1(3) 'welfare checklist'.

*The Paramountcy Principle (s.1(1))*   The child's welfare is the paramount consideration in an application for a residence order because this principle must be applied when the court determines any question with respect to the upbringing of a child (see 11.3).

*The Welfare Checklist (s.1(3))*
Section 1(3) contains a list of factors, (a) to (g), which the court must take into account in contested proceedings for a residence order (and other s.8 orders). The list is not exhaustive – other factors can be taken into account – and the factors are not in any hierarchy of importance. Under s.1(3) the court must take into account the following factors:

*Section 1(3)(a) The Child's Wishes in the Light of the Child's Age and Understanding*   If the child is intelligent and mature enough to make an informed decision, then the child's wishes may determine the matter, all other things being equal. The child's wishes are ascertained by a CAFCASS Children and Family Reporter or a Welsh family proceedings officer, who has a duty to report to the court and to consider the best interests of the child, and who may be cross-examined on the report. The court has the power to appoint a Children's Guardian to represent the child, and to permit the child to be represented by his or her own solicitor without a Children's Guardian (see 9.6). There has been increasing recognition that older children should have a right to have their own voices heard by the court, independently of their parents (see 9.6).

*Section 1(3)(b) The Child's Physical and Emotional Needs*   The courts have held that it is usually better for young children, particularly young babies, to be brought up by their mother, but judges have stressed that this is not a legal principle, or even a legal presumption, but merely a consideration. In *Re S (A Minor) (Custody)* [1991] 2 FLR 388 and *Re A (A Minor) (Custody)* [1991] 2 FLR 394 Butler-Sloss LJ said that where children were very young the unbroken relationship of mother and child would be difficult to displace, unless the mother was unsuitable to care for them. This approach was endorsed by the House of Lords in *Brixey* v. *Lynas* [1996] 2 FLR 499. In *Re W (Residence)* [1999] 2 FLR 390 the Court of Appeal held that the emotional and psychological attachment of the child to the parent is a consideration of very great importance to be included in the balancing exercise. It held that the flexibility and availability of the primary-carer were important considerations, particularly where a child was young and required constant and consistent care.

In recent years, however, fathers have claimed that the family justice system discriminates against them because residence orders are too often made in favour of mothers, and because courts have inadequate powers for enforcing contact. Pressure groups, such as Fathers 4 Justice, have brought these grievances to public attention. The Government has investigated fathers' claims, but has found that the family justice system is not consciously biased against them. However, the courts have over the years given increased recognition to the important role that fathers perform in their children's lives and upbringing, and courts today are unlikely to make statements like those of Butler-Sloss LJ above (that it is usually better for young children to be brought up by their mother) for fear of inflaming strong feelings in fathers.

In respect of the child's needs under s.1(3)(b) the court will not necessarily make the order in favour of the wealthier parent.

*Section 1(3)(c) The Likely Effect on the Child of a Change of Circumstances*    This is similar to the 'continuity of care' or 'status quo' factor which was an important consideration in the case-law before the Children Act came into force. In *D* v. *M (Minor) (Custody Appeal)* [1982] 3 WLR 891 Ormrod LJ stated:

> 'It is generally accepted by those who are professionally concerned with children that, particularly in the early years, continuity of care is a most important part of a child's sense of security and that disruption of established bonds is to be avoided whenever it is possible to do so.'

The court may be unwilling to disturb arrangements which have been satisfactorily in place for some time. For example, in *Re B (Residence Order: Status Quo)* [1998] 1 FLR 368 the Court of Appeal held that the status quo prevailed over the maternal preference factor (see above) and allowed the father's appeal against the residence order made in favour of the child's mother, as the father had cared for the eight-year-old child since the age of two.

Under s.(1)(3)(c) the court may also be unwilling to split up brothers and sisters where this would disturb existing arrangements, and it may also be concerned about disrupting schooling arrangements and the possibility of a child losing contact with friends and relatives if existing residence arrangements are disturbed.

*Section 1(3)(d) The Age, Sex, Background and Any of the Child's Characteristics Which the Court Considers Relevant*    The child's religious preferences, racial and cultural background, health and disabilities can, for example, be considered under s.1(3)(d).

*Section 1(3)(e) Any Harm the Child Has Suffered or is at Risk of Suffering*    'Harm' has the same meaning as it has in s.31 of the Act (see 15.7) and now includes harm caused by 'witnessing the ill treatment of another person'. Witnessing domestic violence can therefore constitute harm. Domestic violence in the context of contact is now recognised as a serious problem (see 12.5, below).

*Religious Beliefs*    Making a residence order in favour of a parent with extreme religious beliefs will not necessarily constitute harm. In *Re R (A Minor) (Residence: Religion)* [1993] 2 FLR 163, for example, a residence order was made in favour of the father, as the mother had died, even though he was a member of the Exclusive Brethren, an extreme religious sect in which members are not allowed to mix socially with anyone outside the fellowship (but the court also made a supervision order in favour of the local authority to ensure the child's safety).

A refusal to make a residence order in favour of a parent on the grounds of his or her religious beliefs may constitute a breach of the European Convention for the Protection of Human Rights. In *Palau-Martinez* v. *France (Application No. 64927/01)* [2004] 2 FLR 810 the ECtHR held that an order granting residence to the child's father, because of the mother's religious convictions (she was a Jehovah's Witness), breached the mother's right to a private and family life under art. 8 ECHR and was discriminatory under art. 14. This decision must now be 'taken into account' by a court in England and Wales as a result of its obligations under s.2 Human Rights Act 1998.

*Same-Sex Partners and Residence*    The fact that a parent is living with a same-sex partner will not necessarily constitute harm and preclude a residence order being made. In *C* v. *C (A Minor) (Custody: Appeal)* [1991] 1 FLR 223 and *B* v. *B (Minors) (Custody, Care and Control)* [1991] 1 FLR 402 the Court of Appeal refused to accept the fathers' arguments that their children would develop emotional problems and be stigmatised by their peers if they were allowed to live with their mother and her lesbian partner on family breakdown. Evidence given by psychologists showed that this was not likely to happen.

*Steps the Court Can Take When There is a Risk of Harm*    If the court is concerned about making a residence order because of a risk of harm, it can make an interim residence order, or back up the residence order with another order, such as a specific issue order, a prohibited steps order, a family assistance order, or a s.37 direction that the local authority investigate the case. In *Re H (A Minor) (Section 37 Direction)* [1993] 2 FLR 541, for example, an interim residence order was made in favour of a lesbian couple where the child was not their own but where the natural parent had agreed to them bringing up the child. A supervision order and a s.37 direction that the local authority investigate the case were also made. CAFCASS now has a duty to make risk assessments where it believes that a child might be at risk of significant harm (see 12.5).

*Section 1(3)(f) How Capable Each Parent is of Meeting the Child's Needs*    The court might consider, for example, whether a parent can provide accommodation, love, emotional security, intellectual stimulation, and care during working hours.

*Section 1(3)(g) The Range of Powers Available to the Court Under the Children Act 1989*    As proceedings for a residence order are themselves family proceedings (s.8(3)), the court can make other orders on application or of its own motion, for example: any other s.8 order; a s.16 family assistance order; an order appointing a guardian; or a s.37 direction that a local authority investigate the child's circumstances (for more on all these orders, see Chapter 11).

## 12.5   Contact Disputes

> **Article 9(3) United Nations Convention on the Rights of the Child 1989**
>
> 'States Parties shall respect the right of the child . . . to maintain personal relations and direct contact with both parents on a regular basis, except if it is contrary to the child's best interests.'

Disputes about contact are more common than residence disputes. In 2006, 66,075 contact orders were made in private law proceedings in England and Wales (*Judicial and Court Statistics 2006*, Cm 2723, Ministry of Justice, 2007). Contact disputes are 'among the most difficult and sensitive cases' which the courts have to deal with (see Wall LJ at [2005] Fam Law 26). Cases sometimes drag on for years, which not only takes up court time but is contrary to the best interests of children.

Despite the high number of contact orders most parents (about 90 per cent of them) make their own contact arrangements, and it is better that they do so, for research shows that parents who turn to the law to settle serious contact disputes risk making matters worse (see Trinder *et al*, *Making Contact: How Parents and Children Negotiate and Experience Contact After Divorce*, Joseph Rowntree Foundation, [2002] Fam Law 872). In fact it has been increasingly recognised by the judiciary and by the Government that contact cases are best dealt with outside the courts (see below).

Wall J (as he was then), speaking at a conference on contact, said (at [2003] Fam Law 275):

'The law, which of necessity, operates within the discipline of defined orders is, in my judgment, ill-suited to deal with the complex family dynamics inherent in disputed contact applications. Arrangements for contact stand more prospects of enduring if they are consensual. Wherever possible, contact disputes should be dealt with outside the courtroom.'

Legislative changes have been made to improve the facilitation and enforcement of contact (see below).

*Contact – Difficult Areas*   Difficulties in respect of the law of contact have occurred in certain areas. One area has concerned contact and domestic violence. In the last few years the courts have come to realise that children may suffer harm from violence in the home on contact visits, and that allegations of domestic violence must be taken seriously and be investigated (see below). Another area of difficulty is that of enforcing and facilitating contact. Fathers, in particular, suffer injustices when contact orders cannot be enforced. The senior judiciary and the Government have been concerned about the problem of enforcement, and proposals for reform have been made (see below). There has also been increasing pressure by proponents of children's rights, including the United Nations Committee on the Rights of the Child (see 9.2), for children's views to be heard more in contact cases, and for some children to be represented by their own solicitor (see below). (For a rare case where the child's views prevailed over the presumption of contact, see *Re S (Contact: Children's Views)* [2002] EWHC 540 (Fam), where a contact order was refused because of the views of the children who were aged 14 and 16.)

*Human Rights and Contact*   The European Court of Human Rights (ECtHR) recognises a presumption in favour of contact between parent and child (see, for example, *Johansen* v. *Norway* (1997) 23 EHRR 33). In *Kosmopolou* v. *Greece (Application No. 60457/00)* [2004] 1 FLR 800 the ECtHR held that:

> '[T]he mutual enjoyment by parent and child of each other's company constitutes a fundamental element of family life, even if the relationship between the parents has broken down, and domestic measures hindering such enjoyment amount to an interference with the right protected by Art. 8 of the Convention.'

As the Human Rights Act 1998 requires courts in the UK to take account of the decisions of the European Court of Human Rights, they must ensure that they order contact and enforce it, unless contrary to the child's best interests, for otherwise they may be in breach of the ECHR and liable in damages.

### (a) Contact Orders

A **contact order** is an order 'requiring the person with whom a child lives, or is to live, to allow the child to visit or stay with the person named in the order, or for that person and the child otherwise to have contact with each other' (s.8(1)).

Where a contact dispute cannot be settled by agreement, with or without the help of mediation, an application can be made for a contact order which the High Court, county courts and magistrates' family proceedings courts have jurisdiction to make under s.8 Children Act 1989 (see further at 11.6). The term 'contact' was introduced by the Children Act to replace that of 'access', because 'contact' was considered to be a more child-centred term than 'access'. A contact order allows a child to have contact rather that giving a parent a right to have access. This change of emphasis also accorded with the approach of the courts in pre-Children Act cases, where judges had taken the view that it was children, not parents, who had rights of access (see, for example, Wrangham LJ in *M* v. *M* [1973] 2 All ER 81).

*Applicants*   These are the same as those who can apply for residence orders (see above, and at 11.5). The Government has discussed the possibility of grandparents being allowed to apply for contact orders without having to obtain leave of the court (see the report published by the House of Commons Constitutional Affairs Select Committee (March 2004), *Family Justice: The Operation of the Family Courts*, HC 116-1), but there have been no proposals to do so.

*Applicable Principles*   These are the same as for residence orders (see above, and at 11.3).

*Other Powers*   The court can: attach a condition to a contact order (s.11(7)); order a welfare report on the child (s.7); and direct that a local authority investigate the child's circumstances (s.37).

*Duration*  A contact order cannot be made to last beyond the child's sixteenth birthday, unless there are exceptional circumstances (s.9(7)). Exceptional circumstances were found in *A* v. *A (Shared Residence)* [2004] EWHC 142 (Fam), [2004] 1 FLR 1195.

*A Welfare Report*  The court may require a welfare report from a CAFCASS Children and Family Reporter (or a Welsh family proceedings officer) under s.7 Children Act 1989. The recommendations in the welfare report are an important consideration for the court when reaching its decision.

### (b)   How the Court Exercises its Discretion

When considering whether to make a contact order and, if so, in what manner, the court must apply the welfare principle (s.1(1)), the no-order principle (s.1(5)), the no-delay principle (s.1(2)) and, in a contested application, the s.1(3) welfare checklist (see 11.3). In *Re M (Contact: Welfare Test)* [1995] 1 FLR 274 Wilson J said that it was helpful to cast the relevant principles on contact into the framework of the s.1(3) welfare checklist and ask whether the fundamental emotional need for every child to have an enduring relationship with both of his parents was outweighed by the depth of harm which, in the light, *inter alia*, of his wishes and feelings, the child would be at risk of suffering by virtue of a contact order.

*The Presumption in Favour of Contact*  Contact is presumed to be beneficial for children, unless it is contrary to the child's welfare. As Sir Stephen Brown P said in *Re W (A Minor) (Contact)* [1994] 2 FLR 441, it is 'quite clear that contact with a parent is a fundamental right of a child, save in wholly exceptional circumstances'. Cogent reasons will therefore be needed to deprive a child of contact (see *Re H (Contact Principles)* [1994] 2 FLR 969). In *Re R (A Minor) (Contact)* [1993] 2 FLR 762 Butler-Sloss LJ stated that it 'is a right of a child to have a relationship with both parents wherever possible' and that 'in general the parent with whom the child does not live has a continuing role to play, which is recognised by s.2(1) of the Children Act 1989'. The decision whether or not to grant contact is therefore child-centred. As the welfare of the child is the court's paramount consideration parental interests are only relevant in so far as they impact on the child's welfare. In most cases the court will decide that it is in the child's best interests for the non-resident parent to have contact. Because of the importance attached to a child knowing his natural parent, the court may even order contact where the father is absent, for instance, because he is in prison (see *Re R (A Minor) (Contact)* [1993] 2 FLR 762; and *A* v. *L (Contact)* [1998] 1 FLR 361).

Because of the importance of contact for children, and the presumption in favour of ordering contact, the Court of Appeal has emphasised that the court should explore all options before contact is terminated (see *Re W (Contact)* [2007] EWCA Civ 753).

The presumption in favour of contact is not, however, adopted by the courts in applications by other family members, for example grandparents (see *Re A (Section 8 Order: Grandparent Application)* [1995] 2 FLR 153). In *Re W (Contact: Application by Grandparent)* [1997] 1 FLR 793 Hollis J stated that, while grandparents have a very great role to play in the life of children, particularly young children, they must remember that they are grandparents, not parents. Hollis J said, however, that their influence could be extremely beneficial to children – provided it was exercised with care and not too frequently. The European Court of Human Rights has also recognised a presumption in favour of contact between parent and child (see 12.2, above).

## (c)  Types of Contact

Different types of contact can be ordered depending on the circumstances. Section 8(1) provides that the child can visit, stay or otherwise have contact with the parent or other named person. Direct contact (visiting or staying contact) will be ordered, unless there are cogent reasons to the contrary affecting the child's welfare (such as where there is violence, see *Re D (Contact: Reasons for Refusal)* [1997] 2 FLR 48).

Sometimes, however, the court will order indirect or supervised contact (the word 'otherwise' in s.8(1) allows the court to do this). The court can specify what arrangements are to take place, for instance by directing that there be indirect contact by letter, birthday cards, Christmas cards or telephone conversations (see s.11(7) and *Re O (Contact: Imposition of Conditions)* [1995] 2 FLR 124). Indirect contact was ordered in *Re P (Contact: Indirect Contact)* [1999] 2 FLR 893 (as the father was a former drug addict who had just been released from prison); and in *Re L (Contact: Genuine Fear)* [2002] 1 FLR 621 (as the mother was genuinely and intensely frightened of the father, and the child would suffer marked emotional harm as a result of the effect of direct contact on the mother). Where there is a risk that contact may harm the child, supervised contact can be ordered, whereby contact takes place in the presence of a third party (see, for example, *Re P (Contact: Supervision)* [1996] 2 FLR 314).

**Contact Centres**   In difficult contact cases where support and supervision are needed Contact Centres can provide a useful service. Run under the auspices of the National Association of Child Contact Centres they provide neutral meeting places where children can enjoy contact with one or both parents (and other family members) in a comfortable and safe environment. Most are staffed by volunteers, but some are run by social services and Children and Family Reporters. Most centres provide only 'supported' contact but a few provide supervised contact, with a high degree of vigilance. The Government has recognised the invaluable facilities that Contact Centres provide and has recommended that the services they provide be extended to help enforce and facilitate contact (see the report, *Making Contact Work*, Department for Constitutional Affairs, 2002).

## (d)  Parental Hostility to Contact

As contact is considered to be a right of the child and beneficial for the child, the courts will not allow contact to be thwarted because of parental hostility to it. In *Re H (A Minor) (Contact)* [1994] 2 FLR 776 Butler-Sloss LJ said that it was important that there should not be 'a selfish parents' charter' whereby a parent could make such a fuss about contact that it could prevent the court ordering it. Only in highly exceptional cases will contact be refused because of a parent's strong opposition and hostility to contact. In *Re J (A Minor) (Contact)* [1994] 1 FLR 729 a contact order was refused as the court found that the mother's hostility to contact with the father caused the child stress. Balcombe LJ emphasised, however, the exceptional nature of the case and said that judges should be very reluctant to allow the implacable hostility of one parent to deter them from making a contact order where they believed the child's welfare required it (see also *Re D (A Minor) (Contact: Mother's Hostility)* [1993] 2 FLR 1).

If there is good reason for parental hostility to contact, however, the courts may refuse it. In *Re H (Contact: Domestic Violence)* [1998] 2 FLR 42 the Court of Appeal held that, although the term 'implacable hostility' was often used as an 'umbrella term' in the context of parents who refused to permit contact, a distinction should be drawn between cases where there was no good reason for hostility (when the court would be very reluctant to deny contact) and those where hostility was based on genuine and rational fear (when the court would have to ask whether contact would be in the child's best interests).

Over the years, however, the courts have increasingly realised that parents may have genuinely held reasons for being intractably hostile to contact, for instance because of fears that the child may suffer violence if contact is granted. For this reason courts now take allegations of domestic violence seriously in contact cases.

In some cases hostility to contact is so great that the parent will refuse to comply with a contact order, and steps to enforce it will have to be taken (see below).

### (e) Contact and Domestic Violence

Over the years there has been growing concern about the harmful impact of ordering contact in the context of domestic violence. Until about ten years ago, domestic violence in the context of contact had been a rather neglected area. There were several reasons for this. First, research on domestic violence had tended to concentrate on adults rather than children. Secondly, the courts had taken the view that children had a right to contact, and that there should be a presumption in favour of contact. Thirdly, the courts were distrustful of mothers who made allegations of violence by fathers, and considered that they were merely being hostile to contact. The courts were keen to ensure that children were brought up having a positive image of a father, even where there were allegations of domestic violence (see, for example, *Re M (Contact: Family Assistance: McKenzie Friend)* [1999] 1 FLR 75).

Increasing concern began to be voiced, however, that the courts had perhaps created too high a threshold for a denial of contact, and that contact was being ordered in cases even though there was a risk of violence. One impetus for a change of approach was research by psychiatrists which showed the harmful effects of domestic violence on children. Another was that in 1999 a report by Radford, *Unreasonable Fears? Child Contact in the Context of Domestic Violence: A Survey of Mothers' Perception of Harm*, published by Women's Aid, provided evidence of children being physically and sexually abused as a result of contact being ordered. The report stated that changes in court practice were overdue, and recommended the introduction of a rebuttable presumption against residence, and direct or unsupervised contact, in cases where there was a risk of violence.

In June 1999 a Consultation Paper by the Children Act Sub-Committee of the Advisory Board on Family Law (*Contact Between Children and Violent Parents: The Question of Parental Contact in Cases where there is Domestic Violence*) was published, proposing guidelines for good practice in contact cases where there were allegations of domestic violence. But it was not in favour of introducing a legislative presumption against contact in domestic violence cases, which exists in some countries.

The Government began to acknowledge that domestic violence had not been fully or appropriately handled by the courts in contact cases, and that something needed to be done. In a *Report to the Lord Chancellor on the Question of Parental Contact in Cases where there is Domestic Violence* (Lord Chancellor's Department, 2002) it recommended that guidelines for good practice should be laid down, that professionals involved needed to be better informed and better trained, and that there should be more research into contact and domestic violence.

As a result of concerns about contact and domestic violence the courts began to take violence more seriously in contact cases and would order indirect contact, supervised contact, or even refuse contact, where there was violence (see, for example, *Re M (Contact: Violent Parent)* [1999] 2 FLR 321; and *Re K (Contact: Mother's Anxiety)* [1999] 2 FLR 703). The courts began to take the view that, where there was evidence of domestic violence, a father would have to show a future track record of proper behaviour, including taking up the offer of indirect contact, before successfully gaining direct contact (see *dicta* of Wall J in *Re O (Contact: Imposition of Conditions)* [1995] 2 FLR 124, approved by Cazalet J in *Re S (Violent Parent: Indirect Contact)* [2000] 1 FLR 481).

The following case had a particularly important impact on contact and domestic violence. In this case the Court of Appeal considered the Report by the Children Act Sub-Committee (see above) and a joint report by two distinguished child psychiatrists on the issue of contact and domestic violence:

▶ *Re L (Contact: Domestic Violence); Re V (Contact: Domestic Violence); Re M (Contact: Domestic Violence); Re H (Contact: Domestic Violence)* [2000] 2 FLR 334

In each appeal the fathers appealed against the judge's refusal to allow them direct contact with their children against a background of domestic violence. The violence or threats of violence had been proved, the fears of the resident parents were reasonable, and serious issues arose as to the risk of emotional harm to the children.

The Court of Appeal, dismissing all four appeals, laid down the following principles which should be applied in contact cases where there are allegations of domestic violence:

▶ Judges and magistrates need to have a heightened awareness of the existence, and consequences for children, of exposure to domestic violence.
▶ Allegations of domestic violence which might affect the outcome of a contact application must be adjudicated upon and found proved or not proved.
▶ Where domestic violence is proved, there is not, nor should be, a presumption of no contact. As a matter of principle, domestic violence cannot of itself constitute a bar to contact.
▶ Domestic violence is a highly relevant and important factor, among others, which must be taken into account by the judge when carrying out the difficult and delicate balancing exercise of discretion, applying the welfare principle in s.1(1) Children Act 1989, and the welfare checklist in s.1(3).
▶ Where domestic violence is proved, the court should weigh in the balance the seriousness of the violence, the risks involved and the impact on the child against the positive factors, if any, of contact between the parent found to have been violent and the child.
▶ Where domestic violence is proved, the following factors, among others, are of particular significance: the extent of the violence; its effect upon the primary-carer; its effect upon the child; and, in particular, the ability of the offender to recognise his past behaviour, to be aware of the need for change, and to make genuine attempts to change it.
▶ In respect of art. 8 ECHR (the right to family life), where there is a conflict between the rights and interests of a child and those of a parent, the child's interests must prevail under art. 8(2).
▶ On an application for interim contact, when allegations of domestic violence have not been adjudicated upon, the court should give particular consideration to the likely risk of harm (physical or emotional) to the child if contact is granted or refused. The court should ensure, as far as it can, that any risk of harm to the child is minimised, and that the safety of the child and the residential parent is secured before, during and after any such contact.

The message to come out of *Re L* was that courts and lawyers needed to be more aware of domestic violence and its effect on children. As a result of *Re L*, courts now take allegations of violence in contact cases seriously, and may, where violence is proved, order indirect or supervised contact, or, in an extreme case, order no contact. As Kaganas said ([2000] CFLQ 311, at 311), *Re L* 'reins back, in domestic violence cases, what was a very strong trend to prioritise contact between children and non-resident parents and to downgrade the risks to which such contact might expose mothers and children'.

In April 2002 the Children Act Sub-Committee of the Lord Chancellor's Advisory Board on Family Law published a set of *Guidelines for Good Practice on Parental Contact in Cases where there is Domestic Violence* (reproduced as Annex 1 in *Re H (Contact: Domestic Violence)* [2005] EWCA Civ 1404, [2006] 1 FLR 943). The guidelines require courts to give early consideration to allegations of domestic violence and, when ordering a s.7 welfare report, to give directions for the CAFCASS Children and Family Reporter to address the issue of domestic violence and to make a risk assessment of the harm which the child might suffer if contact is ordered. The *Guidelines* also lay down the following matters which the courts should, in particular consider, where a finding of domestic violence is made. Paragraph 1.6 provides that the courts should consider the conduct of both parents towards each other and towards the children; and in particular should consider:

'(a) the effect of the domestic violence which has been established on the child and on the parent with whom the child is living;

(b) whether or not the motivation of the parent seeking contact is a desire to promote the best interests of the child or as a means of continuing a process of violence against or intimidation or harassment of the other parent;

(c) the likely behaviour of the parent seeking contact during contact and its effect on the child or children concerned;

(d) the capacity of the parent seeking contact to appreciate the effect of past and future violence on the other parent and the children concerned;

(e) the attitude of the parent seeking contact to past violent conduct by that parent; and in particular whether that parent has the capacity to change and/or to behave appropriately.'

The *Guidelines* provide (see para. 1.7) that, when the court makes a finding of domestic violence but nonetheless considers that direct contact is in the best interests of the child, the court should consider what directions (under s.11(7) Children Act 1989) are required to enable the order to be carried into effect, and in particular consider: whether contact should be supervised; what conditions should be complied with by the person in whose favour the order is made; whether the court should exercise its powers under s.42(2)(b) of Part IV of the Family Law Act 1996 to make a non-molestation order (see 6.4); whether such contact should be for a specified period; and setting a date for the order to be reviewed.

A failure to have regard to *Re L (Contact: Domestic Violence); Re V (Contact: Domestic Violence); Re M (Contact: Domestic Violence); Re H (Contact: Domestic Violence)* (above) or the *Guidelines* prepared by the Children Act Sub-Committee of the Lord Chancellor's Advisory Committee on Family Law are grounds for appeal and may result in a contact order being set aside (which is what happened in *Re H (Contact: Domestic Violence)* [2005] EWCA Civ 1404, [2006] 1 FLR 943, above).

In *Safety and Justice: The Government's Proposals on Domestic Violence* (Cm 5847, Home Office, June 2003) the Government said that it intended to make sure that child contact arrangements in domestic violence cases guaranteed the safety of all parties (see para. 76). It said that an unpublished survey by the Lord Chancellor's Department in 2001 indicated that domestic violence featured in 19 per cent of child contact applications. Steps have been taken to give greater protection to victims of domestic violence and their families (see Chapter 6).

In response to concerns about domestic violence, the definition of 'harm' for the purposes of the welfare checklist (see 11.3) and for making a care or supervision order (see 15.7) now includes 'impairment suffered from seeing or hearing the ill-treatment of another'. This means that courts now have a statutory obligation to consider domestic violence in a contact case. However, Women's Aid and the National Society for the Prevention of Cruelty to Children (NSPCC) continue to voice concerns about the risk of harm to children from domestic violence on contact visits. According to a press release issued by the NSPCC in November 2005, 29 children have died on contact visits in the last 10 years.

*Risk Assessments (s.16A Children Act 1989)*   CAFCASS or Welsh family proceedings officers when exercising any of their functions in respect of any of the orders under Part II of the Children Act 1989, and who suspect that the child concerned is at risk of harm, must make a risk assessment in relation to the child and make that assessment available for the court (ss.16A(1), (2)). A risk assessment, in relation to a child who is at risk of suffering harm of a particular sort, is an assessment of the risk of that harm being suffered by the child (s.16A(3)). The officer must provide the report to the court irrespective of the outcome of the assessment (that is, even if the officer concludes that there is no risk of harm to the child); as the fact that a risk assessment has been carried out is a material fact which should be placed before the court (see *Practice Direction: Children Act 1989: Risk Assessments Under Section 16A* [2007] 2 FLR 625). Section 16A came into force on 1 October 2007.

(f)   Enforcing and Facilitating Contact

> ▶ **Baroness Hale in *Re G (Children) (Residence: Same-Sex Partner)* [2006] UKHL 43, at para. 41:**
>
> 'Making contact happen and, even more importantly, making contact work is one of the most difficult and contentious challenges in the whole of family law. It has recently received a great deal of public attention. Courts understandably regard the conventional methods of enforcing court orders as a last resort: fining the primary carer will only mean that she has even less to spend on the children; sending her to prison will deprive them of their primary carer and give them a reason to resent the other parent who invited this. Nor does punishment address the real sources of the problem, which may range from a simple failure to understand what the children need, to more complex fears resulting from the parents' own relationships.'

The courts in England and Wales must take effective steps to enforce contact otherwise they risk being in breach of the European Convention for the Protection of Human Rights (see 12.2, above).

Despite the obligation to enforce contact, enforcement has created difficulties for the courts. Some parents refuse to comply with contact orders, even though breach is punishable as contempt of court. The courts' inability to enforce contact in some cases has fostered the mistaken perception that the courts discriminate against fathers. Because of these problems, the Government has proposed legislative changes to improve the enforcement (and facilitation) of contact (see below).

*Dealing with Breach*   As the law currently stands, the courts have the following options available when a person fails to comply with a contact order.

*(i) Contempt of Court*   Breach of a contact order is contempt of court, which is punishable by fine or imprisonment. However, contempt can be an unsatisfactory measure in the family sphere. Imposing a fine reduces the amount of money available for the child, and sending a parent to prison may be emotionally damaging for the child. Despite these disadvantages, the courts have been increasingly willing to impose fines and prison sentences for breaches of contact orders (see, for example, *Re S (Contact Dispute: Committal)* [2004] EWCA Civ 1790, [2005] 1 FLR 812). However, the Court of Appeal has warned that a custodial sentence should not be imposed where a fine would be appropriate (see *Re M (Contact Order)* [2005] EWCA Civ 615, [2005] 2 FLR 1006).

Contempt proceedings must comply with art. 6 ECHR (the right to a fair trial) and art. 8 (right to family life). In *Re K (Contact: Committal Order)* [2002] EWCA Civ 1559 a mother successfully appealed against her committal to prison for 42 days for contempt of court because she had breached contact orders. The Court of Appeal held that her failure to have legal representation in the contempt proceedings breached art. 6, and the sentencing court had also breached art. 8 as it should have had regard to the effect of art. 8 on the decision to separate her from her children (following *R (P and Q and QB) v. Secretary of State for the Home Department and Another* [2001] EWCA Civ 1151, [2001] 2 FLR 1122).

*(ii) Transfer Residence to the Other Parent*   Where there are difficulties enforcing contact the court may decide to transfer the child's residence arrangements from the parent who is hostile to contact to the non-resident parent. Residence was transferred from the mother to the father by Bracewell J in *V v. V (Contact: Implacable Hostility)* [2004] EWHC 1215 (Fam), [2004] 2 FLR 851, as the mother had shown continuing hostility to contact and had made unsubstantiated allegations that the father had abused the children. In *Re C (A Child)* [2007] EWCA Civ 866 the Court of Appeal upheld the decision of the judge at first instance who had taken a robust approach to the mother's resistance to contact – by transferring residence from her to the father.

However, a transfer of residence will be ordered only as a last resort, and where it is not contrary to the child's best interests. Transferring residence may disrupt the child's life, and the child may not wish to live with the other parent. The non-resident parent may not have suitable accommodation, may not be able to care for the child full-time, and may not even know the child well.

*(iii) Family Assistance Order*   The court has the power under s.16 Children Act 1989 to make a family assistance order, which may be useful in a difficult contact case (see 12.5). The amendments to s.16 (to make family assistance orders more flexible and more useful in contact cases) came into force on 1 October 2007.

*(iv) Section 37 Order*    Where a court considers that the child is, or is at risk of, suffering significant harm it can make an order under s.37 Children Act 1989 that the local authority investigate the child's circumstances (see 11.12). In *Re M (Intractable Contact Dispute: Interim Care Order)* [2003] EWHC 1024 (Fam), [2003] 2 FLR 636 Wall J made a s.37 order, as the mother had falsely alleged that the children had been sexually abused by the father.

*(v) Direct a Psychiatric Assessment*    In *Re S (Contact: Promoting Relationship with Absent Parent)* [2004] 1 FLR 1279 the Court of Appeal directed that a psychiatrist should assess the family and report on the prospects for contact.

### (g)    Facilitating and Enforcing Contact – The Children and Adoption Act 2006

Over the years, the judiciary and the Government have recognised the injustices that parents (particularly fathers) can suffer when contact orders are not enforced. Part 1 of the Children and Adoption Act 2006 has inserted new provisions into the Children Act 1989 (see below) to improve the facilitation and enforcement of contact. These changes are based on the principle that children benefit from having contact with both parents, but they do not introduce a presumption that parents should have equal contact.

*The Background to the Children and Adoption Act 2006*    In February 2002 the Children Act Sub-Committee of the Lord Chancellor's Advisory Board on Family Law, chaired by Wall J, published *Making Contact Work: A Report to the Lord Chancellor on the Facilitation of Arrangements for Contact Between Children and Their Non-Residential Parents and the Enforcement of Court Orders for Contact*. It made various recommendations, including: providing more information about contact; giving Contact Centres extra funding to facilitate contact; promoting mediation, conciliation and negotiation; amending the provisions governing family assistance orders; giving courts the power to refer a parent to a psychiatrist or psychologist, or to an education programme; to impose community service orders for breach of a contact order; and to award financial compensation to parents who suffer financial loss as a result of loss of contact. Many of these recommendations were incorporated in the Children and Adoption Act 2006.

Two years later, in July 2004, the Government published a consultation paper, *Parental Separation: Children's Needs and Parents' Responsibilities* (Cm 6273) in which it acknowledged that the current way in which the courts intervene in disputed contact cases was not working well. This was followed in January 2005 by the Government publishing a White Paper, *Parental Separation: Children's Needs and Parents' Responsibilities, Next Steps* (Cm 6452), setting out the responses to the consultation paper and outlining proposals: to make changes in respect of the facilitation and enforcement of contact; to provide a wider range of services to support contact, including additional funding for Contact Centres, and advice and parenting support to help parents have meaningful contact with their children; to give CAFCASS a greater role in the promotion and enforcement of contact; to give courts additional powers before making contact orders; to make family assistance orders more flexible so that they could be used effectively in difficult contact cases; to ensure that s.11(7) Children Act 1989 provided sufficient flexibility to the courts' power to attach conditions to contact orders; and to promote the increased use of mediation.

Some of these recommendations were enacted in Part 1 of the Children and Adoption Act 2006, which inserted new provisions into the Children Act 1989.

*The New Contact Provisions*    The following new provisions in the Children Act 1989 have been enacted with the aim of improving and facilitating contact. At the time of writing (2008) they are not yet in force.

*(i) Contact Activity Directions and Conditions (ss.11A –G)*    The court can make a 'contact activity direction' (directing a party to the proceedings to take part in a specified activity that promotes contact with the child) (ss.11A(1), (3)). The direction must specify the contact activity and the activity provider (s.11A(4)). Types of contact activities will include, in particular, classes, and counselling or guidance sessions; and information and advice sessions about arrangements for contact, including information about mediation (s.11A(5)). The court has no power to require a person to have a medical or psychiatric examination, assessment or treatment, or to take part in mediation (s.11A(6)); and cannot make a contact activity direction and dispose finally of the contact proceedings at the same hearing (s.11A(7)). When considering whether to make a contact activity direction, the child's welfare is the court's paramount consideration (s.11A(9)).

The court has jurisdiction (when making or varying a contact order) to make a 'contact activity condition' requiring the person with whom the child lives (or is to live), or a person with a right of contact under a contact order or under a condition in a contact order under s.11(7)(b), to take part in an activity that promotes contact with the child (ss.11C(1), (2)). The condition will specify the activity and the activity provider (s.11C(4)).

Before making a contact activity direction or condition, the court must be satisfied that (s.11E(1)): the activity is appropriate in the circumstances (s.11E(2)); the activity provider is suitable to provide the activity (s.11E(3)); and that the proposed activity is in a place to which the person subject to the direction or condition can reasonably be expected to travel (s.11E(4)). Before making the direction or condition, the court must obtain and consider information about the person who is to be subject to the direction or condition, and consider the likely effect of the direction or condition on that person (s.11E(5)). The information may include information as to any conflict with the person's religious beliefs and any interference with the times (if any) at which that person normally works or attends an educational establishment (s.11E(6)). The court can ask a CAFCASS officer or a Welsh family proceedings officer to provide information on the matters specified in ss.11E(2)–(5) (s.11E(7)).

Financial assistance may be available to assist persons who are required to undertake a contact activity (s.11F). The court may ask a CAFCASS officer or Welsh family proceedings officer to monitor a person's compliance with a contact activity direction or condition, and to report to the court on failure to comply (s.11G).

*(ii) Monitoring Contact Orders (s.11H)*    The court can ask a CAFCASS officer or Welsh family proceedings officer to monitor compliance with a contact order (or an order varying contact) and to report to the court on such matters relating to compliance as the court may specify (ss.11H(1) and (2)). The court can make the request on making or varying a contact order or at any time in subsequent contact proceedings (s.11H(5)). The court can only ask for this monitoring role to be carried out for a period of up to twelve months (s.11H(6)).

*(iii) Warning Notices (s.11I)*    When a court makes or varies a contact order, it must attach a notice warning of the consequences of failing to comply with the contact order.

*(iv) Enforcement Orders (ss.11J–11N)* If the court is satisfied beyond reasonable doubt and without reasonable excuse that a contact order has been breached, it may make an 'enforcement order' imposing an unpaid work requirement on the person in breach (ss.11J(1), (2)), unless that person can prove on the balance of probabilities that he has a reasonable excuse for failing to comply with the contact order (ss.11J(3), (4)).

The following persons can apply for an enforcement order: the person who for the purpose of the contact order is the person with whom the child lives, or is to live; the person whose contact with the child is provided for in the contact order; any person subject to a s.11(7)(b) contact condition or contact activity condition; or the child concerned (s.11J(5)). A child needs leave to apply for an enforcement order, which the court can only grant if the child has sufficient understanding to make the application (ss.11J(6), (7)). Schedule A1 to the Children Act 1989 makes further provision for the enforcement of orders.

An enforcement order cannot be made for failure to comply with a contact order unless the person concerned has received a copy of a notice under s.11I (s.11K(1)), and it cannot be made against a person aged under 18 at the time of the breach (s.11K(2)). Before making an enforcement order, the court must be satisfied that (s.11L(1)): the order is necessary to secure compliance with the contact order; and that the likely effect of the order on the person in breach is proportionate to the seriousness of the breach. It must also be satisfied that the provision for the person to work under an unpaid work requirement can be made in the local justice area in which the person in breach resides, or will reside (s.11L(2)). The court must obtain and consider information about the person and the likely effect of the enforcement order on that person before making the order (s.11L(3)). The provisions about seeking information are the same as those for obtaining information before making a contact activity or direction (see above and see ss.11L(4)–(6)). When making an enforcement order, the court must take into account the welfare of the child who is the subject of the contact order (s.11L(7)).

*(v) Contact Orders – Compensation for Financial Loss (s.11O)* If certain persons suffer financial loss as a result of the breach of a contact order, the court can make an order requiring the person in breach to compensate that person in respect of the financial loss (ss.11O(1), (2)). The following persons can apply for compensation: the person who, for the purposes of the contact order, is the person with whom the child lives, or is to live; the person for whom contact is provided for in the contact order, or a person subject to a s.11(7)(b) contact condition or contact activity condition; or the child concerned (s.11O(6)). The child needs leave of the court to apply, which can only be granted if the child has sufficient understanding to make the application (ss.11O(7), (8)). The amount of compensation must not exceed the amount of the applicant's financial loss (s.11O(9)). In determining the amount of compensation payable, the court must take into account the financial circumstances of the person in breach (s.11O(10)). In exercising its powers, the court must take into account the welfare of the child (s.11O(14)). An order to pay compensation cannot be made against a person where the failure occurred before that person attained the age of 18 (s.11P(2)).

*(vi) Family Assistance Orders (s.16)* As a result of amendments to s.16 (by s.6 Children and Adoption Act 2006), family assistance orders are now better suited to being used in difficult contact cases (see 11.12).

### 12.6 Enforcing Residence and Contact Orders in Other Parts of the UK

Residence and contact orders made in England and Wales can be enforced in other parts of the UK (that is, in Scotland and Northern Ireland) under the Family Law Act 1986 (see s.25). The order can be registered in the court in the other part of the UK, whereupon that court has the same powers for the purpose of enforcing the order as if it had made the order (s.29). The court has the power, however, to refuse to enforce the order if enforcement is contrary to the child's best interests.

### 12.7 Changing a Child's Name on Family Breakdown

*(i) Surnames* On family breakdown the residential parent may wish to change the child's surname, perhaps because of a desire to sever ties with the other parent, or for the child to acquire the step-parent's surname.

A child's surname can be changed by a person with parental responsibility for the child, provided every other person with parental responsibility consents. Oral consent is sufficient, except where a residence order is in force, when written consent is required (see s.13(1)(b) Children Act 1989). Written consent is also required if the child is in local authority care (s.33(7), and see *Re S (Change of Surname)* [1999] 1 FLR 672). Where consent (oral or written) is not forthcoming, the court's consent will be needed.

A dispute about the child's surname can be settled by applying for a specific issue order under s.8 Children Act 1989, or, if a residence order is in force, by applying under s.13. Where a change of name seems imminent, a s.8 prohibited steps orders may be necessary to stop the change of surname. When considering an application, the child's welfare is the court's paramount consideration (s.1(1)), and the s.1(3) welfare checklist will apply if the application is by way of a specific issue or prohibited steps order (see s.1(4)). Although, the Children Act does not require the court to consider the welfare checklist in an application for a change of surname under s.13, the court is likely to perform the same sort of exercise.

The courts take the view that changing a child's surname is a serious matter (*Dawson v. Wearmouth* [1999] AC 308, [1999] 1 FLR 1167), and the child's wishes, not parental wishes, prevail. In *Re C (Change of Surname)* [1998] 2 FLR 656 the Court of Appeal held that good reasons have to be shown before the judge will allow a change of name. In *Re W; Re A; Re B (Change of Name)* [1999] 2 FLR 930 Butler-Sloss LJ said that a desire to change a child's name because the applicant parent did not have the same name as the child will generally not carry much weight.

The court will take into account cultural and religious circumstances when deciding whether to permit a change of surname. In *Re S (Change of Names: Cultural Factors)* [2001] 2 FLR 1005 a mother applied to have her child's Sikh names changed to Muslim names after she had moved back into a Muslim community on family breakdown. Wilson J ordered an informal change of name so that the mother and child would be able to integrate into the Muslim community, but held that there was no benefit for the child to have his names formally changed by deed poll, as his Sikh name represented the reality of his heritage.

In *Re R (Surname: Using Both Parents')* [2001] EWCA Civ 1344, [2001] 2 FLR 1358 Thorpe LJ suggested that parents should be encouraged to use the Spanish custom of combining the paternal and maternal surnames as a way of avoiding surname disputes. Hale LJ said that, in appropriate cases, parents and courts should be more prepared to contemplate using both surnames. It was no longer consistent with modern law that the child should bear only the father's name.

*(ii) First Names*    The Court of Appeal held in *Re H (Child's Name: First Name)* [2002] EWCA Civ 190, [2002] 1 FLR 973 that the rules about surnames (see above) do not apply to disputes about first names.

### 12.8    Removing a Child from the UK

On relationship breakdown, one parent may wish to leave the UK with the child. In this situation, the consent of all persons with parental responsibility is needed, otherwise the person taking the child out of the UK commits a criminal offence (see 14.5). If a residence order is in force, the child cannot be removed from the UK (except for a period of up to one month) without the written consent of all those with parental responsibility, or otherwise the permission of the court (s.13(1)(b)). (See further at 14.4.)

### 12.9    The Voice of the Child in Residence and Contact Proceedings

See 9.6.

## Summary

1   Many children experience parental relationship breakdown.

2   On divorce, the district judge under s.41 Matrimonial Causes Act 1973 must consider the Statement of Arrangements for Children, and consider whether to exercise his powers under the Children Act 1989. In exceptional circumstances a decree absolute of divorce can be postponed.

3   Parents retain parental responsibility for their children on relationship breakdown.

4   Maintenance for children on family breakdown can be sought from the Child Support Agency (and in some cases in the courts) and lump sum and property orders can be sought from the courts (see Chapter 13).

5   Disputes about arrangements for children on family breakdown are best settled by parents (with or without the help of a mediator), rather than by the court.

6   Disputes about with which parent the child should live on family breakdown can be settled by making an application for a s.8 residence order under the Children Act 1989 (see also Chapter 11). The welfare of the child is the court's paramount consideration (s.1(1)) and the other welfare principles in s.1 apply. A shared residence order can be made (s.11(4)). Once a residence order is made, no person can change the child's surname or remove the child from the UK (except for up to one month) without the written consent of all persons with parental responsibility, or otherwise with permission of the court (ss.13(1), (2)).

7   The child has a right to contact. Contact orders can be made under s.8 Children Act 1989. There is a presumption of contact unless there are cogent reasons against it. The court must apply the welfare principles in s.1 Children Act 1989. Direct contact, indirect contact, supervised contact and an order of no contact are possible options for the court. Hostility to contact by residential parents has caused difficulties for the court. Domestic violence is a serious factor to be considered by the court, but there is no presumption against contact where violence is proved.

## Summary cont'd

**8** Difficulties in respect of facilitating and enforcing contact have led to the enactment of new provisions in the Children Act 1989 (by Part 1 of the Children and Adoption Act 2006) which aim to improve and resolve contact difficulties on family breakdown.

**9** Other disputes on family breakdown can be settled by an application for a s.8 specific issue or prohibited steps order.

**10** A child's surname is an important issue to be determined by the court where there is parental conflict. A dispute can be decided by making an application for a specific issue order, or, if a residence order is in force, by making an application under s.13. The child's welfare, not the parents' wishes, prevail.

**11** There is increasing recognition that children should be allowed to participate in private law proceedings.

## Further Reading and References

Bailey-Harris, 'Contact – challenging conventional wisdom' [2001] CFLQ 361.

Bainham *et al* (eds.), *Children and their Families: Contact, Rights and Welfare*, 2003, Hart Publishing.

Butler *et al*, *Divorcing Children: Children's Experience of Their Parents' Divorce*, 2003, Jessica Kingsley.

Cantwell, 'What is contact for?' [2005] Fam Law 299.

Collier, 'Fathers 4 Justice, law and the new politics of fatherhood' [2005] CFLQ 511.

Douglas and Ferguson, 'The role of grandparents in divorced families' (2003) *International Journal of Law, Policy and the Family* 41.

Fortin, Richie and Buchanan, 'Young adults' perceptions of court-ordered contact' [2007] CFLQ 211.

Fretwell-Wilson, 'Fractured families, fragile children – the sexual vulnerability of girls in the aftermath of divorce' [2002] CFLQ 1.

Gilmore, 'Court decision-making in shared residence order cases: a critical examination' [2006] CFLQ 478.

Gosden, 'Children's surnames – how satisfactory is the current law?' [2003] Fam Law 186.

Hayes, '*Dawson* v. *Wearmouth* – What's in a name? A child by any other name is surely just as sweet?' [1999] CFLQ 423.

Humphreys and Harrison, 'Focusing on safety – domestic violence and the role of child contact centres' [2003] CFLQ 237.

Kaganas, '*Re L (Contact: Domestic Violence); Re V (Contact: Domestic Violence); Re M (Contact: Domestic Violence); Re H (Contact: Domestic Violence)*: Contact and domestic violence' [2000] CFLQ 311.

Kaganas and Diduck, 'Incomplete citizens: changing images of post-separation children' (2004) 67(6) *Modern Law Review* 959.

Kaganas and Piper, 'Grandparents and contact: "Rights v. welfare" revisited' (2001) *International Journal of Law, Policy and the Family* 250.

Kaganas and Piper, 'Shared Parenting – A 70% solution?' [2002] CFLQ 365.

Masson, 'Thinking about contact – A social or legal problem?' [2000] CFLQ 15.

Murch *et al*, *Safeguarding Children's Welfare in Uncontentious Divorce: A Study of Section 41 of the Matrimonial Causes Act 1973*, Department of Constitutional Affairs, and see also [1999] Fam Law 682.

Murch with Keehan, *The Voice of the Child in Private Family Law Proceedings*, 2003, Family Law.

## Further reading cont'd

Piercy, 'Intractable contact disputes' [2004] Fam Law 815.

Prest, 'The right to respect for family life: obligations of the state in private law children cases' [2005] Fam Law 124.

Reece, 'UK women's groups' child contact campaign: "so long as it is safe"' [2006] CFLQ 538.

Smart and May, 'Residence and contact disputes in court' [2004] Fam Law 36.

Smart, Wade and Neale, 'Objects of concern? Children and divorce' [1999] CFLQ 365.

Van Krieken, 'The "best interests of the child" and parental separation: on the "civilising of parents"' (2005) 68(1) *Modern Law Review* 25.

Wall J, 'Making contact' [2003] Fam Law 275.

Wall, The Right Hon Lord Justice, 'Enforcement of contact orders' [2005] Fam Law 26.

## Websites

**Association for Shared Parenting**: www.sharedparenting.org.uk

**Families Need Fathers**: www.fnf.org.uk

**Family and Parenting Institute**: www.familyandparenting.org

**HM Courts' Service**: www.hmcourtsservice.gov.uk

**National Association of Child Contact Centres**: www.nacc.org.uk

**National Youth Advocacy Service**: www.nyas.net

**One Parent Families**: www.oneparentfamilies.org.uk

# Chapter 13

## Child Support and Financial Provision and Property Orders for Children

---

**The Legislation**

**Child Support Acts 1991 and 1995** Make provision in respect of the powers and duties of the Child Support Agency and provision in respect of the assessment and enforcement of child support maintenance.

**Section 15 and Schedule 1 to the Children Act 1989** Give the court power to make finance and property orders to or for the benefit of children, and also dependent children after they have reached majority.

**Part II of the Matrimonial Causes Act 1973** Gives the divorce court power to make financial provision orders (periodical payments and lump sums) and property adjustment orders to or for the benefit of children.

**Domestic Proceedings and Magistrates' Courts Act 1978** Gives the magistrates' family proceedings court the power to make financial provision orders (periodical payments and lump sums) to or for the benefit of children (but only if the parents are married and the marriage is subsisting).

---

### 13.1  Finance and Property for Children

---

**Article 27(3)  United Nations Convention on the Rights of the Child 1989**

'States Parties shall take all appropriate measures to secure the recovery of maintenance for the child from the parents.'

---

All parents have a duty to provide financial support for their children, and this obligation continues when parental relationships break down. If financial provision is sought in the courts it may take the form of maintenance (a regular contribution to the upkeep of a child) or a lump sum payment. Property orders can also be made to or for the benefit of children.

As far as child maintenance disputes are concerned, cases are dealt with by the Child Support Agency, although the courts have some limited jurisdiction to make orders for child maintenance. The courts, not the Agency, however, can only make orders for capital sums and property orders for children.

Parents can make their own arrangements about financial provision for their children, and it is best that they do so, because an application to the Child Support Agency can be a protracted affair, and bringing court proceedings can be costly, unpredictable and time-consuming. Hostility and bitterness between parents can also be detrimental to children. It should be noted that the Child Support Agency is to be abolished and replaced by a new system for dealing with child support maintenance (see 13.2). Information on the reforms can be found on the Child Support Agency and Department for Work and Pensions websites.

## 13.2    Child Support Maintenance – The Child Support Agency

Where a parent is unwilling to pay child maintenance, or sufficient child maintenance, an application can be made to the Child Support Agency which has powers and duties under the Child Support Act 1991, and in regulations, to calculate and review child maintenance, and to collect and enforce payment. Parents are under no obligation to apply to the Agency. They can make their own child maintenance arrangements, although any written agreement about maintenance is void if it purports to oust the jurisdiction of the Agency. Divorcing parents can opt to have an agreement about child maintenance incorporated into a court order known as a 'consent order'.

### (a)    The Background

The Child Support Act 1991 came into force on 5 April 1993. Before that date, disputes about child maintenance were heard by the courts which had wide discretionary powers to make periodical payments orders for children according to the circumstances of each case. However, in 1990, as a result of dissatisfaction with the court-based system, the Conservative Government published a White Paper, *Children Come First* (Cm 1264), in which it made proposals for a radically new child maintenance system which would be run by a Government Agency (the Child Support Agency).

In the White Paper the Government put forward various arguments in favour of reform. It claimed that the discretionary court system was resulting in arbitrary and unpredictable awards of child maintenance. Many fathers were failing to fulfil their maintenance obligations, and the cost of this was being thrown onto the State, and consequently onto the taxpayer. Increasing divorce and increasing one-parent families were resulting in many parents, particularly women, being increasingly dependent on State benefits. The welfare needs of children were also not being sufficiently protected. According to the Government, the court-based system was 'unnecessarily fragmented, uncertain in its results, slow and ineffective' (para. 2, *Children Come First*). It therefore proposed the introduction of a new child maintenance system based on systems in Australia and the USA. The aims of the new system would be: to enforce parental support obligations effectively, cheaply and quickly; to introduce certainty and predictability; to reduce the potential for inter-parental conflict; and to reduce dependency on social security and cost to the taxpayer.

The Government's proposals were rapidly passed into law under the Child Support Act 1991, which was based, according to the Government, on a recognition that children have a right to be maintained, and that parents, not the State, have a responsibility to maintain them. The 1991 Act made three radical changes. It transferred the task of assessing, reviewing, collecting and enforcing child maintenance from the courts into a new Government body, the Child Support Agency; it prohibited the courts from making maintenance orders for children in any case where the Child Support Agency had jurisdiction to make a maintenance assessment; and it introduced a formula for calculating maintenance.

*Reaction to the New Scheme*   Despite receiving all-party support, the scheme provoked immediate and intense hostility. Not only was the formula for calculating maintenance complex and difficult to understand, but the scheme was perceived by many fathers as being unjust and grossly unfair because they were required to pay much higher levels of maintenance than under the previous court-based scheme. Step-fathers felt especially aggrieved, as the amount of maintenance they were required to pay made it difficult for them to support their new families. Some fathers thought the new system was unfair, because Agency assessments failed to take account of 'clean break' arrangements which had been made on divorce before the new scheme came into force (see *Crozier* v. *Crozier* [1994] Fam 114). Another absurdity of the new scheme was demonstrated in *Phillips* v. *Pearce* [1996] 2 FLR 230, where the mother was forced to apply to the court for a lump sum for the child, because, although the father lived in a house worth £2.6 million and owned and controlled a company, the Child Support Agency had said it was impossible to calculate child support because he had no income.

*Amendments to the Scheme ('Departures' or 'Variations')*   Because of dissatisfaction, minor amendments were made in order to mitigate some of the hardships and anomalies created by the new scheme. In February 1994 minor changes were made to the formula, and in April 1995, after the publication of the White Paper, *Improving Child Support* (Cm. 2745), a 'departures' system was introduced by the Child Support Act 1995, whereby the Agency was given power to depart from the formula in certain situations where an assessment had produced unfair results. (This later became known as 'variations', see below.) These minor reforms, which modified rather than radically altered the scheme, did not, however, staunch the flow of criticism. Dissatisfaction with the formula continued to be voiced, and there was also concern about delays, errors of calculation and difficulties of enforcement on the part of the Agency.

*Continuing Dissatisfaction*   Because of continuing dissatisfaction with the scheme, the Labour Government published a consultation paper in 1998 (*Children First: A New Approach to Child Support*, Cm 3992), followed by a White Paper in 1999 (*A New Contract for Welfare: Children's Rights and Parents' Responsibilities*, Cm 4349) in which it proposed to simplify and speed up the calculation of child support.

In the White Paper the Government acknowledged that the child support system had failed to improve the position of children living apart from their parents. Not only did parents find the system difficult to understand, but they were required to provide a considerable amount of information in order for a maintenance assessment to be made. The Government acknowledged that the scheme was prone to errors, and needed constant amendment to keep up with changes to welfare benefit levels. It therefore proposed that the system be replaced with 'a simple and more deliverable system focused on the needs of children and good, responsible parents' (Introduction, para. 9). Parents would be able to see more clearly how much maintenance was due, and children would receive maintenance more quickly and more regularly.

The changes, which were considerably more radical than any previous amendments to the scheme, were introduced by way of amendment to the Child Support Act 1991 by the

Child Support, Pensions and Social Security Act 2000. The most radical change was the simplification of the formula for calculating maintenance to make it more comprehensible and accessible to parents, and easier and quicker for the Agency to administer.

*Problems Continue* Despite the changes which have been made over the years, the child support system has continued to have problems. Enforcement and delays in making assessment have been major problems, in particular. In *Smith* v. *Secretary of State for Work and Pensions* [2004] EWCA Civ 1343, [2005] 1 FLR 606 Ward LJ said that it was 'appalling' to think that the effective date for the assessment in this case was September 2001 and that three years later it had still not been made. He said that the family had suffered from delay and uncertainty, which was another stain on the Agency's reputation.

The House of Commons Work and Pensions Select Committee on Child Poverty in its *Third Report* on the Agency (July 2004) was highly critical of the huge administrative and equipment inefficiencies which had led to a huge backlog of cases (170,000 cases, increasing at 30,000 per quarter) and to many cases which for a variety of reasons were 'stuck' and going nowhere.

In January 2005, the House of Commons Work and Pensions Committee published a report, *The Performance of the Child Support Agency*, in which it described the Agency as a failing organisation, currently in crisis. It said that there was a lack of adequate staff training and monitoring. It said that there should be a greater focus on compliance and enforcement, which should include more frequent use of deductions from earnings orders, removal of driving licences and consideration of travel bans or the removal of passports. It said that a strategy must urgently be developed to progress cases that were still waiting for a maintenance calculation. The committee said that, if the responses to the report did not provide the information necessary to make a judgment as to whether the Agency as currently constituted could be rescued, then consideration should be given to the option of winding up the Agency. Before his retirement as Minister for Welfare and Pensions, David Blunkett MP described the Child Support Agency as a 'shambles'.

In 2005, Resolution (an organisation of family law solicitors) published a report on the Child Support Agency in which it criticised the system and made proposals for reform. It recommended that the courts' jurisdiction should be re-established for cases which used the court process for other issues, such as pension sharing, spousal maintenance and capital provision (see Chapter 8). It recommended the introduction of a Child Maintenance Arbitrator system to promote settlements, and a special enforcement body which might work separately from the Agency.

In sum, there has been a catalogue of failures and the Agency had failed many children. Non-resident parents have refused to pay maintenance and the Agency has failed to enforce payment. By July 2006, £3 billion was owed in unpaid child support. There have been errors in maintenance calculations (in July 1997, the National Audit Office found that estimated bills sent to fathers were wrong in eight out of ten cases). In 2003, the Government introduced a new £456 million computer system but this had major problems. There have been delays in dealing with cases (by July 2006, the Agency had a backlog of 300,000 cases).

As a result of this catalogue of failings, the Government proposes to make radical changes to the child support system, which includes abolishing the Child Support Agency.

(b)   Reform of the Child Support System

Because of the failings of the system, in February 2006 the Government commissioned an investigation by Sir David Henshaw into the child support scheme with the remit of suggesting reforms. His report (*Recovering Child Support: Routes to Responsibility*, Cm 6894, Department for Work and Pensions, July 2006) identified major failings in the system and recommended the introduction of a completely new system, where the emphasis would be on parents making private agreements about maintenance, and with difficult cases being dealt with by a new body with tougher enforcement powers. The report also recommended that fathers should be automatically named on birth certificates to encourage them to accept responsibility for their children.

In July 2006 the Government's response to the Henshaw Report was presented to Parliament (*A Fresh Start: Child Support Redesign*, Cm 6895, Department for Work and Pensions). This was followed in December 2006 by a White Paper (*A New System of Child Maintenance*, Cm 6979, Department for Work and Pensions) setting out a new child support system which would empower parents to take responsibility for making their own maintenance agreements but with radically strengthened enforcement powers in cases of non-compliance. It also proposed joint birth registration to encourage more fathers to pay maintenance. In May 2007 the Government published its responses to the Child Maintenance White Paper. This was followed in June 2007 by the publication of the Child Maintenance and Other Payments Bill.

*The Child Maintenance and Other Payments Bill 2007*   The Bill proposes the following main changes to the child support system:

- the Child Support Agency will be replaced by a new body, the Child Maintenance and Enforcement Commission (C-MEC);
- the C-MEC will have increased enforcement powers (such as surrender of passports, taking money out of accounts held by financial institutions, curfews);
- parents on low incomes will be permitted to keep more of the maintenance owed to them;
- parents will be empowered to make and maintain their own private maintenance arrangements;
- parents with care on benefit will no longer be obliged to use the CSA (or C-MEC) – so that they have more choice over their maintenance arrangements;
- assessment will be simplified by using latest available tax-year information and, where possible, fixing the award for a year, so that there is more certainty for parents about the amount of maintenance to be paid;
- assessment will be based on gross (not net) weekly income, in order to provide a quicker, and more accurate calculation process;
- the C-MEC will be given the power to operate a charging scheme so that defaulting parents can be fined, to help cover the costs of enforcement;
- new powers for information-sharing between credit reference agencies in respect of defaulting parents will be introduced – so that non-payment could potentially affect future loan or mortgage applications.

In short, the main thrust of the new scheme is to encourage more parents to make their own private agreements about child maintenance and for the C-MEC to focus on hard cases where parents refuse to make payment. The power of the C-MEC to use harsher penalties will, the Government hopes, act as an incentive for non-resident parents to enter into voluntary agreements.

The Government expects the C-MEC to become operational in 2010.

*Problems With the Proposed New System?*  The new system is unlikely to provide an immediate and complete remedy for the problems that exist. The emphasis on encouraging parents to make their own agreements seems somewhat idealistic, when the main reason for establishing the Child Support Agency in the first place was to remedy the problem that many parents were not reaching agreement about child maintenance and were wasting considerable amounts of court time and public money litigating over the matter. One of the consequences of the reforms is that there is likely to be an upsurge of cases reaching the courts. In fact, the Government has recognised that this is likely to happen (see *Judicial and Court Statistics 2006*, Cm 7273, 2007, Ministry of Justice).

Resolution (an organisation of family law solicitors) has expressed concern (see [2007] Fam Law 762) about the enforceability of private maintenance agreements. Resolution has said that it is difficult to see what incentive there will be for parents to use them (because they will not be enforceable) and for this reason it is 'likely that this proposal will have little impact on reducing the administrative burden faced by the new system'. Resolution also warns of the danger that parents may decide that some maintenance is better than none, and consequently enter into inadequate agreements. It would like to see private agreements registered in, and enforced by, the courts or via the C-MEC.

Another concern is in respect of the severity of the penalties for non-compliance. The penalties for failing to pay child maintenance may not be a proportionate response, and for that reason may not be human rights compliant.

Enforcement is likely to continue to cause problems, as parents who are unable to agree to or enforce voluntary agreements will still have to go through the C-MEC, so that the burden on the commission is likely to remain high. Resolution has said that 'if the Government is serious about empowering parents and reducing the burden on C-MEC, they should ensure that those, who choose to, are free to use the court process to enforce their own maintenance agreements' ([2007] Fam Law 762). Resolution says that, as thousands of children have been failed by the Child Support Agency, it is important that the Government gets it right this time.

## 13.3  The Child Support Scheme

Child support maintenance is an amount of money which a non-resident parent must pay towards the cost of bringing up a child. The framework for the child support scheme is found in the Child Support Act 1991 (as amended).

### (a)  The Child Support Agency

The Child Support Agency (CSA) is an executive agency of the Department for Work and Pensions. It has a legal duty under the Child Support Act 1991 to calculate child support for a qualifying child living in the UK if it receives an application for a child maintenance calculation, and it has jurisdiction to deal with it. Besides calculating and reviewing maintenance, and making arrangements for collecting payments, its other principal activities include: tracing and contacting non-resident parents; sorting out paternity disputes; collecting and passing on maintenance payments and taking action to enforce payment; preparing and presenting appeals to be heard by the independent Child Support Appeal Tribunal Service; and working with the Benefits Agency (if clients receive social security) to ensure correct payments and to protect against fraud.

Most Agency decisions are non-discretionary, but some are discretionary. When exercising any discretionary power, Agency decision-makers must take account of the welfare of any child likely to be affected (s.2).

*Jurisdiction*  The CSA has jurisdiction to calculate and collect child maintenance if the person with care (PWC) and the qualifying child are habitually resident in the UK (s.44). The non-resident parent (NRP) must normally be resident in the UK, but there are exceptions, for example, for members of the British civil service, naval, military or air forces, or parents who are employed in certain companies or bodies working overseas (s.44(2A)). There is no definition of 'habitual residence' in the Act – this is determined by case-law. There is a right of appeal to an independent tribunal against a decision on the CSA's jurisdiction (s.20).

A person not in receipt of certain welfare benefits (see below) who has a written maintenance agreement in force made before 5 April 1993 cannot apply to the Agency. An application cannot be made to the Agency in a non-benefit case where a court order is in force until one year has elapsed after the order was made (s.4(10)(aa)). If the Agency does not have jurisdiction, the court may have jurisdiction to decide the matter (see below).

### (b) The Basic Principles of the Child Support Act 1991

The basic principles of the Child Support Act 1991 are as follows:

- Each parent of a qualifying child is responsible for maintaining his or her child (s.1(1)).
- A non-resident parent (NRP) is taken to have met his responsibility to maintain a qualifying child by making periodical payments of maintenance with respect to the child of such amount, and at such intervals, as may be determined under the provisions of the Act (s.1(2)).
- Where a maintenance calculation is made, it is the duty of the NRP with respect to whom the calculation is made to make those payments (s.1(3)).
- The person with care (PWC) or the NRP may apply to the Agency for a maintenance assessment to be made (s.4(1)).
- Special rules apply where parents are in receipt of certain welfare benefits (s.6(1)).
- The court retains a residual role to make maintenance orders for children (see s.8).
- The provisions of the Act do not prevent any person from entering into an agreement for the making of periodical payments by way of maintenance to or for the benefit of any child (s.9(2)).
- An application to the Child Support Agency for a maintenance assessment is referred to a child support officer and the amount of child support maintenance is determined in accordance with the formula laid down in Sched. 2 to the Act (s.11).

**(c)**  Definitions for the Purposes of the Child Support Act 1991

A *'Child'* is a child aged under 16, or aged between 16 and 19 and receiving full-time non-advanced education (that is, not doing a course higher than 'A'-level) (s.55(1)).

A *'Qualifying Child'* is a child for whom the non-resident parent has (or both non-resident parents have) to pay maintenance (s.3(1)). A child who is, or has been, married is not a qualifying child (even if the marriage is void or has been annulled) (s.55(2)). A qualifying child includes an adopted child; and a child born to a married couple by artificial insemination by donor (unless the husband did not consent to the treatment) (s.28(2) Human Fertilisation and Embryology Act 1990).

A *'Relevant Other Child'* is a child who lives with the non-resident parent. This can be the non-resident parent's own child or the child of a person who lives with the non-resident parent.

A *'Parent'* is any person who is in law the mother or father of the child (s.54). In addition to biological parents, it also includes adoptive parents and persons with a parental order made under s.30 Human Fertilisation and Embryology Act 1990 (s.54).

The *'Non-Resident Parent' (NRP)* is the parent who is not living in the same household with the child; and who is not the child's main day-to-day carer (s.3(2)). If the child stays with both parents, the non-resident parent is the one who spends fewer nights with the child. If the child spends equal numbers of nights with each parent, the non-resident parent is normally the one who is not in receipt of Child Benefit for the child.

The *'Person With Care'* is the person with whom the child has his home and who usually provides day-to-day care for the child (whether exclusively or in conjunction with any other person) (s.3(3)). It includes parents with care. Local authorities and local authority foster-parents are not persons with care (s.3(3)(c)).

**(d)**  The Welfare of the Child

When the Agency is considering the exercise of any discretionary power, it must 'have regard to the welfare of any child likely to be affected by its decision' (s.2). A discretionary power would include, for example, a decision whether or not to pursue a claim for child support against a parent on benefits, or whether or not to take enforcement action. The welfare principle does not apply to any duty (for example, to calculate child support).

**(e)**  Applicants

Different rules apply to parents, depending on whether they are receiving welfare benefits (Income Support or income-based Jobseeker's Allowance).

*(i) Parents not on Income Support and Income-Based Jobseeker's Allowance*   Provided the parent with care (PWC) is not on Income Support or income-based Jobseeker's Allowance, then the PWC or the non-resident parent (NRP) can apply for a maintenance calculation in respect of the child (or children) (s.4(1)), and either party can apply for collection and enforcement (s.4(2)). There is, however, no obligation to apply. Parents are free to agree between themselves about child maintenance, but they cannot exclude

any right to apply to the Agency under the terms of a maintenance agreement or a consent order, and any provision purporting to restrict an application is void (ss.9(3), (4)).

*(ii) Parents on Welfare Benefits*    Parents with care who claim Income Support or income-based Jobseeker's Allowance are treated as applying for child support unless they opt out (see below) (ss.6(3), (5)). This also applies to PWCs who are living with someone who is claiming one of these benefits for them.

Parents with care on benefits are required to provide the Agency with information to enable the non-resident parent to be traced and for child maintenance to be calculated and collected (s.6(7)). Failure to provide the required information is a criminal offence, and can result in a reduced benefits decision being made.

*Opting Out for 'Good Cause'*    A PWC on Income Support or income-based Jobseeker's Allowance can opt out of the child support scheme (s.6(5)) provided he or she can show 'good cause' – that is, applying for child maintenance will put him or her or any child living with him or her at risk of suffering harm or undue distress.

## (f)    Disputed Parentage

Only a non-resident parent (NRP) is liable to pay child support maintenance. If a person named as the NRP denies that he (or she) is the parent of a qualifying child, the Agency cannot make a maintenance calculation, unless parentage can be proved. The Agency can, however, presume parentage and calculate maintenance where the alleged NRP (s.26(2)): was married to the child's mother at any time between the child's conception and the child's birth; is registered as the child's father on the child's birth certificate; refuses to take a DNA test (within the meaning of s.27A) or has taken a test which shows that there is no reasonable doubt that the NRP is a parent; has adopted the child; is the child's parent under ss.20, 27 and 30 Human Fertilisation and Embryology Act 1990; is declared to be the parent by a declaration of parentage made under s.55A Family Law Act 1986; or has been judged as the father by the court.

If a maintenance calculation is made on the basis of one of the presumptions above, a person can appeal against the calculation on the basis that he or she is not the parent (s.20(1)(a)).

The court has the power to direct a scientific test to establish parentage (see 10.3), and voluntary DNA testing is also available from the Agency.

## (g)    Calculating Child Support – The Formula

The original formula for calculating child support maintenance, which was so complex as to be almost unintelligible, was replaced by a new formula which came into force on 3 March 2003 (see Part 1 of Sched. 1 to the Child Support Act 1991, as amended).

The maintenance calculation is based on the NRP's net income or benefit status, and takes no account of the child's age or individual needs. The amount of child maintenance depends on the following factors: the number of children who qualify for child maintenance; the NRP's income and circumstances; and the number of any relevant 'other children' living with the NRP. In most cases, maintenance is worked out as a percentage of the NRP's net weekly income (income after National Insurance, tax and pension contributions have been deducted). No account is taken of the PWC's income or the income of either person's current partner.

In *Secretary of State for Work and Pensions* v. *M* [2006] UKHL 11, where the mother (the NRP) was living with her lesbian partner, and the father was the PWC, the Court of Appeal held that the provisions of the child support regulations should be read so as to include persons of the same sex – in order to ensure that there is no discrimination under art. 14 European Convention for the Protection of Human Rights taken in conjunction with art. 8 (right to family life). However, the House of Lords allowed the appeal of the Secretary of State (Baroness Hale dissenting) and held that art. 8 was not engaged.

### Child Support Rates

There are four child support rates. In most cases the basic rate applies, but, if the NRP does not earn much, or is in receipt of certain benefits, the reduced rate or flat rate applies. A nil rate applies to certain categories of persons. Special rules apply to special cases. For example, if care of the child (or children) is shared, the level of maintenance paid by the NRP is reduced.

**The Basic Rate (NRP's weekly net income is £200 or more)**   The NRP pays the following percentage of net weekly income as child support maintenance (para. 2(1) of Part 1 of Sched. 1):

- 15 per cent for one qualifying child;
- 20 per cent for two qualifying children;
- 25 per cent for three or more qualifying children.

**Example**  A NRP with a weekly net income of £400 will pay £60 for one child, and £100 for three or more children.

There is a maximum amount of net weekly income that can be taken into account when calculating child maintenance (currently £2,000), but the PWC can apply to the court for 'top-up' maintenance if the NRP's net weekly income exceeds £2,000. 'Top up' maintenance granted by the court can be collected by the Agency with child support.

**The Reduced Rate (NRP's net weekly income is more than £100 but less than £200)**   The NRP pays a flat rate of £5 a week on the first £100 of net income, plus a percentage of net weekly income over £100. The percentage is different from the basic rate. It depends on the number of qualifying children and the number of relevant other children (para. 3 of Part 1 of Sched. 1). The rates are available on the Child Support Agency's website.

**The Flat Rate (NRP has a net weekly income of £100 or less, or the NRP or his or her partner is in receipt of certain prescribed benefits, pensions and allowances)**   The flat rate is £5 a week for any number of children (para. 4 of Part 1 of Sched. 1). If the NRP has a partner, the NRP pays half the flat rate (£2.50 a week). If both members of a couple, in receipt of Income Support or Jobseeker's Allowance, are NRPs and both have a child maintenance calculation, they each pay child maintenance at a flat rate of £2.50.

*The Nil Rate*   Some NRPs have a nil rate of liability, such as those with a net weekly income of less than £5, children in full-time non-advanced education, people engaged in work-based training, full-time students, prisoners, 16- or 17-year-olds in receipt of Income Support or income-based Jobseeker's Allowance (para. 5 of Part 1 of Sched. 1).

*The Default Rate*   Where the information needed to calculate child maintenance cannot be obtained straightaway, the default rate applies, which is £30 per week for one qualifying child, £40 for two qualifying children and £50 for three or more children. When the information needed to complete a maintenance calculation is provided, the new liability will come into effect.

### Deductions for Relevant 'Other Children'

Less child maintenance is paid by the NRP where there are relevant 'other children' living with the NRP (for example, step-children or the NRP's children from a new relationship) (para. 10C(2) of Part 1 of Sched. 1). In such cases a lower amount of net weekly income is used for calculating child maintenance. Thus, the NRP's income is reduced by: 15 per cent if there is one relevant other child; 20 per cent if there are two relevant other children; and 25 per cent if there are three or more relevant other children.

**Example**  If the NRP has a net weekly income of £400 and one relevant other child, 15 per cent is deducted from his or her net weekly income, leaving £340 for the purpose of calculating child maintenance. Fifteen per cent of £340 is £51, so the qualifying child gets £51 instead of £60.

### Shared Care

Where the care of a qualifying child is shared between both parents for 52 or more nights a year, a discount is made when calculating the basic or reduced rate of maintenance (para. 7 of Part 1 of Sched. 1). Thus, in basic rate or reduced rate cases the amount of child maintenance payable each week is reduced for the child by: one-seventh for 52–103 nights; two-sevenths for 104–155 nights; three-sevenths for 156–174 nights; and one-half for 175 nights or more. There is an additional reduction in maintenance of £7 for each child that the NRP looks after for more than 175 nights or more a year.

If a NRP pays maintenance at the basic or reduced rate, maintenance cannot be reduced below £5 as a result of shared care. NRPs who pay the flat rate (because they receive a benefit, pension or allowance) will pay no maintenance if they share care of the qualifying child for a minimum of 52 nights a year.

### Variations from the Formula

The Child Support Act 1991 was amended by the Child Support Act 1995 to allow a variation from the formula in certain exceptional and clearly defined circumstances (see Part 1 of Sched. 4B). A variation can lead to an increase or reduction in the amount of child maintenance. A variation can be applied for at any time (s.28A). The grounds for permitting a variation fall into three categories:

- *Special Expenses* The NRP can apply to have certain special expenses taken into account in the calculation of maintenance payable (that is, contact costs; costs arising from the long-term illness or disability of a relevant other child; boarding school fees; prior debts; payments in respect of certain mortgages, loans, and insurance polices) (para. 2 of Part 1 of Sched. 4B). 'Prior debts' does not include, for example, credit card debts, business debts, fines, certain loans and debts relating to divorce or separation. The special expenses must be more than a specified amount each week, except in the case of costs arising from the long-term illness or disability of a relevant other child.
- *Pre-April 1993 Property or Capital Transfers* A reduction in maintenance may be allowed if the NRP transferred property or capital to the person with care before 5 April 1993 partly or wholly in lieu of child maintenance (para. 3 of Part 1 of Sched. 4B).
- *Additional Cases* A PWC can apply for an increase in child maintenance if the simple system of rates leads to an amount of maintenance which does not properly reflect the NRP's true circumstances (para. 4 of Part 1 of Sched. 4B). Thus, a PWC may be eligible for a variation if the NRP has a lifestyle which is inconsistent with the level of income which has been (or would be) used for the maintenance calculation.

An application for variation can be made at any time. An application is subject to a preliminary consideration (s.28B). On a preliminary consideration, the Agency can reject the application if there are no grounds, insufficient information, or other prescribed circumstances prevail (s.28B(2)). Once it has passed the preliminary stage, the application will be considered in detail by a decision-maker, or, in a complex case, by a tribunal. The person considering the application must be satisfied that the case falls into one of the categories above, and that it is just and equitable in all the circumstances to agree to a variation (ss.28F(1), (2)). Any appeal against the decision must be brought within one calendar month of notification of the variation decision, but this one-month period can be extended if there are special circumstances.

### (h) Appeals

The first level of appeal against a decision made under the child support scheme is to the Child Support Appeal Tribunal (s.20(4)). The Tribunal may make a decision itself or remit the matter to the Secretary of State (s.20(8)). The person aggrieved, or the Secretary of State, has a right of appeal from the Child Support Appeal Tribunal to a Child Support Commissioner, but only on a question of law (s.24), and a right to a further appeal on a question of law to the Court of Appeal (s.25). Appeals must be made in writing.

### (i) Collection and Enforcement of Child Support Maintenance

*Collection Arrangements* The Agency provides a collection service for the payment of child maintenance on behalf of the PWC. Those PWCs who are on benefit are obliged to use this service (s.6(1)), but non-benefit PWCs can, if they wish, make their own arrangements about payment (ss.4(1), (2)). If the collection service is used, the Agency will usually give the NRP the choice of paying by direct debit or standing order, or by voluntary deduction from earnings order, and will stipulate the intervals at which payment is to be made (s.29(2)). The Agency can direct that the NRP try and open a bank or building society account for the purpose of making payment easier. If payment is not made, a deduction from earnings order can be made.

*Financial Penalties and Deduction from Earnings Orders*　A NRP who fails to make payment, or who makes insufficient payment, can be charged a financial penalty of up to 25 per cent of the maintenance due and which may be charged for each week that is unpaid (s.41A). This money goes to the Exchequer, not the PWC.

If the NRP fails to pay, and is in employment, the Agency can make a deduction from earnings order (s.31), whereby the payer's employer is instructed to make deductions of maintenance from the payer's earnings at source and send them to the Agency. When deciding whether to make an order, the Agency must have regard to the welfare of any child likely to be affected. There is a limited right of appeal to the magistrates' court against the making of an order (s.32(5)).

*Enforcement Measures in the Court*　If the person liable for child maintenance fails to make payment, and it is 'inappropriate' to make a deduction from earnings order, or if that order is ineffective, the Child Support Agency (in the guise of the Secretary of State) may apply to the magistrates' court for a liability order (s.33), which the magistrates can make if satisfied that the payments in question have become payable and have not been paid (s.33(3)). The magistrates cannot question the Agency's maintenance assessment (s.33(4)). A liability order can be enforced by distress (sale and seizure of goods by bailiffs to meet payment) (s.35); or in the county court by means of a garnishee order (on funds in a bank or building society) or a charging order (whereby property is sold to make payment) (s.36). An order can be enforced in other parts of the UK.

The House of Lords in *Farley* v. *Secretary of State for Work and Pensions* [2006] UKHL 31, [2006] 2 FLR 1243 examined the role of magistrates' courts in respect of their power in applications for liability orders under s.33 (as there was some uncertainty as to whether or not the magistrates' court had an adjudicative power under s.33 Child Support Act 1991 to determine whether a NRP was a liable person for child support purposes). Their Lordships unanimously held that the language of s.33(4) was clear. On an application for a liability order, the magistrates' court must proceed on the basis that the CSA's maintenance assessment was lawfully and properly made. The court was precluded from questioning any aspect of that assessment. Any challenge to a child support assessment should be made through the statutory appeals machinery. Lord Nicholls stated (at para. 25) that it would have been 'surprising and undesirable if the magistrates' court were to have a parallel jurisdiction to adjudicate upon the same question'.

If enforcement measures fail, more severe measures can be imposed. Thus, magistrates can have the NRP's driving licence removed, or stop the NRP obtaining one, if there is wilful refusal or culpable neglect in respect of paying child maintenance (ss.39A and 40B). In the last resort, a defaulting NRP may be committed to prison, on proof of wilful refusal or culpable neglect in making payment (see s.40).

### Parents Cannot Institute Court Proceedings to Enforce Payment

In the following case the House of Lords held that parents cannot take steps to enforce child maintenance payments in the courts – only the Child Support Agency can do so:

▶ *R (On the Application of Kehoe)* v. *Secretary of State for Work and Pensions* [2005] UKHL 48, [2005] 2 FLR 1249

The father (the NRP) failed to make payments of child maintenance to the mother. Various enforcement measures were taken by the Agency, but these failed. The mother brought judicial review proceedings seeking a declaration of incompatibility under s.4(2) Human Rights Act 1998 on the basis that the enforcement provisions of the Child Support Act 1991 were incompatible with art. 6 of the European Convention for the Protection of Human Rights (the right to a fair trial), because they precluded a parent from bringing enforcement proceedings in the court in her own name or on behalf of her children. She also sought a declaration that the delay by the Agency constituted a breach of her art. 6 rights. She claimed damages under s.7 Human Rights Act 1998. Wall J dismissed the application for a declaration of incompatibility but held that the claimant's inability personally to enforce arrears of child maintenance engaged her rights under art. 6. The Court of Appeal allowed the Secretary of State's appeal in relation to art. 6. The mother appealed to the House of Lords.

The House of Lords dismissed the mother's appeal (Baroness Hale dissenting) and affirmed the decision of the Court of Appeal, holding that the system under the Child Support Act 1991 which prevented the claimant from playing any part in the process of enforcing her entitlement to child support was not incompatible with art. 6(1). The claimant had no substantive right in domestic law which was capable in Convention law of engaging the guarantees that were afforded with regard to 'civil rights and obligations' by art. 6(1). The Child Support Act 1991 had deliberately avoided conferring on the PWC a right to enforce a child maintenance assessment against the NRP. Enforcement was exclusively a matter for the Agency. As art. 6(1) was not engaged, the Agency could not be said to have acted unlawfully within the meaning of s.7 Human Rights Act 1998, and accordingly the claimant had no remedy under that Act.

**BARONESS HALE** (dissenting): '[I]f I am right that the children's civil rights to be properly maintained by their parents are engaged, it follows that the public authority which is charged by Parliament with securing the determination and enforcement of their rights is under a duty to act compatibly with their art. 6 right to the speedy determination and effective enforcement of those rights. . . . Just as the courts, as public authorities, have to act compliantly with the Convention rights, so does the Agency.'

*Note:* The *'Henshaw Report'* (see 13.2, above) suggests that the effects of this case might be reversed, thereby ending the monopoly of the Agency in respect of enforcement actions. Resolution has also called for a reversal of the decision in *Kehoe* to enable parents to take their own enforcement actions (see [2006] Fam Law 892).

The Child Support Act 1991 was also held to constitute a complete code in respect of enforcement measures in *Department of Social Security* v. *Butler* [1995] 1 WLR 1528 (heard before the Human Rights Act 1998 came into force), where the Court of Appeal held that the court has no jurisdiction to grant a *Mareva* injunction (an order freezing a person's property assets) to the Secretary of State against a NRP who fails to make payment of child support.

*Bringing an Action in Negligence Against the CSA*   A negligence claim is unlikely to succeed as the following case (the first negligence claim to be brought against the CSA) shows:

> ▶ *R (Rowley) v. Secretary of State for Work and Pensions* [2007] EWCA Civ 598, [2007] 2 FLR 945
>
> A mother and her three children brought an action in negligence against the CSA seeking damages for its negligent failure to deal with the assessment, collection and enforcement of maintenance owed by the non-resident father. At first instance, the Secretary of State was successful in having the claim struck out on the ground that the claimants were owed no duty of care. The claimants appealed to the Court of Appeal.
>
> The Court of Appeal held, dismissing their appeal, that there was no assumption of responsibility on the part of the Secretary of State, and that to impose a duty of care in negligence would not be an incremental development of the law but a massive extension of it. The remedies provided by s.20 Child Support Act 1991 (right of appeal) and s.41 (right to receive interest) and the right to seek judicial review provided a parent with care with substantial protection and a sufficiently comprehensive remedy. To impose a duty of care in negligence would be inconsistent with the statutory scheme.

Thus, in *Rowley*, a similar approach was taken to that taken by the House of Lords in *Kehoe* (above), in other words that sufficient remedies were available within the statutory scheme of the Child Support Act 1991. However, in *Kehoe*, Baroness Hale (dissenting) had stated that the case was one which had been presented to the House of Lords 'largely as a case about adults' rights when in reality it [was] a case about children's rights'. The same can perhaps be said about the *Rowley* case. In other negligence claims involving children the courts have held that there is a duty of care, at least in the area of child protection (see 15.12). *Rowley* is essentially a policy decision to stop a flood of claims being brought against the Agency by aggrieved parents and children.

### (j) Making a Complaint

Any person dissatisfied with the service provided by the Agency can make a complaint to the Agency. If still not satisfied, a complainant can write to the Independent Case Examiner, who has a duty to investigate the complaint (but not if it involves a matter of law). A complaint can also be made to the Ombudsman (the Parliamentary Commissioner for Administration). The Agency can make special payments to persons who have suffered financial loss, inconvenience, or whose health has been affected as a result of a mistake and/or delay by the Agency. Independent advice about child maintenance can be sought from Citizens Advice Bureaux, Members of Parliament and solicitors. Appeals against a maintenance assessment are also available (see above).

### (k) The Role of the Courts

*(i) Court Order in Force*  Where a court order (or a written maintenance agreement made before 5 April 1993) provides for regular payment of child maintenance by the NRP for a qualifying child, any variation of the amount of child maintenance must be decided by the court, subject to the following two exceptions:

1. First, in benefits cases, a court order (or written agreement) in respect of child maintenance ceases to have effect (from when the maintenance calculation comes into force), if the PWC claims Income Support or income-based Jobseeker's Allowance, or is living with someone who claims these benefits.

2. Secondly, in non-benefit cases, if the parties agree about the amount of child maintenance and that agreement is confirmed by the court under the terms of a consent order made on or after 3 March 2003, and it has been in force for at least one year, either party may give the other party two months' notice of his or her intention to resile from that agreement and to apply to the Agency (s.4(10)(aa)). In such a case, the Agency calculation comes into effect two months and two days after the date of the application, whereupon the court order ceases to have effect. If no application is made to the Agency in these circumstances, the court retains jurisdiction to vary the court order.

*(ii) Residual Role of the Courts*   The court retains a residual role in respect of child maintenance – as the general principle of the child support scheme is that, where the Agency has jurisdiction to make a maintenance assessment, then the court is barred from exercising any power it would otherwise have to make, vary, or revive any maintenance order in respect of a child (s.8(3)).

However, the court retains the power to make child maintenance orders in the following situations:

- *To 'Top Up' a Maintenance Assessment (s.8(6))* Where a maximum Agency assessment is in force (see p.327, above), the PWC may apply for a 'top-up order' for periodical payments from the court.
- *For School Fees and Fees for Advanced Education or Training for a Trade, Profession or Vocation (s.8(7))* A court order for schools fees or educational expenses can be made whether or not there has been a child support calculation, but the court order must be made solely for the purpose of requiring provision of some or all of the expenses incurred in connection with the provision of the instruction or training. (For an example of a school fees case, see *T* v. *T (Financial Provision: Private Education)* [2005] EWHC 2119 (Fam), [2006] 1 FLR 903.)
- *For a Disabled Child (s.8(8))* The court can make an order whether or not a child support calculation is in force, but the order must be made solely to meet some or all of any expenses attributable to the child's disability. A child is disabled if he is blind, deaf or dumb, or is substantially and permanently handicapped by illness, injury, mental disorder or congenital deformity, or any prescribed disability (s.8(9)).
- *For a Child Who is Not a 'Qualifying Child' as Defined by s.55* For example: a child aged 17 or 18 who is not in full-time education, or who is in advanced education (at university or undergoing training for a profession or vocation); a 'child' aged over 18 in higher education; or a step-child.
- *When Making, Varying and Enforcing a Consent Order Which Embodies Periodical Payments for a Child (ss.8(5)–(11))* A party to a consent order made before 3 April 2003 (who is not in receipt of prescribed welfare benefits) cannot apply to the Agency – the court retains jurisdiction. Different rules apply to consent orders made after that date (see above).
- *When Enforcing a Maintenance Agreement Made Between Parents for the Benefit of Their Child* But such an agreement cannot prevent a person from applying to the Agency for a maintenance assessment, and the court does not have jurisdiction to vary the agreement if the Agency would have jurisdiction to make an assessment (ss.9(3), (4) and (5)).

▷ *Where Maintenance is Required from the Caring Parent (s.8(10))*
▷ *Where the Agency Has No Jurisdiction to Make a Maintenance Calculation* For example, because a parent is not habitually resident in the UK.

In addition, the courts retain their jurisdiction to make lump sum and property orders for children (see below), and these orders may be used for maintenance purposes if the child support scheme has not been invoked (see *V* v. *V (Child Maintenance)* [2001] 2 FLR 799).

## 13.4 Finance and Property Orders for Children from the Courts

In addition to maintenance for children, which is available from the courts in a residual category of cases (see above), the court can make lump sum orders and property orders to or for the benefit of a child. These powers can be exercised in divorce (nullity and judicial separation) proceedings, and in proceedings for the dissolution (annulment or separation) of a civil partnership. Section 15 and Sched. 1 to the Children Act 1989 also give the court power to make orders irrespective of the parents' marital status (see 13.5, below). The courts have a wide discretion, but they must apply certain statutory criteria when exercising their discretion to decide whether to make an order, and, if so, in what manner.

### (a) Orders for Children on Divorce and Dissolution of a Civil Partnership

Under Part II of the Matrimonial Causes Act 1973 the divorce court can make periodical payments orders (maintenance) and lump sum orders for a child in proceedings for divorce (or annulment or judicial separation) (s.23). A 'child of the family' includes the parents' own child, any step-child and a privately fostered child (but not a child in local authority care). The divorce court can also make the following property orders to or for the benefit of a child of the family (s.24): a transfer of property order; a settlement of property order; an order varying an ante-nuptial agreement; a post-nuptial settlement for the benefit of the child; and an order for the sale of property (s.24A). (For more on the divorce court's powers, see Chapter 8.)

The above orders can be made to or for the benefit of (s.29): a child under 18; and a child over 18 who is, will be, or would be (if an order were made), receiving instruction at an educational establishment or undergoing training for a trade, profession or vocation, or where special circumstances justify an order being made.

When exercising its discretion to decide whether to make an order and, if so, in what manner, the court must consider all the circumstances of the case, including in particular (s.25(3)): the child's financial needs, income, earning capacity (if any), property and other financial resources; any physical or mental disability of the child; and the manner in which the child is expected to be educated or trained. It must also take into account factors (a)–(d) of s.25(2) Matrimonial Causes Act 1973 checklist, that is, the spouses' resources and financial needs, the standard of living enjoyed by the family before marriage breakdown and any disability of either spouse (see 8.4).

Where the court is exercising its powers against a spouse in favour of a child of the family who is not a child of that party (such as a step-child) the court must also have regard to (s.25(4)): whether that party assumed any responsibility for child maintenance, and, if so, the extent to which, and the basis upon which, that party assumed such responsibility and the length of time for which that party discharged such responsibility; whether in assuming and discharging such responsibility that party did so knowing that the child was not his or her own; and the liability of any other person to maintain the child.

Similar provisions apply in respect of the dissolution (or annulment or separation) of a civil partnership (see s.72(1) and Sched. 1 to the Civil Partnership Act 2004).

### (b)    Orders for Children During a Marriage or Civil Partnership

Orders can be sought from (i) the family proceedings court, or (ii) the county court. These provisions are rarely invoked, however, because child maintenance in most cases must be sought from the Child Support Agency (see above), and, in any event, it is rare for married couples (and civil partners) to seek such orders during the subsistence of their relationship.

*(i) In the Family Proceedings Court*    Under the Domestic Proceedings and Magistrates' Courts Act 1978 the magistrates in the family proceedings court can make periodical payments orders and lump sum orders for parties to a marriage and children of the family. Lump sums are currently limited to a maximum of £1,000 (s.2(3)).

An application can be brought by either spouse on the grounds that the other spouse (s.1): (a) has failed to provide reasonable maintenance for the applicant; (b) has failed to provide, or to make a proper contribution towards, reasonable maintenance for any child of the family; (c) has behaved in such a way that the applicant cannot reasonably be expected to live with the applicant; or (d) has deserted the applicant.

The statutory criteria which the court must apply when exercising its discretion are similar to those in s.25 Matrimonial Causes Act 1973 which must be applied by the divorce court in proceedings for ancillary relief (see above, and 8.4), but with the additional requirement that the magistrates must consider whether to exercise any of the powers they have under the Children Act 1989 (s.8) (see Chapter 11).

Similar provisions apply to civil partnerships under s.72(3) and Sched. 6 to the Civil Partnership Act 2004.

*(ii) In the County Court*    Under s.27 Matrimonial Causes Act 1973 either spouse can apply to the county court for reasonable maintenance (periodical payments and lump sums) on the ground that the other spouse has (a) failed to provide reasonable maintenance for the applicant, or (b) has failed to provide, or to make a proper contribution towards, reasonable maintenance for any child of the family (s.27(1)). The statutory criteria under s.25 which apply to applications for ancillary relief on divorce must be applied (see 8.4).

Similar provisions apply to civil partnerships under s.72(1) and Sched. 5 to the Civil Partnership Act 2004.

### 13.5    Finance and Property Orders for Children Under the Children Act 1989

Under s.15 and paras. 1 and 2 of Schedule 1 to the Children Act 1989 magistrates' family proceedings courts, county courts and the High Court can make periodical payments orders, lump sum orders and property orders for children aged under 18, and for some children aged over 18. The court can only make these orders on an application, unless it is making, varying or discharging a residence order (para. 1(6)), or the child is a ward of court (para. 1(7)), when it can make any of these orders of its own motion.

### (a) Orders Under Paragraph 1

On an application by a parent, guardian or special guardian of a child, or by any person in whose favour a residence order is in force with respect to a child, the court may make any of the following orders against either or both parents of a child (including a step-parent) (paras. 1(1), (2)):

- a periodical payments order (secured or unsecured);
- a lump sum order, provided that such an order may be made to enable expenses in connection with the birth or maintenance of the child, which were reasonably incurred before the making of the order, to be met (Sched. 1, para. 5(1));
- a settlement of property order;
- a transfer of property order.

These orders can be made in favour of the applicant for the benefit of the child, or in favour of the child – except for a settlement of property order which can only be made for the benefit of the child. The High Court and the county court can make any of these orders (para. 1(1)(a)), but the powers of the magistrates in the family proceedings court are limited (see below). The powers conferred under para. 1 may be exercised at any time (para. 1(3)). Periodical payments (unsecured and secured) can be varied and discharged (see below). The court can make further periodical payments orders (unsecured or secured) and lump sum orders with respect to a child who has not reached the age of 18, but it cannot make more than one settlement of property order and more than one transfer of property order (para. 1(5)). This is so, even though para. 1(3) provides that the power to make such orders can be 'exercised at any time' (see *Phillips* v. *Peace* [2004] EWHC 3180 (Fam), [2005] 2 FLR 1212).

### (b) Orders Under Paragraph 2

The court may make periodical payments orders and lump sum orders for a child aged over 18 against one or both parents (but not against a step-parent or foster-parent, para. 16). The court can make these orders on the application of a child aged over 18 who is, will be, or (if an order were made) would be, receiving instruction at an educational establishment or undergoing training for a trade, profession or vocation (whether or not while in gainful employment). The court can also make an order where special circumstances exist. An application under para. 2 cannot be made by any person, if immediately before the child reached the age of 16, a periodical payments order was in force with respect to the child (para. 2(3)). No order can be made under para. 2 if the applicant's parents are living with each other in the same household (para. 2(4)).

### (c) Variation and Discharge of Periodical Payments

Periodical payments orders made under Sched. 1 can be varied or discharged on the application of any person by or to whom payments were required to be made (paras. 1(4) and 2(5)). In exercising its powers of variation or discharge, the court must have regard to all the circumstances of the case, including any change in any of the matters to which the court was to have regard when making the order (para. 6(1)).

### (d) Limits on the Magistrates' Jurisdiction

The magistrates in the family proceedings court have limited powers. Thus, they cannot order the transfer and settlement of property and can only make unsecured, not secured, periodical payments orders. They can make lump sum orders but these are limited to a maximum of £1,000. County courts and the High Court, on the other hand, can make the whole range of orders.

### (e) The Exercise of Discretion

Each case depends on it own facts, but when deciding whether to exercise its powers to make orders under paras. 1 and 2, and if so in what manner, the court must have regard to all the circumstances, including (para. 4(1)):

'(a) the income, earning capacity, property and other financial resources which the applicant, parents and the person in whose favour the order would be made has, or is likely to have, in the foreseeable future;
(b) the financial needs, obligations and responsibilities which the persons named in (a) have or are likely to have in the foreseeable future;
(c) the financial needs of the child;
(d) the income, earning capacity (if any), property and other financial resources of the child;
(e) any physical or mental disability of the child; and
(f) the manner in which the child is being, or is expected to be, educated or trained.'

Where the court is exercising its powers under para. 1 against a person who is not the child's mother or father (such as in the case of a step-child), the court must also consider (para. 4(2)):

'(a) whether that person has assumed responsibility for the child's maintenance and, if so, the extent to which and the basis on which that responsibility was assumed and the length of the period during which he met that responsibility;
(b) whether he did so knowing that the child was not his child;
(c) the liability of any other person to maintain the child.'

### (f) The Approach of the Courts

The following approaches have been adopted by the courts in applications under Sched. 1:

▶ *The Child's Welfare* Although para. 4(1) of Sched. 1 does not expressly refer to the child's welfare, and the paramountcy principle in s.1(1) Children Act 1989 does not apply (see s.105(1) Children Act 1989), the child's welfare is nonetheless taken into account as part of the court's general duty to have regard to all the circumstances; and the child's welfare is 'a constant influence on the discretionary outcome' (Thorpe LJ in *Re P (Child: Financial Provision)* [2003] EWCA Civ 837, [2003] 2 FLR 865, approving Hale J in *J v. C (Child: Financial Provision)* [1999] 1 FLR 152).

▷ *The 'No-Order' Principle in s.1(5) Children Act 1989 (see 11.3)* This does not apply to applications under Sched. 1 (*K v. H (Child Maintenance)* [1993] 2 FLR 61).

▷ *The Child's Standard of Living* Although para. 4 of Sched. 1 makes no mention of the child's standard of living as a factor to be taken into account, the court may take it into account in an appropriate case (see *Re P (Child: Financial Provision)* [2003] EWCA Civ 837, [2003] 2 FLR 865, where Thorpe LJ, approving Hale J in *J v. C (Child: Financial Provision)* (above), said that the child was entitled to be brought up in circumstances which bore some sort of relationship to the father's current resources and present standard of living). (See also *F v. G (Child: Financial Provision)* [2004] EWHC 1848 (Fam), [2005] 1 FLR 261.)

▷ *The Child's Entitlement Under Sched. 1* The entitlement to financial provision under Sched. 1 arises only during the child's dependency or until the child has finished full-time education, unless the child's circumstances are special (for example if the child has a disability). For this reason, the court will usually only make orders to last during the child's dependency or until the child has finished full-time education. This also applies to the provision of a home for the child.

▷ *A Home for the Child* In respect of the home, the court will usually make a settlement of property order (a '*Mesher* type' property adjustment order, see p.190) settling the home on the primary-carer for the benefit of the child, so that ownership will revert back to the owner at the end of the child's dependency or full-time education. Even where the parent who owns the home is incredibly wealthy, the court will not usually order an outright transfer of the home to the other parent (see *A v. A (Financial Provision)* [1994] 1 FLR 657). In *T v. S (Financial Provision for Children)* [1994] 2 FLR 883 an order was made that the property revert back to the father when the youngest child reached the age of 21. In *J v. C* (above), where the father had won £1.4 million on the national lottery, Hale J made an order requiring the father to purchase a house for the child to live in with her mother, which would be held on trust for the child's benefit throughout her dependency and revert to her father when she reached the age of 21 or finished full-time education, whichever was the later.

▷ *Financial Provision for the Benefit of the Child* The courts will guard against claims disguised as being for the benefit of a child when they are really for the benefit of the parent who is caring for the child (see Thorpe LJ in *Re P (Child: Financial Provision)*, above approving Hale J in *J v. C*, above). However, in *Re S (Child: Financial Provision)* [2004] EWCA Civ 1685, [2005] 2 FLR 94 the Court of Appeal held that the words 'for the benefit of the child' in Sched. 1 should be given a wide construction, and could include the cost of the mother travelling to the Sudan to see her child, and to pursue legal proceedings there, even though this might be for the benefit of the mother, as well as the child. The Court of Appeal distinguished *W v. J (Child: Variation of Financial Provision)* [2003] EWHC 2657 (Fam), [2004] 2 FLR 300, where Bennet J had held that the court had no jurisdiction under Sched. 1 to order a parent to pay the applicant a sum to cover the applicant's legal fees in relation to litigation about a child – as such payment was not 'for the benefit of the child' as required by para. 1(2)(a) of Sched. 1. In *Haroutnian v. Jennings* [1980] FLR 62 it was held that it was not wrong for the court to augment a periodical payments order for a child to include an allowance for the mother, especially if the mother had had to give up work, or was unable to work, because she had to look after the child.

▶ *A Broad-Brush Approach* In *Re P (Child: Financial Provision)* [2003] EWCA Civ 837, [2003] 2 FLR 865 the Court of Appeal held that a broad-brush assessment should be adopted in claims under Sched. 1, but that the starting point is to decide on the home that the respondent should provide for the child. It also held that a broad common-sense assessment of the amount of periodical payments should be taken, but that in making that assessment the judge should recognise the responsibility, and often the sacrifice, of the parent who was the primary, or perhaps the exclusive, carer of the child.

▶ *Separate Representation of the Child* In *Morgan* v. *Hill* [2006] EWCA Civ 1602, [2007] 1 FLR 1480 Thorpe LJ said that in exceptional cases brought under Schedule 1 the court should consider separate representation of the child. In *Re S (Unmarried Parents: Financial Provisions)* [2006] EWCA Civ 479, [2006] 2 FLR 950 Thorpe LJ reiterated this point, and said that the facts of that case provided, in his opinion, 'a neat illustration of the advantages of ensuring separate representation for the child in some cases brought under s.15 of the Children Act 1989'. Here the child's father and mother were engaged in an intense and bitter battle and Thorpe LJ said that it was easy to see how in such circumstances 'the crux of the case can be lost to view unless there is some advocate there to urge constantly the needs and interests of the child' – for whom the award is largely designed to satisfy.

*Agreements About Maintenance*    Under para. 10(3) of Schedule 1 the court has the power to alter the terms of an agreement about maintenance where it appears just to do so having regard to all the circumstance in cases: where there has been a change of circumstances; or where the agreement does not contain proper financial arrangements with respect to the child. In *Morgan* v. *Hill* (above) the Court of Appeal held that it was not necessary to demonstrate that such an agreement was massively inadequate in order to obtain a judicial award greater than the agreed settlement.

## Summary

1 All parents have a duty to maintain their children, and all children have a right to be maintained.

2 If a parent fails to provide maintenance, an application can be made for child support from the Child Support Agency, which has the power under the Child Support Act 1991 to calculate, collect and enforce child support maintenance payments. The calculation is not based on discretion, but on percentages of the non-parent's net weekly income and the number of qualifying and relevant other children. Deductions are made for shared care. Variations are permitted in certain limited and exceptional circumstances. The Agency is responsible for enforcing payments, and so a parent cannot apply for enforcement in the court. The Child Support Agency has been criticised since its inception, because of delays, errors and its inadequate enforcement powers.

3 The Government is proposing to make radical reforms to the child support system whereby parents will be encouraged to make their own maintenance agreements and a new body (the Child Maintenance and Enforcement Commission) will concentrate on hard cases and use much tougher enforcement measures.

## Summary cont'd

4   Maintenance can be sought from the courts in certain cases (for example, in school fees cases, where a child is disabled, where the parents are wealthy, or where the Agency does not have jurisdiction).

5   Periodical payments orders, lump sum orders and property adjustment orders can be sought for children on divorce (and on nullity and judicial separation) under Part II of the Matrimonial Causes Act 1973. These orders can also be sought under s.72(1) and Sched. 5 to the Civil Partnership Act 2004 on the dissolution (annulment or separation) of a civil partnership.

6   During marriage, a parent may seek periodical payments (maintenance) and lump sums for a child from the magistrates' family proceedings courts under the Domestic Proceedings and Magistrates' Courts Act 1978. Civil partners can do the same under s.72(3) and Sched. 6 to the Civil Partnership Act 2004. The same orders for children (and also property adjustment orders) can be sought during marriage from the county court and the High Court under s.27 Matrimonial Causes Act 1973 (and also during a civil partnership under s.72(1) and Sched. 5 to the Civil Partnership Act 2004).

7   Orders for financial relief (periodical payments, lump sums, settlements and transfers of property) can be sought under s.15 and para. 1 of Sched. 1 to the Children Act 1989 by parents, guardians, special guardians and persons with a residence order in their favour. Children aged over 18 can apply under para. 2 for periodical payments and lump sums against their parents.

## Further Reading and References

Gilmore, 'Re P (Child) (Financial Provision) – shoeboxes and comical shopping trips – child support from the affluent to fabulously rich' [2004] CFLQ 103.

Sheldon, 'Unwilling fathers and abortion – terminating men's child support obligations' (2003) MLR 175.

Wikeley, 'R (Kehoe) v. Secretary of State for Work and Pensions: no redress when the Child Support Agency fails to deliver' [2005] CFLQ 113.

Wikeley, Child Support: Law and Policy, 2006, Hart Publishing.

## Websites

**Child Support Agency**: www.csa.gov.uk

**Department for Work and Pensions**: www.dwp.gov.uk

# Chapter 14
## Child Abduction

> **Article 11  United Nations Convention on the Rights of the Child 1989**
>
> '1. States Parties shall take measures to combat the illicit transfer and non-return of children abroad.
> 2. To this end, States Parties shall promote the conclusion of bilateral or multilateral agreements or accession to existing agreements.'
>
> **The Legislation**
>
> **Child Abduction Act 1984**  Creates a criminal offence of taking children out of the UK without consent.
>
> **Child Abduction and Custody Act 1985**  Ratifies the 'Hague Convention' and the 'European Convention', two international conventions which make provision for facilitating the return of abducted children.
>
> **Family Law Act 1986**  Provides legal mechanisms for returning children abducted within the different parts of the UK.
>
> **Children Act 1989**  Provides for a range of orders which can be used to prevent abduction, and to permit the lawful movement of children to countries outside England and Wales.

This chapter deals with child abduction both at the national and international levels. It concentrates mainly on the civil, rather than the criminal, law, and deals, in particular, with two international conventions on child abduction, the Hague Convention and the European Convention. It also considers the law governing abductions into England and Wales from 'non-convention' countries. The steps that parents can take to prevent abduction and how parents can legally take a child out of the UK are also addressed.

## 14.1  Introduction

Child abduction is a distressing consequence of family breakdown. It is also a widespread problem arising from increases in family breakdown, the increasing numbers of international marriages and the greater and easier movement of persons.

The courts deal with a range of issues relating to child abduction. Not only do they deal with international abduction cases where a child has been brought into the UK from abroad, but they hear cases where a parent wishes to take a child out of the UK but the other parent objects. The courts can make orders preventing a parent, or other person, taking a child out of the UK, and orders declaring that the removal of a child from the UK is wrongful. They can also make orders asking for information about an abducted child to be disclosed to the court.

Advice about child abduction is available from the Child Abduction Unit (based at the Ministry of Justice, formerly the Department for Constitutional Affairs) and from the Foreign and Commonwealth Office. The Passport Office can provide information about issuing passports where there is a risk of abduction.

The Office of the Head of International Justice deals with queries about international family matters including abduction and relocation, and issues arising under Brussels II Revised (Council Regulation (EC) (No. 2201/ 2003)). The Rt Hon Lord Justice Thorpe is the Head.

## 14.2　Tracing a Child

Tracing a child can be a distressing, difficult and lengthy process. Furthermore, the longer it takes to trace a child, the more settled the child will be in his new environment, so that effecting return may be even more difficult. There are various ways of tracing a child. Where a child has been abducted within or into the UK, information which may help in tracing a child can be obtained from various Government departments, such as the Passport Office, the NHS Central Register, the Child Support Agency and the Ministry of Defence. Where a child has been abducted from the UK to a foreign country, the Foreign and Commonwealth Office and foreign Embassies can help. In order to help trace a child, the court can make orders requiring a person to disclose information about a child. Using the media to publicise a case of abduction may also yield results.

## 14.3　Preventing Abduction

Where there is a risk of abduction, preventative measures should be urgently taken, as once a child has left the UK, the chances of finding and returning the child are more difficult. Where there is a danger of removal, a parent should be vigilant. The following steps can be taken to prevent abduction:

### (a)　Police Assistance: The 'All Ports Warning'

As child abduction is a criminal offence, a parent, or any other person, who believes that a child has been abducted, or may be about to be, can inform the police. The police have various powers. They can arrest any person who is abducting or is suspected of abducting a child. They can also bring into effect an 'All Ports Warning', whereby details of the child and the abductor are sent by the police national computer to ports and airports across the UK to prevent the child leaving the country. The application for a port alert must be *bona fide*, and there must be a real and imminent danger of removal. The person seeking assistance will be required to provide the police with as much information as possible, for example about the child, the abductor, the likely time of travel, the port of departure and so on.

### (b)　A Court Order

Where there is a risk of abduction it may be advisable to obtain a court order. A court order is useful for several reasons. Not only is breach of an order contempt of court, but it may be useful if a parent wishes to institute proceedings or seek the help of various agencies abroad. Furthermore, although an order is not needed to institute a port alert, it provides useful evidence of a genuine risk of abduction.

*Orders Under s.8 Children Act 1989*　A useful range of orders is available under s.8 Children Act 1989 (see 11.4). For example, where there is a risk of an abduction, a prohibited steps order could be sought prohibiting the child's removal from the UK. A dispute about whether the child should be allowed to leave the UK could be settled by an application for a s.8 specific issue order. A residence order can also be used, because, if a residence order is made, the child cannot be removed from the UK without the written consent of every person with parental responsibility, or otherwise the consent of the court (s.13(1)(b) Children Act 1989) – except for a period of up to one month by the person with the residence order (s.13(2)). Similar restrictions exist in respect of taking a child in local authority care out of the UK (s.33(7)).

The court can make a s.8 order (see 11.4) even if the child has been abducted, but it may be reluctant to do so where there may be problems enforcing the order abroad (*Re D (Child: Removal from Jurisdiction)* [1992] 1 WLR 315). Where urgent action is needed the court can make a s.8 order without the respondent being given notice of the proceedings (see, for example, *Re B (A Minor) (Residence Order: Ex Parte)* [1992] Fam 162). Orders without notice do not breach art. 6 of the European Convention for the Protection of Human Rights (the right to a fair trial) (*Re J (Abduction: Wrongful Removal)* [2000] 1 FLR 78).

In an exceptional case, where there is a danger that a parent may attempt to remove a child out of England and Wales, or the UK, the court can impose a direction on a residence order (under s.11(7) Children Act 1989) requiring a parent to live in a defined geographical area (see *B v. B (Residence: Condition Limiting Geographic Area)* [2004] 2 FLR 979, where the children who were living with their mother had told the CAFCASS Children and Family Reporter that their mother wanted to go to Australia to get away from their father). However, such restrictions are rarely imposed.

*Wardship*   As an alternative to a s.8 order, an application can be made to the High Court for the child to be made a ward of court (see 9.7, and, for example, *Re B (Child Abduction: Wardship: Power to Detain)* [1994] 2 FLR 479). The advantage of wardship is that the situation is frozen immediately the application is made, so that any attempt to remove the child from the UK without the court's consent may be contempt of court. The court continues to have a supervisory role over the ward, so that no major step in the child's life can be taken without its consent.

*Other Powers of the Court*   Under the inherent jurisdiction and under statute, the court can order a person to disclose a child's whereabouts (s.33 Family Law Act 1986 and s.24A Child Abduction and Custody Act 1985; and see *Re H (Abduction: Whereabouts Order to Solicitors)* [2000] 1 FLR 766). The county court can authorise an officer of the court, or a police constable, to take charge of a child and deliver him to a named person. The High Court can make a 'seek and find' order requiring the tipstaff (a court official) to find the child and deliver him as directed by the court, or a 'seek and locate' order requiring that the child be located. The High Court can also make an order permitting media publicity about the child, or requiring any person to disclose information about the child to the court, or requesting the disclosure of an address from a Government department or agency. The court can also order the surrender of passports (s.37 Family Law Act 1986).

*Court Orders and the Unmarried Father*   An unmarried father without parental responsibility whose child has been abducted, or is about to be, should consider acquiring parental responsibility (see 10.6), a prohibited steps order and/or a residence order (see 11.7 and 11.5).

### (c) Passport Control

Since 5 October 1998, children under 16 are required to have their own passport (to make it more difficult for parents to abduct children). Children on parents' passports before that date are permitted to travel on that passport until they reach 16 or the passport expires. The Passport Service will issue a passport for a child at the request of either parent or a person with parental responsibility. To prevent abduction, a parent or person with parental responsibility can contact the UK Passport Service and object to the child being issued with a passport. The Passport Service will require the objector to have one of the following orders: a prohibited steps order; an order confirming that the child's removal from the UK is contrary to the wishes of the court; a residence order in his favour; an order stating that the objector's consent is needed to the child's removal from the UK; or an order upholding the objector's objections to the child having a passport or leaving the UK.

In cases where there is a risk of abduction, a restriction can be placed on the child's or likely abductor's passport. Where a child has a UK passport (or is included on a parent's UK passport) the court can order the surrender of that passport where an order restricting removal is in force (s.37 Family Law Act 1986; and see *Re A (Return of Passport)* [1997] 2 FLR 137). The court can order the surrender of a non-UK passport under its inherent jurisdiction (see 9.7, and *Re A-K (Foreign Passport: Jurisdiction)* [1997] 2 FLR 569). The passport can be ordered to be surrendered to the court or to a solicitor. A s.8 order under the Children Act 1989 can be made conditional on a suspected abductor depositing his passport with a solicitor.

## 14.4 Removing a Child Lawfully from the UK

On family breakdown, a parent (usually the primary-carer of the child) may wish to take the child temporarily or permanently out of the UK. A parent can do this, provided he or she is not in breach of any statutory provision or court order.

*Obtaining the Necessary Consents*  A parent who wishes to take a child out of the UK must obtain the consent of all persons who have parental responsibility for the child, otherwise he or she may commit a criminal offence under the Child Abduction Act 1984 (see below), or be in contempt of court if there is a court order prohibiting the child's removal. Oral consent to take the child abroad is usually sufficient, except where a residence order is in force (see 11.5) when written consent is needed of all persons with parental responsibility – unless the holder of the residence order intends to go abroad for less than one month.

### (a) Relocation Applications

After family breakdown the primary-carer (often the mother) may wish to take the child out of the UK, perhaps to start a new relationship, or to take up a new job, or to move back to his or her country of origin. The other parent (often the father) may refuse to agree to this, perhaps because of the difficulty of maintaining contact, or because of a fear that the child will not be returned. Where the necessary consents to take the child out of the UK (see above) are not forthcoming, the court's permission must be sought in order to avoid a conviction for child abduction (see 14.5) or contempt of court.

Permission to leave the UK (that is, to relocate) can be sought by applying for a s.8 specific issue order (see 11.8), or, if a residence order is in force, by applying under s.13(1)

Children Act 1989. The court will apply the welfare principle in s.1(1) Children Act 1989 and the other s.1 welfare principles (see 11.3).

The approach of the courts in relocation cases has been to permit a reasonable and properly thought-out relocation application, unless this is clearly incompatible with the child's welfare. This approach was laid down by the Court of Appeal nearly forty years ago in *Poel* v. *Poel* [1970] WLR 1469. There had to be a compelling reason to justify refusing a reasonable decision to take the child to live outside the UK (see *Re H (Application to Remove from Jurisdiction)* [1998] 1 FLR 848). The rationale for the presumption in favour of allowing a reasonable application was that the primary-carer might become bitter and resentful if the application to relocate was refused, and this could detrimentally impact on the child's welfare. Relocation applications were therefore usually successful (see, for example, *Re K (Application to Remove from Jurisdiction)* [1998] 2 FLR 1006; and *Re M (Leave to Remove Child from Jurisdiction)* [1999] 2 FLR 334; although permission was sometimes refused (see *Re C (Leave to Remove from Jurisdiction)* [2000] 2 FLR 457; and *Re T (Removal from Jurisdiction)* [1996] 2 FLR 252).

With the coming into force of the Human Rights Act 1998, however, parents (mostly fathers) began to argue that the presumption in favour of permitting a reasonable relocation application breached their human rights under the European Convention for the Protection of Human Rights (ECHR). They also argued that the presumption was contrary to the welfare principle in s.1(1) Children Act 1989 – because it failed to treat the child's welfare as the court's paramount consideration:

▶ *Re A (Permission to Remove Child from Jurisdiction: Human Rights)* [2000] 2 FLR 225

The father argued that, if the court gave the mother permission to take their child to New York, it would be a breach of his right to family life under art. 8 ECHR. The Court of Appeal refused to accept his argument, holding that, while art. 8 gave the father and the child a right to family life, it gave the mother a right to a private life, and art. 8(2) required the court to balance such rights where they were in conflict. It held that the test laid down in *Poel* v. *Poel* was not in conflict with the ECHR. In fact, Buxton LJ doubted whether difficult balancing questions of this nature fell within the purview of the ECHR at all.

In the following case, the leading case, the Court of Appeal reviewed the long line of authority on relocation applications in the light of the new obligations imposed on the courts by the Human Rights Act 1998:

▶ *Payne* v. *Payne* [2001] EWCA Civ 1166, [2001] 1 FLR 1052

The mother (the primary carer) applied for permission to remove her daughter (aged 4) permanently from the UK to live with her in New Zealand. The child's father opposed the application and applied for a residence order. The father and the paternal grandmother had regular and exceptionally good staying contact with the child. The mother's application was granted at first instance, applying the principle in *Poel* v. *Poel* (above) that the move would be in the child's best interests because it would make her mother happy. The father appealed to the Court of Appeal, arguing: that contact between children and non-residential parents had increased in importance since the decision in *Poel* v. *Poel*; that the principles in relocation applications were inconsistent with the Children Act 1989 as they created a presumption in favour of the applicant; and that the court's approach was inconsistent with the Human Rights Act (HRA) 1998.

The Court of Appeal dismissed his appeal, holding that there was no conflict between the case-law governing relocation applications and the European Convention for the Protection of Human Rights (ECHR), and the Children Act 1989. It said that the proposition in *Poel* (that a reasonable application would be allowed) did not amount to a presumption in favour of the primary-carer. It held that the child's welfare is always the court's paramount consideration, and that the welfare checklist in s.1(3) Children Act 1989 (see 11.3) should be used by a judge when carrying out the welfare test.

Butler-Sloss P said that, although the reasonable proposals of the residential parent wishing to live abroad carried great weight, they had to be scrutinised carefully so that the court could be satisfied that there was a genuine motivation for the move and not an intention to terminate contact between the child and the other parent. Her Ladyship said that the effect on the child of a denial of contact with the non-resident parent and his family was an important consideration, and that the opportunity for continuing contact between the child and the parent left behind in the UK might be a very significant factor.

Thorpe LJ agreed with Ward LJ in *Re A (Permission to Remove Child from Jurisdiction: Human Rights)* (above) that the advent of the ECHR in domestic law by the HRA 1998 did not necessitate a revision of the fundamental approach to relocation applications formulated by the Court of Appeal and consistently applied over so many years. His Lordship said that 'in a united family the right to family life is a shared right', but that 'once a family unit disintegrates the separating members' separate rights can only be to a fragmented family life'. In the present case the mother's right to mobility under art. 2 of Protocol 4 of the European Convention was another relevant right to be considered.

While each relocation case turns on its own facts, the following are likely to be important factors: housing, education and contact arrangements; potential cultural difficulties for the child; and the nature of the child's bond with the parents. The child's wishes will also be important, as they were in *M v. A (Wardship: Removal from Jurisdiction)* [1993] 2 FLR 715 where the mother's application to relocate was refused as her plans were not reasonable and did not accommodate the needs and wishes of the children who did not wish the status quo to be changed. In *Re H (A Child)* [2007] EWCA Civ 222, [2007] 2 FLR 317 Thorpe LJ said that a fundamentally important part of the judge's task in deciding a finely balanced relocation case was to assess the impact on the caring parent of a decision to refuse permission to relocate. He said that this was 'often the most important single task that confronts the judge'.

An applicant is not required to prove that he or she will suffer psychiatric damage if permission to relocate is refused – all that is required is that a refusal will have an impact on the applicant's sense of well-being and that this will be transmitted to the children (see *Re G (Removal from Jurisdiction)* [2005] EWCA Civ 170, [2005] 2 FLR 166 where the Court of Appeal granted the mother permission to remove the children to Argentina, subject to a condition that continued contact arrangements, the children's schooling and the cessation of the mother's periodical payments be agreed, or, in the absence of agreement, be remitted to the county court and settled there before departure). (For another application of *Payne v. Payne* see *L v. L (Leave to Remove Children from Jurisdiction: Effect on Children)* [2002] EWHC 2577 (Fam), [2003] 1 FLR 900.)

### Case-Law Examples

▶ *Re B (Leave to Remove: Impact of Refusal)* [2004] EWCA Civ 956, [2005] 2 FLR 239

The Court of Appeal allowed the mother's appeal against a refusal by the judge to allow her to go to Australia with the children, and remitted the case for a retrial, as the judge had erred in not giving full consideration to the impact that a refusal of her realistic proposal would have on the mother. Thorpe LJ, with whom May and Scott Baker LJJ agreed, said that it was important to give great weight to the emotional and psychological well-being of the primary-carer, and not merely take note of the impact on the primary-carer of refusing the application to relocate. Thorpe LJ said that 'each case turned on its own facts, but that the applicant's explanation for fundamental relocation is the core of every case'.

▶ *Re B (Removal from Jurisdiction); Re S (Removal from Jurisdiction)* [2003] EWCA Civ 1149, [2003] 2 FLR 1043

Relocation applications were granted, but subject to orders reflecting generous contact. The Court of Appeal held that, where a mother cared for a child within a new family, the impact of a refusal to allow her to leave the jurisdiction on the new family and step-father, or prospective step-father, must be carefully analysed and evaluated. Thorpe LJ said that this consideration applied with even greater force where a step-father was a foreign national. To jeopardise the new family's survival or blight its potential for fulfilment and happiness would be manifestly contrary to the welfare of any child of the family.

▶ *R v. R (Leave to Remove)* [2004] EWHC 2572 (Fam), [2005] 1 FLR 687

Baron J refused the application to remove the children to France, as: the mother (who had psychiatric problems) did not have the necessary emotional stability to establish a new life in another country; the children's contact with their father would be adversely affected; and the mother's plans had not been sufficiently or carefully considered. Baron J applied the paramountcy principle in s.1(1) Children Act 1989, and the factors in the 'welfare checklist' in s.1(3), and, applying *Poel* v. *Poel* and *Payne* v. *Payne* (above), considered the short-, medium-, and long-term welfare of the children.

▶ *Re Y (Leave to Remove from Jurisdiction)* [2004] 2 FLR 330

The child's mother, an American, had married a Welshman and lived in Wales. They divorced, but had an informal shared-care arrangement for their son who had made good progress at his Welsh school and who was bilingual with Welsh as his preferred language. The mother wished to return to the USA with the boy. The mother's application for permission to take the child to the USA was refused, as Hedley J held, applying the observations of Dame Elizabeth Butler-Sloss P in *Payne* v. *Payne* (above), that her case fell well outside the ambit of well-established authorities. In the circumstances, applying the principle that the child's welfare is the paramount consideration (s.1(1) Children Act 1989), the course of least detriment to the child would be for him to continue to live in Wales.

▶ *Re F (Leave to Remove)* [2005] EWHC 2705 (Fam)

The mother's application to remove the child to Jamaica was refused, as her plans were genuine but ill-conceived. Her plans to support herself and the child were wildly speculative. The research into schools had been poor and the school chosen was unsuitable because neither parent could afford it. There were insufficient funds to provide for regular airfares for contact visits, and the mother's hostility to the father might make contact difficult. As Jamaica was not a party to the Hague Convention (see below), the father might have difficulties enforcing a contact order. There would be no benefit to the child in relocating, and the close bond with his father would be severed. If the mother remained here in the jurisdiction her life would not be thwarted.

(See also *Re H (Removal from Jurisdiction)* [2007] EWCA Civ 222.)

*Cultural and Religious Objections to Relocation*  Cultural and religious objections to a parent relocating outside the UK will not usually be allowed to prevail over the primary consideration in relocation cases, which is the welfare of the child. In *Re A (Leave to Remove: Cultural and Religious Considerations)* [2006] EWHC 421 (Fam), [2007] 2 FLR 572 Hedley J allowed the child's mother to relocate with her son (aged 9) to The Netherlands, where she lived with her new husband, despite the father's arguments that his son should remain in England for religious and cultural reasons (in particular, so that he could succeed to the mantle head of the family group).

Payne v. Payne *May be Hardly Relevant in an Unusual Case*  In an unusual fact situation, the principles in *Payne* v. *Payne* may hardly be relevant, as the following case shows:

> ▶ *Re J (Leave to Remove: Urgent Case)* [2006] EWCA Civ 1897, [2007] 1 FLR 2033
>
> The parents had three children, two of whom were living with the father, and the youngest with the mother. Both parents were applying for residence orders. Because of the father's financial situation, the judge granted the father permission to relocate to Bulgaria. The mother appealed to the Court of Appeal on the basis that the father had not made satisfactory practical arrangements for the children.
>
> The Court of Appeal dismissed her appeal. Thorpe LJ (who gave judgment in *Payne* v. *Payne* ) said that, in the circumstances of this unusual case (where the judge had to consider whether a mother's proposals for a residence order should be implemented in this country and the father's residence order be implemented in another) the principles in *Payne* v. *Payne* hardly applied. However, in so far as *Payne* applied, the principles strongly pointed to the father's application being granted.

*Is the Approach in Relocation Cases the Correct One?*  Concern has been expressed that the approach of the courts in relocation cases is wrong – because it places too much emphasis on the reasonable wishes and proposals of the applicant parent, rather than looking at the best interests of the child from the point of view of having the benefit of maintaining a relationship with both parents with the psychological, educational and emotional advantages which that can bring. There is also concern that the courts are denying children their contact rights with the non-resident parent (usually the father).

Spon-Smith (2004) claims that the conventional approach to relocation applications is not supported by American research (by Braver *et al*, 2003) which shows that children do not necessarily benefit from moving with the residential parent to a new location which is distant from the other parent. Worwood (2005) says that in New Zealand the 'emerging trend is for the courts to deny relocation' (p.623), and she states (at p.627) that this area of family law 'is extremely problematic'.

Hayes (2006) argues that trial judges are being prevented by strong rulings from the Court of Appeal from exercising their discretion in relocation cases in a broad and principled manner. She claims that the 'discipline' recommended in *Payne* v. *Payne*, and entrenched as a ruling of law by subsequent Court of Appeal judgments, is misguided because the gloss *Payne* places on the welfare principle narrows the proper application of that principle and is biased in favour of the residential parent (who is almost invariably the mother).

Herring and Taylor (2006) argue that in relocation cases the courts have failed to take into account adequately enough the impact of human rights' reasoning. They say that the Human Rights Act 1998 requires the court to assess the competing interests of all the parties, not just the welfare of the child. However, they argue that, even if a human rights-based approach was adopted, permission to leave should normally be granted to a resident parent who has good reason to relocate.

### (b)  Relocation Within the UK

In respect of relocations from England and Wales to another part of the UK, the Court of Appeal held in *Re H (Children: Residence Order: Condition)* [2001] EWCA Civ 1338, [2001] 2 FLR 1277 that the court must adopt a similar approach to that in *Payne* v. *Payne* (above). The Court of Appeal held that, while the test for internal relocations was less stringent than that for external relocations, relocation within the UK could be highly problematic, and, following *Payne*, the court must always apply the welfare test as the paramount consideration.

### (c)  Temporary Removals

Sometimes a parent may wish to take the child temporarily, not permanently, out of the UK. In some cases the court's permission will be needed. In the following case, the Court of Appeal considered how the courts should deal with applications for temporary removal:

> ▶ *Re A (Temporary Removal from Jurisdiction)* [2004] EWCA Civ 1587, [2005] 1 FLR 639
>
> The child (aged 4) spent five nights a week with the mother, and two nights with the father under the terms of a shared residence order. The mother applied for permission to take the child to South Africa for two years to carry out research for her doctorate. The judge, applying the principles in *Payne* v. *Payne* (above), which apply to permanent removals, refused the application. The Court of Appeal allowed the mother's appeal, as the judge had erred in holding that the considerations which govern decisions about applications for permanent removal of the child should also apply, without modification, to applications for temporary removal. The considerations relevant to an application for permission to relocate permanently were not automatically applicable to applications for temporary removal. Thorpe LJ said: 'The more temporary the removal, the less regard should be paid to the principles stated in *Payne* v. *Payne*.'

*Practical Safeguards to Ensure the Child's Return*    If there is a risk that a parent will not return after a temporary stay outside the UK, the court in England and Wales can impose certain safeguards. Thus, it may: impose a condition on a court order; require an undertaking to be given to the court; require the parties to enter into a notarised agreement containing provisions about returning the child; require 'mirror' orders (orders equivalent to English orders) to be applied for in the foreign court; order a parent to swear on the Holy Qur'an before a Shariah Court that the child will be returned; and/or order a parent to provide a sum of money as surety for the child's return (see, for example, *Re L (Removal from Jurisdiction: Holiday)* [2001] 1 FLR 241).

The following case provides a good example of the court imposing a range of practical safeguards to ensure return:

▶ *Re S (Leave to Remove from Jurisdiction: Securing Return from Holiday)* [2001] 2 FLR 507

The court wished to ensure that the mother would return the children after taking them to India on holiday. She was ordered to: return them by a certain date and not to return them to India without the father's written permission; to deposit the children's passports with her solicitors in India; to provide the father with copies of the airline tickets and the children's visas from the Indian High Commission; to seek only short tourist visas (that order to be served on the Indian High Commission); and not to seek Indian passports or Indian citizenship for the children while in India. The children were made wards of court, and the court made declarations that their habitual residence was England and Wales and that they were British citizens.

## 14.5 Abduction – The Criminal Law

A person who abducts, or attempts to abduct, a child from the UK may commit a criminal offence under: (a) the Child Abduction Act 1984; or (b) the common law.

### (a) The Child Abduction Act 1984

Persons 'connected with a child' (s.1) and 'other persons' (s.2) can commit a criminal offence under the Child Abduction Act (CAA) 1984.

*(i) Persons 'Connected with a Child'* Under s.1 CAA 1984 it is an offence for a person 'connected with a child' under 16 to take or send the child out of the UK without the 'appropriate consent'. A person 'connected with a child' is: a parent (including an unmarried father if there are reasonable grounds for believing he is the father); a guardian; a special guardian; any person with a residence order in their favour; and any person with custody of the child (s.1). 'Appropriate consent' means the consent of: the mother; the father (with parental responsibility); a guardian; a special guardian; any person with a residence order in force in their favour; and any person with custody of the child (s.1(2)(a)).

'Appropriate consent' can include the court's consent where it is required under Part II of the Children Act 1989 (ss.1(2)(b), (c)) (for example, where a residence order is in force, see s.13). However, a person with a residence order in force with respect to the child does not commit a criminal offence if he or she takes the child out of the UK for less than one month, unless this is in breach of another s.8 order (s.1(4)).

It is a defence under the Act if the accused believed that the other person consented to the abduction, or would have consented had he or she been aware of all the circumstances; or the accused was unable to communicate with the other person despite taking reasonable steps to do so (s.1(5)). It is also a defence if the other person unreasonably refused consent to the child being taken out of the UK (but this defence does not apply if the person refusing consent has a residence order in his or her favour; or the person taking or sending the child out of the UK did so in breach of a court order) (s.1(5A)).

*(ii) 'Other Persons'*  Under s.2 a person who is not 'connected with a child' under s.1 commits the offence of child abduction if, without lawful authority or reasonable excuse, he or she takes or detains a child under the age of 16 so as to remove the child from the lawful control of any person having lawful control of the child, or so as to keep the child out of the lawful control of any person entitled to lawful control (s.2(1)). An unmarried father without parental responsibility comes under s.2, unless he is the child's guardian, or has a residence order in his favour, or has custody of the child. An unmarried father, however, has a defence if he can prove that he is the child's father, or that at the time of the alleged offence he reasonably believed that he was the child's father (s.2(3)(a)). It is also a defence if the accused believed that at the time of the alleged offence the child had attained the age of 16 (s.2(3)(b)).

In *Foster and Another* v. *Director of Public Prosecutions* [2004] EWHC 2955 (Admin), [2005] 1 FCR 153 it was held that the mental state for an offence under s.2 is an intentional or reckless taking or detention of a child under the age of 16, but that the offence cannot be proved if the child is no longer in the lawful custody of the person from whom he has been removed.

### (b)  The Offence of Kidnapping

A person who abducts a child unlawfully may commit the common law offence of kidnapping (see, for example, *R* v. *D* [1984] AC 778). Where the child is under 16 and the person removing the child is a person 'connected with' the child under s.1 Child Abduction Act 1984 (above), the consent of the Director of Public Prosecutions is needed to bring a prosecution (s.5 CAA 1984). The offence of kidnapping is rarely used, but may be relevant where an abduction involves a child aged over 16 – as such a child does not come within the scope of the 1984 Act (above).

### 14.6  Child Abduction Within the UK

Under the Family Law Act 1986 a court order relating to a child made in one part of the UK can be recognised and enforced in another part. Thus, for example, a s.8 order made under the Children Act 1989 in a court in England and Wales can be registered in, and enforced by, the Scottish or Northern Ireland courts as if the court there made the order. There is no need to consider the merits of the case afresh. Once registered, the court in that part of the UK has the same powers of enforcement as if it had made the original order. However, a parent and any other interested party can object to enforcement on the ground that the original order was made without jurisdiction; or, because of a change of circumstances, the original order should be varied. Although the court in the other part of the UK can stay proceedings or dismiss the application (ss.30 and 31), it is likely to enforce the order. Under the Act, the court has other powers which may be useful in abduction cases. It can order disclosure of a child's whereabouts (s.33), order recovery of a child (s.34), restrict removal of a child from the jurisdiction (s.35) and order the surrender of passports (s.37).

### 14.7  The Hague Convention on Abduction

#### (a)  Introduction

The UK is a Contracting State to the Hague Convention on the Civil Aspects of International Child Abduction 1980 (the 'Hague Convention'), which was implemented into UK law by Part I of the Child Abduction and Custody Act 1985. The text of the Convention can be found in Sched. 1 to the 1985 Act, and a list of Contracting States is available on Reunite's website (see below). States which are conspicuously absent from the list of Contracting States are those governed by Shariah law, a form of Islamic law.

The scheme of the Convention is to provide a speedy extradition-type remedy whereby Contracting States agree to return abducted children to their country of habitual residence so that the matter can be dealt with there. In this sense it is a provisional remedy, for Hague Convention proceedings are not concerned with the merits of a custody issue – that is a matter for the court in the child's country of habitual residence.

---

**Article 1 of the Hague Convention on the Civil Aspects of International Child Abduction 1980**

'The objects of the present Convention are –
(a) to secure the prompt return of children wrongfully removed to or retained in any Contracting State; and
(b) to ensure that rights of custody and of access under the law of one Contracting State are effectively respected in the other Contracting States.'

---

*Policy Considerations in the Hague Convention*  Various policy considerations are enshrined in the Convention. One is that children should be swiftly returned to their country of habitual residence. Another is the principle of 'comity', a principle of international law which requires courts to have respect for the courts and legal systems of foreign jurisdictions. Thus, the presumption lies in favour of returning a child, and it is generally assumed that if a country is a party to the Hague Convention, then the child's case will be dealt with in a welfare-oriented way. Baroness Hale has pointed to another policy of the Convention which 'is to deter abduction in the first place' and she states that '[t]he message should go out to potential abductors that there are no safe havens among the Contracting States' (para. 42 in *Re M and Another (Minors)* [2007] UKHL 55).

*How the Hague Convention Works*  The Convention works by establishing a network of Central Authorities who must co-operate with each other, and promote co-operation among the competent authorities in their respective States, in order to secure the prompt return of children and to achieve the other objects of the Convention (art. 7). Central Authorities have various duties under the Convention which include: discovering the child's whereabouts; preventing further harm to the child by taking provisional measures; securing the child's voluntary return; exchanging information; providing information and so on. The Central Authority for England and Wales for the purposes of the Convention (and the European Convention, see below) is the Child Abduction Unit, which is based in the Ministry of Justice. The Unit is responsible for making administrative arrangements under the Convention, in order to secure the return of abducted children, and to enforce rights of access. It also provides advice and assistance.

The Hague Convention is concerned with breaches of custody rights, not custody orders, and in this respect is quite different from the European Convention (below). Applications under the Hague Convention are heard by the Family Division of the High

Court (s.4 Child Abduction and Custody 1985), which can also make declarations that a removal or retention of a child outside the UK is wrongful under art. 3 of the Hague Convention (see below). If proceedings are brought under the Hague Convention and the European Convention, the Hague application takes precedence and must be heard first (s.16(4)(c) Child Abduction and Custody Act 1985).

As a decision under the Hague Convention is not a decision on the merits of a custody issue (art. 19), a decision made in Convention proceedings does not determine the child's long-term future – which will be decided by the court of the child's habitual residence (if a return order is made), or (if a return order is not made) in the court in England and Wales. The central question in Convention proceedings is whether the child should be returned to the court of his habitual residence, not whether the child should be returned to a particular person. The policy of the Convention is that disputes about children should be determined in the courts of the country of their habitual residence. In *C* v. *B (Abduction: Grave Risk)* [2005] EWHC 2988 (Fam), [2006] 1 FLR 1095 Sir Mark Potter P said that it was essential that the court hearing a return application did not usurp the function of the 'home' court by considering broader welfare considerations instead of confining itself to those matters which went to the establishment of the defence being relied upon under art. 13 of the Convention.

*The Hague Convention and Abductions Within the EU*    Many cases involve abductions within the European Union. In EU abductions, in addition to the Hague Convention, it is also necessary to take into account the provisions of Council Regulation (EC) (No. 2201/2003) *Concerning Jurisdiction and the Recognition and Enforcement of Judgments in Matrimonial Matters and in Matters of Parental Responsibility* (Brussels II Revised).

Where a judgment has been made in respect of a child in another EU Member State, Brussels II Revised takes precedence over the Hague Convention. For this reason, in *Re T and J (Abduction: Recognition of Foreign Judgment)* [2006] EWHC 1472 (Fam), [2006] 2 FLR 1290 a Spanish judgment (granting care and control of the children to the father, who was living in England) had to be taken into account, with the result that the mother's application for summary return of the children to Spain was refused by Sir Mark Potter P in the High Court.

The following case shows how Brussels II Revised can be relevant in a Hague Convention case:

▶ *Vigreux v. Michel* [2006] EWCA Civ 630, [2006] 2 FLR 1180

The child (a boy aged 14) had been brought to England from France by his father, after a French court had granted sole parental responsibility to the mother. McFarlane J in the High Court refused the mother's application for return, on the basis that the child's wishes, his sufficient age and maturity and certain welfare considerations weighed heavier in the balance than the policy objective of the Hague Convention (that children should be returned to their country of habitual residence). The mother appealed to the Court of Appeal.

The Court of Appeal allowed her appeal, holding that McFarlane J had erred in law in refusing to order return. Thorpe LJ held that the case was one in which the policy of the Hague Convention buttressed by the provisions of Brussels II Revised powerfully outweighed the child's objection defence raised under art. 13 of the Hague Convention. He held that, as the mother had been granted sole responsibility for the child, the French court, not the English court, had jurisdiction to take all the necessary decisions about the child's welfare. It was a French case and the father had refused to return to France only because of his breach of French orders and for fear of the consequences of the French legal system.

Brussels II Revised also imposes an obligation on the courts to hear return applications under the Hague Convention within six weeks (see further below).

*Speed is of the Essence*   In abduction cases any delay is contrary to the child's best interests – because the longer the situation remains undecided the more difficult it will be to disturb the status quo. Because of the importance of speed, Convention proceedings are summary. The court will not, for example, investigate the parent's marital situation or examine the child's welfare (Sir Stephen Brown P in *Re D (Abduction: Custody Rights)* [1999] 2 FLR 626). Cases are usually heard and decided upon on the basis of written evidence. Oral evidence is only sparingly permitted (see Butler-Sloss LJ in *Re F (A Minor) (Child Abduction: Rights of Custody Abroad)* [1995] Fam 224, [1995] 2 FLR 31). (For a case where oral evidence was permitted, see *Re M (Abduction: Leave to Appeal)* [1999] 2 FLR 550, where there was considerable violence against the mother by the father.)

Article 11(3) of Brussels II Revised (see above), which applies to EU Member States, requires proceedings for the return of a child to be completed within 6 weeks 'except where exceptional circumstances make this impossible'.

*The Welfare of the Child*   The welfare of the child is not paramount in Hague Convention cases. This is because 'it is presumed under the Convention that the welfare of children who have been abducted is best met by return to their habitual residence' (Butler-Sloss LJ in *Re M (A Minor) (Child Abduction)* [1994] 1 FLR 390). However, as Baroness Hale has emphasised (in *Re M and Another (Minors)* [2007] UKHL 55, see further below), the Convention is child-centred – as it is principally directed not towards the protection of adults, but of children. As Baroness Hale points out, the Preamble to the Convention refers to the fact that the Contracting States are 'firmly convinced that the interests of children are of paramount importance in matters relating to the custody of children'.

*Human Rights and the Hague Convention*   The European Court of Human Rights has held that a failure by a national authority (under domestic or international law) to secure the return of an abducted child can amount to a breach of art. 8 of the European Convention for the Protection of Human Rights (ECHR) (right to family life, see 1.5), and that national authorities must take positive measures to enable parents to be reunited with the child, unless contrary to the child's best interests. Breaches of art. 8 were found in *Gil and Aui v. Spain (Application No. 56673/00)* [2005] 1 FLR 190 and in *Maire v. Portugal (Application No. 48206/99)* [2004] 2 FLR 653, as the authorities had failed to take appropriate measures under the Hague Convention to secure the return of the abducted child.

In *S v. B (Abduction: Human Rights)* [2005] EWHC 733 (Fam), [2005] FLR 878 Sir Mark Potter P held that the driving policy of the Hague Convention is respect for family life within the meaning of art. 8 ECHR, in the sense that its underlying purpose is to protect children internationally from the harmful effects of their wrongful removal or retention from the care of the parent with custody rights.

*Access (Contact) Rights*   Although art. 21 of the Hague Convention provides that access rights may be secured, it confers no power on the courts to determine access matters, or to recognise or enforce foreign access orders. It merely provides for executive co-operation between Central Authorities for the recognition and enforcement of such access rights as national laws allow. Thus, in England and Wales the Child Abduction Unit (based at the Ministry of Justice) will provide assistance in finding a solicitor, help with legal aid and help in instituting proceedings for s.8 orders under the Children Act 1989 (see *Re G (A Minor) (Hague Convention: Access)* [1993] 1 FLR 669; and *Practice Note (Child Abduction – Lord Chancellor's Department)* [1993] 1 FLR 804). If a foreign access order is in force, an application can be made to have it recognised and enforced in the English court under the European Convention (see below, and see *Re A (Foreign Access Order: Enforcement)* [1996] 1 FLR 561).

Because of concerns about the difficulty of enforcing access rights at the international level, there has been strong support for the Hague Conference on Private International Law to investigate the feasibility of adding a Protocol to the Hague Convention to deal more specifically with the protection of access rights. In New Zealand the courts have adopted an approach whereby contact arrangements can amount to rights of custody, but this approach has not been adopted by the courts in England and Wales (see *H v. M (Abduction: Rights of Custody)* [2005] EWCA Civ 976).

## (b)   The Voice of the Child

***The Voice of the Child in Hague Convention Proceedings***   The usual way in which the voice of the child is heard in abduction proceedings is by means of a written report compiled by a CAFCASS officer (see 1.4), or by another professional, after having conducted an interview with the child (see, for example, *Re M (Abduction: Child's Objections)* [2007] EWCA Civ 260, [2007] 2 FLR 72; and *C v. B (Abduction: Grave Risk)* [2005] EWHC 2988 (Fam), [2006] 1 FLR 1095). There is no obligation on the judge to hear oral evidence even in a case where the art. 13(b) child's objection defence (see below) is being argued (Sir Mark Potter P in *Re M (Abduction: Child's Objections)* [2007] EWCA Civ 260, [2007] 2 FLR 72). In some cases the judge may wish to speak to the child, but this is not a common practice. In exceptional circumstances the child may have separate legal representation.

Although the child's voice may be put before the court, it does not necessarily mean that those views will be taken into account. Thus, in *C v. B (Abduction: Grave Risk)* [2005] EWHC 2988 (Fam), [2006] 1 FLR 1095, for example, the views of the 9-year-old child, whose mother did not wish to return to Australia, were put before the court by means of a CAFCASS report, but Sir Mark Potter P held that, while the child was of sufficient maturity to have his views taken into account, those views (anger with his father and concerns about his mother) did not provide a sufficient basis on which to withhold an order of return for him and his 5-year-old sister.

***Separate Legal Representation for the Child***   Children are not usually separately represented in Hague Convention proceedings. Although the court has the power to give permission for a child to intervene in proceedings, permission is rarely given. The Court of Appeal and a long line of authority has emphasised that a grant of permission to intervene is exceptional (see, for example, Wall LJ in *Re J (Abduction: Child's Objections to Return)* [2004] EWCA Civ 428, [2004] 2 FLR 64).

The age of the child is not of itself sufficient to constitute exceptional circumstances to justify separate representation, as the following case shows:

---

▶ *Re H (Abduction)* [2006] EWCA Civ 1247, [2007] 1 FLR 242

The trial judge refused to allow a 15-year-old girl to be made a party to Hague Convention proceedings. She appealed to the Court of Appeal. Counsel for the child argued (relying on *Mabon* v. *Mabon and Others* [2005] EWCA Civ 634, [2005] 2 FLR 1011, see 9.6) that, because greater freedom had been given to children to participate in private law proceedings, then the same freedom ought to be given in Hague Convention cases.

The Court of Appeal dismissed the appeal, referring to *dicta* of Sir Thomas Bingham MR in *Re M (A Minor)(Child Abduction)* [1994] 1 FLR 390, who had stated that, while there is jurisdiction to permit a child to be joined as party, 'it would rarely be right to exercise it, and compelling grounds would be needed'. The argument based on *Mabon* v. *Mabon* (see p.234) was rejected by the Court of Appeal because Hague Convention proceedings are summary proceedings where speed is of the essence. Wall LJ said that there were, in his judgment, 'material differences between the question of separate representation for a child in a welfare enquiry and separate representation in summary proceedings under an international convention, where the welfare enquiry is to take place elsewhere'.

---

A rare case where a child was given permission to be a party to Hague Convention proceedings was *Re L (Abduction: Child's Objections to Return)* [2002] EWHC 1864 (Fam), [2002] 2 FLR 1042 where a 14-year-old boy was given permission to be separately represented – because he had a distinctive point of view which needed to be heard independently from that of the defaulting parent.

*Are Children Being Heard Enough in Hague Convention Proceedings?* It has been increasingly recognised in Hague Convention cases that children may not be being heard enough. Baroness Hale, in particular, has voiced concern about this, and has called for more children to be separately represented. In *Re D (A Child)(Abduction: Rights of Custody)* [2006] UKHL 51, [2007] 1 FLR 961 Baroness Hale said that, 'whenever it seems likely that the child's views and interests may not be properly presented to the court, and in particular where there are legal arguments which the adult parties are not putting forward, then the child should be separately represented'.

In respect of abductions within the European Union, a failure to hear a child may breach art. 11(2) of Brussels II Revised (Council Regulation (EC) (No. 2201/2003) *Concerning Jurisdiction and the Recognition and Enforcement of Judgments in Matrimonial Matters and in Matters of Parental Responsibility*), which provides that:

'When applying articles 12 and 13 of the 1980 Hague Convention, it shall be ensured that the child is given the opportunity to be heard during the proceedings unless this appears inappropriate having regard to his or her age or degree of maturity'.

Although Brussels II Revised strictly applies only to cases between Member States within the European Union, Baroness Hale in *Re D* (above) held that, as the obligation to hear a child is a principle of universal application and consistent with the UK's obligations under art. 12 of the United Nations Convention on the Rights of the Child (see 9.2), the obligation to hear a child applies not just to European Union cases but to all Hague Convention cases. Her Ladyship held that it created a presumption that a child would be heard unless this appeared inappropriate. She warned, however, that listening to a child does not mean that the court should necessarily give effect to the child's views.

In *Re F (Abduction: Joinder of Child as Party)* [2007] EWCA Civ 393, [2007] 2 FLR 313

Thorpe LJ said that *Re D* (see above) was not to be interpreted as having the effect of lowering the bar with respect of granting party status to the child and he said that there remained a need to demonstrate that the case was sufficiently exceptional. Thorpe LJ said that '[h]earing the child is one thing and giving the child party status is quite another'. In *Re F* the Court of Appeal refused leave for the child (aged 7) to be joined in the proceedings, despite the mother's argument that the judge had not observed her obligation to hear the child under art. 11 Brussels II Revised. The Court of Appeal held that this refusal did not breach the child's human rights under arts. 6 (right to a fair hearing) and 8 (right to family life) of the European Convention for the Protection of Human Rights.

*Hearing the Child Must Not Delay Proceedings*   The Court of Appeal has held that the obligation to hear the wishes and feelings of the child must not be allowed to interfere with the principle that speed is of the essence in abduction cases. In *Re F (Abduction: Child's Wishes)* [2007] EWCA Civ 468, [2007] 2 FLR 697, which involved an EU abduction (from Spain to the UK), the Court of Appeal held that the failure to hear the child had been a fundamental deficiency but that, although there was an obligation to ascertain the child's wishes and feelings (under art. 11(2) of Brussels II Revised), this provision did not override the obligation in the same article to conclude the proceedings within 6 weeks. (See also *Re F (Abduction: Joinder of Child as Party)*, above.)

### (c)   Construing the Convention

As the Convention is an international legal instrument, the courts in England and Wales have stressed the importance of it being construed uniformly by courts in Contracting States (see Lord Browne-Wilkinson in *Re H (Minors) (Abduction: Acquiescence)* [1998] AC 72 at 87). To promote uniformity of construction, the Hague Conference has established the International Child Abduction Database (INCADAT) of leading Convention case-law from the Contracting States.

The courts in England and Wales adopt a purposive approach when construing the Convention. In *Re B (A Minor) (Abduction)* [1994] 2 FLR 249, at 257, Waite LJ said that the Convention was 'to be construed broadly as an international agreement according to its general tenor and purpose, without attributing to any of its terms a specialist meaning which the word or words in question would have acquired under the domestic law of England'.

In *Hunter v. Murrow (Abduction: Rights of Custody)* [2005] EWCA Civ 976, [2005] 2 FLR 1119 the Court of Appeal held that the Convention was a living instrument to be interpreted and applied as necessary to keep pace with social and other trends. It also held that questions involving the construction or interpretation of the Convention were to be answered according to the international jurisprudence of the Contracting States, not simply according to the law of a particular jurisdiction. In *Hunter v. Murrow* the Court of Appeal held that a declaration made under art. 15 of the Hague Convention by the New Zealand court (that the father enjoyed rights of custody prior to the child's removal to London and that the child's removal had been wrongful) was persuasive, but not binding on the court in England and Wales. The question of whether or not the father exercised rights of custody immediately prior to removal was one of domestic law in New Zealand and had to be distinguished from the separate question of whether those rights amounted to rights of custody within the autonomous meaning of the articles of the Hague Convention.

In respect of construing the Convention, in *Re M and Another (Minors)* [2007] UKHL 55 the House of Lords warned that the courts should not add additional words into the Convention (in that case, an additional test of 'exceptionality' to the circumstances under which a court should refuse to order the return of an abducted child, see further below). Baroness Hale, who gave the leading opinion, said (at para. 48):

> 'The Convention itself contains a simple, sensible and carefully thought out balance between various considerations, all aimed at serving the interests of children by deterring and, where appropriate, remedying international child abduction. Further elaboration with additional tests and checklists is not required.'

Baroness Hale said (at paras. 43 and 44) that, while the court is entitled to take into account the various policy aspects of the Convention (see above), that was 'the furthest one should go in seeking to put a gloss on the terms of the Convention'.

## 14.8 The Hague Convention – Jurisdiction

To come within the jurisdiction of the Convention the child must be under 16 and have been habitually resident in one Contracting State and taken to another. If the child has reached the age of 16 by the time of the hearing the High Court can consider the case under its inherent jurisdiction (*Re H (Abduction: Child of 16)* [2000] 2 FLR 51). The Convention does not apply to an unborn child (see *Re F (Abduction: Unborn Child)* [2006] EWHC 2199 (Fam), [2007] 1 FLR 627 – which involved a pregnant mother – where Hedley J said that, as the law of England and Wales conferred no independent rights or status on a foetus, it was not possible in law to abduct a foetus so as to constitute a wrongful removal for the purpose of art. 3 of the Hague Convention).

To come within the scope of the Convention, there must also have been a breach of a right of custody (art. 4) (see 14.9, below).

### (a) Habitual Residence

Habitual residence, not domicile, is the connecting factor used in the Hague Convention. In order for the Convention to apply, the child must have been resident in one Contracting State and moved to another one. If the child is not, or has ceased to be, habitually resident in a Contracting State, there can be no wrongful removal or retention of the child for the purposes of art. 3(a), and the child will fall outside the scope of the Convention. 'Habitual residence' is not defined in the Convention – its meaning must be determined from the case-law. In the following case Lord Brandon in the House of Lords laid down the principles which apply to the question of habitual residence:

---

▶ *Re J (A Minor) (Abduction: Custody Rights)* [1990] 2 AC 562, *sub nom C v. S (A Minor) (Abduction)* [1990] 2 FLR 442

The parents cohabited in Australia and had a young son (aged about 2). The parents' relationship broke down, and, without informing the father, the mother left Australia and flew to England with the child. It was her settled intention not to return to Australia, but to make a long-term home for herself and the child in England. Five days after her departure the father applied to the Australian court for sole custody and guardianship of the child, which was granted. The Australian court later made a declaration that the child's removal from Australia was wrongful under art. 3 of the Hague Convention. A month after the mother's departure, the Australian authorities applied to the English High Court under the Hague Convention for the child's immediate return to Australia.

The House of Lords refused the application for return on the ground that there had been no wrongful removal or retention for the purposes of art. 3. There had been no wrongful removal because, under the law of Western Australia, the father possessed no custody rights capable of being breached at the time when the mother left Australia. Neither was there wrongful retention, as the child had ceased to be habitually resident in Australia before the Australian court had made the custody order. This was because the mother had a unilateral right to determine the child's place of habitual residence (as the father had no custody rights when she left Australia), and her settled intention to come to England had terminated the child's habitual residence in Australia.

In respect of habitual residence Lord Brandon said that:

▶ Habitual residence is to be understood according to its ordinary and natural meaning.
▶ Whether a person is or is not habitually resident in a particular country is a question of fact to be decided by reference to all the circumstances of the case.
▶ There is a significant difference between a person ceasing to be habitually resident in country A, and subsequently becoming resident in country B. A person may cease to be habitually resident in country A in a single day, if he leaves it with a settled intention not to return but to take up long-term residence in country B. But an appreciable period of time and a settled intention are needed for a person to become habitually resident in country B. During that 'appreciable period of time' the person will have ceased to be habitually resident in country A, but not yet have become habitually resident in country B.
▶ In the case of a child of the same age as the child in this case, and who is in the sole lawful custody of his mother, the child's habitual residence will be the same as hers.

In *R* v. *Barnet London Borough Council ex parte Shah* [1983] 2 AC 309 Lord Scarman said that habitual residence is the country adopted voluntarily and for a settled purpose as part of the regular order of a person's life, whether of short or long duration. In *Al Habtoor* v. *Fotheringham* [2001] EWCA Civ 186, [2001] 1 FLR 951 Thorpe LJ said that habitual residence could be acquired 'even if the person's move was intended to be fulfilled within a comparatively short duration, or was only on a trial basis'.

There have been many reported abduction cases involving the issue of habitual residence, from which the following conclusions can be drawn:

**Habitual Residence – Some Conclusions from the Case-Law**

*Habitual residence may be established even after a short period of residence, provided there is a settled intention to reside in that country* (see, for example, *V* v. *B (A Minor) (Abduction)* [1991] 1 FLR 266, where two months' residence was held to be enough; and *Re AF (A Minor) (Child Abduction)* [1992] 1 FLR 548, where one-month's residence was enough).

*A short visit to a country does not necessarily start a period of habitual residence* (see, for example, *Re A (Abduction: Habitual Residence)* [1998] 1 FLR 497, where a three-week visit to Greece for what was akin to a holiday was held not to be an 'appreciable period of time' to create a new habitual residence).

*A child may have no habitual residence at all* (see *W and B* v. *H (Child Abduction: Surrogacy)* [2002] 1 FLR 1008, where a Californian couple's application in England for the return of twins born of an English surrogacy arrangement was refused under the Hague Convention as the twins were not habitually resident in California or England).

*A dependent child will not necessarily have the same habitual residence as a parent* (see *Al Habtoor* v. *Fotheringham* [2001] EWCA Civ 186, [2001] 1 FLR 951, a case brought in wardship, not under the Hague Convention, where the High Court refused jurisdiction as the applicant mother's nine-year-old child remained habitually resident in Dubai, even though she herself was habitually resident in England).

*It is not necessary for a person to remain continuously present in a particular country in order for him or her to retain residence there* (Millet LJ in *Re M (Abduction: Habitual Residence)* [1996] 1 FLR 887).

### (b) Wrongful Removal and Retention

There must be wrongful removal from, or wrongful retention in, a Contracting State in order for the case to come within the scope of the Convention. Wrongful removal and wrongful retention are mutually exclusive concepts (*Re H; Re S (Minors) (Abduction: Custody Rights)* [1991] 2 FLR 262). Wrongful removal occurs when a child is wrongfully removed from his place of habitual residence in breach of a right of custody. Wrongful retention occurs when, at the end of a period of lawful removal, a parent refuses to return a child. However, under art. 3, removal and retention are only wrongful if the removal or retention is in breach of a right of custody (see 14.9, below).

*A Declaration of Wrongful Removal*    Under s.8 Child Abduction and Custody Act 1985 the High Court, on an application made for the purposes of art. 15 of the Hague Convention by any person appearing to the court to have an interest in the matter, may make a declaration that the removal of the child from, or his retention outside, the UK is wrongful within the meaning of art. 3 of the Hague Convention. In *Re C (Child Abduction) (Unmarried Father: Rights of Custody)* [2002] EWHC 2219 (Fam), [2003] 1 FLR 252 Munby J said that the grant of declaratory relief under art. 15 is always a matter of discretion, but in the normal case where an applicant succeeds in persuading the court that a child has been wrongfully removed, and seeks a declaration to assist his prospects of obtaining substantive relief in the requested State, he can normally expect to have the court's discretion exercised in his favour.

A removal or retention is considered wrongful if it is in breach of a custody right (see below).

### 14.9 The Hague Convention – Rights of Custody

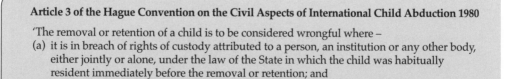

**Article 3 of the Hague Convention on the Civil Aspects of International Child Abduction 1980**

'The removal or retention of a child is to be considered wrongful where –
(a) it is in breach of rights of custody attributed to a person, an institution or any other body, either jointly or alone, under the law of the State in which the child was habitually resident immediately before the removal or retention; and
(b) at the time of removal or retention those rights were actually exercised, either jointly or alone, or would have been so exercised but for the removal or retention.'

The rights of custody mentioned in sub-para. (a) of art. 3 (above) may arise in particular by operation of law, or by reason of a judicial or administrative decision. Article 5(a) provides that for the purposes of the Convention, 'rights of custody' 'shall include rights relating to the care of the person of the child and, in particular, the right to determine the child's place of residence'.

In *Re P (Abduction: Consent)* [2004] EWCA Civ 971, [2004] 2 FLR 1057 the Court of Appeal held that the court's task under art. 3 is to establish the custody rights of the parent under the law of the relevant State, and then to consider whether those rights are rights of custody for the purposes of the Hague Convention (see also *Hunter* v. *Murrow*, above).

(a) A Purposive Construction of Custody

Under art. 5 there must be a breach of a custody right, otherwise the child's removal or retention is not wrongful for the purposes of art. 3. However, in order to give effect to the overriding policy objective of the Convention – which is that children should be expeditiously returned to their country of habitual residence – the English courts have adopted a purposive construction of the expression 'rights of custody' and have interpreted it broadly to include not just legal custody, but *de facto* (factual) custody. Thus, where a person has no custody rights in law, but is exercising rights of a parental or custodial nature, this can constitute custody. In this way, unmarried fathers without legal custody (or without parental responsibility) have been held to have custody rights, despite *Re J (A Minor) (Abduction: Custody Rights)* [1990] 2 AC 562, *sub nom C* v. *S (A Minor) (Abduction)* [1990] 2 FLR 442 (see 14.8, above), where the House of Lords took a narrow view of rights of custody. A broad view of custody was taken by the Court of Appeal in the following case:

▶ *Re B (A Minor) (Abduction)* [1994] 2 FLR 249

The parents were cohabitants living in Australia. The mother, who was a heroin addict, left Australia and went to England, leaving the child with the father and maternal grandmother. Later, the grandmother took the child to England and failed to return the child to Australia, which was in breach of an agreement made between the mother and father that the child would be returned within six months. The father, who had been an exemplary parent (but who had no legal custody), applied to the English High Court for an immediate return order under art. 12. The judge ordered the child's immediate return to Australia. The mother appealed to the Court of Appeal.

The Court of Appeal, by a majority, dismissed her appeal, and held that, as the purposes of the Convention were, in part, humanitarian, the Convention was to be construed broadly as an international agreement according to its general tenor and purpose, without attributing to any of its terms a specialist meaning which the sort of words in question might have acquired under the domestic law of England. The expression 'rights of custody', in most cases, had to be interpreted to give it the widest sense possible in order to accord with the objective of returning children to their country of habitual residence. Rights of an inchoate nature were sufficient to create rights of custody. The removal and retention of the child were held to be wrongful, and the child was ordered to be returned to Australia.

Although the facts in *Re B* were similar to those in *Re J (A Minor) (Abduction: Custody Rights)*, *sub nom C v. S (A Minor) (Abduction)* (see above), the majority of the Court of Appeal adopted a purposive construction and held that the father possessed *de facto* custody rights (he had cared for the child), which were sufficient to bring him within the scope of the Convention. Peter Gibson LJ, however, dissented as he considered that the Court of Appeal was bound by the decision of the House of Lords in *Re J (A Minor) (Abduction: Custody Rights)*, *sub nom C v. S (A Minor) (Abduction)* (see p.358, above) – as the facts of that case were indistinguishable other than for the fact that the mother in *Re B* had perpetuated a cruel deceit on the father.

Although a purposive approach to 'rights of custody' has been adopted by the English courts, they will not always hold that an unmarried father has rights of custody for Convention purposes, even if he has shared care of the child for a considerable length of time (see *Re J (Abduction: Acquiring Custody Rights by Caring for Child)* [2005] 2 FLR 791). (See also *Re G (A Child) (Custody Rights: Unmarried Father)* [2002] EWHC 2219; and *Re F (Abduction: Unmarried Father: Sole Carer)* [2002] EWHC 2896 (Fam).) In *Re O (Child Abduction: Custody Rights)* [1997] 2 FLR 702 a grandparent was held to have custody rights for Hague Convention purposes.

Rights of custody have also been held to arise where there is no legal or *de facto* custody right, but there is a right of veto on the child's removal (*C v. C (Minor: Abduction: Rights of Custody Abroad)* [1989] Fam Law 228). Removal or retention of a child can also be wrongful where it breaches a 'right of custody' possessed by the court, as the following case shows:

---

▶ *Re H (Abduction: Rights of Custody)* [2000] 1 FLR 374

The unmarried mother abducted the child from Ireland and took him to England. The unmarried father who had an interim order for access (contact) applied for the child's return under the Hague Convention, but his application was dismissed, as he possessed no custody rights.

The House of Lords held that the Irish court possessed custody rights, and ordered return of the child to Ireland. The House of Lords held that a court is 'an institution or other body' to which rights of custody can be attributed within the meaning of art. 3. It held that 'rights' should be given a wide interpretation and that the power to determine a child's place of residence could itself be characterised as a right.

---

Where a child's removal is not wrongful within art. 3 (because the applicant has no custody rights which have been breached), the retention of a child may become wrongful if an order granting rights of custody is made with which such retention is incompatible (*Re S (Custody: Habitual Residence)* [1998] 1 FLR 122).

In *Re L (A Child)* [2005] EWHC 1237 (Fam), [2006] 1 FLR 843 Bennett J held that the father had rights of custody of the child within the meaning of art. 3 of the Hague Convention even though he could not exercise them because he was detained in a Spanish prison; and even though the child was accommodated in a children's home by the Spanish local authority.

**(b)**   Seeking a Determination About Rights of Custody from the Country of the Child's Habitual Residence (Art. 15)

Under art. 15 of the Convention the court in England and Wales can seek a determination from the authorities of the State of the child's habitual residence as to whether or not removal of the child was a breach of a right of custody under the law of that country.

**The Status of an Art. 15 Ruling**   The House of Lords held in *Re D (Abduction: Rights of Custody)* [2006] UKHL 51, [2007] 1 FLR 961 that an art. 15 ruling from a requesting State is conclusive as to the parties' rights under the law of the requesting State, *unless* the circumstances are exceptional (for example where a ruling was obtained by fraud or in breach of the rules of natural justice). It held that a foreign court was much better placed than the English court to understand the true meaning and effect of its own laws in Hague Convention terms; and only if its characterisation of the parent's rights was clearly out of line with international understanding of the Convention's terms should the court in the UK decline to follow it. In *Re D* the House of Lords held that the Court of Appeal had been wrong not to consider itself bound by a ruling of the Romanian court (that the mother's removal had not been wrongful, as the father had lost rights of custody on divorce under Romanian law), and was therefore wrong to have ordered jointly-instructed expert evidence on the issue. (Baroness Hale in *Re D* also ruled that children ought to be heard far more frequently in Hague Convention cases, see above.)

**(c)**   Rights of Access (Contact) Do Not Constitute Rights of Custody

In *S v. H (Abduction: Access Rights)* [1998] Fam 49, [1997] 1 FLR 971 Hale J held that rights of access (contact) do not constitute rights of custody; and so she refused to order the child's return to Italy, as the unmarried father applicant had no custody rights under Italian law or under the Convention. Although he had a right to watch over his child's education and living conditions and had rights of access, and despite the need to construe the Convention broadly and purposively, Hale J held that the Convention drew a clear distinction between rights of custody and rights of access. Access rights can, however, be enforced in other ways under the Convention (see below). In *Hunter v. Murrow (Abduction: Rights of Custody)* [2005] EWCA Civ 976, [2005] 2 FLR 1119 the Court of Appeal held that simple contact arrangements did not constitute 'rights of custody' for Convention purposes, even though the New Zealand court had held that the father had enjoyed rights of custody and that there had been a wrongful removal of the child from New Zealand to London.

**(d)**   Rights of Custody and Unmarried Fathers

Unmarried fathers living in England and Wales may find themselves in a vulnerable position if they have no parental responsibility and their child has been, or is at risk of being, abducted. The English courts have taken a broad view of 'custody rights'. In *Re W; Re B (Child Abduction: Unmarried Father)* [1999] Fam 1, [1998] 2 FLR 146 the unmarried fathers sought declarations (under s.6 Child Abduction and Custody Act 1985) that their children had been wrongfully removed or wrongfully retained under the Hague Convention. Hale J held that in the case of an unmarried father whose child is habitually resident in England and Wales, removal of a child is wrongful for Hague Convention purposes if: the unmarried father has parental responsibility; or a court order is in force prohibiting removal; or relevant proceedings are pending in a court in England and Wales; or the unmarried father is the primary-carer of the child, at least if the mother had delegated such care to him; or the court is actively seized of proceedings to determine rights of custody (in which case, removal will be in breach of the rights of custody attributed to the court provided the proceedings remain pending).

Hale J said that 'relevant proceedings' for the purpose of these rules were proceedings relating to residence, parental responsibility or prohibiting removal of a child. Proceedings were 'pending' if interim orders had been made and directions had been given for a full hearing, but not where proceedings had merely been issued. These rules were subsequently incorporated into the *Practice Note ( Hague Convention – Application by Fathers without Parental Responsibility) 14 October 1997* [1998] 1 FLR 491. The question of whether the unmarried father had custody rights arose in the following cases:

---

▶ *Re G (Abduction: Rights of Custody)* [2002] 2 FLR 703

The exercise of parental rights for four months by the unmarried father (who had no parental responsibility) was held to be sufficient to create rights of custody. Sumner J, applying the decision of the Court of Appeal in *Re B (A Minor) (Abduction)* (above) and referring to Hale J in *Re W; Re B* (above), held that, although a significant time should usually pass before custody rights could be established, regard had to be paid to the child's age, the nature of the care and how the father came to exercise those rights. As the father was held to have custody rights for Hague Convention purposes, Sumner J was able to grant a declaration under s.8 Child Abduction and Custody Act 1985 that the child's removal from South Africa to the UK was wrongful under the Convention. (The grandmother was also held, on the facts, to have joint custody of the child with the father.)

▶ *Re C (A Child) (Custody Rights: Unmarried Fathers)* [2002] EWHC 2219 (Fam), [2003] 1 FLR 252

The unmarried father was concerned that the mother might take the child to Ireland, and so he sought a residence order under s.8 Children Act 1989. A few days later the mother took the child to Ireland and did not return, whereupon the father issued proceedings for a specific issue order for the child's return and a prohibited steps order preventing the child's removal from the jurisdiction. He subsequently issued a summons in the High Court, seeking: a declaration (under s.8 Child Abduction and Custody Act 1985) that the child's removal was wrongful; an order that the mother return the child to the jurisdiction; and an order not to remove the child without the father's consent or that of the court.

Munby J held, refusing the declaration and the other orders, that there was nothing in the case-law to suggest that an unmarried father without parental responsibility could acquire rights of custody within the meaning of the Hague Convention in circumstances where a mother had remained the primary-carer. The case was distinguishable from *Re B (A Minor) (Abduction)* (above); *Re O (Child Abduction: Custody Rights)* [1997] 2 FLR 702; and *Re G (Abduction: Rights of Custody)* (above) where the mother was no longer the child's primary-carer. After the father left the family home, he merely had contact, not custody, rights within the meaning of the Convention. His position was indistinguishable from that of the father in *Re J, sub nom C v. S* (above). Neither was the court sufficiently seised of the matter to have custody vested in it. Except for wardship, the mere issue of proceedings that have not yet been served will normally not be enough. Munby J said that an unmarried father without parental responsibility who had reason to fear that his cohabitant might be thinking of removing the child from the jurisdiction must issue proceedings and immediately apply to a judge for relief, otherwise he might find himself deprived of any effective right of recourse to the Convention.

*Unmarried Fathers and Human Rights*  The European Court of Human Rights held in *B* v. *UK* [2000] 1 FLR 1 that it is not discriminatory (under art. 14 ECHR) in conjunction with the right to family life (under art. 8 ECHR) for the English courts to hold that an unmarried father without parental responsibility does not come within the scope of the Hague Convention because he does not have rights of custody. In this case an unmarried father without parental responsibility, whose child had been removed from the UK without his consent, argued that the UK Government was in breach of arts. 14 and 8 because he was treated differently from other fathers. His application failed. The ECtHR held that there was an objective and reasonable justification for the different treatment of the father in this case.

Beevers (2006) has expressed the view that, had the father in *B* v. *UK* been more involved in sharing the care of the child (rather than being involved merely for the first few months of the child's life), then the outcome of the case might have been different.

For cases where unmarried fathers were granted a declaration of wrongful removal, see, for example, *Re J (Abduction: Declaration of Wrongful Removal)* [2000] 1 FLR 78; and *Re C (Abduction: Wrongful Removal)* [1999] 2 FLR 859.

## 14.10  The Hague Convention – Return of Children

A person (institution or other body) claiming that a child has been removed or retained in breach of a right of custody can apply for assistance in securing the child's return from the Central Authority in the Contracting State of the child's habitual residence, or in any other Contracting State (art. 8). The Central Authority of the State where the child is present must take all appropriate measures to effect the voluntary return of the child (art. 10). But, if effecting a voluntary return is not possible, then court proceedings will have to be brought.

As the Convention is based on the presumption that an abducted child should be returned to his country of habitual residence, so that the court there can decide on his future, the court hearing a return application must order the child's return if the application is made during the first 12 months after the wrongful removal or retention (art. 12). After that 12-month period, the court must also order the child's return, unless the child is 'settled in its new environment' (art. 12) (see below). The duty to return a child is, however, subject to any defence being successful (see below). Because speed is of the essence in abduction cases, judicial and administrative authorities in a Contracting State are required to act expeditiously in return proceedings (art. 11).

*Undertakings*  Instead of making a return order, the English courts have sometimes adopted the practice of accepting an undertaking from a party to the proceedings. An undertaking is a promise to the court (for example, to return the child, to provide accommodation, travel costs or maintenance), and breach of the undertaking can be contempt of court. The Court of Appeal, however, has warned that undertakings 'must not be used by parties to try to clog or fetter, or, in particular, to delay the enforcement of a paramount decision to return the child' (Butler-Sloss LJ in *Re M (Abduction: Undertakings)* [1995] 1 FLR 1021). The problem with undertakings, however, is that, compared with court orders, they are not easily understood by foreign courts and enforcement abroad may be difficult.

**14.11** The Hague Convention – Defences to a Return Application

**(a)** Introduction

There are various defences available to a return application. In addition to defences based on the court having no jurisdiction to hear the application (for example, because the child is not habitually resident in a Contracting State, or there is no wrongful removal or retention in breach of a custody right), there are certain defences expressly laid down in the Convention. These are as follows:

---

**Defences Under the Hague Convention**

► The child is now settled in his new environment (art. 12).
► Consent (art. 13(a)).
► Acquiescence (art. 13(a)).
► Grave risk that return will expose the child to physical or psychological harm or otherwise place him in an intolerable situation (art. 13(b)).
► The child objects to being returned and has attained an age and degree of maturity at which it is appropriate to take account of his views (art. 13).

---

In EU abduction these defences may have to be considered in the light of Council Regulation (EC) (No. 2201/2003) *Concerning Jurisdiction and the Recognition and Enforcement of Judgments in Matrimonial Matters and in Matters of Parental Responsibility* (Brussels II Revised).

*A High Threshold for Defences*   The courts have set a high threshold for these defences in order not to frustrate the Convention's primary objective which is to effect the return of abducted children. A long line of Court of Appeal authority has held that the policy of the Hague Convention requires the courts to exercise their discretion in favour of ordering the child's return save in the most exceptional cases. In *Re S (A Minor)(Abduction: Custody Rights)* [1993] Fam 242, *sub nom S* v. *S (Child Abduction: Child's Views)* [1992] 2 FLR 492 Balcombe LJ had stated that only in exceptional cases should the court exercise its discretion to refuse to order an immediate return, and this approach has been endorsed in later cases (see, for example, by Thorpe LJ in *Zaffino* v. *Zaffino (Abduction: Children's Views)*[2005] EWCA Civ 1012, [2006] 1 FLR 410). Furthermore, Sir Mark Potter P in *S* v. *B (Abduction: Human Rights)* [2005] EWHC 733 (Fam), [2005] 2 FLR 878 said that it might also be contrary to the right to family life in art. 8 of the European Convention for the Protection of Human Rights if the threshold were set lower.

The courts are reluctant to refuse to order return, and constantly emphasise that the underlying thesis of the Convention is that the welfare of children is best determined by the court of the child's habitual residence (see, for example, Ward LJ in *Re C (Abduction: Grave Risk of Psychological Harm)* [1999] 1 FLR 1145). Thus, the alleged abductor has a heavy burden to establish a defence. Even if a defence is proved, the court retains an overriding discretion under art. 18 to order the child's return (see below).

*A Lowering of the Threshold?*   In *Re M and Another (Minors)* [2007] UKHL 55 Baroness Hale was of the opinion that the long line of Court of Appeal cases which had held that return applications should be refused save in the most exceptional cases was wrong. Her Ladyship said (at para. 40):

'I have no doubt at all that it is wrong to import any test of exceptionality into the exercise of discretion under the Hague Convention. The circumstances in which return may be refused are themselves exceptions to the general rule. That in itself is sufficient exceptionality. It is neither necessary or desirable to import an additional gloss into the Convention.'

### (b)   The Child is Now Settled in His or Her New Environment (art. 12)

It is possible to argue by way of defence that the child is now settled in his or her new environment. This defence arises under art. 12 which provides that a court hearing a return application must order the child's return after 12 months have passed since the wrongful removal or retention, *unless* the child is 'settled in its new environment'.

However, even though it is proved that the child is settled in his or her new environment, the court has an overriding discretion to order return. The Court of Appeal so held in *Cannon* v. *Cannon* [2004] EWCA Civ 1330, [2005] 1 FLR 169, overruling Singer J in *Re C (Abduction: Settlement)* [2004] EWHC 1245 (Fam), [2005] 1 FLR 127, who had held that there was no such discretionary power in the court. This approach was endorsed by Baroness Hale who gave the leading opinion in the House of Lords in *Re M and Another (Minors)* [2007] UKHL 55.

In *Re M and Another (Minors)*, Baroness Hale also said that, in terms of the child being settled in his or her new environment for the purposes of art. 12, 'the further away one gets from the speedy return envisaged by the Convention, the less weighty those general Convention [policy] considerations must be'. In other words, her Ladyship said that the policy considerations of swift return and comity would carry less weight the longer the abducted child had been in the UK. She said that in settlement cases 'the policy of the Convention would not necessarily point towards return'. Applying this approach to the facts of the case in *Re M and Another (Minors)*, the House of Lords allowed the mother's appeal and refused to order that the children be returned to Zimbabwe.

### (c)   Consent (art. 13(a))

This defence requires the defendant to prove that return of the child should not be ordered as the applicant had consented to the child's removal or retention. Consent is a question of fact, but it must be clear, unequivocal and informed (*Re P (Abduction: Consent)* [2004] EWCA Civ 971, [2004] 2 FLR 1057). The principles that apply to acquiescence (see below) also apply to consent.

Each case turns on its own facts. In *M* v. *M (Abduction: Consent)* [2007] EWHC 1404 (Fam) Sumner J refused to order the return of two children to Greece as the mother had proved by clear and cogent evidence that the applicant father had consented to her bringing the children to the UK. Return was also refused in *Re A (Abduction: Habitual Residence: Consent)* [2005] EWHC 2998 (Fam), [2006] 2 FLR 1, as consent (and acquiescence) had been established.

For other cases on consent, see, for example: *Re K (Abduction: Consent)* [1997] 2 FLR 212; *Re R (Abduction: Consent)* [1999] 1 FLR 828; *Re M (Abduction: Consent: Acquiescence)* [1999] 1 FLR 171; and *Re P (Abduction: Consent)* [2004] EWCA Civ 971, [2004] 2 FLR 1057.

Acquiescence (art. 13(a))

Acquiescence is commonly argued as a defence to a return application. The following is the leading case:

---

▶ *Re H (Abduction: Acquiescence)* **[1997] 1 FLR 87, HL**

The parents were strict Orthodox Jews, who were married and lived in Israel. The mother took the children to England without the father's consent. The father contacted his local Beth Din (a religious court of law), and it entered its own summons for the children's return, which the mother ignored. The Beth Din later ordered the father to take whatever steps he saw fit, and six months after the children had been removed from Israel he invoked Hague Convention proceedings in the High Court in England. The mother argued that he had acquiesced in the children's removal by failing to make a prompt application. The High Court ordered the children's return, but the Court of Appeal allowed the mother's appeal, holding that the father had acquiesced, applying its earlier decision in *Re A (Minors) (Abduction: Custody Rights)* [1992] Fam 106, *sub nom Re A (Minors) (Abduction: Acquiescence)* [1992] 2 FLR 14, where by a majority it had applied an objective test to establish acquiescence, and had held that acquiescence could be signified by a single act or communication, even though that act or communication appeared to be at variance with the general course of a parent's conduct. The father appealed to the House of Lords.

The House of Lords held, allowing his appeal and ordering the children's return to Israel, that the objective test of acquiescence laid down by the Court of Appeal in *Re A* was wrong. The correct approach was that adopted by Balcombe LJ who had dissented in *Re A*. Applying this approach, it was clear that the father had not acquiesced in the children's retention in England.

Lord Browne-Wilkinson laid down the following principles:

▶ Whether the wronged parent had acquiesced in the removal or retention of a child depends on his or her actual state of mind. The test is subjective.
▶ The subjective intention of the wronged parent is a question of fact for the trial judge to determine in all the circumstances of the case, the burden of proof being on the abducting parent.
▶ But there is one exception: where the wronged parent's words or actions clearly and unequivocally show and have led the other parent to believe that the wronged parent is not asserting or going to assert his right to the summary return of the child and are inconsistent with such return, justice requires that the wronged parent be held to have acquiesced.

---

For an example of the 'exception' mentioned by Lord Browne-Wilkinson (above), see *Re D (Abduction: Acquiescence)* [1998] 1 FLR 686 where the father was held to have acquiesced as he had consented to full and final residence orders being made in England and Wales.

---

**Approaches to Acquiescence in the Case-Law**

A custody application made in the child's country of habitual residence is a strong indication that there is no acquiescence (*Re A and Another (Minors: Abduction)* [1991] 2 FLR 241; *Re F (A Minor) (Child Abduction)* [1992] 1 FLR 548).

Making long-term plans for contact may indicate acquiescence (*Re S (Abduction: Acquiescence)* [1998] 2 FLR 115).

Bringing proceedings for contact in the English courts, even though brought in ignorance of the Convention, may indicate acquiescence (*Re B (Abduction: Acquiescence)* [1999] 2 FLR 818).

Acquiescence does not require an applicant to have specific knowledge of the Convention (*Re AZ (A Minor) (Abduction: Acquiescence)* [1993] 1 FLR 682).

A willingness to be involved in negotiations to sort out what is best for a child and the parties does not necessarily amount to acquiescence, even if no agreement is reached (*Re I (Abduction: Acquiescence)* [1999] 1 FLR 778); as the Court of Appeal has held that negotiations at the early stage of a difficult broken relationship are to be encouraged (*P v. P (Abduction: Acquiescence)* [1998] 2 FLR 835).

### (e) Grave Risk of Physical or Psychological Harm, or Otherwise Placing the Child in an Intolerable Situation (art. 13(b))

The burden of establishing this defence, like the other defences, is a heavy one – in order not to frustrate the dominant purpose of the Convention which is to ensure the prompt return of abducted children. The court will require clear and compelling evidence of the grave risk of harm or other intolerability which must be 'substantial, not trivial, and of a severity which is much more than is inherent in the inevitable disruption, uncertainty and anxiety which follows an unwelcome return to the jurisdiction of the court of habitual residence' (Ward LJ in *Re C (Abduction: Grave Risk of Psychological Harm)* [1999] 1 FLR 1145, at 1154). A high degree of intolerability must be established (Balcombe LJ in *Re A (Minors) (Abduction: Custody Rights)* [1992] Fam 106, *sub nom Re A (Minors) (Abduction: Acquiescence)* [1992] 2 FLR 14; and Sir Stephen Brown P in *B v. B (Abduction)* [1993] 1 FLR 238).

In *Re C (A Minor) (Abduction)* [1989] 1 FLR 403 the Court of Appeal held that the defence cannot succeed where the abducting parent has created the psychological harm by his or her own conduct in abducting the child. Butler-Sloss LJ said that the grave risk of harm arises from the refusal to return a child, not by an abducting parent creating a psychological situation and then attempting to rely on it (see also *Re S (Abduction: Custody Rights)* [2002] EWCA Civ 908, [2002] 2 FLR 815). However, in *S v. B (Abduction: Human Rights)* [2005] EWHC 733 (Fam), [2005] 2 FLR 878 Sir Mark Potter P stated that the proposition articulated in *Re C* (that the abducting parent cannot rely upon adverse conditions brought about by a situation created by his or her own conduct) is not a principle articulated in the Hague Convention and should not be applied to the effective exclusion of the art. 13(b) defence, as the words in art. 13(b) are directed to the question of risk of harm to the child and not to the wrongful conduct of the abducting parent. Thus, if the situation would place the child at grave risk of harm, the defence can be established despite the proposition laid down in *Re C*.

The art. 13(b) grave risk defence was successful in *Re D (Article 13b: Non-Return)* [2006] EWCA Civ 146, [2006] 2 FLR 305 where the Court of Appeal dismissed the appeal of the father against the judge's refusal to return the children to Venezuela as the mother had been shot at in the family home in Venezuela at close range by a hired gunman, whose attack the mother suspected had been initiated by the father. The Court of Appeal held that in the exceptional circumstances of the case (strong evidence of extreme violence and danger of physical harm to the children and emotional harm) the children should not be returned.

*Separating Brothers and Sisters*   The court will be aware of the potential harm to children if a return order will result in brothers and sisters being separated. However, separating brothers and sisters will not necessarily be held to constitute psychological harm (see *Re C (Abduction: Grave Risk of Physical or Psychological Harm)* [1999] 2 FLR 478). The courts have recognised that some psychological harm to a child is inherent in any abduction case (Lord Donaldson MR in *Re C (A Minor) (Abduction)* [1989] 1 FLR 403; and see *E v. E (Child Abduction: Intolerable Situation)* [1998] 2 FLR 980).

In *S v. B (Abduction: Human Rights)* [2005] EWHC 733 (Fam), [2005] 2 FLR 878 where the mother was ordered to return the child to New Zealand, even though the teenage half-brother, who was not the subject of the application, did not wish to return, Sir Mark Potter P held that, while it was relevant to take into account the position of the half-sibling who was not the subject of the application, the imperative of the Hague Convention is to safeguard the right to family life as between the child who is the subject of the application and the aggrieved parent. Sir Mark Potter P held, however, that an order which interfered with a mother and a sibling's enjoyment of family life together would be a violation of the sibling's right to family life under art. 8 ECHR, unless it was in accordance with the law, in pursuit of a legitimate aim and necessary and proportionate in a democratic society.

*Allegations of Domestic Violence*   Because of the high threshold for the defence, and the fact that the evidence must support a grave risk of harm to the *child*, not to the parent, it may be difficult for the grave hardship defence to succeed where domestic violence is alleged, even if the violence alleged is serious. Domestic violence is not usually enough on its own to justify a refusal to order a child's return, and the courts in the UK will presume that the courts in the foreign jurisdiction will provide remedies to protect and support a parent who claims that she (or he) will suffer domestic violence if return is ordered. This approach was taken in *Re W (Abduction: Domestic Violence)* [2004] EWHC 1247 (Fam), [2004] 2 FLR 499 where Baron J ordered the child's return to South Africa even though the mother's evidence showed that she had been subjected to regular abuse, which included violence, threats with a firearm and demeaning sexual practices. There were photographs showing extensive bruising, supported by contemporaneous medical records. As there was no real evidence, however, that the child had suffered distress and there was no evidence about the psychological impact of the life that she had led, Baron J held that the grave hardship defence had not been made out. The child's objection to return defence was also dismissed principally because her objection was more to do with concerns about her mother than an objection to returning to South Africa.

---

**Case-Law Examples Where the Article 13(b) Defence Has Been Argued**

▶ *Re S (Abduction: Intolerable Situation: Beth Din)* [2000] 1 FLR 454

The mother argued that if the children were ordered to be returned to Israel, it would result in an intolerable situation under art. 13(b) (as women who were orthodox Jews were discriminated against under Israeli religious law), and this would result in her rights and those of the children being breached under art. 8 (right to family life) ECHR. Connell J refused to accept her argument and ordered their return.

▶ *Re S (Abduction: Custody Rights)* [2002] EWCA Civ 908, [2002] 2 FLR 815

The mother argued that if she was ordered to return the child to Israel, the child would suffer a grave risk of harm because of the political tension and terrorist attacks in Israel. The Court of Appeal held that, although this was a real risk of harm to the child, it was not a grave risk. The fact of terrorism in Israel was not sufficient to justify a refusal to return the child, which would defeat the predominant aim of the Convention to return children to their country of habitual residence.

▶ *TB v. JB (Abduction: Grave Risk of Harm)* [2001] 2 FLR 515

The mother argued that if she was ordered to be returned to New Zealand, her mental condition and ability to look after the children would deteriorate, which would expose the children to a grave risk of physical or psychological harm. She said she was too frightened to return because her second husband had been physically and sexually violent towards her, and he had physically abused the children. Singer J accepted her defence, and refused to order the children's return. The Court of Appeal (Hale LJ dissenting) allowed the father's appeal, holding that, although the word 'harm' in art. 13 could include harm caused by the deterioration of the mother's condition and consequently her ability to care for the children, Singer J had erred because his evaluation of the risk to the children of returning home to New Zealand had not been carried out on the basis that the mother would take all reasonable steps to protect herself and the children. The court was obliged to take the view, in the absence of evidence to the contrary brought by the mother, that the New Zealand courts would make appropriate orders to protect the mother and children from her husband, and punish any non-compliance.

For cases where the grave hardship defence has succeeded, see, for example: *Re F (Child Abduction: Risk if Returned)* [1995] 2 FLR 31; *Re L (Child Abduction) (Psychological Harm)* [1993] 2 FLR 401; and *Re M (Abduction: Psychological Harm)* [1997] 2 FLR 690.

### (f)   Child Objects to Being Returned (art. 13)

The court can refuse to order return if the child objects to being returned and has attained an age and degree of maturity at which it is appropriate to take account of the child's views (art. 13). The court has a discretion as to the amount of weight to be given to the child's views, but will always bear in mind the policy of the Convention, which is that abducted children should be returned to their country of habitual residence. The weight to be attached to the child's objections will depend on the age and maturity of the child.

As Hague Convention proceedings are summary and speed is of the essence, the court will usually be unwilling to hear oral evidence in respect of a child's wishes (see *Re K (Abduction: Child's Objections)* [1995] 1 FLR 977). If the court is put on inquiry that a child objects to being returned, it is the role of the Children and Family Reporter from CAFCASS (see 1.4) to assess whether the child has sufficient maturity, and to convey the child's views to the court. The court can permit the child to be made a party to the proceedings and be separately represented, if it is satisfied that the child has an independent viewpoint which needs to be put before the court (see *Re M (A Minor) (Abduction: Child's Objections)* [1994] 2 FLR 126, where the dispute was between the mother and child, not the mother and father; and *Re L (Abduction: Child's Objections to Return)* [2002] EWHC 1864 (Fam), [2002] 2 FLR 1042). However, it is highly unusual for a child to be separately represented. The Court of Appeal so held in *Re J (Abduction: Child's Objections to Return)* [2004] EWCA Civ 428, [2004] 2 FLR 64 where it also held that a discrete finding as to age and maturity is necessary to determine whether it is appropriate to take account of the child's views, and that the court must be sure that the child's views have not been shaped or coloured by the undue influence and pressure directly or indirectly exerted by the abducting parent.

The child's objections to return were considered in the following cases:

> ▶ *Re S (A Minor) (Abduction: Custody Rights)* [1993] Fam 242, *sub nom S v. S (Child Abduction) (Child's Views)* [1992] 2 FLR 492
>
> A girl aged 10 with a severe stammer and associated behaviour problems was taken from France to England by her mother, where her stammer and behaviour problems disappeared. The father applied for the child's return, but the mother argued, *inter alia*, that the child objected to being returned and had reached an age and degree of maturity at which it was appropriate to take into account her views. The trial judge accepted this defence and refused to return the child. The father's appeal to the Court of Appeal was dismissed. Balcombe LJ laid down the approach to be taken in respect of the defence:
>
> ▶ Whether the child had attained an age and degree of maturity at which it is appropriate to take account of his views are questions of fact to be determined by the trial judge.
> ▶ It will usually be necessary for the judge to find out why the child objects to being returned, and if the only reason is because the child wishes to remain with the abducting parent, who is also asserting that he or she was unwilling to return, then this is a highly relevant factor for the judge when exercising his discretion.
> ▶ There was no age below which a child is to be considered as not having attained sufficient maturity for his views to be taken into account. If the court should come to the conclusion that the child's views have been influenced by some other person, for example the abducting parent, then it is probable that little or no weight will be given to the child's views.
> ▶ It would be contrary to the peremptory nature of the Convention to allow the abducting parent to insist, as of right, that the Convention's mandatory procedures for a child's return should be suspended while detailed investigation is made as to the child's views, their terms and circumstances, and the medical and psychological factors involved in gauging the child's degree of maturity.
>
> ▶ *Re T (Abduction: Child's Objections to Return)* [2000] 2 FLR 192
>
> The Court of Appeal refused to order the return of an 11-year-old girl and her 6-year-old brother to Spain, as the 11-year-old's objections to return had been made out. Although the girl's 6-year-old brother was held to be too young and immature for his views to be taken into account, the Court of Appeal refused to order his return, as there was a grave risk that if he were ordered to be returned to Spain without his sister it would place him in an intolerable position under art. 13(b). Ward LJ identified the proper approach to the question of the child's consent and listed the principles to be derived from the judgment of Balcombe LJ in *Re S (A Minor) (Abduction: Custody Rights)* (above). His Lordship also made the following points:
>
> ▶ The proper approach was to establish whether the child objected to being returned to the country of habitual residence, bearing in mind that there might be cases where that was so inevitably and inextricably linked with an objection to living with the other parent that the two factors could not be separated.
> ▶ It was next necessary to ascertain the age and degree of maturity of the child in order to establish whether it was appropriate to take account of the child's views.

> ▶ In determining whether it was appropriate to take account of the child's views, it was necessary to examine, *inter alia*: the child's own perspective of what was in his short-, medium- and long-term interests; to what extent, if at all, were the objections rooted in reality; to what extent those views had been shaped or even coloured by undue pressure directly or indirectly exerted by the abducting parent; and to what extent it could be mollified on return, and, where it was the case, on removal from any pernicious influence from the abducting parent.

The principles above were endorsed by Sir Mark Potter P in *Re M (Abduction: Child's Objections)* [2007] EWCA Civ 260, [2007] 2 FLR 72 where he held that the court must conduct a three-stage exercise. Thus, the court must first consider whether the child's objections are made out. Next, it must decide whether the child's age and maturity are such that it is appropriate for the court to take account of those objections. And finally it must decide whether it should exercise its discretion in favour of return or not. In *Re M* the Court of Appeal accepted the objections of the child (an intelligent eight-year-old girl) and refused to order her return to Serbia on the basis of her objections being exceptional in the context of the unusual circumstances of the case (the child had been traumatised by her personal experiences in Serbia where drugs had been planted on her mother (possibly by the father) in persistent attempts to incriminate her). Sir Mark Potter P, with whom Rix and Wilson LJJ agreed, held that the general welfare considerations in the case strongly militated in favour of refusing to order return.

There is no fixed age below which the child's views will not be taken into account. Although the views of the 6-year-old child in *Re T* (above) were not taken into account, children as young as six and seven have sometimes been held to be mature enough to have their wishes taken into account (see *Re R (Child Abduction: Acquiescence)* [1995] 1 FLR 716; and *Re K (Abduction: Child's Objections)* [1995] 1 FLR 977). However, although children's views may be taken into account, they are not necessarily decisive of the matter. This is because the court must decide what weight to give those objections when exercising its overriding discretion to decide whether or not to order return (see, for example, *Re J and K (Abduction: Objections of Child)* [2004] EWHC 1985 (Fam), [2005] 1 FLR 273 where the 9-year-old child's wishes not to return were ascertained by the CAFCASS officer, but where Wilson J nevertheless ordered return).

The court will be 'vigilant to ascertain and assess the reasons for the child not wishing to return to the parent living in the State of habitual residence' (Butler-Sloss LJ in *Re M (A Minor) (Child Abduction)* [1994] 1 FLR 390). Although art. 12 requires the child to be returned to the *State* of habitual residence, not to the person requesting the child's return, the court can consider the objections of a child returning to a parent rather than to a State (*Re M (A Minor) (Child Abduction)* [1994] 1 FLR 390).

Enforcing a return order may prove difficult where a child has strong objections to return. In *Re HB (Abduction: Children's Objections)* [1998] 1 FLR 422, despite the 11-year-old girl's strong objections to being returned to Denmark, the High Court ordered her return. However, she refused to board the plane from England to Denmark. Subsequently, after having been granted permission to be joined as party to Convention proceedings, the Court of Appeal held that the court was no longer bound to order her return, because 12 months had passed for the purposes of art. 12, and because of her strong objections to return.

For cases where children have not been returned because of their objections, see, for example: *S* v. *S (Child Abduction: Child's Views)* [1992] 2 FLR 492; *Re R (A Minor: Abduction)* [1992] 1 FLR 105; and *Re B (Abduction: Children's Objections)* [1998] 1 FLR 667. In *Zaffino* v. *Zaffino (Abduction: Children's Views)* [2005] EWCA Civ 1012, [2006] 1 FLR 410 Munby J refused to order the return of two children to Canada on the basis of their objections to return, but the Court of Appeal allowed the father's appeal against the decision.

### 14.12 The Hague Convention – The Overriding Discretion of the Court

A successful defence based on habitual residence or lack of a custody right will mean that the case does not come within the scope of the Convention, and that will be the end of the matter.

In respect of the other defences, a successful defence will not necessarily result in the court refusing to order the child's return. This is because art. 18 gives the court an overriding discretion to decide whether or not to order return.

Once a defence to a return application is established, the court will not usually order return unless there is something special about the case. The case of *Re D (Abduction: Discretionary Return)* [2000] 1 FLR 24 provides an example. Here the defence of consent to the children's removal from France had been proved, but Wilson J nevertheless ordered the children's return to France, as the French court was already seized of the issue and it was a better forum in which to resolve the question of residence. The principles of comity and appropriate forum justified their return. In *Cannon* v. *Cannon* [2004] EWCA Civ 1330, [2005] 1 FLR 169 return was ordered by the Court of Appeal (but later overruled), even though the child had been in England for more than 12 months and was settled in her new environment for the purposes of art. 12. (See also *Re R (Child Abduction: Acquiescence)* [1995] 1 FLR 716; and *Re J and K (Abduction: Objections of Child)* [2004] EWHC 1985 (Fam), [2005] 1 FLR 273.)

### 14.13 The European Convention

The European Convention on the Recognition and Enforcement of Decisions Concerning Custody of Children 1980 (the 'European Convention') was implemented into UK law by Part II of the Child Abduction and Custody Act 1985. The text of the Convention is laid down in Sched. 2 to the Act.

Under the European Convention, a custody decision given in a Contracting State must be recognised and, where it is enforceable in the State of origin, made enforceable in every other Contracting State (art. 7). Like the Hague Convention, the European Convention creates an international network of Contracting States who must work together to effect the return of abducted children. Unlike the Hague Convention, however, it deals with the enforcement of custody (and access) orders, not custody rights.

Although the European Convention is rarely invoked, because it has largely been superseded by the Hague Convention, it is useful for enforcing access (contact) orders, particularly as access rights are not enforceable by Hague Convention proceedings (see above). The European Convention may also be useful where the Hague Convention does not apply, for example, where the person who wrongly removed or retained the child has sole custody.

The European Convention deals with the recognition and enforcement of custody decisions where there has been 'improper removal of a child', by allowing any person who has obtained a custody decision in a Contracting State to apply to a central authority in another Contracting State to have that decision recognised or enforced in that State (art. 4). The Convention applies to custody decisions made before or after the child's wrongful removal across an international frontier from one Contracting State to another (art. 12). A 'custody decision' is a decision made by any judicial or administrative authority relating to the care of a child, including a right to determine the child's place of residence or a right of access to the child (art. 1(c)).

'Improper removal' is defined as 'the removal of a child across an international frontier in breach of a decision relating to his custody which has been given in a Contracting State and which is enforceable in such a State' and includes: (i) the failure to return a child across an international frontier at the end of a period of the exercise of the right of access to the child or at the end of any other temporary stay in a territory other than that where the custody is exercised; and (ii) a removal which is subsequently declared unlawful within the meaning of art. 12 (art. 1(d)).

Decisions on access, and custody decisions dealing with access, can also be recognised and enforced under the Convention subject to the same conditions which apply to custody decisions, but the competent authority of the State addressed may fix the conditions for the implementation and exercise of the right of access, taking into account, in particular, undertakings given by the parties on this matter (art. 11). Where there is no decision as to access or where recognition or enforcement of a custody decision has been refused, the central authority of the State addressed may apply to its own competent authorities for a decision on the right of access if the person claiming a right of access so requests (art. 11(3)). In *Re A (Foreign Access Order: Enforcement)* [1996] 1 FLR 561 an order was made giving recognition to a French access order and making it enforceable in England.

A person wishing to have a custody or access decision recognised or enforced in another Contracting State may apply to the central authority in any Contracting State (art. 4) (in England and Wales, the Child Abduction Unit of the Ministry of Justice), which must take various appropriate steps without delay. These steps include instituting proceedings, discovering the child's whereabouts, securing the recognition or enforcement of the decision, securing delivery of the child to the applicant where enforcement is granted, and informing the requesting authority of the measures taken and their results (art. 5).

Before a custody decision made in another Contracting State can be recognised and enforced in England and Wales it must be registered (ss.15(2)(b) and 16 Child Abduction and Custody Act 1985). An application for registration can be made to the High Court by any person who has rights under the custody decision. The High Court can refuse to register a decision, thereby refusing recognition and enforcement, on certain procedural and/or substantive grounds (see below), or where an application for the child's return is pending under the Hague Convention (s.16(4) Child Abduction and Custody Act 1985). In no circumstances may the original foreign custody decision be reviewed as to its substance (art. 9(3)).

## Grounds for Refusal to Register an Order

Under arts. 9 and 10, the court can refuse to register an order, and thereby fail to recognise and enforce it. However, it is unlikely to do so, as the aim of the European Convention, like that of the Hague Convention, is to foster international co-operation to effect the return of abducted children.

Article 9 lays down procedural grounds for refusing to register an order, namely: (a) where the decision was made in the absence of the defendant or his lawyer, and they were not given sufficient notice of the proceedings; (b) where the decision was made in the absence of the defendant or his lawyer and the competence of the authority giving the decision was not based on the habitual residence of the defendant, the parents, or the child; or (c) where the decision is incompatible with a decision made in the State addressed before the child's removal, unless the child has had his habitual residence in the territory of the requesting State for one year before his removal.

Article 10 lays down substantive grounds for refusing to recognise and enforce an order, namely that a court may refuse to recognise and enforce an order:

(a) if the effects of the decision are manifestly incompatible with the fundamental principles of family and child law in the State addressed;
(b) if the effects of a custody decision are no longer manifestly in accordance with the child's welfare because of a change of circumstances, including the passage of time, but not a mere change of the child's residence after an improper removal;
(c) if at the time proceedings were instituted in the State of origin: (i) the child was a national of, or habitually resident in, the State addressed and no such connection existed with the State of origin; (ii) the child was a national both of the State of origin and of the State addressed and was habitually resident in the State addressed; or
(d) if the decision is incompatible with a decision given in the State addressed or enforceable in that State after being given in a third State, pursuant to proceedings begun before the submission of the request for recognition or enforcement, and if the refusal is in accordance with the welfare of the child.

Where the court is considering whether to refuse to register an order on the basis of (b) above (no longer in accordance with the child's welfare and so on), it must ascertain the child's views (unless it is impracticable to do so having regard to his age and understanding), and it may request appropriate enquiries to be carried out (art. 15(1)).

There are very few reported cases on the Convention:

▶ *Re L (Abduction: European Convention: Access)* [1999] 2 FLR 1089

Grandparents invoked the Convention in order to enforce a French access order in England, after their grandchildren had been taken from France. They were unsuccessful, as there had been a change of circumstances so that the access order was no longer appropriate under art. 10(b). It had been made by the French court on the basis that the children would be living in France, but they were now living in England. Although the English court had jurisdiction under art. 11(2) to vary the order, Bennett J felt that variation was not appropriate in the circumstances.

▶ *T v. T (Abduction: Forum Conveniens)* [2002] 2 FLR 544

The father applied under the European Convention, not the Hague Convention, because the mother had sole custody under a Swedish court order. He was subsequently granted sole custody under a Swedish court order (the mother had disappeared) and so he applied to the English High Court for the order to be recognised, registered and enforced under the European Convention. He also sought an order for the immediate return of the child. The mother argued that the Swedish order should not be recognised under arts. 10(1)(a) and (b) (above). The High Court held that art. 10(1)(a) did not apply as the Swedish approach to the case was not incompatible with the approach to residence and contact in England and Wales. However, the higher prospect that the mother, having been found, would take a full and proper part in Swedish proceedings, and the fact that the child's roots had become more firmly rooted in England, constituted a change of circumstances under art. 10(1)(b), and accordingly under s.16(4)(a) Child Abduction and Custody Act 1985 the Swedish order was refused.

## 14.14  Non-Convention Cases

If a child is abducted out of the UK to a country which is not party to the Hague or European Conventions, the wronged parent is in a precarious position because there is no network of Contracting States which can work together to effect the child's return. There are no international mechanisms in place. A parent will therefore have to try to reach an amicable settlement with the abducting parent, or commence legal proceedings in the country to which the child has been taken. Bringing legal proceedings in a foreign country, however, can be difficult and expensive, and return is not guaranteed, because in some countries fathers are favoured over mothers and the best interests of the child may not be the primary consideration. Bringing proceedings in countries with Islamic legal systems can be particularly difficult.

Where a child is brought into the UK from a non-Convention country, the application for return must be brought in the High Court in wardship proceedings or under its inherent jurisdiction. A s.8 specific issue order under the Children Act 1989 can be sought (see 11.8). The court has a wide discretion in these proceedings, and, unlike Hague Convention proceedings, there is no presumption in favour of ordering return, and the court can, if it wishes, decide to investigate the merits of the case. However, the court can exercise a 'summary' jurisdiction – in other words it can, in accordance with the welfare principle, order the immediate return of the child to a foreign country without conducting a full investigation of the merits of the case.

In some cases the High Court in England and Wales may not have jurisdiction. Thus, there is no jurisdiction to make an order in wardship if the child is not resident in England and Wales on the date of the application (see, for example, *Al Habtoor* v. *Fotheringham* [2001] EWCA Civ 186, [2001] 1 FLR 951 where the mother's application in wardship was refused by the Court of Appeal as the child was resident in Dubai, not England, and because jurisdiction in wardship did not arise just because a child was a British national).

*The Governing Principles in Non-Convention Cases*  The principles applicable in non-Convention cases were laid down by the House of Lords in the following case:

▶ *Re J (A Child) (Child Returned Abroad: Convention Rights)* [2005] UKHL 40, [2005] 2 FLR 802

The mother took the child to England from Saudi Arabia. The father applied under s.8 Children Act 1989 for a specific issue order for the return of the child to Saudi Arabia, but the trial judge refused the application. The father appealed to the Court of Appeal which unanimously allowed his appeal. The mother appealed to the House of Lords, which allowed her appeal, and restored the orders made by the trial judge. The House of Lords held that the trial judge and the Court of Appeal had been wrong to leave out of account the absence of a jurisdiction in the home country to enable the mother to bring the child back to England without the father's consent.

Baroness Hale, who gave the leading opinion, laid down the following principles and approaches to be applied in non-Convention cases for the summary return of children:

- The child's welfare is paramount and the specialist rules and concepts of the Hague Convention are not to be applied by analogy in non-Convention cases.
- Each case depends on its facts. In some cases summary return will be in the child's best interests but in others it will not.
- In having to make a decision whether or not to order summary return, a judge might find it convenient to start from the proposition that it was likely to be better for a child to return to his home country for any dispute about his future to be decided there. Any case against his doing so had to be made.
- It should not be assumed that allowing a child to remain in the UK while his future was decided here inevitably means that he will remain here for ever.
- An important variable is the degree of connection of the child with each country. This does not involve applying the technical concept of habitual residence, but to ask in a common-sense way with which country the child has the closer connection. In determining this issue of the child's 'home country' the child's nationality, where he has lived for most of his life, first language, race or ethnicity, religion, culture and education are relevant matters. A closely related factor is the length of time that the child has spent in each country. Uprooting a child from one environment and bringing him to a completely unfamiliar one, especially if that has been done clandestinely, may well not be in the child's best interests. But, if the child is already familiar with the UK, and had been here for some time without objection, it might be less disruptive for him to remain a little longer while his medium- and longer-term future are decided.
- The relevance of the fact that the legal system of the other country is different from that in the UK depends on the facts of each case. It is wrong to say that the future of the child should be decided according to the conception of child welfare which exactly corresponds with that which is current in England and Wales. In a world which values difference, one culture is not inevitably to be preferred to another. For this reason, English law does not start from any *a priori* assumptions about what is best for any individual child. The court must consider the individual child and weigh in the balance the checklist of factors in s.1(3) Children Act 1989. If there is a genuine issue between the parents as to whether it is in the best interests of the child to live in the UK or elsewhere, it is relevant whether that issue is capable of being tried in the courts of the country to which he is to be returned. If those courts have no choice but to do what the father wishes, without hearing the mother, then the English courts must ask themselves whether it is in the child's best interests to enable the dispute to be heard. The absence of a 'relocation' jurisdiction in the other country may be a decisive factor, unless it appears that the mother may not be able to make a good case for relocation. There may be cases where the connection of the child and the family with the other country is so strong that any difference between the legal systems in the UK and the other country should carry little weight.
- These considerations above must not, however, stand in the way of a swift and unsentimental decision to return the child to his home country, even if that country is very different from the UK. The concept of welfare in the UK is capable of taking cultural and religious factors into account in deciding how a child should be brought up. It also gives great weight to the child's need for a meaningful relationship with both parents.

However, although the child's welfare is the paramount consideration in non-convention cases, Baroness Hale stated *obiter* in *Re M and Another (Minors)* [2007] UKHL 55 (a Hague Convention case), that in non-convention cases the court 'does have the power to order the immediate return of the child to a foreign jurisdiction without conducting a full investigation of the merits' (at para. 38). Her Ladyship said (at para. 39):

> 'Thus there is always a choice to be made between summary return and a further investigation. There is also a choice to be made as to the depth into which the judge will go in investigating the merits of the case before making that choice. One size does not fit all. The judge may well find it convenient to start from the proposition that it is likely to be better for a child to return to his home country for any disputes about his future to be decided there. A case against his doing so has to be made. But the weight to be given to that factor and to all the other relevant factors, some of which are canvassed in *Re J*, will vary enormously from case to case.'

The principles laid down in *Re J* (above) were applied in the following non-convention case:

▶ *Re H (Abduction: Non-Convention Application)* [2006] EWHC 199 (Fam), [2006] 2 FLR 314

Bracewell J, applying the welfare principle, refused to return three children to Dominica after the mother had brought them from there to England without the knowledge or agreement of the father. The children had confirmed the mother's allegations about the father's cruelty and the two eldest children had made it clear to the CAFCASS officer that they did not wish to return. There was no suggestion that the children had been coached or influenced by their mother in what to say. Bracewell J said that it was necessary to consider what protection the courts in Dominica could give the children if they were returned, but she found that the evidence showed that it was acceptable in Dominica to treat children with physical violence. In the circumstances of the case, Bracewell J held that the court should not order the children's return.

However, the Court of Appeal allowed the father's appeal and remitted the case for a rehearing, on the basis that there had not been a sufficiently full investigation of the children's welfare, see *Re H (Abduction: Dominica: Corporal Punishment)* [2006] EWCA Civ 871, [2007] 1 FLR 72.

# Summary

1 Child abduction is a worldwide problem, caused by increasing family breakdown and increasing international mobility.

2 A child can be lawfully taken out of the UK provided there is no court order prohibiting removal and every person with parental responsibility consents. If consent is not forthcoming, a s.8 specific issue order can be sought under the Children Act 1989. Where a residence order is in force, there is an automatic prohibition against removing a child from the UK for more than one month unless all those with parental responsibility give written consent to the removal, or the court grants permission (s.13 Children Act 1989).

3 The following can be used to prevent abduction: a court order; passport control; and police assistance, including the 'All Ports Warning'.

4 Child abduction is a criminal offence under the Child Abduction Act 1984. Abduction can also constitute the criminal offence of kidnapping.

## Summary cont'd

5  If a parent who wishes to take a child out of the UK cannot obtain the consent of the other parent and/or other persons with parental responsibility, then he or she will have to make a relocation application in order to avoid committing a criminal offence or being in contempt of court.

6  The Family Law Act 1986 enables a court order made in one part of the UK to be enforced in another part.

7  The Hague Convention (to which the UK is a party) enables Contracting States to work together to return children wrongfully removed from their country of habitual residence or wrongfully retained in another Contracting State, subject to certain defences, but defences are rarely successful. Once a defence is made out, the court has an overriding discretion to decide whether or not it is in the child's best interests to order return.

8  In abductions within the European Union, in addition to the Hague Convention, it is also necessary to take into account the provisions of Council Regulation (EC) (No. 2201/2003) *Concerning Jurisdiction and the Recognition and Enforcement of Judgments in Matrimonial Matters and in Matters of Parental Responsibility* (Brussels II Revised).

9  The European Convention (to which the UK is a party) enables custody and access orders made in one Contracting State to be recognised, registered and enforced in another when the child has been improperly removed. Certain defences are available. The Convention is rarely invoked.

10 Where a child is wrongfully brought into England and Wales from a non-Convention country, the court will decide whether the welfare of the child requires it to order the child's return. There is no presumption in favour of return, as there is in Hague Convention cases.

## Further Reading and References

Bainham, 'Taking children abroad: human rights, welfare and the courts' [2001] *Cambridge Law Journal* 489.

Beevers, 'Child abduction: inchoate rights of custody and the unmarried father' [2006] CFLQ 499.

Brasse, District Judge, 'The *Payne* threshold: leaving the jurisdiction' [2005] Fam Law 780.

Braver *et al*, 'Relocation of children after divorce and children's best interests: new evidence and legal considerations' (2003) 17(2) *Journal of Family Psychology* 206.

Freedman, 'International terrorism and the grave risk defence of the Hague Convention on International Child Abduction' [2002] IFLJ 60.

Hayes, 'Relocation cases: is the Court of Appeal applying the correct principles?' [2006] CFLQ 351.

Herring and Taylor, 'Relocating relocation' [2006] CFLQ 517.

Longrigg, 'The leave to remove debate' [2005] Fam Law 911.

Perry, '*Payne* v. *Payne* – leave to remove from the jurisdiction' [2001] CFLQ 455.

Schuz, 'Habitual residence of children under the Hague Child Abduction Convention – theory and practice' [2001] CFLQ 1.

Spon-Smith, 'Relocation revisited' [2004] Fam Law 191.

Worwood, 'International relocation – the debate' [2005] Fam Law 621.

## Websites

**Foreign and Commonwealth Office**: www.fco.gov.uk/travel

**Hague Conference Website**: www.hcch.net

**INCADAT (Hague Convention Child Abduction Database)**: www.incadat.com

**International Child Abduction and Contact Unit (IACU)**:
www.officialsolicitor.gov.uk/os/iacu.htm

**Reunite (the International Child Abduction Centre)**: www.reunite.org

**UK Passport Service**: www.ukpa.gov.uk

# Chapter 15

## Child Protection

This chapter deals mainly with the legal provisions governing child protection which are laid down in the Children Act 1989. However, before considering that Act, the practice of child protection and other general matters are considered.

## 15.1  The Practice of Child Protection

### (a)  Personnel Involved in Child Protection

A wide range of different personnel are involved in the task of providing protection for children and services for children in need. The emphasis is on an inter-agency approach.

*Social Workers*  Social workers are responsible under the Children Act 1989 and the Children Act 2004 for working together with other agencies and relevant partners in order to protect children and to make provision for children in need. They work in departments headed by a Director of Social Services. Local authorities are required to set up strategic partnerships ('children's trusts') with health, educational and other bodies in order to co-ordinate children's services in their area. Local authorities also have duties and powers in respect of adoption (see Chapter 16). Local authority social services departments' responsibilities for child protection are laid down in the Children Acts 1989 and 2004, in rules of practice, in regulations and in various guidances, the main one being *Working Together to Safeguard Children: A Guide to Inter-Agency Working to Safeguard and Promote the Welfare of Children* (DfES, 2006) (available on the Every Child Matters website).

*Solicitors*  Solicitors who appear in public law children's cases under the Children Act 1989 are required to be accredited members of The Law Society's Children's Panel. The

Law Society's guidance, *Good Practice in Child Care Cases*, provides a set of good practice guidelines for solicitors.

*CAFCASS Officers*  Children's Guardians are officers of CAFCASS (see 1.4) who are experienced social workers appointed by the court in public law proceedings under the Children Act 1989 (and in adoption proceedings, see Chapter 16). They are independent of the local authority and their role is to safeguard the welfare of the child in the proceedings. The court has a duty to appoint a Children's Guardian on behalf of the child in proceedings for care and supervision orders, emergency protection orders and child assessment orders, unless it is satisfied that it is not necessary to do so in order to safeguard the child's interests. The Children's Guardian is responsible for instructing the lawyer on the child's behalf, but in certain circumstances the child can instruct the lawyer.

*Independent Reviewing Officers*  Each local authority is required to appoint an Independent Reviewing Officer (IRO), an experienced social worker who is responsible for reviewing the case of each child being 'looked after' by the local authority (that is, those children who are the subject of a full or interim care order or who are accommodated by the local authority). The IRO has the power to refer cases to CAFCASS, where appropriate, and CAFCASS can, if necessary, bring proceedings against the local authority.

*Voluntary Groups*  Voluntary agencies, such as the National Society for the Prevention of Cruelty to Children (NSPCC), also provides specialist services to protect and assist children and their families.

### (b)  The Practice of Child Protection – An Overview

*Children's Trusts*  Under the Children Act 2004 Children's Trusts have been created in order to bring together all the services for children and young people in an area, with the aim of improving outcomes for all children and young people by providing a better integrated and responsive service for them. Children's Trust partners include National Health Service Primary Care Trusts, Connexions, Youth Offending Teams and Sure Start local programmes.

*Local Safeguarding Children Boards (LSCBs)*  These have been established by local authorities under the Children Act 2004 to replace area child protection committees (which were non-statutory bodies). LSCBs are the key statutory mechanism for agreeing how the relevant organisations in each local area are to co-operate to safeguard and promote the welfare of children and for ensuring the effectiveness of what they do. LSCBs have a duty to co-ordinate local arrangements and services to safeguard children and to ensure their effectiveness. The partners who work together to safeguard children are prescribed by the Children Act 2004, and include local authorities, National Health Service bodies, the police, CAFCASS and other agencies. LSCBs are responsible for co-ordinating the child death review process which must take place when a child dies in the local authority area.

*The* Guidance – Working Together to Safeguard Children *(2006)*  This *Guidance*, which was revised in 2006 in order to incorporate the changes brought about by the Children Act

2004 (see 15.2), sets out how individuals and organisations working in the child protection system should work together to safeguard and promote the welfare of children. Part 1 is statutory guidance issued under s.7 Local Authority Social Services Act 1970 and must be complied with by local authorities carrying out their social service functions, unless local circumstances indicate exceptional reasons which justify a variation. Part 2 provides non-statutory practice guidelines. The *Guidance* is available on the Every Child Matters website.

*Encouraging the Adoption of Children in Care*   The Government has a policy of encouraging the adoption of more children in care (see Chapter 16). It hopes that the new provision in the Adoption and Children Act 2002 to allow cohabitants to make joint applications for adoption will also result in more children in care being adopted (see 16.7).

### (c)   The Task of Child Protection – Getting the Balance Right

Social workers engaged in the task of child protection have a difficult task in that they must tread a fine line between taking sufficient steps to protect children, while ensuring that they are not over-zealous in their task, and thereby too intrusive into family life. The law has to get this balance right. Social services departments are public authorities for the purposes of the Human Rights Act 1998 (see s.6), and must therefore exercise their duties and powers in line with the European Convention for the Protection of Human Rights (see below). They must respect the right of children and parents to enjoy a private and family life under art. 8 ECHR, while at the same time ensuring that children do not suffer inhuman and degrading treatment under art. 3. Local authorities can have their acts or omissions challenged in the courts (see 15.12, below).

Social workers are usually criticised, however, for not intervening enough, and there is considerable media coverage and concern when children are let down by the system. The Victoria Climbié case was such a case. Sometimes, but less often, social workers and other agencies working to protect children are criticised for being too interventionist. Thus, in the Cleveland affair in the 1980s, social workers were criticised for being too interventionist and too intrusive into family life, when more than one hundred children suspected of being sexually abused were taken away from their homes on the evidence of two paediatricians without other agencies being consulted. The report of the public enquiry set up in the aftermath of the Cleveland affair (*Report of the Enquiry into Child Abuse in Cleveland 1987*, Cm 412, 1987) recommended, *inter alia*, better inter-agency co-operation to protect children and better safeguards for parents and children where emergency intervention was needed. The *Report* had a considerable impact on the drafting of the Children Act 1989, in particular on the aim to achieve the correct balance between family autonomy and State intervention.

### (d)   Child Abuse

Local authorities are responsible for protecting children who have suffered, or who are at risk of suffering, child abuse. However, the Children Act 1989, the key statute making provision in respect of the powers and duties of social workers (and other persons), does not use the term 'child abuse'. Instead it uses the concept of 'significant harm' as the test for determining the legitimacy and appropriateness of State intervention to protect children. Guidance on what constitutes child abuse, however, is provided in various documents governing social work practice, in particular *Working Together to Safeguard Children* (2006). Child abuse can be categorised as: physical abuse; sexual abuse; emotional abuse; and neglect. These categories are used by social workers for the purpose of reporting abuse in child abuse registers. Child abuse can include a wide range of behaviour, for example bullying, harm caused by experiencing violence in the home, mental illness or drug or alcohol abuse on the part of a child's parent, and prostitution and other forms of commercial sexual exploitation.

According to statistics from the Department for Children, Schools and Families (20 September 2007), up till the end of March 2007 in respect of the 27,900 children who were subject to a Child Protection Plan or on a Child Protection Register, neglect was the most common category of abuse (approximately 40 per cent of children). The number of children subject to emotional abuse increased from about 21 per cent in 2006 to 23 per cent in 2007, and the number of children subject to physical abuse dropped slightly – from about 16 per cent to 15 per cent.

### (e) Taking a Child into Care

Despite the need to respect the right to family life, it will sometimes be necessary for a child to be removed from his home and placed in local authority care. This may be with a foster-carer, or in a children's home, or with the child's own parent, or a relative, or a family friend. However, taking a child into care can have its own set of problems, as children in care usually fare less well socially and educationally than other children. Many turn to crime. Some children have even suffered abuse at the hands of those working in the care system (see the Waterhouse Report, *Lost in Care*, 2000). One of the main aims of the Adoption and Children Act 2002 is for more children in care to be adopted so that they can reap the benefits of living in a permanent family (see Chapter 16).

### (f) The Problem of Delay

Delay in child care cases is a serious problem, which is contrary to the best interests of children and their families. The child is left uncertain as to his or her future, and the family is engaged in protracted proceedings. The *Scoping Study on the Causes of Delay* was published by the Lord Chancellor's Department in March 2002, identifying the causes of delay, and in November 2003 a *Protocol for Judicial Case Management in Public Law Children Act Cases* [2003] 2 FLR 719 was introduced with the aim of speeding things up. The *Protocol* sets a guideline of 40 weeks for care cases to be concluded. The focus in the *Protocol* is on the early identification of issues and effective case-management. It is available on the Ministry of Justice website. Because of continuing concerns about delay in child care cases, the Government published the *Review of the Child Care Proceedings System in England and Wales*. In order to improve care proceedings and reduce delay, the procedures laid down in the *Protocol* are to be replaced by a new streamlined and simpler procedure, laid down in the *Public Law Outline*, which will be implemented by means of a *Practice Direction* from April 2008.

## 15.2 The Children Act 2004

The Children Act 2004 was, in part, a response to the tragic death in February 2000 of Victoria Climbié, aged 8, who died from malnutrition and hypothermia after suffering months of torture and neglect, despite being in regular contact with social workers and other agencies. When she died she was found to have 128 injuries on her body. The inquiry, chaired by Lord Laming, found grave errors on the part of social services and criticised social workers and other agencies for failing to intervene (see the *Laming Report on the Inquiry into the Death of Victoria Climbié*, Cm 5730, January 2003). Lord Laming found the Children Act 1989 to be fundamentally sound, but that there had been gaps in its implementation. The problem lay not in the legislation, but in the practice of child protection. It was persons working in the child protection system who were at fault. In fact, the key social worker for Victoria and the senior supervising social worker had not read the guidance for social work practice (*Working Together to Safeguard Children*). The concerns in the *Laming Report* related to lack of good practice; and organisational and management problems. There was poor co-ordination and a failure to share information, and no one with a strong sense of accountability. In all, Lord Laming made some 108 recommendations.

In September 2003, alongside its response to the recommendations of the *Laming Report*, the Government published a consultation paper, *Every Child Matters* (Cm 5960, 2003, DfES), in which it proposed radical changes to the whole system of children's services. Following the consultation, the Government published a White Paper (*Every Child Matters: The Next Steps*). (See also *Keeping Children Safe*, 2003, DfES.) These proposals were subsequently enacted as part of the Children Act 2004.

A main aim of the Children Act 2004 is to improve the life chances for all children by providing better integrated services, and by improving multi-disciplinary practices. A greater emphasis is placed on inter-agency working in combating child abuse. Key developments include: the creation of Children's Trusts under the duty to co-operate; the setting up of Local Safeguarding Children's Boards; and imposing a duty on all agencies to make arrangements to safeguard and promote the welfare of children.

A key provision of the Act is s.10 which requires each local authority to make arrangements to promote co-operation between the authority, each of the authority's relevant partners and such other persons or bodies working with children in the local authority area, as the authority considers appropriate. The arrangements are to be made with a view to improving the well-being of children in the authority's area, which includes protection from harm or neglect alongside other outcomes. Section 10 is the legislative basis for Children's Trusts arrangements. Section 11 places duties on organisations and individuals to ensure that their functions are discharged with regard to the need to safeguard and promote the welfare of children. A range of organisations is required to take part in Local Safeguarding Children Boards (LSCBs) (see ss.13–16). The role of LSCBs is to co-ordinate and ensure the effectiveness of what is done by each person or body represented on the board to safeguard and promote the welfare of children in the area (s.14).

Section 12 of the Act makes provision for the creation of a nationwide database of children, which will enable local authorities, the National Health Service and other agencies to share information on suspected abuse or neglect in families, with the aim of achieving early intervention. This database (called 'ContactPoint') will contain the name, address, medical and school details of children and be used by vetted headteachers, doctors, youth and social workers and fire and rescue staff. It will enable professionals to see the contacts that children have had with statutory agencies and flag up regular contact that needs attention.

**15.3** The European Convention for the Protection of Human Rights and Child Protection

As local authorities and courts are public authorities under the Human Rights Act (HRA) 1998, they must exercise their powers and duties in compliance with the European Convention for the Protection of Human Rights and Fundamental Freedoms (ECHR) (see 1.5). As the case-law of the European Court of Human Rights (ECtHR) must be taken into account by the courts in England and Wales (s.2(1) HRA 1998), this case-law is also relevant to social work practice. A local authority social services department which is found to be in breach of the ECHR can be made to pay damages under the HRA 1998, although damages are not automatic, as the court must be satisfied 'that the award is necessary to afford just satisfaction to the person in whose favour it is made' (s.8).

*The Right to Family Life – The Presumption in Favour of Parents*    Article 8 ECHR guarantees a right to respect for family life. The essential aim of art. 8 is to protect individuals against arbitrary action by public authorities. There are also positive obligations inherent in 'respect' for family life (see 1.5).

In order to comply with the right to family life guaranteed by art. 8, public authorities must ensure that any interference into family life is: in accordance with the law; is for a legitimate aim; and is necessary in a democratic society.

The presumption in favour of keeping children in their families unless contrary to their best interests, which is a presumption recognised by the courts in the UK (see 10.1), is also recognised by the ECtHR as part of the right to family life in art. 8 ECHR. In *Haase v. Germany (Application No. 11057/02)* [2004] 2 FLR 39 the ECtHR held that:

- authorities should make a careful assessment of the impact of proposed care measures on parents and children, and of the alternatives to taking children into public care;
- following a removal into care, a stricter scrutiny is called for in respect of any further limitations by the authorities, for example in respect of restrictions on parental rights and access;
- taking a child into care should normally be regarded as a temporary measure to be discontinued as soon as circumstances permit, and any measures of implementation of temporary care should be consistent with the ultimate aim of reuniting the natural parent;
- taking a newborn baby into public care at the moment of its birth is an extremely harsh measure, for which there must be extraordinarily compelling reasons.

In *Hokkanen* v. *Finland* (1995) 19 EHRR 139, [1996] 1 FLR 289 the ECtHR held that a 'fair balance has to be struck between the interests of the child in remaining in public care and those of the parent in being reunited with the child', but that in carrying out that balancing exercise 'the best interests of the child . . . may override those of the parent'.

The ECtHR has only rarely held that taking a child into care violates art. 8, but it has done so in the case of newborn babies (see *K and T* v. *Finland* (2001) 36 EHRR 255, [2001] 2 FLR 707; and *P, C and S* v. *UK* (2002) 35 EHRR 31, [2002] 2 FLR 631). However, when children are taken into care, the ECtHR has held that public authorities must aim to seek to restore the child to his or her family as soon as is practicable, and that any measure which hinders this (such as prohibiting contact or placing the child a long way away) may violate art. 8 (see, for example, *KA* v. *Finland* [2003] 1 FLR 696).

*The Right to Family Life – The Principle of Proportionality*    An important principle in respect of the right to family life in art. 8 ECHR is that of proportionality (see 1.5). Local authorities and courts must ensure that any intervention into family life, by court order or otherwise, is a proportionate response to a legitimate aim, otherwise they risk being in breach of art. 8. Thus, for example, it might be a disproportionate response for a local authority to remove a child from his home under a care order before having first exhausted its support functions, or to remove a baby shortly after birth without giving the mother an opportunity to improve her parenting skills.

In *Johansen* v. *Norway* (1997) 23 EHRR 33 the ECtHR held that the mother's right to family life had been breached, because she had been deprived of her parental rights and her access rights when her daughter had been taken into care and placed with foster-parents with a view to adoption. However, each case depends on its facts. In *Söderbäck* v. *Sweden* [1999] 1 FLR 250, on the other hand, the ECtHR distinguished *Johansen* on its facts, and found no breach of art. 8.

The principle of proportionality was considered in the following cases:

▶ *Re C and B (Care Order: Future Harm)* [2001] 1 FLR 611

The mother's eldest child was subject to a care order, and her two younger children subject to interim care orders. When the mother gave birth to a fourth child, an emergency protection order was made. The judge later made full care orders in respect of the two younger children and gave the local authority permission to refuse contact between the parents and all four children. The Court of Appeal allowed the appeal in respect of the two younger children, holding that the action taken must be a proportionate response to the nature and gravity of the feared harm. The local authority should have taken time to explore other options. There had been too much speed in the circumstances. Hale LJ referred to the decisions of the ECtHR on the requirement that interference must be necessary and proportionate to the legitimate aim, and held that, while intervention in the family can be appropriate, cutting off contact and a relationship between a child and his family is only justified by the overriding necessity of the best interests of the child.

▶ *Re B (Care: Interference with Family Life)* [2003] EWCA Civ 786, [2003] 2 FLR 813

The Court of Appeal found that the threshold criteria for a care order had been satisfied, but that the interim care order was not a proportionate response under art. 8, as the children would have been sufficiently protected by an order adjourning the application for an interim care order with liberty to renew at short notice. Here the parents had been denied the opportunity of challenging or testing the evidence of a psychiatrist who had alleged that their daughter had been sexually abused by her grandfather.

▶ *Re W (Removal into Care)* [2005] EWCA Civ 642, [2005] 2 FLR 1022

Care orders were made in respect of 5-year-old twins on the basis of a care plan whereby they would remain at home with their parents. As this did not work well, a decision was taken to remove them from their home, and the local authority applied to free them for adoption. The parents, in response, applied to discharge the care orders and sought an injunction under s.8 HRA 1998 to enable the twins to return. Their applications failed. The judge held that there had been no breach of s.8, as the local authority's response was a proportionate and legitimate response to the deterioration of the home situation. The decision was upheld by the Court of Appeal, but it held that parents must issue a HRA 1998 challenge prior to the removal of children and not as a reaction to their removal.

*Procedural Fairness and Human Rights*   A recurring issue in child care cases is that of procedural fairness. Parents sometimes claim that they have not been sufficiently involved in the decision-making process and that, as a result, a decision is in breach of their right to family life. They may argue that they were not allowed to attend meetings with social workers, or were not given reasons for a decision that was made. Lack of procedural fairness can be both a breach of art. 6 ECHR (right to a fair trial) and art. 8 (right to family life). Parents must be fully involved in the decision-making process.

The case-law shows that professionals, particularly local authorities engaged in care and supervision proceedings under Part IV of the Children Act 1989 (see 15.7), may infringe the rights of parents and other parties to proceedings under arts. 6 and 8 of the ECHR 'unless overall they conduct themselves with such integrity, transparency and inclusiveness as to satisfy their rights, necessarily to be construed in a wide sense, to a fair hearing and to respect for their private and family life' (Wilson LJ in *Re J (Care: Assessment: Fair Trial)* [2006] EWCA Civ 545, [2007] 1 FLR 77).

Procedural fairness was considered in the following cases:

▶ *Re L (Care: Assessment: Fair Trial)* **[2002] EWHC 1379 (Fam), [2002] 2 FLR 730**

The mother whose child was the subject of care proceedings was not permitted to attend meetings between the local authority, the psychiatrist and the guardian when concerns about her parenting were expressed. No minutes of the meeting were taken, and the mother was not informed of the outcome. Munby J held that the right to procedural fairness under art. 6 ECHR was not confined to the judicial process, but that a local authority when taking a child into care was under a heavy obligation in respect of a transparent and fair procedure at all stages of the process, both in and out of court. Munby J emphasised certain principles of good social work practice. He said that social workers must notify parents of material criticisms, and advise them how to remedy their behaviour. All professionals involved should keep clear, accurate and full notes and the local authority should make full and frank disclosure of all key documents at an early stage of proceedings. They should provide reports, and parents should be able to make representations, and have the right to attend meetings held by the professionals involved.

▶ *Re V (Care: Pre-Birth Actions)* **[2004] EWCA Civ 1575, [2005] 1 FLR 627**

A care order was made on the application of the local authority (and the child was freed for adoption) almost immediately after the child's birth (the other three children were already in care). The judge held that there had been a breach of the parents' art. 6 rights (rights to procedural fairness) in respect of the local authority's handling of the pre-birth management of the case, as they should have said more to the parents about how to improve their parenting. The judge awarded damages of £100 to each parent. The local authority appealed to the Court of Appeal arguing that: any failure of communication lay with the parents (the mother had cancelled six pre-arranged visits); and that, even if there had been a failure of communication, it could not possibly amount to unlawfulness under the HRA 1998, and could not constitute a breach, since it pre-dated the birth of the child.

The Court of Appeal allowed the appeal, holding that there was no breach of the ECHR and no unlawfulness under the HRA 1998. It said that, when deciding whether or not there had been a breach of the ECHR, the court had to ascertain whether the proceedings taken as a whole were fair (see, for example, *Mantovanelli v. France* (1997) 24 EHRR 370). It was manifestly impermissible to isolate one alleged incident and use it as a basis for finding that there had been a breach of art. 6. Trial judges should be extremely cautious in reading too much into Munby J's judgment in *Re L* (see above), in which he intended merely to draw attention to certain principles of practice that deserved emphasis, but which he did not intend to be taken as a statement of good practice. It was difficult to postulate a case in which the acts or omissions of a social worker acting in that role exclusively at a period before the birth of the relevant child and at a period prior to the initiation of proceedings could constitute a breach of art. 6, or could amount to unlawfulness under the HRA 1998.

▶ *P, C and S* v. *United Kingdom* (2002) 35 EHRR 31, [2002] 2 FLR 631

The ECtHR held that the removal of the baby at birth under an emergency protection order breached the parents' right to family life (under art. 8 ECHR) and their right to a fair trial (under art. 6 ECHR), as they did not have legal representation in the care and freeing for adoption proceedings. The child's right to family life was also held to be breached even though she was represented in the proceedings. The ECtHR stressed that emergency measures to remove a child from a situation of danger must be properly justified by the circumstances, and parents must have procedural protection, as part of the right to family life under art. 8, not just under art. 6.

▶ *Re J (Care: Assessment: Fair Trial)* [2006] EWCA Civ 545, [2007] 1 FLR 77

The Court of Appeal held that the way in which the local authority had reached its decision and communicated its care plan had fallen short of the proper standard of fairness and transparency expected of a local authority in care proceeding. This was because the mother should have been invited to comment on the concerns that were inclining the local authority towards adoption rather than a residential assessment; and the local authority had failed to make clear that the decision was one to which neither the family centre nor the guardian were party. However, while the local authority's conduct lacked fairness and transparency it was not sufficient to constitute an infringement of the mother's rights under art. 6 or art. 8 ECHR. Neither of the two failings by the local authority were sufficiently substantial to affect the fairness of the proceedings.

The European Court of Human Rights has held that parents must have access to the information which the local authority relies on for taking measures of protective care (*Venema* v. *The Netherlands (Application No. 35731/97)* [2003] 1 FLR 551). It has also held that a care order must be capable of convincing an objective observer that it is based on a careful and unprejudiced assessment of all the evidence with the distinct reasons for the care measures being explicitly stated and with all the case material being available to the parents concerned, even if they have not requested it (*KA* v. *Finland* [2003] 1 FLR 696; and see also *K and T* v. *Finland* (2001) 36 EHRR 255, [2001] 2 FLR 707).

*Procedure for Human Rights Claims*    A complaint arising under the Human Rights Act 1998 before a final care order is made should normally be made in the care proceedings by the court dealing with those proceedings (Sir Mark Potter P in *Westminster City Council* v. *RA, B and S* [2005] EWHC 970 (Fam), [2005] 2 FLR 1309, endorsing the approach of Munby J in *Re L (Care Proceedings: Human Rights Claims)* [2003] EWHC 665 (Fam), [2003] 2 FLR 160, and Butler-Sloss P in *Re V (Care Proceedings: Human Rights Claims)* [2004] EWCA Civ 54, [2004] 1 FLR 944).

In *Re S and W (Care Proceedings)* [2007] EWCA Civ 232, [2007] 2 FLR 275 Wall LJ endorsed this approach and said that 'it would be wholly undesirable to have separate proceedings for a care or supervision order under Part IV of the Children Act 1989 running concurrently with proceedings for judicial review'. (See also Wilson LJ in *Re J (Care: Assessment: Fair Trial)* [2006] EWCA Civ 545, [2007] 1 FLR 77.)

However, an application under the Human Rights Act 1998 should not be allowed to unnecessarily delay the trial of a care case (Munby J in *Re L*, above).

## 15.4  The United Nations Convention on the Rights of the Child 1989

The United Nations Convention on the Rights of the Child 1989 (UNCRC) (see 9.2) contains various articles which are relevant to child protection. The courts sometimes refer to the UNCRC when making decisions about children and families. Under the UNCRC States Parties must:

- take all measures to protect children from all forms of abuse while in the care of their parents, guardians and any other person (art. 19);
- ensure the child such protection and care as are necessary for the child's well-being, taking into account the rights and duties of his or her parents or others with parental responsibility, and to this end take all appropriate legislative and administrative measures (art. 3(2));
- ensure that a child shall not be separated from his or her parents against their will, except when competent authorities subject to judicial review determine that such separation is necessary for the best interests of the child; and all interested parties must be given an opportunity to participate in the proceedings and make their views known (art. 9(1)).

Other articles are also relevant, for example art. 34 (right to be protected from sexual exploitation and abuse), and art. 40(4) (right to care, guidance, supervision, counselling and foster-care).

## 15.5  The Children Act 1989

The Children Act 1989 provides local authorities and the courts with various powers and duties relating to State provision for, and State protection of, children. Thus, if a child is in need, local authorities have various powers and duties to provide support under Part III of the Children Act 1989. Local authorities have inquiry and investigative duties and powers (s.47). Where emergency action is needed, local authorities can apply for an emergency protection order (s.44). If a local authority suspects that a child is being ill-treated or is failing to develop properly, and some form of assessment is needed, it can apply for a child assessment order (s.43). If, having investigated the case, it considers that the child is, or is likely to suffer, significant harm, it can apply for a care or supervision order (s.31). In certain limited situations, a local authority can invoke the inherent jurisdiction of the High Court (see 9.7).

Local authority social services departments and the courts must exercise their powers and duties under the Children Act 1989 in accordance with the European Convention for the Protection of Human Rights – as they are public authorities for the purposes of the Human Rights Act 1998 (see 1.5, and 15.3, above).

(a) The Policy Objectives of the Children Act 1989

The practice of child protection under the Children Act 1989 is based on certain important policy objectives.

*(i) Keeping Children in Their Families*    A major policy objective of the Act is that parents, not local authorities, have primary responsibility for their children, and that children should be kept in their families, except where this is contrary to their best interests. Social services and the courts carry out their functions on the basis of the presumption that intervention into family life is a serious matter and is only justified where it is a legitimate and proportionate response in the circumstances. As Johnson J said in *B* v. *B (A Minor) (Residence Order)* [1992] 2 FLR 327:

> 'It is inherent to the philosophy underlying the Children Act 1989 that Parliament has decreed that the State, whether in the guise of a local authority or the court, shall not intervene in the life of children and their families unless it is necessary to do so.'

Wall LJ in *Re L and H (Residential Assessment)* [2007] EWCA Civ 213, [2007] 1 FLR 1370 (see further at 15.7, below) held that the following words of Lord Templeman in *Re KD (A Minor)(Ward: Termination of Access)* [1988] AC 806, [1988] 2 FLR 139 underlie the Children Act 1989:

> 'The best person to bring up a child is the natural parent. It matters not whether the parent is wise or foolish, rich or poor, educated or illiterate, provided the child's moral and physical health are not endangered. Public authorities cannot improve on nature. Public authorities exercise a supervisory role and interfere to rescue a child when the parental tie is broken by abuse or separation. In terms of the English rule [compared with the European rule under art. 8 ECHR] the court decides whether and to what extent the welfare of the child requires that the child shall be protected against harm caused by the parent, including harm which could be caused by the resumption of parental care after separation has broken the parental tie.'

The Children Act 1989 reinforces this policy of keeping children in their families, where possible, in the following ways:

▷ Under s.1(5) the court can only make an order (for example, a care or supervision order) if 'it considers that doing so would be better for the child than making no order at all'.
▷ Rules of social work practice require local authorities to work in partnership with parents to promote and safeguard the welfare of children to prevent them being taken into care. Parents must be allowed to participate in decisions about their children, and so must children who are intelligent and mature enough to do so.
▷ Removing a child from his parents is a serious matter, which can only be effected by a court order and only on proof of certain grounds, for example that the child is suffering, or is likely to suffer, significant harm, and only after a thorough investigation and consideration of all the evidence.

*Re D (Care: Natural Parent Presumption)* [1999] 1 FLR 134 provides a good example of the parental presumption being applied. Here the court had to decide whether the child who was subject to a care order should be placed with his father or with his grandmother with whom the elder siblings were living. The Court of Appeal held that the child should be placed with his father even though this would separate him from his siblings, on the basis of the presumption in favour of parents. Where the court has to consider which of two persons shall look after a child subject to a care order, and one of these persons is a parent, it will first consider the natural parent as the potential carer, and then decide whether any compelling factors exist which displace the presumption in favour of the parent.

The presumption in favour of keeping children in their families is also recognised by the European Court of Human Rights (see 15.3, above).

*(ii) Working in Partnership with Parents*    In order to promote the presumption that children are best kept in their families, local authorities are required to work in partnership with parents and to involve parents as fully as possible. The guidance, *Working Together to Safeguard Children*, establishes two key policy objectives governing good social work practice: the importance of inter-agency co-operation; and the importance of encouraging partnership and participation with parents. Social workers are therefore required to consult with teachers, the police, doctors, probation officers and other people involved with the child, and to consider their views. A key principle of good practice is therefore the promotion of positive partnerships between families and social services and other agencies. Families are encouraged to participate in the decision-making process, and only in exceptional circumstances will parents be excluded from meetings. If they are excluded, they must be permitted to express their views in other ways. A failure to involve parents sufficiently in the process could be a breach of art. 8 or of art. 6 of the European Convention for the Protection of Human Rights (see 15.3, above).

*(iii) Inter-Agency Co-operation*    Another policy aim of the Children Act 1989 is that of inter-agency co-operation, whereby the various agencies (for example, social services, local education authorities and health authorities) must consult with each other and be willing to provide help if this is in the best interests of a child (see ss.27 and 47 Children Act 1989). As part of this emphasis on inter-agency co-operation, s.27 provides that local authorities, local education authorities, local housing authorities and local health authorities (or National Health Service Trusts) have a right to request help from each other and have a reciprocal duty to provide it, except where this is incompatible with their own statutory obligations. Under s.27, for example, a social services department could ask a local housing department to provide accommodation for a child leaving care (see 4.13). The importance of communication and information-sharing about children was emphasised in the *Cleveland Report* (see p.384, above). It was emphasised again in the *Laming Report on the Victoria Climbié Inquiry* (Cm 5730) even where the evidence justified no more than a suspicion of harm. The findings of the *Laming Report* led ultimately to the enactment of the Children Act 2004, where an even greater emphasis has been placed on inter-agency co-operation (see 15.2, above). Inter-agency co-operation is facilitated by Local Safeguarding Children Boards (set up under the Children Act 2004 to replace Area Child Protection Committees).

### (b)  Local Authority Powers and Duties Under the Children Act 1989 – An Overview

Local authority social services departments have a wide range of powers and duties under the Children Act 1989.

An important task for social services departments is to decide whether a child is a 'child in need' or is suffering, or is at risk of suffering, significant harm. If social services are alerted about a child, it conducts an initial assessment. If, after the initial assessment, social services have reasonable cause to suspect that the child is suffering, or is likely to suffer, significant harm, then it must under s.47 Children Act 1989 make such inquiries as are necessary to enable it to decide whether to take any action to safeguard or promote the welfare of the child (s.47(1)). This will mean visiting the child to make an assessment, unless there is already sufficient information available (s.47(4)). If access to the child is thwarted and social services are concerned about the child, it can consider applying for an emergency protection order under s.44 or invoking police powers under s.46. In respect of their s.47 investigative functions, local authorities are not required to make a finding on the balance of probabilities as to past conduct before assessing risk and taking any necessary protective steps (see *Re S (Sexual Abuse Allegations: Local Authority Response)* [2001] EWHC Admin 334, [2001] 2 FLR 776).

If, following initial inquiries, the child is assessed as not being at risk of harm, social services will consider whether the child and family need support under Part III of the Children Act. If, however, it is established that the child is, or is at risk of, suffering significant harm, then a child protection conference will be convened. This takes the form of a multi-agency meeting at which information is assessed and plans made to safeguard and promote the child's welfare. If the child is, or will be, at risk, his name will be placed on the child protection register. Following the decision to register the child, the conference must formulate a child protection plan, which may mean initiating care proceedings. A key worker for the child must be appointed. Regular reviews must be carried out, and if the child is no longer at risk of significant harm, the child will be deregistered. If the initial assessment reveals a likelihood of serious immediate harm, emergency protection measures will have to be taken.

## 15.6 Part III of the Children Act 1989 – Support for Children in Need

### (a) Introduction

Under Part III of the Children Act 1989 local authorities have a duty to provide support for children in need and their families. 'Family' for this purpose includes not just parents and children, but any person with parental responsibility or any other person with whom the child is living (s.17(10)). Services can only be provided, however, with a view to safeguarding or promoting the welfare of a child in need (s.17(3)). Part III duties include the provision of services (ss.17–19) and the provision of accommodation (ss.20 and 21). Local authorities have duties to children 'looked after' by them (ss.22 and 23) and must provide advice and assistance (s.24), and in some cases secure accommodation (s.25). Local authorities must hold case-reviews, co-operate with each other and consult with and request help from other authorities within the local area (such as housing authorities, local education authorities, heath authorities and health service trusts) (see ss.26–30). Schedule 2 to the Children Act lists the services which local authorities can supply for children in need and their families.

The provision of support under Part III may obviate the need to bring care or supervision proceedings. Help and support for the child in his own home is the preferred option, with compulsory intervention by court order only as the last resort. However, although the Children Act lays down a duty to safeguard and promote the welfare of children, the provision of services is only a discretionary matter. The provision of services is ultimately a question of local authority policy and depends on the allocation and availability of resources, which are often limited. For this reason, it is difficult to bring a successful challenge against a local authority.

Local authorities have various duties to children in need under Part III of the Children Act 1989, but these include in particular the duty:

- to safeguard and promote the child's welfare (s.22(3));
- to consult the wishes and feelings of the child, his parents, any person who has parental responsibility for the child, and any other person who the local authority considers relevant (s.22(4));
- to provide accommodation and maintenance for a child (s.23(2));
- to maintain the child in other respects apart from providing accommodation (s.23(1)(b));
- to promote contact (Sched. 2, para. 4);
- to provide 'after care' for children who leave care (s.24(1)).

### (b) Who is a 'Child in Need'?

A child is a 'child in need' for the purposes of Part III if (s.17(10)):

'(a) he is unlikely to achieve or maintain, or to have the opportunity of achieving or maintaining, a reasonable standard of health or development without the provision of services by a local authority under [Part III];
(b) his health or development is likely to be significantly impaired, or further impaired, without the provision for him of such services; or
(c) he is disabled.'

A child is 'disabled' if he is blind, deaf or dumb or suffers from mental disorder of any kind or is substantially and permanently handicapped by illness, injury or congenital deformity or such other disability as may be prescribed; and 'development' means physical, intellectual, emotional, social or behavioural development; and 'health' means physical or mental health (s.17(11)).

### (c) The Part III General Duty

The general duty of local authorities in respect of children in need is laid down in s.17(1):

---

**Section 17(1)  Children Act 1989**

'It shall be the general duty of every local authority, in addition to the other duties imposed on them by [Part III]:
(a) to safeguard and promote the welfare of children within their area who are in need; and
(b) so far as is consistent with that duty, to promote the upbringing of such children by their families,
by providing a range and level of services appropriate to those children's needs.'

---

For the purpose of facilitating the discharge of their general duty under s.17(1), every local authority is required to have regard to the specific duties and powers set out in Part I of Sched. 2 to the Children Act 1989 (s.17(2)).

The scope of the general duty in s.17(1) was considered by the House of Lords in the following case. All three appeals raised the question of whether social services departments were obliged to provide accommodation for children in need and their families under the Children Act 1989 when the local housing authority was unable to house or rehouse them:

---

▶ *R (G)* v. *Barnet London Borough Council; R (W)* v. *Lambeth London Borough Council; R (A)* v. *Lambeth London Borough Council* [2003] UKHL 57, [2004] 1 FLR 454

In each appeal the mother argued that s.17(1) required a local authority to assess and meet the needs of an individual child in need. One local authority had adopted a policy of making accommodation available for a child in need (but not his parents). A second question therefore arose as to whether a local authority could meet a child's needs for accommodation by providing accommodation for the child alone, as distinct from providing accommodation for both mother and child, when it would cost no more to provide accommodation for them both.

The House of Lords held, dismissing all three appeals, that s.17(1) set out duties of a general character which were intended to be for the benefit of all the children in need in the local social services authority's area in general, and not for each and every individual child in need. Consequently, a local social services authority was not under a duty to provide residential accommodation for families so that children could be housed with their families. Although social services could provide accommodation for a child in need and his family, this was not the principal or primary purpose of the legislation. Housing was the function of the local housing authority. An obligation under s.17(1) to provide housing would turn social services departments into housing authorities and thereby subvert the powers and duties of housing authorities under the housing legislation.

---

(d)  Services for Children in Need

The general duty of local authorities laid down in s.17(1) above is facilitated by the performance of specific duties and powers laid down in Part I of Sched. 2 (s.17(2)), such as the identification and assessment of children in need, advertising available services, keeping a register of and providing services for disabled children, preventing neglect and abuse, providing accommodation for those who are ill-treating or are likely to ill-treat children in order to reduce the need for criminal or civil proceedings, reintegrating children in need with their families, promoting contact between a child and his family and so on. Where a child in need is living with his family, appropriate services must be provided, such as advice, activities, home help, travelling assistance and assistance to enable the child and his family to have a holiday. Local authorities must establish 'family centres', where children and families can go for advice, guidance or counselling, and for various social and cultural activities. Local authorities must also, when making day-care arrangements or recruiting local authority foster-parents, consider the different racial groups to which children belong.

Before determining what (if any) services to provide for a particular child in need, a local authority must, so far as is reasonably practicable and consistent with the child's welfare, ascertain the child's wishes and feelings regarding the provision of those services, and give due consideration to those wishes and feelings, having regard to the child's age and understanding (s.17(4A)). Services can include the provision of accommodation, and assistance can be assistance in kind or in exceptional circumstances in cash (s.17(6)). Conditions can be imposed as to repayment of cash, unless a person is receiving Income Support or Family Credit (s.17(7)). Before providing assistance or imposing conditions, the financial means of the child and his parents must be considered (s.17(8)). Local authorities have a duty to facilitate the provision of similar services by others bodies, including in particular voluntary organisations, and may delegate their powers to those bodies (s.17(5)).

In addition to the duties above, the Children Act has been amended to allow parents to purchase services from the local authority for their disabled children and for a voucher scheme to be established for this purpose (see ss.17A and 17B).

### (e)  The Provision of Day Care

Local authorities must provide appropriate day care for pre-school children in need, and, at their discretion, for children who are not in need (ss.18(1), (2) and (4)). Schoolchildren in need must be provided with care or supervised activities outside school hours or during school holidays (s.18(5)), and children not in need may be provided with care or supervised activities (s.18(6)). The Act contains lengthy provisions for the review of day care, in particular in respect of child-minders.

### (f)  The Provision of Accommodation

Some families may need help, for instance, when a parent dies, or a parent is ill, or for some other reason cannot care for a child. Local authorities have a power under s.17(6) to provide accommodation for children in need, and ss.20–25 of the Children Act 1989 lay down various duties in respect of the provision of accommodation for children in need.

The duty to provide children in need with accommodation is laid down in s.20(1):

---

**Section 20(1)  Children Act 1989**

'Every local authority shall provide accommodation for any child in need within their area who appears to them to require accommodation as a result of –
(a)  there being no person who has parental responsibility for him . . .;
(b)  his being lost or having been abandoned; or
(c)  the person who has been caring for him being prevented (whether or not permanently, and for whatever reason) from providing him with suitable accommodation or care.'

---

Although s.20 provides that there is a duty to provide accommodation if the conditions (a) to (c) are satisfied, there is no duty if the local authority's assessment of the case finds that accommodation is not required (for example, where the child requires only help with accommodation, see *R (S)* v. *Sutton London Borough Council* EWHC 1196 (Admin), [2007] 2 FLR 849).

Before providing accommodation under s.20 the local authority must, so far as is reasonably practicable and consistent with the child's welfare, ascertain the child's wishes and feelings regarding the provision of accommodation; and give due consideration (having regard to his age and understanding) to those wishes and feelings (s.20(6)). The local authority must also draw up a written care plan for the child. A child who is accommodated by a local authority is described as being 'looked after' by the local authority, whereupon it has certain statutory duties in respect of the child (ss.23–30). Children who are in care under a court order are also described as being 'looked after' and similar duties are owed to them under the same provisions.

Accommodation can be provided by the local authority by placing the child with another family, with a relative, with some other suitable person, or in a children's home (s.23(2)). Any family member, relative and any other person providing accommodation for a child is described as being a local authority foster-parent (s.23(3)).

Accommodation must also be provided for a child aged 16 or over if a local authority considers the child's welfare is likely to be seriously prejudiced without it (s.20(3)). Accommodation in a community home can be provided for someone aged 16 to 21 if it will safeguard or promote his or her welfare (s.20(5)) (see, for example, *Re T (Accommodation by Local Authority)* [1995] 1 FLR 159, where a 17-year-old girl successfully challenged by way of judicial review a refusal of accommodation, as the court held that the director of social services had erred in considering only her past circumstances and not her future welfare).

A local authority has no duty, however, to provide accommodation if a person with parental responsibility objects, and is able to provide accommodation or arrange for it to be provided (s.20(7)). The only exception is where a person with a residence order or who has care of the child under a court order agrees to the child being accommodated by the local authority (s.20(9)). Any person with parental responsibility may remove the child from local authority accommodation at any time without giving notice (s.20(8)), except where the child is aged 16 or over and agrees to being provided with accommodation (s.20(1)). As the arrangement is voluntary the local authority must comply with the wishes of persons with parental responsibility, unless the child is suffering, or is likely to suffer, significant harm, in which case a care or supervision order or an emergency protection order will be applied for. The right to decide where the child lives remains with the parents, so that a local authority has no power to remove a child to different accommodation if this is contrary to parental wishes (see *R v. Tameside Metropolitan Borough Council ex parte J* [2000] 1 FLR 942, where the parents of a seriously disabled 13-year-old girl successfully challenged by way of judicial review a local authority's decision to move their daughter from a residential home into foster-care, as the court held that the local authority has no power to move the child to different accommodation where it was contrary to parental wishes).

The extent of the duty to provide children in need with accommodation as part of the general duty under s.17 Children Act 1989 was considered by the House of Lords in *R (G) v. Barnet London Borough Council; R (W) v. Lambeth London Borough Council; R (A) v. Lambeth London Borough Council* [2003] UKHL 57, [2004] 1 FLR 454 (above). However, a local authority cannot opt out of its duty to provide accommodation under s.20 Children Act 1989 (see above) by claiming that the duty is merely a general duty to act under s.17; or that it is merely a power (Holman J in *H, Barhanu and B v. London Borough of Wandsworth, London Borough of Hackney, London Borough of Islington and Secretary of State for Education and Skills (Interested Party)* [2007] EWHC 1082 (Admin), [2007] 2 FLR 822).

### (g) The Duty to Provide Accommodation for Children Leaving Care

If a child has been looked after by a local authority for more than a prescribed period of 13 weeks when he or she attains the age of 18, then at that date he or she becomes a 'former relevant child' in respect of whom the local authority has a range of powers and duties under the leaving care provisions, which include the provision of accommodation until the age of 21 or, in some cases, until the age of 24 (see 15.11, and see s.24B Children Act 1989).

### (h)  Accommodating Children in Need – Relationship with Local Housing Authorities

Local authority social services and local authority housing departments are required to co-operate with each other in respect of providing accommodation (see ss.27 and 47 Children Act 1989; and s.213A Housing Act 1996). Sometimes the interface between the obligations to provide accommodation under the children legislation and the housing legislation can create difficulties which may result in litigation (see , for example, *R (M)* v. *London Borough of Hammersmith and Fulham* [2008] UKHL 14 where an 18-year-old girl unsuccessfully applied in judicial review proceedings for a declaration that the local authority had obligations to her under the Children Act 1989, not the Housing Act 1996, because she was a former 'relevant child' under the Children Act 1989 when she had applied for accommodation at the age of 17).

## 15.7  Part IV of the Children Act 1989 – Care and Supervision

Voluntary arrangements provided under Part III of the Children Act 1989 may not work in some cases, or it may come to the notice of a local authority that a child is being, or is at risk of being, harmed. In such circumstances a local authority social services department may have to intervene by bringing proceedings for a care or supervision order under Part IV of the Act, and/or by taking emergency action under Part V.

*Care Order or Supervision Order?*  Although the same threshold criteria apply to the making of care and supervision orders (see further below), the two orders are totally different. A care order places a child in the care of a designated local authority. A supervision order places a child under the supervision of a designated local authority or a probation officer. A care order is a stronger and more serious order than a supervision order, and will be made in preference to a supervision order only where it is really necessary for the child's protection (*Re B (Care or Supervision Order)* [1996] 2 FLR 693). There must be cogent and strong reasons to make a care order rather than a supervision order, as a care order is a more draconian order (Hale J in *Oxfordshire County Council* v. *L (Care or Supervision Order)* [1998] 1 FLR 70). In *Re O (Care or Supervision Order)* [1996] 2 FLR 755 Hale J said that it is right to approach the question of the child's interests from the point of view of the non-intervention principle in s.1(5) Children Act 1989 (see 11.3), and the court should start from the premise that less, rather than more, intervention is generally in a child's best interests.

A care order must be a proportionate and legitimate response to the circumstances of the case, otherwise a local authority may be in breach of the European Convention for the Protection of Human Rights, and the Human Rights Act 1998. Thus, for example, making a care order where a supervision order would be adequate to protect the child might offend the principle of proportionality and be a breach of the right to family life under art. 8 ECHR (see Hale LJ in *Re C and B (Care Order: Future Harm)* [2001] 1 FLR 611; and *Re O (Supervision Order)* [2001] EWCA Civ 16, [2001] 1 FLR 923).

However, despite the more draconian nature of care orders, they are more commonly made than supervision orders. In 2006 7,849 care orders were made in the courts in England and Wales compared with 3,296 supervision orders (*Judicial and Court Statistics 2006*, Cm 7273, Ministry of Justice, 2007).

The court has the power to make a different order from the one applied for (see, for example, *Re C (Care or Supervision Order)* [1999] 2 FLR 621 where a supervision order was made, instead of the care order the local authority had requested). Furthermore, as Part IV proceedings are 'family proceedings' for the purposes of the Children Act (s.8(3)), the court can make a s.8 order (see 11.4) instead of a care or supervision order, either on an application or of its own motion (see *Re K (Care Order or Residence Order)* [1995] 1 FLR 675).

*Jurisdiction*  The court has jurisdiction to hear an application for a care or supervision order if the child is habitually resident, or resident, in England and Wales (ss.1 and 3 Family Law Act 1986), and the child is under the age of 17 (s.31(3) Children Act 1989).

*The Court Cannot Dictate How a Care Order is Implemented*  If the court makes a care order, it cannot dictate how the local authority should implement it (*Re T (A Minor) (Care Order: Conditions)* [1994] 2 FLR 423), as to do so would circumscribe the wide discretionary powers entrusted to local authorities by Parliament. However, there are certain controls on local authorities' powers. Thus, the local authority must supply the court with a care plan containing proposals for future arrangements for the child, and the local authority must review the plan and amend or renew it accordingly (ss.31A(1), (2)). As the court, like a local authority, is a public authority for the purposes of the Human Rights Act 1998, it must ensure compliance with the European Convention for the Protection of Human Rights by considering a care plan carefully to make sure that going into care is the best solution for the child. (See *Hokkanen* v. *Finland* (1995) EHRR 139, [1996] 1 FLR 289.)

*The Court Has No Power to Compel a Local Authority to Institute Care or Supervision Proceedings*  The court has no power to compel a local authority to institute care or supervision proceedings. All it can do is make a direction under s. 37 that the local authority investigate the child's circumstances. Judicial concern has been voiced at the courts' lack of power to compel a local authority to take action (see Stephen Brown P in *Nottinghamshire County Council* v. *P* [1994] Fam 18, at 43). The position was different, however, before the Children Act came into force, as the divorce courts and the High Court in wardship could make care and supervision orders in exceptional circumstances of their own motion (that is, without an application having been made for one).

*Case Management*  Care and supervision proceedings must be managed so as to give effect to the overriding objective in accordance with the *Practice Direction (Judicial Case Management in Public Law Children Act Cases)* [2003] 2 FLR 719 which is (see para. 3): to enable the court to deal with every care case justly, expeditiously, fairly and with the minimum of delay; in ways which ensure, so far as is practicable, that the parties are on an equal footing, the welfare of any children involved is safeguarded, and distress to all parties is minimised; and so far as is practicable, in ways which are proportionate to the gravity and complexity of the issue, and to the nature and extent of the intervention proposed in the private and family life of the children and adults involved. The *Protocol* (resulting from the 2003 *Practice Direction*) is to be replaced by a new protocol, the *Public Law Outline*, in April 2008 in order to improve the way in which child protection cases are dealt with in the courts.

*Human Rights*　The European Court of Human Rights has held that it is a guiding principle that a care order should be regarded as a temporary measure, to be discontinued as soon as circumstances permit, and that any measures implementing temporary care should be consistent with the ultimate aim of reuniting the natural parent and the child (see, in particular, *Olsson v. Sweden (No. 1)* (1988) 11 EHRR 259). However, this principle is subject to the best interests of the child. The European Court also takes the view that there is a positive duty to facilitate family reunification, but that after the passage of a considerable period of time, the interest of a child not to have his or her *de facto* family changed might override the interest of parents to have the family reunited.

　　The ECtHR has also held that, whereas authorities enjoy a wide margin of appreciation in assessing the necessity of taking a child into public care, a stricter scrutiny is required in respect of any further limitations, including restrictions placed on parental rights of access (see *K and T v. Finland* (2001) 36 EHRR 255, [2001] 2 FLR 707; *R v. Finland (Application No. 34141/96)* [2006] 2 FLR 923).

*The Children and Young Persons' Bill 2007*　In June 2007 the Government published a White Paper, *Care Matters: Time for Change* (Cm 7137) in order to improve the statutory framework for children in care. The Children and Young Persons' Bill, which followed on from the White Paper, aims to improve the quality and stability of placements for children in care and includes reforms to increase the focus on the transparency and quality of care placing and to ensure that the voice of the child is heard when important decisions affecting their future are made. The Bill aims to prevent children in local authority care from moving schools mid-way through their GCSE course and to ensure that young people are not forced out of care until they are ready.

### (a)　Who Can Apply for Care and Supervision Orders?

Only local authorities or 'authorised' bodies can institute care or supervision proceedings. The National Society for the Prevention of Cruelty to Children (NSPCC) is the only 'authorised' body (s.31(9)), but, in practice, applications are brought by local authorities as they have a duty to investigate cases where children are suffering, or are at risk of suffering, significant harm (ss.37 and 47).

### (b)　A 'Two-Stage Exercise'

When deciding whether or not to make a care or supervision order, the court performs a two-stage exercise.

　　At the first stage (the 'threshold stage') the court must be satisfied that one of the 'threshold criteria' in s.31(2) is proved. This is largely an adversarial process. This inquiry 'has to be treated as a clinical issue of fact, determined in the light of the circumstances prevailing when the process was initiated' (Waite LJ in *Re S (Discharge of Care Order)* [1995] 2 FLR 639).

Once the threshold stage is crossed, the court must decide at the second stage (the 'welfare stage' or disposal stage) what would best promote the welfare of the child. In conducting this exercise, the court must apply the welfare principle (s.1(1)), the welfare checklist (s.1(3)), the no-order presumption (s.1(5)) and the no-delay principle (s.1(2)) (see 16.8). The threshold stage is, as its name says, only a threshold, so that even if it is crossed, the court is under no obligation to make a care or supervision order. It may, if appropriate, make a residence order, but if it decides to do this, it must also make an interim supervision order, unless the child's welfare is safeguarded without it (s.38(3)). In *Lancashire County Council* v. *B* [2000] 1 FLR 583 the House of Lords held that it by no means follows that because the threshold conditions are satisfied that the court will proceed to make a care or supervision order. Whether it does so will depend on a detailed assessment of the child's welfare in all the circumstances of the case.

In *Re K; A Local Authority* v. *N and Others* [2005] EWHC 2956 (Fam), [2007] 1 FLR 399, although the threshold criteria were satisfied, Munby J refused to make a supervision order, applying the 'no order' principle in s.1(5) Children Act 1989. Munby J held that, given the clear opposition of the young woman (a girl aged 16) and her family to the making of the order, an order would be likely to have a detrimental effect on their future relationship and co-operation with social services. This would also make it difficult for the local authority to fulfil their responsibilities to the young woman under any supervision order if it were made.

At the welfare stage the court must also consider the arrangements that the local authority has made, or proposes to make, in respect of contact (see below) and invite the parties to the proceedings to comment on those arrangements (s.34(11)). Expert evidence is important and the court will also consider the recommendations of the child's guardian. The facts of cases do not create precedents for later cases. Each case depends on its own facts.

**(c)   The 'Threshold Criteria' for Making a Care or Supervision Order**

The threshold criteria for making a care or supervision order are laid down in the following section of the Children Act 1989:

---

**Section 31(2)  Children Act 1989**

'A court may only make a care order or a supervision order if it is satisfied –
(a) that the child concerned is suffering, or is likely to suffer, significant harm; and
(b) that the harm, or likelihood of harm, is attributable to –
   (i)  the care given to the child, or likely to be given to him if the order were not made, not being what it would be reasonable to expect a parent to give him; or
   (ii) the child's being beyond parental control.'

---

Section 31(9) defines the terms used in s.31(2) above. 'Harm' means ill-treatment or the impairment of health or development including, for example, impairment of the child's health or development as a result of witnessing the ill-treatment of another person. This could include, for example, domestic violence (see Chapter 6). 'Development' means physical, intellectual, emotional, social or behavioural development. 'Health' means physical or mental health, and 'ill-treatment' includes sexual abuse and forms of ill-treatment which are not physical. Abandonment of a child can constitute 'ill-treatment' for the purposes of s.31(9) (see *Re M (Care Order: Parental Responsibility)* [1996] 2 FLR 84).

The word 'significant' for the purposes of 'significant harm' is not defined in the Act. Whether harm is 'significant' depends on the circumstances of the case. *Working Together to Safeguard Children*, however, provides social workers with guidance on what constitutes 'significant harm'.

Section 31(10) provides that, where the question of whether harm suffered by a child is significant turns on the child's health or development, his health or development must be compared with that which could reasonably be expected of a similar child. In *Re O (A Minor) (Care Proceedings: Education)* [1992] 1 WLR 912 Ewbank J held that 'a similar child' meant a child of equivalent intellectual and social development. As far as lack of parental control in the threshold criteria is concerned, it does not matter whether this is the fault of the parent or child (*Re O*, above), and harm, or likelihood of harm, attributable to the child being beyond parental control is capable of describing a state of affairs in the past, the present or the future (Stuart-White J in *M v. Birmingham City Council* [1994] 2 FLR 141).

In *Re K; A Local Authority v. N and Others* [2005] EWHC 2956 (Fam), [2007] 1 FLR 399 Munby J said that the court, when considering the threshold criteria, may be required to evaluate parental performance by reference to the objective standard of the hypothetical 'reasonable' parent. But Munby J said that the court 'must always be sensitive to the cultural, social and religious circumstances of the particular child and family, particularly when the parents have recently, or comparatively recently, arrived from a foreign country with different standards and expectations from those in this country'. In this case the young girl (aged 16) and her family were Kurdish Muslims from Iraq.

### (d)   When Must the Threshold Criteria be Satisfied?

In *Re M (A Minor) (Care Order: Threshold Conditions)* [1994] 2 AC 424 the House of Lords held that the date on which the threshold criteria under s.31(2) have to be satisfied is the date of the application or, if temporary protective arrangements (such as an emergency protection order) have continuously been in place, the date on which those arrangements were initiated. In other words, the date for the establishment of the threshold criteria is that date on which the local authority first took protective measures in relation to the child. However, the Court of Appeal has held that, if there is other material upon which the threshold criteria can be satisfied, the local authority has a duty to put such material before the court, even if that material did not represent the basis on which the local authority initially intervened (*Re G (Care Proceedings: Threshold Conditions)* [2001] EWCA Civ 968, [2001] 2 FLR 1111). Thus, later events can be relied on where they are capable of proving what the position was at the relevant time (that is, when the local authority first took protective measures). However, the Court of Appeal has held that such material must have been in existence on the date on which the local authority instituted the proceedings; and the process of introducing such material must be fair, and the parents or carers must be given the opportunity to address it (*Re A (Children: Split Hearing)* [2006] EWCA Civ 714, [2007] 1 FLR 905).

### (e)   The Standard of Proof in Care Proceedings

As proceedings for care and supervision orders are civil proceedings, the local authority must prove the fact(s) alleged (the threshold criteria) on the basis of the civil law standard of proof (the balance of probabilities), not the criminal standard of proof (beyond reasonable doubt).

The House of Lords considered the standard of proof in the following case:

> ▶ *Re H and Others (Minors) (Sexual Abuse: Standard of Proof)* **[1996] AC 563**, *sub nom Re H and R (Child Sexual Abuse: Standard of Proof)* **[1996] 1 FLR 80**
>
> The local authority applied for care orders in respect of three girls (aged 13, 8 and 2) after the eldest daughter (aged 14) had alleged that she had been sexually abused by her mother's cohabitant. He had been charged with rape but acquitted. The applications for care orders were dismissed, as the threshold conditions in s.31(2) were not satisfied. It could not be established to the requisite high standard of proof that the 14-year-old daughter's allegations were true.
>
> The House of Lords held by a majority that the standard of proof in care proceedings was the ordinary civil standard of balance of probability, but that the more improbable the event, the stronger the evidence had to be before, on the balance of probability, the occurrence of the event would be established. Lord Nicholls said that a conclusion that a child is suffering, or is likely to suffer, harm 'must be based on facts, not just suspicion'. The House of Lords unanimously rejected, however, a submission that 'likely' in the phrase 'likely to suffer harm' meant probable, but held that 'likely' meant likely in the sense of a real possibility, a possibility that could not sensibly be ignored having regard to the nature and gravity of the feared harm in the particular case.
>
> **LORD NICHOLLS**: 'The balance of probability standard means that a court is satisfied an event occurred if the court considers that, on the evidence, the occurrence of the event was more likely than not. When assessing the probabilities the court will have in mind as a factor, to whatever extent is appropriate in the particular case, that the more serious the allegation the less likely it is that the event occurred and, hence, the stronger should be the evidence before the court concludes that the allegation is established on the balance of probability.... Built into the preponderance of probability standard is a generous degree of flexibility in respect of the seriousness of the allegation.
>
> Although the result is much the same, this does not mean that where a serious allegation is in issue the standard of proof required is higher. It means only that the inherent probability or improbability of an event is itself a matter to be taken into account when weighing the probabilities and deciding whether, on balance, the event occurred. The more improbable the event, the stronger must be the evidence that it did occur before, on the balance of probability, its occurrence will be established.'

Lord Nicholls' approach in *Re H* has been endorsed in subsequent cases, even where the court is trying an issue which involves a serious criminal act (see *Re U (Serious Injury: Standard of Proof); Re B* [2004] EWCA Civ 567, [2004] 2 FLR 263).

In *Re W (Care: Threshold Criteria)* [2007] EWCA Civ 102, [2007] 2 FLR 98 Wall LJ said that the distinction between the two limbs of s.31(2) was 'not academic', and he stated that '[t]he permanent removal of children from their parents' care ... requires a careful adherence by the courts and local authorities to the criteria which have been laid down by Parliament for the exercise of those powers'. In *Re W* the Court of Appeal held, allowing the mother's appeal and ordering a rehearing, that it had not been open to the judge on the facts of the case to hold that the threshold criteria were satisfied on the basis that the mother had failed to protect the child from sexual abuse (or the risk of it) by the father.

The test applies even though a jury in criminal proceedings has come to a different conclusion (see *A Local Authority* v. *S, W and T (By His Guardian)* [2004] EWHC 1270 (Fam), [2004] 2 FLR 129 where, despite the father having been acquitted of the manslaughter of his elder child, the local authority successfully sought a care order in respect of the surviving child as the threshold criteria were held by Hedley J to be satisfied). The inability of medical experts to make a confident diagnosis about whether a child has been harmed does not preclude the court from finding that the threshold criteria have been satisfied on the balance of probabilities (see *Re B (Non-Accidental Injury)* [2002] EWCA Civ 752, [2002] 2 FLR 1133).

Some commentators have criticised the decision of the majority in *Re H* (above). McCafferty (1999) said that it created a complicated standard of proof for allegations of serious abuse, and that the decision was wrong because it had the effect of taking the non-intervention principle enshrined in the Children Act too far, particularly in the light of the right not to be subject to inhuman and degrading treatment under art. 3 ECHR and its interpretation by the ECtHR in *A* v. *United Kingdom (Human Rights: Punishment of Child)* [1998] 2 FLR 959 (see 9.5). McCafferty argued that the child's welfare should be paramount not just at the welfare stage, but also at the threshold stage. Hemingway and Williams (1997) described the reasoning in *Re H* as flawed, and said that the decision would create a real danger that some children would not be afforded the protection that they deserved.

The Court of Appeal has held that, where a local authority is seeking to satisfy the threshold criteria on a variety of bases, it is necessary to define with clarity precisely what findings of fact the local authority is inviting the court to make, particularly where the court has directed a split hearing of the proceedings (Wall LJ in *CL* v. *East Riding Yorkshire Council, MB and BL (A Child)* [2006] EWCA Civ 49, [2006] 2 FLR 24).

### (f) Shared Care, Uncertain Perpetrators and the Threshold Criteria

In the following case the House of Lords had to decide how the threshold criteria should be applied where a child has suffered significant harm, but it is not possible to identify the perpetrator of the harm:

> ▶ *Lancashire County Council* v. *B* [2000] 1 FLR 583
>
> A young baby (child A) suffered harm as a result of being shaken, but it was impossible to prove whether A's parents or the child-minder, who also had a child (child B), was responsible. The Court of Appeal held that the threshold criteria in s.31(2)(b)(i) (lack of reasonable care) were satisfied in respect of child A, but not in respect of child B (because she had suffered no harm), even though it was unclear whether the parents or the child-minder were responsible for A's injuries. Child A's parents appealed to the House of Lords arguing that the harm suffered to their child had to be attributable to their care, and that the continuation of the care proceedings infringed their right to family life under art. 8 of the European Convention on Human Rights.
>
> The House of Lord unanimously dismissed their appeal, as the threshold conditions had been met. A majority of the House of Lords said that, under s.31(2)(b)(i) the court had to be satisfied that the harm suffered by the child was attributable to 'the care given to the child', which normally referred to the care given by parents or other primary-carer. However, their Lordships said that different considerations applied in cases of shared care where the child suffers harm but the court is unable to identify which of the carers provided the deficient care. They held that the words 'care given to the child' in s.31(2)(b)(i) embraced the care given by any of the carers, and that the threshold conditions could be satisfied where there was no more than a possibility that the parents were responsible for inflicting the injuries. This

interpretation, their Lordships said, was necessary to permit the court to intervene to protect a child at risk where the individual responsible for harming the child could not be identified. In other words, the interpretation was necessary to avoid the risk of a child remaining wholly unprotected. Lord Clyde, on the other hand, said that s.31(2)(b)(i) simply defined the standard of care and did not require the identification of the person who caused the harm.

The House of Lord stressed that in cases like this the fact that it had not been proved that the parents had been responsible for the child's injuries could be taken into account at the 'welfare stage,' once the threshold conditions had been met. The House of Lords held that there had been no breach of art. 8 ECHR as the steps taken by the local authority had been those reasonably necessary to pursue the legitimate aim of protecting the child from injury.

Hall (2000) has questioned how the decision squares with that in *Re H (Minors) (Sexual Abuse: Standard of Proof)* (above), where the House of Lords had held that significant harm had to be based on a real possibility of risk, not mere suspicion. In the *Lancashire* case, the threshold conditions in respect of child A were met even though it was not clear which person had caused the harm. (See also Perry [2000] CFLQ 301.)

***The Welfare Stage and Several Possible Perpetrators*** In *Re O and N; Re B (Minors)* [2003] UKHL 18, [2003] 1 FLR 1169 the House of Lords unanimously held that in uncertain perpetrator cases, where the judge had found that the child had suffered significant harm at the hands of his parents or carer but was unable to identify which parent or carer had caused the harm, the preferred interpretation of the Children Act was that the court should proceed at the welfare stage of care proceedings on the footing that each of the possible perpetrators be treated as such. It held that the approach to the standard of proof laid down in *Re H (Minors) (Sexual Abuse: Standard of Proof)* (above) (that is, that there be a real possibility that a person was a perpetrator) was not appropriate at the welfare stage in cases involving uncertain perpetrators.

### (g) The Local Authority's Care Plan

Where an application is made on which a final, not interim, care order (see s.31A(5)) might be made with respect to a child, the local authority must, within such time as the court may direct, prepare a 'care plan' for the future care of the child (s.31A(1)). A care plan will include information, for example, about the child's needs, the placement, and about the management and support to be provided by the local authority. It will also provide details about contact – as before making a care order the court must consider the arrangements, or proposed arrangements, for contact (see s.34(11)).

In *Re J (Minors) (Care: Care Plan)* [1994] 1 FLR 253, at 261,Wall J stressed the importance of care plans:

'A properly constructed care plan is not only essential to enable the court to make its decision based on all the known facts; it will or should have been compiled either in consultation with the parents and other interested parties, including where appropriate the child or children involved, or at the very least after taking their views and wishes into account. It will thus enable the other parties to focus on the relevant issues. Much court time and costs may thereby be saved.'

***The Court Must Scrutinise the Care Plan*** The court must carefully scrutinise the care plan in order to be satisfied that giving parental responsibility to the local authority will not do more harm than good for the child's welfare (see Hale J in *Berkshire County Council* v. *B* [1997] 2 FLR 171). If the court considers that the care plan is not in the child's best interests, or that more information is needed, it may decide to make an interim care order even though it is not completely happy with the plan (*Re L (Sexual Abuse: Standard of Proof)* [1996] 1 FLR 116, approving Wall J's views in *Re J (Minors) (Care: Care Plan)* [1994] 1 FLR 253).

*Duty to Keep a Care Plan Under Review*    While the application is pending the local authority must keep the care plan under review, and revise it, or renew it, if some change is required (s.31A(2)). Once a child is in care, the local authority must continue to keep the care plan under review, and renew or revise the care plan if some change is required, and must consider whether to apply or discharge the care order (s.26(2)). However, the court has held that, even if the child is in care, the local authority is not entitled to make significant changes to the care plan, or to change the child's living arrangements without properly involving the child's parents (and in some cases the child) in the decision-making process and without giving the parents a proper opportunity to make their case before a decision is made (see *Re G (Care: Challenge to Local Authority's Decision)* [2003] EWHC 551 (Fam), [2003] 2 FLR 42; and *X Council* v. *B (Emergency Protection Orders)* [2004] EWHC 2015 (Fam), [2005] 1 FLR 341).

*Involving Parents*    A failure to involve a parent in the decision-making process in respect of a care plan or a change in care plan constitutes a breach of a parent's human rights, and may, depending on the circumstances of the case, result in a local authority having to pay compensation to the wronged parent in the form of damages (see, for example, *Re C (Breach of Human Rights: Damages)* [2007] EWCA Civ 2, [2007] 1 FLR 1957, but where damages were not awarded in the circumstances of the case).

*Challenging a Care Plan*    If a local authority fails to comply with its care plan, a parent (and / or child) has various options available. An application can be made to discharge the care order, a complaint can be made under the Complaints Procedure, a challenge can be brought under the Human Rights Act 1998, and a claim in negligence can be brought. Independent Reviewing Officers can also provide assistance (see below). In the following case, a care plan was challenged in proceedings for judicial review, but this procedure was held not to be the best way of making a challenge:

▶ *R (CD)* v. *Isle of Anglesey County Council* [2004] EWHC 1635 (Admin), [2005] 1 FLR 59

The local authority had drawn up a care plan without giving due consideration to the clearly and consistently expressed views of the young person, a 15-year-old disabled girl, in respect of the number of nights she should spend with her foster-carers. The care plan required her to board for longer at her new school and stay in respite care. The care plan was challenged in judicial review. Wilson J held that the care plan was unlawful and set it aside, because, *inter alia*, the local authority had failed to give due consideration to her clear and consistent wishes. Wilson J held that it is generally preferable for issues relating to care plans to be resolved in the Family Division of the High Court within an application for a care order, rather than by way of judicial review in the Queen's Bench Division, as in the Family Division the emphasis is on the child's best interests, whereas in judicial review proceedings the emphasis is on the lawfulness or otherwise of the local authority.

*Problems with Care Plans*   Before new provisions for the appointment of Independent Reviewing Officers were introduced (see below) there was judicial concern about the fact that, once a child was in care, a local authority could choose not to implement the proposals in its care plan, to the detriment of the child, and with the court having no power to intervene. The judiciary was concerned that children could drift in care with nobody, including the child, having the right to review the promises made by the local authority in its care plan. Young children with parents with no interest in them were in a particularly vulnerable position, even though local authorities had a duty to conduct regular case reviews, at which the views of the parents were relevant.

Concerns about care plans were voiced by the House of Lords in the following case, but these concerns have now been addressed by the legislature, and amendments inserted into the Children Act 1989:

▶ *Re S (Care Order: Implementation of Care Plan); Re W (Minors) (Care Order: Adequacy of Care Plan)* [2002] UKHL 10, [2002] 1 FLR 815

In each appeal the local authority had failed to implement the proposed arrangements it had made for the child in its care plan. The Court of Appeal recognised that there were gaps in the Children Act 1989 in respect of care plans, and proposed ways in which the court could fill these gaps, such as by having wider powers to make interim care orders, and by starring essential milestones in the care plan which if not met would enable the child's guardian or local authority to apply to the court for directions.

The House of Lords allowed the appeals, because the Court of Appeal had exceeded the bounds of judicial jurisdiction when interpreting the Children Act 1989, and because it was not possible for judges to continue to exercise supervision over a local authority once the child is in care. The House of Lords held that the Children Act 1989 was not incompatible with the Human Rights Act 1998, but that there was a statutory gap in the Act, as a child, whose parents were not interested in the matter, might be left without an effective remedy (as required by art. 6 ECHR) to challenge a local authority's failure to implement its proposals in its care plan. There was a statutory lacuna, but no statutory incompatibility with the ECHR.

*Independent Reviewing Officers and Care Plans*   The gaps in the Children Act 1989 which were identified by the House of Lords in *Re S; Re W* (above) were filled by amendments made to s.26 Children Act 1989. These amendments, which came into force in September 2004, require local authorities to appoint Independent Reviewing Officers (s.26(2)(k)). These officers are responsible for participating in case reviews, for monitoring the local authority's functions in respect of case reviews, and for referring a case to a CAFCASS officer (or a Welsh family proceedings officer) (see 1.4) where appropriate (s.26(2A)). It is then open to the CAFCASS officer to seek a court order against the local authority to put right its failings in relation to the care plan (for example, by bringing an application to discharge the care order, or for contact between the child and another person, or for a declaration under the Human Rights Act 1998 that the local authority's plans are contrary to the child's human rights). But before bringing court proceedings, a CAFCASS officer will try to reach a negotiated settlement and will refer the case to mediation, if appropriate.

**(h)** Effect of a Care Order – Obligations of the Local Authority

If a care order is made statutory responsibility for the child passes to the local authority, and the court has no power (unless expressly provided by statute) to interfere with the local authority's powers (*A* v. *Liverpool City Council* [1982] AC 363). Because power passes to the local authority, the court has no power to impose conditions on a care order in respect of the child's accommodation arrangements, or to direct how the local authority should look after the child (*Re T (A Minor) (Care Order: Conditions)* [1994] 2 FLR 423; and *Re S and D (Children: Powers of Court)* [1995] 2 FLR 456). Neither can the court direct that the Children's Guardian be allowed to continue his involvement with a child (*Kent County Council* v. *C* [1993] 1 FLR 308).

If a care order is made, the child is described as being 'looked after' by the local authority, whereupon it has various duties and powers in respect of the child. The court no longer monitors the administrative arrangements for the child and has no say in these arrangements unless there is an application before the court. The Children's Guardian's involvement in the case also terminates.

A care order imposes a duty on the local authority to receive and keep the child in its care (s.33(1)), and the local authority has a general duty to safeguard and promote the child's welfare (s.22). A care order discharges any s.8 order, a supervision order and a school attendance order, and terminates wardship (s.91). A care order remains in force until the child reaches 18, unless brought to an end earlier (s.91(2)), but the Government is proposing to change the law so that children are not forced to move out of care until they are ready (see the Children and Young Persons' Bill 2007).

*Local Authorities – Parental Responsibility*   A care order gives the local authority parental responsibility for the child and the power to determine the extent to which the child's parent(s) or guardian may meet their parental responsibility where it is needed to safeguard and promote the child's welfare (ss.33(3), (4)).

However, a local authority's parental responsibility is not absolute, and does not deprive the child's parents of their parental responsibility. A local authority is not entitled to take decisions about the child without reference to, or over the heads of, the parents. It is not entitled to make significant changes to its care plan. Neither is it entitled to make changes to the child's living arrangements without first discussing the matter with the parents, and, in some cases, the child. It has no power to give or refuse consent to the child's adoption, or to appoint a guardian, or to change the child's religion (s.33(6)), and it cannot prevent the child's unmarried mother entering into a parental responsibility agreement with the child's father (*Re X (Parental Responsibility Agreement: Children in Care)* [2000] 1 FLR 517).

A local authority must exercise its parental responsibility in a way which complies with the European Convention on Human Rights, in particular with the substantive and procedural requirements of art. 8. Thus, it must inform parents of decisions it makes, give parents opportunities to be heard and to make representations, and involve them in the decision-making process.

*Parents – Parental Responsibility*   The child's parents do not lose parental responsibility while a care order is in force; and there is a presumption of reasonable contact between the child and his family (see below). Thus, a parent remains entitled to do what is reasonable in all the circumstances for the purpose of safeguarding and promoting the child's welfare (s.33(5)), and retains any rights, duty, power and responsibility in relation to the child and his property under any other enactment (s.33(9)), for example, to make decisions about education and medical treatment.

While a care order is in force no person can change the child's surname or remove the child from the UK without the written consent of every person who has parental responsibility for the child, or the leave of the court (s.33(7)). However, a local authority can allow the child to be taken out of the UK for up to one month (s.33(8)(a)) and can under Sched. 2, para. 19 arrange (or assist in arranging) for the child to live outside England and Wales, subject to the court's approval. In *Re L (Care Order: Immigration Powers to Remove)* [2007] EWHC 158 (Fam), [2007] 2 FLR 789, however, Holman J held that the restriction on removing a child in care out of the UK (in s.33(7)) did not apply to the Home Secretary in respect of his immigration powers and duties. For this reason, Holman J held that it was not possible for the local authority to include a provision in an order requiring the Home Secretary to apply to the High Court if he were to seek the removal of the child from the UK.

*Placement of the Child*   Most children who are the subject of a care order are not returned home to their parents. The court will instead approve a plan to place them outside the immediate family. There are various options here. Thus, the child may be placed with foster-parents, remain with existing short-term foster-carers, or be placed with members of the extended family (such as a grandparent or other relative). Placing the child can be implemented under the terms of the care order, or under a residence order (see 11.5) or under a special guardianship order (see 16.20). In some cases, the child may be placed for adoption (see Chapter 16).

### (i)   Effect of a Supervision Order

A supervision order does not give the local authority parental responsibility, but places the child under the supervision of a designated local authority officer or a probation officer (s.31(1)(b)). With a supervision order, unlike a care order, safeguarding the child's interests remains the primary responsibility of the parents. Under a supervision order the local authority merely assists and befriends the child (ss.35(1)(a), (b)) and the operation of any conditions or undertakings depends on parental agreement (see *Re B (Supervision Order: Parental Undertaking)* [1996] 1 FLR 676). A supervisor can, however, apply to have the supervision order varied or discharged where the order is not complied with, or the supervisor considers the order is no longer necessary (s.35(1)(c)).

Parts I and II of Sched. 3 to the Children Act 1989 list specific powers in respect of supervision, for example the supervisor can give directions that the child live in a certain place, attend at a certain place and participate in certain activities. A supervision order can require a child to have a medical or psychiatric examination, but only with the child's consent if the child has sufficient understanding to make an informed decision, and only if satisfactory arrangements have been, or can be, made for the examination. A supervision order can be made in the first instance for up to one year, but the supervisor can apply to have the order extended for up to a maximum of three years in total (Sched. 3, para. 6). The court has no power to impose conditions on a supervision order (*Re S (Care or Supervision Order)* [1996] 1 FLR 753).

## (i)    Interim Care and Supervision Orders

The court has the power to make interim care orders and interim supervision orders (s.38). In practice, the court usually makes a series of interim orders before a final order. The purpose of interim orders is to enable the court to maintain the status quo pending the final hearing, and for it to obtain any information it needs before making a final decision. Although an interim care order is a 'holding' order, it is regarded as a form of care order, so that, once it is made, care of the child passes to the local authority and the manner in which the child is cared for passes out of the court's control. For this reason the court has no more power to impose conditions on an interim order than it has on a final order, except in respect of medical or psychiatric assessment (see *Re L (Interim Care Order: Power of Court)* [1996] 2 FLR 742).

The power to make interim orders can be exercised only where care and supervision proceedings are to be adjourned (such as for inquiries or reports to be made), or where the court makes an order under s.37(1) directing a local authority to investigate the child's circumstances (s.38(1)). An interim order cannot be made unless there are reasonable grounds for believing that the threshold criteria for making a care or supervision order are satisfied (s.38(2)). An interim order must be used for its intended purpose. It cannot be used to provide the court with continuing control over the actions of a local authority (as the Court of Appeal had wrongly suggested in *Re S; Re W*, see p.408, above).

If the court decides to make a residence order in care or supervision proceedings, an interim supervision order must also be made, unless the child's welfare is otherwise satisfactorily safeguarded (s.38(3)). There is no limit on the number of interim orders that can be made, but, as delay is detrimental to a child (s.1(2)) and it is important for a final decision to be made, interim orders are limited to a maximum of eight weeks in the first instance and four weeks subsequently (ss.38(4), (5)). There must be good reason for the continuation of an interim care order (*C v. Solihull Metropolitan Borough Council* [1993] 1 FLR 290; and *Hounslow London Borough Council v. A* [1993] 1 FLR 702).

## (k)    Directing a Medical or Psychiatric Examination or Other Assessment of the Child

Where the court makes an interim care or supervision order it may make a direction under s.38(6) as appropriate with regard to the medical or psychiatric examination or other assessment of the child. The direction can be to the effect that there is to be no such examination or assessment; or that there is to be no such examination or assessment unless the court directs otherwise (s.38(7)).

Section 38(6) provides that a child with sufficient understanding to make an informed decision can refuse to consent to the medical or psychiatric examination or other assessment. However, as the child's welfare prevails, the court can override a child's refusal to consent, even if the child has sufficient understanding to make an informed decision (see *South Glamorgan County Council v. W and B* [1993] 1 FLR 574, at 9.4).

*Directing a Residential Assessment*    Under s.38(6) the court may decide that there should be a residential assessment of the child and/or parent(s). In *Re C (A Minor) (Interim Care Order: Residential Assessment)* [1997] AC 489, [1997] 1 FLR 1 the House of Lords held that the court can direct a residential assessment even if the local authority objects (for example, because of the cost), as the purpose of ss.38(6) and (7) is to enable the court to obtain the information it needs so that it can decide what final order to make. Lord Browne-Wilkinson said, however, that when exercising its discretion to order a particular examination or assessment, the court will take into account 'the cost of the proposed assessment and the fact that local authorities' resources are notoriously limited'. *Re C* was applied in *Re B (Interim Care Order: Directions)* [2002] EWCA Civ 25, [2002] 1 FLR 545.

In *Sheffield City Council* v. *V (Legal Services Commission Intervening)* [2006] EWHC 1861 (Fam), [2007] 1 FLR 279 Bodey J held that a direction under s.38(6) should not be made until the court had had the opportunity to examine in appropriate, but not excessive, detail the scope and nature of the proposed assessment.

*The Importance of Obtaining Evidence by Means of a s.38(6) Assessment*  In *Re L and H (Residential Assessment)* [2007] EWCA Civ 213, [2007] 1 FLR 1370 the Court of Appeal, allowing the appeal against a refusal to direct a s.38(6) assessment by the judge at first instance, emphasised the importance of making a s.38(6) direction in order to ensure that all the evidence is put before the court before a child is removed permanently from his or her home by means of a care order. Wall LJ held that, before moving children permanently from their families and placing them for adoption, the court must ensure that the case had been fully investigated and that all the relevant evidence necessary for the decision is in place. Article 6 of the European Convention for the Protection of Human Rights (the right to a fair hearing) required it and so did the underlying policy of the Children Act 1989, which was that, wherever possible children should be brought up by their parents or within their natural families. Wall LJ held that there were no general guidelines as to when the court should or should not order an assessment under s.38(6), but that the proceedings must be fair. If an expert brought in to advise the court strongly recommended that a residential assessment should take place, that was a powerful pointer to the propriety of such an order. On the facts of the case, the judge had been plainly wrong to characterise the assessment as one involving therapy. Wall LJ held that, although the local authority and guardian might be right in their view that the parents were unable to parent satisfactorily, it was manifestly in the interests of the child to obtain evidence on the issue.

*Residential Assessment for Therapeutic Purposes*  In the following case, the House of Lords held that an assessment under s.38(6) above cannot include therapeutic treatment:

▶ *Re G (A Child) (Interim Care Order: Residential Assessment)* [2005] UKHL 68, [2006] 1 FLR 601

The local authority sought a care order after the child's birth, as the mother posed a significant risk to the child (her first child had been at risk, and her second child had died of multiple non-accidental injuries). The judge made an interim care order and directed a residential assessment of the mother at a hospital, despite the local authority's objections. The hospital strongly recommended that the mother be offered intensive psychotherapy, but the trial judge refused to order an assessment under s.38(6) as this was therapy, not assessment. The parents successfully appealed to the Court of Appeal, which held that 'assessment' under s.38(6) can include therapy.

The House of Lords (allowing the local authority's appeal and upholding the decision of the trial judge) held that the purpose of ss.38(6) and (7) was to provide the court with information. If the framers of the Children Act had meant the court to be in charge not only of the examination and assessment of the child, but also of the medical or psychiatric treatment to be provided for the child and her parents, the Act would have said so.

*Apportioning the Costs of an Assessment* In *Lambeth London Borough Council v. S, C, V and J (By His Guardian) (Legal Services Commission Intervening)* [2005] EWHC 776 (Fam), [2005] 2 FLR 1171 Ryder J in the High Court held that the costs of a residential assessment could be apportioned between the parties, rather than being borne automatically by the local authority which had brought the care proceedings. He also held that the funding of an assessment was not beyond the powers of the Legal Services Commission.

## (I) Discharge and Variation of Care and Supervision Orders

A supervision order can be varied or discharged, but a care order can only be discharged – as variation would undermine a local authority's responsibility for a child.

*(i) Discharge of a Care Order* An application for discharge can be made by: any person with parental responsibility for the child; the child; or the local authority (s.39(1)). A child does not need permission to apply for discharge (*Re A (Care: Discharge Application by Child)* [1995] 1 FLR 599). Persons without parental responsibility cannot apply for discharge, but can with the permission of the court apply for a s.8 residence order, which (if granted) will automatically discharge the care order (s.91(1)). In practice, applications to discharge a care order are made by the local authority, which at every statutory case conference must consider whether to apply for discharge. As an alternative to discharge, the court can substitute the care order with a supervision order, without the need to satisfy the threshold criteria (ss.39(4), (5)). The court also has the power to discharge the care order and make the child a ward of court (*Re RJ (Fostering: Person Disqualified)* [1999] 1 FLR 605).

In a discharge application the court must apply the s.1(1) welfare principle and the other s.1 provisions (see 11.3). There is no need to prove that the threshold conditions for a care order no longer apply (see *Re S (Discharge of Care Order)* [1995] 2 FLR 639). A further application to discharge the care order, or to substitute it with a supervision order, cannot be made for six months after the original application, except with leave of the court (s.91(15)).

*(ii) Variation or Discharge of a Supervision Order* A supervision order can be varied or discharged on the application of: any person with parental responsibility for the child; the child; or by the person supervising the child (s.39(2)). An order can also be varied on the application of a person with whom the child is living, if the original order imposes a requirement which affects that person (s.39(3)). When exercising its powers, the court must apply the s.1(1) welfare principle and the other s.1 provisions (see 11.3). A further application to discharge or vary the supervision order cannot be made for six months after the original application, except with leave of the court (s.91(15)).

### (m) Procedure in Care and Supervision Proceedings

Care or supervision proceedings commence in the magistrates' family proceedings court, but can be transferred to a county court or the High Court, or to another family proceedings court. An application for a care or supervision order can also be made in any family proceedings (s.31(4)) (see 11.9). The local authority, the child and any person with parental responsibility are automatically parties to the proceedings, but other persons can be joined as parties with leave of the court. When considering whether to grant leave, the court will exercise its powers in the same way as it does in leave applications for s.8 orders (see s.10(9), and 11.4). (See *Re W (Care Proceedings: Leave to Apply)* [2004] EWHC 3342 (Fam), [2005] 2 FLR 468, where an aunt applied for leave to be a party to the care proceedings in relation to her niece, but was refused at first instance and by Sumner J on appeal.)

A father without parental responsibility has no automatic right to be joined as a party to the proceedings, but he is entitled to notice of the proceedings and is likely to be given leave by the court to take part. In *Re B (Care Proceedings: Notification of Father Without Parental Responsibility)* [1999] 2 FLR 408 Holman J said that an unmarried father should be permitted to participate in proceedings unless there is some justifiable reason to the contrary. A refusal to allow an unmarried father without parental responsibility to participate in care or supervision proceedings may breach his right to family life under art. 8 ECHR (see, for example, *McMichael* v. *United Kingdom (Application No. 16424/90)* (1995) 20 EHRR 205 where the ECtHR held that the failure to allow an unmarried father without parental responsibility to participate in a Scottish children's hearing was a breach of art. 8).

The child will be represented by a Children's Guardian (see below) and a solicitor. Parties to the proceedings have a general duty of full and frank disclosure (see *Re BR and C (Care: Duty of Disclosure: Appeals)* [2002] EWCA Civ 1925).

### (n) The Children's Guardian

In care and supervision proceedings the court must appoint a Children's Guardian, an officer of CAFCASS (or a Welsh family proceedings officer) (see 1.4), unless a guardian is not needed to safeguard the child's interests (s.41(1)). The role of the guardian is to protect and safeguard the best interests of the child in the proceedings. In *Re S and W (Care Proceedings)* [2007] EWCA Civ 232, [2007] 2 FLR 275, Wall LJ said:

'[T]he guardian is appointed by the court as the children's representative, and . . . one of the guardian's functions is fearlessly to protect the children concerned against local authority incompetence and maladministration, as well as poor social work practice.'

The guardian must be independent of the parties, to prevent a conflict of interest arising. In addition to having a general duty to safeguard the child's interests in the manner prescribed by the rules of court (s.41(2)(b)), the guardian has specific duties, for example: to ascertain the child's wishes and whether the child has sufficient understanding; to investigate all the circumstances; to interview people involved; to inspect records; and to appoint professional assistance. The rules of court provide that, in carrying out his duties, the guardian must have regard to the principle that delay should be avoided. The guardian has a right to examine and copy local authority records relating to a child, which can be admitted in evidence (s.42), such as minutes of a child protection conference, or a report compiled by an area child protection committee (*Re R (Care Proceedings: Disclosure)* [2000] 2 FLR 75). When the investigation has been completed, the guardian must make a written report advising what should be done in the best interests of the child. The report (unless the court directs otherwise) must be filed at the court before the hearing date and copies served on all the parties. This report usually has a considerable influence on the court.

Rules of court provide that the guardian must appoint a solicitor to act for the child (if not already appointed), and that the guardian must give instructions on the child's behalf, except where the child is capable of giving instructions and those instructions conflict with those of the guardian (when the solicitor must take instructions from the child).

### (o)    Care and Supervision Orders – Appeals

Any party to care or supervision proceedings can appeal against the making of, or refusal to make, a final or interim care or supervision order. Appeals from family proceedings courts are to the High Court and from county courts and the High Court to the Court of Appeal. The appeal court will not, however, interfere with a discretionary decision made by a lower court unless the judge has erred in law, or is under a misapprehension of fact, or the decision is outside a band of reasonable discretion within which reasonable disagreement is possible (*G v. G (Minors) (Custody Appeal)* [1985] 1 WLR 647, (1985) FLR 894). As this is a high threshold, it is sometimes difficult for an appeal to succeed.

## 15.8    Contact in Care

**Article 9(3)  United Nations Convention on the Rights of the Child 1989**

'States Parties shall respect the right of the child who is separated from one or both parents to maintain personal relations and direct contact with those parents on a regular basis, except if it is contrary to the child's best interests.'

As contact between children and parents is considered to be mutually beneficial, and children have a right of contact (see 12.5), the courts have held that cogent reasons are required for terminating contact (see Balcombe LJ in *Re J (A Minor) (Contact)* [1994] 1 FLR 729, at 735). The European Court of Human Rights has also recognised the importance of children in care having contact with their parents and family. In *K and T v. Finland* (2000) 31 EHRR 484, [2000] 2 FLR 793 it held that, while there is a wide margin of appreciation in care cases, it nevertheless remains important to scrutinise any restrictions placed by authorities on parental rights of contact (see also *Scott v. UK* [2000] 1 FLR 958). Contact is important for children in care, because it improves their chances of being rehabilitated with their families.

Section 34 Children Act 1989 deals with contact. It lays down a duty of contact, and gives the court power to make orders permitting and terminating contact. It also requires the court, before it makes a care order, to consider the arrangements that the local authority has made, or proposes to make, for contact; and it must invite the parties to the proceedings to comment on those arrangements (s.34(11)).

*The Duty to Provide Contact*   Section 34(1) provides that a local authority must allow a child in care reasonable contact with: parents; any guardian or special guardian; any person with parental responsibility for him under s.4A; any person with a residence order in his favour in respect of the child; and a person who has care of the child under an order made by the High Court under its inherent jurisdiction. Despite this requirement, a local authority can as a matter of urgency refuse contact for up to seven days without obtaining a court order where such action is needed to promote the child's welfare (s.34(6)). Regulations provide that in such a case written notice of the decision must be given to any child who has sufficient understanding, and to any person in respect of whom there is a presumption of reasonable contact.

*Section 34 Orders*   Under s.34 the court can make: (i) orders in respect to contact; and (ii) orders permitting a local authority to refuse contact. They can be made on an application, or by the court of its own motion when making a care order, or in any family proceedings in connection with a child in care (s.34(5)). They can be made when the care order is made, or subsequently (s.34(10)). The orders can be varied or discharged on the application of the local authority, the child, or any person named in the order (s.34(9)). The court can impose conditions on an order (s.34(7)). When exercising its powers, the court must apply the s.1(1) welfare principle and the other s.1 provisions in the Children Act (see 11.3).

*(i) Orders in Respect to Contact*   Under s.34(2) the court, on the application of the local authority or the child, can make such order as it considers appropriate in respect to the contact which is to be allowed between the child and any named person. The court has no power under s.34(2), however, to make an order prohibiting the local authority from permitting parental contact with a child (*Re W (Section 34(2) Orders)* [2000] 1 FLR 502).

Not many orders are made in respect of contact – only 571 were made in 2006 (*Judicial and Court Statistics 2006*, Cm 7273, 2007, Ministry of Justice).

Under s.34(3) the court may also make an order in respect of contact on the application of any person who has a right to reasonable contact under s.34(1) (see above), or by any person who has been granted leave to apply. Although grandparents, relatives or friends of a child are not allowed contact with a child as of right (unless they have a residence order in their favour, or an order made under the High Court's inherent jurisdiction), they can apply for the court's leave to apply for an order in respect to contact with a child in care (s.34(3)(b)). The test which the court must apply when considering leave applications is the same as that laid down in s.10(9) Children Act 1989 which applies to leave applications for s.8 orders (see 11.4, and *Re M (Care: Contact: Grandmother's Application for Leave)* [1995] 2 FLR 86). The court is not, however, restricted to considering only those matters set out in s.10(9), but must conduct a full judicial inquiry into the application in accordance with arts. 6 and 8 of the European Convention for the Protection of Human Rights (see Sumner J in *Re W (Care Proceedings: Leave to Apply)* [2004] EWHC 3342 (Fam), [2005] 2 FLR 468, where the child's aunt was refused permission to apply under s.34(3)). A frivolous or vexatious application, or one where the prospects of success are remote, will be dismissed. An applicant for leave to apply must prove that there is a serious issue to be tried and that he has a good arguable case. As contact between a child and his relatives is assumed to be beneficial, local authorities must file evidence to justify why it is not consistent with the child's welfare to promote such contact (*Re M (Care: Contact: Grandmother's Application for Leave)* [1995] 2 FLR 86).

The court can order that parents have contact with their children, even though the local authority's long-term care plan is eventually to terminate contact with a view to adoption (*Berkshire County Council* v. *B* [1997] 1 FLR 171).

*(ii) Section 34(4) Orders Authorising a Local Authority to Refuse Contact* Under s.34(4) the court can make an order (on the application of the local authority or the child) authorising the authority to refuse to allow contact between the child and any person entitled to reasonable contact under s.34(1) (see above). The court has the power to make an interim s.34(4) order. If the court refuses to make a s.34(4) order, a further application cannot be made for six months except with leave of the court (s.91(17)). The court can insert conditions into an order (s.34(7)).

In 2006, 1,135 orders refusing contact were made under s.34(4) (*Judicial and Court Statistics 2006*, Cm 7273, 2007, Ministry of Justice).

The courts have adopted a restrictive approach to applications under s.34(4), and have held that contact between a parent and child in care is only to be terminated where there is no likelihood of rehabilitation and where post-adoption contact is not considered to be in the child's best interests (see *Re T (Termination of Contact: Discharge of Order)* [1997] 1 FLR 517; *Re L (Sexual Abuse: Standard of Proof)* [1996] 1 FLR 116; and *Re H (Termination of Contact)* [2005] EWCA Civ 318, [2005] 2 FLR 408). The Court of Appeal has held that an order cannot be made under s.34(4) just because circumstances might change in the future (*Re S (Care: Parental Contact)* [2004] EWCA Civ 1397, [2005] 1 FLR 469).

In *Re B (Minors) (Termination of Contact: Paramount Consideration)* [1993] Fam 301, *sub nom Re B (Minors) (Care: Contact: Local Authority's Plans)* [1993] 1 FLR 543 Butler-Sloss LJ said that, while Parliament had given the court, not the local authority, the duty to decide on contact, the proposals of a local authority had to command the court's greatest respect and consideration. However, while the practical convenience of the local authority was relevant, the child's welfare was the paramount consideration.

*Domestic Violence and Contact* As in private law (see 12.5) the courts have become increasingly aware of the danger of permitting a child in care to have contact where there is a risk of the child witnessing domestic violence. In *Re G (Domestic Violence: Direct Contact)* [2000] 2 FLR 865 it was held that the reluctance of a child to see a parent in a case involving serious domestic violence requires careful consideration by the court, and the local authority was given permission to terminate direct contact.

*Human Rights* Parents sometimes use human rights arguments in s.34(4) proceedings, in particular art. 6 (right to a fair trial) and art. 8 (right to family life) of the European Convention for the Protection of Human Rights (see 1.5). In terms of art. 8, an order terminating contact must be proportionate (see 1.5).

*Discharging a s.34(4) Order* An order can be discharged (s.34(9)) if there has been a change of circumstances, and its discharge will promote the child's welfare. However, as one of the policies of the Children Act is for local authorities to work in partnership with children and their families, regulation provides that the local authority and the person in whose favour the order was made can make an agreement about contact (instead of applying for variation or discharge), provided the child, if of sufficient understanding, agrees.

## 15.9  Part V of the Children Act 1989 – Emergency Protection

Part V of the Children Act 1989 provides the legal framework for dealing with children who need protection in an emergency or otherwise. It does so by making provision, *inter alia*, for child assessment orders (CAOs) and emergency protection orders (EPOs). These orders are subject to certain safeguards so as to prevent unjustifiable intrusion into family life. For example, they are of short duration and are open to challenge. In some cases, emergency action will be followed by an application for a care or supervision order (see above).

Under Part V a local authority has various investigative duties when it is informed that a child who lives, or is found in its area, is the subject of an EPO or is in police protection (see below), or the local authority has reasonable cause to suspect that such child is suffering, or is likely to suffer, significant harm (see s.47(1)). Once a local authority has obtained an order under Part V, enquiries must be made to decide what action should be taken to safeguard or promote the child's welfare (s.47(2)).

As Part V proceedings are not 'family proceedings' for the purposes of the Children Act (see s.8(4)), the court cannot make any s.8 order in the proceedings. When considering whether to make an order under Part V the child's welfare is the court's paramount consideration (s.1(1)) and the other s.1 principles apply (see 11.3), except for the s.1(3) welfare checklist, because conducting the s.1(3) exercise is lengthy and would defeat the purpose of a Part V application, which is for immediate short-term emergency protection.

The following are available for emergency protection under Part V of the Children Act: (a) a child assessment order (CAO); (b) an emergency protection order (EPO); and (c) police protection. In practice, however, local authority social workers often prefer to make agreements with parents that children be accommodated with the local authority under s.20 Children Act 1989 (see 15.6, above), rather than seeking an EPO or requesting police protection (see research by Masson, 2005). By doing this, local authorities comply with the important policy objective of the Children Act that local authorities should work in partnership with parents.

### (a)  Child Assessment Orders

Under s.43 the court has jurisdiction to make a child assessment order (CAO), which is an order enabling a medical or psychiatric assessment of the child to take place so that it can be established whether or not the child is suffering, or is likely to suffer, significant harm. A CAO allows a local authority to intervene to protect a child where the circumstances are not sufficiently urgent or serious enough to justify other intervention, for example, by means of an emergency protection order (EPO). With a CAO order the child can remain at home, and so it is less severe than an EPO. CAOs are not commonly made. In 2006, only 22 orders were made (*Judicial and Court Statistics 2006*, Cm 7273, 2007, Ministry of Justice).

*The Grounds for an Order*    The court can make a child assessment order on the application of a local authority (or the NSPCC) if it is satisfied that (s.43(1)): the applicant has reasonable cause to suspect that the child is suffering, or is likely to suffer, significant harm; and an assessment of the state of the child's health or development, or of the way in which he has been treated, is required to enable the applicant to determine whether or not the child is suffering, or is likely to suffer, significant harm; and it is unlikely that such an assessment will be made, or be satisfactory, in the absence of an order under this section.

The court can treat the application as an application for an EPO (s.43(3)). The court cannot make a CAO if there are grounds for making an EPO, and it considers it ought to make an EPO rather than a CAO (s.43(4)). The CAO must specify when the assessment is to begin and it must last no longer than seven days from that date (s.43(5)). The effect of an order is to order any person in a position to do so to produce the child to the person named in the order and to comply with any directions in the order (s.43(6)). The order authorises the person carrying out the assessment, or part of it, to do so in accordance with the terms of the order (s.43(7)). A child of sufficient understanding to make an informed decision may refuse to submit to a medical or psychiatric examination, or other assessment, regardless of any term in the order authorising assessment (s.43(8)), although in *South Glamorgan County Council* v. *W and B* (see 9.4) it was held that the court can override the child's wishes.

A child can be kept away from home for an assessment but only where that is really necessary for the assessment, and only in accordance with directions and for the period(s) of time specified in the order (s.43(9)). The CAO must contain directions about contact (s.43(10)). Before the application is heard, the local authority (or the NSPCC) must take reasonably practicable steps to ensure that notice of the application is given to: the child's parents; any person with parental responsibility; any person caring for the child; any person who has contact with the child either under a s.8 contact order or a s.34 order; and the child (s.43(11)). This notice requirement is to ensure that, where possible, the hearing takes place between the parties in order to prevent unjustifiable intervention. The rules of court make provision for variation and discharge (s.43(12)). The court is required to appoint a CAFCASS officer for the child unless it is satisfied that it is not necessary to do so in order to safeguard the child's interests (ss.41(1) and (2), as amended).

## (b)  Emergency Protection Orders

Under s.44 Children Act 1989 the court can make an emergency protection order (EPO), which is an order providing an immediate but temporary remedy in a genuine emergency. In an emergency, an application can be heard by a single justice and may, with leave of the clerk of the court, be made without notice being given to the other party – although, wherever possible, proceedings must be heard *inter partes*. In 2006, 1,639 EPOs were made (*Judicial and Court Statistics 2006*, Cm 7273, Ministry of Justice, 2007).

*Applicants*    Section 44 provides that 'any person' may apply for an EPO, but in practice it is local authority social services departments who do so. According to Masson (2005), local authorities often prefer to make agreements with parents that the child at risk be provided with accommodation under s.20 Children Act 1989 (see 15.6), rather than bring proceedings for an EPO.

*The Grounds for Making an EPO*    The applicant must satisfy the court that there is reasonable cause to believe that the child is likely to suffer harm if: he is not removed to accommodation provided by or on behalf of the applicant; or he does not remain in the place in which he is being accommodated (s.44(1)(a)). The court can also make an EPO on the application of a local authority (or the NSPCC) if enquiries in respect of the child are being made under s.47(1)(b) and those enquiries are being frustrated by access to the child being unreasonably refused to a person authorised to seek access, and the applicant has reasonable cause to believe that access to the child is required as a matter of urgency (ss.44(1)(b), (c)). Local authorities must keep parents informed about what is happening at the hearing, and they have a continuing duty to keep the case under review (s.44).

*The Approach of the Courts*    The following principles will be applied by the court when it is considering whether or not to make an EPO:

- As an EPO is regarded as a severe and extremely harsh measure requiring exceptional justification and extraordinarily compelling reasons, the court will not make an EPO unless it is satisfied that it is both necessary and proportionate, and that no other less radical form of order will promote the child's welfare. (The European Court of Human Rights so held in *P, C and S* v. *UK* (2002) 35 EHRR 31, [2002] 2 FLR 631, which involved the removal of a newborn baby.) Separation of the child will only be contemplated if immediate separation is essential to secure the child's safety. Imminent danger must be established. (See also *Re M (Care Proceedings: Judicial Review)* [2003] EWHC 850 (Admin), [2003] 2 FLR 171.)
- An EPO should not be made for any longer than is absolutely necessary to protect a child.
- The evidence in support of an EPO has to be full, detailed, precise and compelling.
- Save in wholly exceptional cases, parents must be given adequate prior notice of the date, time and place of the application for an EPO, and the evidence relied on.
- A without notice (*ex parte*) application will normally only be considered appropriate if the case involves a genuine emergency, great urgency or some other compelling reason to believe that the child's welfare will be compromised if the parents are alerted in advance (but even then some kind of informal notice to the parents may well be possible). As a result of their obligations under the Human Rights Act 1998, the courts must ensure that making an EPO without notice does not breach art. 6 of the ECHR (right to a fair trial), or that making an EPO is not in breach of the principle of proportionality and therefore in breach of the right to family life under art. 8.
- A Children's Guardian, an officer of CAFCASS, must be appointed immediately upon issue of proceedings for an EPO.

The above principles (and others) were set out and applied by Munby J in the following case, where he described an EPO summarily removing a child from his parents as a 'terrible and drastic remedy':

▶ *X Council* v. *B (Emergency Protection Orders)* [2004] EWHC 2015 (Fam), [2005] 1 FLR 341

Three children were taken into foster-care under without notice (*ex parte*) EPOs. Munby J held that, while child assessment orders, and possibly even very short-term EPOs, had been appropriate to enable medical tests and examinations to take place, it was not clear that there had been any justification for removing the children into foster-care. He said that the local authority had failed to address itself adequately to the requirements of ss.44(5) or (10) Children Act 1989, and it was not clear that it had exercised the exceptional diligence called for by art. 8 of the European Convention on Human Rights. The distress suffered by the children and parents due to their separation had been exacerbated by the unacceptably limited amount of contact permitted, and by the interventionist manner in which contact had been supervised. Munby J said that the Court of Appeal had repeatedly emphasised that any intervention under Parts V (and IV) of the Children Act should be proportionate to the legitimate aim of protecting the welfare and interests of the child. As Hale LJ had said in *Re O (Supervision Order)* [2001] EWCA Civ 16, [2001] 1 FLR 923, 'proportionality . . . is the key'.

In *Re X (Emergency Protection Order)* [2006] EWHC 510(Fam), [2006] 2 FLR 701 McFarlane J held that the list of factors relating to the making of EPOs laid down by Munby J in *X Council* v. *B* (above) was required reading for every magistrate and justices' clerk in any EPO application. McFarlane J emphasised that EPOs should be made only in a genuine emergency and contain only what was necessary to provide immediate short-term protection. He said lack of information or a need for assessment could never, of themselves, establish the existence of a genuine emergency sufficient to justify an EPO – evidence establishing the threshold under s.44 Children Act 1989 was necessary. In *Re X Council* (above) the child had been taken into care and one year later significant flaws were found in the process of making the original EPO – it had been made on the basis of flawed evidence.

*Duration of an EPO*   An order can be made in the first instance to last for up to eight days, but can be extended for up to a further seven days on application if the court has reasonable cause to believe that the child is likely to suffer significant harm if the order is not extended (s.45).

*Effect of an EPO*   While an EPO is in force it operates as a direction to any person who is in a position to do so to comply with any request to produce the child to the applicant (s.44(4)(a)). It authorises the child's removal to accommodation provided by or on behalf of the applicant and the child being kept there; or it prevents the child's removal from any hospital, or other place, in which he was being accommodated immediately before the order was made (s.44(4)(b)). It is a criminal offence intentionally to obstruct a person authorised to remove the child, or to prevent the removal of the child (s.44(15)). The EPO gives the applicant limited parental responsibility (s.44(4)(c) and s.44(5)(b)). The applicant must comply with regulations made by the Secretary of State (s.44(5)).

While an EPO is in force, the applicant cannot remove the child from his home or retain him in a place for longer than is necessary to safeguard the child's welfare, and must return the child or allow him to be removed when safe to do so (s.44(10)). The child can be returned to the care of the person from whom he was removed or, if that is not reasonably practicable, then to a parent, a person with parental responsibility or to such other person as the applicant with the agreement of the court considers appropriate, although while the order is in force the applicant can exercise his powers with respect to the child where it is necessary to do so (ss.44(11), (12)). Local authorities must make arrangements (subject to directions in the order as to contact and medical assessment or examination) to allow the child reasonable contact with the following persons and any person acting on his or her behalf: parents; any other person with parental responsibility; any person with whom the child was living immediately before the order was made; and any person with a right to contact under a s.8 order or a s.34 contact order (s.44(13)). Local authorities should continue to consider less drastic emergency removal of the child even though an EPO has been obtained.

*Imposing Directions on an EPO* When the order is made, or while it is in force, the court can give directions and impose conditions as to contact and/or may give directions with respect to the medical or psychiatric examination or other assessment of the child, which can include a condition that no examination or assessment be carried out unless the court directs (ss.44(6), (8) and (9)). Where a direction as to medical or psychiatric examination or assessment is made, a child of sufficient understanding to make an informed decision may refuse the examination or assessment (s.44(6)). Directions in an order can be varied at any time (s.44(9)(b)).

*Challenging an EPO* There is no right of appeal against the making, or refusal, of an EPO. However, an application to discharge the order can be heard 72 hours or more after it was made (ss.45(9), (10)) on the application of: the child; his parent; any person who has parental responsibility for the child; or any person with whom the child was living immediately before the order was made (s.45(8)). An EPO can be challenged under the Human Rights Act 1998, and judicial review proceedings may provide a useful way of challenging an order. In *X Council* v. *B (Emergency Protection Orders)* (see p.420, above), Munby J held, that while an application for judicial review is not normally an appropriate remedy for challenging an EPO, it is not necessarily precluded in an appropriate case to correct an error or injustice. He said that, as the effect of an EPO was to remove a child from a parent for up to 15 days without a statutory right of appeal, judicial review might provide a mechanism for review of an unreasonable decision by the family proceedings court. Habeas corpus has been held not to be an appropriate remedy (*Re S (Habeas Corpus); S* v. *Haringey London Borough Council* [2003] EWHC 2734 (Admin), [2004] 1 FLR 590).

### (c) Police Protection

Under s.46 Children Act 1989 the police have various powers in emergency cases involving children. Thus, any constable who has reasonable cause to believe that a child would otherwise be likely to suffer significant harm can remove the child to suitable accommodation, or take reasonable steps to prevent the child's removal (s.46(1)). This power lasts for up to 72 hours, during which time the police must ensure that inquiries are conducted by a designated officer and that the child is accommodated by the local authority (ss.43(3)(e), (f)). The police must inform the local authority, the parents and the child of any steps it proposes to take. While the child is in police protection, the police do not have parental responsibility for the child but must do what is reasonable to safeguard or promote the child's welfare. While the child is accommodated under s.46, the parents cannot remove the child, but they are permitted to have contact.

According to Masson (2005, at p.78) police protection is widely used, despite the lack of attention given to police protection in the literature on child protection.

### 15.10 Excluding an Abuser from the Home

The court can include an exclusion requirement in an interim care order (s.38A) and in an emergency protection order (s.44A), so that a person who abuses a child can be moved from the home. An exclusion requirement can only be made if the grounds for an interim care order or emergency protection order are proved, and the court is satisfied that there is reasonable cause to believe that if the relevant person is excluded from the home the child will cease to suffer, or cease to be likely to suffer, significant harm. The court must also be satisfied that another person living in the home (whether or not a parent) is able and willing to give the child the care which it would be reasonable to expect a parent to give, and that that person consents to the exclusion requirement (s.38A(2)). The exclusion requirement may provide that the abuser leave the house, be prevented from entering the house and/or be excluded from a defined area around the house (s.38A(3)). A power of arrest may be attached to an exclusion requirement (s.38A(5)). The court may accept an undertaking from an abuser, instead of making an exclusion requirement.

## 15.11   Local Authorities' Duties Towards 'Looked After' Children

Local authorities have duties under the Children Act 1989 towards children 'looked after' by them, whether accommodated under a voluntary arrangement or under a care order (s.22(1)). A local authority must safeguard and promote the child's welfare and make such use of services available for children cared for by their own parents as appears reasonable in the case of the particular child (s.22(3)). Before making a decision about a child being looked after, or proposed to be looked after, the local authority must ascertain the wishes and feelings of the child, his parents, any person with parental responsibility and any other relevant person (s.22(4)). It must also consider their wishes in respect of the child's religion, racial origin and cultural and linguistic background (s.22(5)). It must advise, assist and befriend the child, with a view to promoting his welfare when he ceases to be looked after by them (s.24(1)). A local authority must encourage rehabilitation by allowing the child to live with his family, unless contrary to his welfare (s.23(6)), and ensure that the accommodation provided is near the child's home, and that brothers and sisters remain together (s.23(7)). A local authority's general duties to a child are facilitated by more specific duties, such as by the inspection of foster-parents, and children's homes. Local authorities also have a duty to promote contact (Sched. 2, para. 15, and see above).

### Care in Care – The Care Standards Act 2000
The aim of the Care Standards Act 2000 is to regulate and improve standards in children's homes, care homes, private and voluntary health-care and other care services. The Act also establishes the National Care Standards Commission (NCSC), which has power to inspect children's homes, fostering agencies, local authority and voluntary adoption agencies and boarding schools. It establishes the post of Children's Rights Director within the NCSC to oversee child care services.

### Children Leaving Care
The Children (Leaving Care) Act 2000 has amended the Children Act 1989 (see ss.23 and 24 and Sched. 2, paras. 19A–C) to impose a duty on local authorities in respect of children who leave care. Each local authority is required to provide a comprehensive after-care service to ease the passage of looked after children into adulthood. A local authority looking after a child has a duty to advise, assist and befriend the child with a view to promoting his welfare when it has ceased to look after him (para. 19A). It must keep in touch with a care leaver and prepare needs assessments and formulate 'pathway plans'

in respect of education, training, careers and financial support until the person leaving care reaches the age of 21 (para. 19B). A local authority is required to appoint a personal adviser to keep in touch with the person leaving care (para. 19C). According to the *Children Leaving Care Act Guidance*, the personal adviser plays a 'negotiating role on behalf of the child'. A local authority is also required to provide financial support, including the cost of education and training up to the age of 24. The Children and Young Persons Bill 2007 makes provision to prevent young people being forced from care until they are ready.

If a local authority fails to comply with these statutory requirements, a challenge can be made in judicial review proceedings (see, for example, *R (J) v. Caerphilly County Borough Council* [2005] EWHC 586 (Admin), [2005] 2 FLR 860 where Munby J held that a local authority has a duty to carry out its statutory obligations even if the person leaving care is unco-operative and unwilling to engage, or refuses to engage, with the local authority). In *R (Berhe and Others) v. Hillingdon London Borough Council* [2003] EWHC 2075 (Admin), [2004] 1 FLR 439 Sullivan J held that asylum-seeking minors who had been looked after by a local authority were entitled on reaching adulthood to benefit from the provisions of the Children (Leaving Care) Act 2000.

A new Bill, the Children and Young Persons' Bill 2007, has been put before Parliament with the aim of improving care for children in care.

## 15.12 Challenging Local Authority Decisions About Children

Parents, relatives, children, foster-parents and others may sometimes be dissatisfied with action taken, or not taken, by a local authority. It may be possible to resolve a grievance informally, particularly as a policy aim of the Children Act 1989 is to encourage co-operation and agreement, but, if this is not possible, then the following procedures can be invoked.

*(i) Using the Children Act 1989*   One way of challenging a local authority is to appeal against a care or supervision order or apply to have it discharged (see above). In respect of an emergency protection order, a discharge application can be made, but there is no right of appeal. A decision about contact with a child may also be challenged (see above). A care order can also be challenged by making an application for a s.8 residence order, which, if granted, automatically discharges the care order (s.91(1)). However, the court is unlikely to grant a residence order, or grant leave to apply for one, where it interferes with a local authority's plans (see, for example, *Re A and W (Minors) (Residence Order: Leave to Apply)* [1992] Fam 182, [1992] 2 FLR 154 where a foster-mother's application for leave to apply for a residence order as a means of challenging a local authority decision forbidding her to foster children was refused).

It is not possible to apply to make a child a ward of court as a way of challenging a care order, as a child cannot simultaneously be a ward of court and the subject of a care order (ss.100(2)(c) and 91(4)). Another option is to make a complaint to the Secretary of State, who has the power to declare a local authority to be in default, if it fails without reasonable cause to comply with a duty under the Children Act 1989, and who can require compliance within a specified period (s.84). A further option is to use the complaints procedure (below).

*(ii) The Complaints Procedure*   The Children Act 1989 requires local authorities to establish a complaints procedure (see s.26, as amended). Until recently, complaints could only be

made in respect of Part III duties and powers, but the procedure has been extended to care and supervision, and emergency protection, and children are now entitled to advocacy services (see below, and *Getting the Best from Complaints*, 2005, DfES). The following persons can make a complaint: a 'looked after' child or a child in need; a parent; a person with parental responsibility; a foster-parent; any person whom the local authority considers has sufficient interest in the child's welfare to warrant representation being considered; a young person who considers he has been given inadequate preparation for leaving care or for after-care; and a child who is the subject of a placement order for the purposes of adoption.

*(iii) Advocacy Services for Children*    Sections 24D and 26A Children Act 1989 (inserted by the Adoption and Children Act 2002) introduce a more child-centred approach to complaints. Section 26A allows children making complaints to have access to an independent advocacy service (see *Get it Sorted: Providing Effective Advocacy Services for Children and Young People Making a Complaint Under the Children Act 1989*, 2003, DfES). Local authorities must make arrangements to provide assistance (such as advocacy services and representation) for children and young persons who make, or intend to make, complaints under the Children Act procedures (s.26A(1)). This duty applies to the standard complaints procedure in s.26 (above), and to the procedure for young people leaving care under s.24D (inserted by the Children (Leaving Care) Act 2000). The assistance which local authorities must put in place must include representation (s.26A(2)). Local authorities may choose to provide the assistance themselves or may come to an agreement with a national or local advocacy service provider.

*(iv) A Challenge Under the Human Rights Act 1998*    Local authorities are 'public authorities' for the purposes of the Human Rights Act (HRA) 1998 and must therefore act in a way which is compatible with the European Convention for the Protection of Human Rights (s.6 HRA 1998) (see 1.5). Any person who is a victim of an unlawful act (or proposed act) of a local authority may bring an application under s.7 HRA 1998, either by way of a free-standing application against a local authority, or by relying on a Convention right in any legal proceedings (s.7). European Convention challenges are usually brought in legal proceeding (such as care proceedings) rather than being brought under the HRA 1998 itself. Damages can be awarded for a breach of a Convention right by a public authority (s.8 HRA 1998).

Claims against local authorities have often been brought in respect of procedural unfairness under art. 6 ECHR or the right to family life under art. 8:

**Case-Law Examples**

▶ *Re G (Care: Challenge to Local Authority's Decision)* [2003] EWHC 551 (Fam), [2003] 2 FLR 42

The parents applied for discharge of care orders and an injunction under s.7 HRA 1998 to prevent their children's removal into care, as the local authority had delayed in making a decision about the children, and had kept no minutes or written records of meetings and decisions made. Munby J held that the local authority was in breach of the right to family life under art. 8.

▶ *Re M (Care: Challenging Decisions by Local Authority)* [2001] 2 FLR 1300

The child was in care and her parents, who were separated, had a long history of alcohol and drug abuse. At a planning meeting, to which the parents and their solicitors were not invited, the local authority finally ruled out any prospect of the child living with the father. Each parent commenced separate free-standing applications under s.7 HRA 1998 arguing that they were victims of an unlawful act of the public authority, and that the placement should be set aside. Holman J held that the local authority had acted unlawfully under s.6 HRA 1998 in respect of the way in which it had conducted the planning meeting, which was contrary to the parents' right to respect for their family life under art. 8. The local authority had failed sufficiently to involve the parents at a critical moment, and so the decision made at the planning meeting was quashed by Holman J.

▶ *Re W (Removal into Care)* [2005] EWCA Civ 642, [2005] 2 FLR 1022

The parents challenged the removal of twins from their care by means of an application to discharge the care orders and by way of injunction under s.8 HRA 1998. Thorpe LJ in the Court of Appeal held that an application under the HRA 1998 was the right remedy, not the application to discharge the care orders, as what they were challenging was the lawfulness of the local authority's decision to remove the twins.

▶ *Re C (Breach of Human Rights: Damages)* [2007] EWCA Civ 2, [2007] 1 FLR 1957

At first instance the judge made a declaration under the HRA 1998 that there had been a significant breach of the mother's human rights caused by the local authority's decision to abandon the care plan without giving the mother an opportunity to participate in the decision-making process. However, the judge did not make an order for damages, as the declaration of a breach provided just satisfaction. The mother's appeal on the issue of damages was dismissed by the Court of Appeal, which held that she was not entitled to compensation because this was a case of lawful removal of the child, and because the procedural breach had not been significant. The evidence strongly suggested that the mother had not had the capacity to participate at the material time and the local authority had mitigated the breach by going to considerable lengths to keep her lawyer informed.

(See also *Re L (Care: Assessment: Fair Trial)* [2002] EWHC 1379 (Fam), [2002] 2 FLR 730; and *C v. Bury Metropolitan Borough Council* [2002] EWHC 1438 (Fam), [2002] 2 FLR 868.)

*(v) Judicial Review* Judicial review is an administrative law remedy which may be made against a local authority (or other public body, such as a Government department, court or health authority) by an aggrieved person, including a child. The application must be made to the Administrative Court. The court can grant the following remedies: a 'mandatory order' (directing the respondent to take a particular course of action); a 'prohibitory order' (prohibiting the respondent from taking a particular course of action); and a 'quashing order' (quashing the decision of the respondent). It can order damages in conjunction with one of these orders. The Administrative Court can also issue declarations and injunctions.

Strict rules govern judicial review applications. Thus leave must be obtained from the court for the case to proceed to a full application on its merits, which will be granted only if the court considers that there is a reasonable chance of the court deciding that the local authority's decision was so unreasonable that no reasonable authority could have ever come to it. Leave to apply must be sought within three months from the date on which the grounds for the application arose. Leave will not be granted unless the applicant has a sufficient interest in the matter to which the application relates. The grounds on which judicial review may be granted are: illegality; procedural impropriety (breach of the rules of natural justice); and irrationality (*Council of Civil Service Unions* v. *Minister for the Civil Service* [1985] AC 374). To succeed on the ground of irrationality (unreasonableness), the local authority must have acted irrationally, in other words it must be proved that the local authority took into account matters which it ought not to have taken into account, or failed to take into account matters which it ought to have taken into account, or came to a conclusion that was so unreasonable that no authority would have come to it. However, as judicial review is a discretionary remedy, the court may refuse a remedy even if a ground is proved.

As local authorities are public authorities for the purposes of the Human Rights Act 1998, and as judicial review is a means of challenging local authority action or inaction, challenges by way of judicial review are often based on, or supported by, human rights' arguments under the European Convention for the Protection of Human Rights:

> ▶ *The Queen on the Applications of L and Others* v. *Manchester City Council; The Queen on the Application of R and Another* v. *Manchester City Council* [2001] EWHC 707 (Admin)
>
> Children (by their litigation friend) successfully applied for judicial review of the local authority's policy whereby it paid substantially lower fostering payments to short-term foster-parents who were friends or relatives of children. Munby J held that the local authority's policy was irrational, and also breached art. 8 ECHR (right to family life), as under art. 8(2) it was neither a necessary nor proportionate response. The local authority had a positive obligation when exercising its duties under Part III of the Children Act to secure respect for family life under art. 8. The policy was also held to be discriminatory under art. 14 ECHR, as the reference in art. 14 to 'other status' included family status.

Where a local authority has wide discretion in a particular matter (as it has under the Children Act 1989) it is difficult to succeed in an action for judicial review, and, where there is another procedure for challenging a local authority, the court may not grant judicial review before that has been pursued (see, for example, *R* v. *Royal Borough of Kingston upon Thames ex parte T* [1994] 1 FLR 798, where an application for judicial review was refused as a remedy should have been sought under the Children Act complaints procedure). Judicial review is therefore a remedy of last resort, and will be refused where there is another equally effective and convenient remedy.

A considerable disadvantage of judicial review is that, even if a quashing order (the more likely remedy) is granted, the local authority's obligation is merely to reconsider its original decision, and, provided that decision is not illegal, procedurally improper or irrational, then it can come to the same decision as it did the first time.

The drawbacks of the court's powers in judicial review proceedings were referred to in *Re T (Judicial Review: Local Authority Decisions Concerning Child in Need)* [2003] EWHC 2515 (Admin), [2004] 1 FLR 601 where Wall J held that, while the court was in a position to direct the local authority to reconsider the question of the services it should provide under Part III Children Act 1989 for the child in question, it could not direct the local authority in respect of what to decide, or to direct that it make any special provision for him. Wall J said that the power to direct the local authority to implement a particular course of action would require a specific statutory authority.

There are many reported cases involving applications for judicial review in the context of local authorities' powers under the Children Act 1989, for example in respect of: placing a child's name on the child protection register (*R* v. *Hampshire County Council ex parte H* [1999] 2 FLR 359); failing to allow a solicitor to attend a child protection conference and failing to supply the applicant with the minutes (*R* v. *Cornwall County Council ex parte LH* [2000] 1 FLR 236); failing to obtain parental permission to move a child from residential care to foster care (*R* v. *Tameside Metropolitan Borough Council ex parte J* [2000] 1 FLR 942); and refusing to carry out assessments of children in need (*R (On the Application of S)* v. *Wandsworth, Hammersmith and Lambeth London Borough Council* [2002] 1 FLR 469).

In *Re M (Care Proceedings: Judicial Review)* [2003] EWHC 850 (Admin), [2003] 2 FLR 171, where the parents sought an injunction in judicial review proceedings to restrain the local authority from commencing emergency protection or care proceedings in respect of their unborn child, Munby J dismissed the application and held that the greatest possible caution is called for where the purpose of judicial review proceedings is to restrain what are on the face of it proper proceedings in a domestic court. He said that, although the European Court of Human Rights had made clear that removing a child from his mother at or very shortly after birth was a draconian measure requiring exceptional justification, there are cases where the need for such highly intrusive intervention is imperatively demanded in a baby's interests.

*(vi) Commissioner for Local Administration*   A complaint can be made to the Commissioner for Local Administration (the Local Government Ombudsman), who has a duty to investigate complaints of maladministration by local authorities. This is a lengthy and limited remedy.

*(vii) An Application to the Children's Commissioner*   A complaint can be made to the Children's Commissioner (see 9.1).

*(viii) An Application to the European Court of Human Rights*   Despite the implementation of the Human Rights Act 1998, it is still open to a parent, child or other aggrieved party, who has exhausted all the remedies available in the courts in the UK, to apply to the European Court of Human Rights in Strasbourg, alleging that the UK is in breach of the European Convention for the Protection of Human Rights.

*(ix) An Action in Negligence*   Social workers and other persons working in the child protection system are not immune from a claim in negligence, although the courts are aware of the difficult task social workers have and that local authorities have limited resources. A claim may therefore be struck out on the ground that there is no duty of care in negligence for reasons of public policy. There has, however, been a change of attitude in respect of negligence claims against local authorities working in the child protection area, and the courts are now more willing to allow claims to proceed to trial, particularly since the coming into force of the Human Rights Act 1998. The following cases are examples of claims brought in negligence:

▶ *X (Minors)* v. *Bedfordshire County Council and Related Appeals* **[1995] 2 AC 633, [1995] 2 FLR 276**

The case involved conjoined appeals against local authorities in respect of their statutory powers in the field of child protection and education. The House of Lords had to consider whether a common law duty of care in negligence could be imposed on a local authority in respect of its statutory powers.

In the first appeal ('the *Bedfordshire* case') a negligence claim was brought by five children who had suffered years of abuse and serious neglect because the defendant local authority had failed to take steps to protect them, even though it had been informed on several occasions that they were suffering harm. The House of Lords struck their claim out on policy grounds, holding that the defendant authority owed them no duty of care.

In the second appeal ('the *Newham* case') the child had been taken into care after a child psychologist employed by the local authority had wrongly identified the mother's cohabitant as having abused the child, when it was someone else who had abused the child. As a result, the child was taken away from the mother for about a year. The House of Lords held that the defendant local authority owed the mother and daughter no duty of care in negligence on policy grounds.

(**Note**: Four of the children in 'the *Bedfordshire* case' subsequently took their case to the ECtHR in Strasbourg (see *Z and Others* v. *United Kingdom* [2001] 2 FLR 603), which held that the UK Government was in breach of the ECHR as the children had suffered inhuman and degrading treatment (under art. 3) and had lacked an effective remedy (under art. 13). The ECtHR awarded them damages in just satisfaction. The child and the mother in 'the *Newham* case' also took their case to the ECtHR which held that there had also been breaches of art. 3 and art. 13 and awarded them damages (see *TP and KM* v. *United Kingdom* [2001] 2 FLR 545). After these two decisions, the courts in the UK became more willing to allow cases in negligence to proceed to trial and for negligence claims to succeed, particularly where the claimants were children, or adults who had suffered as children.)

▶ *Barrett* v. *Enfield London Borough Council* **[2001] 2 AC 550**

The House of Lords held that the defendant local authority owed a duty of care in negligence to the claimant who alleged he had suffered serious personal consequences during his time in care, because he had been moved from foster-home to foster-home and the local authority had made no attempt to rehabilitate him with his mother or to have him adopted. He was therefore allowed to pursue his negligence claim.

▶ *W* v. *Essex County Council* **[2000] 1 FLR 657**

The House of Lords held that a duty of care in negligence was owed by the defendant local authority to parents who had suffered psychiatric illness as a result of their daughters being sexually assaulted by a 15-year-old boy, who had been placed with them as a foster-child, despite the social worker knowing that the boy posed a risk because he had assaulted his own sisters. The social worker had assured the parents (wrongly) that the boy was no risk. The case could therefore proceed to trial.

▶ *A* v. *Essex County Council* **[2003] EWCA Civ 1848, [2004] 1 FLR 749**

Parents sought damages in negligence (including damages for psychiatric injury) against the defendant local authority for failing to give them sufficient information about a brother and sister who had been placed with them for adoption. During the adoption placement, and after the adoption, the boy attacked the claimants and their natural child and was diagnosed with attention deficit hyperactivity disorder. The judge held the defendant authority liable in negligence for failing to provide the claimant parents with all relevant information about the two children they were preparing to adopt, but the judge held that the local authority was only liable for injury, loss and damage during the adoption placement, but not after the adoption orders were made. The decision was upheld by the Court of Appeal.

▶ *D* v. *East Berkshire Community NHS Trust; MAK* v. *Dewsbury Healthcare NHS Trust; RK* v. *Oldham NHS Trust* [2005] UKHL 23, [2005] 2 FLR 284

In each of the three appeals the parents alleged that medical professionals had negligently misdiagnosed child abuse rather than the actual cause of the child's health problems, and that this had disrupted their family life and caused them psychiatric injury. The parents sought damages in negligence against the defendant NHS Trusts. The House of Lords held by a majority (Lord Bingham dissenting) that the defendants owed no duty of care in negligence to the parents – because to impose such a duty would result in a conflict of interests. As the doctors were concerned with the protection of children, not parents, they must be free to act single-mindedly in the interests of children. There were cogent reasons of public policy for holding that no duty of care was owed to the parents.

▶ *Lawrence* v. *Pembrokeshire County Council* [2007] EWCA Civ 446, [2007] 2 FLR 705

The claimant sued the defendant in negligence because social workers had placed her four children on the Child Protection Register where they had remained registered for 14 months. The only difference between the claimant's case and the *East Berkshire* case (above) was that the facts of her case post-dated the coming into force of the Human Rights Act 1998. At first instance her claim was struck out as the defendant authority owed no duty of care. The Court of Appeal dismissed her appeal, holding that the right to respect for family life guaranteed by art. 8 of the European Convention for the Protection of Human Rights did not outweigh the duty of a local authority to protect children at risk by placing them on the Child Protection Register. The Court of Appeal held that the cogency of the reasoning in *East Berkshire* remained untouched and was compatible with the jurisprudence of the European Court of Human Rights. The same principles in *East Berkshire* (where the defendants were health professionals) applied to social workers investigating child abuse.

(See also *D* v. *Bury Metropolitan Borough Council; B* v. *Bury MBC* [2006] EWCA Civ 1, [2006] 2 FLR 147 where *D* v. *East Berkshire* (above) was applied so that the mother's appeal against a refusal to find that she was owed a duty of care in negligence was dismissed by the Court of Appeal (her child had been wrongly assessed by the local authority as suffering significant harm when in fact the child had suffered injuries as a result of suffering from brittle bone disease).)

## Summary

1 Local authorities have duties and powers under the Children Act 1989 to safeguard and promote the welfare of children. Local authorities must work in partnership with families and children, with compulsory intervention by court order in the last resort – as parents have primary responsibility for their children.

2 As local authorities are public authorities for the purposes of the Human Rights Act 1998, they must abide by the European Convention for the Protection of Human Rights.

3 Local authorities must co-operate with other professionals and other agencies in the task of child protection.

4 Under Part III of the Children Act 1989 local authorities have a duty to provide services for children in need and disabled children, including in particular the provision of day care and accommodation. A child 'accommodated in care' under a voluntary arrangement can be removed at any time.

## Summary cont'd

5    Under Part IV of the Children Act 1989 local authorities can apply for care and supervision orders, which may be granted by the court if the 'threshold criteria' in s.31(2) are satisfied, and the court considers the child's welfare requires such an order to be made. In assessing welfare, the court must apply the welfare principle (s.1(1)), the no-delay principle (s.1(2)), the welfare checklist (s.1(3)) and the no-order presumption (s.1(5)). A care order gives the local authority parental responsibility for the child, but a parent does not lose parental responsibility. A supervision order places the child under the supervision of a designated local authority officer or a probation officer. A care order can be discharged. A supervision order can be varied or discharged. There is a presumption of continuing reasonable contact between parents and others and the child in care, unless terminated or restricted by court order (s.34).

6    Under Part V of the Children Act 1989 a child assessment order (s.43) and an emergency protection order (s.44) can be made where children need emergency protection. The police have powers to provide protection for children where they have reasonable cause to believe that a child is likely to suffer significant harm (s.46).

7    Local authorities have certain duties to children 'looked after' by them whether under a voluntary arrangement or under a court order.

8    Local authorities can be challenged under the Children Act 1989 complaints procedure or under the general law by bringing a tort action or by seeking judicial review. An application may also be made to the local ombudsman. Challenges can be brought under the Human Rights Act 1998.

## Further Reading and References

Bailey-Harris and Harris, 'Local authorities and child protection – the mosaic of accountability' [2002] CFLQ 117.

Brophy, 'Diversity and child protection' [2003] Fam Law 674.

Conway, 'The Laming Inquiry – Victoria Climbié's legacy' [2003] Fam Law 513.

Fairgreave and Green (eds.), *Child Abuse Tort Claims Against Public Bodies: A Comparative View*, 2004, Ashgate.

Hall, 'What price the logic of proof of evidence?' [2000] Fam Law 423.

Harwin and Owen, 'The implementation of care plans, and its relationship to children's welfare' [2003] CFLQ 71.

Hayes, 'Child protection – from principles and policies to practices' [1998] CFLQ 119.

Hemingway and Williams, '*Re M and R; Re H and R*' [1997] Fam Law 740.

Hollingsworth and Douglas, 'Creating a children's champion for Wales? The Care Standards Act 2000 (Part V) and the Children's Commissioner for Wales Act 2001' (2002) MLR 58.

Keating, 'Shifting standards in the House of Lords: Re H and Others (Minors) (Sexual Abuse: Standard of Proof)' [1996] CFLQ 157.

Lindley and Richards, '*Working Together 2000* – how will parents fare under the new child protection process?' [2000] CFLQ 213.

Lyon, *Child Abuse* (3rd edn), 2003, Family Law.

Masson, 'Emergency protection, good practice and human rights' [2004] Fam Law 882.

Masson, 'Emergency intervention to protect children: using and avoiding legal controls' [2005] CFLQ 75.

Masson *et al*, *Care Profiling Study*, 2008, Ministry of Justice.

McCafferty, 'A duty to act – article 3 of the Human Rights Convention *v.* the non-intervention principle?' [1999] Fam Law 717.

## Further reading cont'd

Miles, 'Z and Others v. United Kingdom; TP and KM v. United Kingdom – human rights and child protection' [2001] CFLQ 431.

Murphy, 'Children in need: the limits of local authority accountability' (2003) Legal Studies 104.

Parkinson, 'Child protection, permanency planning and children's right to family life' (2003) IJLP&F 147.

Perry, 'Lancashire County Council v. B: Section 31 – threshold or barrier?' [2000] CFLQ 301.

Rees, 'Beyond the hype – a year in the life of the Children's Commissioner for Wales' [2002] Fam Law 748.

Williams, 'The practical operation of the Children Act complaints procedure' [2002] CFLQ 25.

## Websites

**Department for Children, Schools and Families**: www.dcsf.gov.uk

**Every Child Matters**: www.everychildmatters.gov.uk

**Ministry of Justice**: www.justice.gov.uk

**National Council of Voluntary Childcare Organisations**: www.ncvcco.org

**NSPCC (National Society for the Prevention of Cruelty to Children)**: www.nspcc.org.uk

# Chapter 16

## Adoption and Special Guardianship

This chapter deals with adoption and special guardianship. Although special guardianship is not part of the adoption legislation, it is dealt with in this chapter as it may provide a better alternative for a child than adoption.

---

**The Legislation**

**Adoption and Children Act 2002** Lays down the powers and duties of adoption agencies and the courts in respect of adoption. It replaces the Adoption Act 1976.

**Children Act 1989** Provides a range of alternatives to adoption, in particular special guardianship orders, residence orders, and parental responsibility agreements and parental responsibility orders.

---

The Government website, Every Child Matters, contains useful information on adoption and on special guardianship.

## 16.1 Adoption – Introduction

Adoption of a child is effected by a court order known as an adoption order which extinguishes the parental responsibility of the child's birth parents, and other persons, and vests it in the adopters. Adoption therefore involves the complete legal transference of parental responsibility and makes the child a full legal member of the new family.

The law of adoption is laid down in the Adoption and Children Act 2002, which came fully into force on 30 December 2005. This Act introduced a radically new law of adoption in place of the 'old' law which had been contained in the Adoption Act 1976. It also made important changes to the Children Act 1989 (see Chapter 11). At the international level, the Hague Convention on the Protection of Children and Co-operation in Respect of Intercountry Adoption 1993 is also part of adoption law in the UK. The European Convention for the Protection of Human Rights is also relevant.

*(i) Adoption and Human Rights* As adoption agencies and courts are public authorities for the purposes of the Human Rights Act 1998 they must exercise their powers and duties in compliance with the European Convention for the Protection of Human Rights (ECHR) (see 1.5). They must ensure, in particular, that adoption is in the child's best interests, and that it does not breach the right to family life of the child and the natural parents under art. 8 ECHR. Any interference with the right to family life of children and parents must be legitimate, necessary and proportionate (art. 8(2)). The following case was decided by the European Court of Human Rights, and must be taken into account by the courts in the UK as result of its obligations under s.2(1) Human Rights Act 1998:

▶ *Johansen* v. *Norway* **(1997) 23 EHRR 33**

The child, who was in care, had been placed in a foster-home with a view to her adoption, and the mother had been deprived of contact. The ECtHR held that: 'the mutual enjoyment by parent and child of each other's company constitutes a fundamental element of family life and that domestic measures hindering such enjoyment amount to an interference with the right protected by art. 8.' The ECtHR held that there had been a breach of the ECHR, as the far-reaching measures taken were inconsistent with the aim of reuniting the mother and child and should only have been taken in exceptional circumstances where they could be justified in the best interests of the child.

But each case depends on its facts. In *Söderbäck* v. *Sweden* [1999] 1 FLR 250, for instance, an adoption order was held not to breach art. 8 ECHR.

The ECtHR has held that legislation permitting the placing for adoption of a child by a mother shortly before the child's birth without the natural father's knowledge or consent may be a breach of the right to family life guaranteed by art. 8 ECHR (see *Keegan* v. *Ireland* (1994) 18 EHRR 342), but it depends on the facts of the case. In *Eski* v. *Austria (Application No. 21949/03)* [2007] 1 FLR 1650 the ECtHR held that the father's art. 8 rights had not been breached because his consent to adoption had been dispensed with, as the domestic court had carefully examined the case and given reasons. It held that the assessment of the interests of the child and the father's limited relationship with her lay within the margin of appreciation of the domestic court and justified a proportionate interference with the father's art. 8 rights.

The UN Convention on the Rights of the Child is also relevant (see 9.2).

*(ii) The Role of CAFCASS in Adoptions* The role of the CAFCASS officer (or Welsh family proceedings officer) (see 1.4) in adoption depends on whether or not the birth-parents agree to the adoption. If it appears to the court that the birth-parents do agree, then the court will appoint a CAFCASS Reporting Officer who has a duty to make sure that consent to the adoption has been freely given. If a parent does not agree, or there are special circumstances, then the court will appoint a Children's Guardian, if needed, who will usually be the Reporting Officer who was already engaged in the case. The case will then be investigated in more depth. Under s.22 Adoption and Children Act 2002 a CAFCASS officer is responsible for witnessing pre-court consent to adoption and reporting back to the adoption agency prior to the court application for an adoption order. These duties mirror those of the Reporting Officer, but the CAFCASS officer reports to the adoption agency.

*(iii) Adoption Procedure* Rules of procedure for adoption are laid down in the Family Procedure (Adoption) Rules 2005 and in Practice Directions (see in particular, *President's Guidance (Adoption: The New Law and Procedure)* [2006] 1 FLR 1234). All three tiers of family courts (High Court, county courts and magistrates' courts) have jurisdiction to hear adoptions. Certain county courts are designated as adoption centres and any application for an adoption order to a county court must be commenced in such a centre. The overriding objective in all adoption proceedings is 'to enable the court to deal with cases justly, having regard to the welfare issues involved' (r.1 Family Procedure (Adoption) Rules 2005). 'Dealing with a case justly' includes, so far as is

practicable: ensuring that it is dealt with expeditiously and fairly; dealing with the case in ways which are proportionate to the nature, importance and complexity of the issues; ensuring that the parties are on an equal footing; saving expense; and allotting to the case an appropriate share of the court's resources, while taking into account the need to allot resources to other cases.

## 16.2  Adoption Trends

*(i) Numbers of Adoptions*  Adoptions were once much more common than they are now. For example, in 1968 there were 24,800 adoptions, but by the late 1990s there were fewer than 9,000 a year. The decline in the number of adoptions was due partly to the shortage of babies available for adoption as a result of improved methods of contraception, the legalisation of abortion, and the fact that single motherhood was no longer stigmatised so that mothers were no longer under pressure to give up their babies. Children who are adopted today are often older children who have been taken into local authority care. In fact, the Government has adopted a policy of increasing the numbers of children who are adopted from the care system.

Figures from the Office for National Statistics show that in 2006 there were 4,764 children entered into the Adopted Children Register following the making of adoption orders. This was 516 fewer than in 2005, representing a decrease of 9.8 per cent. Compared with 1996, the number of adoptions has fallen by 17 per cent and in 2006 was at its lowest since 1998.

*(ii) Adoptions by Step-Parents and Relatives*  Some adoptions are 'in family' adoptions, in other words adoptions by step-parents and relatives. Step-parent adoptions are common because of the high incidence of family breakdown, and because step-parents often wish to acquire parental responsibility for their step-children (23 per cent of adoptions in 2004 were made in favour of step-parents, 11 per cent more than in 2003). 'In family' adoptions can have drawbacks. In particular, they can sever the child's legal and social relationship with the other birth-parent and the other side of the family. Before the Adoption and Children Act 2002 came into force, a step-parent who wished to adopt a step-child had to do so jointly with his or her spouse – because the law required married couples to make joint applications for adoption. This meant, rather bizarrely, that the child's birth-parent had to adopt his or her own child. However, this anomaly had been removed by the Adoption and Children Act 2002 as step-parents can now make a sole application to adopt a step-child. Furthermore, step-parents now have a wider range of alternatives to adoption available whereby they can obtain parental responsibility. Thus, they can acquire parental responsibility for a step-child either by agreement or court order (see 10.7), and special guardianship and residence orders also provide alternative ways for a step-parent to acquire parental responsibility (see 11.5, and 16.20, below).

*(iii) Adoption with Contact – 'Open' Adoption*  Attitudes to contact after adoption have changed over the years. At one time, adoption was 'closed' in the sense that contact after adoption was not considered a possibility – it was thought best if children permanently severed their links with their birth-family. However, it is now accepted that contact may be beneficial to some adopted children, particularly older ones. Thus, the court has the power to order contact between an adopted child and a member of his

or her birth-family, or a foster-parent, and must in certain circumstances review existing and proposed contact arrangements and invite the parties to comment on them (see 16.12, below). The importance of children maintaining links with their birth-family is also recognised in the welfare checklist in s.1(4) Adoption and Children Act 2002 (see 16.8, below).

## 16.3 Adoption – The Development of the Law

The process of reforming adoption law (which is now contained in the Adoption and Children Act 2002) has taken many years. Pressure for reform initially arose because adoption law had not kept up-to-date with changes in adoption practice. The Adoption Act 1976 (which governed the law before the Adoption and Children Act 2002) was rooted in the philosophy and practice of adoption in the 1960s and 1970s, namely an exclusive model of adoption which focused on the adoption of babies rather than older children. The outdatedness of the law was also exacerbated by the fact that the 1976 Act was not fully implemented until 1988.

In the late 1980s and early 1990s the Conservative Government conducted an inter-departmental review of adoption and various research and consultation documents were published, which included a consultation paper, *Review of Adoption Law: Report to Ministers of An Inter-Departmental Working Group*, 1992, and a White Paper, *Adoption: The Future*, Cm 2288, 1993. In 1996 a consultation paper was published (*Adoption: A Service for Children*) which contained a draft Adoption Bill making fundamental changes to adoption law (for example, placement orders to replace freeing orders; a new welfare principle; and changes to the grounds for dispensing with consent). However, in 1997 the Conservative Government lost the general election, with the result that the Adoption Bill was not presented to Parliament.

When the Labour Government came into power, it announced that it was committed to improving adoption (see para. 1.5, *Supporting Families*, Home Office, 1998). However, it began to realise that adoption could provide a better alternative for some children in care, because of major failings in the child care system. In the year 2000 the *'Waterhouse Report'* (*Lost in Care – Report of the Tribunal of Inquiry into the Abuse of Children in Care in the Former County Council Areas of Gwynedd and Clwyd*) was published, in which it identified 'drift' in care as one of the major failings of the child protection system. In February 2000 Tony Blair, the Prime Minister, reacted to the *Waterhouse Report* by announcing that he would personally lead a thorough review of adoption policy in order to ensure that the Government was making the best use of adoption as an option to meet the needs of children looked after by local authorities. In July 2000 the *Prime Minister's Review: Adoption* (a study of the use of adoption for children in care by the Performance and Innovation Unit of the Cabinet Office) was published, the clear message of which was that too many children were in care for too long and that these children needed a family who could meet their needs on a permanent basis. Adoption, the *Review* concluded, could provide children with the permanency they needed, and the Government should promote an increase in adoption for looked after children. In December 2000 the Government published a White Paper, *Adoption: A New Approach* (Cm 5017), building on the Prime Minister's *Review* and setting out the Government's plans to promote the greater use of adoption, improve the performance of the adoption service and put children at the centre of the adoption process.

In March 2001 the Adoption and Children Bill was presented to Parliament. It received the Royal Assent in November 2002, and the Adoption and Children Act 2002 came fully into force on 30 December 2005.

*The Main Changes to Adoption Law*   The Adoption and Children Act 2002 made the following changes to adoption law:

- Aligned adoption law with the Children Act 1989 by making the child's welfare the paramount consideration in all decisions relating to adoption.
- Provided a new welfare-based ground for dispensing with parental consent.
- Abolished freeing for adoption orders and provided new measures for placement for adoption either with parental consent or under a placement order.
- Overhauled eligibility to apply for adoption orders by enabling single persons, married couples, civil partners, and, for the first time, unmarried couples (opposite-sex and same-sex) to apply. Introduced new provisions to enable step-parents to make a sole application for adoption.
- Strengthened the restrictions on arranging adoptions and advertising children for adoption other than through adoption agencies, and introduced new restrictions relating to reports.
- Widened the range of options for providing permanence for children by amending the Children Act 1989 to introduce a new concept called special guardianship.
- Amended the Children Act 1989 to introduce new provisions for step-parents to acquire parental responsibility.
- Required courts to draw up timetables for resolving adoption cases without delay.
- Placed a duty on local authorities to maintain an Adoption Service, including new arrangements for the provision of Adoption Support Services.
- Provided for a new and more consistent approach to access to information about adoptions held in adoption agency records and by the Registrar-General.
- Established an Independent Reviewing Mechanism to enable prospective adopters who had been turned down for adoption to be entitled to an independent review.
- Introduced Independent Reviewing Officers responsible for chairing reviews of all looked after children (and for reviewing care plans, see 15.7).
- Incorporated the Adoption (Intercountry Aspects) Act 1999 in respect of inter-country adoptions, and provided additional restrictions on bringing a child into the UK.
- Established an Adoption and Children Act Register to suggest matches between children waiting to be adopted and approved prospective adopters.

*More Adoptions for More Children in Care*   A major aim of the Act is to encourage the wider use of adoption for children in care. With a view to encouraging more adoptions of children in care, and to make them succeed, the 2002 Act places a duty on local authorities to provide comprehensive support services, including financial support.

*Tackling Delay*   The 2002 Act introduces new measures to tackle the problem of delay. To prevent delay in matching children with adoptive families, the Adoption and Children Act Register suggests matches between children waiting to be adopted and approved prospective adopters (ss.125–131 Adoption and Children Act 2002). The British Association for Adoption and Fostering (BAAF) is responsible for operating the Adoption Register for England and Wales. To reduce delay, courts are required to draw up timetables to prevent delay, and to give directions to ensure that the timetable is kept to. The Act also introduces a 'no-delay' principle, like that in the Children Act 1989 (see 11.3).

## 16.4    Agency Adoptions and Non-Agency Adoptions

Adoptions are (i) agency adoptions or (ii) non-agency adoptions.

*(i) Agency Adoptions*    These are adoptions where the child is placed for adoption by an adoption agency (that is, a local authority or an approved adoption agency). Adoption agencies have responsibilities for making arrangements for adoption and placing children for adoption (see ss.2–17). Local authorities must maintain an adoption service, and an adoption support service (which includes the provision of financial support) (s.3). Adoption agencies must provide counselling, advice and information about adoption (s.2(6)). Local authorities must advertise these services (s.5). Persons interested in adoption can apply for an assessment of needs for the purposes of adoption support (see s.4), which local authorities have a duty to carry out (s.3(1)). Local authorities are required to notify education and healthcare authorities if a person has educational or healthcare needs (s.4(9)), and they must co-operate with each other in the exercise of their assessment of needs functions (ss.4(11), (12)).

*(ii) Non-Agency Adoptions*    These are adoptions by relatives, step-parents and private foster-parents. They include adoptions by local authority foster-parents who wish to adopt a child but with whom the local authority has not placed a child with a view to adoption.

## 16.5    Illegal Placements and Transactions

It is a criminal offence for persons other than adoption agencies to make arrangements for adoption (ss.92, 93), for unauthorised persons to prepare adoption reports (s.94) and for persons to advertise for adoption (ss.123, 124). Certain payments and rewards made in connection with adoption are also prohibited (s.95). The court may, however, depending on the circumstances, authorise certain payments retrospectively, as it did sometimes under the old law. There are also prohibitions on bringing overseas children into the UK (see below).

## 16.6    The Welfare Principles

Section 1 Adoption and Children Act 2002 lays down the following welfare principles, which must be applied by courts and adoption agencies when coming to a decision relating to the adoption of a child (s.1(1)). These are new principles introduced by the 2002 Act in order to align adoption law with the Children Act 1989.

*(i) The Welfare Principle*    The welfare principle is as follows:

> **Section 1(2)**  The 'paramount consideration of the court or adoption agency must be the child's welfare, throughout his life.'

Under the law of adoption before the Adoption and Children Act 2002 came into force the child's welfare was the 'first', not 'paramount', consideration, and the welfare principle applied only to the child throughout his childhood, not 'throughout his life'. The change from 'first' to 'paramount' brought adoption law into line with the welfare principle in the Children Act 1989 (see 11.3), and into line with art. 21 of the UN Convention on the Rights of the Child 1989 (see 9.2) which provides that 'States Parties that recognise and/or permit the system of adoption shall ensure that the best interests of the child shall be the paramount consideration'.

Although the child's welfare is paramount, the interests of the child's birth-parents and birth-family can be taken into account under the welfare checklist (see below). Factors taken into account under the old law are likely to continue to be taken into account. Thus, for example, if the motive for adoption is to obtain British nationality and immigration rights, then the application may be refused just as it was under the old law (see, for example, *Re K (A Minor) (Adoption Order: Nationality)* [1994] 2 FLR 557, where an adoption order made in favour of a teenage girl from South Africa was discharged on the Home Secretary's appeal, on the grounds of public policy).

The welfare principle in s.1(2) also applies to the issue of dispensing with parental consent (see 16.11, below).

*(ii) The No-Delay Principle*   Section 1(3) provides that 'the court or adoption agency must at all times bear in mind that, in general, any delay in coming to the decision is likely to prejudice the child's welfare'. This brings the law into line with the Children Act 1989 and the requirements of art. 6 of the European Convention for the Protection of Human Rights, which requires cases to be heard promptly.

*(iii) The Welfare Checklist (s.1(4))*   This is a list of factors which must be applied by courts and adoption agencies in determining the best interests of the child in any decision relating to adoption. It is similar to the welfare checklist in s.1(3) Children Act 1989 (see 11.3).

Under s.1(4), courts and adoption agencies must have regard to the following matters (among others):

'(a)  the child's ascertainable wishes and feelings regarding the decision (considered in the light of the child's age and understanding);
(b)  the child's particular needs;
(c)  the likely effect on the child (throughout his life) of having ceased to be a member of the original family and become an adopted person;
(d)  the child's age, sex, background and any of the child's characteristics which the court or agency considers relevant;
(e)  any harm (within the meaning of the Children Act 1989) which the child has suffered or is at risk of suffering;
(f)  the relationship which the child has with relatives, and with any other person in relation to whom the court or agency considers the relationship to be relevant, including –
  (i)   the likelihood of any such relationship continuing and the value to the child of its doing so;
  (ii)  the ability and willingness of any of the child's relatives, or of any such person, to provide the child with a secure environment in which the child can develop, and otherwise to meet the child's needs;
  (iii) the wishes and feelings of any of the child's relatives, or of any such person, regarding the child.'

The term 'relationships' in s.1(4) is not confined to legal relationships (s.1(8)(a)), and 'relatives' includes the child's mother and father (s.1(8)(b)). 'Harm (within the meaning of the Children Act 1989)' includes seeing or hearing the ill-treatment of another (such as witnessing domestic violence).

Although the child's wishes and feelings are important under s.1(4)(a), there is no requirement that older children must consent to adoption, even though the 1992 *Review of Adoption* had recommended that older children should be permitted to give consent.

The child's relationships with his birth-family, including brothers and sisters, will be an important consideration under the checklist. The right to family life in art. 8 of the European Convention for the Protection of Human Rights will be relevant. The Preamble to the United Nations Convention on the Rights of the Child 1989 also recognises the right of the child to grow up in a family environment and to know his real identify. As s.1(4)(c) requires courts and adoption agencies to consider the child 'throughout his life', inheritance and succession interests may be relevant considerations.

*(iv) The Child's Religious, Racial, Cultural and Linguistic Background*   Adoption agencies, when placing children for adoption, must give due consideration to the child's religious persuasion, racial origin and cultural and linguistic background (s.(1(5)). However, despite the respect given to private and family life, to freedom of thought, conscience and religion and any individual belief system, the law does not give religious belief a pre-eminent place in the balance of factors that comprise welfare (Ryder J in *Haringey London Borough Council v. C, E and Another Intervening* [2006] EWHC 1620 (Fam), [2007] 1 FLR 1035). Thus, although religious beliefs of a parent may be taken into account, they can never be determinative of the outcome of adoption proceedings, however profoundly held, as the welfare of the child is the paramount consideration (see also *Re S; Newcastle City Council v. Z* [2005] EWHC 1490 (Fam), [2007] 1 FLR 861, a case heard six months before the 2002 Act came into force, where the mother wished to delay adoption for religious reasons until suitable adopters had been found).

*(v) Duty to Consider Other Powers; and the 'No-Order' Principle*   Courts and adoption agencies must consider the whole range of powers available under the 2002 Act and the Children Act 1989; and the court must not make any order unless doing so would be better for the child than not doing so (s.1(6)). (These principles are also laid down in the Children Act 1989, see 11.3.) If the court were to make an adoption order when another order would be sufficient to protect the child's welfare (for example, a special guardianship order), this might be a breach of s.1(6), and possibly the principle of proportionality which is part of the right to family life under art. 8 ECHR (see 1.5).

## 16.7   Eligibility for Adoption

*(i) Who Can be Adopted?*   The child to be adopted must be under the age of 18 on the date of the adoption application (s.49(4)), but an adoption order can be made if the child reaches 18 before the conclusion of adoption proceedings (s.49(5)). An adoption order cannot be made, however, in any case if the child has reached the age of 19, or is, or has been, married (ss.47(8), (9)).

*(ii) Who Can Adopt?*   A wider range of applicants can apply for adoption under the 2002 Act than under the 'old' law. Under the old law only married couples could make a joint

application for adoption, but under the 2002 Act civil partners and cohabiting couples (opposite-sex and same-sex) can now apply (s.49). This has widened the pool of potential adopters for children in care. Applicants must satisfy certain domicile and age limit requirements (ss.50, 51). Applications for an adoption order can be made by a 'couple' or a sole applicant (s.49):

- ▷ *A Couple* A 'couple' means 'a married couple, or two people who are civil partners of each other, or two people (whether of different sexes or the same sex) living as partners in an enduring family relationship (s.144(4)). A 'couple' does not include two people if one of them is the other's parent, grandparent, sister, brother, aunt or uncle (s.144(5)). Each applicant must have attained the age of 21 (s.50(1)), unless one of the couple is either the mother or father of the child, in which case that person need only have attained the age of 18 (s.50(2)).
- ▷ *A Sole Applicant* The applicant must have attained the age of 21, and must not be married (s.51(1)). However, a married person can make a sole application if the court is satisfied that: his or her spouse cannot be found; or that they are separated permanently and are living apart; or that the other spouse is incapacitated from applying because of physical or mental ill-health (s.51(3)).

*(iii) Step-Parent and Partner Applicants* A step-parent or partner of the parent of the child can make a sole application to adopt a step-child or the child of his or her partner, provided the applicant has attained the age of 21 (s.51(2)). This provision removes the anomaly under the old law which required a step-parent to make a joint application for adoption with the child's parent. As an alternative to adoption, a step-parent or partner might consider becoming a special guardian of the child (see 16.18, below), or obtain parental responsibility for the child (see 10.7), or obtain a residence order in respect of the child (which can be extended until the child reaches the age of 18) (see 16.17).

*(iv) Domicile Requirements* At least one of the couple or the single applicant must be domiciled in part of the British Islands; or both of the couple have been, or the single applicant has been, habitually resident in part of the British Islands for a period of not less than one year ending with the date of the application (s.49).

### 16.8　Preliminaries to Making an Adoption Order

*(i) Probationary Residence Requirements* The child must have had his or her home with the applicant(s) at all times during the relevant period preceding the application for the adoption order (s.42).

*Agency Placements* The child must have had his home with the applicant(s) at all times during the ten weeks preceding the adoption application (s.42(2)).

*Non-Agency Placements* If the adoption application involves a step-parent or partner of the child's parent, the child must have lived with the applicant(s) for a continuous period of at least six months immediately preceding the application (s.42(3)). If the applicants are local authority foster-parents, the continuous minimum period of residence is one year (s.42(4)). In other cases (such as where the applicant is a relative), the child must have had his home with the applicant(s) for a cumulative period of at least three years (whether continuous or not) during the period of five years ending with the application, except where the court grants leave to make the application (ss.42(5), (6)). The aim of the three-year residence requirement in the case of relatives is to provide a disincentive to 'in family' adoptions, because of their potential to distort family relationships.

*(ii) Agency Adoptions – Duty to Provide a Report*   In an agency case, the adoption agency which places the child for adoption must submit to the court a report dealing with the suitability of the applicants and any relevant s.1 welfare issue in respect of the child, and must assist the court in any manner it directs (s.43). A CAFCASS officer or Welsh family proceedings officer (see 1.4) will be responsible for compiling the report.

*(iii) Non-Agency Adoptions – Notice of Intention to Adopt*   In a non-agency case, the proposed adopter(s) must have given notice to the appropriate local authority of their intention to apply for an adoption order not more than two years, or less than three months, before the date on which the application for an adoption order is made (ss.44(2), (3)). On receipt of notification, the local authority must arrange for the matter to be investigated and submit a report to the court, in particular in respect of the prospective adopters' suitability for adoption and any relevant welfare issues under s.1 of the Act (ss.44(5), (6)).

*(iv) Suitability for Adoption*   Under regulations made under the 2002 Act, the adoption agency is required to take into account various matters for determining the suitability of the prospective adopters, and for reporting as to their suitability.

*(v) The 'Consent Condition' or 'Placement Condition' Must be Satisfied*   The 'consent condition' or the 'placement condition' must be satisfied before an adoption order can be made (s.47). Thus the court must be satisfied that: each parent or guardian consents to the making of the adoption order; or that each parent or guardian has given advance consent under s.20 and has not withdrawn that consent and does not oppose the making of the adoption order; or that the consent of each parent or guardian can be dispensed with under s.52 (s.47(2)). In respect of placement for adoption (whether by the consensual route or placement order), the court must be satisfied: that the child has been placed for adoption with the prospective adopters; that the child has been placed with the consent of each parent or guardian or placed under a placement order; and that no parent or guardian opposes the making of the adoption order (s.47(4)).

## 16.9   The Adoption Order

An adoption order is an order which gives parental responsibility for the child to the adopter(s) (s.46(1)). It extinguishes the parental responsibility of the child's mother and father, and any one else with parental responsibility; and terminates any order under the Children Act 1989 (s.46(2)). In the case of a step-parent adoption, however, the adoption order does not affect the parental responsibility or duties of the person who is the natural parent of the adopted child (s.46(3)(b)). An adoption order extinguishes any duty to pay child maintenance (by agreement or court order), except where the maintenance duty arises under a trust or by an agreement which expressly provides that the duty is not to be extinguished (ss.46(2), (4)).

*(i) Requirements for Obtaining an Adoption Order*   The primary ground for making an adoption order is that the order is justified in all the circumstances of the case, with paramount consideration being given to the child's welfare though his or her life (see s.1). The court can make an adoption order only if each of the following requirements is satisfied:

- The applicants (or applicant) are eligible for adoption.
- The child is eligible for adoption.
- The child has had his or her home with the applicant(s) at all times during the relevant period preceding the application for the adoption order.
- The adoption agency has had sufficient time to see the child with the applicant(s) (s.42(7)).
- In an agency placement, a report on the suitability of the applicants has been submitted by the agency, in which there must be proper regard for the need for stability and permanence in their relationship (ss.43 and 45).
- In a non-agency placement, the required notice requirements have been satisfied.
- No previous application for a British adoption order has been made by the same applicant(s) in relation to the same child, unless it appears to the court that either because of the change of circumstances or for any other reason it is proper to hear the application (s.48).
- There has been no contravention by the applicant(s) of the provisions relating to illegal transactions (ss.92–96, 123).
- The requirements regarding consent to adoption are satisfied; or the child has been placed by the adoption agency with the prospective adopters in whose favour the order is proposed to be made; and, either the child was placed with the consent of each parent (and the consent of the mother was given when the child was at least six weeks old); or the child was placed for adoption under a placement order; and in either case that no parent or guardian opposes the making of the adoption order.

*(ii) How the Court Exercises its Powers in Adoption Proceedings*   The welfare test (s.1(2)), and the 'welfare checklist' (s.1(4)), and the other s.1 principles of the Adoption and Children Act 2002 must be applied by the court (see 16.6, above). Before making the adoption order, the court must also be satisfied that the consent conditions (s.47(2)) or placement conditions (s.47(4)) are satisfied; and that the adoption agency or local authority has had sufficient opportunities to see the child with the applicant(s) in the home environment (s.47(2)). Before making the order, the court must also consider whether there should be arrangements for allowing any person to have contact with the child (s.46(6)). As the court has a duty under the welfare checklist to consider whether it should exercise any of its powers under the 2002 Act or the Children Act 1989, it may make a s.8 contact order of its own motion. Parents also have a right at the final adoption hearing to apply for a contact order under s.26 (see below).

*(iii) Removal of the Child*   Where an application for an adoption order has been made, the child cannot be removed from accommodation, except with leave of the court (s.37(a)).

*(iv) The Status of the Adopted Child*   An adopted person is treated in law as if he or she was born as the child of the adopter(s) (s.67(1)). An adopted person is the legitimate child of

the adopter(s), and, if the child is adopted by a couple or by one of a couple under s.51(2) (adoption by partner of parent of adopted child), the child is to be treated as the child of that relationship (s.67(2)). A person who is adopted by one member of a couple under s.51(2) is to be treated in law as not being the child of any person other than the adopter and the other member of the couple (s.67(3)(a)). In any other case, an adopted person is to be treated in law as not being the child of any person other than the adopter(s) (s.67(3)(b)).

*(v) Restrictions on Making a Further Application for an Adoption Order*   Where a previous application for an adoption order has been refused by any court, a second application for an adoption order may not be heard unless it appears to the court that there is a change in circumstances or other reason which makes it proper to hear the application (s.48(1)).

*(vi) Revocation of an Adoption Order*   An adoption order cannot be revoked, except where a child who has been adopted by one natural parent as sole adoptive parent subsequently becomes legitimised by his natural parents' marriage (s.55(1)).

## 16.10   Placement for Adoption

Sections 18–29 of the 2002 Act have introduced a new concept of placement to replace that of freeing for adoption. These provisions only apply to agency placements. The aim of the new provisions is to ensure that consent to adoption is dealt with much earlier in the adoption process than under the old law. The aim is also to provide greater certainty and stability for the child who is to be adopted, and reduce uncertainty for the prospective adopters.

The adoption agency must be satisfied that the child ought to be placed for adoption (s.18(2)). Where a child is placed, or is authorised to be placed, for adoption by a local authority, the child is described as being 'looked after' by the local authority for the purposes of the Children Act 1989, whereupon the local authority has certain obligations to the child (s.18(3)) (see 15.11).

A child can be placed for adoption with (a) the consent of the child's parents or guardian, or (b) by way of a placement order.

### (a)   Placement by Consent of the Birth-Parents

Section 19 Adoption and Children Act 2002 authorises an adoption agency to place a child for adoption (except a baby aged under six weeks), where it is satisfied that each parent or guardian has consented to the child being placed for adoption (with prospective adopters identified in the consent form and/or with any prospective adopters who may be chosen by the agency), and that consent has not been withdrawn.

'Consent' means 'consent given unconditionally and with full understanding of what is involved, but a person may consent to adoption without knowing the identity of the persons in whose favour the order will be made' (s.52). Consent must be given on the prescribed form.

A parent who consents to a child being placed for adoption by an adoption agency may at the same time or at a subsequent time give advance consent to the making of a future adoption order (s.20).

Where a parent is prepared to consent the adoption agency must request CAFCASS (see 1.4) to appoint an officer (or the National Assembly of Wales to appoint a Welsh family proceedings officer) for the purposes of signification by that officer of the consent.

*Withdrawal of Consent*   Where a child is placed with consent, the birth- parents can withdraw their consent at any time up until an *application* for an adoption order has been made. If the child is placed for adoption but consent to adoption is withdrawn before the adoption application, then the child must be returned to the birth-parents within 14 days. If consent is withdrawn before the child is placed for adoption, the child must be returned within one week. Where, however, the child is being accommodated by the local authority and the authority has applied for a placement order, the child may not be removed without the court's leave.

Where consent has not been withdrawn before an adoption application has been made, but the birth-parents do not wish the child to be adopted, they can defend the final adoption order but only with leave (permission) of the court, which it can grant only if there has been a change of circumstances (ss.47(5), (7)). The question of leave to defend was considered in the following case:

▶ *Re P (Adoption: Leave Provisions)* [2007] EWCA Civ 616

The father of a two-year-old girl applied for leave to defend adoption proceedings, asserting a change of circumstances since the placement order had been made (namely that he and the mother had improved the deficiencies in their lives and were successfully caring for their second child). At first instance the judge refused leave as he was not sufficiently satisfied as to the change of circumstances; or that the child's welfare (which was the court's paramount consideration) required her to be adopted. The parents appealed.

The Court of Appeal held, dismissing their appeal, that the welfare test in s.1 Adoption and Children Act 2002 can be applied by the court in an application for leave to defend adoption proceedings under s.45(5) even if, at the first stage, the court had found that there had been no material change of circumstances. The judge had been right to consider that, if he were wrong in finding that the parents' circumstances had not changed sufficiently, he could alternatively consider the application by reference to the welfare criteria in s. 1 of the 2002 Act.

*Parental Responsibility*   Where a child has been placed for adoption under s.19 (that is, by parental consent) or an adoption agency is authorised to place a child for adoption under s.19, parental responsibility for the child is given to the agency concerned (ss.25(1) and (2)). However, if the child is placed with prospective adopters, parental responsibility it is given to them (s.25(3)). During the placement the birth-parents' parental responsibility is not extinguished until the final adoption order is made. Parental responsibility is shared with the prospective adopters and the adoption agency, with the agency determining the extent to which the parental responsibility of the child's parents or of the prospective adopters is to be restricted (s.25(4)), and with the power to remove the child from the placement.

(b)   Placement of the Child by Placement Order

*(i) A Placement Order*   Under s.21 of the 2002 Act the court can make a 'placement order', which is an order 'authorising a local authority to place a child for adoption with any prospective adopters who may be chosen by the authority' (s.21(1)).

The court cannot make a placement order unless (s.21(2)):

(a) the child is subject to a care order;
(b) it is satisfied that the threshold conditions for making a care order under s.31(2) Children Act 1989 are met (see 15.7); *or*
(c) the child has no parent or guardian (s.21(2)).

In addition, the court must be satisfied that (s.21(3)): each of the child's parents or guardian has consented to the child being placed for adoption with any prospective adopters who may be chosen by the local authority and has not withdrawn that consent; or that the parent's or guardian's consent should be dispensed with (see below).

*(ii) Applications for Placement Orders*   In some situations a local authority has a duty to apply for a placement order. In some situations it has a discretion to do so.

*A Duty to Apply*   A local authority *must* apply for a placement order in respect of a child if (s.22(1)):

(a) the child has been placed for adoption by them or is being provided with accommodation by them;
(b) no adoption agency is authorised to place the child for adoption;
(c) the child has no parent or guardian, or the authority considers the threshold criteria in s.31(2) Children Act 1989 for a care order are met; *and*
(d) the authority is satisfied that the child ought to be placed for adoption.

The appropriate local authority *must* apply for a placement order if they are satisfied that the child ought to be placed for adoption and (s.22(2)):

(a) an application has been made (and has not been disposed of) on which a care order might be made in respect of a child; or
(b) the child is subject to a care order and the appropriate local authority is not authorised to place the child for adoption.

*A Discretion to Apply*   A local authority *may* apply for a placement order if (s.22(3)): the child is subject to a care order; and the local authority is authorised to place the child for adoption under s.19 (placement by parental consent, see above).

*No Duty or Discretion*   There is no duty or discretion to apply for a placement order where there is notice of an intention to adopt (unless four months have passed since notification without an application having been made, or the application has been withdrawn or refused) (s.25(2)). There is no duty or discretion if an application for an adoption order has been made but has not been disposed of (s.25(2)).

If a local authority is under a duty to apply for a placement order or has made an
lication but it has not been disposed of, the child is described as being 'looked after
e authority' (s.22(4)).

*Exercise of Discretion*   When considering whether to make a placement order, the
st apply the welfare principle and the other principles in s.1 (see above). Before

making the order, the court has a duty to consider what arrangements for contact the adoption agency has made, or proposes to make, for the child, and must invite the parties to comment on those arrangements (s.27(7)). The court may, in an appropriate case, make an order as to contact (see below). The court cannot make a placement order unless an effort has been made to notify parents or guardians with parental responsibility about the application (s.141).

*Directions*  The court can direct a medical, psychiatric or other assessment of the child where an application for a placement order is pending or no interim care order has been made – but a child of sufficient understanding to make an informed decision can refuse to submit to the examination or assessment (s.22(6)). As this power is similar to that in s.38(6) Children Act 1989 (see 15.7), similar considerations are likely to apply.

*(iv) Duration of the Order*  A placement order remains in force until revoked, or an adoption order is made, or the child marries or becomes a civil partner, or the child reaches the age of 18 (s.21(4)).

*(v) Representation of the Child*  A child is party to placement order proceedings (see s.41 Children Act 1989, as amended) and the court has a duty to appoint a Children's Guardian (see 1.4) to safeguard the child's interests, unless it is not necessary to do so. Separate representation for the child is permitted in some circumstances (s.93 Children Act 1989, as amended).

*(vi) Variation and Revocation*  A placement order can be varied on the application of two local authorities for the purpose of substituting one local authority with the other (s.23). An order can also be revoked by any person (except the child and the local authority) with leave of the court, provided the child has not been placed for adoption by the local authority (ss.24(1), (2)). Leave can be granted only if there has been a change of circumstances since the order was made (s.21(3)). If a placement order is revoked, any pre-existing care order automatically revives, so that the child will continue to be protected.

*(vii) Effect of a Placement Order*  A placement order gives parental responsibility to the local authority (s.25(2)) or to the prospective adopters while the child is with them (s.25(3)). During the placement the parents' parental responsibility is not extinguished until the final adoption order is made. Parental responsibility is shared with the prospective adopters and the adoption agency, with the agency determining the extent to which the parental responsibility of the child's parents or of the prospective adopters is to be restricted (s.25(4)), and with the power to remove the child from the placement. If a placement with prospective adopters breaks down, and the local authority considers adoption is still in the child's best interests, there is no need for it to apply for another placement order before it makes a new adoption placement.

Once a placement order has been made, only the local authority can remove the child. The placement order remains in force until it is revoked (s.24), or an adoption order is made, or the child marries or becomes a civil partner, or attains the age of 18. The parents may not apply to revoke the order unless: the court gives leave on the grounds that the circumstances have changed since the order was made; *and* the child is not placed for adoption by the local authority.

The adoption agency can remove the child from the placement (for example, where the placement is failing), whether or not the birth-parents have requested the child's return (s.30). Once placement for adoption has been authorised, contact provisions under s.8 and s.34 Children Act 1989 cease to have effect (ss.26(1), (6)), but this does not prevent an application for a contact order being made under s.26 of the 2002 Act (see below).

While a placement order is in force:

▷ No one may cause the child to be known by a new surname or remove the child from the UK (except for a period of up to one month by the person who provides the child's home), unless the court has given permission or the child's parents or guardians have given written consent (ss.28(2), (3)).

▷ Any care order ceases to have effect (s.29(1)), and on the making of the placement order any s.8 order or supervision order under the Children Act 1989 ceases to have effect (s.29(2)).

▷ The court has no power to make a s.8 order, a supervision order or a child assessment order (s.29(3)).

▷ A special guardianship order cannot be made until a final adoption order is made, but leave will be needed to apply for one. If a special guardianship order is made it does not automatically discharge the placement order. The court will have to consider whether to revoke the placement order, applying the welfare principle and the other s.1 principles.

There are also restrictions on making contact orders (see below). Parents, guardians and other persons can, however, apply for a residence order if they have obtained the court's leave under s.47(3) or s.47(5) to oppose the making of a final adoption order.

*(viii) Restrictions on Removing the Child Pending a Placement Order*   A child who is being accommodated pending a placement order cannot be removed from that accommodation except with leave of the court or the local authority (s.30(2)). Where a placement order has been made, only the local authority can remove the child (s.34). Thus, parents have no automatic right to have their children returned to them. The only remedy they have is to apply for revocation of the placement order, which may be difficult (see above).

*(ix) Baby Placements*   An adoption agency may place a baby who is less than six weeks old for adoption with the voluntary agreement of the parent or guardian, whereupon the baby becomes a 'looked after' child of the local authority (see 15.11). However, the placement provisions do not apply. Thus, the agency has no power to determine to what extent the parental responsibility of any parent, or of the prospective adopters, can be restricted under s.25(4) of the Act.

## 16.11   Consent to Adoption

### (a)   Consent to Adoption

Consent is relevant to placement and to adoption. Consent is dealt with earlier in the adoption process than it was under the old law, in order to create certainty and stability for the child and to reduce uncertainty for the prospective adopters. Another aim is to reduce the extent to which birth-families are faced with a *fait accompli* at the final adoption hearing, as they sometimes were under the old law.

'Consent' for the purposes of placement and for adoption means (s.52(5)) 'consent given unconditionally and with full understanding of what is involved; but a person may consent to adoption without knowing the identity of the persons in whose favour the order will be made'. The 2002 Act has introduced a new concept of 'advance' consent.

*(i) Whose Consent is Required?* The consent of each parent or guardian of the child (including a special guardian) is required before an adoption agency may place the child for adoption (s.19(1)) or the court can make an adoption order (s.47(2)). As 'parent' for the purposes of consent means a parent with parental responsibility (s.52(6)), the consent of the unmarried father without parental responsibility is not required. However, where an unmarried mother consents to adoption under s.19 (placement by parental consent), a father who subsequently acquires parental responsibility is to be treated as having at that time given consent in accordance with s.52 on the same terms as the mother (ss.52(9), (10)). Where a father acquires parental responsibility after an application for an adoption order has been made, he can, with leave of the court, oppose the adoption order on the basis that there has been a change of circumstances (s.46). Although the consent of the child's relatives is not needed, the court can take their wishes into account under the s.1(4) welfare checklist (see 16.6, above).

For more on consent of the unmarried father and notifying him of the adoption, see further below.

*(ii) Mother's Consent Within Six Weeks of Birth* In respect of an adoption order, any consent given by a mother is ineffective if given less than six weeks after the child's birth (s.52(3)). In respect of a placement order, consent may be given at any time after the child's birth.

*(iii) Formalities* Consent to placement for adoption and to the making of an adoption order (including advance consent) must be given in the prescribed form (s.52(7)). CAFCASS officers and Welsh family proceedings officers are responsible for advising parents on consent and for witnessing consent, and for reporting to the court on matters relating to the child (see s.102).

*(iv) Effect of Consent* If the child is placed for adoption under s.19, it is an offence for the birth-parents to remove the child from the prospective adopters (s.30).

*(v) Withdrawal of Consent* Once an application for an adoption order has been made, any consent given with respect to the placement for adoption or any advance consent cannot be withdrawn (s.52(4)). Parents who wish to oppose the adoption order after the cut-off point must obtain leave to do so, which the court can grant only if it is satisfied that there has been a change of circumstances since the consent was given or the placement order was made (s.47(7)). The question of leave to defend was considered in *Re P (Adoption: Leave Provisions)* [2007] EWCA Civ 616 (see p.445, above).

*(vi) Advance Consent* Section 20 introduces a new concept of 'advance consent', which enables the birth-parents to relinquish their child and have nothing further to do with the adoption process. Unlike freeing for adoption under the old law, where

freeing could take place against parental wishes, parental consent under the new provision is voluntary.

Thus, a parent (or guardian) who consents to his or her child being placed for adoption by an adoption agency under s.19, may, at the same time, or subsequently, consent to the making of a future adoption order (s.20(1)). Advance consent can be withdrawn (s.20(3)), but any withdrawal is ineffective if made after an application for an adoption order has been made (s.52(4)). A parent who gives advance consent can at the same time or subsequently give notice to the adoption agency stating that he does not wish to be informed of any application for an adoption order (or can withdraw such statement) (s.20(4)). If a parent gives advance consent and chooses not to be notified of the application for the adoption order, placement and adoption can proceed without that parent being involved in any way. Parents are given some protection, however, as they have a right to be notified of the date and place of the adoption application (see s.143), whereupon they can apply for leave to oppose the making of the adoption order, which the court can grant if there has been a change of circumstances since consent was given (s.47(7)). Advance consent is subject to the provisions governing dispensing with consent.

*(vii) The Unmarried Father – Consent to and Involvement in Adoption*   There is no requirement in the 2002 Act for an unmarried father without parental responsibility to give his consent to placement for adoption or adoption. However, in the cases decided under the old law the courts were increasingly willing to involve them in the adoption process, particularly with the coming into force of the Human Rights Act 1998 and the risk of breaching a father's human rights under art. 8 ECHR (right to family life) and art. 6 ECHR (right to a fair hearing). In *Re H; Re G (Adoption: Consultation of Unmarried Fathers)* [2001] 1 FLR 646 Dame Elizabeth Butler-Sloss P held that, as a matter of good practice, judges would be expected to give directions so that unmarried fathers were informed of adoption proceedings, unless good reasons to the contrary existed (for instance, where there was no family life between the father and the child).

In *Re R (Adoption: Father's Involvement)* [2001] 1 FLR 302 Thorpe LJ commented on the shift towards unmarried fathers without parental responsibility being accorded greater involvement in adoption proceedings, and held that the unmarried father might have been justified in raising a complaint under art. 6 ECHR if he had not been given notice of the adoption proceedings. (See also *Re J (Adoption: Contacting Father)* [2003] EWHC 199 (Fam), [2003] 1 FLR 933.)

In *Re C (Adoption: Disclosure to Father)* [2005] EWHC 3385 (Fam), [2006] 2 FLR 589 Hedley J, referring to Dame Elizabeth Butler-Sloss P in *Re H: Re G* (above), directed that the father who was serving a prison sentence be informed about adoption proceedings, because the local authority wanted him to be informed despite the mother's wishes to the contrary. Although he had no parental responsibility, Hedley J said that both parents were entitled to be involved in decisions about their children, at least when the decision might have long-term implications for the child concerned. He said that, where family life was established as it has been here (they had parented other children together), then there had to be very compelling reasons indeed why a parent should be shut out from notice of the existence of the child or proposals for the future of the child.

*Notifying the Unmarried Father About an Adoption*   Although in most cases an unmarried father without parental responsibility will be notified about adoption proceedings in respect of his child, the Court of Appeal held in the following case that there is only a duty to inform a father if this is in the best interests of the child:

> ▶ *Re C (A Child)* [2007] EWCA Civ 1206
>
> The child, a baby girl (aged 17 weeks, born as the result of a one-night stand), was put up for adoption by her mother. The local authority wished to approach the father and the extended family to see if they were willing and able to care for her, but the mother wished to keep the identity of the child secret from the father. At first instance the county court judge ordered that the baby's father and extended family should be told. The mother appealed.
>
> The Court of Appeal allowed her appeal, holding that there was no duty on the local authority to make inquiries of the father and of the child's extended family about the possibility of their providing long-term care. Arden LJ held that before the Adoption and Children Act 2002 the courts had made it clear that, while in general terms the views of a father of a newborn baby should be obtained, they had not required the consent of the father to be obtained where the mother and father had had only had a fleeting relationship. The question was whether the 2002 Act had changed that position. In this case her Ladyship said that ss.1(4)(c) and (f) of the welfare checklist were particularly important. Applying these to the case, there was no duty of an absolute kind for inquiries to be made, when a decision needed to be made about the long-term care of a child. Such a duty only arises if it was in the best interests of the child. There was no breach of the father's right to family life under art. 8 of the European Convention for the Protection of Human Rights as he had had no family life with the child. Neither was it a violation of the ECHR to deprive him of the possibility of obtaining a right to family life. The child's grandparents did have a right to family life under art.8, but they would be able to obtain the information by making their own application under the Children Act 1989. Arden LJ held that the courts should not require a preference to be given as a matter of policy to the natural family of a child. Section 1 Adoption and Children Act 2002 did not impose any such policy, but rather it required the interests of the child to be considered.

(b) Grounds for Dispensing with Consent

Section 52 lays down two grounds for dispensing with consent to adoption and to placement for adoption:

- ▶ that a parent or guardian cannot be found or is incapable of giving consent (s.52(1)(a)); or
- ▶ that the welfare of the child requires the consent to be dispensed with (s.52(1)(b)).

The paramountcy of the child's welfare (s.1(2)) and the s.1(4) welfare checklist (see 16.6, above) apply to dispensing with consent.

In respect of the s.52(1)(a) ground, the court is likely, by analogy with the old law, to require that all reasonable steps have been taken to find the parent or guardian (see *Re S (Adoption)* [1999] 2 FLR 374).

Some commentators have expressed concern that the s.52(1)(b) ground may threaten the rights of birth-parents. Bridge and Swindells (2003, at p.152) state that, unless courts are vigilant, it 'has the potential for bringing a strong flavour of social engineering against the birth family and gives rise to the question whether the balance has shifted too far'. Parental interests, however, are taken into account under the welfare checklist, as the court must consider the impact on the child of ceasing to be a member of the birth-family. Parents who are opposed to the court dispensing with their consent can also invoke the right to family life in art. 8 of the European Convention for the Protection of Human Rights (see 1.5).

Contact

The Adoption and Children Act 2002 makes provision in respect of contact in the context of placement for adoption and adoption. However, there is no presumption of contact as there is in the public law provisions of the Children Act 1989 (see 15.8).

Before making a placement order, the court must consider the arrangements which the adoption agency has made, or proposes to make, for allowing any person to have contact with the child, and must invite the parties to the proceedings to comment on them (s.24(7)). Once the adoption agency is authorised to place a child for adoption, it must consider what arrangements it should make for allowing any person to have contact with the child. The court will also have to consider contact between the child and his birth-parents and family when it conducts the welfare exercise.

*Children Act 1989 – Contact Orders Not Effective and Applications Barred*   Where an adoption agency is authorised to place a child for adoption (whether by consent or under a placement order), any provision for contact under s.8 or s.34 of the Children Act 1989 ceases to have effect and any contact activity direction under s.11A Children Act 1989 relating to contact with the child (see 12.5) is discharged (ss.26(1), (6)). While an adoption agency is authorised to place a child for adoption or the child is placed for adoption, an application for contact cannot be made under the Children Act 1989, but the court can make a contact order under s.26 Adoption and Children Act 2002.

*Section 26 Contact Order*   Where an adoption agency is authorised to place a child for adoption (by parental consent or placement order), or the child is placed for adoption, the court can make a contact order under s.26 Adoption and Children Act 2002 requiring the person with whom the child lives, or is to live, to allow the child to visit or stay with the person named in the order, or for the person named in the order and the child otherwise to have contact with each other (s.26(2)). The following persons can apply (s.26(3)): the child; the adoption agency; parents, guardians or relatives; any person with a contact order which has ceased to be effective; any person with a residence order in force with respect to the child; any person who has care of the child under an order made by the High Court under its inherent jurisdiction; and any other person with leave of the court. The court of its own motion can make a s.26 contact order when making a placement order (s.26(4)).

The welfare principle and the other s.1 principles apply to the exercise of the court's discretion. The order may provide for contact on any conditions that the court considers appropriate (s.27(5)). The contact order is only effective while the adoption agency is authorised to place the child for adoption (or the child is less than six weeks old), but it may be varied or revoked by the court on the application of the child, the agency or the person named in the order (s.27(1)). The court may authorise the adoption agency to refuse to allow contact, if necessary to safeguard or promote the child's welfare, provided refusal is decided as a matter of urgency and does not last for more than seven days (s.27(2)).

*Post-Adoption Contact*   A contact application under the Children Act 1989 cannot be made until the final adoption hearing, when the court can make a s.8 contact order for post-adoption contact in an appropriate case (s.26(5)). The court is likely to be unwilling, however, to make a s.8 contact order where there is any opposition by the adopters. The parties themselves can, if they wish, make their own arrangements about contact.

As one of the main aims of the 2002 Act is to encourage adoptions of children in care, many adopted children will be older children. It may be contrary to the best interests of some children to sever their relationship with their birth-family. The court has a duty, before making an adoption order, to consider whether any arrangements should be made for allowing any person contact with the child, and it must consider any existing or proposed arrangements and obtain the views of the parties to the proceedings (s.46(6)). As the s.1(4) welfare checklist requires the court to have regard to the whole range of powers under the Children Act 1989, the court must consider whether to make a s.8 contact order under that Act. An application for a s.8 contact order can be heard concurrently with an application for adoption (s.26(5)).

Once an adoption order is made, the birth-parents lose their automatic right to apply for a contact order (and other orders) under s.8 Children Act, and must obtain leave of the court to apply, which the court may be unwilling to grant because of the possible disruption this may cause for the adopters and the child.

## 16.13   Baby Adoptions

Special provisions exist for the adoption of babies who are less than six weeks old. An adoption agency may place such a baby for adoption without the need for formal consent under s.19 or for a placement order (s.18(1)), but any consent by the mother to a placement or to the making of an adoption order is ineffective for the purpose of making an adoption order if such consent is given less than six weeks after the child's birth (ss.52(3) and 47(4)). This six-week time limit is to enable the mother to recover from the child's birth, and to enable her to be sure that adoption is what she really desires. Contact orders can, however, be made under s.26, if the baby has been placed for adoption, because of the importance of allowing brothers and sisters and relatives to have contact with the child.

## 16.14   Adoption by Step-Parents, Relatives and Foster-Carers

### (a)   Step-Parents and Partner Adoptions

A step-parent, or partner of a couple, can apply for an adoption order (see below), but one of the following options may be considered a better alternative to adoption:

▶ *Acquire Parental Responsibility by Agreement or Court Order Under s.4A Children Act 1989* (see 10.7)   The advantage of this over adoption is that the child's other birth-parent does not lose parental responsibility, so that the child is not legally separated from the other birth-parent's extended family. The disadvantage is that parental responsibility can be revoked.

- *Section 8 Residence Order*  This order (or an extended residence order) (see 16.18) gives the applicant parental responsibility for the duration of the order (see 11.5 and 16.18). This has the same advantages and disadvantages as the option of acquiring parental responsibility (above).
- *Special Guardianship Order* (see 16.20)  The disadvantage of this order is that the child must have been living with the applicant step-parent or partner for at least three years, or the consent of all those with parental responsibility must have been obtained.

*An Adoption Order*  If a step-parent or cohabiting partner wishes to adopt his or her step-child or child of their partner, the child must have had his home with the applicant at all times during the six months preceding the application (s.42(3)). The step-parent or partner must give notice of his or her intention to adopt to the appropriate local authority not more than two years, or less than three months, before applying for the order (ss.44(2), (3)). This enables the local authority to investigate the case and submit a report to the court in respect of the applicant's suitability for adoption and any s.1 welfare issues (ss.44(5), (6)). The consent requirement must have been satisfied. The 2002 Act expressly recognises the status of a child adopted by a couple or one of a couple (see s.67).

### (b)  Adoption by Relatives

A relative can adopt a child to whom he or she is related, provided the child has had his home with the relative for not less than three years (which need not be continuous) during the five years ending with the application (s.42(5)), or the court grants leave to apply for adoption (s.42(6)). The relative must have notified the local authority of his or her intention to apply for adoption not more than two years, or less then three months, before applying for the order (s.44(3)). He or she must be suitable for adoption (s.45), and consent must have been obtained (s.47(2)).

*Alternatives to Adoption*  Although adoption by a relative may be in a child's best interests where the child's parents are dead or where a relative has been caring for a child and the parents are no longer involved, a more appropriate alternative to adoption may be for a relative to obtain parental responsibility by means of a special guardianship order or a residence order (which can be extended until the child reaches 18).

### (c)  Adoption by Local Authority Foster-Carers

Foster-carers can adopt a foster-child in their care, but the rules differ depending on whether the case is an agency case or a non-agency case. An agency case is one where the local authority decides to place a child with foster-carers or to convert a foster placement into an adoption placement. A non-agency case is one where the local authority has not placed the child with the foster-carers for adoption and has refused to give its approval when they have sought approval. In such a case there is nothing to stop the foster-carers giving notice of their intention to adopt as a non-agency case.

*(i) Agency Cases*  Foster-carers can seek local authority approval to become prospective adopters of a foster-child. If the local authority gives approval, the foster-child lives with

them as his prospective adopters, provided the child's parent(s) or guardian have consented to adoption under s.19, or a placement order has been made. Once the child is placed with the foster-carers as prospective adopters, only the local authority may remove the child (ss.30, 34). Preliminary requirements must be satisfied before an adoption order can be made. Thus, the child must have had his or her home with the foster-parent(s) at all times during the 10 weeks preceding the adoption application; and investigation and reports as to their suitability must have been made and satisfied. The placement condition in s.47(4) (see above) for making an adoption order will be satisfied, provided the child's parents or guardian do not oppose the making of an adoption order (for which they need leave of the court).

*(ii) Non-Agency Cases*    The child must have had his home with the foster-parent(s) for a continuous period of not less than one year, although the court can give leave to waive this requirement (ss.42(4), (6)). They must give notice to the local authority of their intention to adopt not more than two years, or less than three months, before the date on which the application is made under s.44. The consent condition in s.47(2) must also be satisfied. Where the local authority foster-carers have given notice of their intention to adopt and the child has had his home with them for at least one year, the child may be removed only with: leave of the court; or by the local authority; or by a person with parental responsibility (if the child is voluntarily accommodated by the local authority under s.20 Children Act 1989) (s.38), unless the child has been living with the foster-carers for five years or more and they have given notice of their intention to adopt or an application for leave to make an application is pending (s.38(2)). If the foster-carers have made an application for adoption, the child may be removed only with leave of the court or by the local authority (s.38(3)).

*Alternatives to Adoption*    As an alternative to adoption, foster-parents can acquire parental responsibility by obtaining a residence order or a special guardianship order.

## 16.15    Adopted Persons – Access to Information

Adoption was once seen as a secretive process whereby it was best for adopted children to have no contact with, or knowledge of, their birth-parents. Today, however, it is recognised that a child's knowledge of his background is crucial to the formation of a sense of identity. As a result, it is now possible for adopted persons, once they reach 18, to investigate their origins, and to make contact with their birth-family. In this respect there has been a move towards greater 'openness' in adoption. In *Gunn-Russo* v. *Nugent Care Society and Secretary of State for Health* [2001] EWHC Admin 566, [2002] 1 FLR 1 Scott-Baker J said that the 'balance has continued to shift towards greater freedom of information to adopted people', but that the issue which will often arise is 'how to resolve the tension between on the one hand maintaining the confidentiality under which the information was supplied and on the other hand providing the information that the adopted person has a real desire, and often need, to have'.

### (a)    Access to Birth Certificates

An adopted child on reaching the age of 18 can obtain a copy of his or her original birth certificate. However, the Registrar-General has a discretion to refuse to provide a copy, for example on the ground of public policy. In *R* v. *Registrar-General ex parte Smith* [1991] 2 QB 393, [1991] 1 FLR 255 the Registrar-General refused to supply a copy of a birth certificate to an adopted person (who was serving a life sentence for murder, who had subsequently killed a fellow prisoner in the mistaken belief that he was his mother) as this might endanger the life of his mother if he were to be released. The court in judicial review proceedings upheld the refusal.

### (b)    Adoption Registers

There are three adoption registers: (i) the Adoption Register for England and Wales; (ii) the Adopted Children Register; and (iii) the Adoption Contact Register.

*(i) The Adoption Register for England and Wales*    This register links children needing new families with people waiting to adopt. The Register holds this information on a computer database and links are made between children and prospective adopters. The British Association for Adoption and Fostering (BAAF) operates the Register.

*(ii) The Adopted Children Register*    The Registrar-General has a duty (under ss.77 and 78 Adoption and Children Act 2002) to maintain the Adopted Children Register, and an index of the register. The Register is not open to public inspection or search, but any person may search the index of the Register and have a certified copy of any entry in the Register (s.78(2)) and thereby trace the original birth registration of an adopted child. Adults who were adopted can obtain a copy of their original birth certificate. Where the adopted person has not attained the age of 18, a person is not entitled to have a certified copy of an entry in the Register, unless the applicant has provided the Registrar with certain prescribed particulars. Counselling is available for adopted adults before they decide to obtain information about their birth records. Local authorities are required to provide a counselling service.

The courts have no power to restrict the information placed in the Register, but the High Court may under its inherent jurisdiction prohibit the Registrar-General from providing details of the adoption to any applicant while the child is under 18 (see, for example, *Re W (Adoption Details: Disclosure)* [1998] 2 FLR 625). The court can also authorise the Registrar-General to disclose information. In *Re H (Adoption: Disclosure of Information)* [1995] 1 FLR 236 the court authorised the Registrar-General to provide information so that a 53-year-old adopted person with a treatable genetic disease could trace her brother so that he could be screened and treated if necessary. Authorisation to disclose information may, however, be refused (see *D* v. *Registrar-General* [1997] 1 FLR 715).

*(iii) The Adoption Contact Register*    The Registrar-General has a duty to maintain this Register (under ss.80 and 81 Adoption and Children Act 2002), which allows an adopted person to register his or her interest in contacting birth relatives (in Part I of the Register); and relatives searching for an adopted person to register their interest in being contacted (in Part II). If there is a match, the Registrar-General gives the adopted person the relative's name and address, but no information is provided to the relative. Thus, the decision to initiate contact is left to the adopted person.

The Registrar-General has a duty (under s.79 Adoption and Children Act 2002) to make traceable the connections between the register of live births or other adoption records and any corresponding entry in the Adoption Contact Register, and to disclose that information, or any other information, which might enable an adopted person to obtain a certified copy of his or her birth record. The Registrar-General is under a duty to give the connecting birth-record information to an adoption agency in respect of a person whose birth record is kept by the Registrar-General.

## 16.16  Disclosure of Information

Sections 56–65 Adoption and Children Act 2002 introduced new provisions governing the disclosure to adopted persons of information held by adoption agencies in connection with adoption, and for access to birth records. These provisions also cover the release of adoption agency information to birth-relatives and other persons. Under these provisions, adoption agencies act as a single point of access to identifying information (including information necessary to access birth records), as they are the bodies best placed to provide support and counselling for the sensitive task of disclosure.

## 16.17  Adopters and the Independent Reviewing Mechanism

The Independent Reviewing Mechanism is a new body set up under the Adoption and Children Act 2002 with the aim of increasing public confidence in the adoption system. The function of the Review Panel is to offer prospective adopters a right to review if an adoption agency will not approve them. The independent panel reviews the information that went before the original adoption panel, and, if necessary, seeks further information. It will make a recommendation about whether the applicants are suitable to become adopters, but the final decision remains with the adoption agency.

## 16.18  Alternatives to Adoption

*(i) Special Guardianship Orders*   See 16.20 (below).

*(ii) Residence Orders*   The advantage of a residence order made under s.8 Children Act 1989 (see 11.5) is that it does not have the finality of an adoption order – the child's birth-parents retain parental responsibility. The drawback is that it lacks the certainty and finality of an adoption order, which may create uncertainty and insecurity for the child. (For cases where a residence order rather than an adoption order was made, see, for example: *Re M (Adoption or Residence Order)* [1998] 1 FLR 570 (the 12-year-old girl did not wish to be adopted); and *Re B (Adoption Order)* [2001] EWCA Civ 347, [2001] 2 FLR 26 (the child maintained regular and good contact with the birth-father).)

Amendments to the Children Act 1989 by the Adoption and Children Act 2002 make it easier for foster-parents to apply for residence orders (and extended residence orders). They no longer require leave of the court to apply, and the requirement that the child must live with them for at least three years immediately preceding the application has been reduced to one year (s.10(5A) Children Act 1989). Foster-parents can apply for special guardianship (see below), provided the child has lived with them for at least one year (s.14A(5)(d)).

*(iii) Extended Residence Orders*   The normal rule is that a residence order remains in force until the child reaches 16, unless the court considers there are exceptional circumstances

to justify it lasting longer (see 11.5). However, the Children Act 1989 has been amended by the Adoption and Children Act 2002 so that a residence order made in favour of a person who is not the parent or guardian of the child may on the request of the applicant remain in force until the child reaches the age of 18 (s.12(5)). The aim of 'extended' residence orders is to provide greater security for children. Such an order would, for example, enable a child to have a legal relationship with a step-parent while retaining the legal relationship with the birth-family, which would be lost by adoption.

*(iv) Parental Responsibility for Step-Parents*   Under s.4A Children Act 1989 (inserted by the Adoption and Children Act 2002) a step-parent can acquire parental responsibility for a step-child by agreement or by court order (see 10.7). The aim of this new provision is to reduce the number of step-parent adoptions.

## 16.19  Inter-Country Adoption

Over the years there have been increasing numbers of inter-country adoptions. Wars and poverty have left many children abandoned and orphaned, and in some countries girls have been considered to be inferior to boys and are unwanted by their families and have become available for adoption. In the 1990s, in particular, there was a sharp increase in adoptions from Romania, Bosnia and some South American countries.

Inter-country adoptions can have their own set of problems, for although adoption may give children from abroad a quality of life they did not have in their country of origin, there is a danger that such adoptions may exploit the needs of children by being too adult-centred. Inter-country adoptions may fail to take account of the importance of children remaining in touch with their own cultural roots and their birth-family, and they may have been arranged privately without the checks and safeguards which exist for adoptions under domestic law.

In response to concerns about inter-country adoption, there have been increasing numbers of safeguards put in place under international law and domestic law. The Hague Convention on the Protection of Children and Co-operation in Respect of Intercountry Adoption 1993 came into force in England and Wales on 1 June 2003, as a result of the Adoption (Intercountry Aspects) Act 1999. The Convention provides a framework for the regulation of inter-country adoption by setting out minimum standards for the control and regulation of the flow of children between the signatory States. The effect of the Convention is that anyone in England and Wales who wishes to adopt a child from overseas must undergo the same procedures as he or she would if adopting a child under domestic law. Under these provisions there are restrictions on inter-country adoption, and stringent penalties, including imprisonment, for those who fail to comply with requirements. Any person who is habitually resident in the UK who wishes to adopt a child from abroad is required to be assessed and approved as eligible and suitable to adopt. (For more on international adoption, see the Government's Every Child Matters website.)

Article 1 of the Hague Convention on Adoption states that the aims of the Convention are:

'1. To establish safeguards to ensure that inter-country adoptions take place in the best interests of the child and with respect for the child's fundamental rights as recognised by international law;

2. To establish a system of co-operation amongst Contracting States to ensure that those safeguards are respected and thereby prevent the abduction, the sale of, or traffic in children;

3. To secure the recognition in Contracting States of adoptions made in accordance with the Convention.'

The underlying rationale of the Convention is for Contracting States to work together to ensure that adoption is in the best interests of the child, and only after possibilities for placement of the child within the State of origin have been given due consideration (art. 4(b)). The aim is for children to stay within their own communities where possible. Where this is not possible, the Convention makes provisions to regulate the adoption process. It does so by requiring Central Authorities to be established whose function it is to work together to protect children during the adoption process and to monitor the operation of the Convention. Central Authorities are responsible, *inter alia*, for exchanging information about the child, ensuring that the child is adoptable, that the relevant consents have been given after appropriate counselling and that they have not been induced by payment or compensation, and that the prospective adopters are eligible and suitable to adopt the child. The Convention also provides for the automatic recognition in all Contracting States of adoptions certified by the Central Authority concerned as having been made in accordance with the Convention. Various regulations govern inter-country adoption.

Part 2 (Adoptions with a Foreign Element) of the Children and Adoption Act 2006 makes changes to inter-country adoption. It makes provision to suspend inter-country adoptions from countries where the Secretary of State has public policy concerns about the practices there in connection with the adoption of children (for example, child trafficking). It gives the Secretary of State the power to charge a fee for adopters or prospective adopters for services provided in relation to inter-country adoptions. It also lays down provisions preventing an overlap of functions by local authorities where a child is brought into the UK for the purposes of inter-county adoption, and it also amends s.83 Adoption and Children Act 2002 to make it harder for inter-country adopters to circumvent restrictions on bringing children into the UK.

## 16.20   Special Guardianship

Sections 14A–G Children Act 1989 (inserted by the Adoption and Children Act 2002) make provision in respect of special guardianship orders (SGOs). The aim of special guardianship is to give a child for whom adoption is not suitable the security and permanence of a legally secure family placement. Special guardianship might be appropriate, for instance, where it is not in a child's best interests to have his legal relationship with his birth-parents and birth-family severed by adoption, or where the child is an older child in foster-care who does not wish to be adopted. It may also provide an alternative to adoption where there are cultural and religious difficulties with adoption. Since the coming into force of the Adoption and Children Act 2002 there have been more reported decisions about special guardianship orders than any other part of the 2002 Act.

### (a)   Special Guardianship Distinguished from Adoption

The following table shows the main differences between special guardianship and adoption:

| | SPECIAL GUARDIANSHIP | ADOPTION |
|---|---|---|
| **Status of Child.** | The child lives with/is cared for by the special guardian but remains the child of the birth-parent. | The child is the child of the adopters. The adopters are the child's parents. |
| **Parental Responsibility.** | Vests in the special guardian but is retained by the birth-parent. But the special guardian can exercise parental responsibility to the exclusion of all other persons. | Vests in the adopters. |
| **Restrictions on the Exercise of Parental Responsibility.** | The special guardian can agree to the following but also needs the agreement of the birth-parent and anyone else with parental responsibility (or otherwise the court): to take the child out of the UK for more than 3 months; to change the child's surname; to consent to the child's adoption; to consent to the child having serious medical treatment (such as sterilisation, circumcision, immunisation). | There are no restrictions on the exercise of parental responsibility by the adopters. |
| **Duration of Each Order.** | A special guardianship order ceases automatically on the child attaining the age of 18, if not revoked earlier by the court. | An adoption order is permanent. |
| **Revocation or Discharge of the Order.** | The birth-parent can apply for discharge of the special guardianship order, but needs leave of the court, which it can grant only if there has been a significant change of circumstances.<br>    The court can discharge a special guardianship order of its own motion in any family proceedings. | An adoption order cannot be revoked (except in a wholly exceptional case, such as where there has been a serious procedural impropriety). |
| **Maintenance of the Child.** | The birth-parent continues to have a maintenance obligation to the child. | Any maintenance obligation owed by the child's birth-parent is extinguished on adoption. |
| **Death of the Child.** | The special guardian must notify the child's parent(s) who have parental responsibility. | The adopters need not notify the birth-parents of the child's death. |
| **Intestacy.** | The child has no right to inherit from a special guardian who dies intestate. | The child has a right to inherit from the adopter(s) on the adopter(s) intestacy. |
| **Birth-Parent Wishes to Apply for a Residence Order.** | The birth-parent does not need leave of the court. | The birth-parent needs leave of the court. |
| **Birth-Parent Wishes to Apply for a Contact Order, Specific Issue or Prohibited Steps Order.** | The birth-parent needs leave of the court to apply for these orders. | The birth-parent needs leave of the court to apply for any of these orders. |

|  | SPECIAL GUARDIANSHIP | ADOPTION |
|---|---|---|
| **Birth-Parent – as Respondent in Future Legal Proceedings In Respect of the Child.** | The special guardian and birth-parent will be parties to proceedings under the Children Act 1989 (such as for s.8 orders, care or supervision orders, and emergency protection orders). | Only the adopters will be automatic respondents, not the birth-parent(s). |

**(b)** Making a Special Guardianship Order

*(i) Applicants* The following persons can apply under the Children Act 1989 for a special guardianship order (SGO) as of right (s.14A(5)):

- a guardian of the child;
- a person with a residence order in force with respect to the child;
- a person who has the consent of all those persons who have a residence order in their favour with respect to the child;
- any person with whom the child has lived for three out of the previous five years, provided he or she has the consent of any person with parental responsibility, or any person with a residence order, or the local authority (if the child is in care);
- any other person who has the consent of all persons with parental responsibility for the child;
- a local authority foster-parent with whom the child has lived for a period of at least one year immediately preceding the application.

The applicant must be at least 18 years old and must not be a parent of the child (s.14A(2)). A joint application can be made (ss.14A(1), (3)).

Other persons can apply for a SGO with leave of the court (s.14A(3)). When considering whether to grant leave, the court applies the same factors as those which apply to leave applications for s.8 orders under the Children Act 1989 (s.14A(12)) (see 11.5). A child can apply for a SGO with leave of the court, which the court can grant but only if it is satisfied that the child has sufficient understanding to make the proposed application (s.14A(12)).

The court can also make a SGO of its own motion in any family proceedings (see 11.9), which includes adoption proceedings (s.14A(6)).

*(ii) Local Authority Duty to Provide a Report* In some circumstances, written notice of an intention to apply for a SGO must be given to the relevant local authority (see s.14A(7)). On receipt of this notice, it has a duty to investigate the matter and prepare a report for the court about the suitability of the applicant(s) for special guardianship, and other matters (s.14A(9)). The court cannot make an order until it has received this report (s.14A(11)) dealing with the matters referred to in s.14A(8). The compulsory nature of these report provisions were emphasised in the following case:

> ▶ *Re S (Adoption Order or Special Guardianship Order) (No. 2)* [2007] EWCA Civ 90, [2007] 1 FLR 855
>
> The judge of her own motion made a SGO in favour of the child's foster-parent (even though the foster-parent wished to adopt the child). She did so without a local authority report being available on the basis that the child's welfare was better served by a SGO than an adoption order. The Court of Appeal held that the reporting requirement in s.14A(11) was unequivocal, and other reports containing relevant information (such as an adoption application report) could not be relied on in the absence of a s.14A(8) report. However, it held that the court should adopt a pragmatic approach, and in any case in which the court was minded to make a SGO of its own motion, then, if much of the relevant information was already before the court, the local authority should be requested to fulfil the terms of s.14A(8) by providing missing information and by cross-referencing existing reports.

*(iii) Making a Special Guardianship Order – The Exercise of Discretion*   The rules governing the exercise of the court's discretion are laid down in s.14B(1). Thus, when considering whether or not to make a SGO, the court must apply the welfare principle and other principles in s.1 Children Act (see 11.3); and before making an order must consider whether or not a contact order should be made in respect of contact between the child and his birth-family. The court must also consider whether to vary or discharge any existing s.8 order. On making the order, the court can permit the child to be known by a new surname or to leave the UK (s.14B(2)). To reduce delay, the court must draw up a timetable and give directions to ensure that the timetable is adhered to (s.14E).

Whether or not the court will make a SGO will depend on the facts of the case, applying the principle that the welfare of the child is the court's paramount consideration (see s.1(1) Children Act 1989). An order is only appropriate if, in the particular circumstances of the case, it is best fitted to meet the needs of the child concerned (see *Re S (Adoption Order or Special Guardianship Order)* [2007] EWCA Civ 54, [2007] 1 FLR 819).

Sometimes the court will have to decide whether to make a SGO or an adoption order (see further below).

*(iv) Effect of a Special Guardianship Order*   The effect of a SGO is that the special guardian acquires parental responsibility for the child, which (subject to any other order in force with respect to the child) can be exercised to the exclusion of any other person(s) with parental responsibility (s.14C) – apart from any other special guardian. Special guardians have a right to local authority support services similar to those available to adopters under the Adoption and Children Act 2002, and they have a right to make representations (including complaints) to the local authority about such support, which local authorities have a duty to provide (ss.14F and G).

A SGO discharges any existing care order or related contact order (s.91(5A)), but does not prevent a care order or a residence order being made while the SGO is in force (s.10(7A) Children Act 1989), whereupon an application will have to be made to have the SGO varied or discharged (see below).

*(v) Where a Placement Order is in Force*   A SGO cannot be made while a placement for adoption order (see 16.10) is in force (s.14A(13)), unless an application has been made for a final adoption order, and the person making the application for the SGO has

obtained leave under s.29(5) Adoption and Children Act 2002; or is the guardian of the child under s.47(5). Written notice of an intention to apply for a SGO must be given to the local authority which is looking after the child or in whose area the applicant is ordinarily resident (s.14A(7) Children Act 1989, and s.29(6) Adoption and Children Act 2002).

*(vi) Restrictions on the Exercise of Special Guardianship*    While a SGO is in force, no one may cause the child to be known by a new surname or remove the child from the UK (except for up to three months) without the written consent of every person with parental responsibility for the child, or with leave of the court (ss.14C(3), (4) Children Act 1989). These restrictions do not apply where a placement order is in force (s.29(7)(b) Adoption and Children Act 2002). A special guardian must take reasonable steps to inform the birth parent(s) of the child's death, should he die (s.14C(5) Children Act 1989).

*(vii) Variation and Discharge*    A SGO can be varied or discharged by the court of its own motion during any family proceedings in which a question arises with respect to the child's welfare (s.14D(2)), or on an application by (ss.14D(1), (3)): the special guardian; a parent or guardian with leave of the court; the child with leave of the court; any person in whose favour a residence order is in force with respect to the child; and any person with leave of the court who has, or immediately before the making of the SGO had, parental responsibility for the child. The court can grant leave to applicants (other than the child) if there has been a significant change in circumstances since the order was made (s.14(D)(5)). If a care order is in force with respect to the child, leave must be obtained from the local authority.

### (c)  Special Guardianship or Adoption?

The court may have to decide whether the child's best interests are better promoted by it making an adoption order or a special guardianship order (SGO). The decision will depend on the facts of the particular case.

The following case is the leading case on the principles to be applied when the court is considering whether to make an adoption order or a SGO:

> ▶ *Re S (Adoption Order or Special Guardianship Order)* [2007] EWCA Civ 54, [2007] 1 FLR 819
>
> The child (aged 6 and in care of the local authority) was placed with a foster-mother but the child's mother had regular contact, and the father had contact. The foster-mother applied to adopt the child but the judge concluded that adoption was not the best way of securing the child's welfare and made a SGO of her own motion. The foster-mother appealed to the Court of Appeal.
>
> The Court of Appeal held, dismissing her appeal, that:
>
> ▶ The key question which the court must ask itself when deciding whether to make a SGO or an adoption order is which order would better serve the welfare of the child, applying the welfare checklists in s.1 Children Act 1989 (see 11.3) and s.1 Adoption and Children Act 2002 (see 16.6).

▶ It is unlikely that the court will need to be concerned with the alternative of making 'no order' (see 11.3 and 16.6), as in most cases the issue will be, not the actual placement of the child, but the form of order that should govern the future welfare of the child.

▶ Because of the importance of such cases to the parties and children concerned, judges must give full reasons and explain their decision with care.

▶ Provided the judge has carefully examined the facts, made appropriate findings and applied the welfare checklists, it is unlikely that the court would be able to interfere with the exercise of judicial discretion, particularly in a finely balanced case.

▶ The risk of prejudice caused by delay is likely to be of less pivotal importance in this type of case; and in many cases it might be appropriate to pause and give time for reflection, particularly in cases where the order is being made of the court's own motion.

▶ The court must be satisfied that the order it decides to make is a proportionate response to the problem, having regard to the right to family life in art. 8 of the European Convention for the Protection of Human Rights (see 1.5). Special guardianship involves a less fundamental interference with existing legal relationships than adoption, and in some cases the fact that the welfare objective could be achieved with less disruption of existing family relationships could properly be regarded as tipping the balance. However, in most cases art. 8 ECHR is unlikely to add anything to the considerations contained in the welfare checklists.

▶ Special guardianship does not provide the same permanency as adoption (as the child's parents can apply for a residence order without leave and other s.8 orders with leave, and the leave threshold is set relatively low) – although a court can make a s.91(14) order under the Children Act 1989 to prevent further applications to the court by the child's parents (see 11.12). The fact that special guardianship cannot give the same permanency as adoption might tip the scales in favour of adoption.

▶ When applying its own motion powers to make a SGO the court can take into account the fact that the person concerned does not wish to be the child's special guardian. But if, applying the welfare checklist under the 1989 Act (including the potential consequences to the child of the refuser implementing the threat to refuse to be appointed a special guardian) the court came to the view that a SGO would best serve the welfare interests of the child, that is the order the court should make.

### Intra-Familial Cases – Special Guardianship or Adoption?

Whether special guardianship will be the preferred option rather than adoption will depend on the facts of the case, applying the principle that the welfare of the child is the court's paramount consideration. A SGO may provide a better alternative to adoption in an intra-familial case (for example, in the case of an applicant grandparent or relative of the child), because it has the benefit of not skewing family relationships. On the other hand, adoption may be a better option because of the security it provides for the child. In *Re AJ (Adoption Order or Special Guardianship Order)* (see below) the Court of Appeal stressed, however, that SGOs had not replaced adoption orders in cases where children were to be placed permanently within their wider families.

In the following cases, the court had to decide whether to make a SGO or an adoption order. They show the fact-based nature of the judicial decision-making process. They also show that appealing against a discretionary decision made at first instance is unlikely to succeed, unless the judge is plainly wrong or there has been an error of law:

▶ *S v. B and Newport City Council; Re K* [2007] FLR 1116

Hedley J made a SGO in favour of the 6-year-old child's grandparents with whom he had been living under a care order since he was 6 months old. He did so despite the grandparents' preference for an adoption order – because he felt that adoption would skew the family relationships. Hedley J also made an order under s.91(14) Children Act 1989 prohibiting any further applications to the court by the child's parents (see 11.12) and an order under s.14B(2)(a) giving leave for the child to be known by the surname of the grandparents. Hedley J said that the case was 'one of those cases for which special guardianship was specifically designed' as it permitted familial carers, who were not the parents, 'to have all the practical authority and standing of parents, whilst leaving intact real and readily comprehensible relationships with the family'.

▶ *Re AJ (Adoption Order or Special Guardianship Order)* [2007] EWCA Civ 55, [2007] 1 FLR 507

The Court of Appeal, with Wall LJ giving judgment, upheld the decision of the judge at first instance who had made an adoption order in preference to a SGO. Adoption by the child's uncle and aunt, not special guardianship, was the best solution, because the child who had been with the aunt and uncle since the age of 6 months needed the assurance that the security of that placement would not be disturbed. A SGO would not provide that assurance, whereas adoption would. The child's father had made aggressive telephone calls to the aunt, and the aunt was concerned that the parents were unpredictable and would litigate issues concerning the child's care. The Court of Appeal agreed with the judge that an adoption order would in the circumstances of the case not unduly distort the family dynamics.

▶ *Re M-J (Adoption Order or Special Guardianship Order)* [2007] EWCA Civ 56, [2007] 1 FLR 691

The child who was subject to a care order had been looked after by his aunt since he was 6 months old (because of the mother's alcohol and drug dependency). The aunt applied to adopt the child but this was opposed by the child's mother. The judge considered that, although many of the child's needs could be met by a SGO combined with a s.91(14) Children Act 1989 order (restricting the child's mother making further applications to the court, see 11.12), those orders did not provide total security. He found that no lesser order would meet the child's welfare, and that an adoption order was a proportionate order to make in the circumstances of the case. The mother appealed to the Court of Appeal on the basis that a SGO was more appropriate in a family placement. The Court of Appeal held, dismissing her appeal, that the adoption order was appropriate in the circumstances of the case.

# Summary

1  Adoption severs the legal link between the birth-parents and the child and creates a new legal link between the adopter(s) and the child.

2  The law on adoption is laid down in the Adoption and Children Act 2002 which came fully into force on 30 December 2005, replacing the old law which was contained in the Adoption Act 1976.

3  A legal adoption can only be effected by an adoption order, which is irrevocable. It transfers parental responsibility from the birth-parents to the adopter(s).

## Summary cont'd

4 In adoption cases the court and adoption agencies must apply the welfare principle which is that the 'paramount consideration of the court or adoption agency must be the child's welfare, throughout his life' (s.1(2) Adoption and Children 2002). Courts and adoption agencies must also apply the welfare checklist in s.1(4) Adoption and Children 2002.

5 The Adoption and Children Act 2002 introduces a new concept of placement for adoption which replaces freeing for adoption.

6 A child under the age of 18 who is not, or has not been, married can be adopted.

7 Joint and sole application for adoption can be made. Married couples can make a joint application, and so can cohabitants (opposite-sex and same-sex). A step-parent can make a sole application for adoption (which was not possible under the old law).

8 Consent to adoption must be given but can be dispensed with under s.52 if: the parent or guardian cannot be found or is incapable of giving consent; or the welfare of the child requires consent to be dispensed with.

9 The Registrar-General is responsible for maintaining the Adopted Children Register, and the Adoption Contact Register.

10 Various provisions are in place to govern inter-country adoption, in particular the Hague Convention on the Protection of Children and Co-operation in Respect of Intercountry Adoption 1993.

11 The Adoption and Children Act 2002 inserts new provisions into the Children Act 1989 which provide alternatives to adoption, in particular special guardianship orders (ss.14A-G Children Act 1989), and extended residence orders (s.12(5) Children Act 1989). Instead of adoption, a step-parent can acquire parental responsibility for a step-child by entering into a parental responsibility agreement or obtaining a parental responsibility order (s.4A CA 1989).

12 In some cases the court may have to decide whether to make a special guardianship order or an adoption order. The governing principle is that the welfare of the child is the court's paramount consideration (applying s.1 Children Act 1989 and s.1 Adoption and Children Act 2002), but the outcome of the case depends on the facts of the case.

## Further Reading and References

Ball, 'The changed nature of adoption: a challenge for the legislators', in Miller (ed.), *Frontiers of Family Law*, 2003, Ashgate.

Ball, 'The Adoption and Children Act 2002 – A critical examination' (2005) vol. 29(2) *Adoption & Fostering* 6.

Bridge and Swindells, *Adoption – The Modern Law*, 2003, Family Law.

Choudhry, 'The Adoption and Children Act 2002, the welfare principle and the Human Rights Act 1998 – a missed opportunity' [2003] CFLQ 119.

Cooke, 'Dispensing with parental consent to adoption – a choice of welfare tests' [1997] CFLQ 259.

Cullen, 'Adoption – a (fairly) new approach' [2005] CFLQ 475.

Harris-Short, 'Legislation: the Adoption and Children Bill – a fast track to failure' [2001] CFLQ 405.

Hayes, 'Giving due consideration to ethnicity in adoption placements – a principled approach?' [2003] CFLQ 255.

Hitchings and Sagar, 'The Adoption and Children Act 2002: a level playing field for same-sex adopters?' [2007] CFLQ 60.

## Further reading cont'd

President's Guidance – *Adoption: The New Law and Procedure*, March 2006 – Judiciary of England and Wales (see website below).

Quinton and Selwyn, 'Adoption: research, policy and practice' [2006] CFLQ 459.

Quinton, Selwyn, Ruston and Dance, 'Contact with birth parents – a response to Ryburn' [1998] CFLQ 349.

Ryburn, 'In whose best interest? – post-adoption contact with the birth family' [1998] CFLQ 53.

Smith and Logan, 'Adoptive parenthood as a "legal fiction" – its consequences for direct post-adoption contact' [2002] CFLQ 281.

Thoburn, 'The risks and rewards of adoption for children in the public care' [2003] CFLQ 391.

## Websites

**British Association for Adoption and Fostering (BAAF)**: www.baaf.org.uk

**Every Child Matters**: www.everychildmatters.gov.uk/adoption

**Judiciary of England and Wales**: www.judicary.gov.uk

# Index